STRUCTURED
COMPUTER ORGANIZATION

STRUCTURED
COMPUTER ORGANIZATION

THIRD EDITION

ANDREW S. TANENBAUM

Vrije Universiteit
Amsterdam, The Netherlands

Prentice-Hall International, Inc.

ISBN 0-13-852872-1

© 1990, 1984, 1976 by **PRENTICE-HALL, INC.**
A Division of Simon & Schuster
Englewood Cliffs, N.J. 07632

Printed in the United States of America

10 9 8 7 6

ISBN   0-13-852872-1

Prentice-Hall International (UK) Limited, *London*
Prentice-Hall of Australia Pty. Limited, *Sydney*
Prentice-Hall Canada Inc., *Toronto*
Prentice-Hall Hispanoamericana, S.A., *Mexico*
Prentice-Hall of India Private Limited, *New Delhi*
Prentice-Hall of Japan, Inc., *Tokyo*
Simon & Schuster Asia Pte. Ltd., *Singapore*
Editora Prentice-Hall do Brasil, Ltda., *Rio de Janeiro*
Prentice-Hall, Inc., *Englewood Cliffs, New Jersey*

To Suzanne, Barbara, Marvin, Bram, Twister, and the memory of Sweetie π

CONTENTS

4 THE MICROPROGRAMMING LEVEL 161

8 ADVANCED COMPUTER ARCHITECTURES   431

9 READING LIST AND BIBLIOGRAPHY   535

APPENDICES

A   BINARY NUMBERS   553

B   FLOATING-POINT NUMBERS   565

PREFACE

The first and second editions of this book were based on the idea that a computer can be regarded as a hierarchy of levels, each one performing some well-defined function. This fundamental concept is as valid today as it was when the first edition came out, so it has been retained as the basis for the third edition. As in the second edition, the digital logic level, the microprogramming level, the conventional machine level, the operating system machine level, and the assembly language are all discussed in detail.

Although the basic structure has been maintained, this third edition contains many changes, both small and large, that bring it up to date in the rapidly changing computer industry. One general change is the replacement of the material on 8-bit microprocessors and batch processing mainframes by new material on advanced personal computers and workstations. The four running examples used in the second edition have been replaced by two modern examples: the Intel 8088/80286/80386 computer family and the Motorola 68000/68020/68030 family (with emphasis on the 80386 and 68030).

Another important development in recent years is the appearance of the RISC machine. This topic is treated in depth, including a detailed look at two of the more popular RISC machines currently on the market, the SPARC and the MIPS. RISC machines are also compared to CISC machines, to provide balance and show the reader the strengths and weaknesses of each.

Multiprocessors and parallel computers have also come in widespread use since the second edition, so these too are discussed here. The treatment covers MIMD machines, including hypercubes, Transputers, bus-based systems, and multistage switching networks, as well as SIMD machines like the Connection Machine and Cray supercomputers. Data flow machines are also examined.

A chapter-by-chapter rundown of the major changes since the second edition follows. Chapter 1 now contains an historical overview of computer architecture, pointing out how we got where we are now and what the milestones were along the way.

In Chapter 2, the material on input/output devices has been completely redone, emphasizing modern devices, such as bit-map terminals, mice, and laser printers.

Chapter 3 (digital logic level) has undergone substantial revision, and now treats computer buses and modern I/O chips. Both the IBM PC bus and the VME bus are described in detail. The Intel and Motorola families are introduced here. Finally, the internal workings of a typical IBM PC clone are described at the chip level, and a circuit diagram is given and discussed at length. The material is presented gradually in such a way that a reader with no previous background in electronics will be able to finish the chapter having a pretty good idea of how a typical PC works inside.

Chapter 4 (microprogramming level) contains a detailed example of what microprogramming is and how it works. This example has proved very popular with readers and has been left intact. However, new material on improving performance has been included, dealing with pipelining and cache memories. Finally, rarely seen material on the microarchitectures of the Intel 8088 and Motorola 68000 chips is presented and discussed.

Chapter 5 (conventional machine level) deals with what many people refer to as "machine language." Since Intel and Motorola chips are being used as the main examples in this edition, they are described in considerable detail here, especially the 80386 and the 68030.

Chapter 6 (operating system machine level) has been reorganized to put the material in a more educationally sound order. The example operating systems used are UNIX® and OS/2™. UNIX is widely known, but OS/2 has a surprisingly large number of features that are not present in UNIX and are well worth examining.

Chapter 7 (assembly language level) has been brought up to date by using examples from the machines we have been studying, but otherwise has not been changed much.

In contrast, Chapter 8 (advanced architectures) has been completely rewritten. This all-new chapter treats up-and-coming ideas in computer architecture, focusing on two topics. The first is RISC machines. Both the theory and practice of these important new computers are covered. As a first example, the SPARC chip, designed by Sun Microsystems, is discussed. This widely used chip is closely based on the Berkeley RISC I and RISC II chips, which have been extensively described and debated in the professional journals and trade press. Following the SPARC is a discussion of the MIPS R2000/R3000 chips. These are compared and contrasted with the SPARC in many ways to provide the reader insight into the various design trade-offs that exist.

The second major topic of this new chapter concerns parallel computers and multiprocessors. Like RISC machines, these computers are beginning to be widely used and have a bright future. Any person interested in computer architecture should know about them. A variety of different types are discussed, including both SIMD and MIMD. Both types are illustrated with a number of practical examples. These include hypercubes, Transputers, bus-based systems such as the DEC Firefly, the Ultracomputer, the Connection Machine, and the Cray supercomputers..

The bibliography and appendices have been revised and brought up to date. In particular, the IEEE floating point standard is discussed in Appendix B.

Finally, many problems have been revised since the second edition. Accordingly, a new problem solutions manual is available from Prentice-Hall.

Prof. Paul Amer of the University of Delaware has written a set of tools (assemblers, disassemblers, simulators, etc.) that go with the microprogramming examples in Chap. 4. Interested parties should contact him by email at amer@dewey.udel.edu.

A number of people have read the manuscript and provided useful suggestions. I am especially indebted to Jennifer Steiner for a large number of valuable remarks and for finding errors that everyone else missed. Stephen Hartley, Alistair Holden, Joseph Hughes, Bob Hummel, Susan Flynn Hummel, Kevin Kitagawa, John McCabe, Ron McCarty, John Mashey, Ann Miller, M. Taghi Mostafavi, Mark Niedelman, Thomas Stevens, Bruce Suter, David Todd, Charles Williams, and Charles Zahn also made numerous helpful comments for which I am grateful. My students, especially Jeroen Belien, Michel Oey, Eigon Willems en Niels Willems have also helped debug the text.

Finally, I once again want to thank Suzanne for her patience for my long hours in front of my PC/AT. From my point of view the PC/AT is a big improvement over my old PC/XT, but from hers, it does not make much difference. I also want to thank Barbara and Marvin for executing a *sleep* primitive within an hour or so of the appointed time, thus giving me the opportunity to "play with the computer" every evening. Finally, I'd like to express my hope that Bram takes after Sweetie π and not after Fluffy.

ANDREW S. TANENBAUM

STRUCTURED
COMPUTER ORGANIZATION

1

INTRODUCTION

A digital computer is a machine that can solve problems for people by carrying out instructions given to it. A sequence of instructions describing how to perform a certain task is called a **program**. The electronic circuits of each computer can recognize and directly execute a limited set of simple instructions into which all its programs must be converted before they can be executed. These basic instructions are rarely much more complicated than:

Add 2 numbers.

Check a number to see if it is zero.

Move a piece of data from one part of the computer's memory to another.

Together, a computer's primitive instructions form a language in which it is possible for people to communicate with the computer. Such a language is called a **machine language**. The people designing a new computer must decide what instructions to include in its machine language. Usually they try to make the primitive instructions as simple as possible, consistent with the computer's intended use and performance requirements, in order to reduce the complexity and cost of the electronics needed. Because most machine languages are so simple, it is difficult and tedious for people to use them.

This problem can be attacked in two principal ways: both involve designing a

1

new set of instructions that is more convenient for people to use than the set of built-in machine instructions. Taken together, these new instructions also form a language, which we will call L2, just as the built-in machine instructions form a language, which we will call L1. The two approaches differ in the way programs written in L2 are executed by the computer, which, after all, can only execute programs written in its machine language, L1.

One method of executing a program written in L2 is first to replace each instruction in it by an equivalent sequence of instructions in L1. The resulting program consists entirely of L1 instructions. The computer then executes the new L1 program instead of the old L2 program. This technique is called **translation**.

The other technique is to write a program in L1 that takes programs in L2 as input data and carries them out by examining each instruction in turn and executing the equivalent sequence of L1 instructions directly. This technique does not require first generating a new program in L1. It is called **interpretation** and the program that carries it out is called an **interpreter**.

Translation and interpretation are similar. In both methods instructions in L2 are ultimately carried out by executing equivalent sequences of instructions in L1. The difference is that, in translation, the entire L2 program is first converted to an L1 program, the L2 program is thrown away, and then the new L1 program is executed. In interpretation, after each L2 instruction is examined and decoded, it is carried out immediately. No translated program is generated. Both methods are widely used.

Rather than thinking in terms of translation or interpretation, it is often more convenient to imagine the existence of a hypothetical computer or **virtual machine** whose machine language is L2. If such a machine could be constructed cheaply enough, there would be no need for having L1 or a machine that executed programs in L1 at all. People could simply write their programs in L2 and have the computer execute them directly. Even though the virtual machine whose language is L2 is too expensive to construct out of electronic circuits, people can still write programs for it. These programs can either be interpreted or translated by a program written in L1 that itself can be directly executed by the existing computer. In other words, people can write programs for virtual machines, just as though they really existed.

To make translation or interpretation practical, the languages L1 and L2 must not be "too" different. This constraint often means that L2, although better than L1, will still be far from ideal for most applications. This result is perhaps discouraging in light of the original purpose for creating L2— relieving the programmer of the burden of having to express algorithms in a language more suited to machines than people. However, the situation is not hopeless.

The obvious approach is to invent still another set of instructions that is more people-oriented and less machine-oriented than L2. This third set also forms a language, which we will call L3. People can write programs in L3 just as though a virtual machine with L3 as its machine language really existed. Such programs can either be translated to L2 or executed by an interpreter written in L2.

The invention of a whole series of languages, each one more convenient than its predecessors, can go on indefinitely until a suitable one is finally achieved. Each language uses its predecessor as a basis, so we may view a computer using this technique as a series of **layers** or **levels**, one on top of another, as shown in Fig. 1-1. The bottom-most language or level is the simplest and the highest language or level is the most sophisticated.

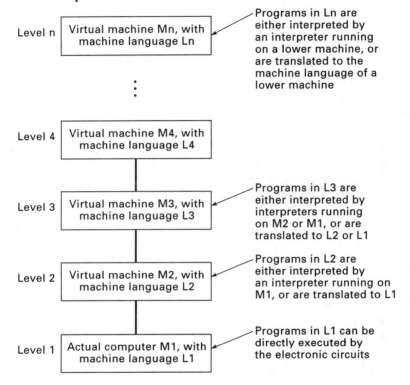

Fig. 1-1. A multilevel machine.

1.1. LANGUAGES, LEVELS, AND VIRTUAL MACHINES

There is an important relation between a language and a virtual machine. Each machine has some machine language, consisting of all the instructions that the machine can execute. In effect, a machine defines a language. Similarly, a language defines a machine—namely, the machine that can execute all programs written in the language. Of course, the machine defined by a certain language may be enormously complicated and expensive to construct directly out of electronic circuits but we can imagine it nevertheless. A machine with C, Pascal, or COBOL as its machine language would be complex indeed but it is certainly conceivable, and perhaps in a few years such a machine will be considered easy to build.

A computer with n levels can be regarded as n different virtual machines, each with a different machine language. We will use the terms "level" and "virtual machine" interchangeably. Only programs written in language L1 can be directly carried out by the electronic circuits, without the need for intervening translation or interpretation. Programs written in L2, L3, ..., Ln must either be interpreted by an interpreter running on a lower level or translated to another language corresponding to a lower level.

A person whose job it is to write programs for the level n virtual machine need not be aware of the underlying interpreters and translators. The machine structure ensures that these programs will somehow be executed. It is of little interest whether they are carried out step by step by an interpreter which, in turn, is also carried out by another interpreter, or whether they are carried out directly by the electronics. The same result appears in both cases: the programs are executed.

Most programmers using an n-level machine are only interested in the top level, the one least resembling the machine language at the very bottom. However, people interested in understanding how a computer really works must study all the levels. People interested in designing new computers or designing new levels (i.e., new virtual machines) must also be familiar with levels other than the top one. The concepts and techniques of constructing machines as a series of levels and the details of some important levels themselves form the main subject of this book. The title *Structured Computer Organization* comes from the fact that viewing a computer as a hierarchy of levels provides a good structure or framework for understanding how computers are organized. Furthermore, designing a computer system as a series of levels helps to ensure that the resulting product will be well structured.

1.2. CONTEMPORARY MULTILEVEL MACHINES

Most modern computers consist of two or more levels. Six-level machines are not at all unusual, as shown in Fig. 1-2. Level 0, at the bottom, is the machine's true hardware. Its circuits carry out the machine language programs of level 1. For the sake of completeness, we should mention the existence of yet another level below our level 0. This level, not shown in Fig. 1-2 because it falls within the realm of electrical engineering (and is thus outside the scope of this book), is called the **device level**. At this level, the designer sees individual transistors, which are the lowest-level primitives for computer designers. (Of course, one can also ask how transistors work inside but that gets into solid-state physics.)

At the lowest level that we will study, the **digital logic level**, the interesting objects are called **gates**. Although built from analog components, such as transistors, gates can be accurately modeled as digital devices. Each gate has one or more digital inputs (signals representing 0 or 1) and computes as output some simple function of these inputs, such as AND or OR. Each gate is built up of at most a

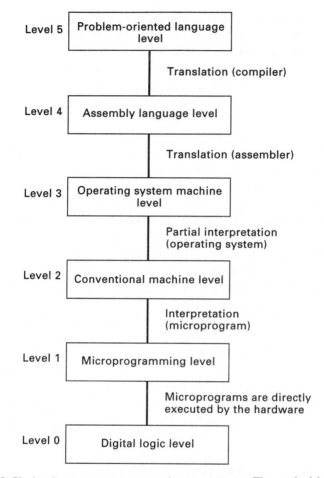

Fig. 1-2. Six levels present on most modern computers. The method by which each level is supported is indicated below it, along with the name of the supporting program in parentheses.

handful of transistors. We will examine the digital logic level in detail in Chap. 3. Although knowledge of the device level is something of a specialty, with the advent of microprocessors and microcomputers, more and more people are coming in contact with the digital logic level. For this reason we have included the latter in our model and devoted an entire chapter of the book to it.

The next level up is level 1, which is the true machine language level. In contrast to level 0, where there is no concept of a program as a sequence of instructions to be carried out, in level 1 there is definitely a program, called a **microprogram**, whose job it is to interpret the instructions of level 2. We will call level 1 the **microprogramming level**. Although it is true that no two computers have identical microprogramming levels, enough similarities exist to allow us to abstract out the essential features of the level and discuss it as though it were well defined. For example, few machines have more than 20 instructions at this level and most of these instructions involve moving data from one part of the machine to another, or making some simple tests.

Each level 1 machine has one or more microprograms that can run on it. Each microprogram implicitly defines a level 2 language (and a virtual machine, whose machine language is that language). These level 2 machines also have much in common. Even level 2 machines from different manufacturers have more similarities than differences. In this book we will call this level the **conventional machine level**, for lack of a generally agreed-upon name.

Every computer manufacturer publishes a manual for each of the computers it sells, entitled "Machine Language Reference Manual" or "Principles of Operation of the Western Wombat Model 100X Computer" or something similar. These manuals are really about the level 2 virtual machine, not the level 1 actual machine. When they describe the machine's instruction set, they are in fact describing the instructions carried out interpretively by the microprogram, not the hardware instructions themselves. If a computer manufacturer provided two interpreters for one of its machines, interpreting two different level 2 machine languages, it would need to provide two "machine language" reference manuals, one for each interpreter.

It should be mentioned that some computers do not have a microprogramming level. On these machines the conventional machine level instructions are carried out directly by the electronic circuits (level 0), without any level 1 intervening interpreter. As a result, level 1 and not level 2 is the conventional machine level. Nevertheless, we will continue to call the conventional machine level "level 2," despite these exceptions.

The third level is usually a hybrid level. Most of the instructions in its language are also in the level 2 language. (There is no reason why an instruction appearing at one level cannot be present at other levels as well.) In addition, there is a set of new instructions, a different memory organization, the ability to run two or more programs in parallel, and various other features. More variation exists between level 3 machines than between either level 1 machines or level 2 machines.

The new facilities added at level 3 are carried out by an interpreter running at level 2, which, historically, has been called an **operating system**. Those level 3 instructions identical to level 2's are carried out directly by the microprogram, not by the operating system. In other words, some of the level 3 instructions are interpreted by the operating system and some of the level 3 instructions are interpreted directly by the microprogram. This is what we mean by "hybrid." We will call this level the **operating system machine level**.

There is a fundamental break between levels 3 and 4. The lowest three levels are not designed for direct use by the average garden-variety programmer. They are intended primarily for running the interpreters and translators needed to support the higher levels. These interpreters and translators are written by people called

systems programmers who specialize in designing and implementing new virtual machines. Levels 4 and above are intended for the applications programmer with a problem to solve.

Another change occurring at level 4 is the method by which the higher levels are supported. Levels 2 and 3 are always interpreted. Levels 4, 5, and above are usually, although not always, supported by translation.

Yet another difference between levels 1, 2, and 3, on the one hand, and levels 4, 5, and higher, on the other, is the nature of the language provided. The machine languages of levels 1, 2, and 3 are numeric. Programs in them consist of long series of numbers, which are fine for machines but bad for people. Starting at level 4, the languages contain words and abbreviations meaningful to people.

Level 4, the assembly language level, is really a symbolic form for one of the underlying languages. This level provides a method for people to write programs for levels 1, 2, and 3 in a form that is not as unpleasant as the virtual machine languages themselves. Programs in assembly language are first translated to level 1, 2, or 3 language and then interpreted by the appropriate virtual or actual machine. The program that performs the translation is called an **assembler**. Assembly language once was important but it is becoming less important as time goes on.

Level 5 consists of languages designed to be used by applications programmers with problems to solve. Such languages are called **high-level languages**. Literally hundreds of different ones exist. A few of the better known ones are BASIC, C, COBOL, FORTRAN, LISP, Modula 2, and Pascal. Programs written in these languages are generally translated to level 3 or level 4 by translators known as **compilers**, although occasionally they are interpreted instead.

Levels 6 and above consist of collections of programs designed to create machines specifically tailored to certain applications. They contain large amounts of information about that application. It is possible to imagine virtual machines intended for applications in administration, education, computer design, and so on. These levels are an area of current research.

In summary, the key thing to remember is that computers are designed as a series of levels, each one built on its predecessor. Each level represents a distinct abstraction, with different objects and operations present. By designing and analyzing computers in this fashion, we are temporarily able to suppress irrelevant detail and thus reduce a complex subject to something easier to understand.

The set of data types, operations, and features of each level is called its **architecture**. The architecture deals with those aspects that are visible to the user of that level. Features that the programmer sees, such as how much memory is available, are part of the architecture. Implementation aspects, such as what kind of chip technology is used to implement the memory, are not part of the architecture. The study of how to design those parts of a computer system that are visible to the programmers is called **computer architecture**. In common practice, computer architecture and computer organization mean essentially the same thing.

1.3. EVOLUTION OF MULTILEVEL MACHINES

To provide some perspective on multilevel machines, we will briefly examine their historical development. The first digital computers, back in the 1940s, had only two levels: the conventional machine level, in which all the programming was done, and the digital logic level, which executed these programs. The digital logic level's circuits were complicated, difficult to understand and build, and unreliable.

In 1951, M. V. Wilkes, in England, suggested the idea of designing a three-level computer in order to drastically simplify the hardware. This machine was to have a built-in, unchangeable interpreter, whose function was to execute conventional machine language programs interpretively. Because the hardware would now only have to execute microprograms, which have a limited instruction repertoire, instead of conventional machine language programs, which have a much larger instruction repertoire, fewer electronic circuits would be needed. Because electronic circuits were made from vacuum tubes at the time, such simplification promised to reduce tube count and hence enhance reliability. A few of these three-level machines were constructed during the 1950s. More were constructed during the 1960s. By 1970 the idea of having the conventional machine level be interpreted by a microprogram, instead of directly by the electronics, was widespread.

Assemblers and compilers were developed during the 1950s to ease the programmer's task. In those days most computers were "open shop," which meant that the programmer had to operate the machine personally. Next to each machine was a sign-up sheet. A programmer wanting to run a program signed up for a block of time, say Wednesday morning 3 to 5 A.M. (many programmers liked to work when it was quiet in the machine room). When the time arrived, the programmer headed for the machine room with a deck of cards in one hand and a sharpened pencil in the other. Upon arriving in the computer room, he† gently nudged the previous programmer toward the door and took over the computer.

If he wanted to run a FORTRAN program, he went through the following steps:

1. He went over to the cabinet where the program library was kept, took out the big green deck labeled FORTRAN compiler, put it in the card reader, and pushed the start button.

2. He put his FORTRAN program in the card reader and pushed the continue button. The program was read in.

3. When the computer stopped, he read his FORTRAN program in a second time. Although some compilers only required one pass over the input, many required two or more. For each pass, a large card deck had to be read in.

---

† "He" should be read as "He or she" throughout this book.

4. Finally, the translation neared completion. The programmer often became nervous near the end because if the compiler found an error in his program, he had to correct it and start all over again. If there were no errors, the compiler punched out the translated machine language program on cards.

5. The programmer then put the machine language program in the card reader along with the subroutine library deck and read them both in.

6. The program began executing. More often than not it did not work and unexpectedly stopped in the middle. Generally, the programmer fiddled with the console switches and looked at the console lights for a little while. If lucky, he figured out the problem, corrected the error, and went back to the cabinet containing the big green FORTRAN compiler to start all over again. If less fortunate, he made a printout of memory and took it home to study.

This procedure, with minor variations, was normal at many computer centers for years. It forced the programmers to learn how to operate the machine and to know what to do when it broke down, which was often. The machine was frequently idle while people were carrying cards around the room or scratching their heads trying to find out why their programs were not behaving the way they were supposed to.

Around 1960 people tried to reduce the amount of wasted time by automating the operator's job. A program called an **operating system** was kept in the computer at all times. The programmer provided certain control cards along with the program that were read and carried out by the operating system. Figure 1-3 shows a sample deck for one of the first widespread operating systems, FMS (FORTRAN Monitor System), on the IBM 709.

The operating system read the *JOB card and used the information on it for accounting purposes. (The asterisk was used to identify control cards, so they would not be confused with program and data cards.) Later, it read the *FORTRAN card, which was an instruction to load the FORTRAN compiler from a magnetic tape. The compiler then read in and compiled the FORTRAN program. When the compiler finished, it returned control back to the operating system, which then read the *DATA card. This was an instruction to execute the translated program, using the cards following the *DATA card as the data.

Although the operating system was designed to automate the operator's job (hence the name), it was also the first step in the development of a new virtual machine. The *FORTRAN card could be viewed as a virtual "compile program" instruction. Similarly, the *DATA card could be regarded as a virtual "execute program" instruction. A level with only two instructions was not much of a level but it was a start in that direction.

In subsequent years, operating systems became more and more sophisticated.

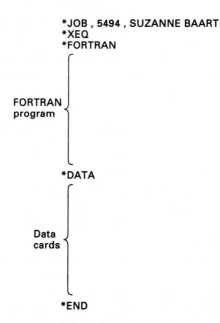

```
*JOB , 5494 , SUZANNE BAART
*XEQ
*FORTRAN


FORTRAN
program



*DATA



Data
cards




*END
```

Fig. 1-3. A sample job for the FMS operating system.

New instructions, facilities, and features were added to the conventional machine level until it began to take on the appearance of a new level. Some of this new level's instructions were identical to the conventional machine level instructions, but others, particularly input/output instructions, were completely different. The new instructions were often known as "operating system macros" or "supervisor calls" and the terms still linger on.

Operating systems developed in other ways as well. The early ones read card decks and printed output on the line printer. This organization was known as a **batch system**. Usually there was a wait of several hours between the time a program was submitted and the time the results were ready. Developing software was difficult under those circumstances.

In the early 1960s researchers at Dartmouth College, MIT, and elsewhere developed operating systems that allowed (multiple) programmers to communicate directly with the computer. In these systems, remote terminals were connected to the central computer via telephone lines. A programmer could type in a program and get the results typed back almost immediately, right in his own office, or in his garage at home, or wherever he kept his terminal. These systems were, and still are, called **time-sharing systems**.

Our interest in operating systems is in those parts that interpret the instructions and features present in level 3 and not present in level 2 rather than in the time-sharing aspects. Although we will not emphasize it, you should keep in mind that operating systems do more than just interpret parts of level 3 programs.

1.4. HARDWARE, SOFTWARE, AND MULTILEVEL MACHINES

Programs written in a computer's machine language (level 1) can be directly executed by the computer's electronic circuits (level 0), without any intervening interpreters or translators. These electronic circuits, along with the memory and input/output devices, form the computer's **hardware**. Hardware consists of tangible objects—integrated circuits, printed circuit boards, cables, power supplies, memories, card readers, line printers, and terminals—rather than abstract ideas, algorithms, or instructions.

Software, in contrast, consists of **algorithms** (detailed instructions telling how to do something) and their computer representations—namely, programs. Programs can be represented on punched cards, magnetic tape, photographic film, and other media but the essence of software is the set of instructions that makes up the programs, not the physical media on which they are recorded.

An intermediate form between hardware and software is **firmware**, which consists of software embedded in electronic devices during their manufacture. Firmware is used when the programs are rarely or never expected to be changed, for example, in toys or appliances. Firmware is also used when the programs must not be lost when the power is off (e.g., when the doll's battery runs down). In many computers, the microprogram is in firmware.

A central theme of this book that will occur over and over again is:

Hardware and software are logically equivalent.

Any operation performed by software can also be built directly into the hardware and any instruction executed by the hardware can also be simulated in software. The decision to put certain functions in hardware and others in software is based on such factors as cost, speed, reliability, and frequency of expected changes. There are no hard and fast rules to the effect that X must go into the hardware and Y must be programmed explicitly. Designers with different goals may, and often do, make different decisions.

On the very first computers, the distinction between hardware and software was clear. The hardware carried out a few simple instructions, such as ADD and JUMP, and everything else was programmed explicitly. If a program needed to multiply two numbers, the programmer had to write his own multiplication procedure or borrow one from the library. As time progressed, it became obvious to hardware designers that certain operations were being performed frequently enough to justify constructing special hardware circuits to execute them directly (to make them faster). The result was a trend toward moving operations downward, to a lower level. What had previously been programmed explicitly at the conventional machine level was later found below it in the hardware.

With the coming of age of microprogramming and multilevel computers, the reverse trend also became apparent. On the earliest computers there was no doubt that the ADD instruction was carried out directly by the hardware. On a microprogrammed computer, the conventional machine level's ADD instruction was interpreted by a microprogram running at the bottom level and was carried out as a series of small steps: fetch the instruction, determine its type, locate the data to be added, fetch the data from memory, perform the addition, and store the result. This was an example of a function that moved upward, from the hardware level to the microprogram. Once again we emphasize: There are no hard and fast rules about what must be in hardware and what must be in software.

When developing a multilevel machine, the designers must decide what to put in each level. This is a generalization of the problem mentioned earlier, of deciding what to put in the hardware and what to put in the software, the hardware merely being the lowest level. It is interesting to note some of the features of some modern computers that are now performed by the hardware or microprogram but that originally were explicitly programmed at the conventional machine level. They include:

1. Instructions for integer multiplication and division.

2. Floating-point arithmetic instructions (see Appendix B).

3. Double-precision arithmetic instructions (arithmetic on numbers with twice as many significant figures as usual).

4. Instructions for calling and returning from procedures.

5. Instructions for speeding up looping.

6. Instructions for counting (adding 1 to a variable).

7. Instructions for handling character strings.

8. Features to speed up computations involving arrays (indexing and indirect addressing).

9. Features to permit programs to be moved in memory after they have started running (relocation facilities).

10. Clocks for timing programs.

11. Interrupt systems that signal the computer as soon as an input or output operation is completed.

12. The ability to suspend one program and start another in a small number of instructions (process switching).

The point of this discussion is to show that the boundary between hardware and software is arbitrary and constantly changing. Today's software is tomorrow's hardware, and vice versa. Furthermore, the boundaries between the various levels are also fluid. From the programmer's point of view, how an instruction is actually implemented is unimportant (except perhaps for its speed). A person programming at the conventional machine level can use its multiply instruction as though it were a hardware instruction without having to worry about it, or even be aware of whether it really is a hardware instruction or not. One person's hardware is another person's software.

The fact that a programmer need not be aware of how the level he is using is implemented leads to the idea of structured machine design. A level is often called a virtual machine because the programmer thinks of it as a real physical machine, even though it does not actually exist. By structuring a machine as a series of levels, programmers working on level n need not be aware of all the messy details of the underlying levels. This structuring enormously simplifies the production of complex (virtual) machines.

1.5. MILESTONES IN COMPUTER ARCHITECTURE

Hundreds of different kinds of computers have been designed and built during the evolution of the modern digital computer. Most have been long forgotten, but a few have had a significant impact on modern ideas. In this section we will give a brief sketch of some of the key historical developments, to get a better understanding of how we got where we are now. Needless to say, this section only touches on the highlights, and leaves many stones unturned. Figure 1-4 lists some of the milestone machines to be discussed in this section. Slater (1987) is a good place to look for additional historical material on the people who founded the computer age.

1.5.1. The Zeroth Generation—Mechanical Computers (1642-1945)

The first person to build a working calculating machine was the French scientist Blaise Pascal (1623-1662), in whose honor the programming language Pascal is named. This device, built in 1642, when Pascal was only 19, was designed to help his father, a tax collector for the French government. It was entirely mechanical, using gears, and powered by a hand operated crank.

Pascal's machine could only do addition and subtraction, but thirty years later the great German mathematician Baron Gottfried Wilhelm von Leibniz (1646-1716) built another mechanical machine that could multiply and divide as well. In effect, Leibniz had built the equivalent of a four-function pocket calculator three centuries ago.

Nothing much happened for 150 years until a professor of mathematics at the University of Cambridge, Charles Babbage (1792-1871), inventor of the speedometer, designed and built his **difference engine**. This mechanical device, which like Pascal's could only add and subtract, was designed to compute tables of numbers useful for naval navigation. The entire construction of the machine was designed to run a single algorithm, the method of finite differences using polynomials. The most interesting feature of the difference engine was its output method: it punched

Year	Name	Made by	Comments
1834	Analytical Eng.	Babbage	First attempt to build a digital computer
1936	Z1	Zuse	First working relay calculating machine
1943	COLOSSUS	British gov't	First electronic computer
1944	Mark I	Aiken	First American general-purpose computer
1946	ENIAC I	Eckert/Mauchley	Modern computer history begins here
1949	EDSAC	Wilkes	First stored-program computer
1951	Whirlwind I	M.I.T.	First real-time computer
1951	UNIVAC I	Eckert/Mauchley	First computer sold commercially
1952	IAS	von Neumann	Most current machines use this design
1960	PDP-1	DEC	First minicomputer (50 sold)
1961	1401	IBM	Enormously popular small business machine
1962	7094	IBM	Dominated scientific computing in early 1960's
1963	B5000	Burroughs	First machine designed for a high-level language
1964	360	IBM	First product line designed as a family
1964	6600	CDC	First machine with extensive internal parallelism
1965	PDP-8	DEC	First mass-market minicomputer (50,000 sold)
1970	PDP-11	DEC	Dominated minicomputers in the 1970's
1974	8080	Intel	First general-purpose CPU on a chip
1974	CRAY-1	Cray	First supercomputer
1978	VAX	DEC	First 32-bit supermini

Fig. 1-4. Some milestones in the development of the modern digital computer.

its results into a copper engraver's plate with a steel die, thus foreshadowing later write-once media such as punched cards and early optical disks.

Although the difference engine worked reasonably well, Babbage quickly got bored with a machine that could only run one algorithm. He began to spend increasingly large amounts of his time and family fortune (not to mention 17,000 pounds of the government's money) on the design and construction of a successor called the **analytical engine**. The analytical engine had four components: the store (memory), the mill (computation unit), the input section (punched card reader) and the output section (punched and printed output). The store consisted of 1000 words of 50 decimal digits used to hold variables and results. The mill could accept operands from the store, add, subtract, multiply or divide them, and return a result to the store. Like the difference engine, it was entirely mechanical.

The great advance of the analytical engine was that it was general purpose. It read instructions from punched cards and carried them out. Some instructions commanded the machine to fetch two numbers from the store, bring them to the mill, be operated on (e.g., added), and have the result sent back to the store. Other instructions could test a number and conditionally branch depending on whether it was positive or negative. By punching a different program on the input cards, it was possible to have the analytical engine perform different computations, something not true of the difference engine.

Since the analytical engine was programmable in a simple assembly language, it needed software. To produce this software, Babbage hired a young woman named Ada Augusta Lovelace, who was the daughter of the famed British poet, Lord Byron. Ada Lovelace was thus the world's first computer programmer. The modern programming language Ada® is named in her honor.

Unfortunately, like many modern designers, Babbage never quite got the hardware debugged. The problem was that he needed thousands upon thousands of cogs and wheels and gears produced to a degree of precision that nineteenth century technology was unable to provide. Nevertheless, his ideas were far ahead of his time, and even today most modern computers have a structure very similar to the analytical engine, so it is fair to say that Babbage was the (grand)father of the modern digital computer.

The next major development occurred in the 1930s, when a German engineering student named Konrad Zuse built a series of automatic calculating machines using electromagnetic relays. Zuse was unaware of Babbage's work, and his machines were destroyed by the Allied bombing of Berlin in 1944, so his work did not have any influence on subsequent machines. Still, he was one of the pioneers of the field.

Slightly later, in the United States, two people also designed calculators, John Atanasoff at Iowa State College and George Stibbitz at Bell Labs. Atanasoff's machine was amazingly advanced for its time. It used binary arithmetic and had capacitors for memory, which were periodically refreshed to keep the charge from leaking out, a process he called "jogging the memory." Modern dynamic RAM chips work exactly the same way. Unfortunately the machine never really became operational. In a way, Atanasoff was like Babbage: a visionary who was ultimately defeated by the inadequate hardware technology of his time.

Stibbitz' computer, although more primitive than Atanasoff's, actually worked. Stibbitz gave a public demonstration at a conference at Dartmouth College in 1940. One of the people in the audience was John Mauchley, an unknown professor of physics at the University of Pennsylvania. The computing world would hear more about Prof. Mauchley later.

While Zuse, Stibbitz, and Atanasoff were designing automatic calculators, a young man named Howard Aiken was grinding out tedious numerical calculations by hand as part of his Ph.D. research at Harvard. After graduating, Aiken recognized the importance of being able to do calculations by machine. He went to the library, discovered Babbage's work, and decided to build out of relays the general-purpose computer that Babbage had failed to build out of toothed wheels.

Aiken's first machine, the Mark I, was completed at Harvard in 1944. It had 72 words of 23 decimal digits each, and had a cycle (i.e., instruction) time of 6 sec. Input and output used punched paper tape. By the time Aiken had completed its successor, the Mark II, relay computers were obsolete. The electronic era had begun.

1.5.2. The First Generation—Vacuum Tubes (1945-1955)

The stimulus for the electronic computer was World War II. During the early part of the war, German submarines were wreaking havoc on British ships. Commands were sent from the German admirals in Berlin to the submarines by radio, which the British could, and did, intercept. The problem was that these messages were encrypted using a device called the **ENIGMA**, whose forerunner, incidentally, was designed by amateur inventor and former U.S. president, Thomas Jefferson.

Early in the war, British intelligence managed to acquire an ENIGMA machine from Polish Intelligence, which had stolen it from the Germans. However, to break a coded message, a huge amount of computation was needed, and it was needed very soon after the message was intercepted to be of any use. To decode these messages, the British government set up a top secret laboratory that built an electronic computer called the COLOSSUS. The famous British mathematician Alan Turing helped design this machine. The COLOSSUS was operational in 1943, but since the British government kept virtually every aspect of the project classified as a military secret for 30 years, the COLOSSUS line was basically a dead end. It is only worth noting because it was the world's first electronic digital computer.

In addition to destroying Zuse's machines and stimulating the construction of the COLOSSUS, the war also affected computing in the United States. The army needed range tables for aiming its heavy artillery and found calculating them by hand to be time consuming and prone to errors.

John Mauchley, who knew of Atanasoff's work as well as Stibbitz', was aware that the army was interested in mechanical calculators. Like many computer scientists after him, he put together a grant proposal asking the army for funding to build an electronic computer. The proposal was accepted in 1943, and Mauchley and his graduate student, J. Presper Eckert, proceeded to build an electronic computer, which they called the **ENIAC (Electronic Numerical Integrator And Computer)**. It consisted of 18,000 vacuum tubes and 1500 relays. The ENIAC weighed 30 tons and consumed 140 kilowatts of power. Architecturally, the machine had twenty registers, each capable of holding a 10-digit decimal number. It was programmed by setting up 6000 multiposition switches and connecting a multitude of sockets with a veritable forest of jumper cables.

The machine was not finished until 1946, when it was too late to be of any use for its original purpose. However, since the war was over, Mauchley and Eckert were allowed to organize a summer school to describe their work to their scientific colleagues. That summer school was the beginning of an explosion of interest in building large digital computers.

After that historic summer school, many other researchers set out to build electronic computers. The first one operational was the EDSAC (1949), built at Cambridge University in the U.K. by Maurice Wilkes. Others included the JOHNIAC at the Rand Corporation, the ILLIAC at the University of Illinois, the MANIAC at Los Alamos Laboratory, and the WEIZAC at the Weizmann Institute in Israel.

Eckert and Mauchley began working on a successor, the **EDVAC** (**Electronic Discrete Variable Automatic Computer**), but that project was fatally wounded when they left Penn to form a startup company, the Eckert-Mauchley Computer Corporation, in Philadelphia (Silicon Valley had not yet been invented). After a series of mergers, this company became the modern Unisys Corporation.

Meanwhile, one of the people involved in the ENIAC project, John von Neumann, went to Princeton's Institute of Advanced Studies to build his own version of the EDVAC, the **IAS machine**. Von Neumann was a genius in the same league as Leonardo Da Vinci. He spoke many languages, was an expert in the physical sciences and mathematics, and had total recall of everything he ever heard, saw, or read. He was able to quote from memory the verbatim text of books he had read years earlier. At the time he became interested in computers, he was already the most eminent mathematician in the world.

One of the things that was apparent to him was that programming computers with huge numbers of switches and cables was slow, tedious, and inflexible. He came to realize that the program could be represented in digital form in the computer's memory, along with the data. He also saw that the clumsy serial decimal arithmetic used by the ENIAC, with each digit represented by 10 vacuum tubes (1 on and 9 off) could be replaced by using parallel binary arithmetic.

His basic design, now known as a **von Neumann machine**, was used in the EDSAC, the first stored program computer, and is still the basis for nearly all digital computers, even now, almost half a century later. This design, and the IAS machine, built in collaboration with Herman Goldstine, has had such an enormous influence, that it is worth describing briefly. A sketch of the architecture is given in Fig. 1-5.

The von Neumann machine had five basic parts: the memory, the arithmetic-logic unit, the program control unit, and the input and output equipment. The memory consisted of 4096 words, a word holding 40 bits (0 or 1). Each word held either two 20-bit instructions or a 39-bit signed integer. The instructions had 8 bits devoted to telling the instruction type, and 12 bits for specifying one of the 4096 memory words.

Inside the arithmetic-logic unit, the forerunner to the modern **CPU** (**Central Processing Unit**) was a special internal 40-bit register called the **accumulator.** A typical instruction added a word of memory to the accumulator or stored the

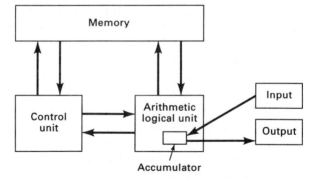

Fig. 1-5. The original von Neumann machine.

accumulator in memory. The machine did not have floating-point arithmetic because von Neumann felt that any competent mathematician ought to be able to keep track of the decimal point (actually the binary point) in his head.

At about the same time von Neumann was building the IAS machine, researchers at M.I.T. were also building a computer. Unlike IAS, ENIAC and other machines of its type, which had long word lengths and which were intended for heavy number crunching, the M.I.T. machine, the Whirlwind I, had a 16-bit word and was designed for real-time control. This project led to the invention of the core memory by Jay Forrester, and then eventually to the first commercial minicomputer.

While all this was going on, IBM was a small company engaged in the business of producing card punches and mechanical card sorting machines. Although IBM had provided some of Aiken's financing, it was not terribly interested in computers until it produced the 701 in 1953, long after Eckert and Mauchley's company was number one in the commercial market with its UNIVAC computer. The 701 had 2K of 36-bit words, with two instructions per word. It was the first in a series of scientific machines that came to dominate the industry within a decade. Three years later came the 704, which had 4K of core memory, 36-bit instructions, and floating-point hardware. In 1958, IBM began production of its last vacuum tube machine, the 709, which was basically a beefed up 704.

1.5.3. The Second Generation—Transistors (1955-1965)

The transistor was invented at Bell Labs in 1948 by John Bardeen, Walter Brattain, and William Shockley, for which they were awarded the 1956 Nobel Prize in physics. Within 10 years the transistor revolutionized computers, and by the late 1950s, vacuum tube computers were obsolete. The first transistorized computer was built at M.I.T.'s Lincoln Laboratory, a 16-bit machine along the lines of the Whirlwind I. It was called the **TX-0** (Transistorized eXperimental computer 0), and was merely intended as a device to test the much fancier TX-2.

The TX-2 never amounted to much, but one of the engineers working at the Laboratory, Kenneth Olsen, formed a company (DEC) in 1957 to manufacture a commercial machine much like the TX-0. It was four years before this machine, the PDP-1, appeared, primarily because the venture capitalists who funded DEC firmly believed that there was no market for computers. Instead, DEC mostly sold small circuit boards.

When the PDP-1 finally appeared in 1961, it had 4K of 18-bit words and a cycle time of 5 microsec. This performance was half that of the IBM 7090, the transistorized successor to the 709, and fastest computer in the world at the time. The PDP-1 cost $120,000; the 7090 cost millions. DEC sold dozens of PDP-1s, and the minicomputer industry was born.

One of the first PDP-1s was given to M.I.T., where it quickly attracted the attention of some of the budding young geniuses so common at M.I.T. One of the PDP-1's many innovations was a visual display (CRT) and the ability to plot points anywhere on its 512 by 512 screen. Before long, the students had programmed the PDP-1 to play spacewar, and the world had its first video game.

A few years later DEC introduced the PDP-8, which was a 12-bit machine, but much cheaper than the PDP-1 ($16,000). The PDP-8 had a major innovation: a single bus, the omnibus, as shown in Fig. 1-6. A **bus** is a collection of parallel wires used to connect the components of a computer. This architecture was a major departure from the memory-centered IAS machine, and has been adopted by nearly all small computers since. DEC eventually sold 50,000 PDP-8s, which established it as the leader in the minicomputer business.

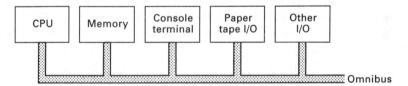

Fig. 1-6. The PDP-8 omnibus.

Meanwhile, IBM's reaction to the transistor was to build a transistorized version of the 709, the 7090, as mentioned above, and later the 7094. The 7094 had a cycle time of 2 microsec and 32K of 36-bit words of core memory. The 7090 and 7094 marked the end of the ENIAC-type machines, but they dominated scientific computing for years in the 1960s.

At the same time IBM had become a major force in scientific computing with the 7094, it was making a huge amount of money selling a little business-oriented machine called the 1401. This machine could read and write magnetic tapes, read and punch cards, and print output almost as fast as the 7094, and at a fraction of the price. It was terrible at scientific computing, but for business record keeping it was perfect.

The 1401 was unusual in that it did not have any registers, or even a fixed word length. Its memory was 4K 8-bit bytes. Each byte contained a 6-bit character, an administrative bit, and a bit used to indicate end-of-word. A MOVE instruction, for example, had a source and a destination address, and began moving bytes from the source to the destination until it hit one with the end-of-word bit on.

In 1964 a new startup company, CDC, introduced the 6600, a machine that was nearly an order of magnitude faster than the mighty 7094. It was love at first sight among the number crunchers, and CDC was launched on its way to success. The secret to its speed, and the reason it was so much faster than the 7094, was that inside the CPU was a highly parallel machine. It had several functional units for doing additions, others for doing multiplication, and still another for division, and all of them could run in parallel. Although getting the most out of it required careful programming, with some work it was possible to have 10 instructions being executed at once.

As if this wasn't enough, the 6600 had a number of little computers inside to help it, sort of like Snow White and the Seven Dwarves. This meant that the CPU could spend all its time crunching numbers, leaving all the details of job management and input/output to the smaller computers. The 6600 was a major milestone in numerical computing.

There were many other computers in this era, but one stands out for quite a different reason and is worth mentioning: the Burroughs B5000. The designers of machines like the PDP-1, 7094, and 6600 were all totally preoccupied with the hardware, either making it cheap (DEC) or fast (IBM and CDC). Software was almost completely irrelevant. The B5000 designers took a different tack. They built a machine specifically with the intention of having it programmed in Algol 60, a forerunner of Pascal, and included many features in the hardware to ease the compiler's task. The idea that software also counted was born. Unfortunately it was forgotten almost immediately.

1.5.4. The Third Generation—Integrated Circuits (1965-1980)

The invention of the integrated circuit allowed dozens of transistors to be put on a single chip. This packaging made it possible to build computers that were smaller, faster, and cheaper than their transistorized predecessors. Some of the more significant computers from this generation are described below.

By 1964 IBM was the leading computer company, and had a big problem with its two highly successful machines, the 7094 and the 1401: they were as incompatible as two machines could be. One was a high-speed number cruncher using parallel binary arithmetic on 36-bit registers, and the other was a glorified input/output processor using serial decimal arithmetic on variable-length words in memory. Many of its corporate customers had both, and did not like the idea of having two separate programming departments with nothing in common.

When the time came to replace these two series, IBM took a radical step. It introduced a single product line, the System/360, based on integrated circuits, that was designed for both scientific and commercial computing. The System/360 contained many innovations, the most important of which was that it was a family of about a half-dozen machines with the same assembly language, and increasing size and power. A customer could replace his 1401 with a 360 Model 30 and his 7094 with a 360 Model 75. The Model 75 was bigger and faster (and more expensive), but software written for one of them could, in principle, run on the other. In practice, software written for a small model would run on a large model without problems, but when moving to a smaller machine, the program might not fit in memory. Still, this was a major improvement over the situation with the 7094 and 1401. The idea of machine families caught on instantly, and within a few years most computer manufacturers had a family of common machines spanning a wide range of price and performance. Some characteristics of the initial 360 family are shown in Fig. 1-7. Other models were introduced later.

Property	Model			
	30	40	50	65
Relative performance	1	3.5	10	21
Cycle time (nsec)	1000	625	500	250
Maximum memory (K)	64	256	256	512
Bytes fetched per cycle	1	2	4	16
Maximum number of data channels	3	3	4	6

Fig. 1-7. The initial offering of the IBM 360 product line.

Another major innovation in the 360 was **multiprogramming**, having several programs in memory at once, so that when one was waiting for input/output to complete, another could compute.

The 360 also was the first machine that could emulate (simulate) other computers. The smaller models could emulate the 1401, and the larger ones could emulate the 7094, so that customers could continue to run their old unmodified binary programs while converting to the 360. Some models ran 1401 programs so much faster than the 1401 itself, that many customers never converted.

The 360 solved the dilemma of binary-parallel versus serial decimal with a compromise: the machine had 16 32-bit registers for binary arithmetic, but its memory was byte-oriented, like that of the 1401, and it had 1401 style serial instructions for moving variable-sized records around memory.

Another major feature of the 360 was a (for that time) huge address space of 2^{24} bytes (16 megabytes). With memory costing several dollars per byte in those days, 16 megabytes looked very much like infinity. Unfortunately, the 360 series was later followed by the 370 series, 4300 series, 3080 series, and 3090 series, all using exactly the same architecture. By the mid 1980s, the 16 megabyte limit became a real problem, and IBM had to partially abandon compatibility when it went to 32-bit addresses needed to address the new 2^{32} byte memory.

With hindsight, it can be argued that since they had 32-bit words and registers anyway, they probably should have had 32-bit addresses as well, but at the time no one could imagine a machine with 16 megabytes. Faulting IBM for this lack of vision is like faulting a modern personal computer vendor for having only 32-bit addresses, because in a few years all personal computers will need more than 4 gigabytes (a gigabyte is 10^9 bytes), at which time the 32-bit addresses will become intolerably small.

The minicomputer world also took a big step forward in the third generation with DEC's introduction of the PDP-11, a 16-bit successor to the PDP-8. In many ways, the PDP-11 was like a little brother to the 360 series just as the PDP-1 was like a little brother to the 7094. Both the 360 and PDP-11 had word-oriented registers and a byte-oriented memory and both came in a range spanning a considerable price/performance ratio. The PDP-11 was enormously successful, especially at universities, and continued DEC's lead over the other minicomputer manufacturers.

1.5.5. The Fourth Generation—Personal Computers and VLSI (1980-199?)

By the 1980s, **VLSI** (**Very Large Scale Integration**) had made it possible to put first tens of thousands, then hundreds of thousands, and finally millions of transistors on a single chip. This development led to smaller and faster computers. Before the PDP-1, computers were so big and expensive that companies and universities had to have special departments called **computer centers** to run them. With the advent of the minicomputer, a department could buy its own computer. By 1980, prices had dropped so low that it was feasible for a single individual to have his own computer. The personal computer era had begun.

Personal computers were used in a very different way than large computers. They were used for word processing, spreadsheets, and numerous highly interactive applications that the larger computers could not handle well.

At present, computers can be divided into roughly five overlapping categories, as shown in Fig. 1-8. These are based on physical size, performance, and application areas. At the low end, we have personal computers, desktop machines using a single chip processor usually dedicated to a single person. They are widely used in offices, in education, and for home use.

Minicomputers are widely used in real time applications, for example, for air traffic control or factory automation. Precisely what constitutes a minicomputer is hard to say, since many companies make a product consisting of a 16- or 32-bit microprocessor, some memory, and some input/output chips, all on a single circuit board. Functionally, such a board is the equivalent of a traditional minicomputer such as the PDP-11.

The supermini is essentially a very large minicomputer, almost always based on a 32-bit processor, and generally equipped with tens of megabytes of memory.

Type	Typical MIPS	Typical megabytes	Example machine	Example use
Personal computer	1	1	IBM PS/2	Word processing
Minicomputer	2	4	PDP-11/84	Real-time control
Supermini	10	32	SUN-4	Network file server
Mainframe	30	128	IBM 3090/300	Banking
Supercomputer	125	1024	Cray-2	Weather forecasting

Fig. 1-8. Five common computer types.

Such machines are used as departmental time-sharing systems, as network file servers, and many other applications. These modern machines are all far more powerful than the IBM 360 Model 75, the most powerful mainframe in the world at the time of its introduction (1964).

Traditional mainframes are the descendants of the IBM 360 and CDC 6600 type machines. The real difference between a mainframe and a supermini is the input/output capacity and the applications for which it is used. A typical supermini might have one or two 1-gigabyte disks. A mainframe might have 100 of them. Superminis are normally used for interactive applications, whereas most mainframes are used for large batch jobs or transaction processing such as banking or airline reservations where huge data bases are required.

At the upper end of the spectrum are the supercomputers. These machines are specially designed to maximize the number of **FLOPS (FLoating point Operations Per Second)**. Anything below 1 gigaflop/sec is not considered to be a supercomputer. Supercomputers have unique, highly parallel architectures in order to achieve these speeds, and are only effective on a small range of problems.

For years, the names supercomputer and Seymour Cray have been almost synonomous. Cray designed the CDC 6600 and its successor, the 7600. Then he formed his own company, Cray Research, to build the Cray-1 and Cray-2. In 1989, Cray left to form yet another company to build the Cray-3.

1.5.6. The Intel Family

In 1968, the Intel Corporation was founded to make memory chips. Shortly thereafter it was approached by a calculator manufacturer that wanted a single chip CPU for its calculator and by a terminal manufacturer that wanted a single chip controller for its terminal. Intel made both of these chips, the 4004, a 4-bit CPU, and the 8008, an 8-bit CPU. These were the world's first single chip CPUs.

Intel did not expect anybody other than the original customers to be interested in them, so they set up a low volume production line. They were wrong. There was a tremendous amount of interest, so they set about designing a general purpose CPU chip that got around the 8008's 16K memory limit (imposed by the number of pins on the chip). This design resulted in the 8080, a small, general-purpose CPU. Much like the PDP-8, this product took the industry by storm, and instantly became a mass market item. Only instead of selling thousands, as DEC had, Intel sold millions.

Two years later, in 1976, Intel came out with the 8085, a repackaged 8080 with some extra input/output features. Then came the 8086, a true 16-bit CPU on a single chip. The 8086 was designed to be somewhat similar to the 8080, but it was not completely compatible with the 8080. The 8086 was followed by the 8088, which had the same architecture as the 8086, and ran the same programs, but had an 8-bit bus instead of a 16-bit bus, making it both slower and cheaper than the 8086. When IBM chose the 8088 as the CPU for the original IBM PC, this chip quickly became the personal computer industry standard.

In subsequent years, Intel came out with the 80186 and 80188, essentially new versions of the 8086 and 8088 respectively, but containing a large amount of input/output circuitry as well. They were never widely used.

Neither the 8088 nor the 8086 could address more than 1 megabyte of memory. By the early 1980s this became more and more of a serious problem, so Intel designed the 80286, an upward compatible version of the 8086. The basic instruction set was essentially the same as that of the 8086 and 8088, but the memory organization was quite different, and rather awkward, due to the requirement of compatibility with the older chips. The 80286 was used in the IBM PC/AT and in the midrange PS/2 models. Like the 8088, it was a huge success.

The next logical step was a true 32-bit CPU on a chip, the 80386. Like the 80286, this one was more-or-less compatible with everything back to the 8008, which was a boon to people for whom running old software was important, but a nuisance to people who would have preferred a simple, clean, modern architecture unencumbered by the mistakes and technology of the past. Like the 80286, this chip is widely used. The 80386SX is a special version of the 80386 designed to fit into an 80286 socket to provide a partial upgrade for existing 80286 machines.

The 80486 is upward compatible with the 80386. All 80386 programs will run on the 80486 without modification. For that reason, almost everywhere in the text where we refer to the 80386, the same holds for the 80486. The primary difference between the 80486 and the 80386 is the presence of a floating-point coprocessor, memory controller, and 8K cache on chip. In addition, the 80486 is typically two to four times faster than the 80386, and is better suited for multiprocessor systems as well.

The evolution in the Intel CPU line reflects the evolution in the computer industry as a whole. In about a decade and a half, we have gone from a 4-bit CPU to a 32-bit CPU with a performance gain of a factor of more than 1000. In another dimension, the 8086 contains 30,000 transistors; the 80486 has over a million of them. The Intel family is shown in Fig. 1-9.

The Intel series of chips forms the heart of all MS-DOS computers, so it is important enough to study in considerable detail. Throughout the book we will use

Name	Year	Register width	Data bus width	Address space	Comments
4004	1971	4	4	1K	First microprocessor on a chip
8008	1972	8	8	16K	First 8-bit microprocessor
8080	1974	8	8	64K	First general-purpose CPU on a chip
8085	1974	8	8	64K	Repackaged 8080
8086	1978	16	16	1M	First 16-bit CPU on a chip
8088	1980	16	8	1M	Processor used in the IBM PC
80186	1982	16	16	1M	8086 + input/output support on a chip
80188	1982	16	16	1M	8088 + input/output support on a chip
80286	1982	16	16	16M	Address space increased to 16 megabytes
80386	1985	32	32	70T	True 32-bit CPU on a chip
80386SX	1988	32	16	70T	80386 with an 80286 bus
80486	1989	32	32	70T	Faster version of the 80386

Fig. 1-9. The Intel CPU family. Note: K = Kilo (2^{10}), M = Mega (2^{20}), G = Giga (2^{30}), and T = Tera (2^{40}).

this CPU family again and again as an example, with our primary emphasis on the 8088, 80286, and 80386, the most important models.

1.5.7. The Motorola Family

Shortly after Intel introduced the 8080, Motorola, a competing semiconductor vendor, brought out the 6800. The 6800 was an 8-bit machine comparable to the 8080. It was well received, and widely used as an embedded controller in industrial equipment in the early 1970s. It was followed by the 6809, which was compatible with the 6800, but added some extra features for facilitating 16-bit arithmetic.

Then in 1979, Motorola did something few companies have done before or since: it introduced a completely new CPU chip that was not compatible with the 6800 or 6809. The idea was that this chip, the 68000, would leapfrog the competition (the 8086) and be attractive to engineers who wanted a clean design, rather than one burdened down with being compatible with obsolete machines.

The 68000 was indeed a radical departure from the past. Although it fetches data from memory 16 bits at time (in other words, the data bus is 16 bits wide), all the registers that the programmer sees are 32 bits wide, and the machine can add and subtract (but not multiply or divide) 32-bit numbers in a single instruction. Thus the 68000 is a hybrid between 16- and 32-bit architectures.

As such, it makes a good litmus test. If you are ever trying to determine if someone is a hardware person or a software person, ask him if the 68000 is a 16- or a 32-bit machine. A hardware engineer will say 16, due to the 16-bit data bus. A programmer will say 32, because the registers are all 32 bits wide. It all depends on one's perspective.

The 68000 was chosen by the designers of the Macintosh, Atari, Amiga and other popular computers due to its clean break with the past and its 32-bit word length. In general, the chip was quite successful, and was the start of a family of chips, like the Intel series. Only, unlike the Intel chips, the members of the **680x0** family, as it is often called, are very similar from the programmer's point of view, with only a few new instructions introduced in each new version. they are members of a family in the sense that when a new machine comes out, it always runs all the existing software.

The second chip in the family was the 68008, which was identical to the 68000 except for the use of an 8-bit data bus for low-end products. Unlike Intel's 8-bit version of the 8086 (the 8088), the 68008 was never widely used.

It did not take long before people wanted to implement sophisticated operating systems like UNIX on the 68000. Many of these systems have virtual memory, a technique for allowing programs to address more memory than the computer actually has. Virtual memory (which we will study later in detail) works by swapping parts of the program from memory to disk automatically as needed. The 68000 could almost support virtual memory, but not quite. There were a small number of features missing from the chip.

Motorola solved this problem by bringing out the 68010 chip, which had the necessary features. Slightly later, it brought out another chip, the 68012, that was the same as the 68010, except that it had more address pins so it could address 2 gigabytes of memory, instead of a mere 16 megabytes.

Both of these chips were effectively killed off a year later when Motorola introduced the 68020, a true 32-bit chip, with a 32-bit bus and 32-bit multiply and divide instructions. The 68020 was a big success, and was the heart of most scientific and engineering workstations, such as those made by Sun Microsystems, Apollo and Hewlett-Packard. The successor to the 68020 was the 68030, which contained not only a complete 68020, but also a complete memory management unit on the same chip.

The 68040, like the 80486, contains a CPU, floating-point coprocessor, memory management unit, and cache on chip. Being about equal in complexity, it is not surprising that the 68040 and 80486 contain about the same number of transistors on chip, 1.2 million for the 68040 and 1.16 million for the 80486. The 68040 runs the same software as the 68030, so our discussion of the 68030 architecture throughout the book also holds for the 68040. The 68040 is roughly comparable to the 80486 in many ways, just as the 68030 is roughly comparable to the 80386. These chips will no doubt continue to compete for years to come. A summary of the Motorola family of chips is given in Fig. 1-10.

Name	Year	Register width	Data bus width	Address space	Comments
68000	1979	32	16	16M	First member of the family
68008	1982	32	8	4M	Low-end chip with 8-bit bus
68010	1983	32	16	16M	Supports virtual memory
68012	1983	32	16	2G	Large-address-space version of 68010
68020	1984	32	32	4G	True 32-bit CPU
68030	1987	32	32	4G	Memory management unit on the CPU chip
68040	1989	32	32	4G	Faster version of the 68030

Fig. 1-10. The Motorola CPU family.

1.6. OUTLINE OF THIS BOOK

This book is about multilevel computers (which includes nearly all modern computers) and how they are organized. We will examine five levels in considerable detail—namely, the digital logic level, the microprogramming level, the conventional machine level, the operating system machine level, and the assembly language level. Some of the basic issues to be examined are:

1. The overall design of the level (and why it was designed that way).

2. The kinds of instructions available.

3. The kinds of data used.

4. The mechanisms available for altering the flow of control.

5. The memory organization and addressing.

6. The relationship between instruction set and memory organization.

7. The method by which the level is implemented.

The study of these topics, and similar ones, is computer organization or computer architecture, as we mentioned earlier.

We are primarily concerned with concepts rather than details or formal mathematics. For that reason, some of the examples given will be highly simplified, to emphasize the central ideas and not the details.

To provide some insight into how the ideas presented in this book can be, and are, applied in practice, we will use the Intel family and the Motorola family as running examples throughout the book. These two have been chosen for several reasons. First, both are widely used and the reader is likely to have access to at least one of them. Second, each one has its own unique architecture, which provides a basis for comparison and encourages a "what are the alternatives?" attitude. Books dealing with only one machine often leave the reader with a "true machine design revealed" feeling, which is absurd in light of the many compromises and arbitrary decisions that designers are forced to make. You are encouraged to study these and all other computers with a critical eye and to try to understand why things are the way they are, as well as how they could have been done differently rather than simply accepting them as given.

It should be made clear from the beginning that this is not a book about how to program the Intel or Motorola chips. These machines will be used for illustrative purposes where appropriate but we make no pretense of being complete. Readers wishing a thorough introduction to one of them should consult the manufacturer's publications.

Chapter 2 is an introduction to the basic components of a computer— processors, memories, and input/output equipment. It is intended to provide an overview of the system architecture.

Chapters 3, 4, 5, 6, and 7 each deal with one specific level shown in Fig. 1-2. Our treatment is bottom-up, because machines have traditionally been designed that way. The design of level k is largely determined by the properties of level $k - 1$, so it is hard to understand any level unless you already have a good grasp of the underlying level that motivated it. Also, it is educationally sound to proceed from the simpler lower levels to the more complex higher levels rather than vice versa.

Chapter 3 is about the digital logic level, the machine's true hardware. It discusses what gates are and how they can be combined into useful circuits. Boolean algebra, a tool for analyzing digital circuits, is also introduced. Computer buses are explained, and the internal workings of a typical PC clone are described at the chip level.

Chapter 4 introduces the concepts of microprogramming and the architecture of the microprogramming level, plus its relation to the conventional machine that it supports. A major part of the chapter consists of a simple example machine worked out in detail. The chapter also contains discussions of the microprogramming level of some real machines.

Chapter 5 discusses the conventional machine level, the one most computer vendors advertise as the machine language. First, we will examine the level in the abstract and then we look at our example machines in detail.

Chapter 6 covers some of the instructions, memory organization, and control mechanisms present at the operating system machine level.

Chapter 7 introduces the assembly language level. Because the assembly language level, unlike the levels below it, is usually implemented by translation instead of interpretation, the emphasis here is on the translation process rather than the details of any specific assembly languages. The related topics of macros (which is itself a particular kind of translation technique) and linking (which is really the last phase of the translation process) are also covered.

Chapter 8 introduces a number of advanced topics. In particular, both the Intel and Motorola families are fairly traditional von Neumann machines. A considerable amount of current research is devoted to looking at alternatives to the von Neumann architecture, and this chapter has been designed to give the flavor of some of this work, and to encourage the reader to investigate it further. Two topics are covered in detail: RISC machines and parallel architectures.

Chapter 9 contains an annotated list of suggested readings, arranged by subject, and an alphabetical list of literature citations. It is the most important chapter in the book. Use it.

The appendices contain brief introductions to finite-precision arithmetic, including binary numbers, and floating-point numbers.

PROBLEMS

1. Explain each of the following terms in your own words:

    a. Translator.
    b. Interpreter.
    c. Virtual machine.

2. What is the difference between interpretation and translation?

3. Is it conceivable for a compiler to generate output for level 1 instead of level 2? Discuss the pros and cons of this proposal.

4. Can you imagine any multilevel computer in which the device level and digital logic levels were not the lowest levels? Explain.

5. Consider a computer with identical interpreters at levels 1, 2, and 3. It takes an interpreter n instructions to fetch, examine, and execute one instruction. A level 1 instruction takes k nanoseconds to execute. How long does it take for an instruction at levels 2, 3, and 4?

6. Consider a multilevel computer in which all the levels are different. Each level has instructions that are m times as powerful as those of the level below it; that is, one level r instruction can do the work of m level $r - 1$ instructions. If a level 1 program requires k seconds to run, how long would equivalent programs take at levels 2, 3 and 4, assuming n level r instructions are required to interpret a single $r + 1$ instruction?

7. Some instructions at the operating system machine level are identical to conventional machine language instructions. These instructions are carried out directly by the microprogram rather than by the operating system. In light of your answer to the preceding problem, why do you think this is the case?

8. In what sense are hardware and software equivalent? Not equivalent?

9. One of the consequences of von Neumann's idea to store the program in memory is that programs can be modified, just like data. Can you think of an example where this facility might have been useful? (Hint: Think about doing arithmetic on arrays.)

10. The performance ratio of the 360 model 75 is 50 times that of the 360 model 30, yet the cycle time is only five times as fast. How do you account for this discrepancy?

11. Two basic system designs are shown in Fig. 1-5 and Fig. 1-6. Describe how input/output might occur in each system. Which one has the potential for better overall system performance?

2

COMPUTER SYSTEMS ORGANIZATION

A digital computer consists of an interconnected system of processors, memories, and input/output devices. This chapter is an introduction to these three components and to their interconnection, as background for the detailed examination of specific levels in the five succeeding chapters. Processors, memories, and input/output are key concepts and will be present at every level, so we will start our study of computer architecture by looking at all three in turn.

2.1. PROCESSORS

The organization of a simple bus-oriented computer is shown in Fig. 2-1. The **CPU (central processing unit)** is the "brain" of the computer. Its function is to execute programs stored in the main memory by fetching their instructions, examining them, and then executing them one after another. The CPU is composed of several distinct parts. The control unit is responsible for fetching instructions from main memory and determining their type. The arithmetic and logical unit performs operations such as addition and Boolean AND needed to carry out the instructions.

The CPU also contains a small, high-speed memory used to store temporary results and certain control information. This memory consists of a number of **registers**, each of which has a certain function. The most important register is the **program counter** (PC), which points to the next instruction to be executed. The

Central processing unit (CPU)

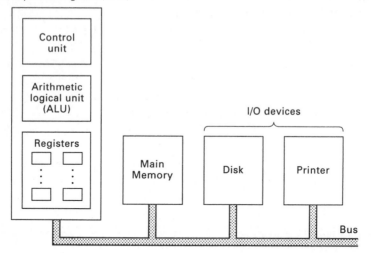

Fig. 2-1. The organization of a simple computer with one CPU and two I/O devices.

name "program counter" is somewhat misleading because it has nothing to do with *counting* anything, but the term is universally used. Also important is the **instruction register** (IR), which holds the instruction currently being executed. Most computers have other registers as well, some of them available to the level 2 and 3 programmers for storing intermediate results.

2.1.1. Instruction Execution

The CPU executes each instruction in a series of small steps:

1. Fetch the next instruction from memory into the instruction register.
2. Change the program counter to point to the following instruction.
3. Determine the type of instruction just fetched.
4. If the instruction uses data in memory, determine where they are.
5. Fetch the data, if any, into internal CPU registers.
6. Execute the instruction.
7. Store the results in the proper place.
8. Go to step 1 to begin executing the following instruction.

This sequence of steps is frequently referred to as the **fetch-decode-execute** cycle. It is central to the operation of all computers.

This description of how a CPU works closely resembles a program written in English. Figure 2-2 shows this informal program rewritten as a Pascal procedure. The very fact that it is possible to write a program that can imitate the function of a CPU shows that a program need not be executed by a "hardware" CPU consisting of a box full of electronics. Instead, a program can be carried out by having another program fetch, examine, and execute its instructions. A program (such as Fig. 2-2) that fetches, examines, and executes the instructions of another program is called an interpreter, as mentioned in Chap. 1.

This equivalence between hardware processors and interpreters has important implications for computer organization. After having specified the machine language, L, for a new computer, the design group can decide whether they want to build a hardware processor to execute programs in L directly or whether they want to write an interpreter instead. If they choose to write an interpreter, they must also provide some machine to run the interpreter.

Because an interpreter breaks the instructions of its target machine into small steps, the machine on which the interpreter runs can often be much simpler than a hardware processor for the target machine would be. For economic as well as other reasons, programs at the conventional machine level of most modern computers are carried out by an interpreter running on a totally different and much more primitive level 1 machine that we have called the microprogramming level.

The collection of all instructions available to the programmer at a level is called the **instruction set** of that level. The number of instructions in the instruction set varies from machine to machine and from level to level. For the conventional machine level, for example, the size of the instruction set is typically in the range 20 to 300. A large instruction set is not necessarily better than a small one. In fact, the opposite tends to be true. A large instruction set often means that the instructions are not very general. Compilers for high-level languages, such as Ada, Modula 2, and Pascal, generally perform better on machines with small, well-chosen instruction sets than on machines with large, unwieldy ones. Machines with very small instruction sets, called **RISC** machines, will be discussed in Chap. 8. These machines do not use microprogramming and are extremely fast.

Be sure you realize that the instruction set and organization of the microprogramming level is, in fact, the instruction set and organization of the hardware (CPU). The instruction set and organization of the conventional machine level, in contrast, is determined by the microprogram, and not by the hardware.

2.1.2. CPU Organization

The internal organization of part of a classical von Neumann CPU is shown in Fig. 2-3 in more detail. This part is called the **data path** and consists of the registers (typically 1 to 16) and the **ALU (Arithmetic Logical Unit)**. The registers feed

```
type word = ... ;
     address = ... ;
     mem = array[0 .. 4095] of word ;
procedure interpreter (memory : mem ; ac : word ; StartingAddress : address );
```

(This procedure interprets programs for a simple machine with 1
instruction per word . The memory consists of a sequence of words
numbered 0, 1, ..., 4095. The machine has a processor register
called the *ac*, used for arithmetic . The ADD instruction adds a
word to the *ac*, for example . The interpreter keeps running until
the run bit is turned off by a HALT instruction . The state of a
process running on this machine consists of memory, the program
counter, the run bit, and the *ac*. The initial state is passed
in via the parameters .)

```
var ProgramCounter, DataLocation : address ;
    InstrRegister, data : word ;
    DataNeeded : boolean ;
    InstrType : integer ;
    RunBit : 0..1;

begin
    ProgramCounter := StartingAddress ;
    RunBit := 1;
    while RunBit = 1 do
        begin
            {Fetch next instruction into the instruction register}
            InstrRegister := memory [ProgramCounter ];

            {Advance the program counter to point to the next instruction}
            ProgramCounter := ProgramCounter + 1;

            {Decode the instruction and record its type}
            DetermineInstrType (InstrRegister, InstrType );

            {Locate data used by instruction.}
            FindData (InstrType, InstrRegister, DataLocation, DataNeeded );

            {Fetch data from memory if need be}
            if DataNeeded then data := memory [DataLocation ];

            {Advance the process by executing the instruction}
            execute (InstrType, data, memory, ac, ProgramCounter, RunBit )
        end
end;
```

Fig. 2-2. An interpreter for a simple computer.

into two ALU input registers, labeled *A* and *B* in the figure. These registers hold the ALU input while the ALU is computing.

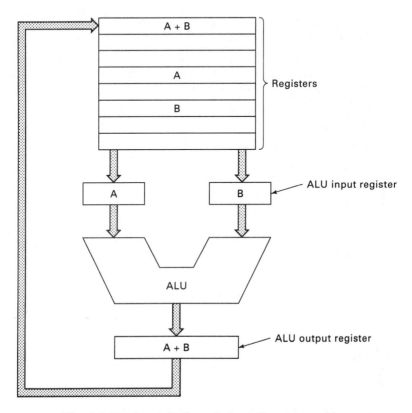

Fig. 2-3. The data path of a typical von Neumann machine.

The ALU itself performs addition, subtraction, and other simple operations on its inputs, yielding a result in the output register. This output register can be stored back into a register, and from there, back into memory, if desired. In the example, addition is illustrated.

Instructions can be divided into three categories: register-memory, register-register, and memory-memory. Register-memory instructions allow memory words to be fetched into registers, where they can be used as ALU inputs in subsequent instructions, for example. A typical register-register instruction fetches two operands from the registers, brings them to the ALU input registers, performs some operation on them, and stores the result back in a register. A memory-memory instruction fetches its operands from memory into the ALU input registers, performs its operation, and then writes the result back into memory. The operation of the data path is the heart of most CPUs. To a considerable extent, it defines what the machine can do. We will come back to this important topic in Chap. 4.

2.1.3. Parallel Instruction Execution

From the earliest days of computing, designers have been trying to make machines go faster. To some extent, machines can be accelerated by just speeding up the hardware. However, various physical limits are beginning to loom on the horizon. For one thing, the laws of physics say that nothing can travel faster than the speed of light, which is about 30 cm per nanosecond in vacuum and 20 cm per nanosecond in copper wire. This means that to build a computer with a 1 nsec instruction time, the total distance that the electrical signals can travel, within the CPU, to memory, and back, cannot be more than 20 cm. Therefore very fast computers have to be very small.

Unfortunately, fast computers produce more heat than slow ones, and fitting the computer into a small volume makes dissipating this heat difficult. Supercomputers are sometimes submersed in liquid freon, a coolant, in order to transfer the heat out as quickly as possible. All in all, making computers go faster and faster is getting harder and harder, and very expensive as well.

However, another approach is possible. Instead of a single high-speed CPU, it is possible to build a machine with many slower (and cheaper) ALUs or even complete CPUs to gain the same computing power at a lower cost. Much research has been devoted to building such parallel machines. In this section we will provide a brief introduction to some of the techniques used.

Parallel machines can be divided into three categories (Flynn, 1972) based on how many instruction and data streams they have:

1. SISD: Single Instruction stream, Single Data stream.

2. SIMD: Single Instruction stream, Multiple Data stream.

3. MIMD: Multiple Instruction stream, Multiple Data stream.

The traditional von Neumann machine is SISD. It has one instruction stream (i.e., one program), executed by one CPU, and one memory containing its data. The first instruction is fetched from memory and then executed. Then the second instruction is fetched and executed.

Nevertheless, even within this sequential model, a limited amount of parallelism is possible by fetching and starting the next instruction before the current one is finished. The CDC 6600 and some of its successors, for example, have multiple functional units (specialized ALUs), each of which can perform a single operation at high speed, as illustrated in Fig. 2-4. In this example, we have five functional units, two each for the common operations of addition and multiplication, and one each for subtraction and division.

The idea behind this design is that the control unit fetches an instruction and then hands it to one of the functional units for execution. Meanwhile, the control unit fetches the next instruction and hands it off to a different functional unit. This

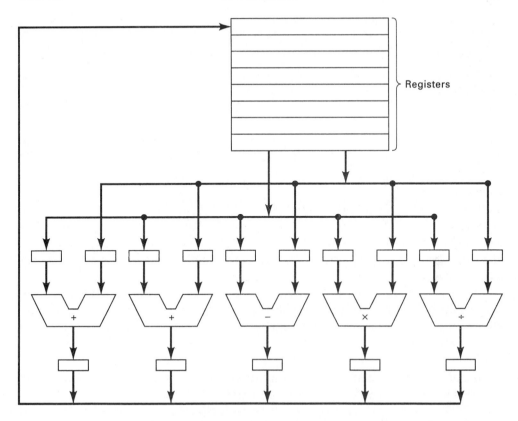

Fig. 2-4. A CPU with five functional units that can run in parallel.

process continues until it can go no further, either because all the functional units of the type needed are busy, or because a needed operand is still being computed.

This general strategy obviously implies that the time to perform an operation is much longer than the time to fetch an instruction, so it is commonly used for floating-point operations, which are complex and slow, rather than integer operations, which are simple and fast.

A variant on this idea is to split the execution of each instruction up into parts, like a car being built on an assembly line. In Fig. 2-5(a) we see a CPU consisting of five processing units, $P1$ through $P5$. During the first time interval, the first instruction is fetched from memory by $P1$, as shown in Fig. 2-5(b). During the second time interval, the first instruction is passed along to $P2$ for analysis, while $P1$ fetches the next instruction. In each subsequent interval, a new instruction is fetched by $P1$ and the other instructions are passed along to the next unit along the path.

The organization of Fig. 2-5(a) is called a **pipeline machine**. If each step (time interval) is n nsec, it takes $5n$ nsec to execute an instruction. Nevertheless, a completed instruction rolls out of $P5$ every n nsec, for a speedup of a factor of five.

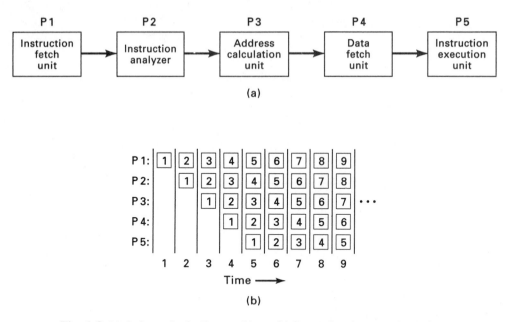

Fig. 2-5. (a) A five-unit pipeline machine. (b) State of each processing unit as a function of time.

Note that although it employs some internal parallelism, a pipeline machine is still an SISD machine, because there is one program and one set of data.

SIMD machines, in contrast, operate on multiple data sets in parallel. A typical application for an SIMD machine is weather forecasting. Imagine computing the daily temperature average for many sites from the 24 hourly averages. For each site, exactly the same computation must be done, but with different data.

One architecture well-suited for this task is the **vector machine**, shown in Fig. 2-6(a). The data path here is similar to that of Fig. 2-3, except that instead of having a single variable for each ALU input, we have a vector with n inputs. Similarly, the ALU is really a vector ALU, capable of performing an operation, such as vector addition [shown in Fig. 2-6(b)], on two input vectors and delivering an output vector as result. Some supercomputers have an architecture similar to this.

An alternative approach to SIMD is the **array processor**, a design pioneered by the University of Illinois ILLIAC IV computer and illustrated in Fig. 2-7 (Hord, 1982). This architecture consists of a square grid of processor/memory elements. A single control unit broadcasts instructions, which are carried out in lockstep by all the processors, each one using its own data from its own memory (loaded during the initialization phase). The array processor is especially well-suited to calculations on matrices.

Flynn's third category is MIMD, in which different CPUs carry out different programs, sometimes sharing some common memory. For example, in an airline reservations system, multiple simultaneous reservations do not proceed in parallel,

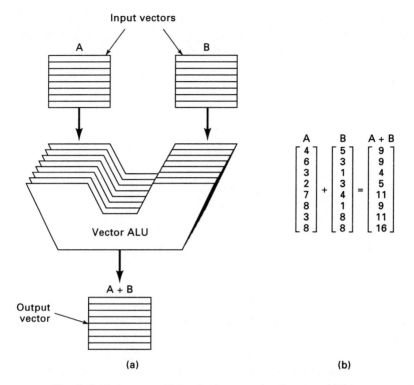

$$
\begin{array}{ccc}
A & B & A+B \\
\begin{bmatrix} 4 \\ 6 \\ 3 \\ 2 \\ 7 \\ 8 \\ 3 \\ 8 \end{bmatrix} + & \begin{bmatrix} 5 \\ 3 \\ 1 \\ 3 \\ 4 \\ 1 \\ 8 \\ 8 \end{bmatrix} = & \begin{bmatrix} 9 \\ 9 \\ 4 \\ 5 \\ 11 \\ 9 \\ 11 \\ 16 \end{bmatrix}
\end{array}
$$

(a) (b)

Fig. 2-6. (a) A vector ALU. (b) An example of vector addition.

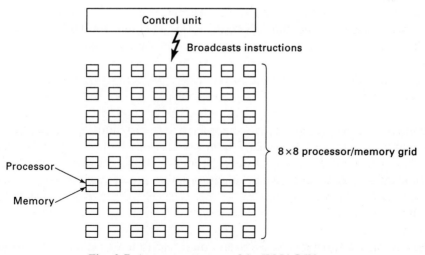

Fig. 2-7. An array processor of the ILLIAC IV type.

instruction by instruction, so we have multiple instruction streams and multiple data streams. Figure 2-8(a) shows a **multiprocessor**, an MIMD machine using shared memory. Each processor has access to the shared memory via the bus.

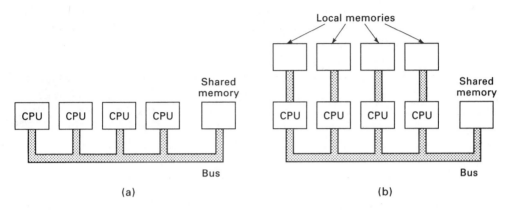

Fig. 2-8. (a) A basic multiprocessor. (b) A multiprocessor with local memories.

It does not take much imagination to realize that with a large number of fast processors constantly trying to access memory over the same bus, conflicts will result. Multiprocessor designers have come up with various schemes to reduce this contention and improve performance. One design, shown in Fig. 2-8(b), gives each processor some local memory of its own, not accessible to the others. This memory can be used for program code and those data items that need not be shared. Access to this private memory does not use the main bus, greatly reducing bus traffic.

Other multiprocessors use not one bus, but multiple buses to reduce the load. Still others use **caching**, a technique for keeping frequently used memory words within each processor. Caching will be discussed in detail in Chap. 4. A survey of multiprocessor architectures is given in (Gajski and Pier, 1985).

2.2. MEMORY

The **memory** is that part of the computer where programs and data are stored. Some computer scientists (especially British ones) use the term **store** or **storage** rather than memory. Without a memory from which the processors can read and write information, there would be no stored-program digital computers.

2.2.1. Bits

The basic unit of memory is the binary digit, called a **bit**. A bit may contain a 0 or a 1. It is the simplest possible unit. (A device capable of storing only zeros could hardly form the basis of a memory system. At least two values are needed.)

People often say that computers use binary arithmetic because it is "efficient." What they mean (although they rarely realize it) is that digital information can be stored by distinguishing between different values of some continuous physical quantity, such as voltage or current. The more values that must be distinguished, the less separation between adjacent values, and the less reliable the memory. The binary number system requires only two values to be distinguished. Consequently, it is the most reliable method for encoding digital information. If you are unfamiliar with binary numbers, see Appendix A.

Some computers, such as the large IBM mainframes, are advertised as having decimal as well as binary arithmetic. This trick is accomplished by using 4 bits to store one decimal digit. Four bits provide 16 combinations, used for the 10 digits 0 through 9, with six combinations not used. The number 1944 is shown below encoded in decimal and in pure binary, using 16 bits in each example:

decimal: 0001 1001 0100 0100   binary: 0000011110011000

Sixteen bits in the decimal format can store the numbers from 0 to 9999, giving only 10,000 combinations, whereas a 16-bit pure binary number can store 65,536 different combinations. For this reason, people say that binary is more efficient.

However, consider what would happen if some brilliant young electrical engineer invented a highly reliable electronic device that could directly store the digits 0 to 9 by dividing the region from 0 to 10 volts into 10 intervals. Four of these devices could store any decimal number from 0 to 9999. Four such devices would provide 10,000 combinations. They could also be used to store binary numbers, by only using 0 and 1, in which case, four of them could only store 16 combinations. With such devices, the decimal system is obviously more efficient.

2.2.2. Memory Addresses

Memories consist of a number of **cells** (or **locations**) each of which can store a piece of information. Each cell has a number, called its **address**, by which programs can refer to it. If a memory has n cells, they will have addresses 0 to $n - 1$. All cells in a memory contain the same number of bits. If a cell consists of k bits, it can hold any one of 2^k different bit combinations. Figure 2-9 shows three different organizations for a 96-bit memory. Note that adjacent cells have consecutive addresses (by definition).

Computers that use the binary number system (including octal and hexadecimal notation for binary numbers) also express memory addresses as binary numbers. If an address has m bits, the maximum number of cells directly addressable is 2^m. For example, an address used to reference the memory of Fig. 2-9(a) would need at least 4 bits in order to express all the numbers from 0 to 11. A 3-bit address would be sufficient for Fig. 2-9(b) and (c), however. The number of bits in the address is related to the maximum number of directly addressable cells in the memory and is

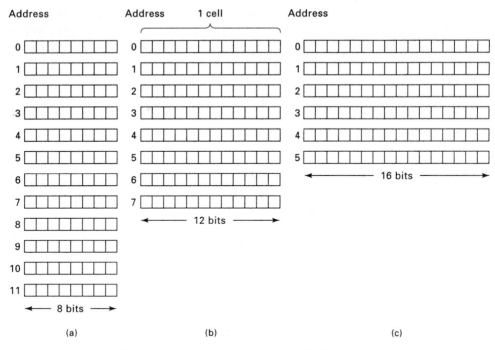

Fig. 2-9. Three ways of organizing a 96-bit memory.

independent of the number of bits per cell. A memory with 2^{12} cells of 8 bits each and a memory with 2^{12} cells of 60 bits each would each need 12-bit addresses.

The number of bits per cell for some computers that have been sold commercially follows.

Burroughs B1700:   1 bit per cell
IBM PC: 8 bits per cell
DEC PDP-8:   12 bits per cell
IBM 1130:   16 bits per cell
DEC PDP-15:   18 bits per cell
XDS 940:   24 bits per cell
Electrologica X8:   27 bits per cell
XDS Sigma 9:   32 bits per cell
Honeywell 6180:   36 bits per cell
CDC 3600:   48 bits per cell
CDC Cyber: 60 bits per cell

The significance of the cell is that it is the smallest addressable unit. In recent years, most computer manufacturers have standardized on an 8-bit cell, which is called a **byte**. Bytes are grouped into **words**. A computer with a 16-bit word has 2 bytes/word, whereas a computer with a 32-bit word has 4 bytes/word. The significance of a word is that most instructions operate on entire words, for example, adding two words together. Thus a 16-bit machine will have 16-bit registers and instructions for manipulating 16-bit words, whereas a 32-bit machine will have 32-bit registers and instructions for moving, adding, subtracting, and otherwise manipulating 32-bit words.

2.2.3. Byte Ordering

The bytes in a word can be numbered from left-to-right or right-to-left. At first it might seem that this choice is unimportant, but as we shall see shortly, it has major implications. Figure 2-10(a) depicts part of the memory of a 32-bit computer whose bytes are numbered from left-to-right, such as the Motorola family. Figure 2-10(b) gives the analogous representation of a 32-bit computer using right-to-left numbering, such as the Intel family. The former system, where the numbering begins at the "big" (i.e., high-order) end is called a **big endian** computer, in contrast to the **little endian** of Fig. 2-10(b). These terms are due to Jonathan Swift, whose *Gulliver's Travels* satirized politicians who made war over their dispute about whether eggs should be broken at the big end or the little end. The term was first used in computer architecture in a delightful article by Cohen (1981).

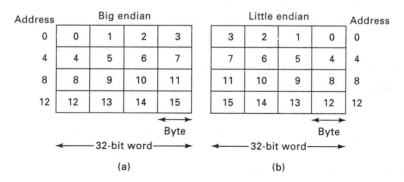

Fig. 2-10. (a) Big endian memory. (b) Little endian memory.

It is important to understand that in both the big endian and little endian systems, a 32-bit integer with the numerical value of, say, 6, is represented by the bits 110 in the rightmost (low-order) 3 bits of a word and zeros in the leftmost 29 bits. In the big endian scheme, these bits are in byte 3 (or 7, or 11, etc.), whereas in the little endian scheme they are in byte 0 (or 4, or 8, etc.). In both cases, the word containing this integer has address 0.

If computers only stored integers, there would not be any problem. However, many applications require a mixture of integers, character strings, and other data types. Consider, for example, a simple personnel record consisting of a string (employee name), and two integers (age and department number). The string is terminated with 1 or more 0 bytes to fill out a word. The big endian representation is shown in Fig. 2-11(a) and the little endian representation is shown in Fig. 2-11(b) for Jim Smith, age 21, department 260 ($1 \times 256 + 4 = 260$).

	Big endian			
0	J	I	M	
4	S	M	I	T
8	H	0	0	0
12	0	0	0	21
16	0	0	1	4

(a)

Little endian				
	M	I	J	0
T	I	M	S	4
0	0	0	H	8
0	0	0	21	12
0	0	1	4	16

(b)

Transfer from big endian to little endian			
	M	I	J
T	I	M	S
0	0	0	H
21	0	0	0
4	1	0	0

(c)

Transfer and swap				
J	I	M		0
S	M	I	T	4
H	0	0	0	8
0	0	0	21	12
0	0	1	4	16

(d)

Fig. 2-11. (a) A personnel record for a big endian machine. (b) The same record for a little endian machine. (c) The result of transferring the record from a big endian to a little endian. (d) The result of byte-swapping (c).

Both of these representations are fine and internally consistent. The problems begin when one of the machines tries to send the record to the other one over a network. Let us assume that the big endian sends the record to the little endian one byte at a time, starting with byte 0 and ending with byte 19. (We will be optimistic and assume the bits of the bytes are not reversed by the transmission, as we have enough problems as is.) Thus the big endian's byte 0 goes into the little endian's memory at byte 0, and so on, as shown in Fig. 2-11(c).

When the little endian tries to print the name, it works fine, but the age comes out as 21×2^{24} and the department is just as garbled. This situation arises because the transmission has reversed the order of the characters in a word, as it should, but it has also reversed the bytes in an integer, which it should not.

An obvious solution is to have the software reverse the bytes within a word after the copy has been made. Doing this leads to Fig. 2-11(d) which makes the two integers fine but turns the string into " MIJTIMS" with the "H" hanging in the middle of nowhere. This reversal of the string occurs because when reading it, the computer first reads byte 0 (a space), then byte 1 (M), and so on.

There is no simple solution. One way that works, but is inefficient, is to include a header in front of each record telling what kind of data follows (string, integer, or other) and how long it is. This allows the receiver to perform the necessary conversions only. In any event, it should be clear that the lack of a standard for byte ordering is a major nuisance when exchanging data between different machines.

2.2.4. Error-Correcting Codes

Computer memories can make errors occasionally due to voltage spikes on the power line or other causes. To guard against such errors, most memories use error-detecting or error-correcting codes. When these codes are used, extra bits are added to each memory word in a special way. When a word is read out of memory, the extra bits are checked to see if an error has occurred.

To understand how errors can be handled, it is necessary to look closely at what an error really is. Suppose that a memory word consists of m data bits to which we will add r redundant, or check bits. Let the total length be n (i.e., $n = m + r$). An n-bit unit containing m data and r check bits is often referred to as an n-bit **codeword**.

Given any two codewords, say, 10001001 and 10110001, it is possible to determine how many corresponding bits differ. In this case, 3 bits differ. To determine how many bits differ, just compute the bitwise Boolean EXCLUSIVE OR of the two codewords, and count the number of 1 bits in the result. The number of bit positions in which two codewords differ is called the **Hamming distance** (Hamming, 1950). Its significance is that if two codewords are a Hamming distance d apart, it will require d single-bit errors to convert one into the other. For example, the codewords 11110001 and 00110000 are a Hamming distance 3 apart because it takes 3 single-bit errors to convert one into the other.

With an m-bit memory word, all 2^m bit patterns are legal, but due to the way the check bits are computed, only 2^m of the 2^n codewords are valid. If a memory read turns up an invalid codeword, the computer knows that a memory error has occurred. Given the algorithm for computing the check bits, it is possible to construct a complete list of the legal codewords, and from this list find the two codewords whose Hamming distance is minimum. This distance is the Hamming distance of the complete code.

The error-detecting and error-correcting properties of a code depend on its Hamming distance. To detect d single-bit errors, you need a distance $d + 1$ code because with such a code there is no way that d single-bit errors can change a valid codeword into another valid codeword. Similarly, to correct d single-bit errors, you need a distance $2d + 1$ code because that way the legal codewords are so far apart that even with d changes, the original codeword is still closer than any other codeword, so it can be uniquely determined.

As a simple example of an error-detecting code, consider a code in which a single **parity bit** is appended to the data. The parity bit is chosen so that the number of 1 bits in the codeword is even (or odd). Such a code has a distance 2, since any single-bit error produces a codeword with the wrong parity. It can be used to detect single errors. Whenever a word containing the wrong parity is read from memory, an error condition is signaled and special action is taken. The program cannot continue, but at least no incorrect results are computed.

As a simple example of an error-correcting code, consider a code with only four valid codewords:

0000000000, 0000011111, 1111100000, and 1111111111

This code has a distance 5, which means that it can correct double errors. If the codeword 0000000111 arrives, the receiver knows that the original must have been 0000011111 (if there was no more than a double error). If, however, a triple error changes 0000000000 into 0000000111, the error will not be corrected properly.

Imagine that we want to design a code with m data bits and r check bits that will allow all single-bit errors to be corrected. Each of the 2^m legal memory words has n illegal codewords at a distance 1 from it. These are formed by systematically inverting each of the n bits in the n-bit codeword formed from it. Thus each of the 2^m legal memory words requires $n + 1$ bit patterns dedicated to it. Since the total number of bit patterns is 2^n we must have $(n + 1)2^m \le 2^n$. Using $n = m + r$ this requirement becomes $(m + r + 1) \le 2^r$. Given m, this puts a lower limit on the number of check bits needed to correct single errors. Figure 2-12 shows the number of check bits required for various memory word sizes.

Word size	Check bits	Total size	Percent overhead
8	4	12	50
16	5	21	31
32	6	38	19
64	7	71	11
128	8	136	6
256	9	265	4
512	10	522	2

Fig. 2-12. Number of check bits needed for single-error correcting code.

This theoretical lower limit can, in fact, be achieved using a method due to Richard Hamming (1950). Before giving Hamming's algorithm, let us look at a simple graphical representation that clearly illustrates the idea of an error-correcting code for 4-bit memory words. The Venn diagram of Fig. 2-13(a) contains three circles, A, B, and C, which together form seven regions. As an example, let us encode the 4-bit memory word 1100 in the regions AB, ABC, AC, and BC, one bit per region (in alphabetical order). This encoding is shown in Fig. 2-13(a).

Next we add a parity bit to each of the three empty regions to produce even parity, as illustrated in Fig. 2-13(b). By definition, the sum of the bits in each of the three circles, A, B, and C is now an even number. In circle A, we have the four numbers 0, 0, 1, and 1, which add up to 2, an even number. In circle B, the numbers are 1, 1, 0, and 0, which also add up to 2, an even number. Finally, in circle C, we have the same thing. In this example all the circles happen to be the same, but sums of 0 and 4 are also possible in other examples. This figure corresponds to a codeword with 4 data bits and 3 parity bits.

Now suppose that the bit in the AC region goes bad, changing from a 0 to a 1, as shown in Fig. 2-13(c). The computer can now see that circles A and C have the

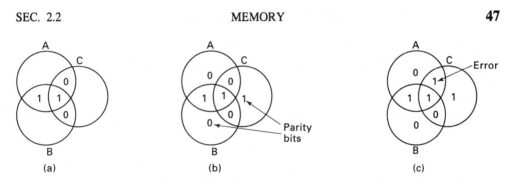

Fig. 2-13. (a) Encoding of 1100. (b) Even parity added. (c) Error in *AC*.

wrong (odd) parity. The only single-bit change that corrects them is to restore *AC* back to 0, thus correcting the error. In this way, the computer can repair single-bit memory errors automatically.

Now let us see how Hamming's algorithm can be used to construct error-correcting codes for any size memory word. In a Hamming code, *r* parity bits are added to an *m*-bit word, forming a new word of length *m* + *r* bits. The bits are numbered starting at 1, not 0, with bit 1 the leftmost (high-order) bit. All bits whose bit number is a power of 2 are parity bits; the rest are used for data. For example, with a 16-bit word, 5 parity bits are added. Bits 1, 2, 4, 8, and 16 are parity bits, and all the rest are data bits. In all, the memory word has 21 bits (16 data, 5 parity). We will (arbitrarily) use even parity in this example.

Each parity bit checks specific bit positions; the parity bit is set so that the total number of 1s in the checked positions is even. The bit positions checked by the parity bits are:

Bit 1 checks bits 1, 3, 5, 7, 9, 11, 13, 15, 17, 19, 21.

Bit 2 checks bits 2, 3, 6, 7, 10, 11, 14, 15, 18, 19.

Bit 4 checks bits 4, 5, 6, 7, 12, 13, 14, 15, 20, 21.

Bit 8 checks bits 8, 9, 10, 11, 12, 13, 14, 15.

Bit 16 checks bits 16, 17, 18, 19, 20, 21.

In general, bit *b* is checked by those bits $b_1, b_2, \cdots, b_j$ such that $b_1 + b_2 + \cdots + b_j = b$. For example, bit 5 is checked by bits 1 and 4 because 1 + 4 = 5. Bit 6 is checked by bits 2 and 4 because 2 + 4 = 6, and so on.

Figure 2-14 shows construction of a Hamming code for the 16-bit memory word 1111000010101110. The 21-bit codeword is 001011100000101101110. To see how error correction works, consider what would happen if bit 5 were inverted by a surge on the power line. The new codeword would be 001001100000101101110 instead of 001011100000101101110. The 5 parity bits will be checked, with the following results:

Parity bit 1 incorrect (1, 3, 5, 7, 9, 11, 13, 15, 17, 19, 21 contain five 1s).

Parity bit 2 correct (2, 3, 6, 7, 10, 11, 14, 15, 18, 19 contain six 1s).

Parity bit 4 incorrect (4, 5, 6, 7, 12, 13, 14, 15, 20, 21 contain five 1s).

Parity bit 8 correct (8, 9, 10, 11, 12, 13, 14, 15 contain two 1s).

Parity bit 16 correct (16, 17, 18, 19, 20, 21 contain four 1s).

The total number of 1s in bits 1, 3, 5, 7, 9, 11, 13, 15, 17, 19, and 21 should be an even number because even parity is being used. The incorrect bit must be one of the bits checked by parity bit 1—namely, bit 1, 3, 5, 7, 9, 11, 13, 15, 17, 19, or 21. Parity bit 4 is incorrect, meaning that one of bits 4, 5, 6, 7, 12, 13, 14, 15, 20, or 21 is incorrect. The error must be one of the bits in both lists, namely, 5, 7, 13, 15, or 21. However, bit 2 is correct, eliminating 7 and 15. Similarly, bit 8 is correct, eliminating 13. Finally, bit 16 is correct, eliminating 21. The only bit left is bit 5, which is the one in error. Since it was read as a 1, it should be a 0. In this manner, errors can be corrected.

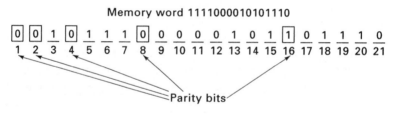

Fig. 2-14. Construction of the Hamming code for the memory word 1111000010101110 by adding 5 check bits to the 16 data bits.

A simple method for finding the incorrect bit is first to compute all the parity bits. If all are correct, there was no error (or more than one). Then add up all the incorrect parity bits, counting 1 for bit 1, 2 for bit 2, 4 for bit 4, and so on. The resulting sum is the position of the incorrect bit. For example, if parity bits 1 and 4 are incorrect but 2, 8, and 16 are correct, bit 5 (1 + 4) has been inverted.

2.2.5. Secondary Memory

Because every word in main memory must be directly accessible in a very short time, main memory is relatively expensive. Consequently, most computers have slower, cheaper, and usually much larger secondary memories as well. Secondary memories are used to hold sets of data far larger than main memory can hold.

Magnetic Tapes

Historically, **magnetic tape** was the first kind of secondary memory. A computer tape drive is analogous to a home tape recorder: a 2400-ft-long tape is wound from the feed reel past a recording head to the take-up reel. By varying the current in the recording head, the computer can write information on the tape in the form of little magnetized spots.

Figure 2-15 shows how information is organized on a magnetic tape. On a computer with 8-bit bytes, each frame contains 1 byte, plus an extra, redundant bit, called a parity bit, to improve reliability. Typical recording density is 1600 frames (bytes) per inch (denoted as 1600 bpi), which means that a frame takes up less than 1/1000 of an inch. Other common densities are 800 bpi and 6250 bpi. After a tape drive has finished writing a **physical record** (a sequence of frames), it leaves a gap on the tape while slowing down. If the program writes short physical records on the tape, most of the space will be wasted in the gaps. By writing physical records that are much longer than the gap, the tape utilization can be kept high.

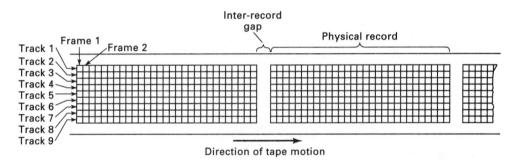

Fig. 2-15. Information on a magnetic tape is recorded as a sequence of rectangular bit matrices.

Magnetic tapes are sequential-access devices. If the tape is positioned at the beginning, to read physical record n, it is first necessary to read physical records 1 through $n - 1$, one at a time. If the information desired is near the end of the tape, the program will have to read almost the entire tape, which may take several minutes. Forcing a CPU that can execute millions of instructions per second to wait 200 sec while a tape is advanced is wasteful. Tapes are most appropriate when the data must be accessed sequentially.

Magnetic Disks

A **disk** is a piece of metal, ranging from about 5 to 10 inches in diameter, to which a magnetizable coating has been applied at the factory, generally on both sides (see Fig. 2-16). Information is recorded on a number of concentric circles, called **tracks**. Disks typically have between 40 and a few hundred tracks per surface. Each disk drive has a movable head that can be moved closer to, or farther from, the center. The head is wide enough to read or write information from exactly one track. A disk drive often has several disks stacked vertically about an inch apart. In such a configuration the arm will have one head next to each surface, all of which move in and out together. The radial position of the heads (distance from the spindle) is called the **cylinder**. A disk drive with n platters will have $2n$ heads, hence $2n$ tracks per cylinder.

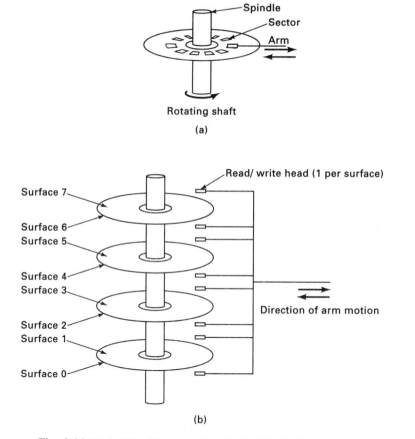

Fig. 2-16. (a) A disk with one platter. (b) A disk with four platters.

Tracks are divided into **sectors**, normally between 10 and 100 sectors per track. A sector consists of a certain number of bytes, usually 512.

To specify a transfer, the program must provide the following information: the cylinder and head, which together specify a unique track, the sector number where the information starts, the number of words to be transmitted, the main memory address where the information comes from or goes to, and whether information is to be read from the disk into memory or written from memory to the disk.

Disk transfers always start at the beginning of a sector, never in the middle. If a multisector transfer crosses a track boundary within a cylinder (e.g., from surface 0 to surface 1 at the same arm position), no time is lost because switching from one head to another is done electronically. However, if the transfer crosses a cylinder boundary, one rotation time may be lost while repositioning the heads to the next cylinder and waiting for sector 0 to come around.

If the head happens to be positioned over the wrong cylinder, it must first be moved. This motion is called a **seek**. A seek typically takes 3 msec between adjacent tracks and 20 to 100 msec to go from the innermost cylinder to the outermost cylinder. Once the head is positioned properly, the controller must wait until the first sector has rotated under the head before beginning the transfer. The time wasted waiting for the right sector varies from 0, if the program is lucky, to the complete rotation time if it just missed. This waiting time is called the **rotational latency**. Most disks rotate at 3600 rotations/min, giving a maximum latency of 16.67 msec. The total access time is the seek time plus the rotational latency plus the transfer time. The information is transferred at a rate of one track per rotation period.

Nearly all computers use multiplatter disks as described above for their main data storage. These are often called **hard disks**. The most common type is the **winchester disk**, which is a sealed unit (to avoid contamination from dust). The heads on a winchester drive are aerodynamically shaped and float on a cushion of air generated by the spinning platters. Their capacities range from about 20 megabytes on low-end personal computers to around 10 gigabytes on large mainframes.

Floppy Disks

With the advent of the personal computer, a way was needed to distribute software. The solution was found in the **diskette** or **floppy disk**, a small, removable medium so called because the early ones were physically flexible. The floppy disk was actually invented by IBM for recording maintenance information about its mainframes for the service staff, but was quickly seized on by personal computer manufacturers as a convenient way to distribute software for sale.

Unlike winchester disks, where the heads float a few microns above the surface, floppy disk heads actually touch the diskettes. As a result, both the media and the heads wear out comparatively quickly. To reduce wear and tear, personal computers retract the heads and stop the rotation when a drive is not reading or writing. Consequently, when the next read or write command is given, there is a delay of about half a second while the motor gets up to speed.

Nowadays, two sizes are commonly used, 5.25 inch and 3.5 inch. Each of these has a low-density and a high density version. The 3.5 inch diskettes come in a rigid jacket for protection, so they are not really "floppy." Since the 3.5 inch disks store more data and are better protected, they will eventually replace the 5.25 inch ones. The most important parameters of all four types are shown in Fig. 2-17.

Size (inches)	5.25	5.25	3.5	3.5
Capacity (bytes)	360K	1.2M	720K	1.44M
Tracks	40	80	80	80
Sectors/track	9	15	9	18
Heads	2	2	2	2
Rotations/min	300	360	300	300
Data rate (kbps)	250	500	250	500
Type	Flexible	Flexible	Rigid	Rigid

Fig. 2-17. Comparison of four common diskette types.

Optical Disks

In recent years, optical (as opposed to magnetic) disks have become available. They have much higher recording densities than conventional magnetic disks. Optical disks were originally developed for recording television programs, but they can be put to more esthetic use as computer storage devices. Television has a bandwidth of 6 MHz, so a 1-hour disk has a theoretical capacity of about 20 gigabits. Practical systems achieve about half that. (**Bandwidth** is an electrical engineering term and refers to the information-carry capacity of a wire or other channel. A bandwidth of 1 Hertz (Hz) is typically, but not always, good for transmitting one bit per second.)

Due to their potentially enormous capacity, optical disks have been the subject of a great deal of research and have gone through an incredibly rapid evolution. The first generation was invented by the Dutch electronics conglomerate, Philips, and further developed in collaboration with Sony. These disks are based on the same technology used in Compact Disc audio players and are called **CD ROMs** (**Compact Disc Read Only Memory**).

A CD ROM is prepared by using a high-power laser to burn 1-micron (10^{-6} of a meter) holes in a master disk. From this master, a mold is made. This mold is used to stamp out copies on plastic disks, the same way phonograph records are made. A thin layer of aluminum is then deposited on the surface, followed by a transparent plastic layer for protection. CD ROMs are read by devices similar to CD audio players, by having a detector measure the energy reflected off the surface when a low-power laser is aimed at the surface. The holes, called **pits**, and the unburned areas between the pits, called **lands**, have different reflectivity, making it possible to distinguish between pits and lands.

This technology has some important consequences. First of all, because the CD ROMs are stamped, rather than recorded like conventional floppy disks, fully automated machinery can mass produce them at a very low price. Second, because stamping aluminum coated plastic disks is not very accurate, the digital information normally contains many errors.

The error problem is attacked two ways. First, the read head in the drive contains a precision mirror driven by a servomechanism that is used for tracking the surface to compensate for manufacturing imperfections. Second, the data are recorded using a complex method called a **crossinterleaved Reed-Solomon** error correcting code. This coding method uses more bits than a Hamming code, but can correct multiple errors.

Furthermore, instead of using pits for 0s and lands for 1s (or vice versa), each pit-land or land-pit transition represents a 1 bit. The interval between two transitions tells how many zeros are present between the 1 bits. Data are recorded in groups of 24 bytes, each of which is first expanded from 8 to 14 bits using the Reed-Solomon code. Three special bits are added between each group and a synchronization byte is added to form a frame. A group of 98 frames forms a block containing 2K bytes of user data, which is the basic addressable unit. Although this scheme is complicated and wastes considerable disk area, it provides extremely high reliability using a low-cost medium.

Information on a CD ROM is written as a single continuous spiral, unlike magnetic disks with their discrete cylinders and tracks. This format is illustrated in Fig. 2-18. Each CD ROM contains 270,000 data blocks, for a total capacity of 553 megabytes. The data are read at a constant linear velocity of 75 inches/sec (by having the rotation speed decrease as the head moves outward), which gives a data rate of 153.60 kbytes/sec.

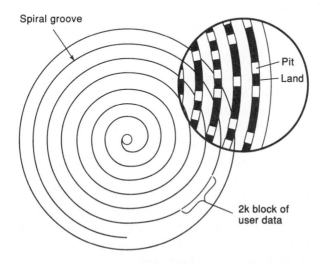

Fig. 2-18. CD ROM format.

CD ROMs are potentially useful for distributing large data bases, especially those mixing text and images. A complete law, medical, or literary library of 250 thick books fits easily on one CD ROM, as does a fully illustrated encyclopedia. A computer aided instruction course consisting of thousands of color slides, each one accompanied by 10 seconds of audio narration, is another candidate for CD ROM. A street map for an entire state could be the base for an automobile navigation system, with a voice synthesizer directing the driver to the destination. The possibilities are limited only by our imagination.

Despite this enormous potential, CD ROMs are not writable, which limits their utility as computer storage devices. The desire to have a writable medium led to the next phase, the **WORM (Write Once Read Many)** optical disk. This device allows users to write information on optical disks themselves. However, once a pit has been burned into the surface, it cannot be erased. Such disks are good for making data archives, accounting audit trails, and other information that is (semi)permanent. They are not well suited for making and erasing temporary scratch files. However, given the large capacity of these disks, a slash-and-burn style of just appending temporary files until the disk is full and then throwing it away is conceivable.

It is clear that the existence of write-once disks has a major impact on the way software is written. Not being able to modify files tends to suggest a different kind of file system, in which a file is really a sequence of **immutable versions**, none of which can be changed, and each of which replaces the previous one. This model is quite different than the usual update-in-place model used on magnetic disks.

The third phase of optical disk evolution is erasable optical media. These use magneto-optical technology. The plastic disk is coated with alloys of metals so exotic, such as terbium and gadolinium, that few people have ever even heard of them. These metals have the interesting property that at low temperatures they are insensitive to magnetic fields, but at high temperatures their molecular structure aligns itself with any magnetic field present.

To use this property to record information, the drive's heads contain a laser and a magnet. The laser fires an ultrashort light burst at the metal, raising its temperature instantaneously, but not pitting the surface. At the same time, the magnet is issuing a field in one of two directions. When the laser pulse is over, the metal has been magnetized in one of two possible directions, representing 0 or 1. This information can be read back the same way as with a CD ROM, using a much weaker laser. The disk can also be erased and overwritten the same way it was written in the first place.

Writable optical disks are not likely to replace conventional winchester disks for some time—probably many years, if ever—for two reasons. First, their seek times are an order of magnitude slower than those of winchester disks. Second, their data rates are also an order of magnitude slower. Together, the overall performance of magnetic disks is simply much better. While optical disks will no doubt improve in time, magnetic disks will probably improve just as fast to keep them ahead. Nevertheless, for applications where a large amount of removable storage is critical, optical disks have a bright future ahead of them.

2.3. INPUT/OUTPUT

Before a computer can get to work solving a problem, it must be given the program and data. After it has found the solution, the computer must communicate this solution to the human beings who posed the problem in the first place. The topic of getting information into and out of computers is called input/output, or usually just **I/O**.

Not all input comes from people and not all output is intended for people. A computer-operated solar telescope may get its input data directly from instruments observing the sun. A computer controlling an automated chemical plant may direct its output to machines throughout the plant that regulate the chemicals being produced.

Two I/O organizations are commonly used in modern computers. Large mainframes use the design shown in Fig. 2-19. In this design, a computer system consists of a CPU (or possible multiple CPUs), a memory, and one or more specialized I/O processors called **data channels**. All the I/O devices are attached to the channels.

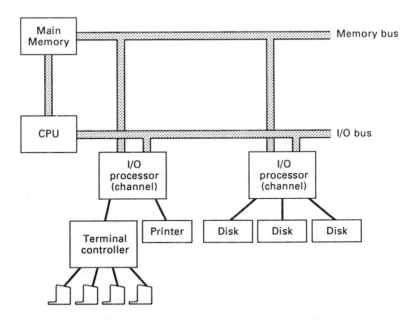

Fig. **2-19.** I/O structure on a large mainframe.

When the CPU wants I/O performed, it loads a special program into one of the channels, and tells the channel to execute it. The channel handles all the I/O to and from main memory by itself, leaving the CPU free to do other things. When the channel is finished, it sends the CPU a special signal called an **interrupt**, to make the CPU stop whatever it is doing and pay attention to the channel. The advantage of this organization is that it allows the CPU to offload all the I/O work to the channel. In this way, computing and I/O can take place at the same time.

Since mainframes typically generate a tremendous I/O load, they are usually equipped with at least three buses. The memory bus allows the channels to read and write words from memory. The I/O bus allows the CPU to issue commands to the channels and allows the channels to interrupt the CPU. Finally, there is a third bus to allow the CPU to access memory without having to use the other buses.

Personal computers use a simpler system structure, as illustrated in Fig. 2-20. Most of these machines have a card cage with a large printed circuit board at the bottom, called the **motherboard**. The motherboard contains the CPU chip, some memory, and various support chips. It also contains a bus etched along its length, and sockets into which the edge connectors of additional memory and I/O boards can be inserted. Minicomputer structure is similar, except that the CPU is also located on a plug-in board, with the motherboard just being a passive receptacle for other boards, in which case it is called a **backplane.**

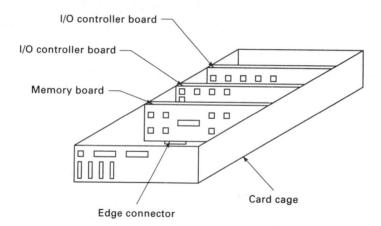

Fig. 2-20. Physical structure of a personal computer.

The logical structure of a personal computer is shown in Fig. 2-21. Most have a single bus used to connect the CPU, memory, and I/O devices. Each I/O device consists of two parts, one containing most of the electronics, called the **controller**, and one containing the I/O device itself, such as a disk drive. The controller is usually contained on a board plugged into the card cage, except for those controllers that are not optional (such as the keyboard), which are often located on the motherboard. Even though the display (monitor) is not an option, the video controller is often located on a plug-in board to allow the user to choose between color, monochrome, high resolution, low resolution, and so on. The controller connects to its device by a cable attached to a connector on the back of the card cage.

The job of a controller is to control its I/O device and handle bus access for it. When a program wants data from the disk, it gives a command to the disk

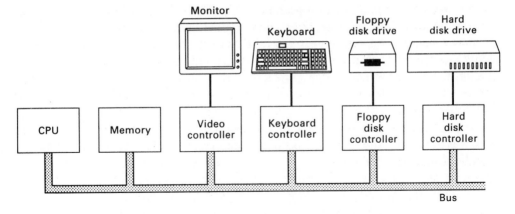

Fig. 2-21. Logical structure of a personal computer.

controller, which then issues seeks and other commands to the drive. When the proper track and sector have been located, the drive begins outputting the data as a serial bit stream to the controller. It is the job of the controller to break the bit stream up into words, and write each word into memory, as it is assembled. A controller that reads or writes a block of data to or from memory without CPU intervention is said to be performing **direct memory access**, better known by its acronym **DMA**.

The bus is not only used by the I/O controllers, but also by the CPU for fetching instructions and data. What happens if the CPU and an I/O controller want to use the bus at the same time? The answer is that a chip called a **bus arbiter** decides who goes next. In general, I/O devices are given preference over the CPU, because disks and other moving devices cannot be stopped, and forcing them to wait would result in lost data. When no I/O is in progress, the CPU can have all the bus cycles for itself to reference memory. However, when some I/O device is also running, that device will request and be granted the bus when it needs it. This process is called **cycle stealing** and it slows down the computer. Mainframes have multiple buses, as we have seen, so they do not suffer from this problem.

Many kinds of I/O devices are available today. A few of the more common ones are discussed below.

2.3.1. Terminals

Computer terminals consist of three elements: a keyboard, a monitor, and some electronics to control the other two. Keyboards come in several varieties. In the cheapest ones, each key is simply a switch that makes electrical contact when depressed. More expensive ones have a magnet under each key that passes through a coil when struck, thus inducing a current that can be detected. Various other methods, both mechanical and electromagnetic, are also used in some keyboards.

A monitor is a box consisting primarily of a **CRT (Cathode Ray Tube)** and its power supplies. The CRT contains a gun that can shoot an electron beam against a phosphorescent screen near the front of the tube, as shown in Fig. 2-22(a). (Color monitors have three electron guns, one each for red, green and blue.) During the horizontal scan, the beam sweeps across the screen in about 50 μsec, tracing out an almost horizontal line on the screen. Then it executes a horizontal retrace to get back to the left-hand edge in order to begin the next sweep. A device like this that produces an image line by line is called a **raster scan** device. If the horizontal retrace is not instantaneous, it is said to be **boustrophedonic** (the way an ox plows a field: left-to-right then right-to-left; oxen do not have instant retrace either).

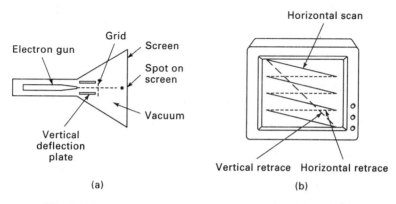

Fig. 2-22. (a) Cross section of a CRT. (b) CRT scanning pattern.

Horizontal sweeping is controlled by a linearly increasing voltage applied to the horizontal deflection plates placed to the left and right of the electron gun. Vertical motion is controlled by a much more slowly linearly increasing voltage applied to the vertical deflection plates placed above and below the gun. After somewhere between 400 and 1000 sweeps, the voltages on the vertical and horizontal deflection plates are rapidly reversed together to put the beam back in the upper left-hand corner. A full screen image is normally repainted between 30 and 60 times a second. The beam motions are shown in Fig. 2-22(b).

To produce a pattern of dots on the screen, a grid is present inside the CRT. When a positive voltage is applied to the grid, the electrons are accelerated, causing the beam to hit the screen and make it glow briefly. When a negative voltage is used, the electrons are repelled, so they do not pass through the grid and the screen does not glow. Thus the voltage applied to the grid causes the corresponding bit pattern to appear on the screen. This mechanism allows an electrical signal to be converted into a visual display.

Three kinds of terminals are in common use: character-map terminals, bit-map terminals, and RS-232-C terminals. They all can use any keyboard type, but they differ in the way the computer communicates with them and how the output is handled. In the following sections we will briefly describe each of these.

Character-map terminals

Most personal computers use the scheme shown in Fig. 2-23 to display output on the monitor. (The keyboard is treated as a completely separate device.) On the serial communication board is a chunk of memory, called the **video RAM**, as well as some electronics for accessing the bus and generating video signals.

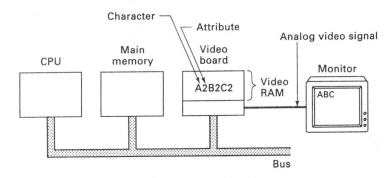

Fig. 2-23. Terminal output on a personal computer.

To display characters, the CPU copies them to the video RAM in alternate bytes. Associated with each character is an **attribute byte** that describes how that character is to be displayed. Attributes can include its color, intensity, whether it is blinking, and so on. Thus a screen image of 25 by 80 characters requires 4000 bytes of video RAM, 2000 for the characters and 2000 for the attributes. Some boards have more memory to hold multiple screen images.

The job of the video board is to repeatedly fetch characters from the video RAM and generate the necessary signal to drive the monitor. An entire line of characters is fetched at once so the individual scan lines can be computed. This signal is a high-frequency analog signal that controls the scanning of the electron beam that paints the characters on the screen. Because the board outputs a video signal, the monitor must be within a few meters of the computer.

Bit-map Terminals

A variation on this idea is to have the screen not be regarded as a 25 by 80 array of characters, but an array of picture elements, called **pixels**. Each pixel is either on or off. It represents one bit of information. On personal computers the screen may contain as few as 200 by 320 pixels, but more commonly 480 by 640. On engineering workstations, the screen is typically 1024 by 1024 pixels. Terminals using a bit map rather than a character map are called **bit-map terminals**. Many video boards can operate either as character-map terminals or bit-map terminals, under software control.

The same general idea is used as in Fig. 2-23, except that the video RAM is just seen as a big bit array. The software can set any pattern it wants there, and that is displayed instantly. To draw characters, the software might decide to allocate, for example, a 9 by 14 rectangle for each character, and fill in the necessary bits to make the character appear. This approach allows the software to create multiple fonts, and intermix them at will. All the hardware does is display the bit array. Color can be handled using multiple arrays, sometimes called **bit planes**. With n bit planes, one out of 2^n colors can be selected per pixel.

Bit-map terminals are commonly used to support displays containing several **windows**. A window is an area of the screen used by one program. With multiple windows, it is possible to have several programs running at the same time, each one displaying its results independent of the other ones.

Although bit-map terminals are highly flexible, they have two major disadvantages. First, they require a considerable amount of video RAM. A 1024 by 1024 display requires 1 million bits, or 128K bytes for monochrome, and half a megabyte for color at 4 bits/pixel (compared to 4K for character-map terminals, either monochrome or color).

The second disadvantage is performance. To display anything, a tremendous amount of copying is needed. Moving a 9 by 14 character to the screen requires moving at least 28 bytes, as well as a lot of work to insert the character into the right place in the bit map. Worse yet, scrolling the screen usually means copying the entire memory. Consequently, bit-map terminals need very fast CPUs to manipulate the bits. Alternatively, they can be equipped with special hardware for managing pixels quickly.

RS-232-C Terminals

Dozens of companies make computers and hundreds of companies make terminals. To allow (almost) any terminal to be used with (almost) any computer, a standard computer-terminal interface, called **RS-232-C**, has been developed. Any terminal that supports the RS-232-C interface can be connected to any computer that also supports this interface.

RS-232-C terminals have a standardized 25-pin connector on them. The RS-232-C standard defines the mechanical size and shape of the connector, the voltage levels, and the meaning of each of the signals on the pins.

When the computer and the terminal are far apart, it is frequently the case that the only practical way to connect them is over the telephone system. Unfortunately, the telephone system is not capable of transmitting the signals required by the RS-232-C standard, so a device called a **modem** (**mo**dulator-**dem**odulator) has to be inserted between the computer and the telephone and also between the terminal and the telephone to perform signal conversion. We will study modems in the next section.

Figure 2-24 shows the placement of the computer, modems, and terminal when a telephone line is used. When the terminal is close enough to the computer that it can be wired-up directly, modems are not used, but the same RS-232-C connectors and cables are still used, although those pins related to modem control are not needed.

To communicate, the computer and terminal each contain a chip called a **UART (Universal Asynchronous Receiver Transmitter**), as well as logic to access the bus. To display a character, the computer fetches a character from its main memory and presents it to the UART, which then shifts it out onto the RS-232-C cable bit-for-bit. In effect, the UART is really a parallel-to-serial converter, since an entire character (1 byte) is given to it at once, and it outputs the bits one at a time at a specific rate. The most common rates are 110, 300, 1200, 2400, 9600 and 19,200 bits/sec.

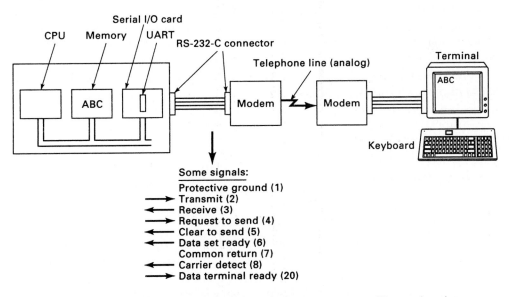

Fig. 2-24. Connection of an RS-232-C terminal to a computer. The numbers in parentheses in the list of signals are the pin numbers.

In the terminal, another UART receives the bits and rebuilds the entire character, which is then displayed on the screen. Input from the terminal's keyboard goes through a parallel-to-serial conversion in the terminal, and is then reassembled by the UART in the computer.

The RS-232-C standard defines almost 25 signals, but in practice, only a few are used (and most of those can be omitted when the terminal is wired directly to the computer without modems). Pins 2 and 3 are for transmitting and receiving data, respectively. Each handles a one-way bit stream, in opposite directions. When the terminal or computer is powered up, it asserts (i.e., sets to 1) the Data Terminal Ready signal to inform the modem that it is on. Similarly, the modem asserts Data Set Ready to signal its presence. When the terminal or computer wants to send data, it asserts Request to Send to ask permission. If the modem is willing to grant that permission, it asserts Clear to Send as a response. Other pins are used for various status, testing, and timing functions.

2.3.2. Modems

With the growth of computer usage in the past years, it is common for one computer to need to communicate with another one. For example, many people have personal computers at home that they use for communicating with their computers at work, with home banking systems, or with electronic bulletin boards. All these applications use the telephone to provide the underlying communication path.

However, a raw telephone line is not suitable for transmitting computer signals, which generally represent a 1 as about 5 volts and a 0 as 0 volts, as shown in Fig. 2-25(a). Two-level signals suffer considerable distortion when transmitted over a voice-grade telephone line, thereby leading to transmission errors. A pure sine wave signal at a frequency of 1000 to 2000 Hz, called a **carrier**, can be transmitted with relatively little distortion, however, and this fact is exploited as the basis of most telecommunication systems.

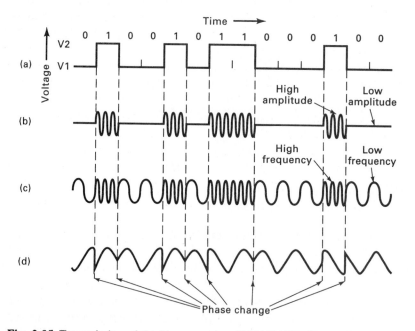

Fig. 2-25. Transmission of the binary number 01001011000100 over a telephone line bit by bit. (a) Two-level signal. (b) Amplitude modulation. (c) Frequency modulation. (d) Phase modulation.

Because the pulsations of a sine wave are completely predictable, a pure sine wave transmits no information at all. However, by varying the amplitude, frequency, or phase, a sequence of 1s and 0s can be transmitted, as shown in Fig. 2-25. This process is called **modulation**. In **amplitude modulation** [see Fig. 2-25(b)], two different voltage levels are used, for 0 and 1, respectively. A person listening to digital data transmitted at a very low data rate would hear a loud noise for a 1 and no noise for a 0.

In frequency modulation [see Fig. 2-25(c)], the voltage level is constant but the carrier frequency is different for 1 and 0. A person listening to frequency modulated digital data would hear two tones, corresponding to 0 and 1. Frequency modulation is often referred to as **frequency shift keying.**

In simple **phase modulation** [see Fig. 2-25(d)], the amplitude and frequency do not change, but the phase of the carrier is reversed 180 degrees when the data switches from 0 to 1 or 1 to 0. In more sophisticated phase-modulated systems, at the start of each indivisible time interval, the phase of the carrier is abruptly shifted by 45, 135, 225, or 315 degrees, to allow 2 bits per time interval, called **dibit** phase encoding. Other schemes, for transmitting 3 or more bits per time interval also exist. The number of time intervals is the **baud** rate. With 2 or more bits per interval, the bit rate will exceed the baud rate. Many people confuse these two terms.

If the data to be transmitted consist of a series of 8-bit characters, it would be desirable to have a connection capable of transmitting 8 bits simultaneously—that is, eight pairs of wires. Because voice-grade telephone lines provide only one channel, the bits must be sent serially, one after another (or in groups of two if dibit encoding is being used). The device that accepts characters from a computer in the form of two-level signals, one bit at a time, and transmits the bits in groups of one or two, in amplitude-, frequency-, or phase-modulated form, is the modem.

The transmitting modem sends the individual bits within one character at regularly spaced time intervals. For example, 1200 baud implies one signal change every 833 μsec. A second modem at the receiving end is used to convert a modulated carrier to a binary number. Because the bits arrive at the receiver at regularly spaced intervals, once the receiving modem has determined the start of the character, its clock tells it when to sample the line to read the values of the individual bits.

Asynchronous and Synchronous Transmission

Two different methods are used for transmitting characters. In **asynchronous** transmission, the time interval between two characters is not fixed, although the time interval between two consecutive bits within a character is fixed. For example, a person typing at a time-sharing terminal will not type at uniform speed, so the time interval between two successive characters will not be constant.

This speed variation raises the problem of how the receiver can recognize the first bit of a character. If the modulation methods of Fig. 2-25 are used, there is no way to distinguish between no data and a 0 bit. A character consisting entirely of 0s would be completely invisible. Furthermore, a character consisting of a 1 followed by seven 0s could not be distinguished from a character consisting of 7 0s followed by a 1, because the receiver would have no way of telling whether the 1 bit was at the start, middle, or end of the character.

In order to permit the receiver to recognize the start of a character, a start bit is transmitted directly before each character. To improve reliability, 1 or 2 stop bits are transmitted directly after each character. Normally, the line is kept in the 1 state while no data are being transmitted to allow a broken circuit to be detected, so the start bit is 0. The stop bits are then 1, to distinguish them from start bits. Between the start and stop bits, the data bits are transmitted at uniformly spaced time intervals. A timer in the receiving modem is started when the start bit arrives, allowing the modem to tell which bit is which. Asynchronous communication is illustrated in Fig. 2-26(a).

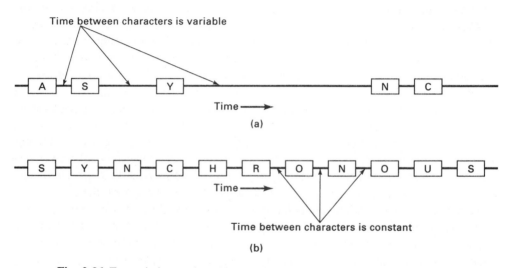

Fig. 2-26. Transmission modes. (a) Asynchronous transmission. (b) Synchronous transmission.

The bit rates used for asynchronous transmission range from 110 bps to 19,200 bps. At 110 bps, two stops are used, so a 7-bit character plus parity bit plus 1 start bit plus 2 stop bits gives 11 bits per character. Therefore, 110 bps corresponds to 10 characters/sec. The higher rates use only 1 stop bit.

In **synchronous** transmission, the need for start and stop bits is eliminated. The result is to speed up data transmission. Synchronous communication often proceeds at bit rates of 4800 bps, 9600 bps, or even higher. In this method, once the modems have synchronized, they continue to send characters in order to remain in synchronization, even if there are no data to transmit. A special "idle" character is sent when there are no data. In synchronous transmission, unlike asynchronous transmission, the interval between two characters is always exactly the same.

Synchronous transmission requires that the clocks in the transmitter and receiver remain synchronized for long periods of time, whereas asynchronous transmission does not, because the start of each character is explicitly indicated by a start bit. The length of time a transmission can be carried on without resynchronizing the receiver to the phase of the transmitter depends on the stability of the clocks. Typically, the clocks are stable enough to allow blocks of thousands of characters to be sent without having to resynchronize. These blocks sometimes use Hamming codes or other techniques to detect and correct transmission errors. Synchronous transmission is illustrated in Fig. 2-26(b).

Simplex, Half-Duplex, and Full-Duplex Transmission

Three modes of transmission are used for communication purposes: simplex, half-duplex, and full-duplex. A **simplex** line is capable of transmitting data in only one direction. The reason is not due to any property of the wires themselves but simply because one end has only a transmitter and the other end has only a receiver. This configuration is rarely used by computers because it provides no way for the receiver to transmit an acknowledgment signal to the sender, indicating that the message was received correctly. Radio and television broadcasting are examples of simplex transmission.

A **half-duplex** line can send and receive data in both directions but not simultaneously. During any transmission, one modem is the transmitter and the other is the receiver. A common situation is for device A, acting as the transmitter, to send a series of characters to device B, acting as the receiver. Then A and B simultaneously switch roles and B sends a message back to A specifying whether the characters were received without error or not. If there were no transmission errors, A and B switch roles again and A sends the next message to B. If there were errors, A retransmits the garbled message again. The "conversation" between the transmitter and the receiver about what to do next is called the **protocol**. The time required to switch a half-duplex line from one direction to the other may be many character times. A railroad track is an example of a half-duplex channel, because it can handle traffic going either way but not at the same time.

A **full-duplex** line can, in contrast, send and receive data in both directions simultaneously. Conceptually, a full-duplex line is equivalent to two simplex lines, one in each direction. Because two transmissions may be proceeding in parallel, one in each direction, a full-duplex line can transmit more information than a half-duplex line of the same data rate. Furthermore, full-duplex lines do not waste any time switching directions.

2.3.3. Mice

As time goes on, computers are being used by people with less expertise in how computers work. Computers of the ENIAC generation were used only by the people who built them. In the 1950s, computers were only used by highly skilled professional programmers. Nowadays, computers are widely used by people who need to get some job done, and do not know (or even want to know) much about how computers work or how they are programmed.

Many of these people perceive typing (frequently cryptic) commands on a keyboard as user-unfriendly, if not downright hostile. They greatly prefer systems in which the computer displays menus on the screen, and they point to the item they want. Using this model requires having a way to point at the screen. The most common way of allowing users to point at the screen is with a device called a **mouse**.

A mouse is a small plastic box that sits on the table next to the terminal. When it is moved around on the table, a little pointer on the screen moves too, allowing users to point at screen items. The mouse has one, two, or three buttons on top, to allow users to select items from menus. Much blood has been spilled as a result of arguments about how many buttons a mouse ought to have. Naive users prefer one (it is hard to push the wrong button if there is only one), but sophisticated ones like the power of multiple buttons to do fancy things.

Three kinds of mice are in use: mechanical mice, optical mice, and optomechanical mice. One kind of mechanical mouse has two rubber wheels protruding through the bottom, with their axles perpendicular to one another, as illustrated in Fig. 2-27. When the mouse is moved parallel to its main axis, one wheel turns. When it is moved perpendicular to its main axis, the other one turns. Each wheel drives a variable resistor (potentiometer). By measuring changes in the resistance, it is possible to see how much each wheel has rotated, and thus calculate how far the mouse has moved in each direction. Another kind of mechanical mouse achieves the same effect using a ball that protrudes slightly from the bottom.

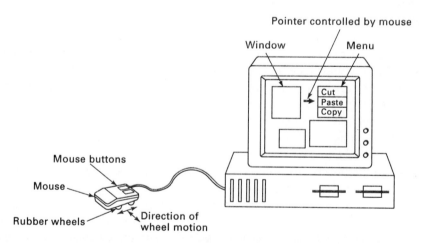

Fig. 2-27. A wheeled mouse being used to point to menu items.

The second kind of mouse is the optical mouse. This kind has no wheels or ball. Instead, it has an **LED (Light Emitting Diode)** and a photodetector on the bottom. The optical mouse is used on top of a special plastic pad containing a rectangular grid of closely spaced lines. As the mouse moves over the grid, the photodetector senses line crossings by seeing the changes in the amount of light being reflected back from the LED. Electronics inside the mouse count the number of grid lines crossed in each direction.

The third kind of mouse is optomechanical. Like the two-wheeled mechanical mouse, it has two rotating wheels mounted at 90 degrees to each other. However, each wheel contains an LED in its center, a set of slits uniformly spaced around the circumference of the wheel, and a detector just outside the wheel. As the mouse moves, the wheels rotate, and light pulses strike the detectors whenever a slit comes between an LED and its detector. The number of pulses detected is proportional to the amount of motion.

Although mice can be set up in various ways, a common arrangement is to have the mouse send a sequence of three bytes to the computer every 100 msec. Usually these characters come in on an RS-232-C line, just as though they had been typed on a keyboard. The first byte contains a signed integer telling how many units the mouse has moved in the x-direction in the last 100 msec. The second byte gives the same information for y motion. The third byte contains the current state of the mouse buttons. Sometimes two bytes are used for each coordinate.

Low level software in the computer accepts this information as it comes in, and converts the relative movements sent by the mouse to an absolute position. It then displays an arrow on the screen at the position corresponding to where the mouse is. When the arrow points at the proper item, the user clicks a mouse button, and the computer can then figure out which item has been selected from its knowledge of where the arrow is on the screen.

2.3.4. Printers

While CRT terminals can suffice for many interactive applications, for others a permanent record of the output is needed on paper. To fullfil this need, many kinds of printers have been devised. Below we will briefly describe the main types of printers and how they work.

Impact Printers

The oldest kind of printer, the impact printer, works like a typewriter: a piece of metal or plastic with a raised letter strikes an inked ribbon against a sheet of paper, leaving an image of the letter on the paper, as shown in Fig. 2-28(a). On modern personal computers, this form of printing is used in **daisy wheel** printers, so called because they contain a spoked wheel like a daisy, with the characters on the petals, as illustrated in Fig. 2-28(b). To print a character, the printer rotates the proper character in front of the electromagnet, and then energizes the magnet, pressing the letter against the ribbon. Printers of this type give good quality, especially when used with a carbon ribbon, and achieve a speed of 20 to 40 characters/sec.

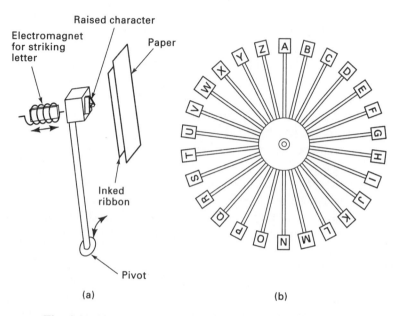

Fig. 2-28. (a) Cross section of impact printing. (b) A daisy wheel.

Large mainframes also use impact printers, but here the letters are embossed on a steel "bicycle" chain that encircles the paper. An 80-column printer will have 80 hammers, one for each column position. A line is printed by instructing each hammer to strike as soon as the proper letter is in front of it. Within one rotation of the chain, each character will appear in each column, thus making it possible to print the entire line. These printers can often print a page in a few seconds or less.

Matrix Printers

Another common type of printer is the **matrix printer**, in which a print head containing between seven and 24 electromagnetically activatable needles is scanned across each print line. A cheap printer might have seven needles, for printing 80 characters in a 5×7 matrix across the line. In effect, the print line then consists of 7 horizontal lines, each consisting of $5 \times 80 = 400$ dots. Each dot can be printed or not printed, depending on the characters to be printed. Figure 2-29(a) illustrates the letter "A" printed on a 5×7 matrix.

The print quality can be increased by two techniques: using more needles and having the circles overlap. Figure 2-29(b) shows an "A" printed using 24 needles that produce overlapping dots. Usually multiple passes over each scan line are required to produce overlapping dots, so increased quality goes hand in hand with

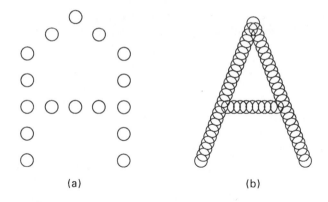

Fig. 2-29. (a) The letter "A" on a 5×7 matrix. (b) The letter "A" printed with 24 overlapping needles.

slower printing rates. Good matrix printers can operate in several modes, offering different trade-offs between print quality and speed.

Laser Printers

Probably the most exciting development in printing since Johann Gutenberg invented movable type in the Fifteenth century is the **laser printer**. This device combines a high quality image, excellent flexibility, good speed, and moderate cost into a single peripheral. Laser printers use almost the same technology as photocopy machines, and will probably be available in combined copier/printer machines before long.

The basic technology is illustrated in Fig. 2-30. The heart of the printer is a rotating precision drum. At the start of each page cycle, it is charged up to about 1000 volts and coated with a photosensitive material. Then light from a laser is scanned along the length of the drum much like the electron beam in a CRT, only instead of achieving the horizontal deflection using a voltage, a rotating octagonal mirror is used to scan the length of the drum. The light beam is modulated to produce a pattern of light and dark spots. The spots where the beam hits lose their electrical charge.

After a line of dots has been painted, the drum rotates a fraction of a degree to allow the next line to be painted. Eventually, the first line of dots reaches the toner, a reservoir of an electrostatically sensitive black powder. The toner is attracted to those dots that are still charged, thus forming a visual image of that line. A little later in the transport path, the toner-coated drum is pressed against the paper, transferring the black powder to the paper. The paper is then passed through heated rollers to bind the toner to the paper permanently, fixing the image. Later in its rotation, the drum is discharged and scraped clean of any residual toner, preparing it for being charged and coated again for the next page.

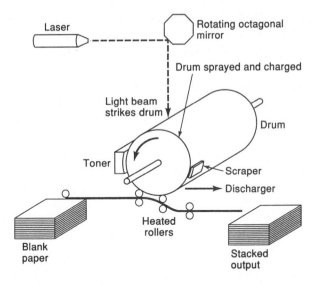

Fig. 2-30. Operation of a laser printer.

That this process is an exceedingly complex combination of physics, chemistry, mechanical engineering, and optical engineering hardly needs to be said. Nevertheless, complete assemblies, called **print engines**, are available from several vendors. Laser printer manufacturers combine the print engines with their own electronics and software to make a complete printer.

A slightly different kind of print engine that does not use a laser is also available. In this type, a row of LEDs is mounted along the length of the drum (or aimed at it via fiber optics). The LEDs are turned on and off in software to form each line. This design has a simpler optical design, but requires more electronics to drive all the LEDs.

Two different approaches are possible for turning a print engine into a complete printer. At one extreme, the computer just feeds in ordinary text, with commands for selecting fonts and perhaps drawing lines, rectangles, and circles. A computer inside the printer builds up the bit map for each page and transfers it to the printer. The advantage of this approach is that a very low bandwidth between the printer and the computer is needed. To print a page of 50 lines of 80 characters in a single font requires 4000 bytes of input. A typical low-end printer running at 12 pages/min requires a computer-to-printer bandwidth of 6400 bps, something that can be supplied by a 9600 baud RS-232-C line. The disadvantage is that a complete computer is needed inside the printer. To store the bit map for an 8.5×11 inch page at 300×300 dots per square inch, requires a megabyte of memory in the computer.

To avoid the expense of the computer and printer, some systems use the main computer and its memory to build up the bit map, just transferring the raw bit image to the printer. This scheme makes the printer much cheaper, but now requires transferring the 1 megabyte image in 5 sec, for a data rate of 1.6 megabits/sec. Alternatively, the printer can be slowed down if this data rate cannot be achieved.

Intermediate designs between these two extremes are also possible, but clearly as we move to 600 dots/inch and higher, considerable memory, computing power, and bandwidth will be needed. Unfortunately, professional typesetting systems need between 1000 and 2000 dots/inch, so at least an order of magnitude performance improvement is required. As an aside, the camera ready copy for this book was printed using an LED printer with an effective resolution of 450 dots/inch. If you compare it to professionally typeset books using a low-power microscope, the difference will be glaringly apparent. Hopefully the high intellectual content offsets the low physical resolution.

The laser printer has spawned a whole new industry called **desktop publishing**. The Apple Macintosh, IBM PC, and other computers have software that allow users to type in documents and have them appear on the screen the same way the final output will appear. This system is often called **WYSIWYG (What You See Is What You Get)**, pronounced "wiz e wig." Many of these systems translate the input text to an intermediate language called **PostScript**, and then download it to the laser printer. Inside the printer is an interpreter that converts the PostScript to pixels and prints them. PostScript is the de facto standard for laser printers.

2.3.5. Character Codes

Each computer has a set of characters that it uses. As a bare minimum, this set includes the 26 capital letters, the 10 digits 0 through 9, and a few punctuation marks, such as space, period, minus sign, comma, and carriage return. More sophisticated character sets include both capital letters and small letters, the 10 digits, a wide assortment of punctuation marks, a collection of special characters useful in mathematics and business, and sometimes even Greek letters.

In order to transfer these characters into the computer, each one is assigned a number: for example, $a = 1$, $b = 2$, ..., $z = 26$, $+ = 27$, $- = 28$. The mapping of characters onto integers is called a **character code**. Present-day computers use either a 6-, 7-, 8- or 9-bit code. A 6-bit code allows only $2^6 = 64$ characters—namely 26 letters, 10 digits, and 28 other characters, mostly punctuation marks and mathematical symbols.

For many applications 64 characters are not enough, in which case a 7- or 8-bit character code must be used. A 7-bit character code allows up to 128 characters. One widely used 7-bit code is called **ASCII (American Standard Code for Information Interchange)**. Figure 2-31 shows the ASCII code. Codes 1 to 37 (octal) are control characters and do not print. The codes from 128 to 255 are not defined. The most widely used 8-bit character code is the IBM **EBCDIC** code used on large IBM mainframes. It is obsolete, but for compatibility reasons, IBM is stuck with it.

Control characters

0	NUL	Null	20	DLE	Data link escape
1	SOH	Start of heading	21	DC1	Device control 1
2	STX	Start of text	22	DC2	Device control 2
3	ETX	End of text	23	DC3	Device control 3
4	EOT	End of transmission	24	DC4	Device control 4
5	ENQ	Enquiry	25	NAK	Negative acknowledge
6	ACK	Acknowledge	26	SYN	Synchronous idle
7	BEL	Bell	27	ETB	End of transmission block
10	BS	Backspace	30	CAN	Cancel
11	HT	Horizontal tab	31	EM	End of medium
12	LF	Line feed	32	SUB	Substitute
13	VT	Vertical tab	33	ESC	Escape
14	FF	Form feed	34	FS	File separator
15	CR	Carriage return	35	GS	Group separator
16	SO	Shift out	36	RS	Record separator
17	SI	Shift in	37	US	Unit separator

40	(Space)	60	0	100	@	120	P	140	`	160	p
41	!	61	1	101	A	121	Q	141	a	161	q
42	"	62	2	102	B	122	R	142	b	162	r
43	#	63	3	103	C	123	S	143	c	163	s
44	$	64	4	104	D	124	T	144	d	164	t
45	%	65	5	105	E	125	U	145	e	165	u
46	&	66	6	106	F	126	V	146	f	166	v
47	'	67	7	107	G	127	W	147	g	167	w
50	(	70	8	110	H	130	X	150	h	170	x
51	)	71	9	111	I	131	Y	151	i	171	y
52	*	72	:	112	J	132	Z	152	j	172	z
53	+	73	;	113	K	133	[	153	k	173	{
54	,	74	<	114	L	134	\	154	l	174		
55	-	75	=	115	M	135	]	155	m	175	}
56	.	76	>	116	N	136	^	156	n	176	~
57	/	77	?	117	O	137	_	157	o	177	(Delete)

Fig. 2-31. The ASCII character code (octal).

2.4. SUMMARY

Computer systems are built up from three types of components: processors, memories, and I/O devices. The task of a processor is to fetch instructions one at a time from a memory, decode them, and execute them. The fetch-decode-execute cycle can always be described as an algorithm and, in fact, is often carried out by a software interpreter running at a lower level.

Systems capable of executing instructions in parallel are becoming increasingly common. Parallel computers of the SIMD type include vector processors and array processors. MIMD computers are multiprocessors, using a variety of schemes to connect the processors and memory.

Memories can be categorized as primary or secondary. The primary memory is used to hold the program currently being executed. Its access time is short—a few hundred nanoseconds at most—and independent of the address being accessed. Many memories are equipped with error correcting codes to enhance reliability. Secondary memories, in contrast, have access times that are much longer (milliseconds or more) and dependent on the location of the data being read or written. Tapes, magnetic disks and optical disks are the most common secondary memories.

I/O devices are used to transfer information into and out of the computer. Examples are terminals, mice, and laser printers. On mainframes, the I/O devices are attached to data channels. On smaller machines they are driven by controllers connected directly to the system bus. Here too, common I/O devices include terminals, modems, mice, and printers. Most I/O devices use the ASCII character code, except on IBM mainframes, where EBCDIC is used.

PROBLEMS

1. What is the purpose of step 2 in the list of Sec. 2.1.1? What would happen if this step were omitted?

2. A certain computation is highly sequential—that is, each step depends on the one preceding it. Would an array processor or a pipeline processor be more appropriate for this computation? Explain.

3. To compete with the newly invented printing press, a certain medieval monastery decided to mass-produce handwritten paperback books by assembling a vast number of scribes in a huge hall. The head monk would then call out the first word of the book to be produced and all the scribes would copy it down. Then the head monk would call out the second word and all the scribes would copy it down. This process was repeated until the entire book had been read aloud and copied. Which of the parallel processor systems of Sec. 2.1.3 does this system most resemble?

4. Estimate how many characters, including spaces, a typical book contains. How many bits are needed to encode a book in ASCII with parity? How many 1600-bpi tapes are needed to store a library of 10^6 books?

5. Estimate the maximum storage capacity of the human brain using the following assumptions. All memory is coded as DNA molecules. A DNA molecule is a linear sequence of the four basic nucleotides: A, C, G, and T. From the average weight of a nucleotide, roughly 10^{-20} gram, and an average brain weight of 1500 grams, deduce the bit capacity of the brain for this encoding form. *Note*: This calculation is only an upper limit, because the brain contains many cells that perform functions other than memory.

6. Which of the following memories are possible? Which are reasonable? Explain.

    a.   10-Bit address, 1024 cells,   8-bit cell size
    b.   10-Bit address, 1024 cells,   12-bit cell size

    c.   9-Bit address, 1024 cells,   10-bit cell size
    d.   11-Bit address, 1024 cells,   10-bit cell size
    e.   10-Bit address,   10 celis, 1024-bit cell size
    f. 1024-Bit address,   10 cells,   10-bit cell size

7. Sociologists can get three possible answers to a typical survey question such as "Do you believe in the tooth fairy?"—namely, yes, no, and no opinion. With this in mind, the Sociomagnetic Computer Company has decided to build a computer to process survey data. This computer has a trinary memory—that is, each byte (tryte?) consists of 8 trits, with a trit holding a 0, 1, or 2. How many trits are needed to hold a 6-bit number? Give an expression for the number of trits needed to hold n bits.

8. A certain computer can be equipped with 262,144 bytes of memory. Why would a manufacturer choose such a peculiar number, instead of an easy-to-remember number like 250,000?

9. The transfer rate between a CPU and its associated memory is orders of magnitude higher than the mechanical I/O transfer rate. How can this imbalance cause inefficiencies?

10. Measure your own reading speed. How does your data rate compare to that of a 300-bps telephone line?

11. Compute the data rate of the human eye using the following information. The visual field consists of about 10^6 elements (pixels). Each pixel can be reduced to a superposition of the three primary colors, each of which has 64 intensities. The time resolution is 100 msec.

12. How long does it take to read a disk with 800 cylinders, each containing five tracks of 32 sectors? First, all the sectors of track 0 are to be read starting at sector 0, then all the sectors of track 1 starting at sector 0, and so on. The rotation time is 20 msec, and a seek takes 10 msec between adjacent cylinders and 50 msec for the worst case. Switching between tracks of a cylinder can be done instantaneously.

13. A computer has a bus with a 250 nsec cycle time, during which it can read or write a 32-bit word from memory. The computer has a disk that uses the bus and runs at 4 Mbytes/sec. The CPU normally fetches and executes one 32-bit instruction every 250 nsec. How much does the disk slow down the CPU?

14. The director of your local computer center has just decided that the appropriate place for all its card punches, card readers, and similar equipment is the Smithsonian Institution. However, just to be on the safe side, it has also been decided to save all existing card decks on magnetic tape. If the interrecord gap on the 1600-bpi tapes used is 0.25 inch, and fifteen 80-column cards are written per physical tape record, how many 2000-card boxes will fit on a 2400-ft tape?

15. Decode the following binary ASCII text: 1001001 0100000 1001100 1001111 1010110 1000101 0100000 1011001 1001111 1010101 0101110.

16. Devise an even-parity Hamming code for the digits 0 to 9.

17. Devise a code for the digits 0 to 9 whose Hamming distance is 2.

18. In a Hamming code, some bits are "wasted" in the sense that they are used for checking and not information. What is the percentage of wasted bits for messages whose total length (data + check bits) is $2^n - 1$? Evaluate this expression numerically for values of n from 3 to 10.

19. Transmission errors on telephone lines often occur in bursts rather than individually. Because the basic Hamming code can only correct single errors within a character, it is of no use if a noise burst garbles n consecutive bits. Devise a method of transmitting ASCII text over a line where noise bursts may garble as many as 100 consecutive bits. Assume that the minimum interval between two noise bursts is thousands of characters. *Hint:* Think carefully about the order of bit transmission.

20. When even-parity ASCII text is transmitted asynchronously at a rate of 10 characters/sec over a 110-bps line, what percent of the received bits actually contain data (as opposed to overhead)?

21. A certain asynchronous ASCII terminal does parity checking and prints at 60 characters/sec. Which speed should it use: 110, 300, 600, or 1200 bps?

22. A bit-map terminal has a 1000×1000 display. The display is redrawn 50 times a second. How long is the pulse corresponding to one pixel?

23. A manufacturer advertises that its color bit-map terminal can display 2^{24} different colors. Yet the hardware only has 1 byte for each pixel. How can this be done?

24. The Hi-Fi Modem Company has just designed a new frequency-modulation modem that uses 16 frequencies instead of just 2. Each second is divided into n equal time intervals, each of which contains one of the 16 possible tones. How many bits per second can this modem transmit, using synchronous transmission?

25. How many characters/sec (7 bits + parity) can be transmitted over a 2400-bps line in each of the following modes?

    a. Synchronous
    b. Asynchronous (1 start bit and 1 stop bit)

26. Write a procedure *hamming*(*ascii*, *encoded*) that converts the low-order 7 bits of *ascii* into an 11-bit integer codeword stored in *encoded*.

27. Write a function *distance*(*code*, *n*, *k*) that takes an array *code*, of *n* characters of *k* bits each as input, and returns the distance of the character set as output.

3

THE DIGITAL LOGIC LEVEL

At the bottom of the hierarchy of Fig. 1-2 we find the digital logic level, the computer's real hardware. In this chapter, we will examine many aspects of digital logic, as a building block for the study of higher levels in subsequent chapters. Our study will emphasize microcomputers not only because they are easy to understand, but because they are becoming increasingly important.

The basic elements from which all digital computers are constructed are amazingly simple. We will begin our study by looking at these basic elements and also at the special two-valued algebra (Boolean algebra) used to analyze them. Next we will examine some fundamental circuits that can be built using gates in simple combinations, including circuits for doing arithmetic. The following topic is how gates can be combined to store information, that is, how memories are organized. After that, we come to the subject of CPUs and especially how single chip CPUs interface with memory and peripheral devices.

3.1. GATES AND BOOLEAN ALGEBRA

Digital circuits can be constructed from a small number of primitive elements by combining them in innumerable ways. In the following sections we will describe these primitive elements, show how they can be combined, and introduce a powerful mathematical technique that can be used to analyze their behavior.

3.1.1. Gates

A digital circuit is one in which only two logical values are present. Typically, a signal between 0 and 1 volt represents one value (e.g., binary 0) and a signal between 2 and 5 volts represents the other value (e.g., binary 1). Voltages outside these two ranges are not permitted. Tiny electronic devices, called **gates**, can compute various functions of these two-valued signals. These gates form the hardware basis on which all digital computers are built.

The details of how gates work inside is really beyond the scope of this book, belonging to the **device level**, which is below our level 0. Nevertheless, we will now digress ever so briefly to take a quick look at the basic idea, which is not difficult. All modern digital logic ultimately rests on the fact that a transistor can be made to operate as a very fast binary switch. In Fig. 3-1(a) we have shown a single bipolar transistor (the circle) embedded in a simple circuit. This transistor has three connections to the outside world: the **collector**, the **base**, and the **emitter**. When the input voltage, V_{in}, is below a certain critical value, the transistor turns off and acts like an infinite resistance, causing the output of the circuit, V_{out}, to take on a value close to V_{cc}, an externally regulated voltage, typically +5 volts. When V_{in} exceeds the critical value, the transistor switches on and acts like a wire, causing V_{out} to be pulled down to ground (by convention, 0 volts).

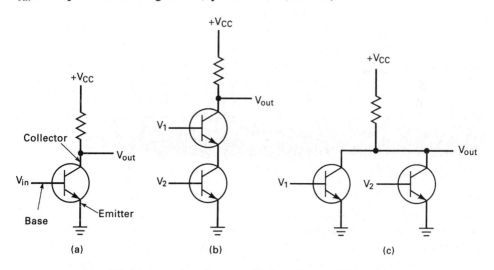

Fig. 3-1. (a) A transistor inverter. (b) A NAND gate. (c) A NOR gate.

The important thing to notice is that when V_{in} is low, V_{out} is high, and vice versa. This circuit is thus an inverter, converting a logical 0 to a logical 1, and a logical 1 to a logical 0. The resistor is needed to limit the amount of current drawn by the transistor. The time required to switch from one state to the other is typically a few nanoseconds.

In Fig. 3-1(b) two transistors are cascaded in series. If both V_1 and V_2 are high, both transistors will conduct and V_{out} will be pulled low. If either input is low, the corresponding transistor will turn off, and the output will be high. In other words, V_{out} will be low if and only if both V_1 and V_2 are high.

In Fig. 3-1(c) the two transistors are wired in parallel instead of in series. In this configuration, if either input is high, the corresponding transistor will turn on and pull the output down to ground. If both inputs are low, the output will remain high.

These three circuits, or their equivalents, form the three simplest gates. They are called NOT, NAND, and NOR gates, respectively. NOT gates are often called **inverters**; we will use the two terms interchangeably. If we now adopt the convention that "high" (V_{cc} volts) is a logical 1, and that "low" (ground) is a logical 0, we can express the output value as a function of the input values. The conventional symbols used to depict these three gates are shown in Fig. 3-2(a)-(c), along with the functional behavior for each circuit.

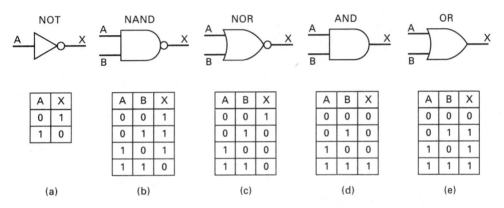

Fig. 3-2. The symbols and functional behavior for the five basic gates.

If the output signal of Fig. 3-1(b) is fed into an inverter circuit, we get another circuit with precisely the inverse of the NAND gate—namely, a circuit whose output is 1 if and only if both inputs are 1. Such a circuit is called an AND gate; its symbol and functional description are given in Fig. 3-2(d). Similarly, the NOR gate can be connected to an inverter to yield a circuit whose output is 1 if either or both inputs is a 1 but 0 if both inputs are 0. The symbol and functional description of this circuit, called an OR gate, are given in Fig. 3-2(e). The small circles used as part of the symbols for the inverter, NAND gate, and NOR gate are called **inversion bubbles**. They are often used in other contexts as well to indicate an inverted signal.

The five gates of Fig. 3-2 are the principal building blocks of the digital logic level. From the foregoing discussion, it should be clear that the NAND and NOR gates require two transistors each, whereas the AND and OR gates require three each. For this reason, many computers are based on NAND and NOR gates rather than the more familiar AND and OR gates. (In practice, all the gates are implemented somewhat differently, but NAND and NOR are still simpler than AND and OR.) In passing it is worth noting that gates may have more than two inputs. In principle, a NAND gate, for example, may have arbitrarily many inputs, but in practice more than eight inputs is unusual.

Although the subject of how gates are constructed belongs to the device level, we would like to mention the major families of manufacturing technology because they are referred to frequently. The two major technologies are **bipolar** and **MOS** (Metal Oxide Semiconductor). The major bipolar types are **TTL** (Transistor-Transistor Logic), which has been the workhorse of digital electronics for years, and **ECL** (Emitter-Coupled Logic), which is used when very high-speed operation is required.

MOS gates are 10 times slower than TTL and 100 times slower than ECL but require almost no power and almost no space, so large numbers of them can be packed together tightly. MOS comes in many varieties, including PMOS, NMOS, and CMOS, with new varieties continually appearing.

3.1.2. Boolean Algebra

To describe the circuits that can be built by combining gates, a new type of algebra is needed, one in which variables and functions can take on only the values 0 and 1. Such an algebra is called a **Boolean algebra**, after its discoverer, the English mathematician George Boole (1815-1864). Strictly speaking, we are really referring to a specific type of Boolean algebra, a **switching algebra**, but the term "Boolean algebra" is so widely used to mean "switching algebra" that we will not make the distinction.

Just as there are functions in "ordinary" (i.e, high school) algebra, so are there functions in Boolean algebra. A Boolean function has one or more input variables and yields a result that depends only on the values of these variables. A simple function, f, can be defined by saying that $f(A)$ is 1 if A is 0 and $f(A)$ is 0 if A is 1. This function is the NOT function of Fig. 3-2(a).

Because a Boolean function of n variables has only 2^n possible sets of input values, the function can be completely described by giving a table with 2^n rows, each row telling the value of the function for a different combination of input values. Such a table is called a **truth table**. The tables of Fig. 3-2 are examples of truth tables. If we agree to always list the rows of a truth table in numerical order (base 2), that is, for two variables in the order 00, 01, 10, and 11, the function can be completely described by the 2^n-bit binary number obtained by reading the result column of the truth table vertically. Thus NAND is 1110, NOR is 1000, AND is 0001, and OR is 0111. Obviously, only 16 Boolean functions of two variables exist, corresponding to the 16 possible 4-bit result strings. In contrast, ordinary algebra has an infinite number of functions of two variables, none of which can be described by giving a table of outputs for all possible inputs because each variable can take on any one of an infinite number of possible values.

Figure 3-3(a) shows the truth table for a Boolean function of three variables: $M = f(A, B, C)$. This function is the majority logic function, that is, it is 0 if a majority of its inputs are 0 and 1 if a majority of its inputs are 1. Although any Boolean function can be fully specified by giving its truth table, as the number of variables increases, this notation becomes increasingly cumbersome. Instead, another notation is frequently used.

To see how this other notation comes about, note that any Boolean function can be specified by telling which combinations of input variables give an output value of 1. For the function of Fig. 3-3(a) there are four combinations of input variables that make M 1. By convention, we will place a bar over an input variable to indicate that its value is inverted. The absence of a bar means that it is not inverted. Furthermore, we will use implied multiplication or a dot to mean AND and + to mean OR. Thus, for example, $A\bar{B}C$ means $A = 1$ and $B = 0$ and $C = 1$. Also, $A\bar{B} + B\bar{C}$ means ($A = 1$ and $B = 0$) or ($B = 1$ and $C = 0$). The four rows of Fig. 3-3(a) producing 1 bits in the output are: $\bar{A}BC$, $A\bar{B}C$, $AB\bar{C}$, and ABC. The function, M, is true if any one of these four conditions is true; hence we can write

$$M = \bar{A}BC + A\bar{B}C + AB\bar{C} + ABC$$

as a compact way of giving the truth table. A function of n variables can thus be described by giving a "sum" of at most 2^n n-variable "product" terms. This formulation is especially important, as we will see shortly, because it leads directly to an implementation of the function using standard gates.

3.1.3. Implementation of Boolean Functions

As mentioned above, the formulation of a Boolean function as a sum of up to 2^n product terms leads directly to a possible implementation. Using Fig. 3-3 as an example, we can see how this implementation is accomplished. In Fig. 3-3(b), the inputs, A, B, and C, are shown at the left edge and the output function, M, is shown at the right edge. Because complements of the input variables are needed, they are generated by tapping the inputs and passing them through the inverters labeled 1, 2, and 3. To keep the figure from becoming cluttered, we have drawn in six vertical lines, three of which are connected to the input variables, and three of which are connected to their complements. These lines provide a convenient source for the inputs to subsequent gates. For example, gates 5, 6, and 7 all use A as an input. In an actual circuit these gates would probably be wired directly to A without using any intermediate "vertical" wires.

The circuit contains four AND gates, one for each term in the equation for M (i.e., one for each row in the truth table having a 1 bit in the result column). Each AND gate computes one row of the truth table, as indicated. Finally, all the product terms are ORed together to get the final result.

The circuit of Fig. 3-3(b) uses a convention that we will need repeatedly

A	B	C	M
0	0	0	0
0	0	1	0
0	1	0	0
0	1	1	1
1	0	0	0
1	0	1	1
1	1	0	1
1	1	1	1

(a)

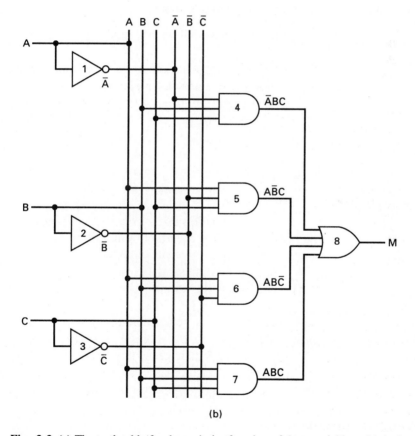

(b)

Fig. 3-3. (a) The truth table for the majority function of three variables. (b) A circuit for (a).

throughout this book: when two lines cross, no connection is implied unless a heavy dot is present at the intersection. For example, the output of gate 3 crosses all six vertical lines but it is connected only to $\overline{C}$. Be warned that some authors use other conventions.

From the example of Fig. 3-3 it should be clear how to implement a circuit for any Boolean function:

1. Write down the truth table for the function.

2. Provide inverters to generate the complement of each input.

3. Draw an AND gate for each term with a 1 in the result column.

4. Wire the AND gates to the appropriate inputs.

5. Feed the output of all the AND gates into an OR gate.

Although we have shown how any Boolean function can be implemented using NOT, AND, and OR gates, it is often convenient to implement circuits using only a single type of gate. Fortunately, it is straightforward to convert circuits generated by the preceding algorithm to pure NAND or pure NOR form. To make such a conversion, all we need is a way to implement NOT, AND, and OR using a single gate type. The top row of Fig. 3-4 shows how all three of these can be implemented using only NAND gates; the bottom row shows how it can be done using only NOR gates. (These are straightforward, but they are not the only possibilities; see Fig. 3-5.)

One way to implement a Boolean function using only NAND or only NOR gates is first follow the procedure given above for constructing it with NOT, AND, and OR. Then replace the multi-input gates with equivalent circuits using two-input gates. For example, $A + B + C + D$ can be computed as $(A + B) + (C + D)$, using three two-input OR gates. Finally, the NOT, AND, and OR gates are replaced by the circuits of Fig. 3-4.

Although this procedure does not lead to the optimal circuits, in the sense of the minimum number of gates, it does show that a solution is always feasible. Both NAND and NOR gates are said to be **complete**, because any Boolean function can be computed using either of them. No other gate has this property, which is another reason they are often preferred for the building blocks of circuits.

3.1.4. Circuit Equivalence

Circuit designers naturally try to reduce the number of gates in their products to reduce component cost, printed circuit board space, power consumption, and so on. To reduce the complexity of a circuit, the designer must find another circuit that computes the same function as the original but does so with fewer gates (or perhaps

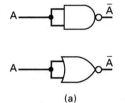

(a)

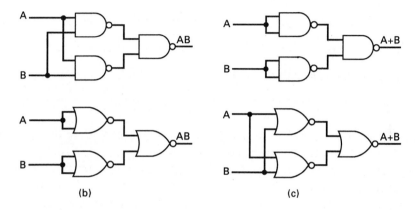

(b)   (c)

Fig. 3-4. Construction of (a) NOT, (b) AND, and (c) OR gates using only NAND gates or only NOR gates.

with simpler gates, for example, two-input gates instead of four-input gates). In the search for equivalent circuits, Boolean algebra can be a valuable tool.

As an example of how Boolean algebra can be used, consider the circuit and truth table for $AB + AC$ shown in Fig. 3-5(a). Although we have not discussed them yet, many of the rules of ordinary algebra also hold for Boolean algebra. In particular, $AB + AC$ can be factored into $A(B + C)$ using the distributive law. Figure 3-5(b) shows the circuit and truth table for $A(B + C)$. Because two functions are equivalent if and only if they have the same output for all possible inputs, it is easy to see from the truth tables of Fig. 3-5 that $A(B + C)$ is equivalent to $AB + AC$. Despite this equivalence, the circuit of Fig. 3-5(b) is clearly better than that of Fig. 3-5(a) because it contains fewer gates.

In general, a circuit designer can represent a circuit as a Boolean function and then apply the laws of Boolean algebra to this representation in an attempt to find a simpler but equivalent one. From the final representation, a new circuit can be constructed.

To use this approach, we need some identities from Boolean algebra. Figure 3-6 shows some of the major ones. It is interesting to note that each law has two forms that are **duals** of each other. By interchanging AND and OR and also 0 and 1, either form can be produced from the other one. All the laws can be easily proven

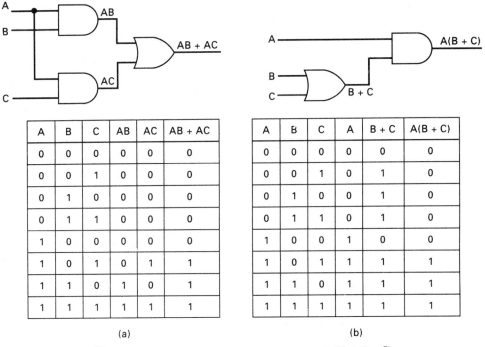

A	B	C	AB	AC	AB + AC
0	0	0	0	0	0
0	0	1	0	0	0
0	1	0	0	0	0
0	1	1	0	0	0
1	0	0	0	0	0
1	0	1	0	1	1
1	1	0	1	0	1
1	1	1	1	1	1

(a)

A	B	C	A	B + C	A(B + C)
0	0	0	0	0	0
0	0	1	0	1	0
0	1	0	0	1	0
0	1	1	0	1	0
1	0	0	1	0	0
1	0	1	1	1	1
1	1	0	1	1	1
1	1	1	1	1	1

(b)

Fig. 3-5. Two equivalent functions. (a) $AB + AC$. (b) $A(B + C)$.

by constructing their truth tables. Except for de Morgan's law, the absorption law, and the AND form of the distributive law, the results are reasonably intuitive. De Morgan's law can be extended to more variables, for example, $\overline{ABC} = \overline{A} + \overline{B} + \overline{C}$.

Name	AND form	OR form
Identity law	$1A = A$	$0 + A = A$
Null law	$0A = 0$	$1 + A = 1$
Idempotent law	$AA = A$	$A + A = A$
Inverse law	$A\overline{A} = 0$	$A + \overline{A} = 1$
Commutative law	$AB = BA$	$A + B = B + A$
Associative law	$(AB)C = A(BC)$	$(A + B) + C = A + (B + C)$
Distributive law	$A+BC = (A+B)(A+C)$	$A(B + C) = AB + AC$
Absorption law	$A(A+B) = A$	$A + AB = A$
De Morgan's law	$\overline{AB} = \overline{A} + \overline{B}$	$\overline{A + B} = \overline{A}\overline{B}$

Fig. 3-6. Some identities of Boolean algebra.

De Morgan's law suggests an alternative notation. In Fig. 3-7(a) the AND form is shown with negation indicated by inversion bubbles, both for input and output.

Thus an OR gate with inverted inputs is equivalent to a NAND gate. From Fig. 3-7(b), the dual form of de Morgan's law, it is clear that a NOR gate can be drawn as an AND gate with negated inputs. By negating both forms of de Morgan's law, we arrive at Fig. 3-7(c) and (d), which show equivalent representations of the AND and OR gates. Analogous symbols exist for the multiple variable forms of de Morgan's law (e.g., an n input NAND gate becomes an OR gate with n inverted inputs).

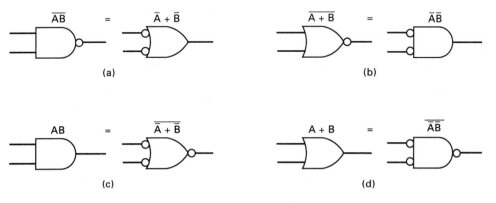

Fig. 3-7. Alternative symbols for some gates: (a) NAND. (b) NOR. (c) AND. (d) OR.

Using the identities of Fig. 3-7 and the analogous ones for multi-input gates, it is easy to convert the sum-of-products representation of a truth table to pure NAND or pure NOR form. As an example, consider the XOR (exclusive or) function of Fig. 3-8(a). The standard sum-of-products circuit is shown in Fig. 3-8(b). To convert to NAND form, the lines connecting the output of the AND gates to the input of the OR gate should be redrawn with two inversion bubbles, as shown in Fig. 3-8(c). Finally, using Fig. 3-7(a), we arrive at Fig. 3-8(d). The variables $\overline{A}$ and $\overline{B}$ can be generated from A and B using NAND or NOR gates with their inputs tied together. Note that inversion bubbles can be moved along a line at will, for example, from the outputs of the input gates in Fig. 3-8(d) to the inputs of the output gate.

As a final note on circuit equivalence, we will now demonstrate the surprising result that the same physical gate can compute different functions, depending on the conventions used. In Fig. 3-9(a) we show the output of a certain gate, F, for different input combinations. Both inputs and outputs are shown in volts. If we adopt the convention that 0 volts is logical 0 and 5 volts is logical 1, called **positive logic**, we get the truth table of Fig. 3-9(b), the AND function. If, however, we adopt **negative logic**, which has 0 volts as logical 1 and 5 volts as logical 0, we get the truth table of Fig. 3-9(c), the OR function.

Thus the convention chosen to map voltages onto logical values is critical. Except where otherwise specified, we will henceforth use positive logic, so the terms logical 1, true, and high are synonyms, as are logical 0, false, and low.

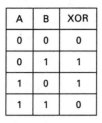

A	B	XOR
0	0	0
0	1	1
1	0	1
1	1	0

(a)

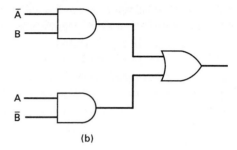

(b)

(c)   (d)

Fig. 3-8. (a) The truth table for the EXCLUSIVE OR function. (b)-(d) Three circuits for computing it.

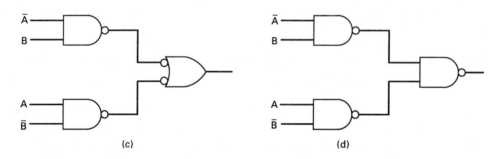

A	B	F
0^V	0^V	0^V
0^V	5^V	0^V
5^V	0^V	0^V
5^V	5^V	5^V

(a)

A	B	F
0	0	0
0	1	0
1	0	0
1	1	1

(b)

A	B	F
1	1	1
1	0	1
0	1	1
0	0	0

(c)

Fig. 3-9. (a) Electrical characteristics of a device. (b) Positive logic. (c) Negative logic.

3.2. BASIC DIGITAL LOGIC CIRCUITS

In the previous sections we saw how to implement truth tables and other simple circuits using individual gates. In practice, few circuits are actually constructed gate-by-gate anymore, although this once was common. Nowadays, the usual building blocks are modules containing a number of gates. In the following sections we will examine these building blocks more closely and see how they are used and how they can be constructed from individual gates.

3.2.1. Integrated Circuits

Gates are not manufactured or sold individually but rather in units called **integrated circuits**, often called **ICs** or **chips**. An IC is a square piece of silicon about 5×5 mm on which some gates have been deposited. ICs are usually mounted in rectangular plastic or ceramic packages measuring 5 to 15 mm wide and 20 to 50 mm long. Along the long edges are two parallel rows of pins about 5 mm long that can be inserted in sockets or soldered to printed circuit boards. Each pin connects to the input or output of some gate on the chip or to power or to ground. The packages with two rows of pins outside and ICs inside are technically known as **dual inline packages** or **DIPs**, but everyone calls them chips, thus blurring the distinction between the piece of silicon and its package. The most common packages have 14, 16, 18, 20, 22, 24, 28, 40, 64, or 68 pins. For large chips, square packages with pins on all four sides are often used.

Chips can be divided into rough classes based on the number of gates they contain, as given below. This classification scheme is obviously extremely crude, but it is sometimes useful. The upper limit on VLSI is currently between 1 and 2 million transistors.

SSI (Small Scale Integrated) circuit: 1 to 10 gates.
MSI (Medium Scale Integrated) circuit: 10 to 100 gates.
LSI (Large Scale Integrated) circuit: 100 to 100,000 gates.
VLSI (Very Large Scale Integrated) circuit: >100,000 gates.

These classes have different properties and are used in different ways.

An SSI chip typically contains two to six independent gates, each of which can be used individually, in the style of the previous sections. Figure 3-10 illustrates a schematic drawing of a common SSI chip containing four NAND gates. Each of these gates has two inputs and one output, requiring a total of 12 pins for the four gates. In addition, the chip needs power (V_{cc}), and ground (GND), which are shared by all gates. The package generally has a notch near pin 1 to identify the orientation. To avoid clutter in circuit diagrams, neither power, nor ground, nor unused gates are conventionally shown.

Figure 3-11 shows some other common SSI chips. These chips belong to the 7400 TTL series developed by Texas Instruments and now produced by many semiconductor manufacturers. They are most appropriate for simple circuits that cannot be realized any other way. The circuit of Fig. 3-3(b) could be constructed from one 7404, two 7411s, and one 7432. No four-input OR gate is available in the 7400 series, but the same function can be computed by ORing pairs of inputs and then ORing the results together. Symbolically, this can be represented as $A + B + C + D$ $= (A + B) + (C + D)$, that is, A and B are ORed together as are C and D, with these

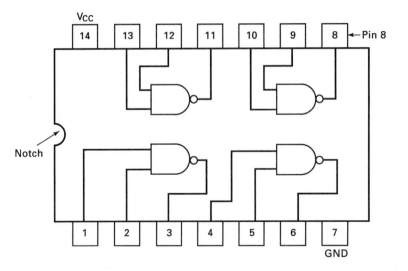

Fig. 3-10. An SSI chip containing four gates.

two sums then being ORed. If the circuit of Fig. 3-3(b) were actually constructed this way, the printed circuit board on which they were mounted would contain conducting wire-like tracks to connect the appropriate pins. Some of the gates would not be used. The 7486 chip contains a gate we have not shown before, the EXCLUSIVE OR gate, which is a one-gate equivalent to the circuit of Fig. 3-8.

For our purposes, all gates are ideal in the sense that the output appears as soon as the input is applied. In reality, chips have a finite **gate delay**, which includes both the signal propagation time through the chip and the switching time. Typical delays are 1 to 20 nsec. In schematics one often sees numbers like 74S00, 74L00, 74H00, and 74LS00. These represent functionally equivalent chips with different delay/power/price trade-offs. The 74C00 series consists of CMOS chips that are functionally identical to the corresponding 7400 TTL ones.

It is within the current state of the art to put a million gates on a single chip. Because any circuit can be built up from NAND gates, you might think that a manufacturer could make a very general chip containing the equivalent of 250,000 chips like the 7400. Unfortunately, such a chip would need 3,000,002 pins. With the standard pin spacing of 0.1 inch, the chip would be over 2 miles long, which might have a negative effect on sales. Clearly, the only way to take advantage of the technology is to design circuits with a high gate/pin ratio. In the following sections we will look at simple MSI circuits that combine a number of gates internally to provide a useful function requiring only a limited number of external connections (pins). After that we will examine two applications requiring thousands of gates (LSI) yet only 20 to 40 pins—namely, memory chips and microprocessor chips. The dividing line between LSI and VLSI is vague, but a typical VLSI chip might have a large microprocessor, some memory, in one form or another, and perhaps a special-purpose floating-point unit.

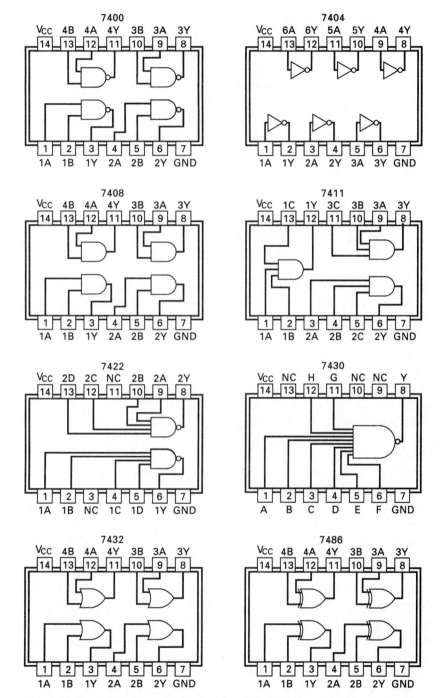

Fig. 3-11. Some SSI chips. Pin layouts from *The TTL Data Book for Design Engineers*, copyright © 1976 Texas Instruments Incorporated.

3.2.2. Combinational Circuits

Many applications of digital logic require a circuit with multiple inputs and multiple outputs in which the outputs are uniquely determined by the current inputs. Such a circuit is called a **combinational circuit**. Not all circuits have this property. For example, a circuit containing memory elements may generate outputs that depend on the stored values as well as the input variables. A circuit implementing a truth table, such as that of Fig. 3-3(a), is a typical example of a combinational circuit. In this section we will examine some frequently used combinational circuits, as examples of MSI chips.

Multiplexers

At the digital logic level, a **multiplexer** is a circuit with 2^n data inputs, one data output, and n control inputs that select one of the data inputs. The selected data input is "gated" (i.e., routed) to the output. Figure 3-12 is a schematic diagram for an eight-input multiplexer. The three control lines, A, B, and C, encode a 3-bit number that specifies which of the eight input lines is gated to the OR gate and thence to the output. No matter what value is on the control lines, seven of the AND gates will always output 0; the other one may output either 0 or 1, depending on the value of the selected input line. Each AND gate is enabled by a different combination of the control inputs.

The circuit of Fig. 3-12 is an ideal candidate for implementation as an MSI chip, as illustrated in Fig. 3-13(a). Such a chip has eight data inputs, three control inputs, and one output. When power and ground are included, the chip could be implemented in a 14-pin package. Using this MSI multiplexer chip, we can implement the circuit of Fig. 3-3(b) on a single chip, as shown in Fig. 3-13(b). For each combination of A, B, and C, one of the data input lines is selected. Each input is wired to either V_{cc} (logical 1) or ground (logical 0). The algorithm for wiring the inputs is simple: input D_i is the same as the value in row i of the truth table. In Fig. 3-3(a), rows 0, 1, 2, and 4 are 0, so the corresponding inputs are grounded; the remaining rows are 1, so they are wired to logical 1. In this manner any truth table of three variables can be implemented using the chip of Fig. 3-13(a).

We have already seen how a multiplexer chip can be used to select one of several inputs and how it can implement a truth table. Another of its applications is as a parallel-to-serial data converter. By putting 8 bits of data on the input lines and then stepping the control lines sequentially from 000 to 111 (binary), the 8 bits are put onto the output line in series. A typical use for parallel-to-serial conversion is in a keyboard, where each keystroke implicitly defines a 7- or 8-bit number that must be output serially over a telephone line.

The MSI chip of Fig. 3-13(a) has eight data inputs. Chips similar to it are commercially available, as are multiplexer chips with 16 data inputs. Furthermore, chips with two independent four-input multiplexers exist, as do chips with four

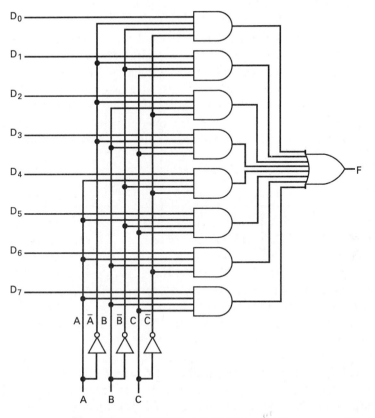

Fig. 3-12. An eight-input multiplexer circuit.

independent two-input multiplexers. Some of these chips provide both the selected output and its complement, and some have an additional input line that forces the output to 0, independent of the inputs (i.e., a chip enable/disable pin).

The inverse of a multiplexer is a **demultiplexer**, which routes its single input signal to one of 2^n outputs, depending on the values of the n control lines. If the binary value on the control lines is k, output k is selected.

Decoders

As a second example of an MSI chip, we will now look at a circuit that takes an n-bit number as input and uses it to select (i.e., set to 1) exactly one of the 2^n output lines. Such a circuit, illustrated for $n = 3$ in Fig. 3-14, is called a **decoder**.

To see where a decoder might be useful, imagine a memory consisting of eight chips, each containing 8K bytes. Chip 0 has addresses 0 to 8191, chip 1 has addresses 8192 to 16383, and so on. When an address is presented to the memory,

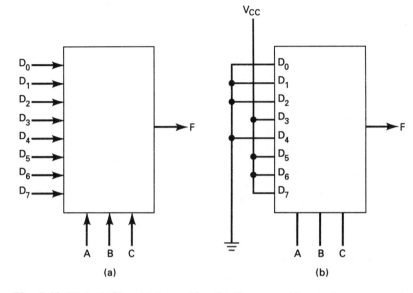

Fig. 3-13. (a) An MSI multiplexer chip. (b) The same chip wired to compute the majority function.

the high-order 3 bits are used to select one of the eight chips. Using the circuit of Fig. 3-14, these 3 bits are the three inputs, A, B, and C. Depending on the inputs, exactly one of the eight output lines, D_0, ..., D_7, is 1; the rest are 0. Each output line enables one of the eight memory chips. Because only one output line is set to 1, only one chip is enabled.

The operation of the circuit of Fig. 3-14 is straightforward. Each AND gate has three inputs, of which the first is either A or $\bar{A}$, the second is either B or $\bar{B}$, and the third is either C or $\bar{C}$. Each gate is enabled by a different combination of inputs: D_0 by $\bar{A}\,\bar{B}\,\bar{C}$, D_1 by $\bar{A}\,\bar{B}\,C$, and so on.

Commercially available MSI decoder chips include 4-to-16, 3-to-8 and dual 2-to-4 (i.e, two 2-to-4 decoders packaged together in a single chip). Furthermore, 4-to-10 decoders for decoding binary-coded decimal numbers are also common.

Comparators

Another useful MSI chip is the **comparator**, which compares two input words. The simple comparator of Fig. 3-15 takes two inputs, A, and B, each of length 4 bits, and produces 1 if they are equal and a 0 if they are not equal. The circuit is based on the EXCLUSIVE OR gate, which puts out a 0 if its inputs are equal and a 1 if they are unequal. If the two input words are equal, all four of the EXCLUSIVE OR gates must output 0. These four signals can then be ORed together; if the result is 0,

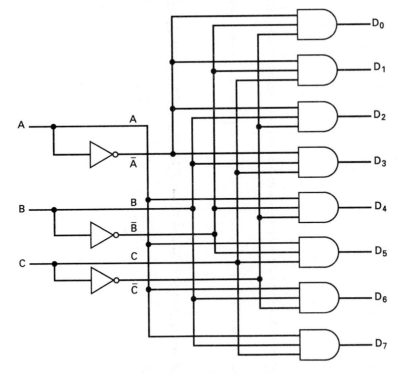

Fig. 3-14. A 3-to-8 decoder circuit.

the input words are equal, otherwise not. In our example we have used a NOR gate as the final stage to reverse the sense of the test: 1 means equal, 0 means unequal. Commercially available MSI comparator chips not only have a pin for $A = B$, but also pins for $A < B$ and $A > B$.

Programmed Logic Arrays

We saw earlier that arbitrary functions (truth tables) can be constructed by computing product terms with AND gates and then ORing the products together. A very general chip for forming sums of products is the **programmed logic array** or **PLA**, a small example of which is shown in Fig. 3-16. This chip, the 74S330, has input lines for 12 variables. The complement of each input is generated internally, making 24 input signals in all. The heart of the circuit is an array of 50 AND gates, each of which can potentially have any subset of the 24 input signals as an input. Which input signal goes to which AND gate is determined by a 24×50 bit matrix supplied by the user. Each input line to the 50 AND gates contains a fuse. When shipped from the factory, all 1200 fuses are intact. To program the matrix the user burns out selected fuses by applying a high voltage to the chip.

The output part of the circuit consists of six OR gates, each of which has up to

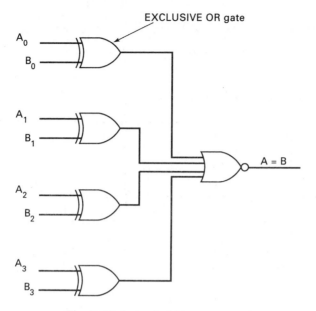

Fig. 3-15. A simple 4-bit comparator.

50 inputs, corresponding to the 50 outputs of the AND gates. Again here, a user-supplied (50×6) matrix tells which of the potential connections actually exist. The chip has 12 input pins, 6 output pins, power, and ground, for a total of 20.

As an example of how a PLA can be used, let us reconsider the circuit of Fig. 3-3(b) once more. It has three inputs, four AND gates, one OR gate, and three inverters. With the appropriate internal connections made, our PLA can compute this function using three of its 12 inputs, four of its 50 AND gates, and one of its six OR gates. (The four AND gates should compute $\overline{A}BC$, $A\overline{B}C$, $AB\overline{C}$, and ABC, respectively; the OR gate takes these four product terms as input.) In fact, the same PLA could be wired up to compute simultaneously a total of four functions of similar complexity. For these simple functions the number of input variables is the limiting factor; for more complicated ones it might be the AND or OR gates.

Although the field-programmable PLAs described above are still in use, for many applications custom-made PLAs are preferable. These are designed by the (large-volume) customer and fabricated by the manufacturer to the customer's specifications. Such PLAs are cheaper than field-programmable ones.

We can now compare the three different ways we have discussed for implementing the truth table of Fig. 3-3(a). Using SSI components, we need four chips. Alternatively, we could suffice with one MSI multiplexer chip, as shown in Fig. 3-13(b). Finally, we could use a quarter of one PLA chip. Obviously, if many functions are needed, the PLA is more efficient than the other two methods. For simple circuits, the cheaper SSI and MSI chips may be preferable.

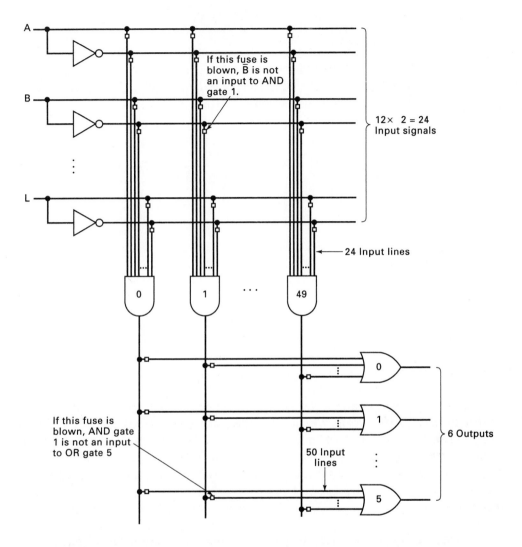

Fig. 3-16. A 12-input, 6-output programmed logic array. The little squares represent fuses that can be burned out to determine the function to be computed. The fuses are arranged in two matrices: the upper one for the AND gates and the lower one for the OR gates.

3.2.3. Arithmetic Circuits

It is now time to move on from the general-purpose MSI circuits discussed above to MSI combinational circuits used for doing arithmetic. We will begin with a simple 8-bit shifter, then look at how adders are constructed, and finally examine arithmetic logical units, which play a central role in any computer.

Shifters

Our first arithmetic MSI circuit is an eight-input, eight-output shifter (see Fig. 3-17). Eight bits of input are presented on lines D_0, ..., D_7. The output, which is just the input shifted one bit, is available on lines S_0, ..., S_7. The control line, C, determines the direction of the shift, 0 for left and 1 for right.

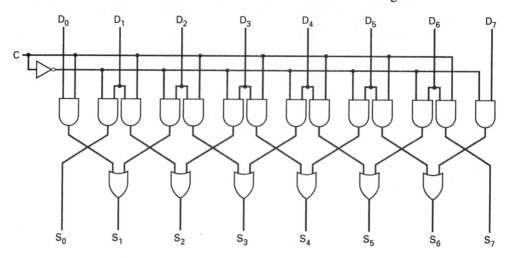

Fig. 3-17. A 1-bit left/right shifter.

To see how the circuit works, notice the pairs of AND gates for all the bits except the gates on the end. When $C = 1$, the right member of each pair is turned on, passing the corresponding input bit to output. Because the right AND gate is wired to the input of the OR gate to its right, a right shift is performed. When $C = 0$, it is the left member of the AND gate pair that turns on, effecting a left shift.

Adders

A computer that cannot add integers is unthinkable. Consequently, circuits for performing addition are an essential part of every CPU. The truth table for 1-bit addition is shown in Fig. 3-18(a). Two outputs are present, the sum of the inputs, A and B, and the carry to the next (leftward) position. A circuit for computing both the sum and the carry is given in Fig. 3-18(b). This circuit is known as a **half adder**.

Although a half adder is adequate for summing the low-order bits of two multi-bit input words, it will not do for a bit position in the middle of the word because it does not handle the carry into the position from the right. Instead, the **full adder** of Fig. 3-19 is needed. From inspection of the circuit it should be clear that a full adder is built up from two half adders. The *Sum* output line is 1 if an odd number of A, B, and the *Carry in* are 1. The *Carry out* is 1 if either A and B are both 1 (left

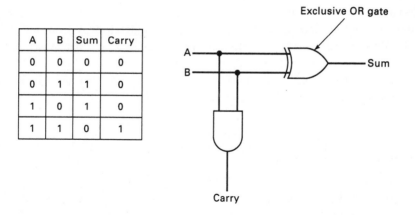

A	B	Sum	Carry
0	0	0	0
0	1	1	0
1	0	1	0
1	1	0	1

Fig. 3-18. (a) Truth table for 1-bit addition. (b) A circuit for a half adder.

input to the OR gate) or exactly one of them is 1 and the *Carry in* bit is also 1. Together the two half adders generate both the sum and the carry bits.

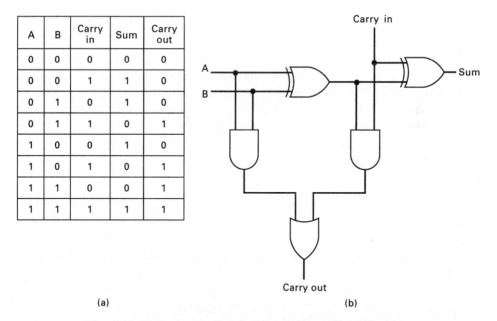

A	B	Carry in	Sum	Carry out
0	0	0	0	0
0	0	1	1	0
0	1	0	1	0
0	1	1	0	1
1	0	0	1	0
1	0	1	0	1
1	1	0	0	1
1	1	1	1	1

(a)   (b)

Fig. 3-19. (a) Truth table for full adder. (b) Circuit for a full adder.

To build an adder for, say, two 16-bit words, one just replicates the circuit of Fig. 3-19(b) 16 times. The carry out of a bit is used as the carry into its left neighbor. The carry into the rightmost bit is wired to 0. This type of adder is called a

ripple carry adder, because in the worst case, adding 1 to 111...111 (binary), the addition cannot complete until the carry has rippled all the way from the rightmost bit to the leftmost bit. Adders that do not have this delay, and hence are faster, also exist.

Arithmetic Logical Units

Most computers contain a single circuit for performing the AND, OR, and sum of two machine words. Typically, such a circuit for n-bit words is built up of n identical circuits for the individual bit positions. Figure 3-20 is a simple example of such a circuit, called an **arithmetic logical unit** or ALU. It can compute any one of four functions—namely, A AND B, A OR B, $\bar{B}$, or $A + B$, depending on whether the function-select input lines F_0 and F_1 contain $00, 01, 10$, or 11 (binary).

The lower left-hand corner of our ALU contains a 2-bit decoder to generate enable lines for the four operations, based on F_0 and F_1. The upper left-hand corner has the logic to compute A AND B, A OR B, and $\bar{B}$, but at most one of these results is passed onto the final OR gate, depending on the enable lines coming out of the decoder. Because exactly one of the decoder outputs will be 1, exactly one of the four AND gates driving the OR gate will be enabled; the other three will output 0, independent of A and B.

The lower right-hand corner of the ALU contains a full adder for computing the sum of A and B, including handling the carries, because it is likely that several of these circuits will eventually be wired in parallel to perform full-word operations. Chips like Fig. 3-20 are actually available and are known as **bit slices**. They allow the computer designer to build an ALU of any desired width. Figure 3-21 shows an 8-bit ALU built up of eight 1-bit ALU slices. Chips containing eight slices packaged together are also available to simplify the design and reduce chip count. Four of these chips can then be connected up to build a 32-bit ALU.

3.2.4. Clocks

In many digital circuits the order in which events happen is critical. Sometimes one event must precede another, sometimes two events must occur simultaneously. To allow designers to achieve the required timing relations, many digital circuits use clocks to provide synchronization. A **clock** in this context is a circuit that emits a series of pulses with a precise pulse width and precise interval between consecutive pulses. The interval between corresponding edges of two consecutive pulses is called the **clock cycle time**. Pulse frequencies are commonly between 1 and 100 MHz, corresponding to clock cycles of 1000 nsec to 10 nsec. To achieve high accuracy, the clock frequency is usually controlled by a crystal oscillator.

In a computer, many events may happen during a single clock cycle. If these events must occur in a specific order, the clock cycle must be divided into

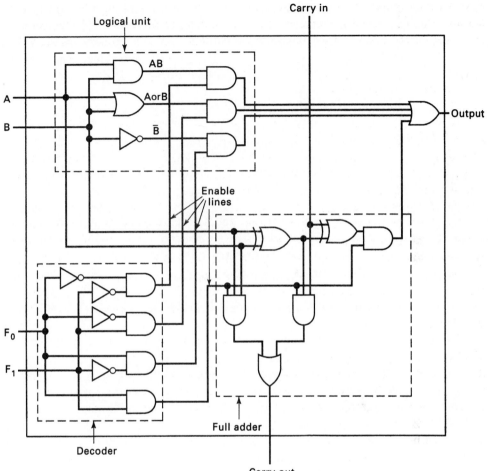

Fig. 3-20. A 1-bit ALU.

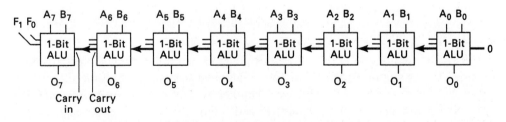

Fig. 3-21. Eight 1-bit ALU slices connected to make an 8-bit ALU.

subcycles. A common way of providing finer resolution than the basic clock is to
tap the primary clock line and insert a circuit with a known delay in it, thus generating a secondary clock signal that is phase-shifted from the primary, as shown in
Fig. 3-22(a). The timing diagram of Fig. 3-22(b) provides four time references for
discrete events:

1. Rising edge of C1

2. Falling edge of C1

3. Rising edge of C2

4. Falling edge of C2

By tying different events to the various edges, the required sequencing can be
achieved. If more than four time references are needed within a clock cycle, more
secondary lines can be tapped from the primary, with different delays.

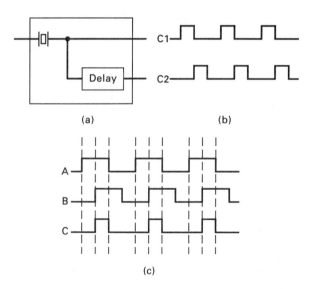

Fig. 3-22. (a) A clock. (b) The timing diagram for the clock. (c) Generation of an
asymmetric clock.

In some circuits one is interested in time intervals rather than discrete instants
of time. For example, some event may be allowed to happen any time C1 is high,
rather than precisely at the rising edge. Another event may only happen when C2 is
high. If more than two intervals are needed, more clock lines can be provided or
the high states of the two clocks can be made to overlap partially in time. In the
latter case four distinct intervals can be distinguished: $\overline{C1}$ AND $\overline{C2}$, $\overline{C1}$ AND C2,
C1 AND $\overline{C2}$, and C1 AND C2.

As an aside, it probably should be pointed out that Fig. 3-22(a)-(b) is really something of a simplification. Real clocks are symmetric, with time spent in the high state equal to the time spent in the low state, as shown by A in Fig. 3-22(c). To generate an asymmetric pulse train, the basic clock is shifted using a delay circuit, as shown by B in Fig. 3-22(c). Finally, these two are ANDed together, to get C in Fig. 3-22(c). It is this signal that is shown as C1 in Fig. 3-22(b). C2 can be generated by delaying C1.

3.3. MEMORY

An essential component of every computer is its memory. Without memory there could be no computers as we now know them. Memory is used for storing both instructions to be executed and data. In the following sections we will examine the basic components of a memory system starting at the gate level to see how they work and how they are combined to produce large memories.

3.3.1. Latches

To create a 1-bit memory, we need a circuit that somehow "remembers" previous input values. Such a circuit can be constructed from two NOR gates, as illustrated in Fig. 3-23(a). Analogous circuits can be built from NAND gates. We will not mention these further, however, because they are conceptually identical to the NOR versions.

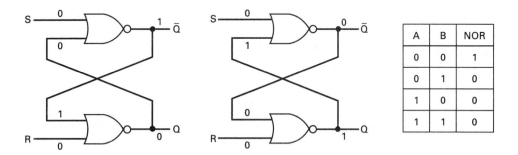

Fig. 3-23. (a) NOR latch in state 0. (b) NOR latch in state 1. (c) Truth table for NOR.

The circuit of Fig. 3-23(a) is called an **SR latch**. It has two inputs, S, for Setting the latch, and R, for Resetting (i.e., clearing) it. It also has two outputs, Q and $\bar{Q}$, which are complementary, as we will see shortly. Unlike a combinational circuit, the outputs of the latch are not uniquely determined by the current inputs.

To see how this comes about, let us assume that both S and R are 0, which they are most of the time. For argument's sake, let us further assume that $Q = 0$. Because Q is fed back into the upper NOR gate, both of its inputs are 0, so its output, $\bar{Q}$, is 1. The 1 is fed back into the lower gate, which then has inputs 1 and 0, yielding $Q = 0$. This state is at least consistent and is depicted in Fig. 3-23(a).

Now let us imagine that Q is not 0 but 1, with R and S still 0. The upper gate has inputs of 0 and 1, and an output, $\bar{Q}$, of 0, which is fed back to the lower gate. This state, shown in Fig. 3-23(b), is also consistent. A state with both outputs equal to 0 is inconsistent, because it forces both gates to have two 0s as input, which, if true, would produce 1, not 0, as output. Similarly, it is impossible to have both outputs equal to 1, because that would force the inputs to 0 and 1, which yields 0, not 1. Our conclusion is simple: For $R = S = 0$, the latch has two stable states, which we will refer to as 0 and 1, depending on Q.

Now let us examine the effect of the inputs on the state of the latch. Suppose that S becomes 1 while $Q = 0$. The inputs to the upper gate are then 1 and 0, forcing the output to 0. This change makes both inputs to the lower gate 0, forcing the output to 1. Thus setting S (i.e., making it 1) switches the state from 0 to 1. Setting R in state 0 has no effect because the output of the lower gate is the same for inputs of 10 and 11.

Using similar reasoning, it is easy to see that setting S in state 1 has no effect but that setting R drives the latch to state 0. In summary, when S is turned on momentarily, the latch ends up in state 1, regardless of what state it was previously in. Likewise, setting R forces the latch to state 0. The circuit "remembers" whether S or R was last on. Using this property we can build computer memories.

Clocked SR Latches

It is often convenient to prevent the latch from changing state except at certain specified times. To achieve this goal, we modify the basic circuit slightly, as shown in Fig. 3-24, to get a **clocked SR latch**.

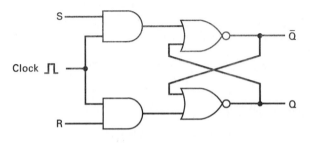

Fig. 3-24. A clocked SR latch.

This circuit has an additional input, the clock, which is normally 0. With the clock 0, both AND gates output 0, independent of S and R, and the latch does not change state. When the clock is 1, the effect of the AND gates vanishes and the latch becomes sensitive to S and R. Despite its name, the clock signal need not be driven by a clock. The terms **enable** and **strobe** are also widely used to mean that the clock input is 1; that is, the circuit is sensitive to the state of S and R.

Up until now we have carefully swept the problem of what happens when both S and R are 1 under the rug. And for good reason: the circuit becomes nondeterministic when both R and S finally return to 0. The only consistent state for $S = R = 1$ is $Q = \overline{Q} = 0$, but as soon as both inputs return to 0, the latch must jump to one of its two stable states. If either input drops back to 0 before the other, the one remaining 1 longest wins, because when just one input is 1, it forces the state. If both inputs return to 0 simultaneously (which is very unlikely), the latch jumps to one of its stable states at random.

Clocked D Latches

A good way to resolve the SR latch's ambiguity is to make sure that it cannot occur. Figure 3-25 gives a latch circuit with only one input, D. Because the input to the lower AND gate is always the complement of the input to the upper one, the problem of both inputs being 1 never arises. When $D = 1$ and the clock is 1, the latch is driven into state logical 1. When $D = 0$ and the clock is 1, the latch is driven into state logical 0. Put in other terms, when the clock is 1, the current value of D is sampled and stored in the latch. This circuit, called a **clocked D latch**, is a true 1-bit memory. The value stored is always available at Q. To load the current value of D into the memory, a positive pulse is put on the clock line.

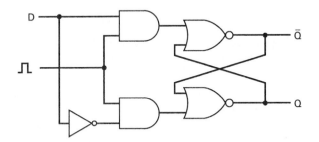

Fig. 3-25. A clocked D latch.

3.3.2. Flip-Flops and Registers

In many circuits it is necessary to sample the value on a certain line at a particular instant in time and store it. In principle, one way to achieve this goal is to use a clocked D latch with a very short pulse on the clock line around the time the sample is to be made. In practice, generating very short pulses can be difficult, so a variation on the latch circuit has been developed. In this variant, called a **flip-flop,** the state transition does not occur when the clock is 1 but during the clock transition from 0 to 1 or from 1 to 0 instead. Thus the length of the clock pulse is unimportant, as long as the transitions occur fast.

For emphasis, we will repeat the difference between a flip-flop and a latch. A flip-flop is **edge triggered**, whereas a latch is **level triggered**. Be warned, however, that in the literature these terms are often confused. Many authors use "flip-flop" when they are referring to a latch, and vice versa.

The standard symbols for latches and flip-flops are shown in Fig. 3-26. Figure 3-26(a) is a latch whose state is loaded when the clock, *CK*, is 1, in contrast to Fig. 3-26(b) which is a latch whose clock is normally 1 but which drops to 0 momentarily to load the state from *D*. Figure 3-26(c) and (d) are flip-flops rather than latches, which is indicated by the pointy symbol on the clock inputs. Figure 3-26(c) changes state on the rising edge of the clock pulse (0 to 1 transition), whereas Fig. 3-26(d) changes state on the falling edge (1 to 0 transition). Many, but not all, latches and flip-flops also have $\overline{Q}$ as an output, and some have two additional inputs *Set* or *Preset* (force state to logical 1) and *Reset* or *Clear* (force state to logical 0).

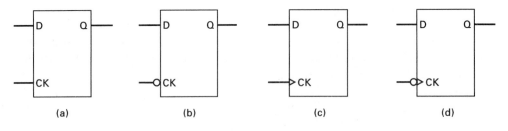

Fig. 3-26. D latches and flip-flops.

Registers

Flip-flops are available in a variety of configurations. A simple one, containing two independent D flip-flops with clear and preset signals, is illustrated in Fig. 3-27(a). Although packaged together in the same 14-pin chip, the two flip-flops are unrelated. A quite different arrangement is the octal flip-flop of Fig. 3-27(b). Here the eight (hence the term "octal") D flip-flops are not only missing the $\overline{Q}$ and preset lines, but all the clock lines are ganged together and driven by pin 11. The flip-flops themselves are of the Fig. 3-26(d) type, but the inversion bubbles on the flip-flops are canceled by the inverter tied to pin 11, so the flip-flops are loaded on the rising transition. All eight clear signals are also ganged, so when pin 1 goes to 0, all the flip-flops are forced to their 0 state. In case you are wondering why pin 11 is inverted at the input and then inverted again at each CK signal, an input signal may not have enough current to drive all eight flip-flops; the input inverter is really being used as an amplifier.

While the obvious reason for ganging the clock and clear lines of Fig. 3-27(b) is to save pins, in this configuration the chip is used in a different way from eight unrelated flip-flops. It is used as a single 8-bit register. Alternatively, two such chips can be used in parallel to form a 16-bit register by tying their respective pins 1 and 11 together. We will look at registers and their uses more closely in Chap. 4.

For the time being, the interesting thing to note is how the scarcity of pins drives chip design inexorably toward circuits with higher and higher gate-to-pin ratios. The simple D latch of Fig. 3-25 requires five gates, so an octal latch chip analogous to Fig. 3-27(b) needs 57 gates, including the eight inverters for CK and the eight inverters for CLR. An edge-triggered flip-flop is more complex than a latch internally, so Fig. 3-27(b) represents the equivalent of something like 100 gates, a far cry from the simple SSI chips of Fig. 3-11. In the next section we will study a different internal organization for memory chips, which allows a much higher gate-to-pin ratio.

3.3.3. Memory Organization

Although we have now progressed from the simple 1-bit memory of Fig. 3-25 to the 8-bit memory of Fig. 3-27(b) we cannot continue this way due to lack of pins on the chip. Each flip-flop requires two pins, D, and Q, in addition to the control pins shared by all the flip-flops. To build large memories a different organization is required.

What we need is a design in which the number of pins grows logarithmically rather than linearly with the memory capacity. A widely used memory organization that meets this criterion is shown in Fig. 3-28. This example illustrates a memory with four 3-bit words. Each operation reads or writes a full 3-bit word. While the total memory capacity of 12 bits is hardly more than our octal flip-flop, it requires fewer pins and most important, the design extends easily to large memories.

While the memory of Fig. 3-28 may look complicated at first, it is really quite simple due to its regular structure. It has eight input lines and three output lines. Three inputs are data: I_0, I_1, and I_2; two are for the address: A_0 and A_1; and three are for control: CS for Chip Select, RD for distinguishing between read and write, and OE for Output Enable. The three outputs are for data: D_0, D_1, and D_2. In principle this memory could be put into a 14-pin package, including power and ground versus 20 pins for the octal flip-flop.

To select this memory chip, external logic must set CS high and also set RD high (logical 1) for read and low (logical 0) for write. The two address lines must be set to indicate which of the four 3-bit words is to be read or written. For a read operation, the data input lines are not used, but the word selected is placed on the data

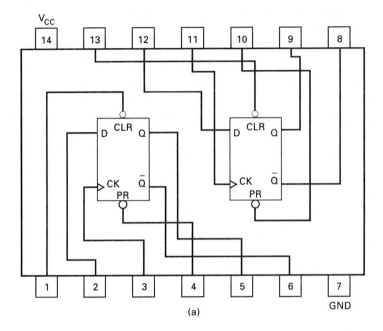

(a)

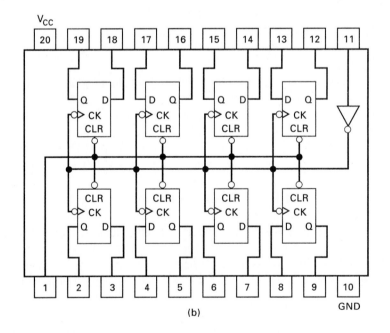

(b)

Fig. 3-27. (a) 7474 dual D flip-flop. (b) 74273 octal flip-flop.

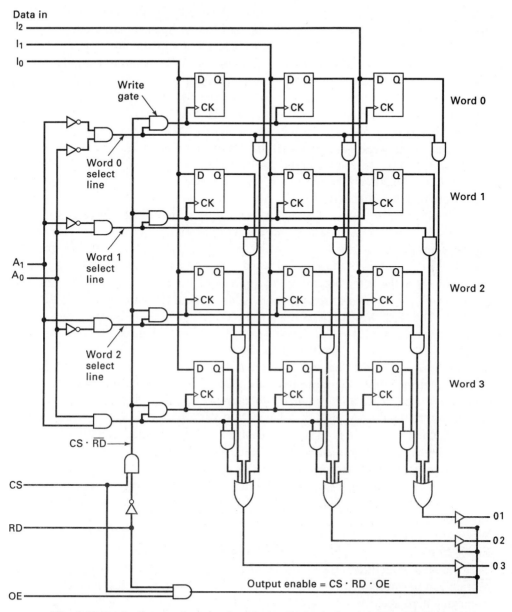

Fig. 3-28. Logic diagram for a 4 × 3 memory. Each row is one of the four 3-bit words. A read or write operation always reads or writes a complete word.

output lines. For a write operation, the bits present on the data input lines are loaded into the selected memory word; the data output lines are not used.

Now let us look at Fig. 3-28 closely to see how it works. The four word-select AND gates at the left of the memory form a decoder. The input inverters have been placed so that each gate is enabled (output is high) by a different address. Each gate drives a word select line, from top to bottom for words 0, 1, 2, and 3. When the chip has been selected for a write, the vertical line labeled CS · $\overline{\text{RD}}$ will be high, enabling one of the four write gates, depending on which word select line is high. The output of the write gate drives all the CK signals for the selected word, loading the input data into the flip-flops for that word. A write is only done if CS is high and RD is low, and even then only the word selected by A_0 and A_1 is written; the other words are not changed.

Read is similar to write. The address decoding is exactly the same as for write. But now the CS · $\overline{\text{RD}}$ line is low, so all the write gates are disabled and none of the flip-flops are modified. Instead, the word select line that is chosen enables the AND gates tied to the Q bits of the selected word. Thus one word outputs its data into the four-input OR gates at the bottom of the figure, while the other three words output 0. Consequently, the output of the OR gates is identical to the value stored in the word selected. The three words not selected make no contribution to the output.

Although we could have designed a circuit in which the three OR gates were just fed into the three output data lines, doing so sometimes causes problems. In particular, we have shown the data input lines and the data output lines as being different, but in actual memories the same lines are used. If we had tied the OR gates to the data output lines, the chip would try to output data, that is, force each line to a specific value, even on writes, thus interfering with the input data. For this reason, it is desirable to have a way to connect the OR gates to the data output lines on reads but disconnect them completely on writes. What we need is an electronic switch that can make or break a connection in a few nanoseconds.

Fortunately, such switches exist. Figure 3-29(a) shows the symbol for what is called a **noninverting buffer**. It has a data input, a data output, and a control input. When the control input is high, the buffer acts like a wire, as shown in Fig. 3-29(b). When the control input is low, the buffer acts like an open circuit, as shown in Fig. 3-29(c); it is as though someone detached the data output from the rest of the circuit with a wirecutter. However, in contrast to the wirecutter approach, the connection can be subsequently restored in a few nanoseconds by just making the control signal high again.

Figure 3-29(d) shows an **inverting buffer**, which acts like a normal inverter when control is high and disconnects the output from the circuit when control is low. Both kinds of buffers are **tri-state devices**, because they can output 0, 1, or none of the above (open circuit). Buffers also amplify signals, so they can drive many inputs simultaneously. They are sometimes used in circuits for this reason, even when their switching properties are not needed.

Getting back to the memory circuit, it should now be clear what the three

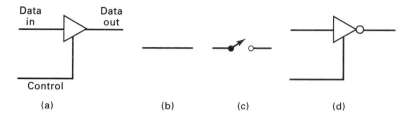

Fig. 3-29. (a) A noninverting buffer. (b) Effect of (a) when control is high. (c) Effect of (a) when control is low. (d) An inverting buffer.

noninverting buffers on the data output lines are for. When CS, RD, and OE are all high, the output enable signal is also high, enabling the buffers and putting a word onto the output lines. When any one of CS, RD, or OE is low, the data outputs are disconnected from the rest of the circuit.

3.3.4. Memory Properties

The nice thing about the memory of Fig. 3-28 is that it extends easily to larger sizes. As we drew it, the memory is 4×3, that is, four words of 3 bits each. To extend it to 4×8 we need only add five more columns of four flip-flops each, as well as five more input lines and five more output lines. To go from 4×3 to 8×3 we must add four more rows of three flip-flops each, as well as an address line A_2. With this kind of structure, the number of words in the memory should be a power of 2 for maximum efficiency, but the number of bits in a word can be anything.

Because integrated circuit technology is well suited to making chips whose internal structure is a repetitive two-dimensional pattern, memory chips are an ideal application for it. As the technology improves, the number of bits that can be put on a chip keeps increasing, typically by a factor of 4 every 3 or 4 years. In the early 1970s, chips had 1K bits; in later years, they had 4K, 16K, 64K, 256K, and so on. By 1990, it was possible to put 4 million bits and more on a chip. The larger chips do not always render the smaller ones obsolete due to different trade-offs in capacity, speed, power, price, and interfacing convenience.

For any given memory size, there are various ways of organizing the chip. Figure 3-30 shows two possible organizations for a medium-size chip (256K-bit): $32K \times 8$ and $256K \times 1$. In the former, 15 address lines are needed to address the selected *byte*, and eight data lines are needed for loading and storing data. In the latter, 18 address lines are needed to address the selected *bit*, but only one line is needed for data in and one for data out. In both cases lines are needed for distinguishing reads from writes and for chip select. The $\overline{OE}$ line is Output Enable; when it is 0 the output is present, when it is 1 it is not present (i.e., the chip output is disconnected from the circuit). The $\overline{WE}$ line is for Write Enable. The bars over $\overline{OE}$, $\overline{WE}$, and $\overline{CS}$ mean that the signal is enabled in the low-voltage state (logical 0) rather than the high-voltage state (logical 1). This convention will be discussed in more detail later.

Note that building a memory with a 16-bit word from 256K × 1 chips requires 16 chips in parallel and gives a total capacity of at least 512K bytes, whereas using 32K × 8 chips requires only two chips in parallel and allows memories as small as 64K bytes.

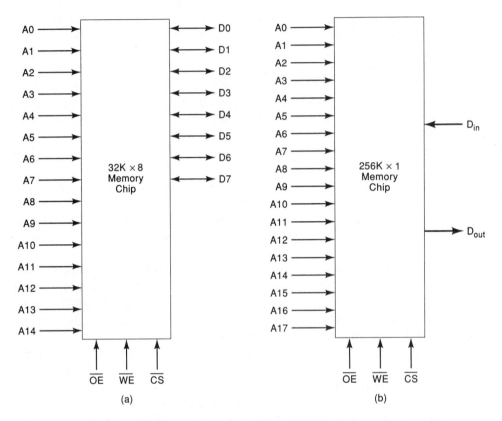

Fig. 3-30. Two ways of organizing a 256K-bit memory chip.

The memories we have studied so far can all be read and written. Such memories are called **RAMs** (Random Access Memories), which is a misnomer because all memory chips are randomly accessible, but the term is well established. RAMs come in two varieties, static and dynamic. **Static RAMs** are constructed internally using circuits similar to our basic D latch. These memories have the property that their contents are retained as long as the power is kept on: seconds, minutes, hours, even days.

Dynamic RAMs, in contrast, do not use latch-like circuits. Instead, a dynamic RAM is an array of tiny capacitors, each of which can be charged or discharged, allowing 0 and 1 to be stored. Because the electric charge tends to leak out, each bit in a dynamic RAM must be **refreshed** every few milliseconds to prevent the data from leaking away. Because external logic must take care of the refreshing, dynamic RAMs require more complex interfacing than static ones, although in many applications this disadvantage is compensated for by their larger capacities. Some dynamic RAMs have on-chip refresh logic, providing both high capacity and simple interfacing. Such chips are said to be **quasi-static**.

RAMs are not the only kind of memory chips. In many applications, such as toys, appliances, and cars, the program and some of the data must remain stored even when the power is turned off. Furthermore, once installed, neither the program nor the data are ever changed. These requirements have led to the development of **ROMs** (Read-Only Memories), which cannot be changed or erased, intentionally or otherwise. The data in a ROM are inserted during its manufacture, essentially by exposing a photosensitive material through a mask containing the desired bit pattern and then etching away the exposed (or unexposed) surface. The only way to change the program in a ROM is to replace the entire chip.

ROMs are much cheaper than RAMs when ordered in large volumes to defray the cost of making the mask. However, they are inflexible, because they cannot be changed after manufacture, and the turnaround time between placing an order and receiving the ROMs may be many weeks. To make it easier for companies to develop new ROM-based products, the **PROM** (Programmable ROM) was invented. This chip is like a ROM, except that it can be programmed (once) in the field, greatly reducing turnaround time.

The next development in this line was the **EPROM** (Erasable PROM), which can not only be field-programmed but also field-erased. When the quartz window in an EPROM is exposed to a strong ultraviolet light for 15 minutes, all the bits are set to 1. If many changes are expected during the design cycle, EPROMs are far more economical than PROMs because they can be reused.

Even better than the EPROM is the **EEPROM** (Electrically Erasable PROM), also called an **EAROM** (Electrically Alterable ROM), which can be erased by applying pulses to it instead of requiring it to be put in a special chamber for exposure to ultraviolet light. EEPROMs differ from RAMs in that both writing a byte and erasing a byte take thousands of times longer, although access times for reading ROMs, PROMs, EPROMs, EEPROMs, and RAMs are comparable (a few hundred nanoseconds at most).

3.4. MICROPROCESSOR CHIPS AND BUSES

Armed with information about SSI chips, MSI chips, and LSI memory chips, we can now tackle the main topic of this chapter—microprocessors. In this section, we will first look at some general aspects of microprocessors as viewed from the digital logic level, including **pinout** (what the signals on the various pins mean). Since microprocessors are so closely intertwined with the design of the buses they use, we will also provide an introduction to bus design in this section. In succeeding sections we will give detailed examples of both microprocessors and their buses.

3.4.1. Microprocessor Chips

For the purposes of this book we will use the term "microprocessor" to mean any CPU that is contained on a single chip, even though some of them have the architecture and computing power of a small mainframe. Our definition is based on packaging, which makes it appropriate for the digital logic level we are now studying.

We have chosen to focus on CPUs contained on a single chip for a good reason: their interface with the rest of the system is well defined. A typical microprocessor chip has between 40 and 132 pins, through which all its communication with the outside world must take place. Some pins output signals from the CPU, others accept signals from the outside world, and some can do both. By understanding the function of all the pins, we can learn how the CPU interacts with the memory and I/O devices at the digital logic level. Although the following material specifically relates to microprocessors, the basic ideas, for example, how CPUs reference memory, how I/O devices are interfaced, and so on, also hold for minicomputers and to some extent for mainframes, albeit in slightly different form.

The pins on a microprocessor chip can be divided into three types: address, data, and control. These pins are connected to similar pins on the memory and I/O chips via a collection of parallel wires called a bus. To fetch an instruction, the microprocessor first puts the memory address of that instruction on its address pins. Then it (usually) asserts a control line to inform the memory that it wants to read a word. The memory replies by putting the requested word on the microprocessor's data pins, and asserting a signal saying that it is done. When the microprocessor sees this signal, it accepts the word and carries out the instruction.

The instruction may require reading or writing data words, in which case the whole process is repeated for each additional word. We will go into the detail of how reading and writing works below, but for the time being, the important thing to understand is that the CPU communicates with the memory and I/O devices by presenting signals on its pins, and accepting signals on its pins. No other communication is possible.

A note on terminology is in order here. On some pins, a high (+5 v) signal causes an action to happen. On others, a low signal causes the action. To avoid confusion, we will consistently say that a signal is **asserted** (rather than saying it goes high or low) to mean that it is set to cause some action. Thus for some pins, asserting it means setting it high. For others, it means setting the pin low. Pins that are asserted low are given signal names containing an overbar. Thus WRITE is asserted high, but $\overline{\text{WRITE}}$ is asserted low. The opposite of asserted is **negated**. When nothing special is happening, pins are negated.

Two of the key parameters that determine the performance of a microprocessor are the number of address pins and the number of data pins. A chip with m address pins can address up to 2^m memory locations. Common values of m are 16, 20, 24, and 32. Similarly, a chip with n data pins can read or write an n-bit word in a single operation. Common values of n are 8, 16, and 32. A microprocessor with 8 data pins will take four operations to read a 32-bit word, whereas one with 32 data pins can do the same job in one operation. Thus the chip with 32 data pins is much faster, but is invariably more expensive as well.

In addition to address and data pins, each microprocessor has some control pins. The control pins regulate the flow and timing of data to and from the microprocessor and have other miscellaneous uses. All microprocessors have pins for power (usually +5 volts), ground, and a clock signal (a square wave), but the other pins vary greatly from chip to chip. Nevertheless, the control pins can be roughly grouped into the following major categories:

1. Bus control.

2. Interrupts.

3. Bus arbitration.

4. Coprocessor signaling.

5. Status.

6. Miscellaneous.

We will briefly describe each of these categories in general terms below. When we look at the Intel and Motorola chips later, we will provide more detail. A generic CPU chip using these signal groups is shown in Fig. 3-31.

The bus control pins are mostly outputs from the microprocessor to the bus (thus inputs to the memory and I/O chips) telling whether the microprocessor wants to read or write memory or do something else.

The interrupt pins are inputs from I/O devices to the microprocessor. In most systems, the microprocessor can tell an I/O device to start operation, and then go off and do something useful while the slow I/O device is doing its work. When the I/O has been completed, the I/O controller chip asserts a signal on one of these pins to interrupt the CPU and have it service the I/O device, for example, to check to see if any I/O errors occurred. Some microprocessors have an output pin to acknowledge the interrupt signal.

The bus arbitration pins are needed to regulate traffic on the bus, in order to prevent two devices from trying to use it at the same time. For arbitration purposes, the CPU counts as a device.

Many microprocessor chips are designed to operate with coprocessors, most commonly floating-point chips, but sometimes graphics or other chips as well. To

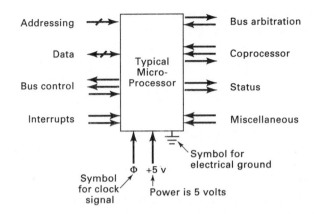

Fig. 3-31. The logical pinout of a typical (hypothetical) microprocessor. The arrows indicate input signals and output signals. The short diagonal lines indicate that multiple pins are used. For a specific microprocessor, a number will be given to tell how many.

facilitate communication between microprocessor and coprocessor, special pins are provided for making and granting various requests.

In addition to these signals, there are various miscellaneous pins that some microprocessors have. Some of these provide or accept status information, others are useful for resetting the computer, and still others are present to assure compatibility with older I/O chips.

3.4.2. Computer Buses

A **bus** is a common electrical pathway between multiple devices. One common example is the system bus present on all microcomputers, which consists of 50 to 100 parallel copper wires etched onto the motherboard, with connectors spaced at regular intervals for plugging in memory and I/O boards. However, buses can also be dedicated to special purposes, such as connecting a microprocessor to one or more coprocessors or local memories. Furthermore, within a microprocessor chip itself there are several buses for connecting internal components, as illustrated in Fig. 3-32. In the literature, buses are sometimes drawn as "fat" arrows, as in this figure.

While the designers of the microprocessor are free to use any kind of bus they want inside the chip, in order to make it possible for boards designed by third parties to attach to the system bus, there must be well-defined rules about how the bus works, and which all devices attached to it must obey. These rules are called the **bus protocol**. In addition, there must be a mechanical and electrical specification, so that third-party boards will fit in the card cage and have connectors that mate with those on the motherboard, both physically and in terms of voltages.

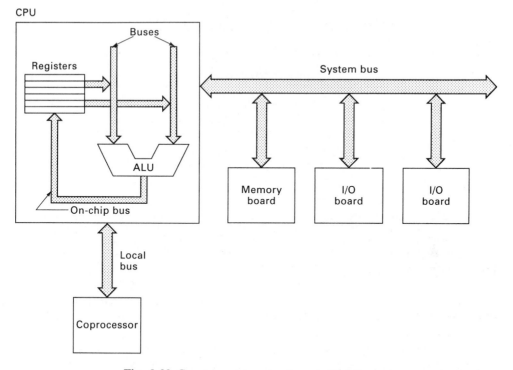

Fig. 3-32. Computer systems can have multiple buses.

A number of buses are in widespread use in the computer world. A few of the better known ones (with examples) are the Camac bus (nuclear physics), EISA bus (80386), Fastbus (high energy physics), IBM PC and PC/AT Buses (IBM PC and PC/AT), Massbus (PDP-11, VAX), Megabus (Honeywell), Microchannel (PS/2), Multibus I (8086), Multibus II (80386), Nubus (Macintosh II), Omnibus (PDP-8), Qbus (LSI-11), S-100 bus (hobby computers), SBI (VAX-11/780), Unibus (PDP-11), Versabus (Motorola), and VME bus (680x0). The world would probably be a better place if all but one would suddenly vanish from the face of the earth. Unfortunately, standardization in this area seems very unlikely as there is already too much invested in all these incompatible systems.

Let us now begin our study of how buses work. Some devices that attach to a bus are active and can initiate bus transfers, whereas others are passive and wait for requests. The active ones are called **masters**; the passive ones are called **slaves**. When the CPU orders a disk controller to read or write a block, the CPU is acting as a master and the disk controller is acting as a slave. However, later on, the disk controller may act as a master when it commands the memory to accept the words it is reading from the disk drive. Several typical combinations of master and slave are listed in Fig. 3-33. Under no circumstances can memory ever be a master.

The binary signals that computer devices output are frequently not strong

Master	Slave	Example
CPU	Memory	Fetching instructions and data
CPU	I/O	Initiating data transfer
CPU	Coprocessor	Handing off floating-point instruction
I/O	Memory	DMA (Direct Memory Access)
Coprocessor	Memory	Fetching operands

Fig. 3-33. Examples of bus masters and slaves.

enough to power a bus, especially if it is relatively long or has many devices on it. For this reason, most bus masters are connected to the bus by a chip called a **bus driver**, which is essentially a digital amplifier. Similarly, most slaves are connected to the bus by a **bus receiver**. For devices that can act as both master and slave, a combined chip called a **bus transceiver** is used. These bus interface chips are often tri-state devices, to allow them to float (disconnect) when they are not needed, or are hooked up in a somewhat different way, called **open collector,** that achieves a similar effect. When two or more devices on an open collector line assert the line at the same time, the result is the Boolean OR of all the signals. This arrangement is often called **wired-OR**. On most buses, some of the lines are tri-state and others, which need the wired-OR property, are open collector.

Like a microprocessor, a bus also has address, data, and control lines. However, there is not necessarily a one-to-one mapping between the microprocessor and bus signals. For example, some microprocessors have three pins that encode whether it is doing a memory read, memory write, I/O read, I/O write, or some other operation. A typical bus will have one line for memory read, a second for memory write, a third for I/O read, a fourth for I/O write, and so on. A decoder chip is needed between the CPU and such a bus to convert the 3-bit encoded signal into separate signals that can drive the bus lines.

The principal bus design issues (in addition to the number of address and data lines), are bus clocking, arbitration mechanism, interrupt handling, and error handling. These issues have a substantial impact on the speed and bandwidth of the bus. In the following sections we will take a closer look at these topics, starting with clocking.

3.4.3. Synchronous Buses

Buses can be divided into two distinct categories depending on their clocking. A **synchronous bus** has a line driven by a crystal oscillator. The signal on this line consists of a square wave with a frequency generally between 5 MHz and 50 MHz. All bus activities take an integral number of these cycles, called **bus cycles**. The other kind of bus, the **asynchronous bus**, does not have a master clock. Bus cycles can be of any length required, and need not be the same between all pairs of devices. We will examine each of these types in turn.

As an example of a how a synchronous bus works, consider the timing of Fig. 3-34(a). In this example, we will use a 4 MHz clock, which gives a bus cycle of 250 nsec. We will further assume that reading a byte from memory takes three bus cycles, for a total of 750 nsec from the start of the T_1 cycle to the end of T_3 cycle. Note that none of the rising or falling edges has been drawn vertically, because no electrical signal can change its value in zero time. In this example we will assume that it takes 10 nsec for a signal to change. The clock, address, data, $\overline{\text{MREQ}}$, and $\overline{\text{RD}}$ lines are all shown on the same time scale.

The start of T_1 is defined by the rising edge of the clock. Part way through T_1 the CPU puts the address of the byte it wants on the address lines. Because the address is not a single value, like the clock, we cannot show it as a single line in the figure; instead, it is shown as two lines, with a crossing at the time that the address changes. Furthermore, the shading prior to the crossing indicates that the shaded value is not important. Using the same shading convention, we see that the contents of the data lines are not significant until well into T_3.

After the address lines have had a chance to settle down to their new values, $\overline{\text{MREQ}}$ and $\overline{\text{RD}}$ are asserted. The former indicates that memory (as opposed to an I/O device) is being accessed, and the latter distinguishes reads from writes. Nothing happens during T_2, to give the memory time to decode the address and put the data on the bus. At the falling edge of T_3 the CPU strobes (i.e., reads) the data lines, latching (i.e., storing) the value in an internal register. Having read the data, the CPU negates $\overline{\text{MREQ}}$ and $\overline{\text{RD}}$. If need be, another memory cycle can begin at the next rising edge of the clock.

In the timing specification of Fig. 3-34(b), eight symbols that occur in the timing diagram are further clarified. T_{AD}, for example, is the time interval between the rising edge of the T_1 clock and the address lines being set. According to the timing specification, $T_{AD} \leq 110$ nsec. This means that the chip manufacturer guarantees that during any operand read cycle, the CPU will output the address to be read within 110 nsec of the midpoint of the rising edge of T_1.

The timing specifications also require that the data be available on the data lines at least 50 nsec before the falling edge of T_3, to give it time to settle down before the CPU strobes (i.e., reads) it in. The combination of the constraints on T_{AD} and T_{DS} means that in the worst case, the memory will have only $250 + 250 + 125 - 110 - 50 = 465$ nsec from the time the address appears until it must produce the data. If memory is unable to respond fast enough, it asserts $\overline{\text{WAIT}}$ (not shown) prior to the falling edge of T_2 when $\overline{\text{WAIT}}$ is strobed. This action will insert **wait states** (extra bus cycles) until the memory is finished and negates $\overline{\text{WAIT}}$.

The timing specification further guarantees that the address will be set up at least 60 nsec prior to $\overline{\text{MREQ}}$ being asserted. This time can be important if $\overline{\text{MREQ}}$ drives chip select on the memory chip because some memories require an address

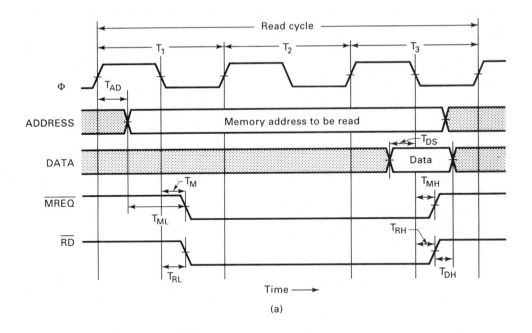

Fig. 3-34. (a) Read timing on a synchronous bus. (b) Specification of some critical times.

Symbol	Parameter	Min	Max	Unit
T_{AD}	Address output delay		110	nsec
T_{ML}	Address stable prior to $\overline{MREQ}$	60		nsec
T_M	$\overline{MREQ}$ delay from falling edge of Φ in T_1		85	nsec
T_{RL}	$\overline{RD}$ delay from falling edge of Φ in T_1		85	nsec
T_{DS}	Data setup time prior to falling edge of Φ	50		nsec
T_{MH}	$\overline{MREQ}$ delay from falling edge of Φ in T_3		85	nsec
T_{RH}	$\overline{RD}$ delay from falling edge of Φ in T_3		85	nsec
T_{DH}	Data hold time from negation of $\overline{RD}$	0		nsec

(b)

setup time prior to chip select. Clearly, the microcomputer designer should not choose a memory chip with a 75-nsec setup time.

The constraints on T_M and T_{RL} mean that $\overline{MREQ}$ and $\overline{RD}$ will both be asserted within 85 nsec from the T_1 falling clock. In the worst case, the memory chip will have only $250 + 250 - 85 - 50 = 365$ nsec after the assertion of $\overline{MREQ}$ and $\overline{RD}$ to get its data onto the bus. This constraint is in addition to the address constraint.

T_{MH} and T_{RH} tell how long it takes $\overline{MREQ}$ and $\overline{RD}$ to be negated after the data have been strobed in. Finally, T_{DH} tells how long the memory must hold the data on the bus after $\overline{\text{RD}}$ has been negated. As far as our example CPU is concerned, the memory can remove the data from the bus as soon as $\overline{\text{RD}}$ has been negated; on some actual microprocessors, however, the data must be kept stable a little longer.

We would like to point out that Fig. 3-34 is a highly simplified version of real timing constraints. In reality, many more critical times are always specified. Nevertheless, it gives a good flavor for how a synchronous bus works.

In addition to read (and write) cycles some synchronous buses support block transfers. When a block read is started, the bus master tells the slave how many bytes are to be transferred, for example, by putting the byte count on the data lines during T_1. Instead of just returning one byte, the slave outputs one byte during each cycle until the count has been exhausted. In this example, a block read of n bytes would take $n + 2$ cycles instead of $3n$.

Another way to make the bus go faster is to shorten the cycle. In our example, one byte is transferred every 750 nsec, for a maximum bandwidth of 1.33 Mbytes/sec. With an 8 MHz clock, the cycle time would be cut in half and we could achieve 2.67 Mbytes/sec. However, shortening the bus cycle can lead to engineering problems. The signals on the various lines do not all travel at exactly the same speed, an effect called **bus skew**. It is essential that the cycle time be long compared to the skew to prevent the nice idea of digitized time intervals from breaking down into analog timing.

Our last point is whether control signals are asserted high or low. It is up to the bus designers to determine which is more convenient, but the choice is essentially arbitrary. One can regard it as the hardware equivalent of a programmer's choice to represent free disk blocks in a bit map as 0s versus 1s.

3.4.4. Asynchronous Buses

Although synchronous buses are easy to work with due to their discrete time intervals, they also have some problems. For one thing, everything works in integral multiples of the bus clock. If a particular CPU and memory are able to complete a transfer in 3.1 cycles, they have to stretch it to 4.0 because fractional cycles are forbidden.

Worse yet, once a bus cycle has been chosen, and memory and I/O cards have been built for it, it is difficult to take advantage of future improvements in technology. For example, suppose a few years after the system of Fig. 3-34 was built, new CPUs and memories became available with cycle times of 100 nsec instead of 250 nsec. Although they could be used, they would run at the same speed as the old ones, since the bus protocol requires the memory to assert the data lines just before the falling edge of T_3.

Putting this fact in slightly different terms, if a bus has a heterogeneous collection of devices, some fast and some slow, the bus has to be geared to the slowest one and the fast ones cannot use their full potential.

Mixed technology can be handled by going to an asynchronous bus, that is, one with no master clock, as shown in Fig. 3-35. Instead of tying everything to the clock, when the bus master has asserted the address, $\overline{\text{MREQ}}$, $\overline{\text{RD}}$, and anything else it needs to, it then asserts a special signal that we will call $\overline{\text{MSYN}}$ (Master SYNchronization). When the slave sees this, it performs the work as fast as it can. When it is done, it asserts $\overline{\text{SSYN}}$ (Slave SYNchronization).

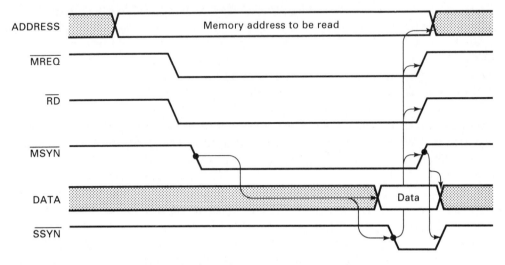

Fig. 3-35. Operation of an asynchronous bus.

As soon as the master sees $\overline{\text{SSYN}}$ asserted, it knows that the data are available, so it latches them, and then negates the address lines, along with $\overline{\text{MREQ}}$, $\overline{\text{RD}}$, and $\overline{\text{MSYN}}$. When the slave sees the negation of $\overline{\text{MSYN}}$, it knows that the cycle has been completed, so it negates $\overline{\text{SSYN}}$, and we are back in the original situation, with all signals negated, waiting for the next master.

Timing diagrams of asynchronous buses (and sometimes synchronous buses as well) use arrows to show cause and effect, as in Fig. 3-35. The assertion of $\overline{\text{MSYN}}$ causes the data lines to be asserted, and also causes the slave to assert $\overline{\text{SSYN}}$. The assertion of $\overline{\text{SSYN}}$, in turn, causes the negation of the address lines, $\overline{\text{MREQ}}$, $\overline{\text{RD}}$, and $\overline{\text{MSYN}}$. Finally, the negation of $\overline{\text{MSYN}}$ causes the negation of $\overline{\text{SSYN}}$, which ends the read.

A set of signals that interlocks this way is called a **full handshake**. The essential part consists of four events:

1. $\overline{\text{MSYN}}$ is asserted.

2. $\overline{\text{SSYN}}$ is asserted in response to $\overline{\text{MSYN}}$.

3. $\overline{\text{MSYN}}$ is negated in response to $\overline{\text{SSYN}}$.

4. $\overline{\text{SSYN}}$ is negated in response to the negation of $\overline{\text{MSYN}}$.

It should be clear that full handshakes are timing independent. Each event is caused by a prior event, not by a clock pulse. If a particular master-slave pair is slow, that in no way affects a subsequent master-slave pair that is much faster.

The advantage of an asynchronous bus should now be clear, but the fact is that most buses are synchronous. The reason is that it is easier to build a synchronous system. The CPU just asserts its signals, and the memory just reacts. There is no feedback (cause and effect), but if the components have been chosen properly, everything will work without handshaking.

3.4.5. Bus Arbitration

Up until now, we have tacitly assumed that there is only one bus master, the CPU. In reality, I/O chips have to become bus master to read and write memory, and also to cause interrupts. Coprocessors may also need to become bus master. The question then arises: "What happens if two or more devices all want to become bus master at the same time?" The answer is that some **bus arbitration** mechanism is needed to prevent chaos.

Arbitration mechanisms can be centralized or decentralized. Let us first consider centralized arbitration. One particularly simple form of centralized arbitration is shown in Fig. 3-36(a). In this scheme, a single bus arbiter determines who goes next. Many microprocessors have the arbiter built into the CPU chip, but in minicomputer systems it is sometimes a separate device. The bus contains a single wired-OR request line that can be asserted by one or more devices at any time. There is no way for the arbiter to tell how many devices have requested the bus. The only categories it can distinguish are: some requests and no requests.

When the arbiter sees a bus request, it issues a grant by asserting the bus grant line. This line is wired through all the I/O devices in series, like a cheap string of Christmas tree lamps. When the device physically closest to the arbiter sees the grant, it checks to see if it made a request. If so, it takes over the bus but does not propagate the grant further down the line. If it has not made a request, it propagates the grant to the next device in line, which behaves the same way, and so on until some device accepts the grant and takes the bus. This scheme is called **daisy chaining**. It has the property that devices are effectively assigned priorities depending on how close to the arbiter they are. The closest device wins.

To get around the implicit priorities based on distance from the arbiter, many buses have multiple priority levels. For each priority level there is a bus request line and a bus grant line. The one of Fig. 3-36(b) has two levels, 1 and 2 (real buses often have 4, 8, or 16 levels). Each device attaches to one of the bus request levels, with more time critical devices attaching to the higher priority ones. In Fig. 3-36(b) device 1 and 2 use priority 1 and devices 3, 4, and 5 use priority 2.

If multiple priority levels are requested at the same time, the arbiter issues a grant only on the highest priority one. Among devices of the same priority, daisy chaining is used. In Fig. 3-36(b), in the event of conflicts, device 3 beats device 4,

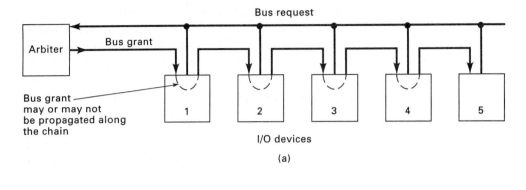

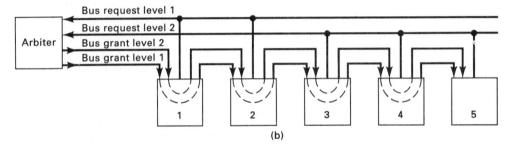

Fig. 3-36. (a) A centralized one level bus arbiter using daisy chaining. (b) The same arbiter, but with two levels.

which beats 5, which beats 1. Device 2 has the lowest priority because it is at the end of the lowest priority daisy chain.

As an aside, it is not technically necessary to wire the level 2 bus grant line serially through devices 1 and 2, since they cannot make requests on it, but as an implementation convenience, it is easier to wire all the grant lines through all the devices, rather than making special wiring that depends on which device has which priority.

Some arbiters have a third line that a device asserts when it has accepted a grant and seized the bus. As soon as it has asserted this acknowledgement line, the request and grant lines can be negated. As a result, other devices can request the bus while the first device is using the bus. By the time the current transfer is finished, the next bus master will have already been selected. It can start as soon as the acknowledgement line has been negated, at which time the following round of arbitration can begin. This scheme requires an extra bus line and more logic in each device, but it makes better use of bus cycles. The PDP-11 and Motorola chips, among others, use this system.

In many systems, the CPU must also contend for the bus, but it has the lowest priority, and only gets the bus when nobody else wants it. The idea here is that the CPU can always wait, but I/O devices frequently must acquire the bus quickly or lose incoming data. Disks rotating at high speed cannot wait.

When decentralized bus arbitration is used, there is no bus arbiter. The VAX SBI, for example, has 16 prioritized bus request lines, one per device. This design limits the number of devices to 16. When a device wants to use the bus, it asserts its request line. All devices monitor all the request lines, so at the end of each bus cycle, each device knows whether it was the highest priority requester, and thus whether it is permitted to use the bus during the next cycle. Compared to centralized arbitration, this arbitration method requires more bus lines, but avoids the potential cost of the arbiter.

Another kind of decentralized bus arbitration is used in the Multibus. This scheme, shown in Fig. 3-37, only uses three lines, no matter how many devices are present. The first bus line is a wired-OR line for requesting the bus. The second bus line is called BUSY, and is asserted by the current bus master. The third line is used to arbitrate the bus. It is daisy chained through all the devices. The head of this chain is held asserted by tying it to the 5 volt power supply.

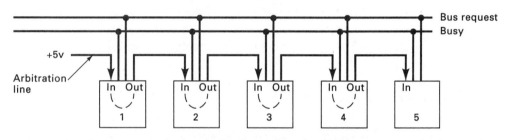

Fig. 3-37. Multibus decentralized bus arbitration.

When no device wants the bus, the asserted arbitration line is propagated through to all devices. To acquire the bus, a device first checks to see if the bus is idle and the arbitration signal it is receiving, IN, is asserted. If IN is negated, it may not become bus master. If IN is asserted, however, the device negates OUT, which requires everyone downstream to negate IN and OUT. When the dust settles, only one device will have IN asserted and OUT negated. This device becomes bus master, asserts BUSY and OUT, and begins its transfer.

A little thought will reveal that the leftmost device that wants the bus always gets it. Thus this scheme is similar to the original daisy chain arbitration, except without having the arbiter, so it is cheaper, faster, and not vulnerable to arbiter failure. The Multibus, incidentally, also offers centralized arbitration, so the system designers have a choice.

One last word about arbitration concerns multiple cycle operations. In multiprocessor systems, it is common practice to use a memory word to protect shared data structures. If this word is 0, a processor may set it to 1 and use the data structure. If it is already 1, the processor must wait until the processor currently using the data structure finishes and sets the word back to 0.

The following sequence of events shows a situation where things go wrong.

1. Processor A reads word x and sees that it is zero (bus cycle 0).

2. Processor B reads word x and sees that it is zero (bus cycle 1).

3. Processor A writes 1 into word x (bus cycle 2).

4. Processor B writes 1 into word x (bus cycle 3).

If this sequence were to happen, two processors would simultaneously think they each had exclusive access to the shared data structure, resulting in chaos. To prevent this situation, some CPUs have an instruction that reads a memory word, and if it is 0, sets it to 1. The trouble is that such an instruction requires two bus cycles, one for the read and one for the write. There is a small, but nonzero, chance that a second processor will sneak in between the read and write and wreak havoc.

The solution to this problem is to add an extra line to the bus, say, LOCK, that can be asserted when such an instruction is started. Once LOCK has been asserted, no other processor is allowed to become bus master until it has been negated. This rule gives the original CPU the possibility of doing multiple bus cycles without interference. On buses that do not have such a feature, it is difficult to build a correctly working multiprocessor system.

3.4.6. Interrupt Handling

Up until now, we have only discussed ordinary bus cycles, with a master reading from a slave or writing to one. Another important bus use is handling interrupts. When the CPU commands an I/O device to do something, it usually expects an interrupt when the work is done. The interrupt signaling requires the bus.

Since multiple devices may want to cause an interrupt simultaneously, the same kind of arbitration problems are present here that we had with ordinary bus cycles. The usual solution is to assign priorities to devices, and use a centralized arbiter to give priority to the most time critical devices. Standard interrupt controller chips exist and are widely used. The IBM PC, PC/AT, PS/2, and all clones (IBM PC compatibles) use the Intel 8259A chip, illustrated in Fig. 3-38.

Up to eight I/O controller chips can be directly connected to the eight IRx (Interrupt Request) inputs to the 8259A. When any of these devices wants to cause an interrupt, it asserts its input line. When one or more inputs are asserted, the 8259A asserts INT (INTerrupt), which directly drives the interrupt pin on the CPU. When the CPU is able to handle the interrupt, it sends a pulse back to the 8259A on INTA (INTerrupt Acknowledge). At that point the 8259A is expected to specify which input caused the interrupt by outputting that input's number on the data bus. The CPU hardware then uses that number to index into a table of pointers, called **interrupt vectors**, to find the address of the procedure to run to service the interrupt.

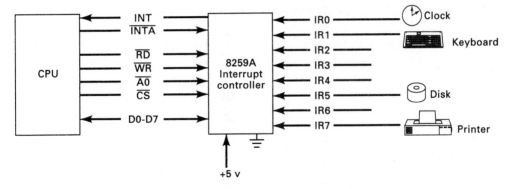

Fig. 3-38. Use of the 8259A interrupt controller.

The 8259A has several registers inside of it that the CPU can read and write using ordinary bus cycles and the $\overline{RD}$ (ReaD), $\overline{WR}$ (WRite), $\overline{CS}$ (Chip Select) and A0 pins. When the software has handled the interrupt and is ready to take the next one, it writes a special code into one of them, which causes the 8259A to negate INT, unless it has another interrupt pending. These registers can also be written to put the 8259A in one of several modes, mask out a set of interrupts, and enable other features.

When more than eight I/O devices are present, the 8259As can be cascaded. In the most extreme case, all eight inputs can be connected to the outputs of eight more 8259As, allowing for up to 64 I/O devices in a two-stage interrupt network. The 8259A has a few pins to handling this cascading, which we have omitted for the sake of simplicity.

While we have by no means exhausted the subject of bus design, the material above should give enough background to understand the essentials of how a bus works, and how microprocessors and buses interact. More material on buses can be found in (Borrill, 1985; and Gustavson, 1984). Let us now move from the general to the specific, and take a look at some examples of actual microprocessors and their buses.

3.5. EXAMPLE MICROPROCESSOR CHIPS

In this section we will examine the Intel and Motorola microprocessor families in some detail at the hardware level. We will also compare the various members of each family, to see how the chips have evolved during the course of time. At the end of the section we will give a brief comparison of two of the chips, the 80386 and the 68030. After that, we will look at two popular buses used with these two families, the IBM PC bus and the VME bus.

3.5.1. The Intel 8088/80286/80386 Microprocessor Chips

In this section we will examine the three most widely used members of the Intel CPU family, the 8088 (used in the IBM PC), the 80286 (used in the IBM PC/AT and midrange PS/2 models), and the 80386 (used in top-of-the-line personal computers). Although these chips share some characteristics, they also differ in various ways. All three are so widely used that it is worth discussing all three of them.

The Intel 8088

The 8088 is an NMOS microprocessor sold in a 40-pin package. Internally it has a 16-bit data path, but it reads and writes memory 8 bits at a time (i.e., the data bus width is 8 bits). It can address 1 megabyte of memory. Whenever possible, the 8088 tries to fetch instructions in advance, so that when the next one is needed, it will already be available.

The 8088 can operate in one of two modes: **minimum mode** or **maximum mode**. Minimum mode is intended for very small systems, with few peripheral devices. For example, an 8088 being used as a washing machine controller would run in minimum mode. The meaning of the pins is different in the two modes, with minimum mode being much simpler. In personal computer systems it virtually always runs in maximum mode, so we will not mention minimum mode any more in this book.

The actual pinout of the 8088 in maximum mode is shown in Fig. 3-39(a). Twenty of the 40 pins contain the memory or I/O address being read or written. These are called A0-A19. Since the 8088 transfers data 8 bits at a time, it might seem logical that an additional eight pins should be used for the data bus. However, to reduce the number of pins needed in order to fit the 8088 into a standard 40 pin package, the data lines D0-D7 are multiplexed onto the same pins as A0-A7. Early in each bus cycle these pins, called, AD0-AD7, contain the address; later in the cycle they contain the data. Precise rules govern the exact timing, so there is never any ambiguity.

Pins 35 - 38 are also multiplexed, containing address lines at the start of each bus cycle and status information at the end. This situation is indicated by the notation A16/S3 (see pin 38). Thus a slash is used to separate two unrelated signals that share a common pin.

On the other hand, pin 33 is called MN/$\overline{\text{MX}}$ (MiNimum/MaXimum), but it does not represent two signals, MN and $\overline{\text{MX}}$, that are present at different times. This pin is asserted to put the chip in minimum mode (MN). In other words, it is asserted to put the chip in not maximum mode ($\overline{\text{MX}}$). The two names on either side of the slash are different ways of saying the same thing. While this notation is highly confusing, it is the official Intel nomenclature, so with some hesitation we will stick to it.

Nevertheless, in an attempt to at least reduce the confusion, we will draw all

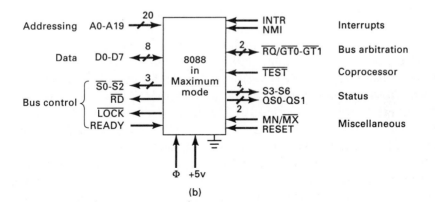

$\overline{S2}$	$\overline{S1}$	$\overline{S0}$	Bus cycle type
0	0	0	Interrupt acknowledge
0	0	1	I/O port read
0	1	0	I/O port write
0	1	1	Halt
1	0	0	Code access
1	0	1	Memory read
1	1	0	Memory write
1	1	1	Release bus

Fig. 3-39. (a) Physical pinout of the 8088. (b) Logical pinout of the 8088. (c) Bus cycle types used on the 8088. Arrows are used to distinguish input, output and input/output signals.

chips henceforth using the logical pinout, rather than the physical pinout. In Fig. 3-39(b) we see the 8088 again, only this time the logical signals are shown, without regard to which signals are located on which pin. Here, for example, we show A0-A19 as being distinct from D0-D7 because logically they are unrelated. The fact that they share some pins is not necessary for understanding how the chip works. A short diagonal line with a number near it tells how many signals are present (e.g., 20 for A0–A19). For completeness, please note that the position in the figure that we have chosen to use for each signal is not based on which pin is used; instead, signals that are related are grouped together for ease of explanation.

Six pins on the 8088 are used for bus control. $\overline{S0}$–$\overline{S2}$ (Status) define the type of bus cycle the 8088 wants. The table in Fig. 3-39(c) shows the possibilities. $\overline{RD}$ (ReaD) indicates that a read cycle is taking place. It is not necessarily used in maximum mode because the same information can be derived from the $\overline{S0}$–$\overline{S2}$ signals, but sometimes it is convenient.

$\overline{LOCK}$ can be asserted by the 8088 to tell other potential masters to leave the bus alone. This signal is needed to gain exclusive access to the memory during certain critical CPU instructions that require multiple bus cycles. It is primarily needed in multiprocessor systems.

Unlike the other five bus control signals, $\overline{READY}$ is an input. When the 8088 asks for a byte from memory, the memory is expected to deliver it within four bus cycles. If the memory can meet this requirement, it asserts $\overline{READY}$ while placing the requested byte on the data bus, and all is well. If, however, the memory is too slow, it must negate $\overline{READY}$ before the fourth bus cycle, and keep it negated until it has put the requested byte on the bus, thus introducing wait states. In this way, the 8088 can be used with either fast or slow memories.

The INTR (INTeRrupt) and NMI (NonMaskable Interrupt) signals are used to cause CPU interrupts. The difference between the two is that software can temporarily mask (disable) the first kind, but not the second kind. A masked interrupt is not lost, but just held waiting, until the software re-enables interrupts. The INTR line is normally used by I/O devices, whereas NMI is used to indicate memory parity error or some other major problem that cannot wait.

The two $\overline{RQ}/\overline{GTx}$ (ReQuest/GranT) lines are used for bus arbitration, for example, between the 8088 and the 8087 floating-point coprocessor chip. Using these lines, a coprocessor can request that the 8088 float all the buses (i.e., electrically disconnect itself from the buses), so that the coprocessor can become bus master to access memory. Unless $\overline{LOCK}$ is currently asserted, the 8088 will normally grant any such request at the end of the current bus cycle. Two lines are provided in order to handle up to two coprocessors.

The $\overline{TEST}$ signal is used to allow the 8088 to test coprocessor status. This test is needed because when a floating-point instruction is encountered, the 8088 starts up the 8087. It can then continue with regular (i.e., not floating-point) instructions in parallel with the coprocessor. When the 8088 needs the result of the floating-point operation, it can test to see if the coprocessor is finished, and if not, wait for it.

The S3–S6 and QSx signals contain information about the internal state of the CPU. It is not entirely clear why they were provided. In practice they are not normally used.

We have already discussed MN/$\overline{MX}$, so the only remaining signal is RESET, which is used to reset the CPU, for example, when the user pushes a reset button on the console. After a reset, the CPU is put in a well-defined initial state.

The Intel 80286

The successor to the 8088 is the 80286. It has three principal advantages over the 8088. First, it has both kernel mode and a protected user mode, making it more suitable for running multiple programs at once. Second, it has a 16-bit data bus (like the 8086), which effectively doubles the memory bandwidth. Third, it is internally faster, and can run at higher clock rates as well. Together, these factors make a typical 80286-based system 5 to 10 times faster than a typical 8088-based system.

The 80286 achieves a considerable amount of its performance from the presence of four independent functional units inside it, as shown in simplified form in Fig. 3-40. The **bus unit** performs all bus operations for the CPU, fetching and storing instructions and data as needed. When it has no other work to do, it attempts to fetch up to six bytes of instructions in advance, feeding them to the instruction unit.

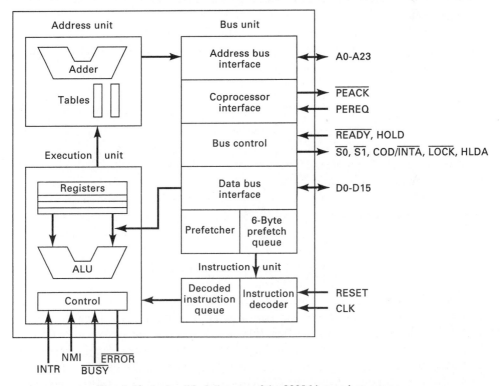

Fig. 3-40. A simplified diagram of the 80286 internal structure.

The **instruction unit** takes the raw bytes fetched by the bus unit and decodes them as instructions for subsequent execution. It can hold up to three fully decoded instructions at once. Having decoded instructions always available means that the CPU rarely has to wait for the next instruction, thus speeding up execution.

The **execution unit** carries out the decoded instructions fed to it by the instruction unit. Some instructions contain memory addresses. These are given to the address unit for further processing.

The **address unit** performs all address computations and handles the virtual memory. (Virtual memory is a technique that lets a program use more memory than the computer has. It is implemented by swapping pieces of the program to and from disk automatically. We will discuss it in detail in Chap. 6.) The address unit feeds its output to the bus unit for reading and writing.

The 80286 requires more than 40 signals, so Intel was forced to go to a different package to accommodate them. Rather than go to 48 pins and continue multiplexing some of the signals, they decided to go to a square 68 pin package with 17 pins on each side. This package allows for the 24 address signals, 16 data signals, and 16 control signals, plus clock, power, and ground, with a few spare pins left unconnected. The logical pinout is shown in Fig. 3-41. The 8088's minimum mode/maximum mode distinction does not exist here; there is only one mode and one pinout.

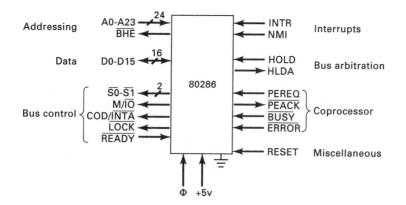

Fig. 3-41. Logical pinout of the 80286.

The 24 address and 16 data signals are straightforward and need no further comment. However, there is one new signal related to addressing that is not present on the 8088, $\overline{BHE}$ (Bus High Enable). The need for $\overline{BHE}$ comes from the 80286's ability to read (and especially write) 16-bit words as a single unit. Nevertheless, CPU instructions exist to read (and write) a single byte. Reading a single byte is not so hard. All the CPU has to do is read a 16-bit word and extract the byte needed. Writing is harder, since writing a single byte must not modify the other half of that byte's word. The $\overline{BHE}$ signal can be negated to prevent the upper byte from being transferred and thus being overwritten in memory. Since A0-A23 may address any byte in the address space, even or odd, by negating $\overline{BHE}$ the 80286 can read or write exactly one byte anywhere in memory.

The 80286's bus control pins are slightly different from the 8088's, but the general idea is the same—namely, to specify whether a bus cycle is for reading from memory, writing to memory, reading from an I/O device, writing to an I/O device, or something else. Intel's naming conventions for $\overline{S0}$, $\overline{S1}$, M/$\overline{IO}$ (Memory/IO), and COD/$\overline{INTA}$ (CODe/INTerrupt Acknowledge) are somewhat arbitrary and not terribly informative. In reality, there is simply a table with 16 entries, corresponding to the 16 bit combinations, telling what each one does. Seven of these are useful, four do nothing, and five are not used. If compatibility with older I/O chips were not so important, a cleaner design would have been possible. $\overline{LOCK}$ and $\overline{READY}$ do the same as on the 8088 (locking the bus and inserting wait states).

Similarly, INTR and NMI are also the same as their 8088 counterparts. On both chips they allow I/O devices to cause CPU interrupts, both maskable and nonmaskable.

The HOLD and HLDA (HoLD Acknowledge) signals are new to the 80286 and provide a general way of doing bus arbitration. When a potential bus master wants the bus, it asserts HOLD. After the 80286 has seen this request and floated its pins, it asserts HLDA, at which time the new bus master takes over. The 80286 continues to stay in floating state and continues to assert HLDA as long as it sees HOLD asserted. When the new master is done, it negates HOLD, and the 80286 continues normally.

The 80286 coprocessor signaling is more elaborate than the 8088's in order to allow coprocessors to utilize the 80286s memory management unit. Using PEREQ (Processor Extension REQuest), a coprocessor can ask the 80286 to fetch the contents of a (virtual) address. When the word is on the bus, the 80286 asserts $\overline{PEACK}$ (Processor Extension ACKnowledge) to allow the coprocessor to grab the word. This whole mechanism is done in hardware, without interrupting the software at all.

The $\overline{BUSY}$ and $\overline{ERROR}$ signals are used to let the 80286 sense the state of the coprocessor and wait for it to complete whatever it is doing. The difference between the two is that $\overline{BUSY}$ is used for normal signaling, while $\overline{ERROR}$ is used to generate a CPU interrupt when something has gone wrong, such as a floating-point overflow error.

The RESET signal works the same way on the 80286 as on the 8088, letting external circuitry reset the computer. In addition, the CLK, power, and ground pins are also the same, although on the 80286 they are present on several pins. Finally, just for completeness, we note that the 80286 also has a pin that must be connected to ground via a 0.047 microfarad capacitor for analog engineering reasons.

The Intel 80386

Intel's first 32-bit CPU on a chip is the 80386. In terms of raw compute speed, it is comparable to a small mainframe. In addition to greater speed, it has several other advantages over the 80286. For one thing, all registers and instructions can handle 8-, 16-, or 32-bit values equally well. For another, it provides programs with a virtual memory of 2^{46} bytes (vs. 2^{32} on the 80286), and it can handle up to 4 gigabytes of physical memory (vs. 16 megabytes on the 80286). Finally, it can emulate both the 8086 and 80286, making it possible to run a great deal of existing software (including operating systems) without any modification. For more information about it, see (El-Ayat and Agarwal, 1985).

With a 32-bit address bus, a 32-bit data bus, and various control signals, the 68-pin package used on the 80286 was too small, so Intel went to a larger standard size. This package consists of a $14 \times 14 = 196$ square pin grid with the middle $8 \times 8 = 64$ subgrid missing, for a total of 132 pins, as shown in Fig. 3-42. Many of these are duplicates of other pins, or unused.

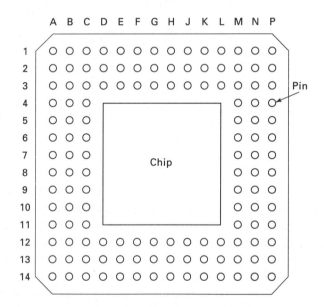

Fig. 3-42. 132-Pin package used on the 80386.

Internally, the 80386, like the 80286, contains a number of functional units that operate in parallel for greater performance. Instead of four of them, there are eight, largely because the address unit and execution unit have been split up into several subunits that can operate independently from one another. Although this design is more complex, the increased performance makes it worthwhile.

The 80386 pinout is similar to that of the 80286, and is shown in Fig. 3-43. Internally, the 80386 works with 32-bit words, and all memory references must be aligned to a four-byte boundary. Thus the CPU can fetch words at addresses 0, 4, 8, and so on, but not words at addresses 1, 2, or 3. As a result, all memory addresses are multiples of four, so the two low-order address bits are always 0, and A0 and A1 do not exist.

Nevertheless, instructions exist to store 8- and 16-bit quantities in memory, so

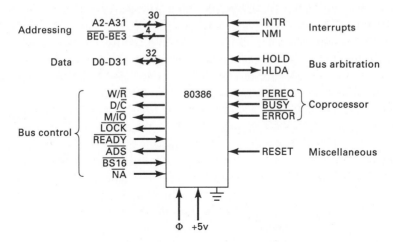

Fig. 3-43. Logical pinout of the 80386.

the problem solved by the $\overline{\text{BHE}}$ signal in the 80286 is present here too, but worse. It has been solved in a straightforward way by simply providing four signals, $\overline{\text{BE0}}$-$\overline{\text{BE3}}$ (Bus Enable) that simply indicate for each of the four bytes in a word, which ones are to be used.

With the 80386, Intel maintained its tradition of redefining all the bus control signals with each new chip. This time they are called W/$\overline{\text{R}}$, (Write/Read), D/$\overline{\text{C}}$ (Data/Code), and M/$\overline{\text{IO}}$ (Memory/IO). However, somebody finally got out a table with the powers of 2 and discovered that $7 \leq 2^3$, so that only three signals are used for the seven kinds of bus cycles needed (code read, data read, data write, I/O read, I/O write, acknowledge, and halt).

$\overline{\text{LOCK}}$ and $\overline{\text{READY}}$ are unchanged, but three new bus control signals are present on the 80386. $\overline{\text{ADS}}$ (ADdress Status) indicates that a valid address is on the bus. When the memory sees this signal, it knows that the address and bus control lines are all valid, so it can start working immediately.

$\overline{\text{BS16}}$ (Bus Size 16) is an input that can be asserted to tell the 80386 that the system contains (older) 16-bit I/O chips. When it sees this signal, the 80386 performs a 32-bit transfer as a sequence of two consecutive 16-bit transfers.

Whereas $\overline{\text{BS16}}$ is used to slow the system down, $\overline{\text{NA}}$ (Next Address) is used to speed it up. By asserting $\overline{\text{NA}}$, the memory can inform the 80386 that it is prepared to accept the next memory address, even though it has not yet asserted $\overline{\text{READY}}$ for the current bus cycle. This feature allows increased pipelining by having the memory start preparing for the next cycle before the CPU has even finished processing the current one.

The INTR, NMI, HOLD, HLDA, PEREQ, $\overline{\text{BUSY}}$, $\overline{\text{ERROR}}$, and RESET signals are all present on the 80286 and have the same function as they do there. $\overline{\text{PEACK}}$ is not present because the 80386 can access its coprocessor directly.

3.5.2. The Motorola 68000/68020/68030 Microprocessor Chips

As a second example of a microprocessor chip family, we will now look at the Motorola 68000, 68020, and 68030 chips. Unlike the three Intel chips we have just studied, which are all quite different CPUs, these three Motorola chips are very similar. The first one, the 68000, has a 32-bit architecture with a 16-bit data bus. The second one, the 68020 (MacGregor et al., 1984; MacGregor and Rubinstein, 1985), differs from the 68000 in that it has a 32-bit data bus and a few additional instructions and other minor features. The 68030 is essentially a 68020 plus a data cache and a memory management unit packaged on the same chip. We will study caches in Chap. 4 and memory management units in Chap. 6.

Rather than go into the pinout of all three chips in detail, we will concentrate on the two most advanced members of the family, the 68020 and 68030, the latter being a superset of the 68020. Conceptually, most of what holds for them also holds for the older 68000. The differences are few (other than the smaller address and data buses) and concern minor issues such as providing support for (now obsolete) 8-bit I/O chips.

The Motorola 68020 and 68030

In the paragraphs below we will describe the pinout of the 68020 and 68030. We will use the term "68030," but the descriptions also hold for the 68020, except for cache control and emulation support, which are not present on the 68020. The 68030 has 32 address pins, A0-A31 and 32 data pins, D0-D31, as shown in Fig. 3-44. Furthermore, the operand size, 1, 2, or 4 bytes, is encoded in SIZ0 and SIZ1.

The Motorola chips have a more elaborate mechanism for bus control than the Intel chips. Furthermore, all the control signals are consistently asserted low. At the start of each bus cycle, the 68030 asserts $\overline{\text{ECS}}$ (External Cycle Start) to indicate the cycle timing to the memory and I/O chips. Reading or writing a word takes multiple bus cycles. $\overline{\text{OCS}}$ (Operand Cycle Start) is asserted on the first one of these only. The type of bus cycle is indicated by $\overline{\text{FC0}}$-$\overline{\text{FC2}}$, analogous to $\overline{\text{S0}}$-$\overline{\text{S2}}$ on the 8088. In addition, R/$\overline{\text{W}}$ indicates whether the cycle is a read or a write cycle. Like $\overline{\text{RD}}$ on the 8088, this information is more for convenience than anything else, since it can be derived from $\overline{\text{FC0}}$-$\overline{\text{FC2}}$.

When all the above signals have been output and are stable, the 68030 asserts $\overline{\text{AS}}$ (Address Strobe) to announce this fact to the rest of the system. During a read cycle, the 68030 asserts $\overline{\text{DS}}$ (Data Strobe) at the point that it is ready to accept the data. On a write cycle the 68030 asserts it when the data bus is valid and stable. $\overline{\text{DBEN}}$ (Data Buffer ENable) can be used by the memory or I/O chips as a signal telling when to enable their data bus buffers. The final bus control output is $\overline{\text{RMC}}$ (Read-Modify-write Cycle), which is used in the same way the Intel chips use $\overline{\text{LOCK}}$—namely, to keep all other bus masters off the bus during a multicycle operation. Like $\overline{\text{LOCK}}$, $\overline{\text{RMC}}$ is used for synchronization in multiprocessor systems.

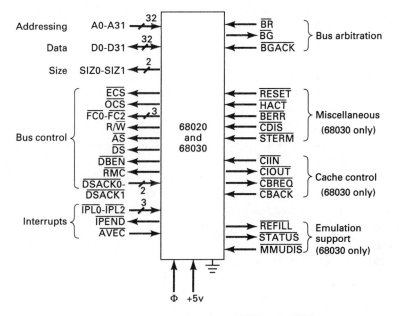

Fig. 3-44. Logical pinout of the 68020 and 68030.

Two bus control signals, $\overline{DSACK0}$ and $\overline{DSACK1}$ (Data and Size ACKnowledgement), are inputs to the 68030 from the bus. They are used to tell when a read or write has been completed, roughly analogous to $\overline{READY}$ on the Intel chips.

The $\overline{IPL0}$-$\overline{IPL2}$ (Interrupt Priority Level) signals are used by I/O chips to generate CPU interrupts. Three bits are available, so any one of seven different priorities can be caused (level 0 is not used). The higher priority levels are used for time-critical devices and take precedence over lower priority levels in the event that two or more interrupts happen simultaneously. When the 68030 has accepted an interrupt signal, it replies by asserting $\overline{IPEND}$ (Interrupt PENDing). Normally an interrupting device specifies the interrupt vector, which tells how to find the interrupt service procedure to run. However, if the device is unable to do so, it can assert $\overline{AVEC}$ (Automatic VECtor) to let the CPU use certain default values.

$\overline{BR}$, $\overline{BG}$, and $\overline{BGACK}$ are used to control who gets to use the bus next, somewhat similar to HOLD and HLDA on the 80286 and 80386, but with an important difference. The $\overline{BR}$ (Bus Request) line is used by I/O devices to request the bus. The $\overline{BG}$ (Bus Grant) line is asserted by the 68030 to announce that the bus has indeed been floated. So far, this protocol is the same as Intel's. A difference, however, is the presence of the $\overline{BGACK}$ line, which is asserted by the requesting device after it sees the bus grant. In principle, a device could request and be granted the bus and then assert $\overline{BGACK}$. At this point $\overline{BR}$ and $\overline{BG}$ are available for another device to request and be granted the bus while the previous device was still using it for transferring data. The second device could not, of course, actually start using the bus until the first one indicated that it was finished by negating $\overline{\text{BGACK}}$. By allowing a second device to begin negotiating for the bus before the first one is done using it, bus cycles are saved.

$\overline{\text{RESET}}$ and $\overline{\text{HALT}}$ allow external devices to reset and stop the CPU, respectively. $\overline{\text{BERR}}$ is used for reporting that something has failed—for example, the 68030 has attempted to access nonexistent memory. $\overline{\text{CDIS}}$ temporarily disables the internal cache. $\overline{\text{STERM}}$ (Synchronous TERMination) is like $\overline{\text{DSACK0}}$ and $\overline{\text{DSACK1}}$ except that it is used on synchronous bus cycles instead of the usual asynchronous ones. This signal is not present on the 68020.

The four cache control signals are not present on the 68020 either. Neither are the three signals used to allow the 68030 to emulate the 68020. Their exact meaning is quite complex and requires an understanding of the chip internals that we have not yet presented, so we will not describe them here.

3.5.3. Comparison of the 80386 and 68030

The 80386 and 68030 chips are both high-performance 32-bit processors of about the same computing power. It is therefore interesting to compare them to see how different designers made different decisions at the hardware level. In subsequent chapters we will see how they differ at higher levels as well.

Both chips use a 32-bit address, but the 80386's always has the 2 low-order bits set to 0, to align transfers on word boundaries. The 68030 does not have this limitation and can address memory starting at any byte. Both chips use a 32-bit data bus. No differences here.

The bus control signals are somewhat different. The 68030 has signals, $\overline{\text{ECS}}$ and $\overline{\text{OCS}}$, that indicate the start of a bus cycle and an operand cycle, respectively, making it easier for external devices to synchronize to the CPU. With the 80386, I/O devices have to synchronize by monitoring the bus themselves. Both chips have signals ($\overline{\text{ADS}}$ and $\overline{\text{AS}}$) announcing that the address bus is valid, but only the 68030 has a similar signal ($\overline{\text{DS}}$) for the data bus. Both use a 3-bit function code to specify the type of bus cycle, and both have an explicit way of letting memory and I/O devices signal completion of a cycle ($\overline{\text{READY}}$ and $\overline{\text{DSACKx}}$). Both also have a way to lock the bus for multicycle operations ($\overline{\text{LOCK}}$ and $\overline{\text{RMC}}$).

Interrupt handling is slightly different. The 80386 has only two priorities, maskable and nonmaskable, whereas the 68030 has seven. They also differ in bus arbitration, with the 68030 making it possible for a second device to request the bus before the first one is done, something the 80386 cannot do.

Although both microprocessors have floating-point coprocessors, the way they interface to them is slightly different. The 80386 regards its coprocessor as being something special, and has specific signals for communicating with it. In contrast, the 68030 regards its coprocessor as just another I/O device, and communicates with it using normal bus cycles. This approach makes it easier to attach additional coprocessors to the 68030. The 68030 processor was, in fact, designed with the idea that users could build their own board-sized coprocessors.

Both chips have a sophisticated memory management unit on chip, but only the 68030 has a substantial data cache. Both use pipelining to improve performance. In summary, the two chips are much more alike than they are different. Both design teams had access to the same technology, both had the same goals, and both were trying to woo the same customers, so it should not be too surprising that the resulting products were fairly similar.

3.6. EXAMPLE BUSES

Buses are the glue that hold computer systems together. In this section we will take a close look at two popular buses: the IBM PC bus (including the closely related PC/AT bus) and the VME bus.

The IBM PC bus is a good example of a bus used on low-end systems. It has 20 address lines and 8 data lines, and is widely used for 8088-based systems. Most PC clones use it, and it forms the basis of the IBM PC/AT and other buses as well.

The VME is a good example of a bus used on high-end, heavy-duty, industrial systems. It supports 32 address lines and 32 data lines. It is used in a number of superminicomputers and many industrial automation applications.

3.6.1. The IBM PC Bus

The IBM PC bus has become the de facto standard on 8088-based systems because nearly all PC clone vendors have copied it in order to allow the many existing third-party I/O boards to be used with their systems. The bus has 62 lines, listed in Fig. 3-45. In this figure, the column labeled *In* refers to signals that are input from the bus to the motherboard, and the column labeled *Out* refers to signals produced on the motherboard and output to the bus.

Physically, the bus is etched onto the motherboard, with about half a dozen connectors spaced 3/4 inch apart into which cards can be inserted. Each card has a tab on it that fits in the connector. The tab has 31 gold-plated strips on each side that make electrical contact with the connector. For the record, IBM calls the bus the **I/O channel**, but nobody else does. We only mention it because two of the bus signals use this name.

The original IBM PC (as well as many clones) is driven by a 14.31818 MHz crystal oscillator. This frequency is not arbitrary. It is required for producing the colorburst signal used on color televisions in North America and Japan. (IBM originally thought that many customers would want to use their existing color televisions as the display device to save the expense of buying a proper monitor. Nobody did, but once they had made this choice, they were stuck with it.) The 14.31818 MHz signal is present on the bus as the OSC (OSCillator) line.

Signal	Lines	In	Out	Description
OSC	1		X	70 nsec Clock signal (14.31818 MHz)
CLK	1		X	210 nsec Clock signal (4.77 MHz)
RESET	1		X	Used to reset the CPU and I/O devices
A0-A19	20		X	20 Address lines
D0-D7	8	X	X	8 Data lines
ALE	1		X	Address latch enable
MEMR	1		X	Memory read
MEMW	1		X	Memory write
IOR	1		X	I/O read
IOW	1		X	I/O write
AEN	1	X		Address enable (asserted to have CPU float the bus)
IO CH CHK	1	X		I/O channel check (parity error)
IO CH RDY	1	X		I/O channel ready (insert wait states)
IRQ2-IRQ7	6	X		Interrupt request lines
DRQ1-DRQ3	3	X		DMA request lines
DACK0-DACK3	4		X	DMA acknowledge lines
T/C	1		X	Terminal/count (indicates DMA completed)
Power	5			±5 Volts, ±12 volts
GND	3			Ground
Reserved	1			(Not used on PC; card select on XT)

Fig. 3-45. Signals on the IBM PC bus.

This frequency is too high for the standard 8088, whose maximum is 5 MHz, so it is divided by 3 to produce a 4.77 MHz signal that actually serves as the master clock that determines the bus cycle. The division of the crystal frequency by 3 is invariably done by an Intel 8284A clock generator chip. The 4.77 MHz signal is also on the bus, where it is called CLK. It is low 2/3 of the time and high 1/3 of the time, unlike OSC which is symmetric. Some PC clones run at 8 MHz, using a faster version of the 8088 chip, so these have a proportionally higher CLK signal.

The 8284A also generates the RESET signal on the bus. To reset the CPU, external circuitry sends a signal to the 8284A, which then asserts RESET to force the CPU and all I/O devices to reinitialize themselves.

The bus also has the 20 address and 8 data lines, as one would expect for a bus designed to be used with the 8088. However, to make sense of many of the other bus lines, it is really necessary to understand not only the 8088 itself, but also some of its support chips and how they are used. In Fig. 3-46 we present a simplified version of the heart of a typical PC clone's motherboard. It consists of seven major chips, as well as some minor chips not shown. The memory subsystem is not shown either since logically it connects to the CPU via the bus, even if it is physically on the motherboard.

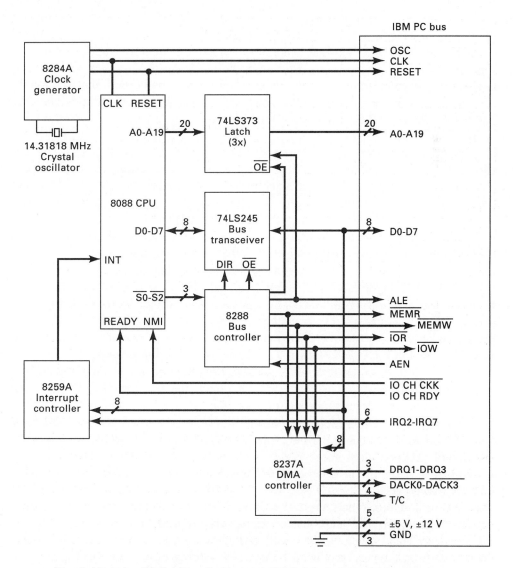

Fig. 3-46. A simplified schematic for a typical PC clone's CPU and support chips.

The first thing to notice about Fig. 3-46 is that the CPU does not drive the address or data lines directly. The address lines are latched by a set of three 74LS373 octal latches, each similar to Fig. 3-27(b). Only 20 of the 24 bits are used.

The need for latching the address lines goes back to Fig. 3-39(a), where we saw that some of the address and data signals are multiplexed onto the same pins. At the start of each CPU bus cycle, the 8088 outputs the address signals. The latches capture these signals and hold them on the address lines for the rest of the cycle, even though they disappear from the 8088's AD0-AD7 shortly thereafter. Thus the latches hide the pin multiplexing and provide pure, demultiplexed address lines to the rest of the system.

The data lines are only sampled or provided by memory and I/O cards at specific instants (e.g., the rising edge of some clock period), so they need not be latched. If the correct signal is present at the moment it is needed, that is enough. Nevertheless, the data lines on the bus are driven by a bus transceiver, the 74LS245. The DIR (DIRection) pin determines whether data are going to the CPU or from the CPU.

However, the real reason for buffering both the address and data lines is that the CPU is a MOS chip, and as such does not put out enough current to drive a whole bus full of boards. The TTL buffer chips put out enough current to drive many boards. Furthermore, when devices other than the CPU want to become bus master (e.g., for DMA), the CPU must float the bus. The simplest way to get the CPU off the bus is to have the external bus request signal, called AEN (Address ENable), be used to negate the output enable signals on the latches and transceivers, thus floating the bus.

Getting back to the bus itself, the next signal in our list is ALE (Address Latch Enable). It is asserted when the address lines are being driven by the CPU, to allow the 74LS373s to know when to latch them. It is also provided on the bus so that the memory and I/O chips know when the address lines have become valid. Before ALE is asserted in each cycle, they are not valid and must not be used.

The next four bus lines are $\overline{\text{MEMR}}$, $\overline{\text{MEMW}}$, $\overline{\text{IOR}}$, and $\overline{\text{IOW}}$ for reading and writing memory and I/O devices, respectively. In effect, the bus provides two distinct address spaces, one for memory and one for I/O. Thus a read from address 0 with $\overline{\text{MEMR}}$ asserted will cause memory location 0 to respond, but a read from address 0 with $\overline{\text{IOR}}$ asserted will cause the I/O chip that has been assigned I/O space address 0 to respond. Memory does not respond when $\overline{\text{IOR}}$ or $\overline{\text{IOW}}$ is asserted.

However, determining when each of these four signals should be asserted is not entirely trivial. As we saw in Fig. 3-39(c), the 8088 outputs the type of bus cycle in encoded form, using signals $\overline{\text{S0}}$-$\overline{\text{S2}}$. To decode this information into the four individual bus signals, the Intel 8288 bus controller chip is used. This chip takes $\overline{\text{S0}}$-$\overline{\text{S2}}$ as input and produces $\overline{\text{MEMR}}$, $\overline{\text{MEMW}}$, $\overline{\text{IOR}}$, and $\overline{\text{IOW}}$ as output, along with ALE. It also takes AEN from the bus (produced by devices wanting to become bus master) and generates the signal that causes the address and data bus drivers to float the bus.

The $\overline{\text{IO CH CHK}}$ (I/O CHannel CHecK) signal is asserted when a parity error is detected on the bus. It is this signal that triggers a nonmaskable interrupt.

The IO CH RDY (I/O CHannel ReaDY) signal is used by slow memories to insert wait states into read and write cycles. It is wired to the 8088's READY pin.

The next set of six signals, IRQ2-IRQ7, are inputs from the bus to the 8259A interrupt controller, as we saw in Fig. 3-38. When one or more devices request an interrupt, the controller keeps track of them, issues the interrupt to the CPU, and puts the interrupt vector number onto the data lines when the CPU asks for it. IRQ0 is normally used by the timer chip and IRQ1 is generally used by the keyboard interrupt. Neither of these uses the bus and neither is shown in Fig. 3-46.

The remaining information signals on the bus relate to DMA. Conceptually, when the CPU asks, say, a disk to read in a block of data, the disk controller chip is supposed to wait for the first byte to arrive from the drive head, and then issue a request to become bus master to write the byte to memory. A similar sequence is required of every device capable of doing DMA.

The logic needed to handle the bus protocol and actually perform the DMA, including incrementing the memory address and decreasing the byte count after each byte transferred, is somewhat complicated. To save the cost of putting this logic into every I/O device, Intel has designed a chip, the 8237A, that can handle the job for other chips, so they need not do it themselves.

In essence, the 8237A is a small CPU with a built-in program. When the 8088 wants to start DMA on some device, it loads the device number, memory address, byte count, direction of transfer and other information into registers inside the 8237A. When the controller chip is ready to read or write the first byte, it asserts one of the DRQx lines on the bus, which are inputs to the 8237A.

Upon seeing this signal, the 8237A requests the bus and sets it up to be ready to transfer a byte. Then it issues a $\overline{\text{DACKx}}$ signal to the controller chip, signaling it to write its byte (for read operations) or read its byte (for write operations). During this one cycle, the controller chip is functioning as bus master and the memory is functioning as slave. This design requires a minimum of logic in the controller chips. The 8237A has four independent channels and can handle up to four transfers simultaneously.

Just as an aside, the 8237A does not have 20 address lines, so it sets up the bus address lines using some dedicated latches, which are not shown in Fig. 3-46. Furthermore, DRQ0 is not output to the bus because it is used for refreshing dynamic RAM.

The T/C is asserted by the 8237A when the byte count is exhausted. This signal lets the controller know that the I/O is done and that it is time to ask the 8259A for an interrupt.

The remaining 8 bus signals are for power and ground. Two lines have +5 volts, and one each have −5, +12, and −12 volts. Three of the lines are grounded. One was reserved for future use, but on the PC/XT it was used for card selection.

Although Fig. 3-46 is far from complete, it is worth studying carefully. The motherboard of most 8088 personal computers uses essentially these chips, augmented with additional ones for the memory subsystem and some critical I/O controllers, such as the keyboard. Furthermore, 80286 and 80386 use analogous chips arranged in a similar way, so the ideas discussed above can be carried over to the other systems as well.

3.6.2. The IBM PC/AT Bus

When IBM introduced the 80286-based PC/AT, it had a major problem on its hands. If it had started from scratch and designed an entirely new 16-bit bus, many potential customers would have hesitated to buy it because none of the vast number of PC plug-in boards available from third-party vendors would have worked using the new machine. On the other hand, sticking with the PC bus and its 20 address lines and 8 data lines would not have taken advantage of the 80286's ability to address 16M of memory and transfer 16-bit words.

The solution chosen was to extend the PC bus. PC plug-in cards have an edge connector with 62 contacts, but this edge connector does not run the full length of the board. The PC/AT solution was to put a second edge connector on the bottom of the board, adjacent to the main one, and design the AT circuitry to work with both types of boards. The general idea is illustrated in Fig. 3-47.

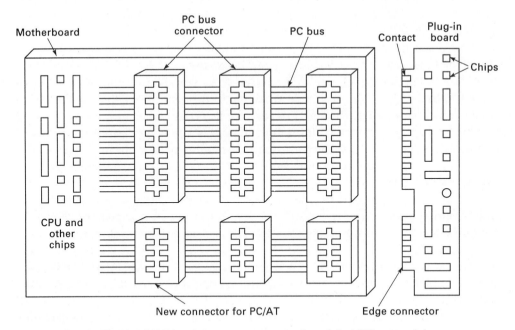

Fig. 3-47. The PC/AT bus has two components, the original PC part and the new part.

The second connector on the PC/AT bus contains 36 lines. Of these, 31 are provided for more address lines, more data lines, more interrupt lines, and more

DMA channels, as well as power and ground. The rest deal with differences between 8-bit and 16-bit transfers. For example, there is a bus line that is driven by the 80286's $\overline{BHE}$ signal to enable/disable the upper byte on transfers.

When IBM brought out the PS/2 series as the successor to the PC and PC/AT, it decided that it was time to start again. Part of this decision may have been technical (the PC bus was by this time really obsolete), but part was no doubt caused by a desire to put an obstacle in the way of companies making PC clones, which had taken over an uncomfortably large part of the market. Thus the mid and upper range PS/2 machines were equipped with a bus, the Microchannel®, that was completely new, and which was protected by a wall of patents backed by an army of lawyers.

The rest of the personal computer industry reacted to this development by adopting its own standard, the **EISA (Extended Industry Standard Architecture)** bus, which is basically an extension of the old PC/AT bus to 32 bits with a few new features thrown in (e.g., for multiprocessing). The advantage of this approach is that it retains compatibility with existing machines and cards, and also that it is based on a bus that IBM had liberally licensed to many companies in order to ensure that as many third parties as possible produced cards for the original PC, something that has come back to haunt it.

3.6.3. The VME Bus

While the IBM PC bus and its descendants are widely used in the personal computer world, in many other applications a more heavyweight bus is needed. In this section we will describe one such bus, the VME bus, and show how it differs from personal computer buses. **VME** stands for **Versa Module Eurocard**, since it is derived from Motorola's earlier Versabus, but uses a standardized double Eurocard format board (160 mm × 200 mm).

Background

In the late 1970s, after Motorola had produced the 68000 chip, it decided to build and sell computer systems based on the 68000. Its first 68000-based system (Exormacs) used a backplane bus that was called the **Versabus**. Shortly after the first Exormacs was shipped, Motorola's European operation suggested adapting the Versabus to use the Eurocard format, which was rapidly becoming the de facto standard for industrial computers in Europe and elsewhere. Motorola agreed that this was a good idea, and signed up Mostek and Signetics/Philips to support this new bus, which was named the **VME** bus. As other companies began producing boards for it, it was decided to set up an IEEE committee to produce an official standard for it (IEEE P1014). VME bus is now one of the most widely used high-performance 32-bit buses, especially for industrial applications. At present over 2000 boards made by more than 250 companies are available for the VME bus.

One of the attractive features of the VME bus is the fact that it has a relatively formal definition in the form of a book that is close to 300 pages. This book describes in great detail exactly how the bus works. It also gives a large number of rules that all VME cards must comply with, as well as many recommendations that any sane designer will observe if he wants to be able to sell the card he is designing. The book also gives numerous observations, comments and examples, so that a customer can buy a VME CPU card from one vendor, a memory card from a second vendor, and an I/O card from a third vendor and they will all work together harmoniously. The IBM PC bus is not nearly so well defined, and it can happen that although cards *A* and *B* both work alone with the CPU, they refuse to work when both are present.

The goals of the VME bus are interoperability, high performance, and high reliability. Interoperability is achieved by having a formal bus standard to which vendors adhere. High performance is achieved by having the bus be asynchronous. No system clock is used to synchronize masters and slaves, allowing individual boards to run at whatever speed current technology allows. In practice, an effective upper limit is one bus cycle every 100 nsec or so, because going faster would give too much skew and other analog engineering problems. With one 4-byte data transfer every 100 nsec, the effective bus bandwidth is 40 Mbytes/sec.

The IBM PC bus, in contrast, has a fixed 4.77 MHz clock, giving a bus cycle of 210 nsec. Since it takes four bus cycles to transfer one byte, the theoretical maximum bandwidth is 1.2 Mbytes/sec. In practice this cannot be achieved because bus arbitration cannot run in parallel with data transfers, as it can on the VME bus.

It is worth saying a little more about synchronous versus asynchronous buses here, because there exist other modern buses such as Multibus II and Nubus that are synchronous at 10 MHz (i.e., have a cycle time of 100 nsec), making them comparable to the VME bus. Consider a CPU working internally at 16, 25, or 30 MHz and running on a synchronous 10 MHz bus. Not all CPU cycles use the bus, but from time to time memory must be referenced.

Since the internal CPU clock is not running in lockstep with the bus, the CPU must simply wait until the start of the next bus cycle before starting its memory operation. This delay will range from 0 to 100 nsec, with an average of 50 nsec. Assuming that one bus cycle is sufficient, the effective access time has been increased from 100 nsec to 150 nsec due to the synchronous nature of the bus. Asynchronous buses can start a cycle at any instant, and do not suffer from this problem.

The VME bus achieves high reliability both through mechanical design and the bus protocols. Instead of using plug-in cards with edge connectors (as does the IBM PC bus), it uses cards with proper connectors consisting of three rows of 32 round metal pins. These connectors mate with proper 96-pin sockets. Although considerably more expensive, this approach virtually eliminates bad connections, one of the main sources of problems in computer systems. Vibration, another big source of trouble, is minimized by requiring precision-machined card cages and guide rails, for handling up to 21 cards. Electrical noise is reduced by using multilayer backplanes and boards.

Reliability is further enhanced by having bus lines that can be used for automatic self-testing and status reporting. Furthermore, the bus has provision for graceful shutdown in the milliseconds available between the moment an impending power failure is noticed and the moment the power has dropped below a usable level.

In addition, the backplane does not contain any active components, the way a motherboard does. Instead, there is a separate system controller board that contains the power-fail monitor, bus arbiter, interrupt controller, and various timers used for testing and utility purposes. This board can be easily replaced if need be.

VME Bus Technical Overview

The VME bus is actually part of a family of three buses that were designed to work in a wide variety of computer systems, from small development systems to complex multiprocessors. Figure 3-48(a) shows a minimal system with three VME cards, one each for the CPU, memory, and an I/O controller.

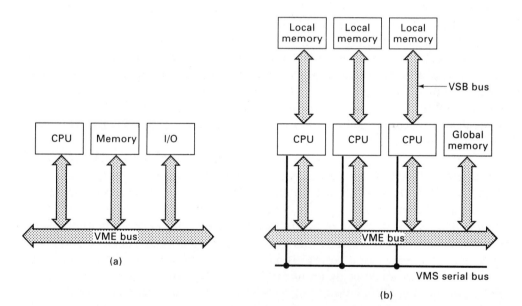

Fig. 3-48. (a) A simple VME system. (b) A VME multiprocessor.

In contrast, Fig. 3-48(b) shows a larger multiprocessor system. In this system, each processor has local memory to which it connects over the **VSB bus**, which is also part of the VME family. By putting all the program code and local data in the local memories, only those instructions that reference the shared global memory have to use the VME bus. This design means that the total bus bandwidth can now greatly exceed the effective 40 Mbyte/sec limit imposed by the VME technology. For example, a multiprocessor with 16 CPUs each requiring a 32-bit word every 200 nsec needs an aggregate bus bandwidth of 320 Mbytes/sec. If 90 percent of these references are for fetching instructions and reading and writing local data (a reasonable assumption for most applications), a system with one VME bus and 16 VSB buses can handle the load.

In addition to the VSB bus, the VME family also supports a bit-serial communication path called the **VMS bus**. This bus runs independently of the other two buses, and can be used for low-bandwidth communication and synchronization among multiple processors, in parallel with data transfers on the main buses. The VMS bus is somewhat like a local area network running on a single coaxial cable.

The VME bus lines can be divided into four groups:

1. Data transfer.

2. Bus arbitration.

3. Priority interrupts.

4. Utilities.

We will now look at each of these in turn.

The VME bus supports 8-, 16-, and 32-bit data transfers, in order to handle small, medium, and large systems. It also supports 16-, 24-, and 32-bit addresses for the same reason. Each bus cycle specifies the address and data width it needs, so that different master/slave pairs can communicate on the same bus with whatever width is most the cost-effective for them, without regard for what other ones are doing.

Several basic types of bus cycles are defined, each operating on various combinations of 1, 2, or 4 bytes. The simplest are ordinary reads and writes of 1, 2, or 4 bytes. Special provision is made for unaligned transfers (e.g., 4 bytes starting at an odd address).

In addition, block transfers (read and write) are also supported, but no transfer may cross a 256-byte boundary. The reason for limiting block transfers in this way is to simplify memory card design. If arbitrary transfers were permitted, then a single block transfer could begin on one card and switch onto a second card partway through, requiring all memory cards to have the ability to pick up a block transfer in the middle. By having each memory card start at a multiple of 256 bytes, this problem is avoided.

The rule about forbidding transfers across 256-byte boundaries is one of the many rules in the bus specification that has been put there to minimize ambiguity about what VME cards are expected to do. One can easily imagine a standard that did not mention the subject resulting in memory boards whose designers never even thought about the possibility of their product having to finish off somebody else's block transfer.

The next type of bus cycle is the indivisible read-modify-write cycle needed to support multiprocessor systems. There is also an interrupt acknowledge bus cycle. We have seen both of these before and will not discuss them further here.

The last type of bus cycle is one we have not seen before: the address-only cycle. No data are transferred during this cycle. Its purpose is to allow a master to announce that it is planning to request a certain address shortly, to allow memory boards to prepare for it and then be able to respond instantly when the real request is made later. By giving slow memories enough advance warning, wait states can sometimes be avoided.

Four types of devices can participate in a data transfer. The master and slave are present, of course, but two other types may also play a role. A **location monitor** may watch the bus and cause a local interrupt on its board whenever an address within a certain range appears. For example, if a certain memory word or I/O register is being written to when it is not supposed to be, a logic analyzer could be attached to the bus to log all bus references, stopping when the word under investigation is touched. The previous n bus cycles can then be displayed, to allow the user to figure out where the bad reference came from.

The fourth type of device that can take part in a data transfer is the **bus timer**, which also monitors the bus constantly. If it notices that a bus cycle is taking too long (e.g., because nonexistent memory has been addressed and there is no slave to respond to it), then it issues an error signal to terminate the bus cycle. Without this facility, an asynchronous bus would hang forever.

Figure 3-49 illustrates a 32-bit VME bus read. When starting a transfer, the master asserts the address lines, A0-A31, the address modifier lines, AM0-AM5, and the $\overline{\text{LWORD}}$ (Long WORD) line. The address lines specify the address, the address modifier lines the bus cycle type, and the $\overline{\text{LWORD}}$ line whether a full 32-bit transfer or a partial transfer is called for.

After all three of these are stable, the master asserts $\overline{\text{AS}}$ (Address Strobe) to tell the slave that the address is now valid and may be latched. It then negates (for a read) or asserts (for a write) $\overline{\text{WRITE}}$. In the figure, a dotted line is provided for $\overline{\text{WRITE}}$ to show the cause-and-effect sequence, but the signal does not necessarily change, depending on what it was already. Finally it asserts $\overline{\text{DS0}}$-$\overline{\text{DS1}}$ to show that it is done and ready to read. The actual coding of $\overline{\text{DS0}}$, $\overline{\text{DS1}}$, $\overline{\text{LWORD}}$, and A1 determines the choice of bytes requested within the selected word. The encoding of these four fields is somewhat obscure.

As soon as the slave sees the assertion of $\overline{\text{DS0}}$-$\overline{\text{DS1}}$, it begins work and puts the data on the D0-D31 lines as soon as it can. After doing so, it asserts $\overline{\text{DTACK}}$ to acknowledge that it is done. When the master sees $\overline{\text{DTACK}}$, it negates most of its signals. Finally it negates $\overline{\text{DS0}}$-$\overline{\text{DS1}}$ as well, which tells the slave to negate $\overline{\text{DTACK}}$, thus ending the cycle. The bus is then ready to perform another cycle.

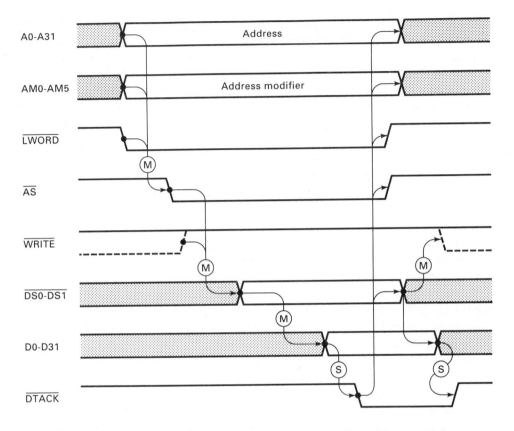

Fig. 3-49. A VME bus read cycle. The arrows labeled with an *M* are internal to the master. Those labeled with an *S* are internal to the slave. The unlabeled ones involve both.

The second group of lines deals with bus arbitration. Three schemes are supported: single-level daisy chaining, fixed priorities, and round robin, although other schemes are not forbidden. For all arbitration schemes, a would-be master makes a request by asserting some line. When it gets the grant and takes the bus, it then asserts a bus busy signal and negates the request. In this way the next master can be chosen while the current one is at work. This facility is also present in the 680x0 chips, so it is hardly surprising that Motorola put it in the bus too. In high-performance systems, it can improve performance considerably.

We have already studied single-level daisy chaining and fixed priorities, so let us look at round robin arbitration. When this method is used, each of the four request lines is considered equal to the others in priority. Each potential master is attached to one of the lines, so with n potential bus masters there will be an average of $n/4$ masters per line. On the first bus cycle, the arbiter grants permission to line

0, on the next cycle, to line 1, and so on. If no one is requesting mastership on a given line, it is skipped. If multiple devices want to be master on the same line, daisy chaining is used among them. Considering that the VME card has two 96-pin connectors, of which about 80 are not used, providing only four request lines seems unduly frugal. Even the old 56-line PDP-11 Unibus had five request lines.

One interesting feature of the VME bus is a line that is used by the bus arbiter to request a low priority master that is engaged in a long block transfer to stop in order to allow a higher priority master to take over.

The third group of VME bus lines deals with priority interrupts. Like the IBM PC bus, the VME bus has a number of interrupt request lines (seven, to be exact) and one daisy-chained interrupt grant line. In a single processor system, interrupt handling is easy—devices raise their hands to cause an interrupt, and some sort of interrupt controller (such as the 8259A) selects one and asserts an interrupt pin on the CPU. When a bus has multiple CPUs and multiple devices, as the VME bus can, the request lines can be partitioned among two or more interrupt controllers, with each controller monitoring specific lines and being responsible for interrupting a specific CPU. For example, lines 1 through 4 could be used to interrupt CPU 1 and lines 5 through 7 could be used to interrupt CPU 2.

Once the interrupt has been requested and granted, the relevant CPU can be interrupted. What the CPU does next is outside the bus protocol. It may, for example, act as master and ask the controller for an interrupt vector number, but it is not required to. If multiple interrupts occur simultaneously, the interrupted CPUs must contend for bus mastership in the normal way.

The final group of bus lines is used for utility functions. One of these lines is a fixed 16 MHz clock signal driven by the system controller board. It is *not* used for delimiting bus cycles, but can be used for measuring time, for example, for timeouts.

Two other lines are used to implement the VMS serial bus. One of these provides clock pulses at 32 MHz so senders will know when to place bits on the other one. Thus the VMS serial bus can run at 32 Mbps, but it can also be run at a submultiple thereof, such as 16 Mbps or 8 Mbps. The two clocks just described are not necessarily synchronized with each other, and they are certainly not synchronized with anything else on the bus.

The remaining lines are concerned with initializing, resetting, and testing the system. A complete list of all the VME signal lines is given in Fig. 3-50. In this figure, *In* and *Out* are with respect to the bus master or system controller.

3.7. INTERFACING

A typical small to medium-sized computer system consists of a microprocessor chip, memory chips and some I/O controllers, all connected by a bus. We have already studied memories, microprocessors, and buses in some detail. Now it is

	Signal	Lines	In	Out	Description
Data transfer	A1-A31	31		X	Address lines. A0 is always 0
	AM0-AM5	6		X	Address modifier defines bus cycle type
	$\overline{\text{LWORD}}$	1		X	Long word. Partially defines data width
	$\overline{\text{AS}}$	1		X	Address strobe. Asserted when address is stable
	$\overline{\text{WRITE}}$	1		X	Asserted on write. Negated on read
	$\overline{\text{DS0}}$-$\overline{\text{DS1}}$	2		X	Data strobe
	$\overline{\text{D0}}$-$\overline{\text{D31}}$	32	X	X	Data lines
	$\overline{\text{DTACK}}$	1	X		Data acknowledge signal
	$\overline{\text{BERR}}$	1	X		Asserted when bus error detected
Bus arbitration	$\overline{\text{BR0}}$-$\overline{\text{BR3}}$	4	X		Bus request lines
	$\overline{\text{BG0IN}}$-$\overline{\text{BG3IN}}$	4		X	Bus grant daisy chain (in)
	$\overline{\text{BG0OUT}}$-$\overline{\text{BG3OUT}}$	4		X	Bus grant daisy chain (out)
	$\overline{\text{BBSY}}$	1	X		Bus busy
	$\overline{\text{BCLR}}$	1		X	Asserted by arbiter to reclaim bus
Interrupts	$\overline{\text{IRQ1}}$-$\overline{\text{IRQ7}}$	7	X	X	Interrupt request lines
	$\overline{\text{IACK}}$	1		X	Head of interrupt acknowledge chain
	$\overline{\text{IACKIN}}$	1		X	Interrupt ack. daisy chain (in)
	$\overline{\text{IACKOUT}}$	1		X	Interrupt ack. daisy chain (out)
Utilities	SYSCLK	1		X	16 MHz system utility clock
	SERCLK	1		X	32 MHz VMS bus bit clock
	$\overline{\text{SERDAT}}$	1	X	X	VMS bus data line
	$\overline{\text{ACFAIL}}$	1		X	AC power failure detected
	$\overline{\text{SYSFAIL}}$	1	X	X	Diagnostic line
	$\overline{\text{SYSRESET}}$	1	X		System reset
	Power	9			± 5 Volts, ± 12 volts
	GND	12			Ground
	Reserved	1			(Not used)

Fig. 3-50. Signals on the VME bus.

time to look at the last part of the puzzle, the I/O chips. It is through these chips that the computer communicates with the external world.

3.7.1. I/O Chips

Numerous I/O chips are already available and new ones are being introduced all the time. Common chips include UARTs, USARTs, CRT controllers, disk controllers, and PIOs. A **UART (Universal Asynchronous Receiver Transmitter)** is a chip that can read a byte from the data bus and output it a bit at a time on a serial line for a terminal, or input data from a terminal. UARTs usually allow speeds from 50 bps to 19.2 kbps; character widths from 5 to 8 bits; 1, 1.5, or 2 stop bits; and provide even, odd, or no parity, all under program control. **USARTs (Universal Synchronous Asynchronous Receiver Transmitters)** can handle synchronous transmission using a variety of protocols as well as performing all the UART functions. Since we already looked at UARTs in Chap. 2, let us now study the parallel interface as an example of an I/O chip.

PIO Chips

A typical **PIO (Parallel Input/Output)** chip is the Intel 8255A, shown in Fig. 3-51. It has 24 I/O lines that can interface to any TTL-compatible device, for example, keyboards, switches, lights, or printers. In a nutshell, the CPU program can write a 0 or 1 to any line, or read the input status of any line, providing great flexibility. A small microprocessor-based system using a PIO can often replace a complete board full of SSI or MSI chips.

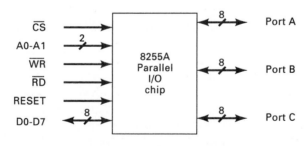

Fig. 3-51. An 8255A PIO chip.

Although the CPU can configure the 8255A in many ways by loading status registers within the chip, we will concentrate on some of the simpler modes of operation. The simplest way of using the 8255A is as three independent 8-bit ports, A, B, and C. Associated with each port is an 8-bit latch register. To set the lines on a port, the CPU just writes an 8-bit number into the corresponding register, and the 8-bit number appears on the output lines and stays there until the register is rewritten. To use a port for input, the CPU just reads the corresponding register.

Other operating modes provide for handshaking with external devices. For example, to output to a device that is not always ready to accept data, the 8255A can present data on an output port and wait for the device to send a pulse back saying that it has accepted the data and wants more. The necessary logic for latching such pulses and making them available to the CPU is included in the 8255A hardware.

From the functional diagram of the 8255A we can see that in addition to 24 pins for the three ports, it has eight lines that connect directly to the data bus, a chip select line, read and write lines, two address lines, and a line for resetting the chip. The two address lines select one of the four internal registers, corresponding to ports A, B, C, and the status register, which has bits determining which ports are for input and which for output, and other functions. Normally, the two address lines are connected to the low-order bits of the address bus.

3.7.2. Address Decoding

Up until now we have been deliberately vague about how chip select is asserted on the memory and I/O chips we have looked at. It is now time to look more carefully at how this is done. Let us consider a simple microcomputer consisting of a CPU, a $2K \times 8$ EPROM for the program, a $2K \times 8$ RAM for the data, and a PIO. This small system might be used as a prototype for the brain of a cheap toy or simple appliance. Once in production, the EPROM might be replaced by a ROM.

The PIO can be selected in one of two ways, as a true I/O device or as part of memory. If we choose to use it as an I/O device, then we must select it using an explicit I/O space address, for example, the $\overline{\text{IORQ}}$ signal on the IBM PC bus. If we use the other approach, **memory-mapped I/O**, then we must assign it four bytes of the address space for the three ports and the control register. The choice is somewhat arbitrary. We will choose memory-mapped I/O because it illustrates some interesting issues in I/O interfacing.

The EPROM needs 2K of address space, the RAM also needs 2K of address space, and the PIO needs 4 bytes. Because our example address space is 64K, we must make a choice about where to put the three devices. One possible choice is shown in Fig. 3-52. The EPROM occupies addresses to 2K, the RAM occupies addresses 32K to 34K, and the PIO occupies the highest four bytes of the address space, 65532 to 65535. From the programmer's point of view, it makes no difference which addresses are used; however, for interfacing it does matter. If we had chosen to address the PIO via the I/O space, it would not need any memory addresses (but it would need four I/O space addresses).

With the address assignments of Fig. 3-52, the EPROM should be selected by any 16-bit memory address of the form 00000xxxxxxxxxxx (binary). In other words, any address whose 5 high-order bits are all 0s falls in the bottom 2K of memory, hence in the EPROM. Thus the EPROM's chip select could be wired to a 5-bit comparator one of whose inputs was permanently wired to 00000.

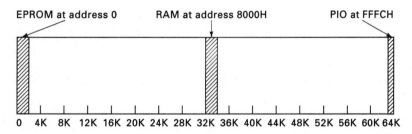

Fig. 3-52. Location of the EPROM, RAM, and PIO in our 64K address space.

A better way to achieve the same effect is to use a five-input OR gate, with the five inputs attached to address lines A11 to A15. If and only if all five lines are 0 will the output be 0, thus asserting $\overline{CS}$ (which is asserted low). Unfortunately, no five-input OR gate exists in the standard SSI series. The closest we can come is an eight-input NOR gate. By grounding three inputs and inverting the output we can nevertheless produce the correct signal, as shown in Fig. 3-53(a). By convention, unused inputs are not shown in circuit diagrams.

The same principle can be used for the RAM. However, the RAM should respond to binary addresses of the form 10000xxxxxxxxxxx, so an additional inverter is needed as shown in the figure. The PIO address decoding is more complicated, because it is selected by the four addresses of the form 11111111111111xx. A possible circuit that asserts $\overline{CS}$ only when the correct address appears on the address bus is shown in the figure. It uses two eight-input NAND gates to feed an OR gate. To build the address decoding logic of Fig. 3-53(a) using SSI requires six chips—the four eight-input chips, an OR gate, and a chip with three inverters.

However, if the computer really consists of only the CPU, two memory chips, and the PIO, we can use a trick to simplify greatly the address decoding. The trick is based on the fact that all EPROM addresses, and only EPROM addresses, have a 0 in the high-order bit, A15. Therefore, we can just wire $\overline{CS}$ to A15 directly, as shown in Fig. 3-53(b). At this point the decision to put the RAM at 8000H may seem much less arbitrary. The RAM decoding can be done by noting that the only valid addresses of the form 10xxxxxxxxxxxxxx are in the RAM, so 2 bits of decoding is sufficient. Similarly, any address starting with 11 must be a PIO address. The complete decoding logic is now two NAND gates and an inverter. Because an inverter can be made from a NAND gate by just tying the two inputs together, a single quad NAND chip is now more than sufficient.

The address decoding logic of Fig. 3-53(b) is called **partial address decoding**, because the full addresses are not used. It has the property that a read from addresses 0001000000000000, 0001100000000000, or 0010000000000000 will give the same result. In fact, every address in the bottom half of the address space will select the EPROM. Because the extra addresses are not used, no harm is done,

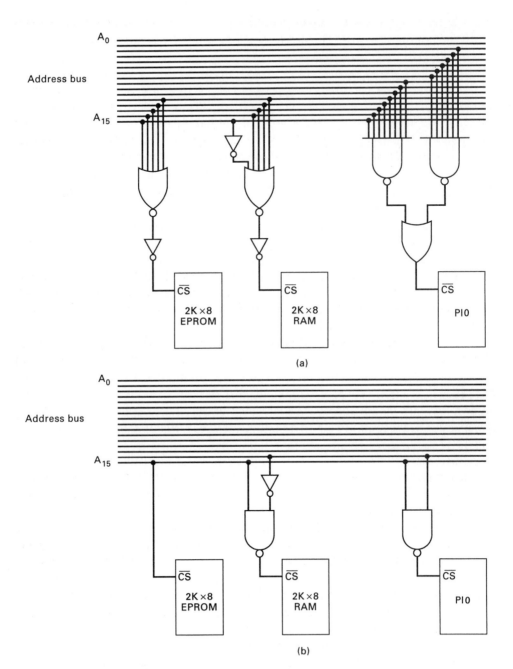

Fig. 3-53. (a) Full address decoding. (b) Partial address decoding.

but if one is designing a computer that may be expanded in the future (an unlikely occurrence in a toy), partial decoding should be avoided because it ties up too much address space.

Another common address decoding technique is to use a decoder chip, such as that shown in Fig. 3-14. By connecting the three inputs to the three high-order address lines, we get eight outputs, corresponding to addresses in the first 8K, second 8K, and so on. For a computer with eight RAMs, each 8K × 8, one such chip provides the complete decoding. For a computer with eight 2K × 8 memory chips, a single decoder is also sufficient, provided that the memory chips are each located in distinct 8K chunks of address space. (Remember our earlier remark that the position of the memory and I/O chips within the address space matters.)

3.8. SUMMARY

Computers are constructed from integrated circuit chips containing tiny switching elements called gates. The most common gates are AND, OR, NAND, NOR, and NOT. Simple circuits can be built up by directly combining individual gates using SSI chips.

More complex circuits are constructed using standard MSI components such as multiplexers, demultiplexers, encoders, decoders, shifters, and ALUs. Arbitrary Boolean functions can be programmed using a PLA. If many Boolean functions are needed, PLAs are much more efficient (i.e., require fewer chips) than using SSI chips. The laws of Boolean algebra can be used to transform circuits from one form to another. In many cases more economical circuits can be produced this way.

Computer arithmetic is done by adders. A single bit full adder can be constructed from two half adders. An adder for a multibit word can be built by connecting multiple full adders in such a way as to allow the carry out of each one feed into its left-hand neighbor.

The components of (static) memories are latches and flip-flops, each of which can store one bit of information. These can be combined linearly into octal latches and flip-flops or logarithmically into full-scale word-oriented memories. Memories are available as RAM, ROM, PROM, EPROM, and EEPROM. Static memories need not be refreshed; they keep their values as long as the power remains on. Dynamic memories, on the other hand, must be refreshed periodically to compensate for leakage from the little capacitors on the chip.

The components of a computer system are connected by buses. Many, but not all, of the pins on a typical microprocessor chip directly drive one bus line. The bus lines can be divided into address, data, and control lines. Synchronous buses are driven by a master clock. Asynchronous buses use full handshaking to synchronize the slave to the master.

The IBM PC bus is a typical personal computer bus. A system using it has an

8088 CPU, a bus controller, an interrupt controller, a DMA chip, some latches and drivers, and other chips. For high-performance industrial applications, the VME bus is often used. It supports 32-bit addresses and 32-bit data transfers, as well as shorter ones.

Switches, lights, printers, and many other I/O devices can be interfaced to computers using parallel I/O chips such as the 8255A. These chips can be configured to be part of the I/O space or the memory space, as needed. They can be fully decoded or partially decoded, depending on the application.

PROBLEMS

1. A logician drives into a drive-in restaurant and says, "I want a hamburger or a hot dog and french fries." The cook flunked out of sixth grade and doesn't know (or care) whether "and" has precedence over "or." As far as he is concerned, one interpretation is as good as the other. Which of the following cases are valid interpretations of the order? (Note that in English "or" means "exclusive or.")

    a. Just a hamburger.
    b. Just a hot dog.
    c. Just french fries.
    d. A hot dog and french fries.
    e. A hamburger and french fries.
    f. A hot dog and a hamburger.
    g. All three.
    h. Nothing—the logician goes hungry for being a wiseguy.

2. A missionary lost in Southern California stops at a fork in the road. He knows that two motorcycle gangs inhabit the area, one of which always tells the truth and one of which always lies. He wants to know which road leads to Disneyland. What question should he ask?

3. There exist four Boolean functions of a single variable and 16 functions of two variables. How many functions of three variables are there? Of n variables?

4. Use a truth table to show that $P = (P \text{ AND } Q) \text{ OR } (P \text{ AND NOT } Q)$.

5. Show how the AND function can be constructed from two NAND gates.

6. Use de Morgan's law to find the complement of $A\bar{B}$.

7. Using the three-variable multiplexer chip of Fig. 3-13, implement a function whose output is the parity of the inputs, that is, the output is 1 if and only if an odd number of inputs are 1.

8. Put on your thinking cap. The three-variable multiplexer chip of Fig. 3-13 is actually capable of computing an arbitrary function of *four* Boolean variables. Describe how, and as an example, draw the logic diagram for the function that is 0 if the English word for the truth table row has an even number of letters, 1 if it has an odd number of letters (e.g., 0000 = zero = four letters → 0; 0111 = seven = five letters → 1; 1101 = thirteen = eight letters → 0). *Hint:* If we call the fourth input variable D, the eight input lines may be wired to V_{cc}, ground, D, or $\overline{D}$.

9. Draw the logic diagram of a 2-bit demultiplexer, a circuit whose single input line is steered to one of the four output lines depending on the state of the two control lines.

10. Draw the logic diagram of a 2-bit encoder, a circuit with four input lines, exactly one of which is high at any instant, and two output lines whose 2-bit binary value tells which input is high.

11. Redraw the PLA of Fig. 3-16 in enough detail to show how the majority logic function of Fig. 3-3 can be implemented. In particular, be sure to show which connections are present in both matrices.

12. What does this circuit do?

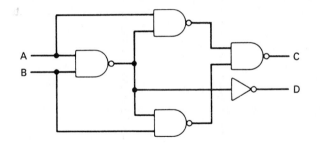

13. A common MSI chip is a 4-bit adder. Four of these chips can be hooked up to form a 16-bit adder. How many pins would you expect the 4-bit adder chip to have? Why?

14. An n-bit adder can be constructed by cascading n full adders in series, with the carry into stage i, C_i, coming from the output of stage $i - 1$. The carry into stage 0, C_0, is 0. If each stage takes T nsec to produce its sum and carry, the carry into stage i will not be valid until iT nsec after the start of the addition. For large n the time required for the carry to ripple through to the high-order stage may be unacceptably long. Design an adder that works faster. *Hint:* Each C_i can be expressed in terms of the operand bits A_{i-1} and B_{i-1} as well as the carry C_{i-1}. Using this relation it is possible to express C_i as a function of the inputs to stages 0 to $i - 1$, so all the carries can be generated simultaneously.

15. If all the gates in Fig. 3-20 have a propagation delay of 10 nsec, and all other delays can be ignored, what is the earliest time a circuit using this design can be sure of having a valid output bit?

16. A 16-bit ALU is built up of 16 1-bit ALUs, each one having an add time of 100 nsec. If there is an additional 10 nsec delay for propagation from one ALU to the next, how long does it take for the result of a 16-bit add to appear?

17. What is the quiescent state of the S and R inputs to an SR latch built of two NAND gates?

18. To help meet the payments on your new personal computer, you have taken up consulting for fledgling SSI chip manufacturers. One of your clients is thinking about putting out a chip containing four D flip-flops, each containing both Q and $\bar{Q}$, on request of a potentially important customer. The proposed design has all four clock signals ganged together, also on request. Neither preset nor clear is present. Your assignment is to give a professional evaluation of the design.

19. The 4×3 memory of Fig. 3-28 uses 22 AND gates and three OR gates. If the circuit were to be expanded to 256×8, how many of each would be needed?

20. As more and more memory is squeezed onto a single chip, the number of pins needed to address it also increases. It is often inconvenient to have large numbers of address pins on a chip. Devise a way to address 2^n words of memory using fewer than n pins.

21. A finite-state machine has 2^n possible states. At each clock pulse, it reads in a k-bit symbol, emits a k-bit output symbol, and switches to a new state. The symbol emitted and the new state depend on the current state and the input symbol. Describe how the machine can be implemented using a ROM, and tell how big the ROM must be.

22. A computer with a 32-bit wide data bus uses $1M \times 1$ dynamic RAM memory chips. What is the smallest memory (in bytes) that this computer can have?

23. Referring to the timing diagram of Fig. 3-34, suppose that you slowed the clock down to a period of 400 nsec instead of 250 nsec as shown but the timing constraints remained unchanged. How much time would the memory have to get the data onto the bus after $\overline{MREQ}$ was asserted, in the worst case?

24. In Fig. 3-34(b), T_{ML} is specified to be at least 60 nsec. Can you envision a chip in which it is negative? In other words, could the CPU assert $\overline{MREQ}$ before the address was stable? Why or why not?

25. Denote the transition times of the address lines of Fig. 3-35 as T_{A1} and T_{A2}, and the transition times of $\overline{MREQ}$ as T_{MREQ1} and T_{MREQ2}, and so on. Write down all the inequalities implied by the full handshake.

26. Most 32-bit buses permit 16-bit reads and writes. Is there any ambiguity about where to place the data? Discuss.

27. The 8088 and other CPUs have a special bus cycle type for interrupt acknowledge. Why?

28. A 10 MHz PC/AT requires four cycles to read a word. How much bus bandwidth does the CPU consume?

29. A 32-bit CPU with address lines A2-A31 requires all memory references to be aligned.

That is, words have to be addressed at multiples of 4 bytes, and half-words have to be addressed at even bytes. Bytes can be anywhere. How many legal combinations are there for memory reads, and how many pins are needed to express them? Give two answers and make a case for each one. Which solution does the 80386 use?

30. The 68030 uses three lines for bus arbitration, vs. only two on the 80386. Suppose bus arbitration takes one cycle and a data transfer four cycles. If the clock rate, internal speed, and all other factors were the same, which machine would be faster and by how much? (*Hint*: Think carefully, this is a sneaky question.)

31. The 68030 has three interrupt lines vs. 1 on the 80386 (excluding NMI). Is this likely to be a significant advantage on small systems? On large ones?

32. The IBM PC bus has 62 lines. Propose a change that would reduce it to 60 without losing any functionality. Your change should not require adding more than a few gates to memory and I/O boards.

33. The circuit of Fig. 3-46 uses 74LS373s and 74LS245s. Why do you think two different kinds are used?

34. A VME card cage contains 16 processors in slots 1 through 16 and a memory card in slot 17. Processor 4 breaks down and the card is removed. After that, interrupts no longer work properly. Explain.

35. A VME multiprocessor has 20 32-bit processors and uses the VSB bus for local memory. Each processor makes n global memory references/sec. Under the best of conditions, what is the theoretical maximum value of n?

36. A computer has instructions that each require two bus cycles, one to fetch the instruction and one to fetch the data. Each bus cycle takes 250 nsec and each instruction takes 500 nsec (i.e., the internal processing time is negligible). The computer also has a disk, with 16 512-byte sectors per track. Disk rotation time is 8.092 msec. To what percent of its normal speed is the computer reduced during a DMA transfer if each DMA transfer takes one bus cycle? Consider two cases: 8-bit bus transfers and 16-bit bus transfers.

37. What would the effect be of adding a third input line to the NAND gate selecting the PIO of Fig. 3-53(b) if this new line were connected to A13?

38. Write a program to simulate the behavior of an $m \times n$ array of two-input NAND gates. This circuit, contained on a chip, has j input pins and k output pins. The values of j, k, m, and n are compile-time parameters of the simulation. The program should start off by reading in a "wiring list," each wire of which specifies an input and an output. An input is either one of the j input pins or the output of some NAND gate. An output is either one of the k output pins or an input to some NAND gate. Unused inputs are logical 1. After reading in the wiring list, the program should print the output for each of the 2^j possible inputs. Gate array chips like this one are widely used for putting custom circuits on a chip because most of the work (depositing the gate array on the chip) is independent of the circuit to be implemented. Only the wiring is specific to each design.

39. Write a program to read in two arbitrary Boolean expressions and see if they represent the same function. The input language should include single letters, as Boolean variables, the operands AND, OR, and NOT, and parentheses. Each expression should fit on one input line. The program should compute the truth tables for both functions and compare them.

40. Write a program to read in a collection of Boolean expressions and compute the 24×50 and 50×6 matrices needed to implement them with the PLA of Fig. 3-16. The input language should be the same as the previous problem. Print the matrices on the line printer.

4

THE MICROPROGRAMMING LEVEL

The boundary between hardware and software is not well defined and, further-more, is constantly shifting. Early computers had instructions for arithmetic, Boolean operations, shifting, comparing, looping, and so on, that were all directly executed by the hardware. For each instruction, a specific hardware circuit was present to carry it out. One could unscrew the back panel and point to the elec-tronic components used by the division instruction, at least in principle.

On a modern multilevel computer, it is no longer possible to isolate the division circuits because there are no division circuits. All the instructions available at the conventional machine level (e.g., instructions for arithmetic, Boolean, shifting, comparing, and looping) are carried out one step at a time by an interpreter running at the microprogramming level. The modern-day equivalent of looking for the divi-sion circuits is to get out a listing of the microprogram and look for that portion of it which interprets division instructions.

Although programs at any level may be carried out by an interpreter, and although this interpreter itself may also be executed by another interpreter, this hierarchy cannot go on indefinitely. At the bottom level, there must be a physical hardware machine, with integrated circuits, power supplies, and similar "hard" objects. These items were the subject of the preceding chapter. In this chapter we will study how the hardware components are controlled by the microprogram and how the microprogram interprets the conventional machine level. In Chap. 8 we will study a class of machines that is not microprogrammed (RISC machines).

Because the architecture of the microprogramming level, called the **microar-chitecture**, is defined by the hardware, it is usually primitive and awkward to program. Timing considerations are frequently important, for example. These considerations led Rosin (1974) to define microprogramming as "the implementation of hopefully reasonable systems through interpretation on unreasonable machines."

The microprogramming level has a specific function: to execute interpreters for other (hopefully, more reasonable) virtual machines. This design goal naturally leads to an organization highly optimized toward fetching, decoding, and executing conventional machine instructions, and, in some cases, more sophisticated instructions. The issues and trade-offs involved in the organization and design for this level will be examined in this chapter.

We will begin our study of the microprogramming level by briefly reviewing the basic building blocks discussed in Chap. 3, because they are part of the architecture of the microprogramming level, hence of concern to the microprogrammer. (A "microprogrammer" is someone who writes microprograms, not a small programmer.) Next, we come to the heart of the subject, how more complex instructions can be built up from sequences of primitive instructions. This topic will be discussed in detail and illustrated by an extensive example. Afterward we will examine the various factors that must be considered when designing a computer's microprogramming level, in order to better understand why it is the way it is. We will also look at ways to improve computer performance. Finally, we will examine the microprogramming level of our two running examples, the Intel and Motorola families.

4.1. REVIEW OF THE DIGITAL LOGIC LEVEL

The microprogrammer's job is to write a program to control the machine's registers, buses, ALUs, memories, and other hardware components. We have studied these devices in the preceding chapter; now we will just review them briefly to put them in perspective. After the review, we will also say a little about the different conceptual ways of packaging the components.

4.1.1. Registers

A register is a device capable of storing information. The microprogramming level always has some registers available to hold information needed for the processing of the instruction currently being interpreted. Conceptually, registers are the same as main memory, the difference being that the registers are physically located within the processor itself, so they can be read from and stored into faster than words in main memory, which is usually off-chip. Larger and more expensive machines usually have more registers than smaller and cheaper ones, which have to use main memory for storing intermediate results. On some computers a group of registers numbered 0, 1, 2, ..., $n - 1$, is available at the microprogramming level, and is called **local storage** or **scratchpad storage**.

Bit number 15 14 13 12 11 10 9 8 7 6 5 4 3 2 1 0

| 0 | 0 | 0 | 0 | 1 | 1 | 0 | 0 | 1 | 0 | 1 | 1 | 0 | 0 | 1 | 0 |

Fig. 4-1. A 16-bit register can hold 16 bits of information.

A register can be characterized by a single number: how many bits it can hold. Figure 4-1 shows a 16-bit register with the bit-numbering convention used in this book. Information placed in a register remains there until some other information replaces it. The process of reading information out of a register does not affect the contents of the register. In other words, when a register is read, a copy is made of its contents and the original is left undisturbed in the register.

4.1.2. Buses

A bus is a collection of wires used to transmit signals in parallel. For example, buses are used to allow the contents of one register to be copied to another one. Unlike the system buses we studied in Chap. 3, these buses only connect two devices, so there is no need for address lines or extensive control lines. The n data lines and one or two control lines are generally sufficient. Buses are used because parallel transfer of all the bits at once is much faster than serial transmission a bit at a time.

A bus may be unidirectional or bidirectional. A unidirectional bus can only transfer data in one direction, whereas a bidirectional bus can transfer data in either direction but not both simultaneously. Unidirectional buses are typically used to connect two registers, one of which is always the source and the other of which is always the destination. Bidirectional buses are typically used when any of a collection of registers can be the source and any other one can be the destination.

Many devices have the ability to connect and disconnect themselves electrically from the buses to which they are physically attached. These connections can be made or broken in nanoseconds. A bus whose devices have this property is called a **tri-state** bus, because each line can be 0, 1, or disconnected. Tri-state buses are commonly used when a bus has many devices attached to it, all of which can potentially put information onto the bus.

In most microarchitectures, some registers are connected to one or more input buses and one or more output buses. Figure 4-2(a) depicts an 8-bit register connected to an input bus and to an output bus. The register consists of eight D-type flip-flops, each connected to the output bus via a noninverting buffer. Each one holds 1 bit. The register has two control signals, CK (ClocK, which really means "load register"), and OE (Output Enable), both of which are connected to all the flip-flops. Normally, both signals are in their quiescent state but occasionally they may be asserted, causing the corresponding action to happen.

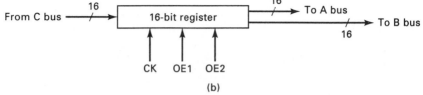

Fig. 4-2. (a) Detail of an 8-bit register connected to an input bus and an output bus. (b) Symbolic representation of a 16-bit register with one input bus and two output buses.

When CK is negated, the contents of the register are not affected by the signals on the bus. When CK is asserted, the register is loaded from the input bus. When OE is negated, the register is disconnected from the output bus and effectively ceases to exist as far as other registers on the bus are concerned. When OE is asserted, the contents of the register are put onto the output bus.

If another register, R, has its input connected to this register's output bus, it may be possible to transfer information from this register to R. To do so, OE must be asserted and kept asserted long enough for the output on the bus to become stable. Then register R's CK line must be asserted, loading R from the bus. The operation of gating a register onto a bus so another register can load the value in occurs often at the microprogramming level, as we will see shortly. As a second example of registers and buses, Fig. 4-2(b) shows a 16-bit register with two output buses, each controlled by a different OE signal.

4.1.3. Multiplexers and Decoders

Circuits that have one or more input lines and compute one or more output values that are uniquely determined by the present inputs are called **combinational circuits**. Two of the most important ones are multiplexers and decoders. A **multiplexer** has 2^n data inputs (individual lines or buses), one data output of the same width as the inputs, and an n-bit control input that selects one of the inputs and routes it to the output. Figure 4-3(a) shows a multiplexer with two buses as input. The 1-bit control signal selects A or B as the output. Figure 3-12 shows the circuit for an 8-input multiplexer.

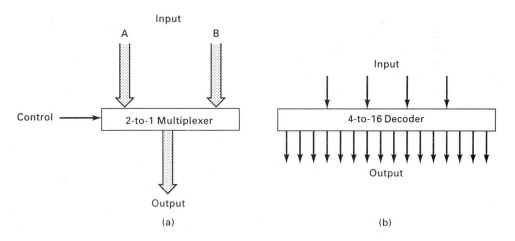

Fig. 4-3. (a) A 2-to-1 multiplexer. (b) A 4-to-16 decoder.

The inverse of a multiplexer is a **demultiplexer**, which routes its single input to one of its 2^n outputs, depending on the value of the n control lines.

Another important combinational circuit is the **decoder** which has n input lines and 2^n output lines, numbered 0 to $2^n - 1$. If the binary number on the input lines is

k, then output line k will be 1 and all the other output lines will be 0. A decoder always has exactly one output line set to 1, with the rest 0. Figure 4-3(b) symbolically illustrates a 4-to-16 decoder; Fig. 3-14 shows the circuit for a 3-to-8 decoder.

The inverse of a decoder is an **encoder**, which has 2^n inputs and n outputs. Only one input line may be 1, and its number, in binary, is presented as the output.

4.1.4. ALUs and Shifters

Every computer needs some way to do arithmetic. The simplest circuit is just an adder, which takes two n-bit inputs and produces their sum as output. A more general arithmetic circuit is the **ALU** or **Arithmetic Logical Unit**. It also has two data inputs and one data output, but it also has some control inputs and outputs. The ALU of Fig. 4-4(a) has two function bits, F_0 and F_1, that determine which function the ALU is to perform. The ALU we will use in our example can compute $A + B$, A AND B, A as well as $\overline{A}$. The first two of these are self-explanatory; the third function just copies A to the output; the fourth one outputs the inverse of A. The third function may seem pointless but later we will see what it is used for. Figure 3-20 shows a four-function ALU that operates on one data bit. By replicating this circuit n times and feeding the carry from bit i into bit $i + 1$, we can make an n-bit wide ALU that performs AND, OR, NOT, and addition.

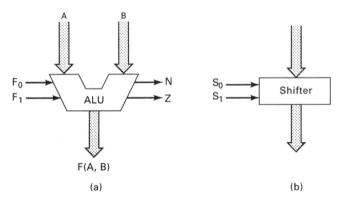

Fig. **4-4.** (a) An ALU. (b) A shifter.

An ALU may also have status outputs. Typical outputs are lines that are 1 when the ALU output is negative, when it is zero, when there is a carry out of the highest bit, or when an overflow occurred. The example of Fig. 4-4(a) has two control outputs, N, which indicates that the ALU output is negative, and Z, which indicates that the ALU output is zero. The N bit is just a copy of the high-order output bit. The Z bit is the NOR of all the ALU output bits.

Although some ALUs can also perform shift operations, most of the time it is necessary to have a separate shift unit. This circuit can shift a multibit input 1 bit left or right, or, alternatively, perform no shift at all. Figure 4-4(b) is the symbol we will use for a shifter; a shift circuit can be found in Fig. 3-17.

4.1.5. Clocks

Computer circuits are normally driven by a **clock**, a device that emits a periodic sequence of pulses. These pulses define machine cycles. During each machine cycle, some activity occurs, such as the execution of a microinstruction. It is often useful to divide a cycle into subcycles, so different parts of the microinstruction can be performed in a well-defined order. For example, the inputs to the ALU must be made available and allowed to become stable before the output can be stored.

Figure 4-5(a) shows a symbolic clock with four outputs. The top one is the primary output; the other three are derived from it by inserting various length delays into the output lines. The primary clock shown in Fig. 4-5(b) (top line) has a pulse width equal to one-fourth of the cycle time. The other three outputs are shown for delays of one, two, and three times the pulse width. The result is a circuit that divides each cycle into four equally long subcycles. For more detail, see Fig. 3-21.

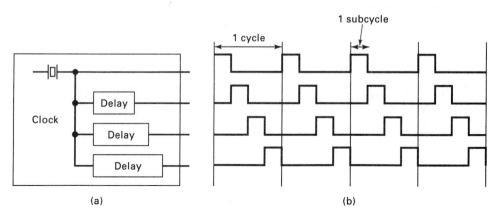

Fig. 4-5. (a) A clock with four outputs. (b) The output timing diagram.

To cause four different transitions that must occur in one cycle to happen in order, the designer could AND the enabling signal for each with a different clock line. The transition tied to the primary clock line would happen first, the transition tied to the clock line with the shortest delay would happen second, and so forth.

4.1.6. Main Memory

Processors need to be able to read data from memory and write data to memory. Most computers have an address bus, a data bus, and a control bus for communication between the CPU and memory. To read from memory, the CPU puts a memory address on the address bus and sets the control signals appropriately, for example, by asserting RD (READ). The memory then puts the requested item on the data bus. In some computers memory read/write is synchronous; that is, the memory must respond within a fixed time. On others, the memory may take as long as it wants, signaling the presence of data using a control line when it is finished.

Writes to memory are done similarly. The CPU puts the data to be written on the data bus and the address to be stored into on the address bus and then it asserts WR (WRITE). (An alternative to having RD and WR is to have MREQ, which indicates that a memory request is desired, and RW, which distinguishes read from write.)

A memory access is nearly always considerably longer than the time required to execute a single microinstruction. Consequently, the microprogram must keep the correct values on the address and data buses for several microinstructions. To simplify this task, it is often convenient to have two registers, the **MAR** (Memory Address Register) and the **MBR** (Memory Buffer Register), that drive the address and data buses, respectively. For our purposes it will be convenient to arrange the buses as indicated in Fig. 4-6. Both registers sit between the CPU and the system bus. The address bus is unidirectional on both sides and is loaded from the CPU side when the control line is asserted. The output to the system address lines is always enabled [or possibly only during reads and writes, which requires an output enable line driven by the OR of RD and WR (not shown)]. The MBR control line causes data to be loaded from the "Data in" bus on the CPU side. The "Data out" line is always enabled. The system data bus is bidirectional, outputting MBR when WR is asserted and loading MBR when RD is asserted.

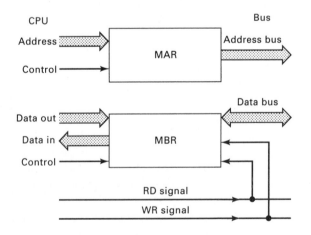

Fig. 4-6. The registers used to drive the address and data buses.

4.1.7. Component Packaging

In the previous sections we have reviewed various circuits that can be combined to form a computer. These circuits are commercially available in several conceptually different forms. The most straightforward way is in MSI (Medium Scale Integration) packages, with each chip containing one component: for example, a register, an ALU, or a shifter. This approach is illustrated in Fig. 4-7(a). The components are then wired together to form the computer. Because a wide variety of high-speed, low-cost MSI chips are available, many computers have been built this way.

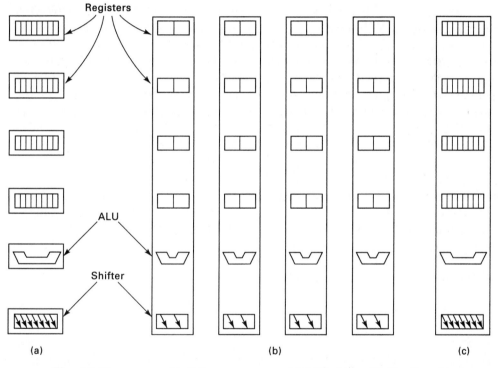

(a)   (b)   (c)

Fig. 4-7. Three ways of building a computer. (a) MSI chips. (b) Bit slice. (c) LSI chip.

The main drawback to building a computer from MSI parts is the large number of chips required, which occupy many boards, consume much power, and dissipate significant heat. Another technique is to use **bit-slice** chips. Each bit-slice chip has, for example, 1 bit of the registers, ALU, and other components. Figure 3-20 shows what a 1-bit ALU slice looks like inside. We could easily extend that design to add, for example, sixteen 1-bit registers, a 1-bit shifter, and other 1-bit-wide components. By taking, say, 32 such chips and putting them side by side, we get a machine with sixteen 32-bit registers, a 32-bit ALU, a 32-bit shifter, and so on.

Alternatively, with only 16 chips we could build a 16-bit machine. Bit slices give the designer the ability to put together a machine of any word length easily. Bit slices with 2 or even 4 bits per slice are also widely available. Figure 4-7(b) depicts an 8-bit-wide machine built out of four 2-bit slices. In general, the bit-slice approach requires fewer chips and much less design time than the MSI approach but usually produces slower machines.

A third approach to combining the components is to put the complete processor on a single chip [see Fig. 4-7(c)]. While this obviously reduces chip count dramatically (to one chip), it also has some disadvantages. To start with, the technology required to pack large numbers of components on a chip is a different one than is used for MSI or bit-slice chips, and it usually produces slower machines. Furthermore, both the design and manufacturing technologies are exceedingly complicated and expensive. In contrast, just about any competent electrical engineer can design a simple computer from MSI or bit-slice chips without too much trouble. From the point of view of a computer manufacturer who expects to be building computers for years, it is probably worth the trouble to master the technologies needed for making single-chip processors; for a company that just needs one special-purpose machine, it is probably not. The choices then become: use a commercially available processor, contract out to have someone else design and manufacture a special-purpose chip, or build it from MSI or bit-slice components.

4.2. AN EXAMPLE MICROARCHITECTURE

Now that we have reviewed all the basic components from which the microprogramming level is constructed, it is time to see how they are connected. Because general principles are few and far between in this area, we will introduce the subject by means of a detailed example.

4.2.1. The Data Path

The **data path** of our example microarchitecture is shown in Fig. 4-8. (The data path is that part of the CPU containing the ALU, its inputs, and its outputs.) It contains 16 identical 16-bit registers, labeled PC, AC, SP, and so on, that form a scratchpad memory accessible only to the microprogramming level. The registers labeled 0, +1, and −1 will be used to hold the indicated constants; the meaning of the other register names will be explained later. (Actually, 0 is never used in our simple examples but it probably would be needed in a more complicated machine, so we have included it because we have more registers than we can use anyway.) Each register can output its contents onto one or both of two internal buses, the A bus and the B bus, and each can be loaded from a third internal bus, the C bus, as shown in the figure.

The A and B buses feed into a 16-bit-wide ALU that can perform four

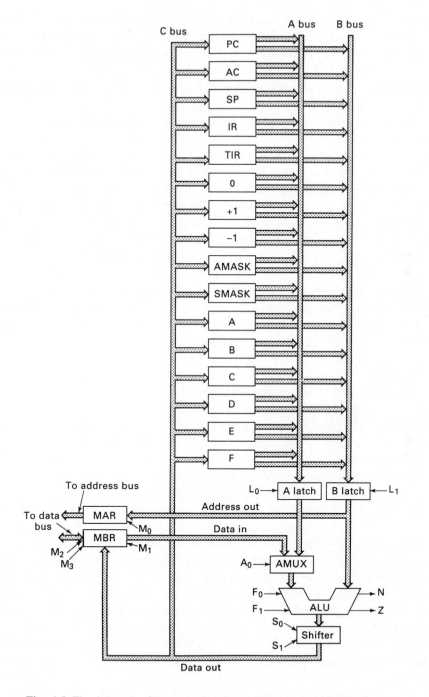

Fig. 4-8. The data path of the example microarchitecture used in this chapter.

functions: A + B, A AND B, A, and NOT A. The function to be performed is specified by the two ALU control lines, F_0 and F_1. The ALU generates two status bits based on the current ALU output: N, which is set when the ALU output is negative, and Z, which is set when the ALU output is zero.

The ALU output goes into a shifter, which can shift it 1 bit in either direction, or not at all. It is possible to perform a 2-bit left shift of a register, R, by computing R + R in the ALU (which is a 1-bit left shift), and then shifting the sum another bit left using the shifter.

Neither the A bus nor the B bus feeds the ALU directly. Instead, each one feeds a latch (i.e., a register) that in turn feeds the ALU. The latches are needed because the ALU is a combinational circuit—it continuously computes the output for the current input and function code. This organization can cause problems when computing, for example, A := A + B. As A is being stored into, the value on the A bus begins to change, which causes the ALU output and thus the C bus to change as well. Consequently, the wrong value may be stored into A. In other words, in the assignment A := A + B, the A on the right-hand side is the original A value, not some bit-by-bit mixture of the old and new values. By inserting latches in the A and B buses, we can freeze the original A and B values there early in the cycle, so the ALU is shielded from changes on the buses as a new value is being stored in the scratchpad. The loading of the latches is controlled by L_0 and L_1.

It is worth pointing out that our solution to this problem (i.e., inserting latches in front of the ALU) is not the only one. If all the registers are flip-flops rather than latches, then a two-bus design is also feasible by loading the operands onto the A and B buses early in the cycle and reading the result from one of the buses late in the cycle. The trade-offs between two and three bus designs involve complexity, parallelism, and amount of wiring. A more detailed treatment of these issues is beyond the scope of this book.

To communicate with memory, we have included an MAR and an MBR in the microarchitecture. The MAR can be loaded from the B latch, in parallel with an ALU operation. The M_0 line controls loading of MAR. On writes, the MBR can be loaded with the shifter output, in parallel with, or instead of, a store back into the scratchpad. M_1 controls loading MBR from the shifter output. M_2 and M_3 control reads and writes from memory. On reads, the data read from memory can be presented to the left input of the ALU via the A multiplexer, indicated by Amux in Fig. 4-8. A control line, A_0, determines whether the A latch or the MBR is fed into the ALU. The microarchitecture of Fig. 4-8 is similar to that of several commercially available bit slices.

4.2.2. Microinstructions

To control the data path of Fig. 4-8 we need 61 signals. These can be divided into nine functional groups, as described below.

　16 signals to control loading the A bus from the scratchpad

　16 signals to control loading the B bus from the scratchpad

　16 signals to control loading the scratchpad from the C bus

　　2 signals to control the A and B latches

　　2 signals to control the ALU function

　　2 signals to control the shifter

　　4 signals to control the MAR and MBR

　　2 signals to indicate memory read and memory write

　　1 signal to control the Amux

Given the values of the 61 signals, we can perform one cycle of the data path. A cycle consists of gating values onto the A and B buses, latching them in the two bus latches, running the values through the ALU and shifter, and finally storing the results in the scratchpad and/or MBR. In addition, the MAR can also be loaded, and a memory cycle initiated. As a first approximation, we could have a 61-bit control register, with one bit for each control signal. A 1 bit means that the signal is asserted and a 0 means that it is negated.

However, at the price of a small increase in circuitry, we can greatly reduce the number of bits needed to control the data path. To begin with, we have 16 bits for controlling input to the A bus, which allows 2^{16} combinations of source registers. Only 16 of these combinations are permitted—namely, each of the 16 registers all by itself. Therefore, we can encode the A bus information in 4 bits and use a decoder to generate the 16 control signals. The same holds for the B bus.

The situation is slightly different for the C bus. In principle, multiple simultaneous stores into the scratchpad are feasible, but in practice this feature is virtually never useful and most hardware does not provide for it. Therefore, we will also encode the C bus control in 4 bits. Having saved $3 \times 12 = 36$ bits, we now need 25 control bits to drive the data path. L_0 and L_1 are always needed at a certain point in time, so they will be supplied by the clock, leaving us with 23 control bits. One additional signal that is not strictly required, but is often useful, is one to enable/disable storing the C bus in the scratchpad. In some situations one merely wishes to perform an ALU operation to generate the N and Z signals but does not wish to store the result. With this extra bit, which we will call ENC (ENable C), we can indicate that the C bus is to be stored (ENC = 1) or not (ENC = 0).

At this point we can control the data path with a 24-bit number. Now we note that RD and WR can be used to control latching MBR from the system data bus and enabling MBR onto it, respectively. This observation reduces the number of independent control signals from 24 down to 22.

The next step in the design of the microarchitecture is to invent a microinstruction format containing 22 bits. Figure 4-9 shows such a format, with two additional fields COND and ADDR, which will be described shortly. The microinstruction contains 13 fields, 11 of which are as follows:

AMUX — controls left ALU input: 0 = A latch, 1 = MBR

ALU — ALU function: 0 = A + B, 1 = A AND B, 2 = A, 3 = $\overline{A}$

SH   — shifter function: 0 = no shift, 1 = right, 2 = left

MBR — loads MBR from shifter: 0 = don't load MBR, 1 = load MBR

MAR — loads MAR from B latch: 0 = don't load MAR, 1 = load MAR

RD   — requests memory read: 0 = no read, 1 = load MBR from memory

WR   — requests memory write: 0 = no write, 1 = write MBR to memory

ENC — controls storing into scratchpad: 0 = don't store, 1 = store

C   — selects register for storing into if ENC = 1: 0 = PC, 1 = AC, etc.

B   — selects B bus source: 0 = PC, 1 = AC, etc.

A   — selects A bus source: 0 = PC, 1 = AC, etc.

The ordering of the fields is completely arbitrary. This ordering has been chosen to minimize line crossings in a subsequent figure. (Actually, this criterion is not as crazy as it sounds; line crossings in figures usually correspond to wire crossings on printed circuit boards or on chips, which cause trouble in two-dimensional designs.)

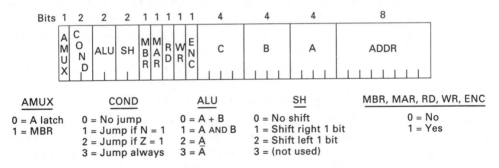

Fig. 4-9. The microinstruction layout for controlling the data path of Fig. 4-8.

4.2.3. Microinstruction Timing

Although our discussion of how a microinstruction can control the data path during one cycle is almost complete, we have neglected one issue up until now: timing. A basic ALU cycle consists of setting up the A and B latches, giving the

ALU and shifter time to do their work, and storing the results. It is obvious that these events must happen in that sequence. If we try to store the C bus into the scratchpad before the A and B latches have been loaded, garbage will be stored instead of useful data. To achieve the correct event sequencing, we now introduce a four-phase clock, that is, a clock with four subcycles, like that of Fig. 4-5. The key events during each of the four subcycles are as follows:

1. Load the next microinstruction to be executed into a register called **MIR**, the MicroInstruction Register.

2. Gate registers onto the A and B buses and capture them in the A and B latches.

3. Now that the inputs are stable, give the ALU and shifter time to produce a stable output and load the MAR if required.

4. Now that the shifter output is stable, store the C bus in the scratchpad and load the MBR, if either is required.

Figure 4-10 is a detailed block diagram of the complete microarchitecture of our example machine. It may look imposing initially but it is worth studying carefully. When you fully understand every box and every line on it, you will be well on your way to understanding the microprogramming level. The block diagram has two parts, the data path, on the left, which we have already discussed in detail, and the control section, on the right, which we will now look at.

The largest and most important item in the control portion of the machine is the **control store**. This special, high-speed memory is where the microinstructions are kept. On some machines it is read-only memory; on others it is read/write memory. In our example, microinstructions will be 32 bits wide and the microinstruction address space will consist of 256 words, so the control store will occupy a maximum of $256 \times 32 = 8192$ bits.

Like any other memory, the control store needs an MAR and an MBR. We will call the MAR the **MPC** (MicroProgram Counter), because its only function is to point to the next microinstruction to be executed. The MBR is just the **MIR** as mentioned above. Be sure you realize that the control store and main memory are completely different, the former holding the microprogram and the latter the conventional machine language program.

From Fig. 4-10 it is clear that the control store continuously tries to copy the microinstruction addressed by the MPC into the MIR. However, the MIR is only loaded during subcycle 1, as indicated by the dashed line from the clock to it. During the other three subcycles it is not affected, no matter what happens to MPC.

During subcycle 2, the MIR is stable, and the various fields begin controlling the data path. In particular, A and B gate onto the A and B buses. The A decoder

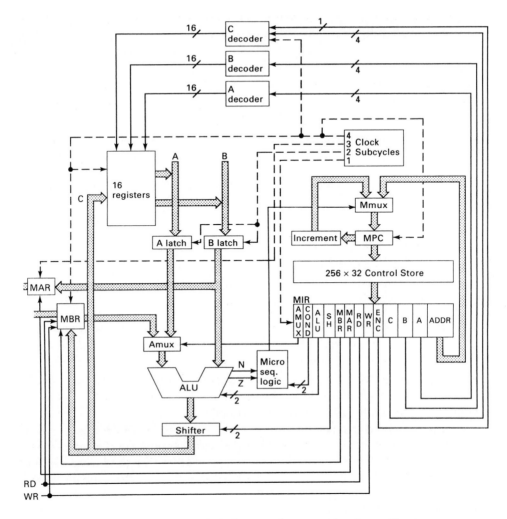

Fig. 4-10. The complete block diagram of our example microarchitecture.

and B decoder boxes in the block diagram provide for the 4-to-16 decoding of each field necessary to drive the OE1 and OE2 lines in the registers [see Fig. 4-2(b)]. The clock activates the A and B latches during this subcycle, providing stable ALU inputs for the rest of the cycle. While data are being gated onto the A and B buses, the increment unit in the control section of the machine computes MPC + 1, in preparation for loading the next sequential microinstruction during the next cycle. By overlapping these two operations, instruction execution can be speeded up.

In the third subcycle, the ALU and shifter are given time to produce valid results. The AMUX microinstruction field determines the left input to the ALU; the right input is always the B latch. Although the ALU is a combinational circuit, the time it takes to compute a sum is determined by the carry-propagation time, not the normal gate delay. The carry-propagation time is proportional to the number of bits in the word. While the ALU and shifter are computing, the MAR is loaded from the B bus if the MAR field in the microinstruction is 1.

During the fourth and final subcycle, the C bus may be stored back into the scratchpad and MBR, depending on ENC and MBR. The box labeled "C decoder" takes ENC, the fourth clock line, and the C field from the microinstruction as inputs, and generates the 16 control signals. Internally, it performs a 4-to-16 decode of the C field, and then ANDs each of these with a signal derived from ANDing the subcycle 4 line with ENC. Thus a scratchpad register is only loaded if three conditions prevail:

1. ENC = 1.

2. It is subcycle 4.

3. The register has been selected by the C field.

The MBR is also loaded during subcycle 4 if MBR = 1.

The two signals that control memory, RD and WR, are asserted as long as they are present in MIR. In effect, the corresponding MIR fields act like latches.

4.2.4. Microinstruction Sequencing

The only remaining issue is how the next microinstruction is chosen. Although some of the time it is sufficient just to fetch the next microinstruction in sequence, some mechanism is needed to allow conditional jumps in the microprogram in order to enable it to make decisions. For this reason we have provided two fields in each microinstruction: ADDR, which is the address of a potential successor to the current microinstruction, and COND, which determines whether the next microinstruction is fetched from MPC + 1 or ADDR. Every microinstruction potentially contains a conditional jump. This decision was made because conditional jumps are very common in microprograms and allowing every microinstruction to have two possible successors makes them run faster than the alternative of setting up some condition in one microinstruction and then testing it in the next. Most existing microarchitectures use our strategy in one form or another.

The choice of the next microinstruction is determined by the box labeled "Micro sequencing logic" during subcycle 4, when the ALU output signals N and Z are valid. The output of this box controls the M multiplexer (Mmux), which routes either MPC + 1 or ADDR to MPC, where it will direct the fetching of the next microinstruction. We have provided the microprogrammer with four choices concerning the the selection of the next microinstruction. The desired choice is indicated by the setting of the COND field as follows:

0 = Do not jump; next microinstruction is taken from **MPC** + 1

1 = Jump to ADDR if N = 1

2 = Jump to ADDR if Z = 1

3 = Jump to ADDR unconditionally

The Micro sequencing logic combines the two ALU bits, N and Z, and the two COND bits, call them L and R for Left and Right, to generate an output. The correct signal is

$$\text{Mmux} = \overline{L}RN + L\overline{R}Z + LR = RN + LZ + LR$$

where + means INCLUSIVE OR. In words, the control signal to Mmux is 1 (routing ADDR to MPC) if LR is 01_2 and N = 1, or LR is 10_2 and Z = 1 or LR is 11_2. Otherwise, it is 0 and the next microinstruction in sequence is fetched. The circuit to compute the Mmux signal can be built from SSI components, as in Fig. 3-3(b), or be part of a PLA, as in Fig. 3-16.

To make our example machine slightly realistic, we will assume that a main memory cycle takes longer than a microinstruction. In particular, if a microinstruction starts a main memory read, by setting RD to 1, it must also have RD = 1 in the next microinstruction executed (which may or may not be located at the next control store address). The data become available two microinstructions after the read was initiated. If the microprogram has nothing else useful to do in the microinstruction following the one that initiated a memory read, the microinstruction just has RD = 1 and is effectively wasted. In the same way, a memory write also takes two microinstruction times to complete.

4.3. AN EXAMPLE MACROARCHITECTURE

To continue our microprogramming level example, we now switch to the architecture of the conventional machine level to be supported by the interpreter running on the machine of Fig. 4-10. For convenience, we will call the architecture of the level 2 or 3 machine the **macroarchitecture**, to contrast it with level 1, the microarchitecture. (For the purposes of this chapter we will ignore level 3 because its instructions are largely those of level 2 and the differences are not important here.) Similarly, the level 2 instructions will be called **macroinstructions**. Thus for the duration of this chapter, the normal ADD, MOVE, and other instructions of the conventional machine level will be called macroinstructions. (The point of repeating this remark is that some assemblers have a facility to define assembly-time "macros," which are in no way related to what we mean by macroinstructions.) We will sometimes refer to our example level 1 machine as Mic-1 and the level 2 machine as Mac-1. Before we describe Mac-1, however, we will digress slightly to motivate its design.

4.3.1. Stacks

A modern macroarchitecture should be designed with the needs of high-level languages in mind. One of the most important design issues is addressing. To illustrate the problem that must be solved, consider the Pascal program of Fig. 4-11(a). The main program initializes two vectors, x and y, with values such that $x_k = k$ and $y_k = 2k + 1$. Then it computes the inner product (also called a dot product) of the two vectors. Whenever it needs to multiply two small positive integers, it calls the function *pmul*. (Imagine that the compiler is for a microcomputer and only implements a subset of Pascal, not including the multiplication operator.)

Block-structured languages like Pascal are normally implemented in such a way that when a procedure or function is exited, the storage it had been using for local variables is released. The easiest way to achieve this goal is by using a data structure called a stack. A **stack** is a contiguous block of memory containing some data and a **stack pointer** (SP) telling where the top of the stack is. The bottom of the stack is at a fixed address and will not concern us further. Figure 4-12(a) depicts a stack occupying six words of memory. The bottom of the stack is at 4020 and the top of the stack, where SP points, is at 4015. Our stacks will grow from high memory addresses to low ones but the opposite choice is equally good.

Several operations are defined on stacks. Two of the most important are PUSH X and POP Y. PUSH advances the stack pointer (by decrementing it in our example) and then puts X into memory at the location now pointed to by SP. PUSH increases the stack size by one item. POP Y, in contrast, reduces the stack size by storing the top item on the stack in Y, and then removing it by incrementing the stack pointer by the size of the item popped. Figure 4-12(b) shows how the stack of Fig. 4-12(a) looks after a word containing 5 has been pushed on the stack.

Another operation that can be performed on a stack is advancing the stack pointer without actually pushing any data. This is normally done when a procedure or function is entered, to reserve space for local variables. Figure 4-13(a) shows how memory might be allocated during the execution of the main program of Fig. 4-11. We have arbitrarily assumed that the memory consists of 4096 16-bit words, and that the words 4021 to 4095 are used by the operating system, and hence not available for storing variables. The Pascal variable k is stored at address 4020. (Addresses are given in decimal.) The array x requires 20 words, from 4000 to 4019. The array y starts at 3980 for $y[1]$ and extends to 3999 for $y[20]$. While the main program is executing outside *pmul*, SP has the value 3980, indicating that the top of the stack is at 3980.

When the main program wants to call *pmul*, it first pushes the parameters of the call, 2 and k, onto the stack, and then executes the call instruction, which pushes the

program *InnerProduct* (*output*);

{This program initializes two vectors, *x* and *y*, of 20 elements each,
  then computes their inner product :
       $x[1] * y[1] + x[2] * y[2] + \dots + x[20] * y[20]$ }

const *max* = 20;   {size of the vectors}

type *SmallInt* = 0..100;
       vec = **array**[1..*max*] **of** *SmallInt* ;

var *k* : *integer* ;
     x , *y* : *vec* ;

function *pmul* (*a* , *b* : *SmallInt*): *integer* ;
{This function multiplies its two parameters together and returns the product.
 It performs the multiplication by repeated addition .}
var *p* , *j* : *integer* ;
begin   {0: reserve stack space for *p* and *j*}
    if (*a* = 0) **or** (*b* = 0) **then**   {1: if either one is 0, result is 0}
      pmul := 0   {2: function returns 0}
    else
      begin
        p := 0;   {3: initialize *p*}
        for *j* := 1 **to** *a* **do**   {4: add *b* to *p* *a* times}
          p := *p* + *b* ;   {5: do the addition}
        pmul := *p*   {6: assign result to function}
      end
  end; {pmul}   {7: remove locals and return value}

procedure *inner* (**var** *v* : *vec* ; **var** *ans* : *integer*);
{Compute the inner product of *v* and *x* and return it in *ans*.}
var *sum* , *i* : *integer* ;
begin   {8: reserve stack space for *sum* and *i*}
    sum := 0;   {9: *sum* will accumulate inner product}
    for *i* := 1 **to** *max* **do**   {10: loop through all the elements}
      sum := *sum* + *pmul* (*x* [*i*], *v* [*i*]);   {11: accumulate one term}
    ans := *sum*   {12: copy result to *ans*}
end; {inner}   {13: remove *sum* and *i* and return}

begin   {14: reserve space for *k*, *x*, and *y*}
    for *k* := 1 **to** *max* **do**   {15: initialization loop}
      begin
        x [*k*] := *k* ;   {16: initialize *x*}
        y [*k*] := *pmul* (2, *k*) + 1   {17: initialize *y*}
      end;
    inner (*y* , *k*);   {18: call *inner*}
    writeln (*k*)   {19: print results}
  end.

Fig. 4-11(a). A Pascal program to compute an inner product.

```
        K = 4020        /DEFINE SOME SYMBOLS              INSP  2         /REMOVE PARAMS
        X = 4000                                         ADDL  SUM       /AC := SUM + PMUL(...)
        Y = 3980                                         STOL  SUM       /SUM := SUM + PMUL(...)
        A = 4                                            LOCO  1         /TEST AT END OF LOOP
        B = 3                                            ADDL  I         /AC := I + 1
        P = 1                                            STOL  I         /I := I + 1
        J = 0                                            SUBD  C20       /AC := I - MAX
        V = 5                                            JNEG  L3        /JUMP IF I < MAX
        ANS = 4                                          JZER  L3        /JUMP IF I = MAX
        SUM = 1                                          LODL  SUM       /12
        I = 0                                            PUSH            /PUSH SUM
                                                         LODL  ANS       /AC := ADDRESS OF ANS
        JUMP  MAIN    /START AT MAIN PROGRAM             POPI            /ANS := SUM
PMUL:   DESP  2       /0                                 INSP  2         /13
        LODL  A       /1                                 RETN            /RETURN
        JNZE  ANOTZ   /JUMP IF A <> 0            MAIN:   DESP  41        /14
        LOCO  0       /2                                 LOCO  1         /15
        JUMP  DONE    /RETURN 0                          STOD  K         /K IS NOT A LOCAL
ANOTZ:  LODL  B       /AC := B                   L4:     LODD  K         /16
        JNZE  BNOTZ   /JUMP IF B <> 0                    PUSH            /PUSH K ONTO STACK
        LOCO  0       /2                                 LOCO  X-1       /AC := (ADDRESS OF X[1])-1
        JUMP  DONE    /RETURN 0                          ADDD  K         /AC := X + K - 1
BNOTZ:  LOCO  0       /3                                 POPI            /X[K] := K
        STOL  P       /P := 0                            LOCO  2         /17
        LOCO  1       /4                                 PUSH            /PREPARE PMUL(2,...)
        STOL  J       /J := 1                            LODD  K         /PREPARE PMUL(2,K)
        LODL  A       /CAN LOOP BE EXECUTED?             PUSH            /BOTH PARAMS PUSHED
        JNEG  L2      /A < 0, DO NOT LOOP                CALL  PMUL      /PMUL(2,K)
        JZER  L2      /A = 0, DO NOT LOOP                INSP  2         /REMOVE PARAMETERS
L1:     LODL  P       /5                                 ADDD  C1        /AC := 2*K + 1
        ADDL  B       /AC := P + B                       PUSH            /PREPARE Y[K] := 2*K+1
        STOL  P       /P := P + B                        LOCO  Y-1       /AC := (ADDRESS OF Y[1])-1
        LOCO  1       /TEST AT END OF LOOP               ADDD  K         /AC := Y + K -1
        ADDL  J       /AC := J + 1                       POPI            /Y[K] := 2*K+1
        STOL  J       /J := J + 1                        LOCO  1         /TEST AT END OF LOOP
        SUBL  A       /AC := J - A                       ADDD  K         /AC := K + 1
        JNEG  L1      /JUMP IF J < A                     STOD  K         /K := K + 1
        JZER  L1      /JUMP IF J = A                     SUBD  C20       /AC := K - MAX
L2:     LODL  P       /6                                 JNEG  L4        /JUMP IF K < 0
DONE:   INSP  2       /7                                 JZER  L4        /JUMP IF K = MAX
        RETN          /RETURN                            LOCO  Y         /18
                                                         PUSH            /PUSH ADDRESS OF Y
INNER:  DESP  2       /8                                 LOCO  K         /AC := ADDRESS OF K
        LOCO  0       /9                                 PUSH            /PUSH IT ALSO
        STOL  SUM     /SUM := 0                          CALL  INNER     /PROCEDURE CALL
        LOCO  1       /10                                INSP  2         /REMOVE PARAMS
        STOL  I       /I := 1                            LODD  K         /19
L3:     LOCO  X-1     /11                                PUSH            /PREPARE WRITELN(K)
        ADDL  I       /AC := X + I - 1                   CALL  OUTNUM1   /LIBRARY ROUTINE
        PSHI          /PUSH X[I]                         INSP  1         /REMOVE PARAM
        LODL  V       /AC := ADDRESS OF VECTOR           CALL  STOP      /END OF JOB
        ADDL  I       /AC := V + I               C1:     1               /CONSTANT 1
        SUBD  C1      /V BEGINS AT 1, NOT 0      C20:    20              /CONSTANT 20
        PSHI          /PUSH V[I]
        CALL  PMUL    /PMUL(X[I],V[I])
```

Fig. 4-11(b). *Innerproduct* in assembly language.

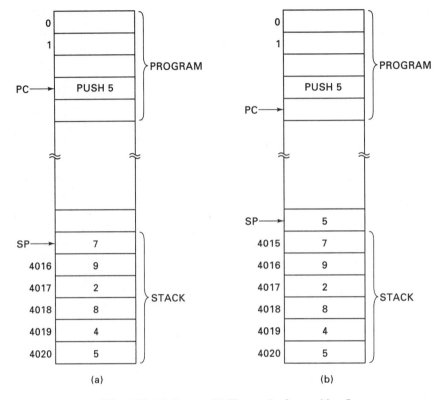

Fig. 4-12. (a) A stack. (b) The stack after pushing 5.

return address onto the stack so that *pmul* will know where to return when it is finished. When *pmul* begins executing, SP is 3977. The first thing it does is advance the stack pointer by 2, to reserve two words for its own local variables, *p* and *j*. At this point SP is 3975, as shown in Fig. 4-13(b). The top five words on the stack constitute the stack frame used by *pmul*; they will be released when it is finished. The words 3979 and 3978 are labeled *a* and *b* because these are the names of *pmul*'s formal parameters but, of course, they contain 2 and *k*, respectively.

When *pmul* has returned and *inner* has been called, the stack configuration is as shown in Fig. 4-13(c). When *inner* calls *pmul*, the stack is as shown in Fig. 4-13(d). Now comes the problem. What code should the compiler generate to access *pmul*'s parameters and locals? If it tries to read *p* using an instruction like MOVE 3976,SOMEWHERE, *pmul* will work when called from the main program but not when called from *inner*. Similarly, MOVE 3971,SOMEWHERE will work when called from *inner*, but not when called from the main program. What is really needed is a way to say "fetch the word 1 higher than the current stack pointer." In other words, the Mac-1 needs an addressing mode that fetches or stores a word at a known distance relative to the stack pointer (or some equivalent addressing mode).

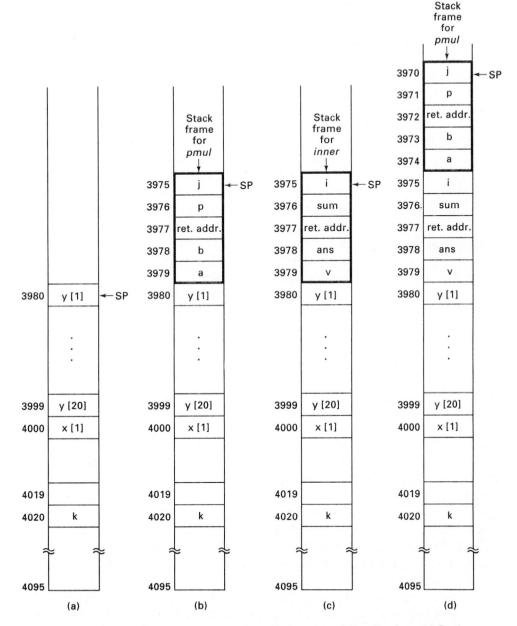

Fig. 4-13. Snapshots of memory during the execution of *InnerProduct*. (a) Stack during execution of the main program. (b) Stack during execution of *pmul*. (c) Stack during execution of *inner*. (d) Stack during execution of *pmul* when called from *inner*.

4.3.2. The Macroinstruction Set

With this addressing mode in mind, we are now ready to look at the Mac-1's architecture. Basically, it consists of a memory with 4096 16-bit words, and three registers visible to the level 2 programmer. The registers are the program counter, PC, the stack pointer, SP, and the accumulator, AC, which is used for moving data around, for arithmetic, and for other purposes. Three addressing modes are provided: direct, indirect, and local. Instructions using direct addressing contain a 12-bit absolute memory address in the low-order 12 bits. Such instructions are useful for accessing global variables, such as x in Fig. 4-11. Indirect addressing allows the programmer to compute a memory address, put it in AC, and then read or write the word addressed. This form of addressing is very general and is used for accessing array elements, among other things. Local addressing specifies an offset from SP and is used to access local variables, as we have just seen. Together, these three modes provide a simple but adequate addressing system.

The Mac-1 instruction set is shown in Fig. 4-14. Each instruction contains an opcode and sometimes a memory address or constant. The first column gives the binary encoding of the instruction. The second gives its assembly language mnemonic. The third gives its name and the fourth describes what it does by giving a Pascal fragment. In these fragments, $m[x]$ refers to memory word x. Thus LODD loads the accumulator from the memory word specified in its low-order 12 bits. LODD is thus direct addressing, whereas LODL loads the accumulator from the word at a distance x above SP, hence is local addressing. LODD, STOD, ADDD, and SUBD perform four basic functions using direct addressing, and LODL, STOL, ADDL, and SUBL perform the same functions using local addressing.

Five jump instructions are provided, one unconditional jump (JUMP) and four conditional ones (JPOS, JZER, JNEG, and JNZE). JUMP always copies its low-order 12 bits into the program counter, whereas the other four only do so if the specified condition is met.

LOCO loads a 12-bit constant in the range 0 to 4095 (inclusive) into AC. PSHI pushes onto the stack the word whose address is present in AC. The inverse operation is POPI, which pops a word from the stack and stores it in the memory word addressed by AC. PUSH and POP are useful for manipulating the stack in a variety of ways. SWAP exchanges the contents of AC and SP, which is useful when SP must be increased or decreased by an amount not known at compile time. It is also useful for initializing SP at the start of execution. INSP and DESP are used to change SP by amounts known at compile time. Due to lack of encoding space, the offsets here have been limited to 8 bits. Finally, CALL calls a procedure, saving the return address on the stack, and RETN returns from a procedure, by popping the return address and putting it into PC.

So far, our machine does not have any input/output instructions. Nor are we about to add any now. It does not need them. Instead, the machine will use

Binary	Mnemonic	Instruction	Meaning
0000xxxxxxxxxxxx	LODD	Load direct	$ac := m[x]$
0001xxxxxxxxxxxx	STOD	Store direct	$m[x] := ac$
0010xxxxxxxxxxxx	ADDD	Add direct	$ac := ac + m[x]$
0011xxxxxxxxxxxx	SUBD	Subtract direct	$ac := ac - m[x]$
0100xxxxxxxxxxxx	JPOS	Jump positive	**if** $ac \geq 0$ **then** $pc := x$
0101xxxxxxxxxxxx	JZER	Jump zero	**if** $ac = 0$ **then** $pc := x$
0110xxxxxxxxxxxx	JUMP	Jump	$pc := x$
0111xxxxxxxxxxxx	LOCO	Load constant	$ac := x \, (0 \leq x \leq 4095)$
1000xxxxxxxxxxxx	LODL	Load local	$ac := m[sp + x]$
1001xxxxxxxxxxxx	STOL	Store local	$m[x + sp] := ac$
1010xxxxxxxxxxxx	ADDL	Add local	$ac := ac + m[sp + x]$
1011xxxxxxxxxxxx	SUBL	Subtract local	$ac := ac - m[sp + x]$
1100xxxxxxxxxxxx	JNEG	Jump negative	**if** $ac < 0$ **then** $pc := x$
1101xxxxxxxxxxxx	JNZE	Jump nonzero	**if** $ac \neq 0$ **then** $pc := x$
1110xxxxxxxxxxxx	CALL	Call procedure	$sp := sp - 1; \, m[sp] := pc; \, pc := x$
1111000000000000	PSHI	Push indirect	$sp := sp - 1; \, m[sp] := m[ac]$
1111001000000000	POPI	Pop indirect	$m[ac] := m[sp]; \, sp := sp + 1$
1111010000000000	PUSH	Push onto stack	$sp := sp - 1; \, m[sp] := ac$
1111011000000000	POP	Pop from stack	$ac := m[sp]; \, sp := sp + 1$
1111100000000000	RETN	Return	$pc := m[sp]; \, sp := sp + 1$
1111101000000000	SWAP	Swap ac, sp	$tmp := ac; \, ac := sp; \, sp := tmp$
11111100yyyyyyyy	INSP	Increment sp	$sp := sp + y \, (0 \leq y \leq 255)$
11111110yyyyyyyy	DESP	Decrement sp	$sp := sp - y \, (0 \leq y \leq 255)$

xxxxxxxxxxxx is a 12-bit machine address; in column 4 it is called x.
yyyyyyyy is an 8-bit constant; in column 4 it is called y.

Fig. 4-14. The Mac-1 instruction set.

memory-mapped I/O. A read from address 4092 will yield a 16-bit word with the next ASCII character from the standard input device in the low-order 7 bits and zeros in the high-order 9 bits. When a character is available in 4092, the high-order bit of the input status register, 4093, will be set. Reading 4092 clears 4093. The input routine will normally sit in a tight loop waiting for 4093 to go negative. When it does, the input routine will load AC from 4092 and return.

Output will be done using a similar scheme. A write to address 4094 will take the low-order 7 bits of the word written and copy them to the standard output device. The high-order bit of the output status register, word 4095, will then be cleared, coming back on again when the output device is ready to accept a new character. Standard input and output may be a terminal keyboard and visual display, or a card reader and printer, or some other combination.

As an example of how one programs using this instruction set, see Fig. 4-11(b), which is the program of Fig. 4-11(a) compiled to assembly language by a compiler that does no optimization at all. (Optimized code would make the example hard to follow.) The numbers 0 to 19 in the comments, indicated by a slash in the assembly language, are intended to make it easier to link up the two halves of the figure. OUTNUM1 and STOP are library routines that perform the obvious functions.

4.4. AN EXAMPLE MICROPROGRAM

Having specified both the microarchitecture and the macroarchitecture in detail, the remaining issue is the implementation: What does a program running on the former and interpreting the latter look like, and how does it work? Before we can answer these questions, we must carefully consider in what language we want to do our microprogramming.

4.4.1. The Micro Assembly Language

In principle, we could write microprograms in binary, 32 bits per microinstruction. Masochistic programmers might even enjoy that; certainly nobody else would. Therefore, we need a symbolic language in which to express microprograms. One possible notation is to have the microprogrammer specify one microinstruction per line, naming each nonzero field and its value. For example, to add AC to A and store the result in AC, we could write

$$\text{ENC} = 1, \text{C} = 1, \text{B} = 1, \text{A} = 10$$

Many microprogramming languages look like this. Nevertheless, this notation is awful and so are they.

A much better idea is to use a high-level language notation, while retaining the basic concept of one source line per microinstruction. Conceivably, one could write microprograms in an ordinary high-level language but because efficiency is crucial in microprograms, we will stick to assembly language, which we define as a symbolic language that has a one-to-one mapping onto machine instructions. Remember that a 25% inefficiency in the microprogram slows the entire machine down by 25%. Let us call our high-level Micro Assembly Language "MAL," which is French for "sick," something you become if you are forced to write too many intricate microprograms for idiosyncratic machines. In MAL, stores into the 16 scratchpad registers or MAR and MBR are denoted by assignment statements. Thus the example in MAL above becomes $ac := a + ac$. (Because our intention is to make MAL Pascal-like, we will adopt the usual Pascal convention of lowercase italic names for identifiers.)

To indicate the use of the ALU functions 0, 1, 2, and 3, we can write, for example,

$$ac := a + ac, \quad a := band\,(ir,\ smask), \quad ac := a, \quad \text{and} \quad a := inv(a)$$

respectively, where *band* stands for "Boolean and" and *inv* stands for invert. Shifts can be denoted by the functions *lshift* for left shifts and *rshift* for right shifts, as in

$$tir := lshift(tir + tir)$$

which puts *tir* on both the A and B buses, performs an addition, and left shifts the sum 1 bit left before storing it back in *tir*.

Unconditional jumps can be handled with **goto** statements; conditional jumps can test n or z; for example,

$$\text{if } n \text{ then goto } 27$$

Assignments and jumps can be combined on the same line. However, a slight problem arises if we wish to test a register but not make a store. How do we specify which register is to be tested? To solve this problem we introduce the pseudo variable *alu*, which can be assigned a value just to indicate the ALU contents. For example,

$$alu := tir;\ \text{if } n \text{ then goto } 27$$

means *tir* is to be run through the ALU (ALU code = 2) so its high-order bit can be tested. Note that the use of *alu* means that ENC = 0.

To indicate memory reads and writes, we will just put *rd* and *wr* in the source program. The order of the various parts of the source statement is, in principle, arbitrary but to enhance readability we will try to arrange them in the order that they are carried out. Figure 4-15 gives a few examples of MAL statements along with the corresponding microinstructions.

4.4.2. The Example Microprogram

We have finally reached the point where we can put all the pieces together. Figure 4-16 is the microprogram that runs on Mic-1 and interprets Mac-1. It is a surprisingly short program—only 79 lines. By now the choice of names for the scratchpad registers in Fig. 4-8 is obvious: PC, AC, and SP are used to hold the

Statement	AMUX	COND	ALU	SH	MBR	MAR	RD	WR	ENC	C	B	A	ADDR
mar := pc; rd	0	0	2	0	0	1	1	0	0	0	0	0	00
rd	0	0	2	0	0	0	1	0	0	0	0	0	00
ir := mbr	1	0	2	0	0	0	0	0	1	3	0	0	00
pc := pc +1	0	0	0	0	0	0	0	0	1	0	6	0	00
mar := ir; mbr := ac; wr	0	0	2	0	1	1	0	1	0	0	3	1	00
alu := tir; if n then goto 15	0	1	2	0	0	0	0	0	0	0	0	4	15
ac := inv (mbr)	1	0	3	0	0	0	0	0	1	1	0	0	00
tir := lshift (tir); if n then goto 25	0	1	2	2	0	0	0	0	1	4	0	4	25
alu := ac; if z then goto 22	0	2	2	0	0	0	0	0	0	0	0	1	22
ac := band (ir, amask); goto 0	0	3	1	0	0	0	0	0	1	1	8	3	00
sp := sp + (-1); rd	0	0	0	0	0	0	1	0	1	2	2	7	00
tir := lshift (ir + ir); if n then goto 69	0	1	0	2	0	0	0	0	1	4	3	3	69

Fig. 4-15. Some MAL statements and the corresponding microinstructions.

three Mac-1 registers. IR is the instruction register and holds the macroinstruction currently being executed. TIR is a temporary copy of IR, used for decoding the opcode. The next three registers hold the indicated constants. AMASK is the address mask, 007777 (octal), and is used to separate out opcode and address bits. SMASK is the stack mask, 000377 (octal), and is used in the INSP and DESP instructions to isolate the 8-bit offset. The remaining six registers have no assigned function and can be used as the microprogrammer wishes.

Like all interpreters, the microprogram of Fig. 4-16 has a main loop that fetches, decodes, and executes instructions from the program being interpreted, in this case, level 2 instructions. Its main loop begins on line 0, where it begins fetching the macroinstruction at PC. While waiting for the instruction to arrive, the microprogram increments PC and continues to assert the RD bus signal. When it arrives, in line 2, it is stored in IR and simultaneously the high-order bit (bit 15) is tested. If bit 15 is a 1, decoding proceeds at line 28; otherwise, it continues on line 3. Assuming for the moment that the instruction is a LODD, bit 14 is tested on line 3, and TIR is loaded with the original instruction shifted left 2 bits, one using the adder and one using the shifter. Note that the ALU status bit N is determined by the ALU output in which bit 14 is the high-order bit, because IR + IR shifts IR left 1 bit. The shifter output does not affect the ALU status bits.

All instructions having 00 in their two high-order bits eventually come to line 4 to have bit 13 tested, with the instructions beginning with 000 going to line 5 and those beginning with 001 going to line 11. Line 5 is an example of a microinstruction with ENC = 0; it just tests TIR but does not change it. Depending on the outcome of this test, the code for LODD or STOD is selected.

For LODD, the microcode must first fetch the word directly addressed by loading the low-order 12 bits of IR into MAR. In this case the high-order 4 bits are all zero but for STOD and other instructions they are not. However, because MAR is only 12 bits wide, the opcode bits do not affect the choice of word read. In line 7, the microprogram has nothing to do, so it just waits. When the word arrives, it is copied to AC and the microprogram jumps to the top of the loop. STOD, ADDD, and SUBD are similar. The only noteworthy point concerning them is how subtraction is done. It uses the fact that

$$x - y = x + (-y) = x + (\overline{y} + 1) = x + 1 + \overline{y}$$

in two's complement. The addition of 1 to AC is done on line 16, which would otherwise be wasted like line 13.

The microcode for JPOS begins on line 21. If AC < 0, the branch fails and the JPOS is terminated immediately by jumping back to the main loop. If, however, AC ≥ 0, the low-order 12 bits of IR are extracted by ANDing them with the 007777 mask and storing the result in PC. It does not cost anything extra to remove the opcode bits here, so we might as well do it. If it had cost an extra microinstruction, however, we would have had to look very carefully to see if having garbage in the high-order 4 bits of PC could cause trouble later.

In a certain sense, JZER (line 23) works the opposite of JPOS. With JPOS, if the condition is met, the jump fails and control returns to the main loop. With JZER, if the condition is met, the jump is taken. Because the code for performing the jump is the same for all the jump instructions, we can save microcode by just going to line 22 whenever feasible. This style of programming would generally be considered uncouth in an application program, but in a microprogram no holds are barred. Performance is everything.

JUMP and LOCO are straightforward, so the next interesting execution routine is for LODL. First, the absolute memory address to be referenced is computed by adding the offset contained in the instruction to SP. Then the memory read is initiated. Because the rest of the code is the same for LODL and LODD, we might as well use lines 7 and 8 for both of them. Not only does this save control store with no loss of execution speed but it also means fewer routines to debug. Analogous code is used for STOL, ADDL, and SUBL. The code for JNEG and JNZE is similar to JZER and JPOS, respectively (not the other way around). CALL first decrements SP, then pushes the return address onto the stack, and finally jumps to the procedure. Line 49 is almost identical to line 22; if it had been exactly the same, we could have eliminated 49 by putting an unconditional jump to 22 in 48. Unfortunately, we must continue to assert WR for another microinstruction.

```
 0: mar := pc; rd;                                    {main loop}
 1: pc := pc + 1; rd;                                 {increment pc}
 2: ir := mbr; if n then goto 28;                     {save, decode mbr}
 3: tir := lshift(ir + ir); if n then goto 19;
 4: tir := lshift(tir); if n then goto 11;            {000x or 001x?}
 5: alu := tir; if n then goto 9;                     {0000 or 0001?}

 6: mar := ir; rd;                                    {0000 = LODD}
 7: rd;
 8: ac := mbr; goto 0;

 9: mar := ir; mbr := ac; wr;                         {0001 = STOD}
10: wr; goto 0;

11: alu := tir; if n then goto 15;                    {0010 or 0011?}

12: mar := ir; rd;                                    {0010 = ADDD}
13: rd;
14: ac := mbr + ac; goto 0;

15: mar := ir; rd;                                    {0011 = SUBD}
16: ac := ac + 1; rd;                                 {Note: x − y = x + 1 + not y}
17: a := inv(mbr);
18: ac := ac + a; goto 0;

19: tir := lshift(tir); if n then goto 25;            {010x or 011x?}
20: alu := tir; if n then goto 23;                    {0100 or 0101?}

21: alu := ac; if n then goto 0;                      {0100 = JPOS}
22: pc := band(ir, amask); goto 0;                    {perform the jump}

23: alu := ac; if z then goto 22;                     {0101 = JZER}
24: goto 0;                                           {jump failed}

25: alu := tir; if n then goto 27;                    {0110 or 0111?}
26: pc := band(ir, amask); goto 0;                    {0110 = JUMP}

27: ac := band(ir, amask); goto 0;                    {0111 = LOCO}

28: tir := lshift(ir + ir); if n then goto 40;        {10xx or 11xx?}
29: tir := lshift(tir); if n then goto 35;            {100x or 101x?}
30: alu := tir; if n then goto 33;                    {1000 or 1001?}

31: a := ir + sp;                                     {1000 = LODL}
32: mar := a; rd; goto 7;

33: a := ir + sp;                                     {1001 = STOL}
34: mar := a; mbr := ac; wr; goto 10;

35: alu := tir; if n then goto 38;                    {1010 or 1011?}

36: a := ir + sp;                                     {1010 = ADDL}
37: mar := a; rd; goto 13;

38: a := ir + sp;                                     {1011 = SUBL}
39: mar := a; rd; goto 16;
```

Fig. 4-16. The microprogram.

40: *tir* := *lshift* (*tir*); **if** *n* **then goto** 46;   {110x or 111x?}
41: *alu* := *tir* ; **if** *n* **then goto** 44;   {1100 or 1101?}

42: *alu* := *ac* ; **if** *n* **then goto** 22;   {1100 = JNEG}
43: **goto** 0;

44: *alu* := *ac* ; **if** *z* **then goto** 0;   {1101 = JNZE}
45: *pc* := *band* (*ir* , *amask*); **goto** 0;

46: *tir* := *lshift* (*tir*); **if** *n* **then goto** 50;

47: *sp* := *sp* + (−1);   {1110 = CALL}
48: *mar* := *sp* ; *mbr* := *pc* ; *wr* ;
49: *pc* := *band* (*ir* , *amask*); *wr* ; **goto** 0;

50: *tir* := *lshift* (*tir*); **if** *n* **then goto** 65;   {1111, examine addr}
51: *tir* := *lshift* (*tir*); **if** *n* **then goto** 59;
52: *alu* := *tir* ; **if** *n* **then goto** 56;

53: *mar* := *ac* ; *rd* ;   {1111000 = PSHI}
54: *sp* := *sp* + (−1); *rd* ;
55: *mar* := *sp* ; *wr* ; **goto** 10;

56: *mar* :=*sp* ; *sp* := *sp* + 1; *rd* ;   {1111001 = POPI}
57: *rd* ;
58: *mar* := *ac* ; *wr* ; **goto** 10;

59: *alu* := *tir* ; **if** *n* **then goto** 62;

60: *sp* := *sp* + (−1);   {1111010 = PUSH}
61: *mar* := *sp* ; *mbr* := *ac* ; *wr* ; **goto** 10;

62: *mar* := *sp* ; *sp* := *sp* + 1; *rd* ;   {1111011 = POP}
63: *rd* ;
64: *ac* := *mbr* ; **goto** 0;

65: *tir* := *lshift* (*tir*); **if** *n* **then goto** 73;
66: *alu* := *tir* ; **if** *n* **then goto** 70;

67: *mar* := *sp* ; *sp* := *sp* + 1; *rd* ;   {1111100 = RETN}
68: *rd* ;
69: *pc* := *mbr* ; **goto** 0;

70: *a* := *ac* ;   {1111101 = SWAP}
71: *ac* := *sp* ;
72: *sp* := *a* ; **goto** 0;

73: *alu* := *tir* ; **if** *n* **then goto** 76;

74: *a* := *band* (*ir* , *smask*);   {1111110 = INSP}
75: *sp* := *sp* + *a* ; **goto** 0;

76: *a* := *band* (*ir* , *smask*);   {1111111 = DESP}
77: *a* := *inv* (*a*);
78: *a* := *a* + 1; **goto** 75;

Fig. 4-16. (cont.)

The rest of the macroinstructions all have 1111 as the high-order 4 bits, so decoding of the "address bits" is required to tell them apart. The actual execution routines are straightforward so we will not comment on them further.

4.4.3. Remarks about the Microprogram

Although we have discussed the microprogram in considerable detail, a few more points are worth making. In Fig. 4-16 we increment PC in line 1. It could equally well have been done in line 0, thus freeing line 1 for something else while waiting. In this machine there is nothing else to do but in a real machine the microprogram might use this opportunity to check for I/O devices awaiting service, refresh dynamic RAM, or something else.

If we leave line 1 the way it is, however, we can speed up the machine by modifying line 8 to read

$$mar := pc; \ ac := mbr; \ rd; \ \textbf{goto} \ 1;$$

In other words, we can start fetching the next instruction before we have really finished with the current one. This ability provides a primitive form of instruction pipelining. The same trick can be applied to other execution routines as well.

It is clear that a substantial amount of the execution time of each macroinstruction is devoted to decoding it bit by bit. This observation suggests that it might be useful to be able to load MPC under microprogram control. On many existing computers the microarchitecture has hardware support for extracting macroinstruction opcodes and stuffing them directly into MPC to effect a multiway branch. If, for example, we could shift the IR 9 bits to the right, clear the upper 9 bits, and put the resulting number into MPC, we would have a 128-way branch to locations 0 to 127. Each of these words would contain the first microinstruction for the corresponding macroinstruction. Although this approach wastes control store, it speeds up the machine greatly, so something like it is nearly always used in practice.

We have not said a word about how I/O is implemented. Nor do we have to. By using memory mapping, the CPU is not aware of the difference between true memory addresses and I/O device registers. The microprogram handles reads and writes to the top four words of the address space the same way it handles any other reads and writes.

4.4.4. Perspective

The time seems appropriate to stop for a minute and reflect on what microprogramming is all about. The basic idea is to start out with a simple hardware machine. In our example, it consists of little more than 22 registers, a small ROM for the control store, a glorified adder, an incrementer, a shifter, and some combinational circuitry for multiplexing, decoding, and sequencing. Using this hardware we were able to construct a software interpreter for carrying out the instructions of a level 2 machine. With the aid of a compiler, we can translate high-level language programs to level 2 instructions and then interpret these instructions one at a time.

Thus to run a program written in a high-level language, we must first translate it to level 2, and then interpret the resulting instructions. Level 2 effectively serves as an interface between the compiler and the interpreter. Although in principle the compiler could generate microcode directly, doing so is complicated and wasteful of space. Each of our macroinstructions occupies one 16-bit word, whereas the corresponding microcode, excluding the instruction decoding logic, requires about four 32-bit microinstructions, on the average. If we were to compile directly to level 1, the total storage needed would increase about eightfold. Furthermore, the increased storage needed is writable control store, which is far more expensive due to its high speed. Using main memory for microcode is not desirable because it results in a slow machine.

In light of these concrete examples, it should be clear why machines are now normally designed as a series of levels. It is done for efficiency and simplicity, because each level deals with another level of abstraction. The level 0 designer worries about how to squeeze the last few nanoseconds out of the ALU by using some spiffy new algorithm to reduce carry-propagation time. The microprogrammer worries about how to get the most mileage out of each microinstruction, typically by exploiting as much of the hardware's inherent parallelism as possible. The macroinstruction set designer worries about how to provide an interface that both the compiler writer and microprogrammer can learn to love, and be efficient at the same time. Clearly, each level has different goals, problems, techniques, and, in general, a different way of looking at the machine. By splitting the total machine design problem into several subproblems, we can attempt to master the inherent complexity in designing a modern computer.

4.5. DESIGN OF THE MICROPROGRAMMING LEVEL

Like just about everything else in computer science, the design of the microarchitecture is full of trade-offs. In the following sections we will look at some of the design issues and the corresponding trade-offs.

4.5.1. Horizontal versus Vertical Microprogramming

Probably the key trade-off is how much encoding to put in the microinstructions. If one were to build the Mic-1 on a single VLSI chip, one could ignore the abstractions such as registers, ALU, and so on, and just look at all the gates. To make the machine run, certain signals are needed, such as the 16 OE signals to gate the registers onto the A bus and the signals that control the ALU function. When we look inside the ALU, we see that the internal circuitry is actually driven by four lines, not two, because in the lower left-hand corner of Fig. 3-20 we find a 2-to-4 decoder circuit. In short, for each machine some set of n control signals applied at the appropriate places can make the machine run, without any decoding.

This point of view leads to a different microinstruction format: just make it n bits wide, one bit per control signal. Microinstructions designed according to this principle are called **horizontal** and represent one extreme of a spectrum of possibilities. At the other end of the spectrum are microinstructions with a small number of highly encoded fields. These are said to be **vertical**. The names come from how an artist might sketch their respective control stores: horizontal designs have a relatively small number of wide microinstructions; vertical ones have many narrow microinstructions.

Between these two extremes lie many mixed designs. Our microinstructions, for example, have a number of bits, such as MAR, MBR, RD, WR, and AMUX, that directly control hardware functions. On the other hand, the A, B, C, and ALU fields require some decoding logic before they can be applied to the individual gates. An extreme vertical microinstruction might just have an opcode, which is merely a generalization of our ALU field, and some operands, such as our A, B, and C fields. In such an organization, opcodes would be needed for reading and writing main memory, making microjumps, and so on, because the fields that control these functions in our machine would no longer be present.

To make the distinction between horizontal and vertical microinstructions clearer, let us now redesign our example microarchitecture to use vertical microinstructions. Each microinstruction will now contain three 4-bit fields, for a total of 12 bits, versus 32 in the original version. The first field is the opcode, OP, which tells what the microinstruction does. The next two fields are two registers, R1 and R2. For jumping they are combined to form a single 8-bit field, R. A typical microinstruction is ADD SP,AC, which means that AC is added to SP.

The complete list of microinstruction opcodes for this new machine, which we will call the Mic-2, is given in Fig. 4-17. From the list it is clear that each microinstruction performs only one function: if it performs an addition, it cannot also shift, load the MAR, or even keep RD asserted. With only 12 bits in the microinstruction there is only room to specify one operation.

Now we must redo Fig. 4-10 to reflect the new microinstructions. The new block diagram is shown in Fig. 4-18. The data path portion, on the left, is identical to the old one. Most of the control portion, on the right, will also remain the same. In particular, we still need MIR and a control store (although the new ones are 12 bits wide instead of 32 bits wide). The sizes and functions of MPC, Mmux, the incrementer, the clock, and the micro sequencing logic are all identical to those in the horizontal design. Furthermore, we need 4-to-16 decoders for the R1 and R2 fields, analogous to those for A, B, and C in Fig. 4-10.

Three main differences between Fig. 4-10 and Fig. 4-18 are the boxes labeled

Binary	Mnemonic	Instruction	Meaning
0000	ADD	Addition	$r1 := r1 + r2$
0001	AND	Boolean AND	$r1 := r1$ AND $r2$
0010	MOVE	Move register	$r1 := r2$
0011	COMPL	Complement	$r1 := inv(r2)$
0100	LSHIFT	Left shift	$r1 := lshift(r2)$
0101	RSHIFT	Right shift	$r1 := rshift(r2)$
0110	GETMBR	Store MBR in register	$r1 := mbr$
0111	TEST	Test register	**if** $r2 < 0$ **then** $n := true$; **if** $r2 = 0$ **then** $z := true$
1000	BEGRD	Begin read	$mar := r2$; rd
1001	BEGWR	Begin write	$mar := r2$; $mbr := r2$; wr
1010	CONRD	Continue read	rd
1011	CONWR	Continue write	wr
1100		(not used)	
1101	NJUMP	Jump if N=1	**if** n **then goto** r
1110	ZJUMP	Jump if Z=1	**if** z **then goto** r
1111	UJUMP	Unconditional jump	**goto** r

$r = 16 * r1 + r2$

Fig. 4-17. The Mic-2 opcodes.

AND, NZ, and OP decode. AND is needed because the R1 field now drives both the A bus and C bus. A problem arises because the A bus is loaded during subcycle 2 but the C bus may not be loaded into the scratchpad until the A and B latches are stable, in subcyle 3. The AND box ANDs the 16 decoded signals with both the sub-cycle 4 line from the clock and a signal coming from OP decode, which is equivalent to the old ENC signal. The result is that the 16 signals that load data into the scratchpad are asserted under the same conditions as before.

The NZ box is a 2-bit register that can be commanded to store the N and Z ALU signals. We need this facility because in the new design the ALU will do work in one microinstruction but the status bits will not be tested until the next one. Because the ALU has no internal storage and N and Z are derived from the current output, N being the high-order bit and Z being the NOR of all the output bits, both status signals would be lost after a microinstruction if they were not latched some-where.

The key element in the new microarchitecture is the OP decoder. This box takes the 4-bit OPCODE field and produces signals that drive the AND box, micro sequencing logic, NZ, Amux, ALU, shifter, MBR, MAR, RD, and WR. The micro

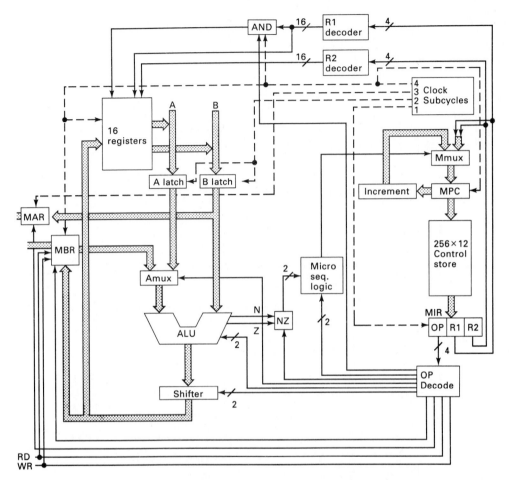

Fig. 4-18. A microarchitecture with vertical microinstructions.

sequencing logic, ALU, and shifter each require two signals, which are identical to what they were in the previous design. In all, the OP decoder generates 13 distinct signals based on the current microinstruction's high-order 4 bits.

For each of the 16 possible microinstruction opcodes, the machine designer must determine which of the 13 signals emanating from the OP decoder are asserted and which are negated. In effect, a 16×13 binary matrix giving the value of each control line for each opcode must be generated. The matrix for the Mic-2 is given in Fig. 4-19. The columns are labeled with the signal names. The suffixes L and H stand for Low and High, respectively, and apply only to the devices with two control lines: the ALU, shifter, and micro sequencing logic.

As an example of a microinstruction opcode, consider BEGRD, which initiates a memory read. It uses ALU function 2 (select A bus), so ALUH = 1 and ALUL =

Control lines

#	Microinstruction opcode	ALUH	ALUL	SHH	SHL	NZ	AMUX	AND	MAR	MBR	RD	WR	MSLH	MSLL
0	ADD					+	+							
1	AND		+			+	+							
2	MOVE	+				+	+							
3	COMPL	+	+			+	+							
4	LSHIFT	+		+		+	+							
5	RSHIFT	+			+	+	+							
6	GETMBR	+				+	+	+						
7	TEST	+				+								
8	BEGRD	+							+		+			
9	BEGWR	+							+	+		+		
10	CONRD	+									+			
11	CONWR	+										+		
12														
13	NJUMP	+												+
14	ZJUMP	+											+	
15	UJUMP	+											+	+

Fig. 4-19. The control signals for each microinstruction opcode. A plus means the signal is asserted; a blank means it is negated.

0. It also latches MAR and asserts RD. All the other control signals are negated. Now consider the jumps. Because we have decided to be compatible with the old micro sequencing logic, we need the MSLH MSLL pair to be 00 for no jump, 01 for jump on N, 10 for jump on Z, and 11 for unconditional jump. (Compatibility has reached such epidemic proportions in the computer industry that even hypothetical machines in textbooks are now compatible with their predecessors.) NJUMP generates 01, ZJUMP generates 10, and UJUMP generates 11. All the other opcodes generate 00.

Now comes the interesting part. How do we build a circuit with four input lines (the 4 opcode bits) and 13 output lines (the 13 control signals) that computes the function of Fig. 4-19? Answer: Use one or more PLAs (or ROMs). Figure 4-19 is actually a slightly peculiar way to represent 13 four-variable truth tables, one per column, with the row number implicitly defining the values of the four variables. Hence the question of how to build the circuit reduces to the question of how one implements a truth table. The best way is with a four-input, 13-output PLA. If that is not available, three 74S330 12-input, six-output PLAs can also be used. If we label the four opcode bits A to D, high to low, then some outputs are:

$$ALUL = \overline{A}\overline{B}\overline{C}D + \overline{A}\overline{B}CD = \overline{A}\overline{B}D$$

$$SHH = \overline{A}\overline{B}\overline{C}\overline{D}$$

$$MAR = A\overline{B}\overline{C}\overline{D} + A\overline{B}\overline{C}D = A\overline{B}\overline{C}$$

$$MSLH = ABC\overline{D} + ABCD = ABC$$

Only 15 of the product terms must be generated internally, because $AB\overline{C}\overline{D}$ does not occur.

With the redesigned hardware now complete, we need to rewrite the microprogram. It is given in Fig. 4-20. The labels have been kept the same to make comparison of the two microprograms easier. So has the syntax. We could have written it using typical assembly language notation (e.g., the opcodes of Fig. 4-17) but instead we have used MAL again because that is much easier to read. Note that MAL statements of the form *alu := reg* use the TEST microinstruction to set the N and Z bits. Be sure that you understand the difference between the microprogram in binary, as it is loaded into the control store, and the assembly language version given in the text.

By and large, this microprogram is simpler than the first one because each line only does one operation. As a consequence, many of the lines in the original one have had to be split up into two, three, or even four lines in this one. Another feature of the vertical design that increases the number of microinstructions is the lack of three-address instructions. See, for example, lines 22 and 27 in the first microprogram.

The original microprogram uses seventy-nine 32-bit words for a total of 2528 bits of control store. The second one uses one hundred sixty 12-bit words, for a total of 1920 bits. This difference represents a saving of 24% in control store. For a single-chip computer, it also represents a 24% saving in the chip area needed for the control store, which makes it easier and cheaper to manufacture. The penalty paid for the smaller control store is more microinstructions have to be executed per macroinstruction. Usually, this makes the machine slower. Consequently, fast, expensive machines tend to be horizontal, and slower, cheaper machines tend to be vertical.

The existence of highly encoded microinstructions, as in the Mic-2, raises some serious philosophical questions about what microprogramming is. The microinstruction set of Fig. 4-17 could almost pass for the *conventional machine language* instruction set of a very simple mini- or microcomputer. The PDP-8, for example, is a minicomputer with a 12-bit word whose instructions are not a whole lot more powerful than these. Considering that the "meaning" of the instructions is largely embedded in hardware (the OP decode PLA or circuit), one might well argue that the Mic-2 is really a nonmicroprogrammed machine that happens to have a software interpreter running on it for yet another machine. If the microprogram for the vertical machine were stored in main memory (as on the IBM 370/145, for example), then the distinction between a highly vertical microprogrammed machine and a hardwired one becomes even less clear. For a more thorough treatment of encoding and parallelism in microcode, see Dasgupta (1979).

4.5.2. Nanoprogramming

The designs discussed so far have had two memories: the main memory (used to hold the level 2 program) and the control store (used to hold the microprogram). A third memory, the **nanostore**, makes interesting trade-offs between horizontal and vertical microprogramming possible. Nanoprogramming is appropriate when many microinstructions occur several times. The microprogram of Fig. 4-16 does not have this property. The most commonly occurring microinstruction is the one containing just *rd*, and it occurs only five times.

Figure 4-21 illustrates the concept of nanoprogramming. In part (a), a microprogram of n microinstructions each w bits wide is shown. A total of nw bits of control store is needed to store the microprogram. Suppose that a careful study of the microprogram revealed that only m different microinstructions of the 2^w possibilities were actually used, with $m \ll n$. A special m-word w-bit nanostore could be used to store each unique microinstruction. Each microinstruction in the original program could then be replaced by the address of the nanostore word containing that microinstruction. Because there are only m words in the nanostore, the control store need only be $\log_2 m$ (rounded up to an integer) bits wide, as shown in Fig. 4-21(b).

The microprogram is executed as follows. The first word is fetched from the control store. It is then used to select a nanostore word, which is fetched and placed in the microinstruction register. The bits of this register are then used to control the gates for one cycle. At the end of the cycle, the next word is fetched from the control store and the process is repeated.

As an example, suppose that the original microprogram is 4096×100 bits but only 128 different microinstructions occur. A 128×100 bit nanostore will suffice to hold all the microinstructions needed. The control store then becomes 4096×7 bits, each word pointing to a nanoinstruction. The memory saving in this example is given by:

$$\text{saving} = 4096 \times 100 - 4096 \times 7 - 128 \times 100 = 368,128 \text{ bits}$$

The price that must be paid for saving control store is slower execution. The machine with the two-level control store will run slower than the original one because the fetch cycle now requires two memory references, one to the control store and one to the nanostore. These two fetches cannot be overlapped.

```
 0:  mar := pc ; rd ;
 1:  rd ;
     pc := pc + 1;
 2:  ir := mbr ;
     tir := lshift (ir );
     if n then goto 28;
 3:  tir := lshift (tir );
     if n then goto 19;
 4:  tir := lshift (tir );
     if n then goto 11;
 5:  alu := tir ;
     if n then goto 9;

 6:  mar := ir ; rd ; {LODD}
 7:  rd ;
 8:  ac := mbr ;
     goto 0;

 9:  mar := ir ; mbr := ac ; wr ; {STOD}
10:  wr ;
     goto 0;

11:  alu := tir ;
     if n then goto 15;

12:  mar := ir ; rd ; {ADDD}
13:  rd ;
14:  a := mbr ;
     ac := ac + a ;
     goto 0;

15:  mar := ir ; rd ; {SUBD}
16:  rd ;
99:  ac := ac + 1;
17:  a := mbr ;
     a := inv (a );
18:  ac := ac + a ;
     goto 0;

19:  tir := lshift (tir );
     if n then goto 25;
20:  alu := tir ;
     if n then goto 23;

21:  alu := ac ; {JPOS}
     if n then goto 0;
22:  pc := ir ;
     pc := band (pc , amask );
     goto 0;
```

```
23:  alu := ac ; {JZER}
     if z then goto 22;
24:  goto 0;

25:  alu := tir ;
     if n then goto 27;
26:  pc := ir ; {JUMP}
     pc := band (pc , amask );
     goto 0;

27:  ac := ir ; {LOCO}
     ac := band (ac , amask );
     goto 0;

28:  tir := lshift (tir );
     if n then goto 40;
29:  tir := lshift (tir );
     if n then goto 35;
30:  alu := tir ;
     if n then goto 33;

31:  a := ir ; {LODL}
     a := a + sp ;
32:  mar := a ; rd ;
     rd ;
     ac := mbr ;
     goto 0;

33:  a := ir ; {STOL}
     a := a + sp ;
34:  mar := a ; mbr := ac ; wr ;
     wr ;
     goto 0;

35:  alu := tir ;
     if n then goto 38;

36:  a := ir ; {ADDL}
     a := a + sp ;
37:  mar := a ; rd ;
     rd ;
     a := mbr ;
     ac := ac + a ;
     goto 0;
```

Fig. 4-20. The microprogram for Mic-2.

38: $a := ir$; {SUBL}
      $a := a + sp$;
39: $mar := a$; rd;
      rd;
      goto 99;

40: $tir := lshift(tir)$;
      if n **then goto** 46;
41: $alu := tir$;
      if n **then goto** 44;

42: $alu := ac$; {JNEG}
      if n **then goto** 22;
43: **goto** 0;

44: $alu := ac$; {JNZE}
      if z **then goto** 0;
45: $pc := ir$;
      $pc := band(pc, amask)$;
      goto 0;

46: $tir := lshift(tir)$;
      if n **then goto** 50;

47: $sp := sp + (-1)$; {CALL}
48: $mar := sp$; $mbr := pc$; wr;
      wr;
49: $pc := ir$;
      $pc := band(pc, amask)$;
      goto 0;

50: $tir := lshift(tir)$;
      if n **then goto** 65;
51: $tir := lshift(tir)$;
      if n **then goto** 59;
52: $alu := tir$;
      if n **then goto** 56;

53: $mar := ac$; rd; {PSHI}
      rd;
54: $sp := sp + (-1)$;
55: $a := mbr$;
      $mar := sp$; $mbr := a$; wr;
      wr;
      goto 0;

56: $mar := sp$; rd; {POPI}
57: rd;
      $sp := sp + 1$;

58: $a := mbr$;
      $mar := ac$; $mbr := a$; wr;
      wr;
      goto 0;
59: $alu := tir$;
      if n **then goto** 62;

60: $sp := sp + (-1)$; {PUSH}
61: $mar := sp$; $mbr := ac$; wr;
      wr;
      goto 0;

62: $mar := sp$; rd; {POP}
63: rd;
      $sp := sp + 1$;
64: $ac := mbr$;
      goto 0;

65: $tir := lshift(tir)$;
      if n **then goto** 73;
66: $alu := tir$;
      if n **then goto** 70;

67: $mar := sp$; rd; {RETN}
68: rd;
      $sp := sp + 1$;
69: $pc := mbr$;
      goto 0;

70: $a := ac$; {SWAP}
71: $ac := sp$;
72: $sp := a$;
      goto 0;

73: $alu := tir$;
      if n **then goto** 76;

74: $a := ir$; {INSP}
      $a := band(a, smask)$;
75: $sp := sp + a$;
      goto 0;

76: $a := ir$; {DESP}
      $a := band(a, smask)$;
77: $a := inv(a)$;
78: $a := a + 1$;
      $sp := sp + a$;
      goto 0;

Fig. 4-20. (cont.)

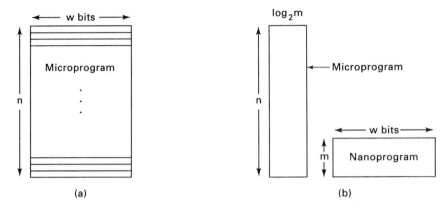

Fig. 4-21. (a) A conventional microprogram. (b) The corresponding nanoprogram if only *m* unique microinstructions occur in the microprogram.

Nanoprogramming is most effective when the same microinstructions are heavily used. If two microinstructions that were almost the same could be counted as really being the same, the microprogram would contain fewer distinct microinstructions, each with a higher usage frequency. A variation on the basic idea allows precisely this. Words in the nanostore may be parameterized. For example, two microinstructions may differ only in the field telling which register is to be gated onto some bus. By putting the register number in the control store instead of in the nanostore (i.e., putting zeros in the register field in the nanoinstructions) the two microinstructions can both point to the same nanoword. When the word is fetched and put into the microinstruction register, the register field is taken from the control store instead of the nanostore. Building up the microinstruction register partly from the control store and partly from the nanostore obviously requires special hardware, but it is not especially complex. Of course, using this approach increases the width of the control store, which may more than offset the gain made by having a smaller nanostore.

4.5.3. Improving Performance

Although the goal of nanoprogramming is to reduce the size of the control store, even at the price of slower execution, a fair amount of time and effort has also gone in the reverse direction: trying to speed up execution, even at the price of more control store. These two seemingly incompatible design goals relate to different marketing goals—producing inexpensive machines and producing fast machines. In this section we will look at some of the ways the straightforward microarchitecture of our examples can be souped up to make the machines run faster.

Up until now we have tacitly assumed that all four subcycles are equally long. While this approach is simple, it rarely results in optimum performance because invariably one of the four inherently takes more time than the other three. Having all subcycles be as long as the worst case slows the machine down. The way to fix this problem is to allow each subcycle to have a duration independent of the other ones. That way the length of each subcycle can be set to the amount of time needed to do the work, and no longer.

Although this is a step in the right direction, it is still too conservative because the length of each subcycle is still determined by the worst case for that subcycle. Consider, for example, subcycle 3 in our examples. If the ALU operation is an addition, the ALU probably needs more time (due to carry-propagation delays) than if the operation is merely select A. If the time devoted to subcycle 3 is a constant determined when the machine is designed, it has to be the time for addition, not for select A. An alternative strategy, is to let the subcycle time be determined by the specific operation to be performed, so it can be set as short as possible.

Once we decide to allow each subcycle to depend on the operation, we must find a way to implement this strategy. Slowing the clock down or speeding it up is technically difficult, so instead a master clock with a period much shorter than the subcycle time is used. Each subcycle then lasts a certain number of pulses. For example, if the ALU time can vary from 75 to 150 nsec, a master clock with a 25-nsec period can be used, with the subcycle taking between three and six periods.

Another question is: How does the machine know how long the subcycle should be? One of two approaches can be used here to tell it. In the first, the microinstruction itself contains one or more fields that explicitly give the timing. The other is to derive the timing based on the operation fields (using a PLA), the same way all the other control signals were generated for the vertical machine. The first approach costs control store bits and the second costs decoding logic and time.

Another way to get more horsepower out of the machine is to increase the flexibility of conditional microjumps. As an example, consider a SKIP LESS macroinstruction that compares AC to a memory word and skips over the next macroinstruction if AC is less. Doing the comparison requires subtracting the memory word from (a copy of) AC, which can result in an overflow, as illustrated in Fig. 4-22.

AC	000100	000100	077777	100001	000010
Mem	000050	170000	177775	000010	100001
	000030	010100	100002	077771	100007
	N = 0	N = 0	N = 1	N = 0	N = 1
	V = 0	V = 0	V = 1	V = 1	V = 1

Fig. 4-22. Some examples of 16-bit two's complement subtraction in octal. The N and V bits for each result are also shown.

Due to the potential for overflow, we cannot tell which operand was smaller by simply looking at the sign bit of the result. In the fourth example of Fig. 4-22, AC is less than memory but AC − memory is positive. The correct condition to be tested is N EXCLUSIVE OR V, where V indicates the presence or absence of overflow. (The hardware sets the V bit whenever the carry *into* the sign bit differs from the carry *out of* the sign bit.)

Fortunately, most ALUs generate not only N and Z but also V and C (carry) as well. However, if only four conditional jumps are available to the microprogrammer, one for each of NZVC, the SKIP LESS macroinstruction will require many microinstructions. To provide more flexibility, many machines do not have the ability to test individual ALU status bits. Instead, a single microinstruction bit causes NZVC to be ORed with the 4 low-order bits of the ADDR field, and the jump taken. Some examples are given in Fig. 4-23. If the 4 low-order bits are all 0, this becomes a 16-way jump. If they are all 1, the jump becomes an unconditional one to a specific address ending in 1111.

ADDR Field	NZVC	Address jumped to
10000000	1001	10001001
10001000	1001	10001001
10001011	1001	10001011
10001011	1000	10001011
10001011	0000	10001011
10001111	0000	10001111
10001111	1100	10001111
10000000	1100	10001100

Fig. 4-23. Some examples of multiway jumping based on NZVC.

With this facility the SKIP LESS instruction becomes much easier to interpret. We choose an ADDR field ending in 0101, for example, 10000101 (binary), and perform the jump. The microinstructions at 10001101 and 10000111 deal with skips that succeed and those at 10000101 and 10001111 deal with skips that fail. No further decoding is needed. We could also have used a base address ending in 0000 instead of 0101 but these are enormously valuable, because they are the only ones available for 16-way jumps. Hence, they should not be chosen lightly.

It should be clear that with this kind of microinstruction sequence control, the placement of microinstructions in the control store can become a real headache. The first microinstruction executed following a 16-way jump must itself contain an unconditional jump because the word following it (except for the last one) is already in use as a possible jump destination. Where should each microinstruction jump to? Certainly not an address of the form xxxx0000, because they are too valuable, but all other addresses, except for those of the form xxxx1111, may also be needed sooner or later. The decision must be made carefully, to avoid running out of some kind of address. Once all the even addresses are gone, for example, it is no longer possible to test the C bit, so the choice of addresses must be done with great care.

4.5.4. Pipelining

Yet another way to speed up the machine is to build the hardware out of several functional units and then pipeline them. In Fig. 2-5 we saw how a five-unit pipeline works. In Fig. 4-24 we see that if instruction 1 is fetched in cycle 1, it will be executed in cycle 5. Similarly, if instruction 4 is fetched in cycle (i.e., time slot) 8, decoded in cycle 9, and so on, it will be executed in cycle 12. Under optimal conditions, in every cycle thereafter, one instruction is executed, for an average execution rate of one instruction per cycle, instead of one instruction per five cycles

	Cycle												
	1	2	3	4	5	6	7	8	9	10	11		
Instruction fetch	1	2	B					4	5	6	7	8	9
Instruction decode		1	2	B					4	5	6	7	8
Address calculation			1	2	B					4	5	6	7
Operand fetch				1	2	B					4	5	6
Execution					1	2	B					4	5

Fig. 4-24. A five-stage pipeline. The numbers are used to label instructions. The instruction marked B is a conditional jump.

Unfortunately, studies have shown that about 30 percent of all instructions are jumps, and these wreak havoc with the pipeline. Jumps can be classified in three categories: unconditional, conditional, and loop. An unconditional jump tells the computer to stop fetching instructions consecutively, and go to some specific address. A conditional jump tests some condition and jumps if the condition is met. A typical example is an instruction that tests some register and jumps if the register contains zero. If the register does not contain zero, the jump is not taken and control continues in the current sequence.

Loop instructions typically decrement an iteration counter and then jump back to the top of the loop if it is nonzero (i.e., there are still more iterations to be done). Loop instructions are an important special case of conditional jumps because it is known in advance that they nearly always succeed.

Consider what happens to the pipeline of Fig. 4-24 when a conditional jump instruction, marked B, is encountered. The next instruction to be executed might be the one following the jump, but it might also be the address jumped to, called the **jump target**. Since the instruction fetcher does not know which until the jump has been executed, it stalls, and cannot go further until the jump has been executed. Consequently, the pipeline empties. Only after cycle 7 has been completed is it known which instruction comes next.

The jump has effectively caused four cycles to be lost, called the **jump penalty**. With one out of every three instructions being a jump, it is clear that the performance loss is substantial.

A great deal of research has gone into the problem of winning back some of this performance (DeRosa and Levy, 1987; McFarling and Hennessy, 1986; Hwu et al., 1989; and Lilja, 1988). The simplest thing to do is hope that the jump will not be taken, and just continue filling the pipeline as though the jump were a simple arithmetic instruction. If it turns out that the jump is indeed not taken, we have lost nothing. If it is taken, we have to kill off the instructions currently in the pipeline, something called **squashing**, and start over.

Squashing causes problems of its own. On some machines, as a byproduct of doing the address calculation, a register can be modified. If the instruction being squashed has modified one or more registers, they must be restored, which means there must be a mechanism for recording their original values.

It is instructive to make a simple model of the performance loss.

Let P_j be the probability that an instruction is a jump.

Let P_t be the probability that the jump is taken.

Let b be the jump penalty.

The average execution time (in cycles) can be computed as the weighted sum of the two cases: regular instructions and jump instructions.

$$\text{average instruction time} = (1 - P_j)(1) + P_j[P_t(1 + b) + (1 - P_t)(1)]$$

Some algebra reveals that the average instruction time is $1 + bP_jP_t$. The execution efficiency is then $1/(1 + bP_jP_t)$. With $b = 4$, $P_j = 0.3$, and a $P_t = 0.65$ (a typical measured value), the machine runs at less than 60 percent of its potential speed.

What can be done to improve performance? To start with, if we could predict which way each jump was going to go, we could fetch the proper instruction and eliminate the penalty. In our formula for the efficiency, we can then replace P_t with P_w, the probability of guessing wrong.

Two kinds of prediction are possible: static (compile time) and dynamic (run time). With static prediction, the compiler makes a guess about each jump instruction it generates. With loop instructions, for example, guessing that it will jump back to the top of the loop is right most of the time. When testing for an unlikely condition, such as a system call returning an error code, jump not taken is most likely. In many cases different instructions are used for these cases, and just looking at the opcode provides a substantial hint.

A more elaborate scheme is for the machine designers to provide two opcodes for each kind of jump, and have the compiler use the first one if it thinks the jump will be taken and the second otherwise. Alternatively, for programs that are to be used heavily, the program can first be run on a simulator, and the behavior of each jump actually recorded. Then the binary program can be patched, replacing each jump with the proper opcode (probably will be taken/probably will not be taken).

The other prediction method is dynamic. During execution, the microprogram builds up a table of addresses containing jumps and keeps track of the behavior of each one. This method tends to slow down the machine with record keeping, so some hardware help may be needed. Measurements have shown that attaining 90 percent accuracy this way is not difficult.

Jump prediction is not the only attack. Another one is attempting to determine which way the jump will go early in the pipeline. Some tests, such as jump on equal, are much easier to make than jump on less than. The former can be done with a comparator, whereas the latter requires a full data path cycle to do a subtraction. With this approach, whenever a jump is encountered, the microprogram makes a quick check in an early stage of the pipeline to see if it can resolve the jump immediately. If so, it knows where to continue fetching.

Compilers can do a great deal to help. For example, when the programmer writes down a loop stepping i from 1 to 10, the compiler can test i to see if i is equal to 10, rather than seeing if it is less than 11, so the microprogram can get away with a comparison instead of a subtraction.

To deal with those jumps that cannot be resolved early, the compiler can try to find something useful for the computer to do while waiting for the jump to be executed. Consider Fig. 4-25(a), an arithmetic statement followed by a test. A very clever optimizing compiler might produce code more like Fig. 4-25(b), which is not legal Pascal, but shows the order of events. First it generates code to make the test, then it does the arithmetic. After the jump has entered the pipeline, several ordinary instructions follow. These have to be done no matter what, so there is no need to make a prediction and there is no need to do squashing. To use this technique effectively, the microprogrammers and the compiler writers had better work together closely during the design.

$a := b + c;$	**if** $b < c$
if $b < c$	$a := b + c;$
then statement;	**then** statement;
(a)	(b)

Fig. 4-25. (a) A Pascal fragment. (b) How the compiler might treat it.

If all else fails, there is always the possibility of following both paths in parallel. Doing so requires having two pipelines in the hardware and does not eliminate the squashing problem. Still on high-end computers, where performance and not price is the issue, this method is sometimes used. Of course, if either path hits another jump before the first one is resolved, life gets even more complicated. Having a few dozen pipelines lying around to deal with the worst case is probably not a good idea.

After all this theorizing about what one could do, let us come back to our example machine for a moment. It does not have distinct hardware units for fetching, decoding, and so on, so not much pipelining is possible, but with minor changes to the microprogram, we can achieve a limited amount of overlap between fetching and executing microinstructions, which is also a form of pipelining.

In Fig. 4-10, for example, if the next microinstruction could somehow be fetched during subcycle 4, subcycle 1 would no longer be needed, and the clock could just generate pulses for subcycles 234234234.... The principal problem occurs in handling conditional jump microinstructions, as we have seen. If the machine waits until the ALU status lines are available before starting to fetch the next microinstruction, it is too late: the cycle is practically over and little overlap can be achieved. On some machines the problem is solved by just using the ALU status lines from the previous cycle, which, of course, have to be latched to keep them from vanishing. These values are available at the start of each microinstruction, so the next fetch can start as soon as the current fetch is finished, long before the execution of the current microinstruction has completed. Needless to say, this way of doing business greatly complicates life for the microprogrammer.

Technically, it is possible to write microprograms for such a machine in a reasonable way. For example, to test some word in the scratchpad and jump if it is negative, the microprogram can run the word through the ALU in a microinstruction *not* containing a jump. The next microinstruction is a no-op with conditional jump; that is, it does nothing except test the latched ALU status bits and jump. The price to be paid for programming in a rational way is doubling the jump time, an undesirable proposition.

The only solution is to get out a jar of aspirins and try to make the best of the situation. For example, the microprogrammer could make a guess which way the conditional jump will usually go, and use the second microinstruction to start doing the work that will probably be needed. Unfortunately, if the jump goes the other way, it will be necessary to do some squashing.

As a simple example, let us rewrite lines 11 to 18 of Fig. 4-16 for a machine with overlapped microinstruction fetching and execution. The results are shown in Fig. 4-26(a). In this example we are lucky because upon executing line 11 we know that the code for either ADDD or SUBD will follow, and both begin with the same microinstruction. Therefore, we just put the common microinstruction in line 12 to keep the machine busy while the jump is being carried out.

A slightly less pleasant example is shown in Fig. 4-26(b). At line 52 we know that either PSHI or POPI will follow but unfortunately these two routines do not have the same first microinstruction. Suppose, however, that a statistical analysis of Mac-1 programs has shown PSHI to be far more common than POPI. Then we could proceed as shown in Fig. 4-26(b). For PSHI everything is fine but for POPI,

11: *alu* := *tir*;
12: *mar* := *ir*; *rd*; **if** *n* **then goto** 16;

13: *rd*;
14: *ac* := *mbr* + *ac*; **goto** 0;

16: *ac* := *ac* + 1; *rd*;
17: *a* : = *inv* (*mbr*);
18: *ac* := *ac* + *a*; **goto** 0;

(a)

52: *alu* := *tir*;
53: *mar* := *ac*; *rd*; **if** *n* **then goto** 56;
54: *sp* := *sp* + (–1); *rd*;
55: *mar* := *sp*; *wr*; **goto** 10;

56: *rd*;
57: *mar* := *sp*; *sp* := *sp* + 1; *rd*;
58: *rd*;
59: *mar* := *ac*; *wr*; **goto** 10;

(b)

Fig. 4-26. Two examples involving overlapped microinstruction fetching and execution.

by the time line 56 is reached, a memory read for the wrong word has already been initiated. Depending on the exact details of the hardware, it may or may not be possible to abort a memory read halfway through without gumming up the works. If we cannot abort it, we just finish it off and then start the correct read. In this example POPI takes 15 microinstructions instead of 13 as in Fig. 4-16. Nevertheless, if the use of overlapping has reduced the basic microinstruction time by even 15%, POPI will be faster now than before.

If multiway jumps formed by ORing NZVC into the low-order bits of ADDR are used instead of individual bit tests, the situation becomes much more complicated. Furthermore, on many machines the overlapping of fetching and executing microinstructions is done in such a way that early during the execution of microinstruction n the choice of microinstruction $n + 1$ has to be made using the ALU status bits previously latched during microinstruction $n - 1$. We will not pursue the matter further here, but at the very least the motivation for Rosin's definition of microprogramming may be clearer now.

4.5.5. Cache Memory

Historically, CPUs have always been faster than memories. As memories have improved, so have CPUs, preserving the imbalance. What this means in practice is that after the CPU issues a memory request, it must remain idle for a substantial time while waiting for the memory to respond. As we have seen, it is common for the CPU to set up a memory read during one bus cycle, and not get the data until two or three cycles later, even if there are no wait states.

Actually, the problem is not technology, but economics. Engineers know how to build memories that are as fast as CPUs, but these are so expensive that equipping a computer with a megabyte or more is out of the question (except perhaps for supercomputers, where the sky's the limit and price is no object). Thus the choice comes down to having a small amount of fast memory or a large amount of slow memory. What we would prefer is a large amount of fast memory at a low price.

Interestingly enough, techniques are known for combining a small amount of fast memory with a large amount of slow memory to get the speed of the fast memory (almost) and the capacity of the large memory at a moderate price. The small, fast memory is called a **cache** (from the French *cacher*, meaning to hide, and pronounced "cash") and is under control of the microprogram. Below we will describe how caches are used and how they work. More information can be found in (Agarwal et al., 1989; Farrens and Pleszkun, 1989; Kabakibo et al., 1987; Kessler et al., 1989; Pohm and Agarwal, 1983; Przybylski et al., 1989; Smith, 1982; and Wang et al., 1989).

For years, people have known that programs do not access their memories completely at random. If a given memory reference is to address A, it is likely that the next memory reference will be in the general vicinity of A. A simple example is the program itself. Except for jumps and procedure calls, instructions are fetched from consecutive locations in memory. Furthermore, most program execution time is spent in loops, in which a limited number of instructions are executed over and over. Similarly, a matrix manipulation program is likely to make many references to the same matrix before moving on to something else.

The observation that the memory references made in any short time interval tend to use only a small fraction of the total memory is called the **locality principle** and forms the basis for all caching systems. The general idea is that when a word is referenced, it is brought from the large slow memory into the cache, so that the next time it is used, it can be accessed quickly. A common arrangement of the CPU, cache, and main memory is illustrated in Fig. 4-27. If a word is read or written k times in a short interval, the computer will need 1 reference to slow memory and $k - 1$ references to fast memory. The larger k is, the better the overall performance.

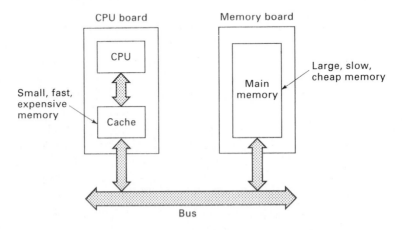

Fig. 4-27. The cache is usually located on the CPU board.

We can formalize this calculation by introducing c, the cache access time, m, the main memory access time, and h, the **hit ratio**, which is the fraction of all references that can be satisfied out of the cache. In our little example of the previous paragraph, $h = (k - 1)/k$. Some authors also define the **miss ratio**, which is $1 - h$.

With these definitions, we can calculate the mean access time as follows:

$$\text{mean access time} = c + (1 - h)\, m$$

As $h \to 1$, all references can be satisfied out of the cache, and the access time approaches c. On the other hand, as $h \to 0$, a memory reference is needed every time, so the access time approaches $c + m$, first a time c to check the cache (unsuccessfully), and then a time m to do the memory reference. On some systems, the memory reference can be started in parallel with the cache search, so that if a cache miss occurs, the memory cycle has already been started. However, this strategy requires that the memory can be stopped in its tracks on a cache hit, making it more complicated. The basic algorithm of looking things up in the cache and starting (or stopping) the main memory reference depending on the result of searching the cache is handled by the microprogram.

Two fundamentally different cache organizations are used, along with a third form that is a hybrid of the first two. For all three types, the memory, assumed to be 2^m bytes, is (conceptually) divided up into consecutive blocks of b bytes, for a total of $2^m/b$ blocks. Each block has an address that is a multiple of b. The block size, b, is normally a power of two.

The first cache type is the **associative cache**, an example of which is shown in Fig. 4-28. It consists of a number of **slots** or **lines**, each containing one block and its block number along with a bit (*Valid*) telling whether that slot is currently in use or not. The example of Fig. 4-28 illustrates a cache with 1024 slots and a memory with 2^{24} bytes divided into 2^{22} 4-byte blocks. In an associative cache, the order of the entries is random.

When the computer is reset, all the *Valid* bits are set to 0, to indicate that no cache entries are valid. Suppose that the first instruction references the 32-bit word at address 0. The microprogram will check all the entries of the cache looking for a valid one containing block number 0. Failing to find one, it will then issue a bus request to fetch word 0 from the memory, and make a valid entry for block number 0 containing the contents of word 0. If this word is needed again, the next time it will be taken from the cache, eliminating the need for a bus operation.

As time goes on, more and more cache entries will be marked as valid. If the program uses fewer than 1024 words of program and data, ultimately the entire program and its data will appear in the cache, and it will run at high speed, without making any memory references over the bus at all. If more than 1024 words are needed, at some point the cache will be full and an old entry will have to be discarded to make room for a new one. In practice, the decision of which one to throw out has to be made very quickly (nanoseconds). The VAX and many other machines pick a slot at random. Other possible algorithms are discussed in Chap. 6 under the heading of virtual memory, where the same problem occurs.

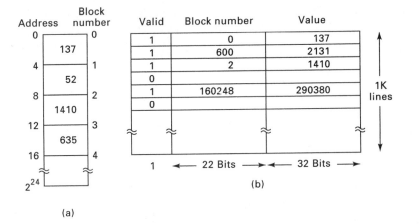

Fig. 4-28. An example caching scheme. (a) Memory with 4-byte blocks. (b) Associative cache with 1024 lines.

The aspect of the associative cache that distinguishes it from the other kinds of caches is that each slot contains a block number and its entry. When a memory address is presented, the microprogram must compute the relevant block number (easy) and then look up that block number in the cache (hard). To avoid a linear search, the associative cache has special hardware that can compare every entry to a given block number simultaneously, rather than in a microprogram loop. This hardware makes the associative cache expensive.

To reduce the cost, a different type of cache was invented, the **direct-mapped cache**. This kind of cache avoids the search by putting each block in a slot whose number can be easily calculated from the block number. For example, the slot number can be the block number modulo the number of slots. With 4-byte (i.e., 1-word) blocks and 1024 slots, for example, the slot number for the word at address A is $(A/4)$ *modulo* 1024. In the example of Fig. 4-29 we see that the words at 0, 4096, 8192, and so on map onto slot 0, the words at 4, 4100, 8196, and so on map onto slot 1, and so forth.

While the direct-mapped cache eliminates the problem of searching, it creates a new problem—how to tell which of the many words that map onto a given slot is currently occupying that slot. In effect, we have created 1024 equivalence classes, based on the block numbers modulo the cache size. In this example, slot 0 might contain any one of words 0, 4096, 8192, etc. The way to tell which is currently in the slot is to put part of the address in the cache, in the *Tag* field. This field contains that part of the address that cannot be computed from the slot number.

To make this point clearer, consider an instruction at address 8192 that moves the word at 4100 to 12296. The block number corresponding to 8192 is computed by dividing it by 4 (our example block size) to get 2048. Next the slot number is computed by taking 2048 modulo 1024, which is the same thing as using the low-

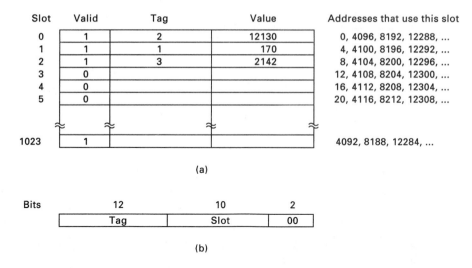

Fig. 4-29. (a) A direct-mapped cache with 1024 slots of 4 bytes each. (b) Calculation of the slot and tag from a 24-bit address.

order 10 bits of 2048. The slot number is 0. The upper 12 bits contain a 2, so that is the tag. Figure 4-29(a) shows the cache after all three addresses have been processed.

Figure 4-29(b) shows how the address is split up. The low-order two bits are always 0 (since the cache works with whole blocks, and these are multiples of the block size, 4 bytes in this example). Next comes the slot number (10 bits), and finally the tag (12 bits). It is straightforward to build hardware that directly extracts the slot number and tag from any memory address.

The fact that multiple blocks map onto the same cache slot can cause problems. Suppose that our move instruction moved 4100 to 12292 instead of to 12296. Both of these addresses map onto slot 1. Depending on the details of the microprogram, whichever one was calculated last would end up in the cache, with the other one purged. In itself, this is not a disaster, but it does degrade the performance of the cache if many words that are being used happen to map to the same slot. The goal, after all, is to improve the performance.

The way out of this difficulty is to expand the direct-mapped cache to have more than one entry per slot. The PDP-11/70, for example, had two entries per slot. A direct-mapped cache with multiple entries per slot is called a **set associative cache** and is illustrated in Fig. 4-30.

Both the associative cache and direct-mapped cache are, in fact, special cases of the set associative cache. If we reduce the number of slots to 1, all the cache entries are in the same slot, and we have to distinguish them entirely by their tags since they all map to the same address. This case is just an associative cache. If $n = 1$, we are back to a pure direct-mapped cache, with one entry per slot.

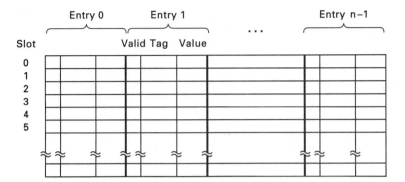

Fig. 4-30. A set associative cache with n entries per slot.

The associative and direct-mapped caches have different strengths and weaknesses. The direct-mapped cache is simpler, cheaper to build, and has a faster access time, since the proper slot can be found by just indexing into the cache using a portion of the address as the index. On the other hand, the associative cache has a higher hit ratio for any given number of slots because there are never conflicts. It cannot happen that k important words cannot be cached simultaneously because they have the bad luck to map onto the same cache slot. When any real computer is being designed, an extensive cache simulation is always made to see how much performance one buys and at what price.

In addition to determining the number of slots, the designers must also choose the block size. We have used one 32-bit word in our examples (for simplicity), but 2, 4, 8, or more words are also possible and frequently used. An advantage of using a large block size is that there is less overhead in fetching one 8-word block than in fetching eight 1-word blocks, especially if the bus allows block transfers. A disadvantage is that not all the words may be needed, so some of the fetches may be wasted.

Another important cache design issue is how to handle writes. Two strategies are commonly used. In the first one, called **write through**, when a word is written to the cache, it is also immediately written back to memory. This approach insures that cache entries are always the same as the corresponding memory entries.

The other write policy, called **copy back**, does not update memory whenever the cache is changed. Instead, memory is only updated when the entry is purged from the cache to allow another entry to take over its slot. When copy back is used, a bit is needed in each cache entry telling whether the cache entry has been changed since it was loaded into the cache.

As with all other aspects of cache design, there are trade-offs here. Write through obviously causes more bus traffic than copy back. On the other hand, if a CPU starts an I/O transfer from memory to disk, and memory is not correct (because recently changed words have not yet been copied back to memory from the cache), incorrect data will be written to disk. This problem can be circumvented, but it adds complexity to the system.

If the ratio of reads to writes is very high, it may be simplest to use write through and just accept the bus traffic. However, if there are many writes, it may be better to use copy back and have the microprogram explicitly purge the entire cache before starting an I/O operation.

Another design issue concerning writes is what to do if a write causes a cache miss. One strategy is to fetch the word into the cache and then update it, writing it back if write through is being used. A different strategy is to write to memory directly, but not fetch a word into the cache except on reads. This issue is called **write allocation policy**. Both of the methods described here are in use.

As integrated-circuit technology improves, it is becoming possible to put very fast caches directly on the CPU chip. These caches are small, due to lack of chip real estate (area), so it may be desirable to have two-level caches, one on the CPU chip and a second one on the CPU board. If a word cannot be found in the on-chip cache, a request is made to the board-level cache. If that also fails, main memory is used.

All things considered, caching is an important technique for improving system performance. Nearly all medium and large-scale computers use some form of caching. Additional information about caches can be found in (Hill, 1988; Przybylski et al., 1988; Short and Levy, 1988; and Smith, 1986, 1987).

4.6. EXAMPLES OF THE MICROPROGRAMMING LEVEL

In this section we will take a look at the microprogramming level of our two running examples, the Intel and Motorola families. These will of necessity be brief because real machines are highly complicated. In both cases, we will examine one of the simpler family members to avoid unnecessary detail.

4.6.1. The Intel 8088 Microarchitecture

The microarchitecture of all the Intel CPUs is similar because they all evolved from the first one, the 8086 (McKevitt and Bayliss, 1979). The 8088 is virtually the same machine as the 8086, except with an 8-bit bus interface instead of a 16-bit interface. The data path, ALU, and register scratchpad are identical. Similarly, the 80286 is also unchanged in terms of the main data path because, like its two predecessors, it is also a 16-bit machine internally. However, the 80286 consists of four multiple independent functional units as shown in Fig. 3-40. The 80386 has a 32-bit data path and eight functional units, so it is somewhat different from the others.

We will focus on the 8088 as the simplest member of the family, but the other designs are similar in spirit, even if they differ in some of the details. The 8088 uses a mixture of microcode and random logic (specialized hardware circuits) to provide good functionality while minimizing the microcode size. The microinstructions are vertical in format, with multibit fields that specify general functions, rather than single bits that control individual gates in the data path.

The heart of the 8088 is the main data path, illustrated in simplified form in Fig. 4-31. The data path has two portions, the lower part, in the bottom half of the figure, and the upper part, in the upper half. The two parts run independently, in parallel.

The lower part is comparable to the data path in most other computers, including our examples. It contains a multifunction ALU, which takes two inputs, computes some simple function of them, and produces one output. The inputs come from three 16-bit registers, TMPA, TMPB, and TMPC, that are loaded in advance of the ALU cycle. The output goes onto the ALU bus, from which it can be routed back into any of the three input registers, or elsewhere within the data path. The ALU can perform both 8-bit and 16-bit operations. The condition codes resulting from an ALU operation can be stored in the PSW under microprogram control.

The lower part of the data path also contains an 8-word scratchpad for AX, BX, CX, DX, SI, DI, BP, and SP. A register can be copied from the scratchpad to the ALU bus, and from there to one of the temporary registers, where it can be used as an ALU input. The ALU output can be routed directly to the scratchpad, without going through a TMP register.

The box marked "cross" between the scratchpad and the ALU bus has the ability to swap bytes as it copies in either direction. This feature is needed to access the 8-bit registers in the scratchpad. For example, to add AL and BH, AX can be copied to TMPA. Then BX can be copied to TMPB, swapping the bytes in the process, so BH occupies the low-order byte of TMPB and BL the high-order byte. An 8-bit addition then adds AL and BH, the sum of which can then be routed back to either AL or BH, depending on the instruction.

The upper part of the data path is concerned with address arithmetic. Remember that on the 8088, a physical memory address is formed by adding a 16-bit address to the appropriate segment register to form a physical 20-bit address that goes out onto the address bus. The upper part contains its own register scratchpad for holding the four segment registers, the program counter, and two holding registers. It also holds the prefetch queue (described below).

The upper part contains an adder that is used to combine 16-bit offsets and segment registers. It is wired up so that the low-order 4 bits of the offset go directly to the address bus, bypassing the adder, whereas bits 4 through 15 of the offset are added to bits 0 through 15 of the segment register to form the upper 16 bits of the bus address. A small ROM is provided for common constants, for example, to add 1 to the program counter after a byte is fetched from memory.

The 8088 is pipelined. Four units are present, for prefetching instructions, decoding instructions, doing address calculations, and executing instructions. The latter three are relatively conventional, but the prefetcher is somewhat unusual. It runs completely independently of the rest of the processor. Whenever the bus is

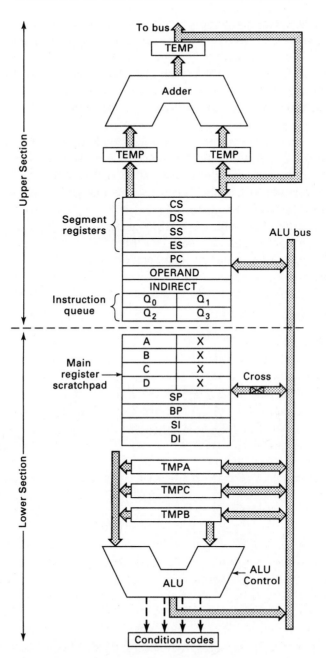

Fig. 4-31. Highly simplified diagram of the 8088 data path.

idle, the prefetcher issues a memory request to read the next byte in the instruction stream. Bytes read are buffered in a queue in the upper scratchpad. When a new instruction byte is needed, it is taken from the queue.

The size of the queue is an interesting design parameter. If it is too small, the CPU will frequently stall waiting for a byte from memory. However, being too large is also no good. The prefetcher does not know what the bytes it fetches mean; it just fetches the next one as long as there is room in the queue. In particular, after a jump, even an unconditional one, it continues fetching bytes that will not be used. If the queue is too large, the prefetcher will waste substantial bus bandwidth fetching bytes behind jump instructions. The 8086 had a 6 byte queue, but this was reduced to 4 bytes with the 8088. Other than the bus width, this is the only difference between the 8088 and the 8086.

In addition to the data path, the 8088 contains a control section that stores the microprogram and drives the data path (see Fig. 4-32). When a new conventional machine level instruction is started, its opcode byte is pulled out of the instruction queue and loaded into IR (Instruction Register).

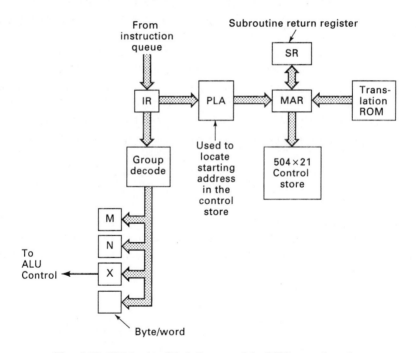

Fig. 4-32. Highly simplified diagram of the 8088 control section.

The hardware unit labeled **group decode** in Fig. 4-32 extracts information from IR and spreads it around the machine. The M and N registers get fields that are used in calculating the source and destination operand addresses. The X register holds the opcode information that is used to tell the ALU what function to perform.

The group decode also extracts the byte/word bit from the opcode. This bit controls whether ALU operations are to be 8 or 16 bits wide, and whether transfers to and from the scratchpad are to be 8 or 16 bits.

The microinstructions are 21 bits wide. A total of 504 of them are needed, and they are stored in a 504×21 ROM in the control section. When a machine instruction is fetched, a PLA converts the opcode into the starting address of the microcode that handles that instruction. Unlike our examples, in which instructions are inspected bit-by-bit, no software decoding is present. It is entirely done in hardware to save time.

The microcode is divided up into **bursts** (sequences) of up to 16 microinstructions, each burst handling one or more machine instructions or providing a general service procedure such as address calculation. Two kinds of microjumps are present: short ones, for jumping around within the current burst (4-bit address) and long ones, for jumping anywhere in the microprogram. Microprocedure calls also exist and are similar to long jumps, except that they deposit their return address in the SR (Subroutine Return) register. Microprocedures may not be nested. In all, the 504-word ROM contains about 90 bursts, averaging 5 or 6 words each.

The general strategy for interpreting many of the arithmetic and logical instructions is as follows. First a microprocedure is called to do the address calculation. This code uses the M and N registers, which already contain the source and destination register fields, where appropriate. When the address calculation microprocedure returns, the operands are available in fixed locations, and the X register contains the ALU code for this machine instruction (put there by the hardware). The main procedure now executes a data path cycle, with the operands and ALU function code coming from registers. It does not even have to know what operation it is performing. In this way, ADD, SUB, AND, OR, and quite a few other instructions can share the same microcode, even though they perform different operations. Of course, PUSH, CALL, and JMP are completely different and each requires its own microcode.

A typical 8088 microinstruction is shown in Fig. 4-33(a). It has two parts, which run in parallel. The left part, consisting of two 5-bit fields, allow every microinstruction to perform a register-to-register move. The 32 registers that can be used as source and destination are the 8- and 16-bit registers in the two scratchpads, and the temporary registers.

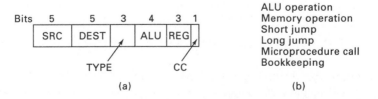

Fig. 4-33. (a) 8088 ALU microinstruction format. (b) Microinstruction types.

The right part is an 11-bit vertically-encoded microinstruction consisting of the type, ALU code, register, and condition code fields. Six microinstruction types are present, as listed in Fig. 4-33(b). They are distinguished by the TYPE field. All microinstructions have 10 bits for moving a source register to a destination register, but the format of the lower 11 bits varies slightly from type to type.

The ALU code can order a specific function to be performed, or instruct the ALU to use the code in the X register. The 3-bit register field supplies the operand, and the final bit tells whether or not the condition codes should be set. Each microinstruction executes in a single clock cycle, so it is not possible to move a value from the scratchpad into a TMP register and then use that register as an ALU operand in the same cycle.

Long jumps and microprocedure calls present a problem, as they require more bits to designate the target than are available in the microinstruction. The solution is to use a **translation ROM** that maps 5-bit addresses onto full microprogram addresses. Long jumps and calls use 5-bit addresses to indicate which target they want. Of course, this strategy means that only 32 addresses may be jumped to or called, but that is enough.

4.6.2. The Motorola 68000 Microarchitecture

As a second example of the microarchitecture of a real machine, let us take a quick look at the Motorola 68000 (Stritter and Tredennick, 1978). The 68000 is a slightly larger chip than the 8088, containing potential space for 68000 transistors (hence its name), although only about 40000 are used, the rest of the space being occupied by wires and so on.

We have mentioned the issue of whether the 68000 is a 16-bit or a 32-bit machine before. That question comes up again in the microarchitecture. The main data path is shown in Fig. 4-34.

As can be seen, the "data path" is, in fact, three separate 16-bit wide data paths, each of which can operate independently of the others, and in parallel. The left part handles the upper 16 bits of address arithmetic. The middle part takes care of the lower 16 bits of address arithmetic. The right part does operations on the data.

Each part has two buses that take data from registers and feed them into the adder or ALU. They also serve to bring ALU output back to the registers. At the top of each of the six buses is a switch, which can be opened or closed in software. By opening the switch, the buses can be electrically connected. If all six switches are open, for example, the registers in the left-hand part can be used as operands to the ALU in the right-hand part

Let us take a look at the registers, starting at the left. The box marked D0–D7 HIGH contains the upper 16 bits of the 8 data registers. The box under it contains the upper 16 bits of the 8 address registers. Next comes the supervisor mode stack pointer, two scratch registers, DT (Data Temporary), and AT (Address Temporary),

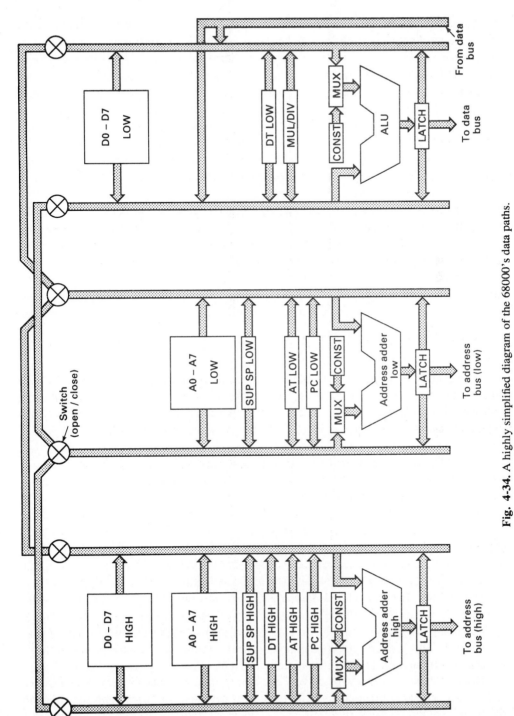

Fig. 4-34. A highly simplified diagram of the 68000's data paths.

and the upper half of the program counter. All 20 of these registers can be put onto either the left bus or the right bus, determined by the microprogram.

Both buses lead into a 16-bit adder. The adder is not a full ALU, and can only add. Since it is primarily used for address arithmetic, it does not need the ability to do anything else, and building a full ALU would have cost more chip area. Note that the left input to the adder is a multiplexer that can select either the left bus or the upper part of a constant ROM, again, under microprogram control.

The ALU output is latched, and can be put on either bus, so that results can be stored in registers. In addition, the latch can drive the external address bus to output the upper half of a 32-bit memory address.

The middle part is essentially the same, except that it does not contain the data scratchpad or the DT register. Of course, its constant ROM holds the low-order 16 bits of the constants, not the high-order bits. The output of its latch can drive the low-order bus address. Both parts can be enabled simultaneously, so a full 32-bit address can be put onto the memory bus at once.

The right-hand part is similar to the other two, containing the low-order part of the data scratchpad and the low-order part of DT. It too has a constant ROM, although this one is on the other bus and contains different constants. Still, the idea is similar.

Three new features appear here. First, the adder has been replaced with a full-function ALU meant to perform arithmetic and Boolean functions on the D registers. Since the ALU is only 16 bits wide, 32-bit operations require two data path cycles. Second, an extra scratch register is present. It is needed for multiplication and division. Third, not only is it possible to send output to the (data) bus, but unlike in the other two parts, it is also possible to accept incoming data.

Not shown in the figure, but worth mentioning, is a set of three instruction registers that hold newly arrived instructions. Three of them are needed because the 68000 is pipelined. The first one holds the instruction being executed; the second one holds the instruction being decoded; the third one holds the instruction being fetched from memory.

Also not shown is the fact that the interface to and from the data bus contains crossover switches in both directions, like the 8088, so the upper and lower bytes of a 16-bit word can be exchanged as they go to the data bus or from the data bus. This facility is needed in order to address and manipulate individual bytes.

The 68000 uses a two-level control store, with a microprogram and a nanoprogram, as shown in Fig. 4-35. The details are somewhat different than the example given in the text, but the goal is the same: to reduce the number of bits in the control store by having the microprogram determine the sequence of nanoinstructions executed, and having the nanoinstructions actually drive the gates in the data paths. The microprogram consists of 544 17-bit words, and the nanoprogram consists of 336 68-bit words, for a total of 32,096 bits. A one-level implementation with 544 68-bit words would have required 36,992 bits, a saving of 13 percent. Since this chip was definitely pushing the state-of-the-art to the limit when it was introduced, the saving was considered worthwhile. For comparison purposes, the 8088's 504×21 microprogram holds 10,584 bits.

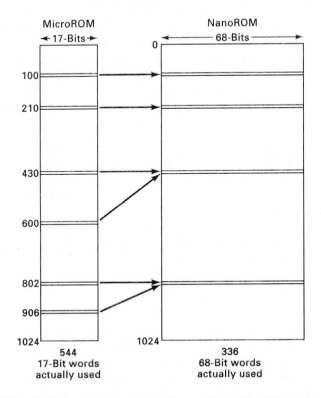

Fig. 4-35. The 68000 has a two-level control store with a microROM and nanoROM.

The ROMs for both the microprogram and nanoprogram are addressed by 10-bit numbers, allowing for up to 1024 entries in each. As we have mentioned, only 544 are needed in the former and only 336 in the latter. In both cases, the entries are scattered throughout the address space in a very careful way. In conventional nanoprogramming, the hardware first fetches a microinstruction, and this microinstruction contains the address of the nanoinstruction to use. The nanoinstruction is then fetched and executed. The process is inherently two stage, since the nanoinstruction cannot be fetched until the microinstruction is available.

The 68000 designers liked the idea of saving chip area using nanoprogramming, but did not like the idea of making the machine slower by having to wait until the microinstruction was available before starting to fetch the nanoinstruction. They used a trick to do everything in one cycle. In most cases, the nanoinstruction corresponding to the microinstruction at address n is also at address n, so they can be fetched simultaneously.

In the cases where a nanoinstruction is shared among two or more microinstructions, a transistor has been removed from the nanoinstruction decoding circuitry to map two or more addresses onto the same word. For example, address 0000011111 can be mapped onto address 0000010111 by leaving out one transistor, so the microinstructions at addresses 31 and 23 both use nanoinstruction 23. Of course, the exact choice of which instruction goes where becomes critical, but the designers had computers to help them put the puzzle together.

Two microinstruction formats are used in the 68000. Both are shown in Fig. 4-36. Microinstructions are not executed sequentially, as on the 8088. Instead, each microinstruction explicitly names its successor. This scheme is necessary given the need to have specific microinstructions map onto specific nanoinstructions.

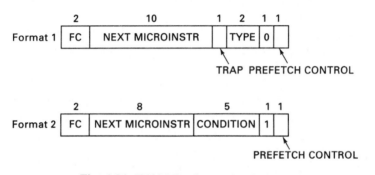

Fig. 4-36. 68000 Microinstruction formats.

Format 1 is used for all microinstructions except conditional jumps. Format 2 is used for the conditional jumps. Both have a bit that is used to begin the prefetching of the next instruction, and both have 2 bits at the other end, FC, for outputting signals to the chip's pins to tell whether a memory reference is instruction space, data space, interrupt acknowledge, or none of the above. Format 1 microinstructions contain a few miscellaneous bits and a 10-bit address telling where to fetch the next microinstruction from. Format 2 microinstructions contain a 5-bit field that selects one of 32 built-in conditions to be tested, such as the condition codes and bits in the instruction register. The test result yields 2 bits that are combined with 8 bits in the microinstruction to select one of four possible successors.

The 68-bit nanoinstructions are horizontally encoded, with 38 distinct fields, most of them 1 or 2 bits. The fields control the gating of all the registers and scratchpads onto the buses, register selection, switch control, condition code setting, ALU function, use of the constant ROMs and multiplexers, and memory operation, which is why so many bits are needed.

4.7. SUMMARY

At the microprogramming level, the CPU consists of two principal components: the data path and the control section. The data path consists primarily of a scratchpad memory and an ALU/shifter portion. A cycle consists of extracting some operands from the scratchpad, running them through the ALU/shifter, and possibly storing the results back in the scratchpad.

The control section holds the control store, where the microprogram is kept. Each microinstruction in the control store controls the gates in the data path during one microcycle. In the example given, the microcycles were divided into subcycles controlled by a clock. During the first subcycle, the microinstruction is fetched from the control store and put into an internal register. In the second subcycle, the ALU inputs are latched to keep them stable throughout the microinstruction. In the third subcycle, the ALU and shifter perform their work. Finally, in the fourth sub-cycle, the result may be stored back in the scratchpad if it is needed for use in a subsequent microinstruction.

Microinstruction sequencing can best be described as bizarre. Few machines have an explicit program counter at the microprogramming level. Instead, microin-structions generally contain the base address of their successors. This base address is typically ORed with a few status bits to produce the final address. On many machines, the base address from one microinstruction is combined with status bits resulting from the previous one to produce a jump address that does not take effect until one instruction later.

Microinstructions can be organized horizontally, with one bit per control signal, vertically, with a few fields requiring complex decoding, or something in between. Horizontal organization leads to long words and fast, highly parallel machines. Vertical organization leads to slower machines and smaller control stores.

Performance can be improved using various techniques. One of these is nanoprogramming, in which the microprogram contains (short) pointers to (long) nanoinstructions that actually control the gates. Nanoprogramming reduces the amount of chip space devoted to ROMS at the expense of slower execution.

Other ways to improve performance are variable cycle times, multiway branch-ing, pipelining, and caching. Each technique brings with it some increased com-plexity, however.

Finally, the microarchitectures of two commercially available chips, the 8088 and 68000, were discussed. The 8088 has a traditional data path, augmented by an upper section for doing arithmetic on the segment registers. It uses 21-bit vertical microinstructions. The 68000 has three independent 16-bit data paths, two for the address and one for the data. It uses a two-level control store with 17-bit microin-structions and 68-bit horizontal nanoinstructions.

PROBLEMS

1. Describe some of the strengths and weaknesses of microprogramming.

2. Translate the following Pascal function to Mac-1 assembly language.

```
function min(i, j, k: SmallInt): SmallInt;
var m: SmallInt;
begin
  if i < j then m := i else m := j;
  if k < m then m := k;
  min := m
end;
```

The type *SmallInt* is the same subrange as in the text.

3. Translate the Pascal statement

   if $i < j$ **then goto** 100;

   to Mac-1 assembly language. Both i and j are 16-bit two's complement integers. Be careful: If $i = 32767$ and $j = -10$, a subtraction will give an undetected overflow.

4. In Fig. 4-11(b) we reload K in the line labeled L4. The two preceding statements ensure that K is in AC after all. Why bother loading it again?

5. Compute the execution time in microinstructions for each Mac-1 instruction running on Mic-1.

6. Repeat the preceding problem but now for Mic-2.

7. Try to compile the Pascal statement

   $n := a[i]$

   directly to Mic-1 instructions, bypassing the Mac-1 level altogether. Discuss your attempt.

8. Consider a possible revision of Mic-1 in which the two sequencing fields, COND and ADDR, are removed, giving 22-bit microinstructions. Microjumps are now handled by distinct 22-bit microinstructions. The ALU N and Z bits are also latched, to make them available to a subsequent microjump. Compare the size of the original Mic-1 program with the one needed for this new design.

9. Do the following two Mic-1 statements perform exactly the same function? Explain.

   $a := a + a$; **if** n **then goto** 0;
   $a := lshift(a)$; **if** n **then goto** 0;

10. Your only listing of a key Mic-1 microprogram was accidentally put into the automatic document feeder for the paper shredder instead of the photocopier next to it. You will now have to reconstruct the source program from a core dump. In the course of the disassembly you come across the binary number

    1100100000010001100100000001000

    Rewrite it in assembly language.

11. How many bit patterns are there for the following Mic-1 instruction?

$ac := mbr + a$; **if** n **then goto** 100;

12. Imagine that you work for a company that is selling a machine with Mic-1 as level 1 and Mac-1 as level 2. The semiconductor vendor that normally supplies your chips has just announced a big clearance sale on one's complement ALUs. Your purchasing department jumped at the chance and bought a whole carload of them. Will the microprogram of Fig. 4-16 continue to work with a one's complement ALU instead of the original two's complement one? In the new machine negative numbers are to be represented in one's complement, of course.

13. If main memory reads and writes took three microinstructions instead of two on Mic-1, would the microprogram size be affected, and if so, by how much?

14. The COND field in the Mic-1 word is 2 bits, which gives four distinct codes. If one of these codes were needed for something else, for example, testing a newly implemented ALU overflow status bit, which of the existing four codes would you recommend sacrificing?

15. Propose adding a simple facility to Mic-1 for calling micro-level procedures. Some way must be found to both call and return from microprocedures, which may not be nested (i.e., a microprocedure may not call another microprocedure). You may modify the Mic-1 architecture but try to minimize the changes needed.

16. Microarchitects are constantly faced with trade-offs between elegance (i.e., ortho-gonality of fields) and control store size. Suppose that you had the job of modifying Mic-1 to add a bit to COND or ADDR and take a bit away from one of the other 11 fields. Make a suggestion of where to find the bit without impairing the functionality of Mic-1 too much.

17. Are there places in the microprogram for Mic-2 where the microprogrammer was forced to choose between time versus memory in a way not required in the micropro-gram for Mic-1? If so, give an example.

18. The microinstructions of Mic-2 are much more compact than those of Mic-1 (12 bits versus 32 bits). Can you envision a Mic-3 with still shorter microinstructions? Dis-cuss.

19. The president of the Nano-Micro-Milli Memory Corporation has been so impressed by the sales of their nanostores that he has considered adding a picostore to the product line. The picostore would be referenced by the nanostore, the same way the nanostore is referenced by the control store; that is, each nanoword would contain the address of a picoinstruction just as the control store contains nanoinstruction addresses. You are the Vice-President in Charge of Getting Rid of Stupid Ideas. What do you think of this proposal?

20. If we were to implement the program of Fig. 4-16 using nanoprogramming, how many bits would the control store plus nanostore require together? Compare this to the number of control store bits in the original design.

21. Suppose we had an *n*-stage pipeline instead of the 5-stage pipeline discussed in the text. What would the jump penalty be then?

22. Consider a machine on which 20 percent of the instructions are conditional jumps and another 10 percent are loop jumps. The conditional jumps can be predicted with 60 percent accuracy and the loop jumps can be predicted with 90 percent accuracy. The penalty for guessing wrong is four cycles. There is no penalty for unconditional jumps or correct guesses. What is the efficiency of the pipeline on this machine?

23. In Fig. 4-28(b), what is the address of the word whose contents is 2131?

24. A cache system has a 95 percent hit ratio, an access time of 100 nsec on a cache hit and an access time of 800 nsec on a cache miss. What is the effective access time?

25. A cache is being designed for a computer with 2^{32} bytes of memory. The cache will have 2K slots and use a 16-byte block. Compute for both an associative cache and a direct-mapped cache how many bytes the cache will occupy.

26. At first glance, the presence or absence of caching does not seem to have anything to do with the decision of whether to map the I/O registers into the memory address space or not. Give it some more thought and see if you can find any potential problems. (*Hint:* If you cannot think of any problems, keep on thinking.)

27. The 68030 has on-chip instruction and data caches. It also has a special kind of bus cycle, read-modify-write, for reading and modifying a memory word in a single indivisible action. Is there any interaction between these two features? Explain.

28. Write a Mac-1 assembly language procedure to multiply two signed integers whose product fits in 16 bits.

29. Write a test program in Mac-1 assembly language to verify that the microprogram is correctly functioning. Check out each instruction with a series of known operands to see if the known result occurs. Such programs are widely used by computer repairmen to try to pinpoint hardware failures.

30. The manufacturer of the Mac-1 has just received a telegram from its most important customer. The telegram reads: "Must have new instruction to shift AC left *n* bits, where *n* is low-order 4 bits of instruction. Need tomorrow morning 8 A.M. Send new microprogram by telegram. Hurry." Your job is to implement the microcode for the shift.

31. Write a Mic-1 simulator in your favorite assembly language. The simulator should read in the microprogram as a series of 32-character (0 and 1) input lines, followed by a blank line. Then it reads in the Mac-1 program, 16 bits per line and runs it.

5

THE CONVENTIONAL MACHINE LEVEL

This chapter introduces the conventional machine level (level 2) and discusses many aspects of its architecture. Historically, level 2 was developed before any of the other levels, and it is still widely (and incorrectly) regarded as "the" machine language. This situation has come about because on many machines the microprogram is in a read-only memory, which means that users (as opposed to the machine's manufacturer) cannot write programs for level 1. Furthermore, even on machines that are user microprogrammable, the enormous complexity of the level 1 architecture is enough to scare off all but the most stouthearted programmers. In addition, because no machines have protection hardware at level 1, it is not possible to allow one person to debug new microprograms while anyone else is using the machine. This characteristic further inhibits user microprogramming.

5.1. EXAMPLES OF THE CONVENTIONAL MACHINE LEVEL

Rather than attempt to define rigorously what the conventional machine level is (which is probably impossible anyway), we will introduce this level by looking at our running examples, first Intel, then Motorola. The purpose of studying two existing CPU families is to show how the ideas discussed here can be applied to the "real world." These machines will be compared and contrasted in various ways to show how different designers make different choices.

You should not draw the conclusion that the remainder of the book is about programming the Intel and Motorola CPUs. Far from it. These machines will be used to illustrate the idea of designing a computer as a series of levels. Various features of their respective architectures will be examined and some information about programming them will be introduced where necessary. However, no attempt will be made to provide a complete description. For a thorough discussion of all the details of these machines, please consult the manufacturer's publications.

Finally, this chapter deals primarily with the architecture and instructions used by ordinary user (i.e., application) programs. Architectural aspects and instructions mostly of interest to operating system writers will be omitted or deferred until our discussion of this topic in Chap. 6.

5.1.1. The Intel 8088/80286/80386 Family

It is fitting to start our discussion of the conventional machine with the Intel 8088, the brain of the IBM PC and its clones, and as such, undoubtedly the most widely used CPU in the world. At the conventional machine level, the 8088 and 8086 are identical, so everything we say about the 8088 also applies to the 8086. The 8088 can address 2^{20} bytes, numbered consecutively starting at 0, as shown in Fig. 5-1.

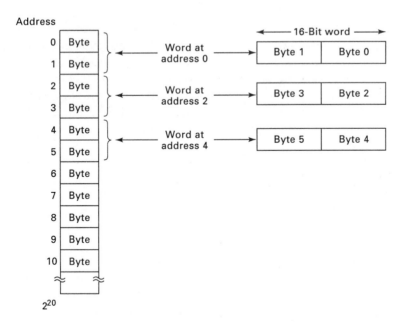

Fig. 5-1. The 8088 memory architecture.

Instructions either operate on these 8-bit bytes, or on 16-bit words. Words need not begin on an even byte, although on the 8086 it is slightly more efficient if words begin at an even byte.

With 2^{20} bytes of memory, the 8088 really needs 20-bit addresses to address memory. Since the registers and everything else about the machine uses 16-bit words, 20-bit numbers are highly inconvenient. To solve this problem, the CPU designers resorted to a *kludge* (computer jargon for an awkward, inelegant way to do something). The kludge consisted of introducing four **segment registers** (code, data, stack, and extra), each one holding a memory address that points to the base of a 64K segment.

Each segment register points somewhere within the 2^{20} byte address space, as shown in Fig. 5-2. All instruction fetches are made relative to the **code segment** register. For example, if this register points at address 96000 and the program counter has the value 1204, then the next instruction will be fetched from address 97204. With this value of the code segment register, instructions located at addresses in the range 96000 to 161,535 can be accessed. To access an instruction outside this range, the code segment register must be changed.

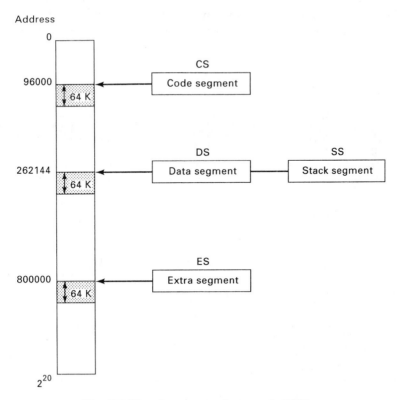

Fig. 5-2. Use of segment registers on the 8088.

Similarly, the **data segment** and **stack segment** registers exist to access the data and the stack segments, respectively. Finally, there is an **extra segment** register that is used as a spare as needed.

This scheme means that at any instant, at most 256K of memory can be accessed without changing a segment register. Some compilers limit programs to 64K for the program text (i.e., the instructions) and another 64K for the combined data and stack, in order to avoid the overhead associated with constantly loading and storing the segment registers or using the extra segment register.

In theory, the segment registers should be 20 bits wide in order to point to an address anywhere within the 2^{20} byte address space. However, as we mentioned above, the 8088 is ill-equipped to deal with 20-bit numbers. This problem was solved by requiring all segment registers to point only to addresses that are multiples of 16 bytes, so that the low-order 4 bits are zero and do not have to be stored. Thus the segment registers contain only the upper 16 bits of the 20-bit addresses.

The 8088 has 14 registers, all 16 bits, but all different. They are listed in Fig. 5-3. AX is primarily used for arithmetic calculations. For example, to compute the sum of two integers, a program can load one of them into AX, then add the second one to AX, and finally store AX in memory. The other registers can also be used, but the instructions for doing so are longer and slower than those using AX.

BX is typically used to hold pointers into memory. CX is used to hold the counter in loop instructions. To iterate through a loop n times, CX is loaded with n. On each iteration, CX is decremented. When it gets to zero, the loop stops.

DX is used as an extension to AX for multiplication and division instructions, where it holds the upper half of a 32-bit product or the upper half of a 32-bit dividend.

Each of these 16-bit registers consists of a lower and an upper half, which can be individually addressed. When used this way, they form a set of eight 1-byte registers that can be used with instructions that manipulate 1-byte quantities. The use of the registers in this manner is a remnant of the way the old 8-bit 8080 worked.

The SI and DI registers are used for string operations. A typical string operation requires a source address, specified by the SI register within the data segment, and a destination, specified by the DI register within the extra segment. The instruction might, for example, move some number of bytes from the source to the destination.

The BP and SP registers are normally used to address the stack. BP points to the bottom of the current stack frame and SP points to the top. A variable local to the current procedure is normally addressed by giving its offset from BP (because it is not possible to specify addresses relative to SP).

Next come the four segment registers, described earlier, followed by the program counter, which points to the next instruction (relative to the start of the code segment).

The last two registers are the IP (Instruction Pointer) and FLAGS registers, which on most other machines are called the program counter and PSW (Program

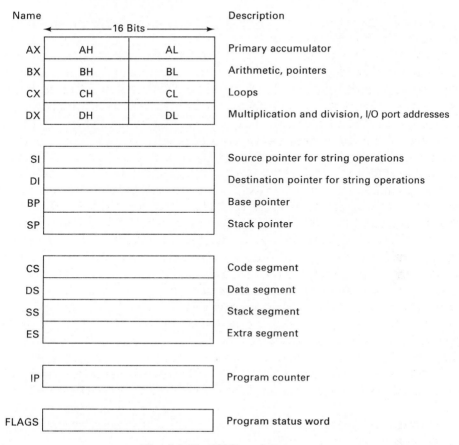

Name			Description
	← 16 Bits →		
AX	AH	AL	Primary accumulator
BX	BH	BL	Arithmetic, pointers
CX	CH	CL	Loops
DX	DH	DL	Multiplication and division, I/O port addresses
SI			Source pointer for string operations
DI			Destination pointer for string operations
BP			Base pointer
SP			Stack pointer
CS			Code segment
DS			Data segment
SS			Stack segment
ES			Extra segment
IP			Program counter
FLAGS			Program status word

Fig. 5-3. The 8088's registers.

Status Word). The program counter points to the next instruction to be executed. We have seen it before, and there is little else to say about it.

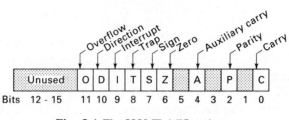

Fig. 5-4. The 8088 FLAGS register.

On the other hand, the FLAGS register (see Fig. 5-4) is new. It is not really a

	Instruction	Description
Moves	MOV dst, src	Move src to dst
	PUSH src	Push src onto the stack
	POP dst	Pop from the stack to dst
	XCHG dst1, dst2	Exchange dst1 and dst2
	LEA dst, src	Load effective address of src into dst
	LDS dst, src	Load data segment register and dst using src
	LES dst, src	Load extra segment register and dst using src
Arithmetic	ADD dst, src	Add src to dst
	SUB dst, src	Subtract src from dst
	MUL src	Multiply AX by src (unsigned)
	IMUL src	Multiply AX by src (signed)
	DIV src	Divide DX:AX by src (unsigned)
	IDIV src	Divide DX:AX by src (signed)
	ADC dst, src	Add src to dst, then add carry bit
	SBB dst, src	Subtract src from dst, then subtract carry bit
	INC dst	Add 1 to dst
	DEC dst	Subtract 1 from dst
	NEG dst	Negate dst (subtract it from 0)
BCD	DAA	Decimal adjust
	DAS	Decimal adjust for subtraction
	AAA	ASCII adjust for addition
	AAS	ASCII adjust for subtraction
	AAM	ASCII adjust for multiplication
	AAD	ASCII adjust for division.
Boolean	AND dst, src	Boolean AND of src into dst
	OR src, dst	Boolean OR of src into dst
	XOR src, dst	Boolean exclusive OR of src into dst
	NOT dst	Replace dst with its 1's complement
Shift Rotate	SAL/SAR dst, count	Shift dst left/right count bits
	SHL/SHR dst, count	Logical shift left/right by count
	ROL/ROR dst, count	Rotate dst left/right count bits
	RCL/RCR dst, count	Rotate dst through carry bits
Test Compare	TST src1, src2	Boolean AND the operands and set FLAGS
	CMP src1, src2	Compare src1 to src2 and set FLAGS

Fig. 5-5. The Intel 8088 instruction set.

Control transfer	JMP addr	Jump to addr
	Jxx addr	Conditional jumps based on FLAGS register
	JCXZ addr	Jump if CX is 0
	CALL addr	Call procedure at addr
	RET	Return from procedure
	IRET	Return from interrupt
	LOOPxx	Loop until condition met
	INT addr	Initiate a software interrupt
	INTO	Interrupt if overflow bit is set

Strings	LODS	Load string
	STOS	Store string
	MOVS	Move String
	CMPS	Compare two strings
	SCAS	Scan strings

Condition codes	STC	Set carry bit in FLAGS register
	CLC	Clear carry bit in FLAGS register
	CMC	Complement carry bit in FLAGS register
	STD	Set direction bit in FLAGS register
	CLD	Clear direction bit in FLAGS register
	STI	Set interrupt bit in FLAGS register
	CLI	Clear interrupt bit in FLAGS register
	PUSHF	Push the FLAGS register onto the stack
	POPF	Pop the FLAGS register from the stack
	LAHF	Load AH from FLAGS register
	SAHF	Store AH in FLAGS register

Miscellaneous	CWD	Convert word in AX to double word in DX:AX
	CBW	Convert byte in AL to word in AX
	XLAT	Translate AL according to a table
	NOP	No operation
	HLT	Halt
	ESC	Escape to (start) floating point coprocessor
	IN port	Input a byte or word from port
	OUT port	Output a byte or word to port
	WAIT	Wait for an interrupt

Fig. 5-5. (cont.)

normal register, but a collection of bits that are set, cleared, and tested by various instructions. Briefly, the bits have the following meanings. The D bit determines the direction of string operations. The I bit enables interrupts. The T bit enables traps for tracing, which is used for debugging.

The remaining bits are often called the **condition codes** because they are set or cleared by various instructions depending on the different conditions that can arise (result negative, zero, and so on). The O bit is set when an arithmetic result overflows. The S bit is set by arithmetic instructions, 1 for negative results, 0 for positive results. Similarly, the Z bit is set to 1 for zero results and cleared to 0 for nonzero results. The A and C bits represent the carries out of the middle and end of the operands respectively. Finally, the P bit gives the parity (odd or even) of the result of an arithmetic instruction. Seven of the bits are unused on the 8088, but some of these are used on its successors.

The 8088 instruction set is listed in Fig. 5-5. Many of the instructions reference one or two operands, either in registers or in memory. For example, the INC instruction increments (adds 1 to) its operand. The ADD instruction adds the source to the destination. Some of the instructions have several closely related variants. For example, the shift instructions can shift either left or right, and can treat the sign bit specially or not. Most of the instructions have a variety of different encodings, depending on the nature of the operands.

In Fig. 5-5, the *src* fields are sources of information, and are not changed. In contrast, the *dst* fields are destinations, and are normally modified by the instruction. There are rules about what is allowed as a source or a destination, which vary somewhat erratically from instruction to instruction, but we will not go into them here. Most instructions have two variants, one that operates on 16-bit words and one that operates on 8-bit bytes. These are distinguished by a bit in the instruction.

For convenience, we have divided the instructions into several groups. The first group contains instructions that move data around the machine, among registers, memory, and the stack. The second group does arithmetic, both signed and unsigned. For multiplication and division, the 32-bit product or dividend is stored in AX (low-order part) and DX (high-order part).

The third group does binary-coded decimal (BCD) arithmetic, treating each byte as two 4-bit **nibbles**. Each nibble holds one decimal digit (0 to 9). Bit combinations 1010 to 1111 are not used. Thus a 16-bit integer can hold a decimal number from 0 to 9999. While this form of storage is inefficient, it eliminates the need to convert decimal input to binary and then back to decimal for output. These instructions are used for doing arithmetic on the BCD numbers.

The Boolean and shift/rotate instructions manipulate the bits in a word or byte in various ways. Several combinations are provided.

The next two groups deal with testing and comparing, and then jumping based on the results. The results of test and compare instructions are stored in various bits of the FLAGS register. Jxx stands for a set of instructions that conditionally jump, depending on the results of the previous comparison (i.e., bits in FLAGS).

The 8088 has several instructions for loading, storing, moving, comparing, and scanning strings of characters or words. These instructions can be prefixed by a special byte called REP, which cause them to be repeated until a certain condition is met, such as CX, which is decremented after each iteration, until reaching 0. In this way, arbitrary blocks of data can be moved, compared, and so on.

The last group is a hodge-podge of instructions that do not fit in anywhere else. These include conversions, I/O, and stopping the CPU.

The 8088 (and also the 80286 and 80386) have a number of instruction **prefixes**, of which we have mentioned one, REP, already. Each of these prefixes is a special byte that can precede most instructions. REP causes the instruction following it to be repeated, as mentioned above. LOCK reserves the bus for the entire instruction, to permit multiprocessor synchronization. Other prefixes are used to force an instruction to fetch its operand from the stack or extra segment, instead of the data segment.

The Intel 80286

Having finished looking at the 8088, let us now turn to the 80286. At the conventional machine level, the 80286 processor is very similar to the 8088. The principal differences as far as user programs are concerned are summarized in Fig. 5-6. To make it easy to run 8088 programs on the 80286, Intel equipped the chip with two modes. In **real address mode** (usually just called real mode) the 80286 pretends that it is an 8088, and does (almost) everything the way an 8088 would have done it. In **protected virtual address mode** (usually just called protected mode), it makes available some additional features not present on the 8088.

8088	80286
Real mode	Real and protected modes
1 MB address space	16384 segments of up to 64K
Segment registers hold pointers	Segment registers hold selectors
No protection mechanism	Protection using rings
No multiprogramming support	Multiprogramming supported
Basic instructions	Basic, extended, and control instructions

Fig. 5-6. Principal differences between the 8088 and 80286 for user programs.

In both modes, the 80286 has the same 14 registers that are shown in Fig. 5-3. The registers have the same lengths and perform the same functions as on the 8088. In addition, all the instructions listed in Fig. 5-5 work on the 80286 in both modes, and in all but a handful of cases have exactly the same semantics. The only differences are in implementation-defined features, such as what happens if you push the SP register onto the stack. The 8088 first decrements SP and then pushes the new value, whereas the 80286 first saves SP and then pushes this saved value. The reason for this difference is due to changes in the microcode. On the whole, nearly all well-behaved 8088 programs will run unmodified on the 80286 in both modes.

Nevertheless, the two modes are not identical. The biggest change at this level is in the memory addressing. In real mode the 80286 has a linear 1M address space, just like the 8088. In protected mode, it has 16,384 segments, each up to 64K bytes long. During the design of the 80286, the question arose of how to allow programs to use this additional memory without radically changing the machine.

One approach would have been to stick to the design of Fig. 5-2, except increase the size of the segment registers to accommodate the larger address space. This approach was not taken as it would have required an awkward size for the segment registers.

Instead a more sophisticated method was used. The segment registers were kept at 16 bits, but instead of representing 20-bit pointers, in protected mode they represent indices (called **selectors**) into system tables. Thus loading the value 2 into DS does not mean that the data segment begins at address 32, but rather that the data segment is pointed to by the second entry in a certain table. Each entry contains a 24-bit pointer and other information. We will study the 80286's and 80386's addressing in detail when we come to virtual memory in Chap. 6.

The 80286 in protected mode has other differences from the 8088 as well. The use of the word "protected" in the name of the mode suggests that it provides some protection. This observation is correct. It is possible to initialize the segment tables in such a way that when the 80286 is used for a multiprogramming system, each process can be prevented from accessing segments belonging to another process. Since this mechanism is so closely tied to the virtual memory, we will defer our discussion of it until Chap. 6 as well.

In addition to the 8088 instruction set, the 80286 has a few additional instructions that the designers forgot the first time around. These are listed in Fig. 5-7.

Instruction	Description
PUSHA	Push all the registers onto the stack
POPA	Pop all the registers from the stack
ENTER count,depth	Set up the stack for procedure entry
LEAVE	Clean up the stack for procedure exit
BOUND reg,addr	Array bounds checking
VERR/VERW	Verify if a segment is readable/writable

Fig. 5-7. Additional instructions present on the 80286.

Most of these instructions make it possible to perform key operations in fewer instructions than on the 8088. Furthermore, some of the more baroque rules about which operands are allowed for which instructions have been relaxed. For example, the PUSH instruction can now have a constant as operand. On the 8088, PUSH can only have register and memory operands, but not constants. This change makes passing constants as parameters to called procedures more efficient. The PUSHA instruction pushes AX, CX, DX, BX, SP, BP, SI, and DI onto the stack, in that order. POPA retrieves the stored registers. These instructions are typically used by interrupt routines to save the state of the machine before handling an interrupt.

The ENTER and LEAVE instructions perform actions that are needed when a procedure is entered or exited. By making special instructions to carry out all the actions at once, procedure entry and exit can be made faster.

BOUND does array bounds checking. Like all the other new instructions, it is provided as an optimization, since the same job can be done by a sequence of 8088 instructions, only more slowly.

Finally VERR and VERW are related to the 80286's segmentation. They allow a program to test the waters before jumping in. By checking first, a program can avoid getting a segmentation error.

The Intel 80386

The 80286 has two fundamental limitations that led Intel to develop the 80386. First, the 80286 is a 16-bit CPU, with 16-bit registers, operands, and instructions. For many applications, a 32-bit CPU is needed. Second, the memory model consisting of many 64K segments is a major nuisance. The problem is not in the number of segments (16,384), which is more than adequate, but in the small size of the segments (64K). The 80386 eliminates these problems, and at the same time adds some additional features that make the 80386 considerably more powerful than the 80286. In addition, it is also much faster.

When designing the 80386, Intel went to great effort to maintain compatibility with the 8088 and 80286, in order to allow 80386s to run existing 8088 and 80286 binary programs. The major differences between the 80286 and 80386 visible to user programs are shown in Fig. 5-8.

Real mode and protected mode are both available on the 80386, and operate pretty much as they do on the 80286. New, however, is **virtual mode,** which is an intermediate form between real and protected modes. Like real mode, it is intended for running old 8088 binary programs.

The difference is that in real mode, a program can do anything that an 8088 can do, including change the segment registers, perform I/O, and so on. This gives it more than enough power to crash the system. In virtual mode, all the normal instructions work as they do on the 8088, but the instructions that can potentially bring the system down, such as I/O, are not executed. Instead they cause traps to the operating system, which can then emulate (simulate) them. As a result, it is possible to have multiple 8088 programs running at the same time, each one protected from the others, and the operating system protected from all of them.

80286	**80386**
Real and protected modes	Real, virtual, and protected modes
16,384 Segments of up to 64K	16,384 Segments of up to 4G
4 Segment registers	6 Segment registers
8– and 16–Bit arithmetic	8–, 16–, and 32–Bit arithmetic
16–Bit registers	32–Bit registers
16–Bit address modes	16– and 32–Bit address modes
8 Prefixes	12 Prefixes
(Not present)	Several new instructions

Fig. 5-8. Principal differences between the 80286 and the 80386 for user programs.

Many 80386-based computers run UNIX as the native operating system, and provide the users with multiple windows. In one or more windows, the user can run old MS-DOS programs. This trick is accomplished by having UNIX switch the 80386 to virtual mode just before starting up an MS-DOS program. All of that program's attempts to do I/O, write on the video RAM, and so on, cause traps to UNIX, which then carries out the desired work and returns control to the MS-DOS program. In this way several old MS-DOS programs can run simultaneously in a UNIX environment and access UNIX files.

One of the main goals of the 80386 was getting rid of the 64K limit per segment, yet retaining compatibility with 80286 programs that expect 64K segments. This seeming impossibility was accomplished in a clever way. Both the 80286 and 80386 use selectors in the segment registers. Each selector is essentially just an index into one of two 8K tables of segment descriptors. Each descriptor contains the segment's address, size, protection code, and other information.

On the 80386, an unused bit in each descriptor has been taken over to indicate whether it is a 16- or 32-bit segment. In 16-bit segments, the maximum address is 64K, and all operations on words manipulate 16-bit words. In 32-bit segments, the maximum address is 4G (2^{32} bytes, about 4 billion), and all operations on words manipulate 32-bit words. It is also possible on an instruction-by-instruction basis to override these defaults by inserting a prefix before the instruction. It is permitted for a program to use a mixture of 16-bit and 32-bit segments.

As a consequence of this architecture, an 80386 program can address a maximum of 16,384 segments of up to 4G each, for a total address space of 2^{46} bytes. This address space is greater than or equal to that of nearly all mainframes and supercomputers. The days of being able to tell a microcomputer from a supercomputer by seeing which one has a bigger address space belong to the past.

One obvious consequence of having an address space of 2^{46} bytes is that pointers have to be at least 46 bits long, a large and inconvenient number. For most

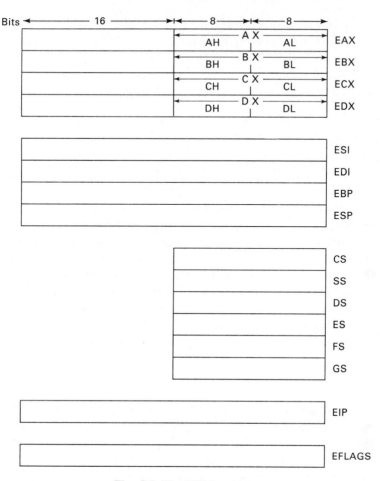

Fig. 5-9. The 80386 registers.

applications this is overkill. Instead, many 80386 programs simply use a single 2^{32} byte segment. This model is often affectionately known as "Motorola mode" because the 680x0's address space consists of a single 2^{32} byte segment.

When using multiple segments, an 80386 program is still restricted to a single segment for code, data, and stack at any instant, just as on the 8088. Also like the 8088, the extra segment register is provided to make it possible to temporarily access another segment. On the 80386, two additional segment registers, FS and GS, have been provided to reduce the number of times segment registers must be loaded. In this way, up to six segments can be accessed without having to change any of the segment registers.

In addition to providing more address space, the other major advance of the 80386 is its ability to do 8-, 16-, and 32-bit arithmetic. The registers have been extended to 32 bits as shown in Fig. 5-9. The extended registers have the same names as the old 16-bit registers, but with an "E" stuck on the front. In a 32-bit segment, an instruction to move a word to AX/EAX will move it to EAX, unless overridden by a special prefix.

Although it was not necessary, Intel decided to change the way instructions address memory on the 80386. In 16-bit segments, everything works the same way as on the 8088 and 80286. However, in 32-bit segments, a whole new set of addressing possibilities (addressing modes) is present. These include efficient ways to access array elements, and other features. We will look at the subject of addressing modes in detail later in this chapter. For the time being it is sufficient to realize that instructions need addressing mode fields to specify where their operands are—registers, memory, the stack, or elsewhere.

The introduction of the FS and GS segment registers required the introduction of two new prefixes, to specify that the next instruction use them instead of the default (usually DS). Furthermore, two prefixes were also introduced to allow an individual instruction in a 16-bit segment to use a 32-bit address or operand, and vice versa. The complete list of prefixes is given in Fig. 5-10.

Prefix	8088	80286	80386	Description
REP	X	X	X	Repeat until CX = 0
REPZ	X	X	X	Repeat until Z flag set
REPNZ	X	X	X	Repeat until Z flag cleared
LOCK	X	X	X	Lock external bus
CS	X	X	X	Use code segment
SS	X	X	X	Use stack segment
DS	X	X	X	Use data segment
ES	X	X	X	Use extra segment
FS			X	Use F segment
GS			X	Use G segment
Operand size			X	Invert operand size (16 or 32)
Address size			X	Invert address size (16 or 32)

Fig. 5-10. 8088, 80286, and 80386 prefixes.

The last item in our list is the presence of a handful of new instructions for bit testing, data conversion, moving, and other things. These new instructions are listed in Fig. 5-11.

In general, these instructions are much more exotic than the ones added to the 80286. The BSF and BSR instructions look at their operands, hunting for 0 bits and setting the FLAGS accordingly. BTx is a group of four instructions that can test,

Instruction	Description
BSF/BSR	Bit scan forward/reverse
BTx	Bit test operations
CDQ/CWDE	Convert one length to another
MOVSX	Move with sign extension
MOVZX	Move with zero extension
SETcc	Set byte from condition codes (flags)
SHLD/SHRD	Shift left/right double
Lxx	Load selector into FS, GS, or SS

Fig. 5-11. Additional instructions present on the 80386.

set, clear, and complement individual bits in a word, without disturbing the other bits. CWDE and CDQ convert a word to a double word and a double word to a quad word (8 bytes), respectively, by doing sign extension. The two MOVxx instructions move small data items to longer ones, with or without sign extension.

SETcc is actually a group of 30 instructions, all of which store a byte at the destination. The byte contains 0 or 1, depending on the state of various condition code bits. This instruction is sometimes of use to compiler writers when evaluating Boolean expressions.

Finally, the SHxD instructions are 32-bit shifts, and Lxx is used for loading segment registers.

5.1.2. The Motorola 68000/68020/68030 Family

As we have pointed out before, the Motorola 68000, 68020, and 68030 are much more alike than are the Intel 8088, 80286, and 80386. That also holds for the conventional machine level. The memory architecture of all three processors, for example, is identical. It is shown in Fig. 5-12. Motorola calls a 16-bit quantity a word and a 32-bit quantity a long word (instead of calling them words and double-words, as does Intel).

It is worth comparing Fig. 5-12 to Fig. 5-1. Both have 16-bit words and 32-bit long or double words (on the 80386), but the byte ordering is different. The Intel CPUs are little endian, that is, they number the bytes starting at the little (low-order) end. The Motorola CPUs are big endians. The two approaches are equally valid, but connecting them in a network is a source of enormous grief.

All the 680x0 processors have 32-bit addresses, so the theoretical address space for all of them goes to 2^{32} bytes. However, on the 68000, there is a one-to-one mapping between the physical memory and the addresses programs see, so the logical limit is the same as the physical limit, namely, 16M. The 68020 and 68030 do

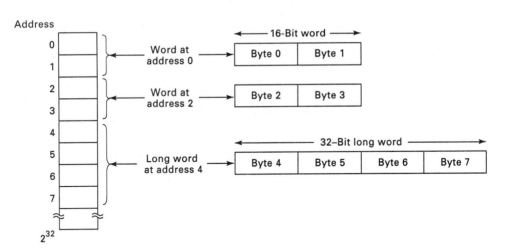

Fig. 5-12. Addressing structure of the 680x0's main memory.

not have this restriction, so programs on them can indeed reference the entire 32-bit address space.

All of the 680x0 machines have 17 32-bit registers available to user programs and a 16-bit register for holding status bits (like the Intel FLAGS register). Eight of the 32-bit registers, A0 to A7, are address registers and normally hold addresses of variables and data structures located in main memory. A0 to A6 have no dedicated function, but A7 is the stack pointer.

The eight 32-bit data registers, D0 to D7, are general-purpose data registers. Most calculations take place using them. They can be used for 8-, 16-, and 32-bit operands. The low-order 8 and 16 bit parts of the D registers do not have special names, as do their Intel counterparts. The 17th 32-bit register is the program counter. The registers are shown in Fig. 5-13.

Like the Intel CPUs, the 680x0 CPUs have a register containing status bits and flags. This register, shown in Fig. 5-14, contains 16 bits. The low-order byte contains 5 bits that are set by most instructions, depending on the results of the operation just performed. The C bit records the carry out of the leftmost bit. The O bit detects overflow. The Z bit is set when the result is zero. The N bit is set when the result is negative. The X bit is a minor variant of the carry bit.

The high-order byte of the status register is used by the operating system to control the machine. It contains fields that deal with the CPU state, interrupts, and tracing. This byte is not used by user programs.

The 68000 instruction set available to user programs is shown in Fig. 5-15. Instructions that only the operating system can execute are not listed. The notation *src* indicates an operand that is not changed, whereas *dst* indicates one that is. Except for the MOVE instruction, if an instruction has both *src* and *dst*, one must refer to a register. Only MOVE can have two memory addresses as operands.

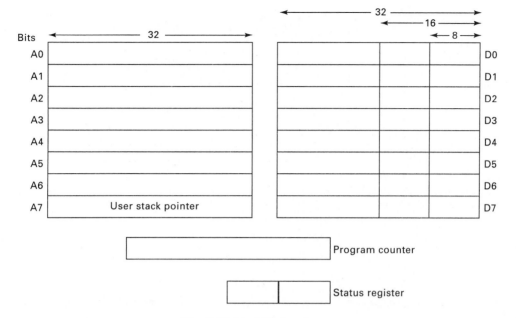

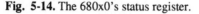

Fig. 5-13. The 680x0 registers.

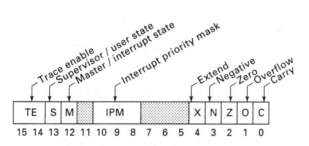

Fig. 5-14. The 680x0's status register.

Note that Motorola chose a different operand order than Intel for its symbolic (i.e., ASCII) assembly language. On the 680x0, the instruction

ADD x,y

means add x to y, whereas on all the Intel machines it means add y to x.

Another notational point is the use of the sharp sign (#) in some instructions, such as

ADDI #n, dst

It indicates that the operand must be an integer constant. An and Dn are used to

	Instruction	Description
Moves	MOVE src, dst	Move src to dst
	MOVEA src, An	Move src to An
	MOVEM src, dst	Move multiple registers to/from memory
	MOVEP src, dst	Move data to/from alternate memory bytes
	MOVEQ #n, dst	Move the constant n to dst (−129 < n < 128)
	LEA src, An	Load effective address of src to An
	PEA src	Push effective address onto the stack
	CLR dst	Move zero to dst
	EXG dst1, dst2	Exchange two 32-bit registers
Arithmetic	ADD src, dst	Add src to dst
	ADDA src, An	Add src to An
	ADDI #n, dst	Add the constant n to dst
	ADDQ #n, dst	Add the constant n to dst (0 < n < 9)
	ADDX src, dst	Add src and extend bit to dst
	SUB src, dst	Subtract src from dst
	SUBA src, An	Subtract src from An
	SUBI #n, dst	Subtract the constant n from dst
	SUBQ #n, dst	Subtract the constant n from dst (0 < n < 9)
	SUBX src, dst	Subtract src and extend bit from dst
	MULU src, Dn	Multiply Dn by src (unsigned)
	MULS src, Dn	Multiply Dn by src (signed)
	DIVU src, dst	Divide dst by src (unsigned)
	DIVS src, dst	Divide dst by src (signed)
	NEG dst	Negate dst (subtract it from 0)
	NEGX dst	Subtract dst and the extend bit from 0
BCD	ABCD src, dst	Add binary coded decimal numbers
	SBCD src, dst	Subtract binary coded decimal numbers
	NBCD dst	Negate binary coded decimal number
Boolean	AND src, dst	Boolean AND of src into dst
	ANDI #n, dst	Boolean AND of the constant n into dst
	OR src, dst	Boolean OR of src into dst
	ORI #n, dst	Boolean OR of the constant n into dst
	EOR src, dst	Boolean exclusive OR of src into dst
	EORI #n, dst	Boolean exclusive OR of the constant n into dst
	NOT dst	Replace dst with its 1s complement

Fig. 5-15. The Motorola 68000 instruction set.

Shift rotate	ASL/ASR #count, dst	Shift dst left/right count bits
	LSL/LSR #count, dst	Logical shift left/right by count
	ROL/ROR #count, dst	Rotate dst left/right count bits
	ROXL/ROXR #count, dst	Rotate with extend bit
	SWAP Dn	Exchange halves of Dn

Test compare	TST src	Compare src to zero
	CMP src1, src2	Compare src1 and src2 and set flags
	CMPA src, An	Compare src to An and set flags
	CMPM (An)+, (Am)+	Compare indirectly and increment registers
	CMPI #n, src	Compare the constant n to src and set flags

Control transfer	JMP addr	JMP to addr
	BRA addr	Branch to addr
	Bcc addr	Conditional branch based on flags
	JSR addr	Jump to subroutine
	BSR addr	Branch to subroutine
	RTS	Return from subroutine
	RTR	Return and restore condition codes
	DBcc dst, addr	Decrement dst and conditional branch
	TRAP #n	Initiate a software trap to vector n
	TRAPV	Trap on overflow

Scc dst	Set dst according to condition codes

Bit ops	BTST src, dst	Test bit specified by src
	BSET src, dst	Test bit specified by src, then set it
	BCLR src, dst	Test bit specified by src, then clear it
	BCHG src, dst	Test bit specified by src, then change it

Miscellaneous	EXT Dn	Sign extend
	LINK An, #n	Allocate n stack bytes upon procedure entry
	UNLK An	Release storage upon procedure exit
	NOP	No operation
	CHK src, Dn	Check array bounds
	TAS dst	Test and set for multiprocessor synchronization

Fig. 5-15. (cont.)

show that a particular operand must be an address or data register, respectively. Finally, the CMPM instruction uses two address registers to locate the operands, and then increments the registers. We will explain the notation later when we come to addressing.

As with the Intel CPUs, we have divided them into several rough groups based on function. The first group deals with moving bytes, words, and long words around the machine. Most of the instructions are straightforward, except for MOVEP, which has to do with performing I/O using certain obsolete peripheral chips.

The next two groups are for arithmetic, both ordinary binary and binary coded decimal, with two decimal digits per byte. Several variants exist for some instructions, each with a different encoding. For example, ADDI, SUBI, ADDQ, and SUBQ all add or subtract a constant, but the first two can handle any constant, whereas the last two are special short instructions for adding or subtracting 3-bit constants. These special instructions drive compiler writers mad because it is often more efficient to get, say, 130 somewhere by adding 5 to 125 than by moving 130 there.

Next come the Boolean instructions and shift/rotate instructions, which operate on operands in registers or memory. They are quite similar to their Intel counterparts. These are followed by several instructions that test or compare their operands and set the flag bits depending on the results.

The following group deals with control transfers. Both branches and jumps are present, the difference between them being the way the target address is encoded. With branches, an offset from the instruction is given, whereas with jumps a more general addressing scheme is used. Procedures can be called and returned from. The instructions containing *cc* come in 16 variants, with different condition code bits being tested. For example, BLT means Branch Less Than and BEQ means Branch EQual, depending on the results of a previous test or comparison.

The four Bxxx instructions are for testing, setting, clearing, and changing individual bits in a 32-bit register or memory location. The first operand is either a constant or a register specifying which bit to use, and the second identifies the operand containing the bit.

The last group is a miscellaneous collection of instructions that do not fit in anywhere else conveniently. The LINK and UNLK instructions are especially important, and are used by compilers to handle the stack setup upon entering and leaving a procedure. Conceptually they are similar to the ENTER and LEAVE instructions on the 80286 and 80386, although the details differ.

Nearly all instructions that use operands can work on 8, 16, or 32-bit values. The operand length is encoded in a 2-bit field within the instruction. Since only three out of the four combinations are needed, the fourth one is often used for a completely different instruction, typically one that can only handle a single length operand. For example, the fourth combination for AND is a multiplication instruction. There is almost no pattern in the way the instructions are encoded.

Differences Between the 68020/68030 and the 68000

So far, everything we have said applies equally well to the 68000, 68020, and 68030. Nevertheless, the three machines are not quite identical at the conventional machine level. Just as Intel decided to add some new instructions later on, so did Motorola. Those instructions present on both the 68020 and 68030 that are available to user programs are listed in Fig. 5-16.

BFxxx src, #n, Dn	Eight-bit field manipulation instructions
BKPT #n	Issue breakpoint cycle on the bus
CAS Dm, Dn, src	Multiprocessor synchronization
CAS2	Complicated multiprocessor synchronization
CHK2 src1, src2	Check array bounds and trap
CMP2 src1, src2	Check array bounds and set flags
DIVUL src, dst	Unsigned long divide
DIVUS src, dst	Signed long divide
EXTB dst	Extend byte to long word
ILLEGAL	Cause an illegal instruction trap
MULU.L src, dst	Unsigned long multiply
MULS.L src, dst	Signed long multiply
PACK Dx, Dy, #n	Pack two BCD digits into one byte
RTD #n	Return from procedure and deallocate stack
TRAPcc	Trap if condition is true
UNPK Dx, Dy, #n	Unpack BCD digits from a byte
cpXXX	Coprocessor command

Fig. 5-16. New user-program instructions present on the 68020 and 68030.

Some of the new instructions provide more efficient ways of doing certain operations, such as array bound checking, manipulating bit fields, converting a byte to a long word, packing and unpacking BCD numbers, returning from a procedure, and synchronizing multiprocessors. None of these are really essential, but chip designers invariably find the urge to add new instructions irresistible.

Other instructions correct problems in the original instruction set, such as the lack of true 32-bit multiply and divide. This was probably omitted originally due to lack of area on the chip.

BKPT is used for communicating with external logic analyzers connected to the system bus. TRAPcc and ILLEGAL both generate traps, the former if a certain condition is true, and the latter always. Finally, cpXXX is a group of instructions for communicating with a floating point or other coprocessor.

There are two instructions, CALLM, for calling a module, and RTM, for returning from a module, that were added to the 68020 and taken out again in the 68030. Companies can change their minds too.

In addition, some 68000 instructions contain a 16-bit constant, for example, the relative distance to branch from the current instruction. Most of these have been modified in the 68020 and 68030 to allow 32-bit constants. Other than the points listed above, for user programs, all three CPUs are the same. For the operating system, however, they have a number of other differences, in particular, memory management and caching.

5.1.3. Comparison of the 80386 and 68030

It is instructive to compare the 80386 and 68030, two of the leading 32-bit chips, to see how different designers made different decisions. We should start out by saying that the two CPUs are more alike at this level than they are different. A glance at the instruction sets will show that they have roughly the same kinds of instructions, although the details differ. Both have instructions for moving data, doing binary and decimal arithmetic, performing Boolean and shift/rotate operations, doing control transfers, and manipulating bit fields. The 80386 has string operations and the 68030 can move multiple registers in one instruction, but in general, most instructions on each machine have a corresponding instruction on the other.

The most significant difference between the two is the addressing. The 80386 has a segmented address space with 16,384 2^{32}-byte segments. The 68030 has one 2^{32}-byte segment. While the idea of a large (46-bit) address space at first sounds attractive, it also means that either pointers have to be 46 bits, which is expensive, or there have to be complicated rules making sure that no data structure can ever point outside its segment. In practice, the Motorola address space is big enough, so the additional 14 bits are not worth much. Intel would never have designed such a machine were it not for the need to be compatible with everything going back ultimately to the 8080.

Another difference is in the registers. The 80386 registers are not all equivalent. For example, the loop instructions always use ECX. While the 80386 is more general than the 80286 in this regard, it is still not as simple as the 68030, all of whose address registers are equivalent and all of whose data registers are equivalent. As a consequence, compilers for the 68030 are simpler than those for the 80386.

Both machines can handle 8-, 16-, and 32-bit quantities. The 68030 does it in a straightforward way: a 2-bit field in the instruction gives the size. The 80386 has only 1 bit, which selects byte or word. Whether "word" means 16 or 32 bits depends on the segment type and the presence or absence of a prefix. The Intel scheme is less elegant, but in practice is probably more efficient, since few programs for a 32-bit machine need 16-bit words.

The method of doing I/O is different on the 80386 and 68030. The former has explicit instructions for reading and writing I/O ports. The latter does not, relying on memory-mapped I/O. Memory-mapped I/O is slightly more general, since any instruction can be used to read or write an I/O register, but this is a minor point.

A final difference between the two machines is the presence of real and virtual modes on the 80386, something the 68030 does not need. Of course, these other modes are only needed for running obsolete software, and a program written specifically for the 80386 is not bothered by them.

5.2. INSTRUCTION FORMATS

A program consists of a sequence of instructions, each one specifying some particular action. Part of the instruction, called the operation code, or **opcode** for short, tells what action is to be performed. Many instructions contain or specify the location of data used by the instruction. For example, an instruction that compares two characters to see if they are the same must specify which characters are to be compared. The general subject of specifying where the operands are (i.e., their addresses) is called **addressing** and is discussed in Sec. 5.3.

Figure 5-17 shows several typical formats for level 2 instructions. On some level 2 machines, all instructions have the same length; on others there may be two or three lengths. Moreover, instructions may be shorter than, the same length as, or longer than the word length.

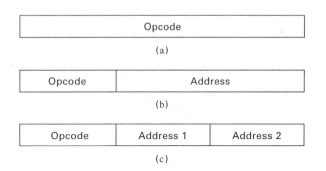

Fig. 5-17. Three typical instruction formats: (a) Zero-address instruction. (b) One-address instruction (c) Two-address instruction.

Some possible relations between instruction length and word length are shown in Fig. 5-18.

5.2.1. Design Criteria for Instruction Formats

When a computer design team has to choose an instruction format (or formats) for their machine, they must consider a number of factors. First, and most important, short instructions are better than long ones. A program consisting of n 16-bit

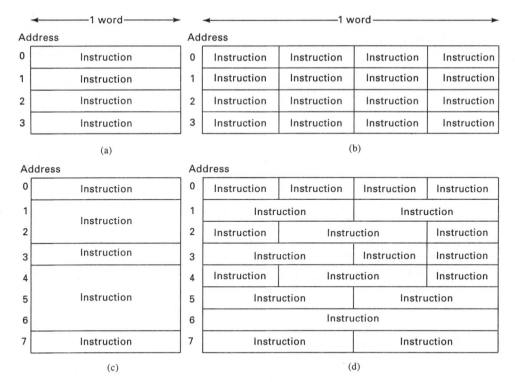

Fig. 5-18. Some possible relationships between instruction length and word length.

instructions takes up only half as much memory space as *n* 32-bit instructions. Memory is not free after all, so designers do not like to waste it.

A second reason is that each memory has a particular transfer rate that is determined by the technology and engineering design of the memory. The transfer rate of a memory is the number of bits per second that can be read out of the memory. A fast memory can give a processor (or an I/O device) more bits per second than a slow memory.

If the transfer rate of a particular memory is *t* bps and the average instruction length is *r* bits, the memory can deliver at most t/r instructions per second. Therefore, the rate at which instructions are executed (i.e., the processor speed) depends on the instruction length. Shorter instructions mean a faster processor. If the time required to execute an instruction is long compared to the time required to fetch it from memory, the instruction fetch time will not be so important. However, with fast CPUs, the memory is often the bottleneck. Increasing the number of instructions fetched per second is therefore an important design criterion.

Sufficient room in the instruction to express all the operations desired is a second design criterion for instruction formats. A machine with 2^n operations and an instruction smaller than n bits is impossible. There simply will not be enough room in the opcode to indicate which instruction is needed.

A third design criterion is that it is highly desirable that the machine's word length be an integral multiple of its character length. If the character code has k bits, the word length should be k, $2k$, $3k$, $4k$, $5k$, ...; otherwise, space will be wasted when characters are stored. Of course, it is possible to store 3.5 characters per word, but doing so causes severe inefficiencies in accessing the characters. The restrictions placed on the word length by the character code affect the instruction length, because either an instruction should occupy an integral number of bytes or words, or an integral number of instructions should fit in a word. A design with a 9-bit character, a 12-bit instruction, and a 31-bit word would be a catastrophe.

A fourth criterion concerns the number of bits in an address field. Consider the design of a machine with an 8-bit character (possibly 7 bits plus parity) and a main memory that must hold 2^{16} characters. The designers could choose to assign consecutive addresses to units of 8, 16, 24, or 32 bits, as well as other possibilities.

Imagine what would happen if the design team degenerated into two warring factions, one advocating making the 8-bit byte the basic unit of memory, and the other advocating the 32-bit word as the basic unit of memory. The former group would propose a memory of 2^{16} bytes, numbered 0, 1, 2, 3, ..., 65535. The latter group would propose a memory of 2^{14} words numbered 0, 1, 2, 3, ..., 16383.

The first group would point out that in order to compare two characters in the 32-bit word organization, the program would not only have to fetch the words containing the characters but would also have to extract each character from its word in order to compare them. Doing so costs extra instructions and therefore wastes space. The 8-bit organization, on the other hand, provides an address for every character, thus making the comparison much easier.

The 32-bit word supporters would retaliate by pointing out that their proposal requires only 2^{14} separate addresses, giving an address length of only 14 bits, whereas the 8-bit byte proposal requires 16 bits to address the same memory. A shorter address means a shorter instruction, which not only takes up less space but also requires less time to fetch. Alternatively, they could retain the 16-bit address to reference a memory four times as large as the 8-bit organization allows.

This example demonstrates that in order to gain a finer memory resolution, one must pay the price of longer addresses, which, in general, means longer instructions. The ultimate in resolution is a memory organization in which every bit is directly addressable (e.g., the Burroughs B1700). At the other extreme is a memory consisting of very long words (e.g., the CDC Cyber series has 60-bit words).

5.2.2. Expanding Opcodes

In the preceding section we saw how short addresses and good memory resolution could be traded off against each other. In this section we will examine trade-offs involving both opcodes and addresses. Consider an $(n + k)$ bit instruction with a k-bit opcode and a single n-bit address. This instruction allows 2^k different operations and 2^n addressable memory cells. Alternatively, the same $n + k$ bits could be broken up into a $(k - 1)$ bit opcode, and an $(n + 1)$ bit address, meaning only half as many instructions but either twice as much memory addressable, or the same amount of memory but with twice the resolution. A $(k + 1)$ bit opcode and an $(n - 1)$ bit address gives more operations, but the price is either a smaller number of cells addressable, or poorer resolution and the same amount of memory addressable. Quite sophisticated trade-offs are possible between opcode bits and address bits as well as the simpler ones just described. The scheme discussed in the following paragraphs is called an **expanding opcode**.

The concept of an expanding opcode can be most clearly seen by an example. Consider a machine in which instructions are 16 bits long and addresses are 4 bits long, as shown in Fig. 5-19. This situation might be reasonable for a machine that has 16 registers (hence a 4-bit register address) on which all arithmetic operations take place. One design would be a 4-bit opcode and three addresses in each instruction, giving 16 three-address instructions.

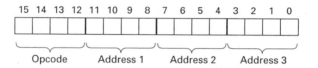

Fig. 5-19. An instruction with a 4-bit opcode and three 4-bit address fields.

However, if the designers need 15 three-address instructions, 14 two-address instructions, 31 one-address instructions, and 16 instructions with no address at all, they can use opcodes 0 to 14 as three-address instructions but interpret opcode 15 differently (see Fig. 5-20).

Opcode 15 means that the opcode is contained in bits 8 to 15 instead of 12 to 15. Bits 0 to 3 and 4 to 7 form two addresses, as usual. The 14 two-address instructions all have 1111 in the leftmost 4 bits, and numbers from 0000 to 1101 in bits 8 to 11. Instructions with 1111 in the leftmost 4 bits and either 1110 or 1111 in bits 8 to 11 will be treated specially. They will be treated as though their opcodes were in bits 4 to 15. The result is 32 new opcodes. Because only 31 are needed, opcode 111111111111 is interpreted to mean that the real opcode is in bits 0 to 15, giving 16 instructions with no address.

As we proceeded through this discussion, the opcode kept getting longer and longer; that is, the three-address instructions have a 4-bit opcode, the two-address instructions have an 8-bit opcode, the one-address instructions have a 12-bit opcode, and the zero-address instructions have a 16-bit opcode.

In practice, expanding opcodes are not quite as clean and regular as in our example. We have assumed that all operands need 4 bits, for example. In reality a variety of different lengths and formats are often required.

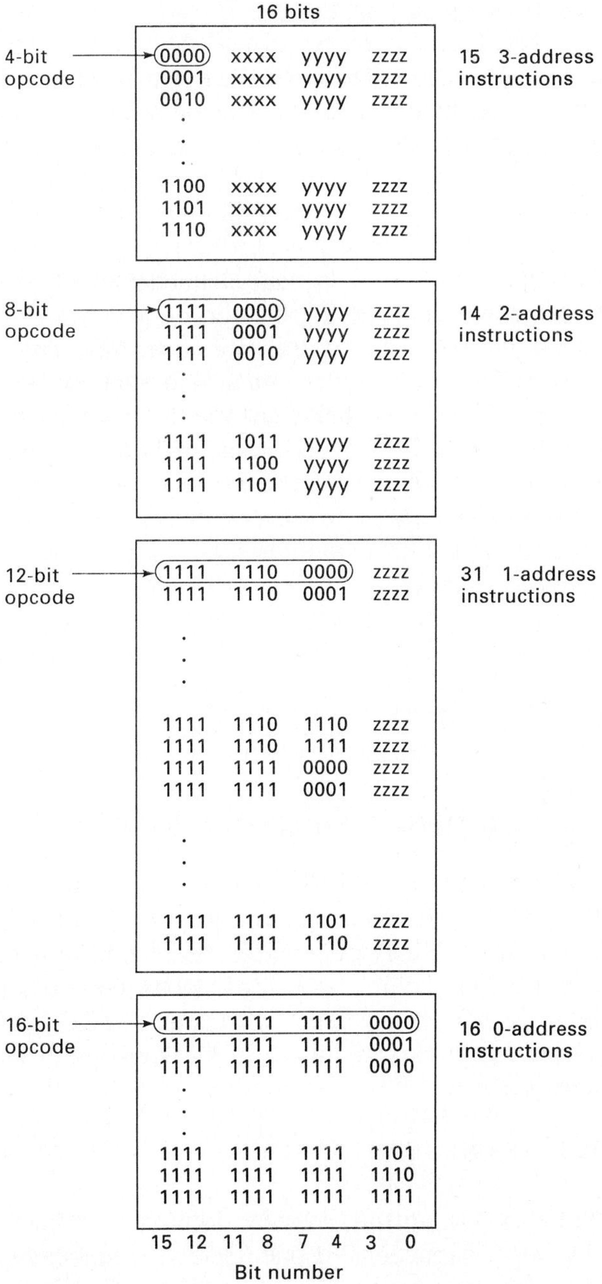

16 bits

4-bit opcode →	(0000)	xxxx	yyyy	zzzz	15 3-address instructions
	0001	xxxx	yyyy	zzzz	
	0010	xxxx	yyyy	zzzz	
	.				
	.				
	1100	xxxx	yyyy	zzzz	
	1101	xxxx	yyyy	zzzz	
	1110	xxxx	yyyy	zzzz	

8-bit opcode →	(1111	0000)	yyyy	zzzz	14 2-address instructions
	1111	0001	yyyy	zzzz	
	1111	0010	yyyy	zzzz	
	.				
	.				
	1111	1011	yyyy	zzzz	
	1111	1100	yyyy	zzzz	
	1111	1101	yyyy	zzzz	

12-bit opcode →	(1111	1110	0000)	zzzz	31 1-address instructions
	1111	1110	0001	zzzz	
	.				
	.				
	1111	1110	1110	zzzz	
	1111	1110	1111	zzzz	
	1111	1111	0000	zzzz	
	1111	1111	0001	zzzz	
	.				
	.				
	1111	1111	1101	zzzz	
	1111	1111	1110	zzzz	

16-bit opcode →	(1111	1111	1111	0000)	16 0-address instructions
	1111	1111	1111	0001	
	1111	1111	1111	0010	
	.				
	.				
	1111	1111	1111	1101	
	1111	1111	1111	1110	
	1111	1111	1111	1111	

15 12 11 8   7   4   3   0
Bit number

Fig. 5-20. An expanding opcode allowing 15 three-address instructions, 14 two-address instructions, 31 one-address instructions, and 16 zero-address instructions. The fields marked xxxx, yyyy, and zzzz are 4-bit address fields.

5.2.3. Examples of Instruction Formats

In this section we will examine the instruction formats of the PDP-11, Intel, and Motorola conventional machine levels. We include the PDP-11 here so its simplicity and regularity can shine out as a beacon to future instruction set architects.

The PDP-11

The majority of the PDP-11 two-operand instructions are encoded as shown in Fig. 5-21. Each instruction contains a 4-bit opcode and two 6-bit address fields. The leftmost opcode bit indicates whether the instruction operates on bytes or words. The address fields are subdivided into a 3-bit mode and a 3-bit register (the PDP-11 has 8 registers). The mode fields tell whether the operand is in a register, is in memory, is a constant, and so on. The same eight modes that are available for source operands are available for destination operands, and any opcode can be used with any source operand and any destination operand. An instruction set in which the method for specifying the operand addresses is independent of the opcode is said to be **orthogonal**. Compiler writers love orthogonal instruction sets.

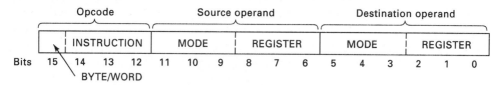

Fig. 5-21. Orthogonal instruction coding on the PDP-11.

For a few other instructions, including one-operand instructions, the PDP-11 uses an expanding opcode scheme, with opcodes x111 (binary) being used as escapes to longer opcodes. These, too, exhibit considerable regularity—for example, with most one-operand instructions using a 10-bit opcode and the same 6-bit mode/register fields as the two-operand instructions. PDP-11 instructions that address memory have one or two additional 16-bit words following the instruction to specify the addresses.

The Intel 8088/80286/80386 Family

With the Intel CPUs, the situation is quite different and much less regular. In general, for two-operand instructions, if one operand is in memory, the other may not be in memory. Thus instructions exist to add two registers, add a register to memory, and add memory to a register, but not to add a memory word to another memory word, something the PDP-11 allows as a direct result of its orthogonality.

On the 8088, each opcode is one byte, but by the time the 80386 came around, the 1-byte opcodes were all used up, so opcode 15 is used as an escape to 2-byte opcodes. The only structure in the opcode field is the use of the low-order bit in some instructions to indicate byte/word, and the use of the adjoining bit to indicate whether the memory address (if present) is the source or the destination.

Following the opcode byte in most instructions is a second byte that tells where the operands are, similar to the two mode/register fields in Fig. 5-21. Since only 8 bits are available, it is split up into a 2-bit mode field and two 3-bit register fields. Thus there are only four ways to address operands (vs. eight on the PDP-11), and one of the operands must always be a register. Logically, any of AX, BX, CX, DX, SI, DI, BP, or SP should be specifiable as either register, but the encoding rules prohibit some combinations and use them for special cases.

On the 80386, in 32-bit segments, the modes are completely different than on the 8088 and 80286. Some of these modes require an additional byte, called **SIB** (**Scale, Index, Base**) giving a further specification. This scheme is not ideal, but they simply ran out of bits.

In addition to all this, some instructions have one, two, or four more bytes specifying a memory address and possibly another one, two, or four bytes used as a constant operand (e.g., to move the number 100 to a register).

The set of all 8088, 80286, and 80386 instruction formats is given in Fig. 5-22. Each instruction potentially has up to six fields, each ranging from 0 to 5 bytes. On the 8088 and 80286, the shortest instruction is 1 byte and the longest is 9 bytes (including the REP, LOCK, and segment override prefixes). On the 80386, the shortest instruction is still 1 byte, but with the addition of the operand size and address size prefixes, an instruction can be up to 17 bytes.

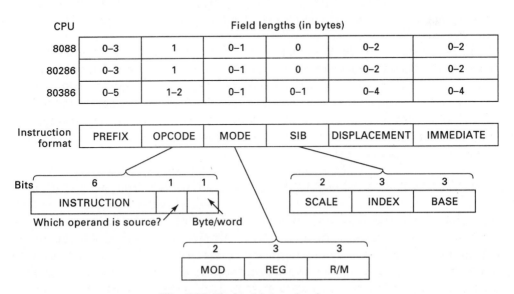

Fig. 5-22. The Intel instruction formats.

The Motorola 68000/68020/68030 Family

The 68000's instruction encoding presents an interesting contrast to that of the PDP-11 and Intel machines. It is clear that in regard to the instruction set and addressing modes, the 68000 designers studied the PDP-11 well and were considerably influenced by it, but when it came to instruction encoding, they went a different route. The basic philosophy behind the PDP-11 instruction encoding is the orthogonality of opcodes and operands—in other words, an instruction should consist of an opcode field and zero, one, or two operand fields, with all operand fields encoded the same way.

With the 68000, this desirable situation is impossible. The 68000 has more instructions than the PDP-11, and three data lengths (byte, word, long) instead of two (byte, word), so the designers could not afford the luxury of orthogonal, or even regular, instruction encoding. Squeezing all the instructions into 16 bits was clearly a struggle, so no bit combinations could be wasted. The result was at least 18 formats (excluding floating-point), depending slightly on precisely where one draws the line between variations of one instruction and two different instructions. The first word of each of these instruction formats is shown in Fig. 5-23. Like the PDP-11, many instructions have additional words following the instruction to provide constants and memory addresses.

Rather than aim for orthogonality, the 68000 designers tried to allocate more opcode space to important (i.e., frequently used) instructions and less opcode space to unimportant ones. In general, this approach leads to more efficient object programs but more complicated compilers. MOVE is unquestionably the most important instruction in any program and is encoded using format 1, with a size field (1 = byte, 2 = long, 3 = word) and two 6-bit operand fields. Each operand field has a 3-bit mode and a 3-bit register field, like the PDP-11, although the set of modes available is somewhat different. The 68000 has 16 A and D registers, not 8, so not every mode can be used with every register; the mode implicitly specifies either an A register or a D register. If bits had not been so tight, the 68000 designers might just have let a MOVE with SIZE = 0 be an illegal instruction for the sake of opcode decoding simplicity. That not being the case, they used SIZE = 0 to encode a variety of instructions in several different formats.

Having allocated nearly a quarter (3/16) of the entire opcode space to one instruction, MOVE, providing two 6-bit operand fields for all the other two-operand instructions was out of the question. Instead, most of the two-operand instructions have one fully general 6-bit operand field (OPERAND) and one 3-bit register field (REG), using formats 2 or 3. This means that the 68000 can add a register to a register, memory to a register, or a register to memory but not memory to memory, as the PDP-11 can. Intel had precisely the same problem. The only difference is that Motorola decided to give up 3/16 of the encoding space to allow MOVE to be orthogonal; Intel did not.

The MOD field in format 2 distinguishes among byte, word, and long, and also

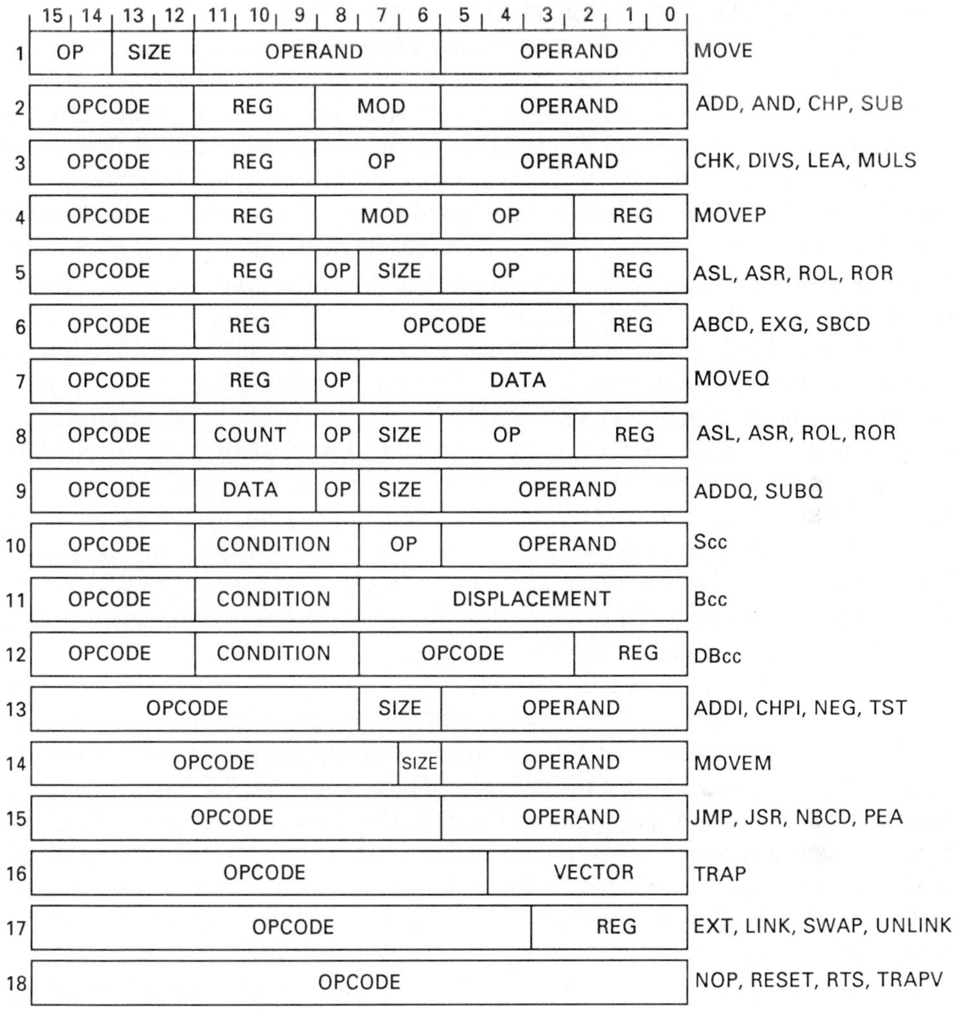

	15 14 13 12	11 10 9 8	7 6	5 4 3 2 1 0	
1	OP / SIZE	OPERAND		OPERAND	MOVE
2	OPCODE	REG	MOD	OPERAND	ADD, AND, CHP, SUB
3	OPCODE	REG	OP	OPERAND	CHK, DIVS, LEA, MULS
4	OPCODE	REG	MOD	OP / REG	MOVEP
5	OPCODE	REG	OP / SIZE	OP / REG	ASL, ASR, ROL, ROR
6	OPCODE	REG	OPCODE	REG	ABCD, EXG, SBCD
7	OPCODE	REG	OP / DATA	DATA	MOVEQ
8	OPCODE	COUNT	OP / SIZE	OP / REG	ASL, ASR, ROL, ROR
9	OPCODE	DATA	OP / SIZE	OPERAND	ADDQ, SUBQ
10	OPCODE	CONDITION	OP	OPERAND	Scc
11	OPCODE	CONDITION	DISPLACEMENT		Bcc
12	OPCODE	CONDITION	OPCODE	REG	DBcc
13	OPCODE	SIZE	OPERAND		ADDI, CHPI, NEG, TST
14	OPCODE	SIZE	OPERAND		MOVEM
15	OPCODE	OPERAND			JMP, JSR, NBCD, PEA
16	OPCODE	VECTOR			TRAP
17	OPCODE	REG			EXT, LINK, SWAP, UNLINK
18	OPCODE				NOP, RESET, RTS, TRAPV

OPCODE, OP determine instruction
OPERAND determines data operated on
REG selects a register
SIZE chooses byte, word, long
MOD determines if operand is source or destination, and length
COUNT, DATA are constants in the range 1-8
CONDITION specifies one of 16 possible conditions to test
DISPLACEMENT is signed offset for branches
VECTOR specifies where to trap

Fig. 5-23. Instruction formats used on the 68000 (first word only).

whether the OPERAND field refers to the source or destination. Because $3 \times 2 = 6$ and 3 bits yield eight possibilities, the other two MOD values are used to indicate completely different instructions.

Some instructions have multiple formats. The shift and rotate instructions, for example, have one variant, format 8, with a constant shift count (COUNT) as part of the instruction, and another variant, format 5, where the count is taken from a specified register. Formats 7 and 9 exist because numerous studies have shown that most constants appearing in programs are small. Format 7 allows an 8-bit constant to be loaded into a register in a single 16-bit instruction. Format 9 allows a number in the range 1 to 8 to be added or subtracted from an operand efficiently. To add 9 to a register, the ADDI instruction (format 13) is needed, with an extra 16-bit word required to store the constant 9.

At first glance it might appear logical that bits 12 to 15 should determine the format, but that is not done because not all formats have equally many instructions. To statically divide the opcode space into 16 equally large groups (which is more or less what the PDP-11 does) would waste too much valuable encoding space. Instead, it is sometimes necessary to examine all 16 bits to separate two unrelated instructions.

An extreme example of this effect is the way Scc (format 10) and DBcc (format 12) are distinguished from ADDQ and SUBQ (format 9). All four instructions have a 5 in the upper four bits, as shown in Fig. 5-24. The latter two are easily differentiated from the former two by the presence of the illegal SIZE = 3 field (the encoding of the lengths is instruction dependent for some peculiar reason; for ADDQ and SUBQ, in contrast to MOVE, 0 = byte, 1 = word, 2 = long, 3 = illegal). Separating Scc from DBcc is tricky because all 16 conditions are legal in both. The solution chosen is to forbid MODE = 1 in Scc. Although not especially elegant, it works, and in any event illustrates the problems that can arise when one tries to pack a lot of information in a limited number of bits.

	15	14	13	12	11	10	9	8	7	6	5	4	3	2	1	0
ADDQ	0	1	0	1		Data		0		Size		Mode			Reg	
SUBQ	0	1	0	1		Data		1		Size		Mode			Reg	
S_{cc}	0	1	0	1		Condition			1	1		Mode			Reg	
DB_{cc}	0	1	0	1		Condition			1	1	0	0	1		Reg	

Fig. 5-24. Four 68000 instructions.

The encoding problem on the 68020 and 68030 is even worse due to the need to support all the 68000 instructions and some new ones. The new instructions were squeezed in here and there, wherever a free bit combination was available. This encoding leads not only to complex compilers and assemblers that have to generate strange formats, but also to convoluted microprograms that have to dismember the formats during execution. Such is the price of progress.

5.3. ADDRESSING

Instructions can be classified according to the number of addresses they use. It should be kept in mind that a collection of numbered CPU registers, in effect, forms a high-speed memory and defines an address space. An instruction that adds register 1 to register 2 should be classified as having two addresses because the instruction must specify which registers are to be added, just as an instruction that adds two memory words must specify which words.

Instructions specifying one, two, and three addresses are all common. On many machines that do arithmetic with only one address, a special register called the **accumulator** provides one of the operands. On these machines, the address is usually the address of a memory word m, in which the operand is located. The instruction for addition specifying the address m has the effect

accumulator := accumulator + memory [m]

Two-address add instructions use one address as the source and the other as the destination. The source is then added to the destination:

destination := destination + source

Three-address instructions specify two sources and a destination. The two sources are added and stored at the destination.

Up to this point we have paid relatively little attention to how the bits of an address field are interpreted to find the operand. One possibility is that they contain the memory address of the operand. Other possibilities also exist, however, and in the following sections we will explore some of them.

5.3.1. Immediate Addressing

The simplest way for an instruction to specify an operand is for the address part of the instruction actually to contain the operand itself rather than an address or other information describing where the operand is. Such an operand is called an **immediate operand** because it is automatically fetched from memory at the same time the instruction itself is fetched; hence it is immediately available for use.

Immediate addressing has the virtue of not requiring an extra memory reference to fetch the operand. It has the disadvantage of restricting the operand to a number that can fit in an address field. In an instruction with a 3-bit address (e.g., register field), the operands would be restricted to 3 bits, which limits their usefulness.

The Intel CPUs do not have an addressing mode for immediate operands. Instead, they have a large collection of distinct instructions in which one of the operands is immediate. In Fig. 5-5, for example, the ADD instruction looks nice and orthogonal, just like the PDP-11. In reality, nine different opcodes are used for ADD, five of them for immediate operands, depending on how the destination is specified and the length of the immediate operand (8, 16, or 32 bits).

The 680x0 has an immediate addressing mode, so any source operand can be a constant. On the 68000, some instructions only permit 8- or 16-bit constants, but on the 68020 and 68030, all three lengths are allowed everywhere. In addition, special instructions such as ADDI, ADDQ and CMPI allow immediate instructions to be coded more efficiently.

5.3.2. Direct Addressing

Another simple method for specifying an operand is to give the address of the memory word where the operand is contained. This form is called **direct addressing**. The details of how the computer knows which addresses are immediate and which are direct will be discussed later. In general, there are two approaches: use different opcodes or use a special addressing mode for each kind of operand.

All the Intel CPUs have direct addressing. The 8088 and 80286 use 16-bit direct addresses. The 80386 uses 16-bit addresses in real and virtual modes, and 16-bit segments in protected mode. In 32-bit protected mode, the direct addresses are 32-bits. Note that in all cases the direct addresses are too short to cover the entire address space.

The 680x0 has two forms of direct addressing, one with a 16-bit address and one with a 32-bit address. Addresses in the first 64K of memory can be referenced with the short form, whereas addresses above 64K need the long form. These two forms are indicated by values in the 3-bit MOD field, and thus apply to all instructions with one or more OPERAND fields in Fig. 5-23.

5.3.3. Register Addressing

Register addressing is conceptually the same as direct addressing. In this form of addressing, the address field contains the number of the register in which the operand is stored. A machine with 16 registers and 65,536 memory words really has two address spaces. One might think of an address on such a machine as having two parts: (a) one bit telling whether a register or a memory word is desired and (b) an address field telling which register or memory word is desired. Because there are fewer registers than memory words, a smaller address is needed, and thus different format instructions are often used for register operands and memory operands.

If there were a corresponding register instruction for every instruction which addressed memory, half the opcodes would be for memory operands and half for register operands. One bit would be needed in the opcode to designate which address space was to be used. If this bit were then removed from the opcode field and placed in the address field, the fact that two address spaces were being used would be clearer. The bit would then indicate which address space to use.

Machines are designed with registers for two reasons: (a) registers are faster than main memory and (b) because there are so few of them, only a few bits are needed to address them. Unfortunately, having 8 or 16 registers also greatly complicates programming because decisions must be made as to which operands and which intermediate results are to be kept in the limited number of registers, and which are to be kept in main memory. W. L. van der Poel (1968) has astutely remarked that computers ought to be provided with either 0, 1, or an infinite number of each feature (infinite meaning sufficiently many that the programmer need not have to waste any time thinking about what to do if something runs out).

The Intel and Motorola chips both have a wide repertoire of instructions that take their operands from registers and leave their results in a register.

5.3.4. Indirect Addressing

Direct addressing is a scheme in which the address specifies which memory word or register contains the operand. Indirect addressing is a scheme in which the address specifies which memory word or register contains not the operand but the address of the operand. As an example, consider an instruction to load a register (which we will call R1) indirectly from memory location 1000, where location 1000 contains 1510, as shown in Fig. 5-25(b).

First, the contents of location 1000 are fetched into an internal CPU register. This 16-bit number (1510) is not put in R1. If it were, as in Fig. 5-25(a), we would have a direct address instruction. Instead, the contents of location 1510 are fetched and put into R1. The number at location 1000 is not the operand but instead it "points to" the operand. For this reason, it is called a **pointer**.

The Intel processors all have indirect addressing via a register. Thus, for example, it is possible to put a pointer in SI and specify that the operand is located in memory at the address pointed to by SI. On the 8088 and 80286, only BX, SI, and DI can be addressed indirectly; on the 80386 all the registers can be used. Indirect addressing using a pointer in memory is not possible on any of them.

The 68000 allows indirect addressing via the address registers. No other forms of indirect addressing are possible. On the 68020 and 68030, indirect addressing is also possible via memory, in several forms. This addition is one of the main differences between the 68000 and the newer CPUs.

Some machines, although neither of our two examples, allow multiple-level indirect addressing. In this addressing mode, a pointer is used to locate a memory word that itself points to another memory word, and so on.

Immediate, direct, indirect, and multiple-level indirect addressing exhibit a certain progression. Immediate addressing requires zero memory references, because the operand was fetched along with the instruction, which we will not count here. Direct addressing requires one memory reference, to fetch the operand. Indirect

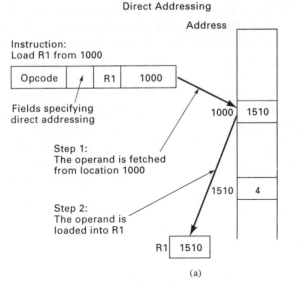

(a)

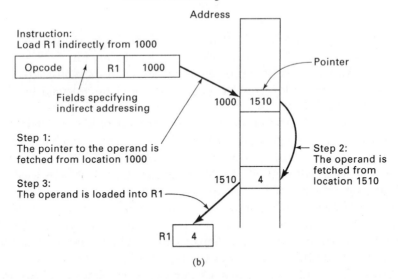
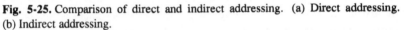

(b)

Fig. 5-25. Comparison of direct and indirect addressing. (a) Direct addressing. (b) Indirect addressing.

addressing requires two memory references, one for the pointer and one for the operand. Multiple-level indirect addressing requires at least three memory references, two or more for pointers and one for the operand. Memory references in this context include register references.

5.3.5. Indexing

Many algorithms require performing some operation on a sequence of data structures stored in consecutive memory locations. For example, consider a block of n machine words occupying locations

$$A, A + 1, A + 2, \cdots, A + n - 1$$

which must be moved to locations

$$B, B + 1, B + 2, \cdots, B + n - 1$$

Assuming that the machine has an instruction

MOVE A,B

that moves the contents of location A to location B, one could execute this instruction, modify the instruction itself to read

MOVE A+1,B+1

execute it again, then modify it again and repeat the cycle until all n words had been copied.

Although programs that modify themselves were once popular, they are now considered bad programming practice. They are difficult to debug and they make sharing of a program among several users of a time-sharing system difficult.

The copying problem can also be solved by indirect addressing. One register or memory word is loaded with the address A; a second one is loaded with B. The MOVE instruction uses these two as pointers. After each word has been copied, the pointers are each increased by one. The pointers are part of the data, not part of the program, of course, and are not shared by simultaneous users.

Another solution is to have one or more registers, called **index registers**, which work as follows. Addresses have two parts, the number of an index register and a constant. The address of the operand is the sum of the constant and the contents of the index register. In the example above, if both addresses are indexed using an index register containing the integer k, the instruction MOVE A, B will move the contents of memory location $A + k$ to $B + k$. By initializing the index register to 0 and incrementing it by the word size after each word is copied, only one register is needed for the copy loop. Furthermore, incrementing a register is faster than incrementing a memory location.

Indexing is also commonly used to address a field at a known offset from the start of a given structure. Local variables in a procedure are accessed this way.

In the example given above it was necessary to explicitly increment the index register by the word size after each use of it. The need to increment or decrement an index register just before or after it is used is so common that some computers provide special instructions or addressing modes, or even special index registers that automatically increment or decrement themselves. Automatic modification of an index register is called **autoindexing**.

Both the Intel and Motorola chips have a variety of different addressing modes that involve indexing. The 680x0 also has autoindexing.

5.3.6. Stack Addressing

We have already noted that making machine instructions as short as possible is highly desirable for saving both CPU time and memory. The ultimate limit in reducing address lengths would be to have instructions with no addresses at all, just opcodes. Surprisingly enough, this situation is possible. It is accomplished by organizing the machine around a data structure called a stack.

A **stack** consists of data items (words, characters, bits, etc.) stored in consecutive order in the memory. The first item pushed onto the stack is said to be at the bottom of the stack. The item most recently pushed onto the stack is said to be on the top of the stack. Associated with each stack is a register or memory word that contains the address of the top of the stack. It is called the **stack pointer**.

Although we have discussed stacks in Chap. 4, we will review that material briefly here because using stacks for arithmetic is quite different from using stacks for holding local variables (both uses can be combined, of course). Figure 5-26 illustrates the operation of a stack. In Fig. 5-26(a) two items are already on the stack. The bottom of the stack is at memory location 1000 and the top of the stack is at memory location 1001. The stack pointer contains the address of the item on the top of the stack, namely, 1001; that is, it "points" to the top of the stack. In Fig. 5-26(b), 6 has been pushed onto the stack and the stack pointer indicates 1002 as the new top of the stack. In Fig. 5-26(c), 75 has been pushed onto the stack, raising the stack pointer to 1003. In Fig. 5-26(d), 75 has been popped off the stack.

Computers that are stack-oriented have an instruction to push the contents of a memory location or a register onto the stack. Such an instruction must both copy the item and increment the stack pointer. Similarly, an instruction to pop the top of the stack into a register or memory location must make a new copy in the proper place and decrement the stack pointer. Some computers have their stacks upside down, with new items being pushed into consecutively lower numbered memory locations rather than consecutively higher numbered locations, as in Fig. 5-26.

Instructions with no addresses are used in conjunction with a stack. This form of addressing specifies that the two operands are to be popped off the stack, one after another, the operation performed (e.g., multiplication or AND) and the result pushed back onto the stack. Figure 5-27(a) shows a stack containing four items. A multiply instruction has the effect of popping the 5 and the 6 off the stack,

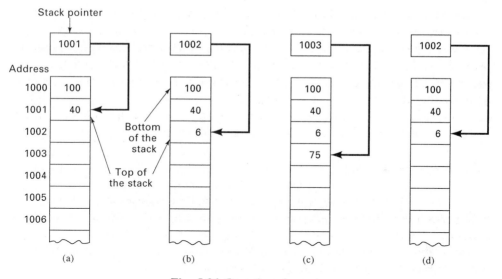

Fig. 5-26. Operation of a stack.

temporarily resetting the stack pointer 1001, and then pushing the result, 30, onto the stack, as shown in Fig. 5-27(b). If an addition is then performed, the result will be as shown in Fig. 5-27(c).

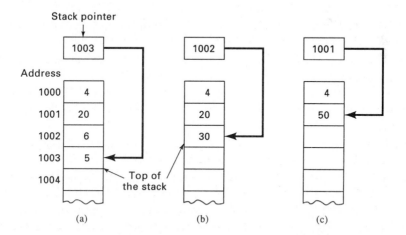

Fig. 5-27. Using a stack for arithmetic. (a) Initial configuration. (b) After a multiplication. (c) After an addition.

Reverse Polish

It is a long-standing tradition in mathematics to write the operator between the operands, as in $x + y$, rather than after the operands, as in $x\ y\ +$. The form with the operator "in" between the operands is called **infix** notation. The form with the operator after the operands is called **postfix** or **reverse Polish**, after the Polish logician J. Lukasiewicz (1958), who investigated the properties of this notation.

Reverse Polish has a number of advantages over infix for expressing algebraic formulas. First, any formula can be expressed without parentheses. Second, it is convenient for evaluating formulas on computers with stacks. Third, infix operators have precedence, which is arbitrary and undesirable. For example, we know that $a \times b + c$ means $(a \times b) + c$ and not $a \times (b + c)$ because multiplication has been arbitrarily defined to have precedence over addition. Reverse Polish eliminates this nuisance.

Several algorithms for converting infix formulas into reverse Polish exist. The one given below is an adaptation of an idea due to E. W. Dijkstra. Assume that a formula is composed of the following symbols: variables, the dyadic (two-operand) operators $+ - * /$, and left and right parentheses. To mark the ends of a formula, we will insert the symbol ⊥ after the last symbol and before the first symbol.

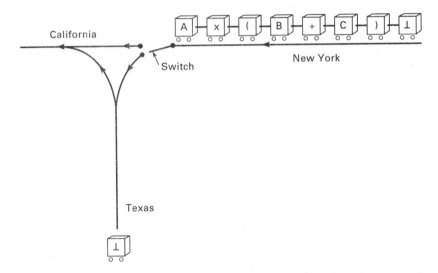

Fig. 5-28. Each railroad car represents one symbol in the formula to be converted from infix to reverse Polish.

Figure 5-28 shows a railroad track from New York to California, with a spur in the middle that heads off toward Texas. Each symbol in the formula is represented by one railroad car. The train moves westward (to the left). When each car arrives at the switch, it must stop and ask if it should go to California directly or take a side trip to Texas. Cars containing variables always go directly to California and never to Texas. Cars containing other symbols must inquire about the contents of the nearest car on the Texas line before entering the switch.

Figure 5-29 shows what happens, depending on the contents of the nearest car on the Texas line and the car at the switch. The first ⊥ always goes to Texas. The numbers refer to the following situations:

1. The car at the switch heads toward Texas.

2. The most recent car on the Texas line turns and goes to California.

3. Both the car at the switch and the most recent car on the Texas line are hijacked and disappear (i.e., both are deleted).

4. Stop. The symbols now in California represent the reverse Polish formula when read from left to right.

5. Stop. An error has occurred. The original formula was not correctly balanced.

Car at the switch

Most recently arrived car on the Texas line		⊥	+	−	×	/	(	)
	⊥	4	1	1	1	1	1	5
	+	2	2	2	1	1	1	2
	−	2	2	2	1	1	1	2
	×	2	2	2	2	2	1	2
	/	2	2	2	2	2	1	2
	(	5	1	1	1	1	1	3

Fig. 5-29. Decision table used by the infix-to-reverse Polish algorithm.

After each action is taken, a new comparison is made between the car at the switch, which may be the same car as in the previous comparison or may be the next car, and the car that is now the last one on the Texas line. The process continues until step 4 is reached. Notice that the Texas line is being used as a stack, with routing a car to Texas being a push operation, and turning a car already on the Texas line around and sending it to California being a pop operation.

The order of the variables is the same in infix and reverse Polish. The order of the operators is different, however. Operators appear in reverse Polish in the order they will actually be executed during the evaluation of the expression. Figure 5-30 gives examples of infix formulas and their reverse Polish equivalents.

Infix	Reverse Polish
A + B x C	ABC x +
A x B + C	AB x C +
A x B + C x D	AB x CD x +
(A + B) / (C – D)	AB + CD – /
A x B/C	AB x C /
((A + B) x C + D) / (E + F + G)	AB + C x D + EF + G + /

Fig. 5-30. Examples of infix formulas and their reverse Polish equivalents.

Evaluation of Reverse Polish Formulas

The following algorithm evaluates a reverse Polish formula.

ALGORITHM

1. Examine each symbol in the reverse Polish formula, starting at the extreme left until you come to an operator.

2. Write down the operator and the two operands immediately to its left on a piece of scratch paper.

3. Erase the operator and the operands from the formula, creating a hole.

4. Perform the operation on the operands and write the result in the hole.

5. If the formula now consists of one value, that is the answer and the algorithm is finished; otherwise, go to step 1.

Figure 5-31 depicts the evaluation of a reverse Polish formula. The order of the operators is the order in which they are actually evaluated.

Reverse Polish is the ideal notation for evaluating formulas on a computer with a stack. The formula consists of n symbols, each one either a variable (i.e., something with a value) or an operator. The algorithm for evaluating a reverse Polish formula using a stack is as follows.

ALGORITHM

1. Set k to 1.

2. Examine the kth symbol. If it is a variable, push it onto the stack. If it is an operator, pop the top two items off the stack, perform the operation, and push the result back onto the stack.

3. If $k = n$, the algorithm terminates and the answer is on the stack; otherwise, add 1 to k and go to step 2.

Figure 5-32 shows the evaluation of the same formula as in Fig. 5-31 but using a

Infix formula (8 + 2 x 5) / (1 + 3 x 2 – 4)

Reverse Polish formula 8 2 5 x + 1 3 2 x + 4 – /

Step	Formula to be evaluated	Leftmost operator	Left operand	Right operand	Result	New formula after performing operation
1	8 2 5 x + 1 3 2 x + 4 – /	x	2	5	10	8 10 + 1 3 2 x + 4 – /
2	8 10 + 1 3 2 x + 4 – /	+	8	10	18	18 1 3 2 x + 4 – /
3	18 1 3 2 x + 4 – /	x	3	2	6	18 1 6 + 4 – /
4	18 1 6 + 4 – /	+	1	6	7	18 7 4 – /
5	18 7 4 – /	–	7	4	3	18 3 /
6	18 3 /	/	18	3	6	6

Fig. 5-31. Evaluation of the formula $(8 + 2 \times 5)/(1 + 3 \times 2 - 4)$ by converting it to reverse Polish and then evaluating the reverse Polish.

stack this time. The number on top of the stack is the right operand, not the left operand. This point is important for subtraction and division since the order of the operands is significant (unlike addition and multiplication).

A computer organized around a stack offers several advantages compared to multiregister machines, such as our examples:

1. Short instructions because many instructions have no addresses.

2. Formulas are easy to evaluate.

3. Complicated algorithms to optimize register use are not needed.

None of the Intel CPUs have stack addressing, but they do have special instructions PUSH and POP to put items onto the stack and remove them, respectively. In contrast, the 680x0 chips all have stack addressing using autoindexing. In predecrement mode the stack pointer (a register) is first decremented and then the register is used as a pointer. In postincrement mode the indirection is first done, and then the register is incremented.

Alternatively, if stacks grow from high addresses to low addresses and the stack pointer always points to the top of the stack (lowest numerical address containing a stack item), predecrement mode can be used for push and postincrement mode can be used for pop. If stacks grow from low addresses to high ones and by convention the stack pointer points to the first empty cell on the stack instead of the last full one, postincrement can be used for push and predecrement for pop. Which system is used is a matter of taste and historical usage.

Infix formula (8 + 2 x 5) / (1 + 3 x 2 – 4)

Reverse Polish formula 8 2 5 x + 1 3 2 x + 4 – /

Step

1	8 2 5 x + 1 3 2 x + 4 – /	Push 8
2	2 5 x + 1 3 2 x + 4 – /	Push 2
3	5 x + 1 3 2 x + 4 – /	Push 5
4	x + 1 3 2 x + 4 – /	Multiply 2 x 5
5	+ 1 3 2 x + 4 – /	Add 8 + 10
6	1 3 2 x + 4 – /	Push 1
7	3 2 x + 4 – /	Push 3
8	2 x + 4 – /	Push 2
9	x + 4 – /	Multiply 3 x 2
10	+ 4 – /	Add 1 + 6
11	4 – /	Push 4
12	– /	Subtract 7 – 4
13	/	Divide 18 / 3

(a)

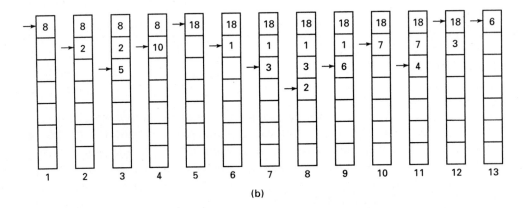

(b)

Fig. 5-32. Use of a stack to evaluate a reverse Polish formula. (a) Steps in the evaluation process. (b) The stack after the corresponding step in (a). The arrow is the stack pointer.

5.3.7. Examples of Addressing

The previous sections discussed a number of different addressing modes—immediate addressing, direct addressing, indirect addressing, indexing, and so on. There still remains the question of how the hardware or level 1 interpreter knows whether an address is immediate, direct, indirect, and so on. One solution is to have a separate opcode for each addressing mode—that is, separate opcodes for ADD IMMEDIATE, ADD DIRECT, ADD INDIRECT, and so on. Another way is to make the mode part of the address. Each instruction could contain a few bits per address specifying which form of addressing was desired.

In this section we will discuss how the addressing modes are specified on our two examples. However, as both examples are large, awkward, and confusing, we will first describe how addressing is done on the PDP-11, which is small, graceful, and clear.

Addressing on the PDP-11

PDP-11 addresses are specified by a 6-bit field, as shown in Fig. 5-33(a). One-address instructions have one such field, and two-address instructions have two such fields, with the same coding used in each. Each 6-bit field consists of a 3-bit addressing mode and a 3-bit register number. The meaning of the modes is given in Fig. 5-33(b). On the PDP-11, register 6 is the stack pointer and register 7 is the program counter. The program counter is advanced by 2 immediately after an instruction word is fetched (before the instruction is executed). This property must be kept in mind when examining some of the addressing modes.

All PDP-11 instructions are actually only 16 bits, but, in some cases one or two extra words directly following the instruction are used by the instruction and can be considered part of it. Mode 6 and mode 7 addressing require a 16-bit constant for indexing. Furthermore, if either mode 2 or mode 3 is specified with register 7 (the program counter), the following sequence of steps occurs.

First, the instruction is fetched and register 7 is increased by 2 (a word is 2 bytes). Then register 7 is used as a pointer to the data (mode 2) or the address of the data (mode 3). In both cases, the word pointed to by R7 is the word following the instruction. After this word is fetched, the autoincrementing of register 7 takes place, increasing register 7 by 2. Autoincrement addressing that specifies the program counter is a clever trick allowing the word following the instruction to be used as data. In mode 2 this word is the operand, yielding immediate addressing. In mode 3 this word is the address of the operand, yielding direct addressing. If both source and destination require an extra word, the first one is for the source.

The PDP-11 has an interesting form of addressing called **self-relative** or **position-independent** addressing. When mode 6 and register 7 are specified, the operand address is found by forming the sum of the index word following the instruction and the program counter. In effect, the index word gives the operand

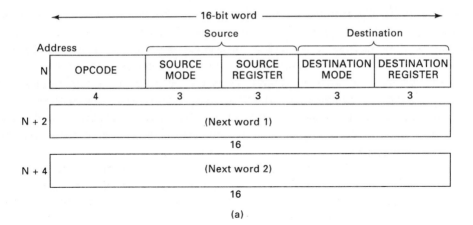

(a)

Mode	Name	How the operand is located
0	Register addressing	The operand is in R.
1	Register indirect	R contains a pointer to the operand.
2	Autoincrement	The content of R is fetched and used as a pointer to the operand. After this step, but before the instruction is executed, R is incremented by 1 (byte instructions) or 2 (word instructions).
3	Autoincrement indirect	The address of a memory word containing a pointer to the operand is fetched from R. Then R is incremented by 1 or 2 before the instruction is executed.
4	Autodecrement	R is first decremented by 1 or 2. The new value of R is then used as a pointer to the operand.
5	Autodecrement indirect	R is first decremented by 1 or 2. The new value of R is then used as the address of a memory location containing a pointer to the operand.
6	Indexing	The operand is at the address equal to the sum of R (the index register) and the 16 bit 2's complement offset in the next word. In modes 6 and 7, the program counter (R7) is incremented by 2 immediately after the next word is fetched.
7	Indexing + indirect addressing	The memory location containing a pointer to the operand is found by adding the contents of R and the next word. In modes 6 and 7, the program counter (R7) is incremented by 2 immediately after the next word is fetched.

(b)

Fig. 5-33. (a) Format of a PDP-11 two-address instruction. (b) Description of the PDP-11 addressing modes. R is the register specified along with the mode.

address by specifying how far away it is from the instruction itself, either in front or behind. In other words, the index word is a relative distance.

If all memory references use this form of addressing instead of direct address-ing (mode 3 with register 7), a program can be loaded anywhere in memory and it will run correctly. In addition, it can also be moved after being loaded, because although the absolute addresses of the needed operands change, their distance from the instructions referencing them remains fixed. However, if any return addresses from procedure calls are on the stack, moving the program is impossible because these addresses are absolute.

As an example of the power of the PDP-11 addressing mechanism, consider the MOV instruction of Fig. 5-34(a). This instruction moves the source operand to register 4. Figure 5-34(b) shows all the different variations of this instruction for different source modes and registers.

Because both the source addressing mode and the destination addressing mode can be independently specified, a single opcode yields a large number of different instructions. For example, the ADD instruction can be used to:

Add a register to another register (0, 0).

Add a register to a memory word (0, 6).

Add a memory word to a register (6, 0).

Add a memory word to another memory word (6, 6).

Pop a word from the stack and add it to a register (2, 0).

Pop a word from the stack and add it to a memory word (2, 6).

Add an immediate operand to a register (2, 0).

Add an immediate operand to a memory word (2, 6).

Add an immediate operand to the top word on the stack (2, 1).

Add a register to the top word on the stack (0, 1).

Add a memory word to the top word on the stack (6, 1).

Add a memory word to an indirectly specified address (6, 7).

Add a register to an indirectly specified address (0, 7).

Add an immediate operand to an indirectly specified address (2, 7).

There are many other possibilities as well. The numbers in parentheses in the list above are the source and destination modes. Note that mode 6 with R7 can always be replaced by mode 3 with R7 (i.e., memory can be addressed self-relative or directly). Also, note that mode 1 with register 6 uses the top word of the stack as a

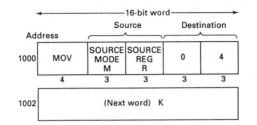

(a)

Source mode M	R = 0 – 5	R = 6	R = 7
0	Move R to R4 (register - register) Example: MOV R3, R4	Move stack pointer to R4 Example: MOV SP, R4	Move program counter to R4 Example: MOV PC, R4
1	Move memory word pointed to by R to R4 Example: MOV *R3, R4	Move top of the stack to R4, but do not remove it from the stack Example: MOV *SP, R4	Move K to R4; program counter is not incremented again so K will be executed as the next instruction Example: MOV *PC, R4
2	Move memory word pointed to by R to R4 and add 2 to R Example: MOV (R3)+, R4	Remove a word from the stack and put it in R4 (pop instruction) Example: MOV (SP)+, R4	Move K to R4 (immediate) addressing) Example: MOV $24, R4
3	Move to R4 the memory word addressed by the word R points to, and add 2 to R Example: MOV *(R3)+, R4	Pop the address of the source operand from the stack, and move the source operand itself to R4 Example: MOV *(SP)+, R4	Load R4 from memory address K (direct addressing) Example: MOV *$24, R4
4	Decrement R by 2 and then load R4 from the address R points to Example: MOV – (R3), R4	M = 4 and R = 6 is not useful as a source; however it is used as a destination in push instructions Example of push: MOV $6, – (SP)	Not used (causes an infinite loop)
5	Decrement R by 2 and then load R4 indirectly from the address R points to Example: MOV *– (R3), R4	Not used	Not used (causes an infinite loop)
6	Load R4 with the memory word at C(R) + K (indexing) Example: MOV 24(R3), R4	Load R4 with the word K/2 words below the top of the stack Example: MOV 24(SP), R4	Load R4 with the word K/2 words from this instruction (self relative addressing) Example: MOV X, R4 Note: The assembler computes the appropriate constant to address X
7	Load R4 with the memory word pointed to by C(R) + K (indexing + indirect addressing) Example: MOV *24(R3), R4	Load R4 from the word whose address is K/2 words below the top of the stack Example: MOV *24(SP), R4	Load R4 with the word pointed to by the word K bytes from this instruction (indirect addressing) Example: MOV *X, R4 Note: The assembler computes the appropriate constant to address X

(b)

Fig. 5-34. (a) A PDP-11 instruction that moves a word to register R4. (b) Different variations for different source modes and registers. R is the register and (R) is its contents. The dollar sign indicates an immediate operand and the asterisk indicates indirection (UNIX assembler notation).

source or destination but does not remove it from the stack, whereas mode 2 with register 6 does remove the top word from the stack.

Although only one opcode is used, the PDP-11 ADD instruction has dozens of distinct and useful variations. If all the variations of all 12 two-address instructions were counted as separate instructions, the PDP-11 would have hundreds of instructions. Due to the extreme flexibility of its addressing modes, the PDP-11 has a powerful instruction set using only a few opcodes.

Addressing on the 8088/80286/80386

The addressing modes on the 8088 and 80286 (and the 80386 within 16-bit segments) are identical. They are also clumsy and highly irregular. The MODE byte in Fig. 5-22 controls the addressing modes. One of the operands is specified by the combination of the MOD and R/M fields. The other is always a register, and is given by the value of the REG field.

The 32 combinations that can be specified by the 2-bit MOD field and the 3-bit R/M field are shown in the table of Fig. 5-35. If both fields are zero, for example, the operand is found by forming the sum of BX and SI, and using that result as a pointer into memory to locate the byte or word to be used as the operand. The choice of byte versus word is controlled by the low-order bit of the opcode (see Fig. 5-22).

		MOD			
		00	01	10	11
	000	M[BX + SI]	M[BX + SI + DISP8]	M[BX + SI + DISP16]	AX or AL
	001	M[BX + DI]	M[BX + DI + DISP8]	M[BX + DI + DISP16]	CX or CL
	010	M[BP + SI]	M[BP + SI + DISP8]	M[BP + SI + DISP16]	DX or DL
	011	M[BP + DI]	M[BP + DI + DISP8]	M[BP + DI + DISP16]	BX or BL
R/M	100	M[SI]	M[SI + DISP8]	M[SI + DISP16]	SP or AH
	101	M[DI]	M[DI + DISP8]	M[DI + DISP16]	BP or CH
	110	Direct addressing	M[BP + DISP8]	M[BP + DISP16]	SI or DH
	111	M[BX]	M[BX + DISP8]	M[BX + DISP16]	DI or BH

Notation: M[. . .] is a memory reference
DISP8 is an 8-bit displacement
DISP16 is a 16-bit displacement

Fig. 5-35. The 8088 and 80286 addressing modes.

As is fairly apparent from Fig. 5-35, the modes are anything but orthogonal. Indirection is possible through BX, SI, and DI, but not through AX, CX, DX, BP, or SP. Direct addressing is allowed, but only by virtue of eliminating indirection through BP. It is possible to use the sum of BX and DI as a pointer, but not the sum of BX and CX or AX and DI. No immediate modes exist, although there are special opcodes for some instructions to permit immediate addressing. Autoindexing is not permitted.

The two middle columns involve modes in which one or two registers are added to an 8- or 16-bit constant called a **displacement** that follows the instruction. If an 8-bit constant is selected, it is first sign-extended to 16 bits before being added. For example, an ADD instruction with R/M = 011, MOD = 01, and a displacement of 6 computes the sum of BP, DI, and 6, and uses the result as the memory address of one of the operands. The REG field specifies a register as the second operand. Bit 1 in the opcode byte tells which operand is the source and which is the destination.

The column for MOD 11 means that the operand is in the indicated register, depending on whether it is a word operand or a byte operand. This value of MOD is used when both operands are in registers.

By the time the 80386 rolled around, Intel had seen the error of its ways. Although the modes in the 16-bit segments are those given in Fig. 5-35, in the 32-bit segments, a new scheme, shown in Fig. 5-36, was introduced. The new modes are more regular than the old ones, and allow indirect addressing through more registers.

		MOD			
		00	01	10	11
R/M	000	M[EAX]	M[EAX + DISP8]	M[EAX + DISP32]	EAX or AL
	001	M[ECX]	M[ECX + DISP8]	M[ECX + DISP32]	ECX or CL
	010	M[EDX]	M[EDX + DISP8]	M[EDX + DISP32]	EDX or DL
	011	M[EBX]	M[EBX + DISP8]	M[EBX + DISP32]	EBX or BL
	100	SIB	SIB with DISP8	SIB with DISP32	ESP or AH
	101	Direct addressing	M[EBP + DISP8]	M[EBP + DISP32]	EBP or CH
	110	M[ESI]	M[ESI + DISP8]	M[ESI + DISP32]	ESI or DH
	111	M[EDI]	M[EDI + DISP8]	M[EDI + DISP32]	EDI or BH

Notation: M[. . .] is a memory reference
DISP8 is an 8-bit displacement
DISP32 is a 32-bit displacement
SIB means Scale, Index, Base byte follows

Fig. 5-36. The 80386 addressing modes.

Furthermore, in some modes an additional byte, called **SIB (Scale, Index, Base)** follows the MODE byte (see Fig. 5-22). The SIB byte specifies a scale factor and two registers. When a SIB byte is present, the operand address is computed by multiplying the index register by 1, 2, 4, or 8 (depending on SCALE), adding it to the base register, and finally possibly adding an 8- or 32-bit displacement, depending on MOD. Almost all the registers can be used as either index or base, a far more general scheme than on the 8088.

The SIB modes are useful for accessing array elements. For example, consider the Pascal statement:

for $i := 0$ to n **do** $a[i] := 0$;

where a is an array of 4-byte integers local to the current procedure. Typically, EBP is used to point to the base of the stack frame containing the local variables and arrays, as shown in Fig. 5-37. The compiler might keep i in EAX. To access $a[i]$, it would use a SIB mode that used as operand address the sum of $4 \times$ EAX, EBP, and 8 to store into $a[i]$ in a single instruction. On the 8088, i would first have to be copied to a scratch register, shifted left 2 bits, have BP added to it, and finally indexed off, for a total of four instructions instead of one.

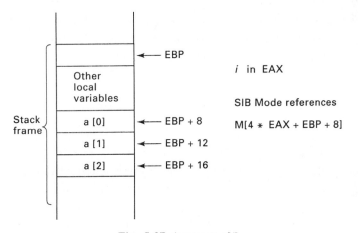

Fig. 5-37. Access to $a[i]$.

Addressing on the 68000/68020/68030

The 68000's addressing modes are similar to those of the PDP-11. They are summarized in Fig. 5-38. On both machines an operand is specified by a 6-bit field consisting of a 3-bit mode and a 3-bit register. The 68000 program counter is not a general register, so the trick used on the PDP-11 for achieving immediate addressing and direct addressing by autoincrementing the program counter does not apply. Instead, explicit addressing modes are provided. The stack pointer is addressable, however (as A7), so all the stack addressing modes do apply to the 68000.

Although Motorola did a better job with the addressing modes on the first round than Intel, it was not content to rest on its laurels for the 68020. The Motorola engineers, too, wanted a way to access array elements in a single instruction, as

Mode	Reg	Extra words	Description
0	D	0	Operand in register D
1	A	0	Operand in register A
2	A	0	Pointer to operand in register A
3	A	0	Pointer in A; autoincrement A after use
4	A	0	Autodecrement A; then use as pointer
5	A	1	Indexed mode with 16-bit displacement
6	A	1	A + index register + 8-bit displacement yields address
7	0	1	Direct addressing with 16-bit address
7	1	2	Direct addressing with 32-bit address
7	2	1	Operand address is PC + 16-bit displacement
7	3	1	Operand address is PC + index + 8-bit displacement
7	4	1 or 2	Immediate data

Fig. 5-38. Addressing modes on the 68000.

well as a way to access other kinds of data structures. This desire led to the addition of several sophisticated new addressing modes. These modes were continued unchanged in the 68030.

A key problem was how to encode them, since all eight of the modes were already in use. The problem was solved by using mode 6, and also mode 7 with register 3. Both of these modes already had an additional 16-bit word present following the instruction word, as shown in Fig. 5-39(a)-(b). Two unused bits were first converted to a scale factor (1, 2, 4, or 8, the same as the 80386) in the one-word format, as shown in Fig. 5-39(c).

To accommodate the new modes, a new format was introduced, indicated by having bit 8 set to 1 instead of 0. In this format, the 8-bit DISPLACEMENT field was replaced by four new fields, and optionally two new displacements as well. While we do not intend to go into this format in all its gory detail, suffice it to say that many combinations of adding (scaled) registers and displacements are possible, including the Intel SIB modes and others. Some of the modes have multiple phases of computation, first adding various components, going to memory to fetch a pointer, and then continuing the addressing computation on the pointer fetched. These modes are sometimes useful for accessing complex data structures passed to procedures as reference parameters.

If you are thinking: "Is all this complexity really necessary?" rest assured, you are not alone. Many computer scientists have come to regard addressing modes such as those of Fig. 5-39(d) as being somewhat akin to the gargoyles in a Gothic cathedral—an overblown way to do something simple (a gargoyle is basically a fancy drainpipe). These people have argued strongly for simple, but fast, computers, known as **RISC** machines. These machines are bare bones devices, designed to have the minimum in complexity and run very fast. They have very few addressing modes, and those they do have are as simple as can be. We will study them in Chap. 8, as mentioned earlier.

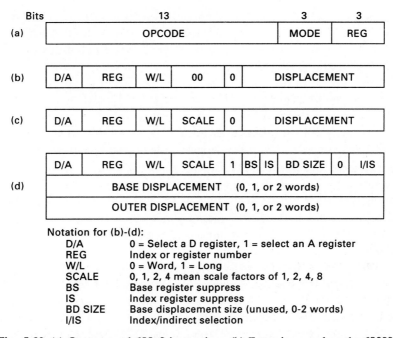

Notation for (b)-(d):
- D/A   0 = Select a D register, 1 = select an A register
- REG   Index or register number
- W/L   0 = Word, 1 = Long
- SCALE   0, 1, 2, 4 mean scale factors of 1, 2, 4, 8
- BS   Base register suppress
- IS   Index register suppress
- BD SIZE   Base displacement size (unused, 0-2 words)
- I/IS   Index/indirect selection

Fig. 5-39. (a) One-operand 680x0 instruction. (b) Extension word on the 68000. (c) Brief format extension word on the 68020 and 68030. (d) Full format extension words on the 68020 and 68030.

5.3.8. Discussion of Addressing Modes

In practice, not all the addressing modes that we have discussed are equally important. Compilers for high-level languages mostly use the following modes:

Autoindex   — Pushing and popping procedure parameters

Direct   — Accessing global variables

Immediate   — Moving constants around

Index   — Accessing local variables

Register   — Holding local variables

Register indirect — Holding pointers to structures

Some of the other modes are also used, but less frequently.

Let us look at our three examples (including the PDP-11) to see how they do. The PDP-11 only has eight addressing modes, but it includes all of the important ones listed above. The remaining PDP-11 modes are present mostly as a result of symmetry (the low-order bit of the address field means indirect, so modes 1, 3, 5, and 7 are the same as 0, 2, 4, and 6, respectively, but with an extra indirection). This scheme is simple, easy to understand, straightforward to implement in microcode, and handles all the normal cases well. DEC gets an A+.

The 68000 designers did their best to copy the PDP-11 addressing modes, but they had a problem: 16 registers instead of 8. Having 16 registers means that 4 bits are needed to address them. With only 6 bits for the mode + register, allocating 4 bits to the register field would have meant only 2 mode bits, considerably weakening the addressing capabilities. (This approach is possible, however. An old Texas Instruments microprocessor, the TI9900, did precisely that.)

The solution they chose was to have one mode for addressing D registers, but have most of the other modes work only with A registers. Like the PDP-11, the 68000 also has modes that address memory relative to the program counter, but unlike the PDP-11, the program counter is not one of the general registers. It probably should have been. Still, the most important addressing modes are present, and the addressing scheme is reasonably orthogonal to the opcodes. Having two full addressing modes per instruction (see Fig. 5-21) would have been nice, but the need to specify a length (8, 16, or 32 bits) in almost every instruction precludes that. All in all, the 68000 is not bad. Motorola gets an A−.

The 68020 and 68030 have more complicated addressing modes for handling arrays, parameters, and complex data structures. These modes improve performance somewhat over the 68000, but they also lead to more complicated microcode and compilers. The jury is still out on the question of whether making addressing modes (and architectures in general) ever more complicated is a good idea. Again, see the discussion of RISC machines in Chap. 8.

The 8088 and 80286 have weak addressing. They have only 2 mode bits (versus 3 on the PDP-11 and 680x0). The eight user registers are all different. Only three of them allow indirect addressing (SI, DI, and BX) and only four allow indexing (SI, DI, BX, and BP). Immediate and autoindex modes do not exist, although there are some special instructions with immediate operands. The only way to access the stack is with the PUSH and POP instructions, and PUSH does not allow immediate operands, so passing a constant as parameter requires two instructions. Let's be generous and give Intel a C for its efforts.

When it came time to design the 80386, the Intel engineers finally decided to build a machine they could be proud of, instead of one compatible with everything going back to the 8080. Consequently, the 80386 32-bit addressing modes are reasonably regular and general, and with the SIB byte quite powerful as well. For most purposes, the addressing power of the 80386 and 68030 chips is about the same.

We have seen how much trouble the lack of bits causes. The 68030, for example, cannot use the D registers for most of the basic addressing modes because a 4-bit field is too big. One other solution is possible, however. It is not used in either the Intel or Motorola lines, but it is used in the DEC VAX—simply use more bits.

The 6-bit mode/register field used in the PDP-11 and 68000 is expanded to a full byte in the VAX, with 4 bits for the mode and 4 bits for the register. This scheme allows all 16 registers to be fully addressed and also allows many modes, but it means that a two operand instruction is a minimum of three bytes, one for the opcode and one each for the operands.

We have now completed our examination of the various trade-offs possible between opcodes and addresses, and various forms of addressing. When approaching a new computer, you should examine the instruction set and addressing possibilities not only to see which ones are available but also to understand why those choices were made and what the consequences of alternative choices would have been.

5.4. INSTRUCTION TYPES

Conventional machine level instructions can be approximately separated into two groups: general-purpose instructions and special-purpose instructions. The general-purpose instructions have wide application. For example, the ability to move data around in the machine is something that is needed by almost every application. The special-purpose instructions have much narrower applications. For example, the 68000 MOVEP instruction takes the contents of a D register and stores it in memory in alternate bytes, with an unused byte between the data bytes. Few applications can make effective use of this instruction and no compiler will ever generate it. (It was included to simplify communication with older, 8-bit-wide peripheral chips.) In the following sections we will discuss the major groups of general-purpose instructions.

5.4.1. Data Movement Instructions

Copying data from one place to another is the most fundamental of all operations. By copying we mean the creating of a new object, with the identical bit pattern as the original. This use of the word "movement" is somewhat different from its normal usage in English. When we say that Marvin Mongoose has moved from New York to California, we do not mean that an identical copy of Mr. Mongoose was created in California and that the original is still in New York. When we say that the contents of memory location 2000 have been moved to some register, we almost always mean that an identical copy has been created there and that the original is still undisturbed in location 2000. Data movement instructions would better be called "data duplication" instructions, but the term "data movement" is already established.

Data can be stored in several places, differing in the way the words are accessed. Three common places are in a particular memory word, in a register, or on the stack. The stack is kept either in special registers or in memory but the way it is accessed is different from standard memory accesses. A memory access requires an address, whereas pushing an item onto the stack does not explicitly address the stack. Data movement instructions require that both the source of the information (i.e., the original) and the destination (i.e., where the copy is to be placed) be specified either explicitly or implicitly.

Data movement instructions must somehow indicate the amount of data to be moved. Instructions exist to move quantities of data ranging from 1 bit to the entire memory. On fixed-word-length machines, the number of words to be moved is usually specified by the instruction—for example, separate instructions to move a word and move a halfword. Variable-word-length machines often have instructions specifying only the source and destination addresses but not the amount. The move continues until an end-of-data field mark is found in the data itself.

The 680x0 has a general-purpose MOVE instruction, with two arbitrary operands, as shown in Fig. 5-23. It can move data between registers, memory, or the stack anywhere. The Intel CPUs have much more limited MOVE instructions, but there are many of them, so it is possible to move anything anywhere as well.

5.4.2. Dyadic Operations

Dyadic operations are those that combine two operands to produce a result. Just about all level 2 machines have instructions to perform addition and subtraction on integers. Except for the 8-bit microcomputers, multiplication and division of integers are standard as well. It is presumably unnecessary to explain why computers are equipped with arithmetic instructions.

Another group of dyadic operations includes the Boolean instructions. Although 16 Boolean functions of two variables exist, few, if any, level 2 machines have instructions for all 16. For example, the function that *computes* TRUE, independent of the arguments is useless. If the bit pattern for TRUE is needed somewhere in the machine, it can simply be moved there rather than be computed. Similar arguments suggest that an instruction to implement $f(P, Q) = P$ would be rather useless.

Three instructions present in many machines are AND, OR, and EXCLUSIVE OR. On fixed-word-length machines, AND computes the bit-by-bit Boolean product of two one-word arguments, the result of which is also a word. Often there exist instructions for bytes and double words as well. Similar remarks apply to the other Boolean operations.

An important use of AND is for extracting bits from words. Consider, for example, a 32-bit-word-length machine in which four 8-bit characters are stored per word. Suppose that it is necessary to separate the second character from the other three in order to print it; that is, it is necessary to create a word which contains that character in the rightmost 8 bits, referred to as **right justified**, with zeros in the leftmost 24 bits.

To extract the character, the word containing the character is ANDed with a constant, called a **mask**. The result of this operation is that the unwanted bits are all changed into zeros—that is, masked out—as shown below.

```
10110111 10111100 11011011 10001011  A
00000000 11111111 00000000 00000000  B (mask)
00000000 10111100 00000000 00000000  A AND B
```

The result would then be shifted 16 bits to the right to isolate the character at the right end of the word.

An important use of OR is to pack bits into a word, packing being the inverse of extracting. To change the rightmost 8 bits of a 32-bit word without disturbing the other 24 bits, first the unwanted 8 bits are masked out and then the new character is ORed in, as shown below.

```
10110111 10111100 11011011 10001011  A
11111111 11111111 11111111 00000000  B (mask)
10110111 10111100 11011011 00000000  A AND B
00000000 00000000 00000000 01010111  C
10110111 10111100 11011011 01010111  (A AND B) OR C
```

The AND operation tends to remove 1s, because there are never more 1s in the result than in either of the operands. The OR operation tends to insert 1s, because there are always at least as many 1s in the result as in the operand with the most 1s. The EXCLUSIVE OR operation, on the other hand, is symmetric, tending, on the average, neither to insert nor remove 1s. This symmetry with respect to 1s and 0s is occasionally useful—for example, in generating "random numbers."

Early computers performed floating-point arithmetic by calling software procedures, but today many computers, especially those intended for scientific work, have floating-point instructions at level 2 for reasons of speed. Some machines provide several lengths of floating-point numbers, the shorter ones for speed and the longer ones for occasions when many digits of accuracy are needed. Floating-point numbers are discussed in Appendix B.

5.4.3. Monadic Operations

Monadic operations have one operand and produce one result. Because one fewer address has to be specified than with dyadic operations, the instructions are sometimes shorter.

Instructions to shift or rotate the contents of a word or byte are quite useful and are often provided in several different variations. Shifts are operations in which the bits are moved to the left or right, with bits shifted off the end of the word being lost. Rotates are shifts in which bits pushed off one end reappear on the other end. The difference between a shift and a rotate is illustrated below.

00000000 00000000 00000000 01110011 A
00000000 00000000 00000000 00011100 A shifted right 2 bits
11000000 00000000 00000000 00011100 A rotated right 2 bits

Both left and right shifts and rotates are useful. If an n-bit word is left rotated k bits, the result is the same as if it had been right rotated $n - k$ bits.

Right shifts are often performed with sign extension. This means that positions vacated on the left end of the word are filled up with the original sign bit, 0 or 1. It is as though the sign bit were dragged along to the right. Among other things, it means that a negative number will remain negative. This situation is illustrated below for 2-bit right shifts.

11111111 11111111 11111111 11110000 A
00111111 11111111 11111111 11111100 A shifted without sign extension
11111111 11111111 11111111 11111100 A shifted with sign extension

An important use of shifting is multiplication and division by powers of 2. If a positive integer is left shifted k bits, the result, barring overflow, is the original number multiplied by 2^k. If a positive integer is right shifted k bits, the result is the original number divided by 2^k.

Shifting can be used to speed up certain arithmetic operations. Consider, for example, computing $18 \times n$ for some positive integer n. Because $18 \times n = 16 \times n + 2 \times n$, $16 \times n$ can be obtained by shifting a copy of n 4 bits to the left. $2 \times n$ can be obtained by shifting n 1 bit to the left. The sum of these two numbers is $18 \times n$. The multiplication has been accomplished by a move, two shifts, and an addition, which is often faster than a multiplication.

Shifting negative numbers, even with sign extension, gives quite different results, however. Consider, for example the one's complement number, -1. Shifted 1 bit to the left it yields -3. Another 1-bit shift to the left yields -7:

11111111 11111111 11111111 11111110 -1 in one's complement
11111111 11111111 11111111 11111100 -1 shifted left 1 bit = -3
11111111 11111111 11111111 11111000 -1 shifted left 2 bits = -7

Left shifting one's complement negative numbers does not multiply by 2. Right shifting does simulate division correctly, however.

Now consider a two's complement representation of -1. When right shifted 6 bits with sign extension, it yields -1, which is incorrect because the integral part of $-1/64$ is 0:

11111111 11111111 11111111 11111111 -1 in two's complement
11111111 11111111 11111111 11111111 -1 shifted right 6 bits = -1

Left shifting does, however, simulate multiplication by 2.

Rotate operations are useful for packing and unpacking bit sequences from words. If it is desired to test all the bits in a word, rotating the word 1 bit at a time either way successively puts each bit in the sign bit, where it can be easily tested, and also restores the word to its original value when all bits have been tested.

All of our example machines have a wide variety of shift and rotate instructions in both directions. Some of them involve the carry bit and some of them do not. It does not really matter much, however, as compilers practically never generate any of them except left shift, as an optimized way to multiply by a power of two.

Certain dyadic operations occur so frequently with particular operands that level 2 machines sometimes have monadic instructions to accomplish them quickly. Moving zero to a memory word or register is extremely common when initializing a calculation. Moving zero is, of course, a special case of the general move data instructions. For efficiency, a CLEAR operation, with only one address, the location to be cleared (i.e., set to zero), is often provided.

Adding 1 to a word is also commonly used for counting. A monadic form of the add instruction is the increment operation, which adds 1. The negate operation is another example. Negating X is really computing $0 - X$, a dyadic subtraction, but again, for efficiency, a separate NEGATE instruction is sometimes provided.

The Intel machines all have INC and DEC instructions for adding or subtracting 1. The 680x0 has slightly more general instructions, ADDQ and SUBQ, which can add or subtract a constant in the range 1 to 8.

5.4.4. Comparisons and Conditional Jumps

Nearly all programs need the ability to test their data and alter the sequence of instructions to be executed based on the results. A simple example is the square root function, $\sqrt{x}$. If x is negative the procedure gives an error message; otherwise, it computes the square root. A function *sqrt* has to test x and then jump, depending on whether it is negative or not.

A common method for doing so is to provide conditional jump (often called conditional branch) instructions that test some condition and jump to a particular memory address if the condition is met. Sometimes a bit in the instruction can be set to 1 or 0, meaning that the jump is to occur if the condition is met or the condition is not met, respectively.

The most common condition to be tested is whether a particular bit in the machine is 0 or not. If an instruction tests the sign bit of a two's complement number and jumps to LABEL if it is 1, the statements beginning at LABEL will be executed if the number was negative, and the statements following the conditional jump will be executed if it was 0 or positive. The same test made on a one's complement number will always jump to LABEL if the tested number is less than or equal to −1, and it will never jump to LABEL if the tested number is greater than or equal to 1. If the number is 0, the jump may happen or not, depending on whether it is +0 or −0. That is obviously rather unpleasant, because mathematically +0 = −0, and is, in fact, one of the strongest arguments against one's complement arithmetic and in favor of two's complement arithmetic.

Many machines have bits that are used to indicate specific conditions. For example, there may be an overflow bit that is set to 1 whenever an arithmetic operation gives an incorrect result. By testing this bit one checks for overflow on the previous arithmetic operation, so that if an overflow occurred, a jump can be made to an error routine. The 68000 even has a special, short instruction, TRAPV, which traps if the overflow bit is on.

Similarly, some processors have a carry bit that is set when a carry occurs from the leftmost bit, for example, if two negative numbers are added. A carry from the leftmost bit is quite normal and should not be confused with an overflow. Testing of the carry bit is needed for multiple-precision arithmetic.

Some machines have an instruction to test the rightmost bit of a word. It allows the program to test if a (positive) number is odd or even in one instruction.

Testing for zero is important for loops and many other purposes. If all the conditional jump instructions tested only one bit, to test a particular word for 0, one would need a separate test for each bit, to ensure that none was a 1. To avoid this situation, many machines have an instruction to test a word and jump if it is zero. Of course, this solution merely passes the buck to level 1. In practice, the hardware usually contains a register all of whose bits are ORed together, to give a single bit telling whether the register contains any 1 bits.

Comparing two words or characters to see if they are equal or, if not, which one is greater is also important, in sorting for example. To perform this test, three addresses are needed, two for the data items, and one for the address to jump to if the condition is true. Computers whose instruction format allows three addresses per instruction have no trouble but those that do not must do something to get around this problem.

One common solution is to provide an instruction that performs a comparison and sets one or more condition bits to record the result. A subsequent instruction can test the condition bits and jump if the two compared values were equal, or unequal, or if the first was greater, and so on. Both of our example machines use this approach.

Some subtle points are involved in comparing two numbers. First, on one's complement machines +0 and −0 are different; for example, on a 32-bit machine,

00000000 00000000 00000000 00000000 +0 in one's complement
11111111 11111111 11111111 11111111 −0 in one's complement

A decision has to be made by the designers whether +0 and −0 are equal and, if not, which is larger. No matter which way it is decided, there are convincing arguments that the wrong decision was made. If the designers make +0 = −0, then the fact that a comparison yields equal does not mean that the bit patterns of the compared data items are the same. Consider a machine with a 32-bit word in which four 8-bit characters are stored. If four characters whose code is 0 are stored in a word, the word will contain 32 zeros. If four characters whose code is 255 are stored in a word, the word will contain 32 ones. If these two words compare as equal because +0 = −0, a text processing program may mistakenly conclude that the two words contain the same four characters.

If, on the other hand, the hardware treats −0 and +0 as unequal, the result of adding −1 to +1 and comparing the result to +0 may well be that they are unequal, because −1 added to +1 may give −0 as the result. Needless to say, this situation is highly undesirable. Two's complement machines, including our examples, do not have problems with +0 and −0, but one's complement machines do have these troubles. The word is gradually getting out to machine architects and, as a result, one's complement machines are slowly dying out.

Another subtle point relating to comparing numbers is deciding whether or not the numbers should be considered signed or not. Three-bit binary numbers can be ordered in one of two ways. From smallest to largest:

Unsigned	Signed	
000	100	(smallest)
001	101	
010	110	
011	111	
100	000	
101	001	
110	010	
111	011	(largest)

The column on the left shows the positive integers 0 to 7 in increasing order. The column on the right shows the two's complement signed integers −4 to +3. The answer to the question "Is 011 greater than 100?" depends on whether or not the numbers are regarded as being signed. Most machines, including the Intel and Motorola ones, have jump instructions for both orderings.

Machines with fewer than three addresses per instruction sometimes handle conditional jumping with an instruction that skips the next sequential instruction if the condition is met. That instruction will frequently be a jump instruction. On some machines several instructions may be skipped, instead of just one, the number of bytes to be skipped being specified in the instruction itself. Typically this is a number from −128 to +127, so it can fit in one byte. The 68000 has several instructions of this type.

The unconditional jump is a special case of the conditional jump in which the condition is always met.

5.4.5. Procedure Call Instructions

A procedure is a group of instructions that performs some task and that can be invoked (called) from several places in the program. The term **subroutine** is often used instead of procedure, especially when referring to assembly language programs. When the procedure has finished its task, it must return to the statement after the call. Therefore, the return address must be transmitted to the procedure.

The return address may be placed in any of three places: memory, a register, or the stack. Far and away the worst solution is putting it in a single, fixed memory location. In this scheme, if the procedure called another procedure, the second call would cause the return address from the first one to be lost.

A slight improvement is having the procedure call instruction store the return address in the first word of the procedure, with the first executable instruction being in the second word. The procedure can then return by jumping indirectly to the first word or, if the hardware puts the opcode for jump in the first word along with the return address, jumping directly to it. The procedure may call other procedures, because each procedure has space for one return address. If the procedure calls itself, this scheme fails, because the first return address will be destroyed by the second call. The ability for a procedure to call itself, called **recursion**, is exceedingly important both for theorists and practical programmers. Furthermore, if procedure A calls procedure B, and procedure B calls procedure C, and procedure C calls procedure A (indirect recursion), this scheme also fails.

A bigger improvement is to have the procedure call instruction put the return address in a register, leaving the responsibility for storing it in a safe place to the procedure. If the procedure is recursive, it will have to put the return address in a different place each time it is called.

The best thing for the procedure call instruction to do with the return address is to push it onto a stack. When the procedure has finished, it pops the return address off the stack and stuffs it into the program counter. If this form of procedure call is available, recursion does not cause any special problems; the return address will automatically be saved in such a way as to avoid destroying previous return addresses. All of our example machines use this method.

5.4.6. Loop Control

The need to execute a group of instructions a fixed number of times occurs frequently and thus some machines have instructions to facilitate doing this. All the schemes involve a counter that is increased or decreased by some constant once each time through the loop. The counter is also tested once each time through the loop. If a certain condition holds, the loop is terminated.

One method initializes a counter outside the loop and then immediately begins executing the loop code. The last instruction of the loop updates the counter and, if the termination condition is not yet satisfied, jumps back to the first instruction of the loop. Otherwise, the loop is finished and it falls through, executing the first instruction beyond the loop. This form of looping is characterized as test-at-the-end type looping, and is illustrated in Fig. 5-40(a).

Test-at-the-end looping has the property that the loop will always be executed at least once, even if n is less than or equal to 0. Consider, as an example, a

```
        i : = 1;                                    i : = 1;

  1: {first statement}                        1: if i > n then goto 2;
     {second statement}                          {first statement}
       .                                          {second statement}
       .                                            .
       .                                            .
     {last statement}                              .
     i : = i + 1;                               {last statement}
     if i < = n then goto 1;                    i : = i + 1;
                                                goto 1;

  2: {first statement after loop}          2: {first statement after loop}

              (a)                                       (b)
```

Fig. 5-40. (a) Test-at-the-end loop. (b) Test-at-the-beginning loop.

program that maintains personnel records for a company. At a certain point in the program, it is reading information about a particular employee. It reads in n, the number of children the employee has, and executes a loop n times, once per child, reading the child's name, sex, and birthday, so that the company can send him or her a birthday present, one of the company's fringe benefits. If the employee does not have any children, n will be 0 but the loop will still be executed once sending presents and giving erroneous results.

Figure 5-40(b) shows another way of performing the test that works properly even for n less than or equal to 0. Notice that the testing is different in the two cases, so that if a single level 2 instruction does both the increment and the test, the designers are forced to choose one method or the other.

Consider the code that should be produced for the Pascal statement

for $i := 1$ **to** n **do begin ... end**

If the compiler does not have any information about n, it must use the approach of Fig. 5-40(b) to correctly handle the case of $n \leq 0$. If, however, it can determine that $n > 0$, for example, by seeing where n is assigned, it may use the better code of Fig. 5-40(a). The FORTRAN standard formerly stated that all loops were to be executed once, to allow the more efficient code of Fig. 5-40(a) to be generated all the time. In 1977, that defect was corrected when even the FORTRAN community began to realize that having a loop statement with outlandish semantics was not a good idea, even if it did save one jump instruction per loop.

All the Intel CPUs iterate a fixed number of times using the LOOP instruction, which decrements CX/ECX by 1, and jumps to a given label if the result is not zero. If it is zero, it falls through and continues execution with the next instruction.

The 680x0 has a somewhat more general instruction that first tests the condition codes for a given condition, falling through the loop if it is true. If the condition is false, a D register is decremented. If the result is 0 or more, the loop is repeated; otherwise the loop is terminated and the instruction following the loop is executed.

5.4.7. Input/Output

No other group of instructions exhibits as much variety from machine to machine as the I/O instructions. Four different I/O schemes are in current use. These are:

1. Programmed I/O with busy waiting.

2. Interrupt-driven I/O.

3. DMA I/O.

4. I/O using data channels.

We will now discuss each of these in turn.

The simplest possible I/O method is **programmed I/O**, which is used in some low-end microprocessors. These microcomputers have a single input instruction and a single output instruction. Each of these instructions selects one of the I/O devices. A single character is transferred between a fixed register in the processor and the selected I/O device. The processor must execute an explicit instruction for each and every character read or written.

As a simple example of this method, consider a terminal with four 1-byte registers, as shown in Fig. 5-41. Two registers are used for input, status and data, and two are used for output, also status and data. Each one has a unique address. If memory-mapped I/O is being used, all four registers are part of the computer's memory address space, and can be read and written using ordinary instructions. Otherwise, special I/O instructions, say, IN and OUT, are provided to read and write them. In both cases, I/O is performed by transferring data and status information between the CPU and these registers.

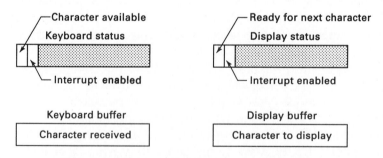

Fig. 5-41. Device registers for a simple terminal.

The keyboard status register has 2 bits that are used and 6 bits that are not used. The leftmost bit (7) is set to 1 by the hardware whenever a character arrives. If the software has previously set bit 6, an interrupt is generated, otherwise it is not (interrupts will be discussed shortly). When using programmed I/O, to get input, the

CPU normally sits in a tight loop repeatedly reading the keyboard status register, waiting for bit 7 to go on. When this happens, the software reads in the keyboard buffer register to get the character. Reading the keyboard data register causes the CHARACTER AVAILABLE bit to be reset to 0.

Output works in a similar way. To write a character to the screen, the software first reads the display status register to see if the READY bit is 1. If not, it loops until the bit goes to 1, indicating that the device is ready to accept a character. As soon as the terminal is ready, the software writes a character to the display buffer register, which causes it to be transmitted to the screen, and also causes the device to clear the READY bit in the display status register. When the character has been displayed and the terminal is prepared to handle the next character, the READY bit is automatically set to 1 again by the controller.

As an example of programmed I/O, consider the Pascal procedure of Fig. 5-42. This procedure is called with two parameters: a character array to be output, and the count of characters present in the array, up to 1K. The body of the procedure is a loop that outputs characters one at a time. For each character, first the CPU must wait until the device is ready, then the character is output. The procedures *in* and *out* would typically be assembly language routines to read and write the device registers specified by the first parameter from or to the variable specified as the second parameter. The division by 128 gets rid of the low-order 7 bits, leaving the READY bit in bit 0.

```
const size = 1023;

type buffer = array [0.. size] of char ;

procedure OutputBuf(b: buffer; count: integer) ;
{Output a block of data to the terminal.}
var status ,i, ready: integer ;
begin
  for i := 0 to count do
    begin                          {For each character execute loop and output 1 char.}
      repeat
        in (DisplayStatusReg, status);  {get the status register}
        ready:= status div 128;         {shift bits 0-6 off the end}
      until ready = 1;

      out (DisplayBufferReg, b [i])   {output one character}
    end
end;
```

Fig. 5-42. An example of programmed I/O.

The primary disadvantage of programmed I/O is that the CPU spends most of its time in a tight loop waiting for the device to become ready. This approach is called **busy waiting**. If the CPU has nothing else to do (e.g., the CPU in a washing machine), busy waiting is fine. However, if there is other work to do, such as running other programs, busy waiting is wasteful, so a different I/O method is needed.

The way to get rid of busy waiting is to have the CPU start the I/O device and tell it to generate an interrupt when it is done. Looking at Fig. 5-41, we show how this is done. By setting the INTERRUPT ENABLE bit in a device register, the software can request that the hardware give it a signal when the I/O is completed. We will study interrupts in detail later in this chapter when we come to flow of control.

It is worth mentioning that in many computers, the interrupt signal is generated by ANDing the INTERRUPT ENABLE bit with the READY bit. If the software first enables interrupts (before starting I/O), an interrupt will happen immediately, because the READY bit will be 1. Thus it may be necessary to first start the device, then immediately afterward enable interrupts. Writing a byte to the status register does not change the READY bit, which is read only.

Although interrupt-driven I/O is a big step forward compared to programmed I/O, it is far from perfect. The problem is that an interrupt is required for every character transmitted. Processing an interrupt is expensive. A way is needed to get rid of most of the interrupts.

The solution lies in going back to programmed I/O, but having somebody else do it. (The solution to many problems lies in having somebody else do the work.) Figure 5-43 shows how this is arranged. Here we have added a new chip, a **DMA** (**Direct Memory Access**) controller to the system, with direct access to the bus.

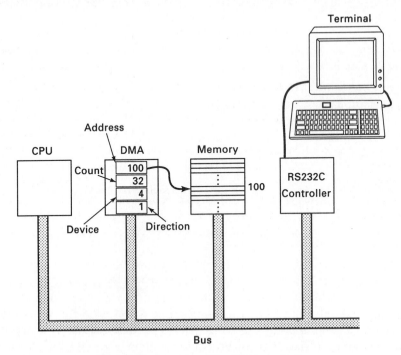

Fig. 5-43. A system with a DMA controller.

The DMA chip has (at least) four registers inside it, all of which can be loaded by software running on the CPU. The first one contains the memory address to be read or written. The second one contains the count of how many bytes (or words) are to be transferred. The third one specifies the device number or I/O space address to use. The fourth one tells whether data are to be read from or written to the I/O device.

To write a block of 32 bytes from memory address 100 to a terminal (say, device 4), the CPU writes the numbers 32, 100, and 4 into the first three DMA registers, and then the code for WRITE (say, 1) in the fourth one, as shown in Fig. 5-43. Once initialized like this, the DMA controller makes a bus request to read byte 100 from the memory, the same way the CPU would read from the memory. Having gotten this byte, the DMA controller then makes an I/O request to device 4, to write the byte to it. After both of these operations have been completed, the DMA controller increments its address register by 1 and decrements its count register by 1. If the count register is still greater than 0, another byte is read from memory and then written to the device.

When the count finally goes to 0, the DMA controller stops transferring data and asserts the interrupt line on the CPU chip. With DMA, the CPU only has to initialize a few registers. After that, it is free to do something else until the complete transfer is finished, at which time it gets an interrupt from the DMA controller. Some DMA controllers have two, or three, or more sets of registers, so they can control multiple simultaneous transfers.

While DMA greatly relieves the CPU from the burden of I/O, the process is not totally free. If a high-speed device, such as a disk, is being run by DMA, many bus cycles will be needed, both for memory references and device references. During these cycles the CPU will have to wait (DMA always has a higher bus priority than the CPU because I/O devices frequently cannot tolerate delays). The process of having a DMA controller take bus cycles away from the CPU is called **cycle stealing**. Nevertheless, the gain in not having to handle one interrupt per byte (or word) transferred far outweighs the loss due to cycle stealing. DMA is the normal method for doing I/O on all personal computers and minicomputers.

On large mainframes, however, the situation is different. These machines typically do so much I/O that cycle stealing would saturate the bus, and even with only one interrupt per block transferred, far too much time would be devoted to interrupt handling. The way out here is to add special I/O processors, called **data channels**, to the architecture, as shown in Fig. 2-19.

A channel is really a specialized computer. It can be given a program to run, and then it goes off and runs the program without any help from the main CPU. When the program has been fully executed, the channel interrupts the CPU. Since a channel program may be quite complicated, involving the transfer of many blocks of data, fewer interrupts are required than with simple DMA transfers.

Since neither the Intel nor Motorola microprocessors use data channels, let us use the I/O structure of the large IBM mainframes as an example here. Two types of channels are present. A **selector channel** controls high-speed devices, such as disks. Due to the high data rate from these devices, a selector channel can only handle one transfer at a time. In contrast, a **multiplexor channel** can handle multiple low-speed devices, such as terminals, at the same time.

To perform I/O on a computer with data channels, the CPU first creates a program for the channel and stores it in main memory. Then it executes a START I/O instruction specifying the channel and the I/O device. The channel then fetches the address of its program from a fixed memory location, puts that address in its program counter, and begins executing its channel program. The various memory words involved are illustrated in Fig. 5-44 for a typical mainframe.

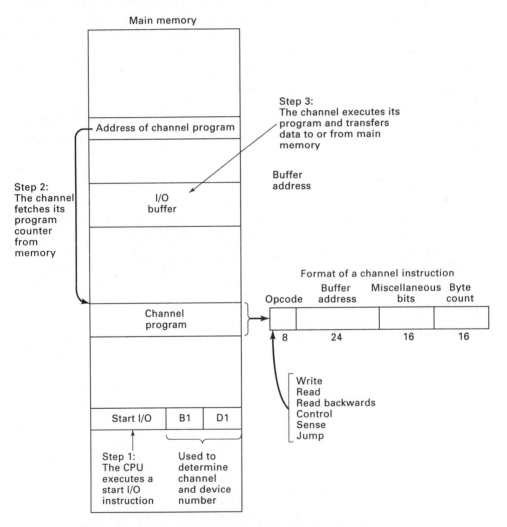

Fig. 5-44. Typical steps involved in performing I/O using a data channel.

A channel program consists of one or more 64-bit instructions for the channel.

Each instruction contains an 8-bit opcode telling which operation is to be performed. These include READ, WRITE, READ BACKWARD (e.g., for rewinding magnetic tapes), CONTROL (e.g., start motor), SENSE (e.g., test for end of file), and CONDITIONAL BRANCH. The channel instructions also contain a 24-bit buffer address telling where the data are to be read from or written into, a count, telling how many bytes are to be transferred, and some flag bits. The flag bits specify such items as no data transmission (good for skipping a record on a tape) and "stop the channel after this instruction is complete."

In addition to the START I/O instruction, the CPU has a few other I/O instructions. The HALT I/O instruction forcibly stops all activity in the selected channel. The TEST I/O and TEST CHANNEL instructions are used to determine the current status of I/O activity. A few other minor I/O instructions are also available.

All the Intel CPUs have explicit I/O instructions to read or write bytes, words, or longs. These instructions specify the I/O port number desired, either directly, as a field within the instruction, or indirectly, using DX to hold it. In addition, of course, DMA chips are frequently used to relieve the CPU of the I/O burden.

None of the Motorola chips have I/O instructions. It is expected that I/O device registers will be addressed via memory mapping. Here, too, DMA is widely used.

5.5. FLOW OF CONTROL

Flow of control refers to the sequence in which instructions are executed. In general, successively executed instructions are fetched from consecutive memory locations. Procedure calls cause the flow of control to be altered, stopping the procedure currently executing and starting the called procedure. Coroutines are related to procedures and cause similar alterations in the flow of control. Traps and interrupts also cause the flow of control to be altered when special conditions occur. All these topics will be discussed in the following sections.

5.5.1. Sequential Flow of Control and Jumps

Most instructions do not alter the flow of control. After an instruction is executed, the one following it in memory is fetched and executed. After each instruction, the program counter is increased by the instruction length. If observed over an interval of time that is long compared to the average instruction time, the program counter is approximately a linear function of time, increasing by the average instruction length per average instruction time. Stated another way, the dynamic order in which the processor actually executes the instructions is the same as the order in which they appear on the program listing, as shown in Fig. 5-45(a).

If a program contains jumps, this simple relation between the order in which instructions appear in memory and the order in which they are executed is no longer true. When jumps are present, the program counter is no longer a

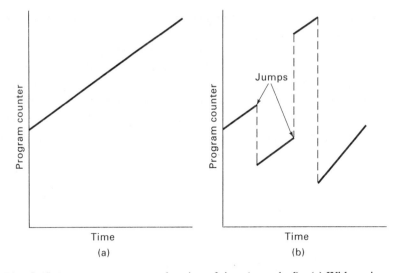

Fig. 5-45. Program counter as a function of time (smoothed). (a) Without jumps. (b) With jumps.

monotonically increasing function of time, as shown in Fig. 5-45(b). As a result, it becomes difficult to visualize the instruction execution sequence from the program listing. When programmers have trouble keeping track of the sequence in which the processor will execute the instructions, they are prone to make errors. This observation led Dijkstra (1968a) to write a then-controversial letter entitled "GO TO Statement Considered Harmful," in which he suggested avoiding GO TO statements. That letter gave birth to the structured programming revolution, one of whose tenets is the replacement of GO TO statements with more structured forms of flow control, such as WHILE loops. Of course, these programs compile down to level 2 programs that may contain many jumps, because the implementation of IF, WHILE, and other high-level control structures require jumping around.

5.5.2. Procedures

The most important technique for structuring programs is the procedure. From one point of view, a procedure call alters the flow of control just as a jump does, but unlike the jump, when finished performing its task, it returns control to the statement or instruction following the call.

However, from another point of view, a procedure body can be regarded as defining a new instruction on a higher level. From this standpoint, a procedure call can be thought of as a single instruction, even though the procedure may be quite complicated. To understand a piece of code containing a procedure call, it is only necessary to know *what* it does, not *how* it does it.

One particularly interesting kind of procedure is the **recursive procedure**, that is, a procedure that calls itself. Studying recursive procedures gives considerable insight into how procedure calls are implemented, and what local variables really are. Now we will give an example of a recursive procedure. The "Towers of Hanoi" is an ancient problem that has a simple solution involving recursion. The problem requires three pegs, on the first of which sit a series of n concentric disks, each of which is smaller in diameter than the disk directly below it. The second and third pegs are initially empty. The object is to transfer all the disks to peg 3, one disk at a time, but at no time may a larger disk rest on a smaller one. Figure 5-46 shows the initial configuration for $n = 5$ disks.

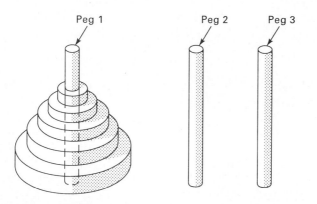

Fig. 5-46. Initial configuration for the Towers of Hanoi problem for five disks.

The solution of moving n disks from peg 1 to peg 3 consists first of moving $n - 1$ disks from peg 1 to peg 2, then moving 1 disk from peg 1 to peg 3, then moving $n - 1$ disks from peg 2 to peg 3 (see Fig. 5-47). To solve the problem we need a procedure to move n disks from peg i to peg j. When this procedure is called, by

   towers (n, i, j)

the solution is printed out. The procedure first tests to see if $n = 1$. If so, the solution is trivial, just move the one disk from i to j. If $n \neq 1$, the solution consists of three parts as discussed above, each being a recursive procedure call.

The complete solution is shown in Fig. 5-48. The call

   towers $(3, 1, 3)$

to solve the problem of Fig. 5-47 generates three more calls, namely

   towers $(2, 1, 2)$
   towers $(1, 1, 3)$
   towers $(2, 2, 3)$

The first and third will generate three calls each, for a total of seven.

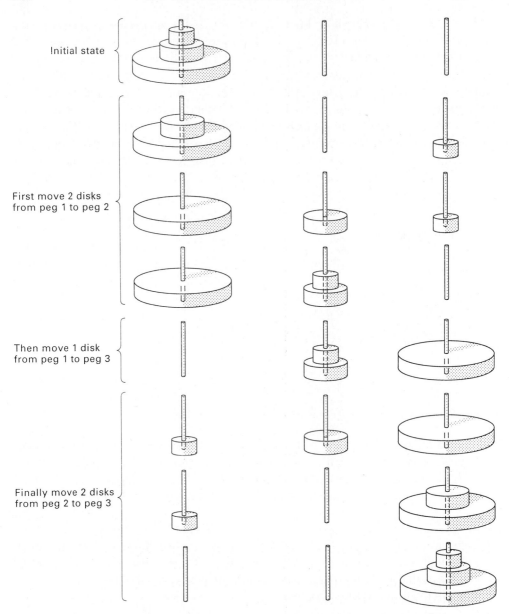

Initial state

First move 2 disks
from peg 1 to peg 2

Then move 1 disk
from peg 1 to peg 3

Finally move 2 disks
from peg 2 to peg 3

Fig. 5-47. The seven steps required to solve the Towers of Hanoi for three disks.

In order to have recursive procedures, we need a stack to store the parameters. Each time a procedure is called, a block of memory called a **stack frame** is reserved on the stack for the parameters, return address, and local variables, if any. The frame most recently created is the current frame. In our examples, the stack

procedure *towers* (*n*, *i*, *j* : *integer*);
{ Towers of Hanoi:

n is the number of disks
i is the starting peg
j is the goal peg
k = 6 − *i* − *j* is the other peg

To move the *n* disks from *i* to *j* first check to see if *n* is 1.
If so, the solution is just one move . If not, decompose the problem
into three subproblems and solve them in sequence :

  1. Move *n* − 1 disks from *i* to *k*
  2. Move 1 disk from *i* to *j*
  3. Move *n* − 1 disks from *k* to *j* }

var *k* : *integer* ;

begin
  if *n* = 1
    then *writeln* (*'Move a disk from peg'*, *i*, *' to peg '*, *j*)
    else
      begin
        k := 6 − *i* − *j*;   {compute the number of the third peg}
        towers (*n*−1, *i*, *k*);   {move *n* − 1 disks from *i* to *k*}
        towers (1, *i*, *j*);   {move 1 disk from *i* to *j*}
        towers (*n*−1, *k*, *j*)   {move *n* − 1 disks from *k* to *j*}
      end
end; { towers }

Fig. 5-48. A procedure for solving the Towers of Hanoi.

always grows downward, from high memory addresses to low ones. We have
chosen this convention because most computers, including the Intel and Motorola
ones, do things this way. A push, therefore, decreases the stack pointer by the word
size and then stores a word at the address given by the stack pointer.

In addition to the stack pointer, which points to the top of the stack (lowest
numerical address), it is often convenient to have a local base pointer, LB, which
points to a fixed location within the frame. Figure 5-49 shows the stack frame for
machine with a 16-bit word. The stack begins at 1000 and grows downward toward
address 0. The original call to *towers* pushes *n*, *i*, and *j*, onto the stack, and then
executes a CALL instruction that pushes the return address onto the stack, at
address 994. On entry, the called procedure stores the old value of LB on the stack,
and then advances the stack pointer to allocate storage for the local variables. With
only one 16-bit local variable, SP is decremented by 2. The situation, after these
things have been done, is shown in Fig. 5-49(a).

With this background, we can now explain what LB is for. In principle, variables could be referenced by giving their offsets from SP. However, as words are

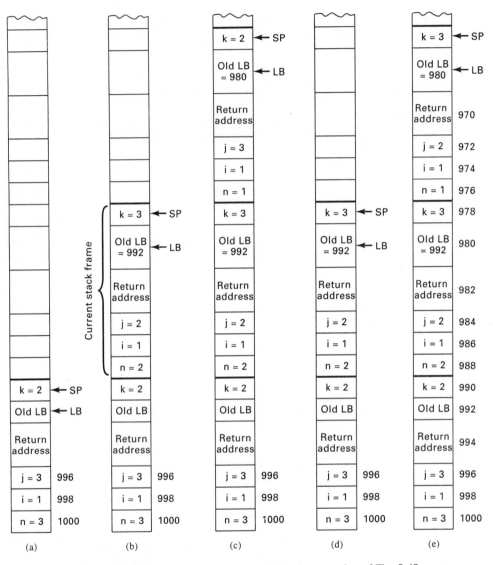

Fig. 5-49. The stack at several points during the execution of Fig. 5-48.

pushed onto the stack and popped from the stack, these offsets change. Although in some cases the compiler can keep track of the number of words on the stack and thus correct the offsets, in some cases it cannot, and in all cases considerable administration is required. Furthermore, on some machines, such as the Intel ones, accessing a variable at a known distance from SP requires multiple instructions.

Consequently, many compilers use a second register, LB, for referencing both local variables and parameters because their distances from LB do not change with pushes and pops. On the Intel CPUs, BP (EBP) is used for this purpose. On the Motorola CPUs, any address register except A7 (the stack pointer) will do. Actual parameters have positive offsets and local variables have negative offsets from LB. The first thing a procedure must do when called is save the previous LB (so it can be restored at procedure exit), copy SP into LB to create the new LB, and advance SP to reserve space for the local variables. This code is called the **procedure prolog**. Upon procedure exit, the stack must be cleaned up again, something called the **procedure epilog**.

One of the most important characteristics of any computer is how short and fast it can make the prolog and epilog. If they are long and slow, procedure calls will be expensive. Programmers who worship at the altar of efficiency will learn to avoid writing many short procedures and write large, monolithic, unstructured programs instead. The Intel ENTER and LEAVE instructions and the Motorola LINK and UNLK instructions have been provided to do most of the procedure prolog and epilog work efficiently.

Now let us get back to the Towers of Hanoi problem. Each procedure call adds a new frame to the stack and each procedure return removes a frame from the stack. In order to illustrate the use of a stack in implementing recursive procedures, we will trace the calls starting with

towers (3, 1, 3)

Figure 5-49(a) shows the stack just after this call has been made. The procedure first tests to see if $n = 1$, and on discovering that $n = 3$, makes the call

towers (2, 1, 2)

After this call is completed the stack is as shown in Fig. 5-49(b), and the procedure starts again at the beginning (a called procedure always starts at the beginning). This time the test for $n = 1$ fails again and the call

towers (1, 1, 3)

is made. The stack then is as shown in Fig. 5-49(c) and the program counter points to the start of the procedure. This time the test succeeds and a line is printed. Next, the procedure returns by removing one stack frame, resetting LB and SP to Fig. 5-49(d). It then continues executing at the return address, which is the second call:

towers (1, 1, 2)

This adds a new frame to the stack as shown in Fig. 5-49(e). Another line is printed; after the return a frame is removed from the stack. The procedure calls continue in this way until the original call completes execution and the frame of Fig. 5-49(a) is removed from the stack.

Parameters can be passed in registers or on the stack. The rules for how they are passed is known as the **calling sequence**.

5.5.3. Coroutines

In the usual calling sequence, there is a clear distinction between the calling procedure and called procedure. Consider a procedure *A*, which calls a procedure *B* in Fig. 5-50.

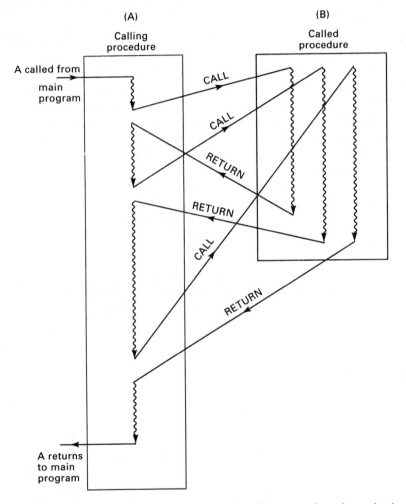

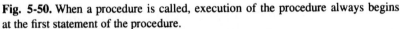

Fig. 5-50. When a procedure is called, execution of the procedure always begins at the first statement of the procedure.

Procedure *B* computes for a while and then returns to *A*. At first sight you might consider this situation symmetric, because neither *A* nor *B* is a main program, both being procedures. (Procedure *A* may have been called by the main program but that is irrelevant.) Furthermore, first control is transferred from *A* to *B*—the call—and later control is transferred from *B* to *A*—the return.

The asymmetry arises from the fact that when control passes from *A* to *B*, procedure *B* begins executing at the beginning; when *B* returns to *A*, execution starts not at the beginning of *A* but at the statement following the call. If *A* runs for a while and calls *B* again, execution starts at the beginning of *B* again, not the statement following the previous return. If, in the course of running, *A* calls *B* many times, *B* starts at the beginning all over again each and every time, whereas *A* never starts over again.

This difference is reflected in the method by which control is passed between *A* and *B*. When *A* calls *B*, it uses the procedure call instruction, which puts the return address (i.e., the address of the statement following the call) somewhere useful, for example, on top of the stack. It then puts the address of *B* into the program counter to complete the call. When *B* returns, it does not use the call instruction but instead it uses the return instruction, which simply pops the return address from the stack and puts it into the program counter.

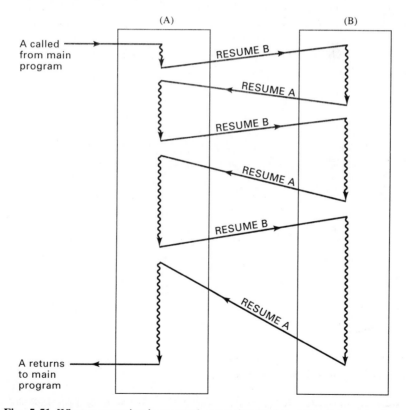

Fig. 5-51. When a coroutine is resumed, execution begins at the statement where it left off the previous time, not at the beginning.

Sometimes it is useful to have two procedures *A* and *B*, each of which calls the other as a procedure, as shown in Fig. 5-51. When *B* returns to *A*, it jumps to the statement following the call to B, as above. When A transfers control to B, it goes not to the beginning (except the first time) but to the statement following the most recent "return," that is, the most recent call of A. Two procedures, each of which regards the other as a procedure (in the sense that it is called, performs some work, and then returns to the statement following the call), are called **coroutines**.

Neither the usual call nor the usual return instruction will suffice to call coroutines, because the address to jump to comes from the stack like a return, but, unlike a return, the coroutine call itself puts a return address somewhere for the subsequent return to it. It would be nice if there were an instruction to exchange the top of the stack with the program counter. In detail, this instruction would first pop the old return address off the stack into a temporary internal register, then push the program counter onto the stack, and finally, transfer the contents of the temporary register into the program counter. Because one word is popped off the stack and one word is pushed onto the stack, the stack pointer does not change. A coroutine calling sequence would be first initialized by pushing the address of one of the coroutines onto the stack. A coroutine call instruction is sometimes called **resume**. It does, in fact, exist on some level 2 machines in the form described here. More often, however, two or three instructions are needed to do the job. Figure 5-52 illustrates RESUME.

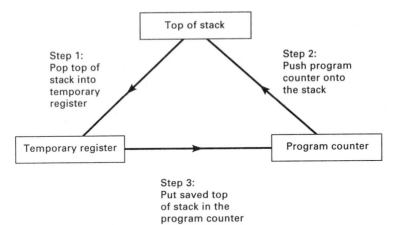

Fig. 5-52. Operation of the RESUME instruction.

As an example of the use of coroutines, consider a very advanced programming package that provides automatic program documentation. At any place in the program, the programmer may insert a comment preceded and followed by #. The program is used by the compiler to produce the object program. The comments are used by the documentation system to produce the manual. The compiler ignores the comments and the documentation system ignores the program. To make the problem interesting we will assume that the documentation part is very clever and parses all the comments to make sure that there are no grammatical errors, because programming manual writers seem to have great difficulties with the English language. A sample input is shown in Fig. 5-53.

```
if seats = 350 #if the plane is full#
  then
      begin
        full = 1; #set a flag#
        NewPlane #request another aircraft#
      end
  else reserve(passenger); #otherwise give this person a seat#
```

Fig. 5-53. A program fragment with code and documentation.

The package described can be written as two coroutines—one for parsing the program and one for parsing the English. The coroutine for the program, the compiler, begins reading the input, parsing as it goes. Eventually, it comes to the first comment symbol, #. At this point it wants to get rid of the comment so that it can continue parsing. To get rid of the comment, the compiler calls the documentation coroutine to skip the comment.

The documentation package begins running and parses the comment. Eventually, it runs across the comment symbol. From its point of view, the program text is to be ignored, so it resumes the compiler to skip the program text. The compiler will be restarted with all its variables and internal pointers intact, from the point it left off, not the beginning. The English parser may be in a complicated state at this point; it is essential that when the compiler has eaten the next piece of program text, the English parser is restarted in the state it was in when it resumed the compiler.

It is worth noting that to implement coroutines, multiple stacks are needed, because each coroutine can also call procedures in the usual way, in addition to making coroutine calls.

5.5.4. Traps

A **trap** is a kind of automatic procedure call initiated by some condition caused by the program, usually an important but rarely occurring condition. A good example is overflow. On many computers, if the result of an arithmetic operation exceeds the largest number that can be represented, a trap occurs, meaning that the flow of control is switched to some fixed memory location instead of continuing in sequence. At that fixed location is a jump to a procedure called the **trap handler**, which performs some appropriate action, such as printing an error message. If the result of an operation is within range, no trap occurs.

The essential point about a trap is that it is initiated by some exceptional condition caused by the program itself and detected by the hardware or micropro-gram. An alternative method of handling overflow is to have a 1-bit register that is set to 1 whenever an overflow occurs. A programmer who wants to check for overflow must include an explicit "jump if overflow bit is set" instruction after every arithmetic instruction. Doing so would be both slow and wasteful of space. Traps save both time and memory compared with explicit programmer-controlled checking. Traps are often implemented by having the microprogram simply make the test.

The trap may be implemented by an explicit test performed by the interpreter at level 1. If an overflow is detected, the trap address is loaded into the program counter. What is a trap at one level may be under program control at a lower level. Having the microprogram make the test still saves time compared to a programmer test, because it can be easily overlapped with something else. It also saves memory, because it need only occur in a few level 1 procedures, independent of how many arithmetic instructions occur in the main program.

A few common conditions that can cause traps are floating-point overflow, floating-point underflow, integer overflow, protection violation, undefined opcode, stack overflow, attempt to start nonexistent I/O device, attempt to fetch a word from an odd-numbered address, and division by zero.

5.5.5. Interrupts

Interrupts are changes in the flow of control caused not by the running pro-gram, but by something else, usually related to I/O. For example, a program may instruct the disk to start transferring information, and set the disk up to provide an interrupt as soon as the transfer is finished. Like the trap, the interrupt stops the running program and transfers control to an interrupt handler, which performs some appropriate action. When finished, the interrupt handler returns control to the inter-rupted program. It must restart the interrupted process in exactly the same state it was in when the interrupt occurred, which means restoring all the internal registers to their preinterrupt state.

The essential difference between traps and interrupts is this: *traps* are synchro-nous with the program and *interrupts* are asynchronous. If the program is rerun a million times with the same input, the traps will reoccur in the same place each time but the interrupts may vary, depending, for example, on precisely when a per-son at a terminal hits carriage return. The reason for the reproducibility of traps and irreproducibility of interrupts is that traps are caused directly by the program and interrupts are, at best, indirectly caused by the program.

To see how interrupts really work, let us consider a common example: a com-puter wants to output a line of characters to a terminal. The system software first collects all the characters to be written to the terminal together in a buffer, initial-izes a global variable *ptr*, to point to the start of the buffer, and sets a second global variable *count* equal to the number of characters to be output. Then it checks to see if the terminal is ready and if so, outputs the first character (e.g., using registers like those of Fig. 5-41). Having started the I/O, the CPU is then free to run another program or do something else.

In due course of time, the character is displayed on the screen. The interrupt can now begin. In simplified form, the steps are as follows.

HARDWARE ACTIONS

1. The device controller asserts an interrupt line on the system bus to start the interrupt sequence.

2. As soon as the CPU is prepared to handle the interrupt, it asserts an interrupt acknowledge signal on the bus.

3. When the device controller sees that its interrupt signal has been acknowledged, it puts a small integer on the data lines to identify itself. This number is called the **interrupt vector**.

4. The CPU removes the interrupt vector from the bus and saves it temporarily.

5. Then the CPU pushes the program counter and PSW (Program Status Word) onto the stack.

6. The CPU then locates a new program counter by using the interrupt vector as an index into a table at the bottom of memory. If the program counter is 4 bytes, for example, then interrupt vector n corresponds to address $4n$. This new program counter points to the start of the interrupt service routine for the device causing the interrupt.

SOFTWARE ACTIONS

7. The first thing the interrupt service routine does is save all the registers so they can be restored later. They can be saved on the stack or in a system table.

8. Each interrupt vector is generally shared by all the devices of a given type, so it is not yet known which terminal caused the interrupt. The terminal number can be found by reading some device register.

9. Any other information about the interrupt, such as status codes, can now be read in.

10. If an I/O error occurred, it can be handled here.

11. The global variables, *ptr* and *count*, are updated. The former is incremented, to point to the next byte, and the latter is decremented, to indicate that one byte fewer remains to be output. If *count* is still greater

than 0, there are more characters to output. Copy the one now pointed to by *ptr* to the output buffer register.

12. If required, a special code is output to tell the device or the interrupt controller that the interrupt has been processed. The 8259A, for example, requires such an acknowledgement.

13. Restore all the saved registers.

14. Execute the RETURN FROM INTERRUPT instruction, putting the CPU back into the mode and state it had just before the interrupt happened. The computer then continues as though no interrupt had happened.

A key concept related to interrupts is **transparency**. When an interrupt happens, some actions are taken and some code runs, but when everything is finished, the computer should be returned to exactly the same state as it was before the interrupt. An interrupt routine that has this property is said to be transparent. Having all interrupts be transparent makes the whole interrupt process a lot easier to understand.

If a computer only has one I/O device, then interrupts always work as we have just described, and there is nothing more to say about them. However, a large computer may have many I/O devices, and several may be running at the same time, possibly on behalf of different users. A nonzero probability exists that while an interrupt routine is running, a second I/O device wants to generate *its* interrupt.

Two approaches can be taken to this problem. The first one is for all interrupt routines to disable subsequent interrupts as the very first thing they do, even before saving the registers. This approach keeps things simple, as interrupts are then taken strictly sequentially, but it can lead to problems for devices that cannot tolerate much delay. For example, on a 9600 bps communication line, characters arrive every 1042 μsec, ready or not. If the first one has not yet been processed when the second one arrives, data may be lost.

When a computer has time-critical I/O devices, a better design approach is to assign each I/O device a priority, high for very critical devices and low for less critical devices. Similarly, the CPU should also have priorities, typically determined by a field in the PSW. When a priority n device interrupts, the interrupt routine should also run at priority n.

While a priority n interrupt routine is running, any attempt by a device with a lower priority to cause an interrupt is ignored until the interrupt routine is finished and the CPU goes back to running a user program (priority 0). On the other hand, interrupts from higher-priority devices should be allowed to happen with no delay.

With interrupt routines themselves subject to interrupt, the best way to keep the administration straight is to make sure that all interrupts are transparent. Let us consider a simple example of multiple interrupts. A computer has three I/O devices, a printer, a disk, and an RS232 line, with priorities 2, 4, and 5, respectively. Initially ($t = 0$) a user program is running, when suddenly at $t = 10$ a printer interrupt occurs. The printer interrupt service routine (ISR) is started up, as shown in Fig. 5-54.

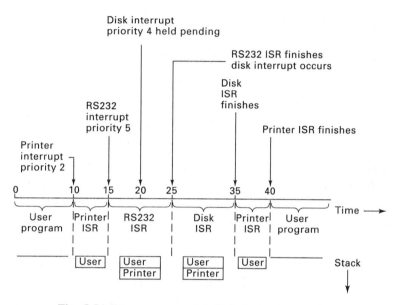

Fig. 5-54. Time sequence of multiple interrupt example.

At $t = 15$, the RS232 line wants attention and generates an interrupt. Since the RS232 line has a higher priority (5) than the printer (2), the interrupt happens. The state of the machine, which is now running the printer interrupt service routine, is pushed onto the stack, and the RS232 interrupt service routine is started.

A little later, at $t = 20$, the disk is finished and wants service. However, its priority (4) is lower than that of the interrupt routine currently running (5), so the CPU hardware does not acknowledge the interrupt, and it is held pending. At $t = 25$, the RS232 routine is finished, so it returns to the state it was in just before the RS232 interrupt happened, namely, running the printer interrupt service routine at priority 2. As soon as the CPU switches to priority 2, before even one instruction can be executed, the disk interrupt at priority 4 now is allowed in, and the disk service routine runs. When it finishes, the printer routine gets to continue. Finally, at $t = 40$, all the interrupt service routines have completed and the user program continues from where it left off.

All the Intel chips have two interrupt levels (priorities), maskable and nonmaskable. Nonmaskable interrupts are generally only used for signaling near-catastrophes, such as memory parity errors. All the I/O devices use the one maskable interrupt.

When an I/O device issues an interrupt, the CPU uses the interrupt vector to index into a 256-entry table to find the address of the interrupt service routine. On the 8088, the table of interrupt vectors starts at absolute address 0, with 4 bytes per entry. On the 80286 and 80386, the interrupt vectors are 8-byte segment descriptors and the table can begin anywhere in memory. A global register points to its start.

With only one usable interrupt level, there is no way for the CPU to let a high-priority device interrupt a medium-priority interrupt service routine while prohibiting a low-priority device from doing so. To solve this problem, the Intel CPUs are normally used with the 8259A interrupt controller (see Fig. 3-38). When the first interrupt comes in, say at priority n, the CPU is interrupted. If a subsequent interrupt comes in at a higher priority, the 8259A interrupts a second time. If the second interrupt is at a lower priority, it is held until the first one is finished. (The interrupt routine must explicitly send a command to the 8259A to tell the 8259A when it is finished, to allow lower-priority interrupts to occur.)

The situation with the Motorola 680x0 is somewhat different. Like the 8088, they have 256 4-byte interrupt vectors starting at absolute address 0. However, unlike all the Intel chips, they all have three pins dedicated to the interrupt level number, 0 through 6, plus 7, which is nonmaskable. In addition, the CPU has a 3-bit priority field in the PSW. When an I/O device wants to cause an interrupt, it puts its priority on the three pins and sends a signal. Depending on its current priority, the CPU may accept the interrupt or not. No 8259A-type chip is needed.

5.6. SUMMARY

The conventional machine level is what most people think of as "machine language." At this level the machine has a byte- or word-oriented memory ranging from tens of kilobytes to tens of megabytes, and instructions such as MOVE, ADD, and JUMP.

Most modern computers have a memory that is organized as a sequence of bytes, with 2 or 4 bytes grouped together into words. There are normally also between eight and 32 registers present, each one containing one word. Many computers come in families, such as the Intel and Motorola families discussed in this chapter.

Instructions generally have one or two operands, which are addressed using immediate, direct, indirect, indexed, or other addressing modes. Some machines have a large number of complex addressing modes. Instructions are generally available for moving data, dyadic and monadic operations, including arithmetic and Boolean operations, jumps, procedure calls, and loops, and sometimes for I/O. Typical instructions move a word from memory to a register (or vice versa), add, subtract, multiply, or divide two registers or a register and a memory word, or compare two items in registers or memory. It is not unusual for a computer to have well over 100 instructions in its repertoire.

Control flow at level 2 is achieved using a variety of primitives, including jumps, procedure calls, coroutine calls, traps, and interrupts. Jumps are used to terminate one instruction sequence and begin a new one. Procedures are used as an abstraction mechanism, to allow a part of the program to be isolated as a unit and called from multiple places. Coroutines allow two threads of control to work simultaneously. Traps are used to signal exceptional situations, such as arithmetic overflow. Finally, interrupts, allow I/O to take place in parallel with the main computation, with the CPU getting a signal as soon as the I/O has been completed.

PROBLEMS

1. Suppose you are working as an 8088 programmer. You have just written a program that has 64K of text and 64K of data + stack, and as such, just barely fits in two segments. Real-time performance of this program is critical. Your boss, who knows little about computers, glances through the 8088 manual and notices that you can set CS, DS and SS separately, to give you access to 64K + 64K + 64K of address space without changing segment registers or using ES prefixes. He suggests you do this. Give one concrete problem with this suggestion.

2. On the Intel CPUs, instructions can contain any number of bytes, even or odd. On the Motorola CPUs, all instructions contain an integral number of words, that is, an even number of bytes. Give one advantage of the Intel scheme.

3. The 80386 has additional segment registers, FS and GS. Since they cannot do anything that ES cannot do equally well, they seem redundant. Why do you think they were added?

4. Design an expanding opcode to allow all the following to be encoded in a 36-bit instruction:

　　7 instructions with two 15-bit addresses and one 3-bit register number
　500 instructions with one 15-bit address and one 3-bit register number
　　50 instructions with no addresses or registers

5. Is it possible to design an expanding opcode to allow the following to be encoded in a 12-bit instruction? A register is 3 bits.

　　4 instructions with 3 registers
　255 instructions with one register
　16 instructions with zero registers

6. A certain machine has 16-bit instructions and 6-bit addresses. Some instructions have one address and others have two. If there are n two-address instructions, what is the maximum number of one-address instructions?

7. Given the memory values below and a one-address machine with an accumulator, what values do the following instructions load into the accumulator?

word 20 contains 40
word 30 contains 50
word 40 contains 60
word 50 contains 70

a. LOAD IMMEDIATE 20
b. LOAD DIRECT 20
c. LOAD INDIRECT 20
d. LOAD IMMEDIATE 30
e. LOAD DIRECT 30
f. LOAD INDIRECT 30

8. Compare 0-, 1-, 2-, and 3-address machines by writing programs to compute

$$X = (A + B \times C) / (D - E \times F)$$

for each of the four machines. The instructions available for use are as follows:

0 Address	1 Address	2 Address	3 Address
PUSH M	LOAD M	MOV (X := Y)	MOV (X := Y)
POP M	STORE M	ADD (X := X+Y)	ADD (X := Y+Z)
ADD	ADD M	SUB (X := X−Y)	SUB (X := Y−Z)
SUB	SUB M	MUL (X := X∗Y)	MUL (X := Y∗Z)
MUL	MUL M	DIV (X := X/Y)	DIV (X := Y/Z)
DIV	DIV M		

M is a 16-bit memory address, and X, Y, and Z are either 16-bit addresses or 4-bit registers. The 0-address machine uses a stack, the 1-address machine uses an accumulator, and the other two have 16 registers and instructions operating on all combinations of memory locations and registers. SUB X,Y subtracts Y from X and SUB X,Y,Z subtracts Z from Y and puts the result in X. Assuming 8-bit opcodes and instruction lengths that are multiples of 4 bits, how many bits does each machine need to compute X?

9. Devise an addressing mechanism that allows an arbitrary set of 64 addresses, not necessarily contiguous, in a large address space to be specifiable in a 6-bit field.

10. Convert the following formulas from infix to reverse Polish.

a. $A + B + C + D + E$
b. $(A + B) \times (C + D) + E$
c. $(A \times B) + (C \times D) + E$
d. $(A - B) \times (((C - D \times E) / F) / G) \times H$

11. Convert the following reverse Polish formulas to infix.

    a. $A B + C + D \times$
    b. $A B / C D / +$
    c. $A B C D E + \times \times /$
    d. $A B C D E \times F / + G - H / \times +$

12. Which of the following pairs of reverse Polish formulas are mathematically equivalent?

    a. $A B + C +$ and $A B C + +$
    b. $A B - C -$ and $A B C - -$
    c. $A B \times C +$ and $A B C + \times$

13. Write three reverse Polish formulas that cannot be converted to infix.

14. Convert the following infix Boolean formulas to reverse Polish.

    a. (A AND B) OR C
    b. (A OR B) AND (A OR B)
    c. (A AND B) OR (C AND D)

15. Convert the following infix formula to reverse Polish and evaluate it using a stack as shown in the text.

    $(2 \times 3 + 4) - (4 / 2 + 1)$

16. The assembly language instruction ADD X,Y means add Y to X on the Intel CPUs, but means add X to Y on the PDP-11 and Motorola CPUs. Why?

17. Suppose a high-performance computer has been designed as a 32-bit machine from beginning to end. All instructions are multiples of 32 bits, the registers are 32 bits, and all bus cycles transfer 32 bits. Can this machine be built as regularly and efficiently as the PDP-11 in terms of opcodes and addressing modes? Discuss the design.

18. It is common in programming for a program to need to determine where a variable X is with respect to the interval A to B. If a three-address instruction were available with operands A, B, and X, how many condition code bits would have to be set by this instruction?

19. The Intel CPUs have a condition code bit that keeps track of the carry out of bit 3 after an arithmetic operation. What good is it?

20. One of your friends has just come bursting into your room at 3 A.M., out of breath, to tell you about his brilliant new idea: an instruction with two opcodes. Should you send your friend off to the patent office or back to the drawing board?

21. Suppose you were designing a machine like the PDP-11, but with only 2 bits per addressing mode instead of 3. Let us assume that you had already decided to include register addressing, indexing, and direct addressing as three of the four modes, and wanted some form of autoindexing as the fourth. Would it be wiser to use autodecrement or autoincrement?

22. Tests of the form

if $n = 0$ **then** ...
if $i > j$ **then** ...
if $k <= 4$ **then** ...

are common in programming. Devise an instruction to perform these tests efficiently. What fields are present in your instruction?

23. For the 16-bit binary number 1001 0101 1100 0011, show the effect of:

a. A right shift of 4 bits with zero fill.
b. A right shift of 4 bits with sign extension.
c. A left shift of 4 bits.
d. A left rotate of 4 bits.
e. A right rotate of 4 bits.

24. How can you clear a memory word on a machine with no CLEAR instruction?

25. Compute the Boolean expression (A AND B) OR C for

A = 1101 0000 1010 1101
B = 1111 1111 0000 1111
C = 0000 0000 0010 0000

26. Devise a way to interchange two variables A and B without using a third variable or register. *Hint*: Think about the EXCLUSIVE OR instruction.

27. On a certain computer it is possible to move a number from one register to another, shift each of them left by different amounts, and add the results in less time than a multiplication takes. Under what condition is this instruction sequence useful for computing "constant × variable"?

28. Why do I/O devices place the interrupt vector on the bus? Would it be possible to store that information in a table in memory instead?

29. A computer uses DMA to read from its disk. The disk has 64 512-byte sectors per track. The disk rotation time is 16 msec. The bus is 16 bits wide, and bus transfers take 500 nsec each. The average CPU instruction requires two bus cycles. How much is the CPU slowed down by DMA?

30. When two local area networks are to be connected, a computer called a bridge is inserted between them, connected to both. Each packet transmitted on either network causes an interrupt on the bridge, to let the bridge see if the packet has to be forwarded. Suppose that it takes 250 μsec per packet to handle the interrupt and inspect the packet, but forwarding it, if need be, is done by DMA hardware without burdening the CPU. If all packets are 1K bytes, what is the maximum data rate on each of the networks that can be tolerated without having the bridge lose packets?

31. Write an assembly language subroutine to convert an infix formula to reverse Polish.

32. Write two assembly language subroutines for N!. The first one should be iterative and the second should be recursive.

33. If you are not convinced that recursion is at times indispensable, try programming the Towers of Hanoi without using recursion and without simulating the recursive solution by maintaining a stack in an array. Be warned, however, that you will probably not be able to find the solution.

34. Write an assembly language subroutine to convert a signed binary integer to ASCII.

6

THE OPERATING SYSTEM MACHINE LEVEL

In the preceding chapters it was shown how an interpreter running at the microprogramming level (level 1) could execute programs written for the conventional machine level (level 2). On a microprogrammed computer, the conventional machine level instructions such as procedure call, multiplication, and loop are not carried out directly by the hardware. Instead, they are fetched, examined, and executed as a series of small steps by the microprogram. The level 2 machine can be programmed by people who know nothing at all about the level 1 machine and its interpreter. As far as they are concerned, the level 2 machine can be used as though it were the real hardware.

Just as an interpreter running on the level 1 machine can interpret programs written in level 2 machine language, an interpreter running on the level 2 machine can interpret programs written in level 3 machine language. For historical reasons (see Sec. 1.3) the interpreter running on the level 2 machine that supports the level 3 machine is called an **operating system**, as shown in Fig. 6-1. Therefore, we will call level 3 the "operating system machine level," for lack of a generally accepted term.

There is an important difference between the way the operating system machine level is supported and the way the conventional machine level is supported. This difference is due to the fact that the operating system machine level has gradually evolved out of the conventional machine level. Most of the operating system machine level's instructions are also present at the conventional machine level. We

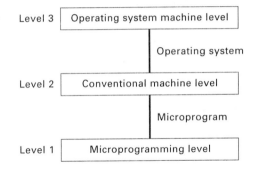

Fig. 6-1. Levels 2 and 3 are both supported by software.

will call these instructions the "ordinary" level 3 instructions, because they include such ordinary operations as arithmetic, Boolean operations, shifting, and so on. We will call the other level 3 instructions (those that are not present at level 2) the OSML instructions, to emphasize their existence only at the Operating System Machine Level.

Although it would be possible to have the operating system interpret all level 3 instructions, doing so is neither efficient nor necessary. The ordinary level 3 instructions can be interpreted directly by the microprogram. This situation is illustrated in Fig. 6-2(a) for the case of a computer with a single memory used to store all programs. As long as only ordinary instructions are being executed, the microprogram fetches instructions directly from the user program, examines them, and executes them.

However, as soon as an OSML instruction is encountered, the situation changes. The microprogram stops interpreting the user program and begins interpreting the operating system instead. The operating system then examines the OSML instruction in the user program and carries it out. When the OSML instruction has been executed, the operating system executes a certain instruction that causes the microprogram to continue fetching and executing user program instructions. Of course, if the next user program instruction is also an OSML instruction, the operating system will be started up again.

This method of executing level 3 programs means that part of the time the computer is functioning as a three-level machine and part of the time as a two-level machine. During the execution of an OSML instruction, three programs are running, one on each (virtual) machine. Each one has its own state, including its own program counter. Conceptually, the level 3 program counter points to the OSML instruction (or its successor, depending on when the program counter is advanced), the level 2 program counter points to that operating system instruction currently executing, and the level 1 program counter tells the actual hardware which microinstruction is to be executed.

In this chapter the operating system will be treated as a single level, for

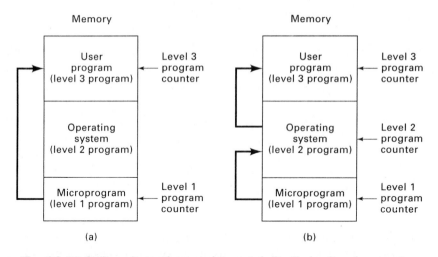

Fig. 6-2. (a) Ordinary instructions are interpreted directly by the microprogram. (b) OSML instructions are interpreted by the operating system, which is interpreted by the microprogram.

simplicity—which does not mean that all operating systems are organized as one level. On the contrary, some advanced operating systems are constructed as a series of several levels. However, the subject of how to design an operating system is beyond the scope of this book. For more information about operating systems, see (Tanenbaum, 1987).

It should be mentioned that most operating systems for large computers are **multiprogramming systems**, which means that rather than supporting only one level 3 virtual machine, the operating system supports several level 3 virtual machines in parallel. If each of these virtual machines is connected to a remote terminal, it is called a time-sharing system. If there are no remote terminals, it is called a batch multiprogramming system. Hybrid forms, in which some virtual machines are being used on line and others are not, are common. A substantial part of the operating system is concerned with managing all the virtual machines rather than with interpreting OSML instructions.

In this book we can only provide the briefest of introductions to the subject of operating systems. We will focus on three topics of importance. The first is virtual memory, a technique provided by many operating systems to make the machine appear to have more memory than it really does. The second is file I/O, a higher-level concept than the I/O instructions that we studied in the previous chapter. The third and last topic is parallel processing—how multiple **processes** can execute simultaneously at level 3. The concept of a process is an important one, and we will describe it in detail later in this chapter. For the time being, a process can be thought of as a running program and all its state information (memory, registers, program counter, I/O status, and so on).

6.1. VIRTUAL MEMORY

In the early days of computers, memories were expensive and small. The IBM 650, the leading scientific computer of its day (late 1950s), had only 2000 words of memory. One of the first ALGOL 60 compilers was written for a computer with only 1024 words of memory. An early time-sharing system ran quite well on a PDP-1 with a total memory size of only 4096 18-bit words for the operating system and user programs. In those days the programmer spent a lot of time trying to squeeze programs into the tiny memory. Often it was necessary to use an algorithm that ran a great deal slower than another, better algorithm simply because the better algorithm was too big—that is, a program using the better algorithm could not be fitted into the computer's memory.

The traditional solution to this problem was the use of secondary memory, such as disk. The programmer divided the program up into a number of pieces, called **overlays**, each of which could fit in the memory. To run the program, the first overlay was brought in and it ran for a while. When it finished, it read in the next overlay and called it, and so on. The programmer was responsible for breaking the program into overlays, deciding where in the secondary memory each overlay was to be kept, arranging for the transport of overlays between main memory and secondary memory, and in general managing the whole overlay process without any help from the computer.

Although widely used for many years, this technique involved much work in connection with overlay management. In 1961 a group of people at Manchester, England, proposed a method for performing the overlay process automatically, without the programmer even knowing that it was happening (Fotheringham, 1961). This method, now called **virtual memory**, had the obvious advantage of freeing the programmer from a lot of annoying bookkeeping. It was first used on a number of computers during the 1960s, mostly associated with research projects in computer systems design. By the early 1970s virtual memory had become available on most computers. Now even microprocessors, including the 80386 and 68030, have highly sophisticated virtual memory systems.

6.1.1. Paging

The idea put forth by the Manchester group was to separate the concepts of address space and memory locations. Consider an example of a computer with a 16-bit address field in its instructions and 4096 words of memory. A program on this computer can address 65536 words of memory. The reason is that 65536 (2^{16}) 16-bit addresses exist. The number of addressable words depends only on the number of bits in an address and is in no way related to the number of memory words actually available. The **address space** for this computer consists of the numbers 0, 1, 2, ..., 65535, because that is the set of possible addresses.

Before virtual memory was invented, people would have made a distinction between the addresses below 4096 and those equal to or above 4096. Although rarely stated in so many words, these two parts were regarded as the useful address space and the useless address space, respectively (the addresses above 4095 being useless because they did not correspond to actual memory addresses). People did not make much of a distinction between address space and actual memory addresses, because the hardware enforced a one-to-one correspondence between them.

The idea of separating the address space and the memory addresses is as follows. At any instant of time, 4096 words of memory can be directly accessed but they need not correspond to addresses 0 to 4095. We could, for example, "tell" the computer that henceforth whenever address 4096 is referenced, memory word 0 is to be used. Whenever address 4097 is referenced, memory word 1 is to be used; whenever address 8191 is referenced, memory word 4095 is to be used, and so forth. In other words, we have defined a mapping from the address space onto the actual memory addresses, as shown in Fig. 6-3.

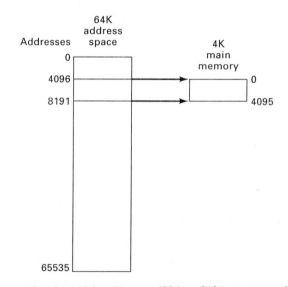

Fig. 6-3. A mapping in which addresses 4096 to 8191 are mapped onto main memory addresses 0 to 4095.

In terms of this picture of mapping addresses from the address space onto the actual memory locations, a 4K machine without virtual memory simply has a fixed mapping between the addresses 0 to 4095 and the 4096 words of memory. An interesting question is: What happens if a program jumps to an address between 8192 and 12287? On a machine without virtual memory, the program would cause an error trap that would print a suitably rude message, such as "Nonexistent memory referenced'' and terminate the program. On a machine with virtual memory, the following sequence of steps would occur:

1. The contents of main memory would be saved in the secondary memory.

2. Words 8192 to 12287 would be located in the secondary memory.

3. Words 8192 to 12287 would be loaded into main memory.

4. The address map would be changed to map addresses 8192 to 12287 onto memory locations 0 to 4095.

5. Execution would continue as though nothing unusual had happened.

This technique for automatic overlaying is called **paging** and the chunks of program read in from secondary memory are called **pages**.

A more sophisticated way of mapping addresses from the address space onto the actual memory addresses is also possible. For emphasis, we will call the addresses that the program can refer to the **virtual address space**, and the actual, hardwired memory addresses the **physical address space**. A **memory map** relates virtual addresses to physical addresses. We presume that there is enough room in the secondary memory (disk) to store the whole program and its data.

Programs are written just as though there were enough main memory for the whole virtual address space, even though such is not the case. Programs may load from, or store into, any word in the virtual address space, or jump to any instruction located anywhere within the virtual address space, without regard to the fact that there really is not enough physical memory. In fact, the programmer can write programs without even being aware that virtual memory exists. The computer just looks like it has a big memory.

This point is crucial and will be contrasted later with segmentation, where the programmer must be aware of the existence of segments. To emphasize it once more, paging gives the programmer the illusion of a large, continuous, linear main memory, the same size as the address space, when, in fact, the main memory available may be smaller (or larger) than the address space. The simulation of this large main memory by paging cannot be detected by the program (except by running timing tests); whenever an address is referenced, the proper instruction or data word appears to be present. Because the programmer can program as though paging did not exist, the paging mechanism is said to be **transparent**.

The idea that a programmer may use some nonexistent feature without being concerned with how it works is not new to us, after all. The instruction set of a level 2 computer is nonexistent in the sense that none of the instructions are hardware primitives, but all of them are, in fact, carried out by software at level 1. Similarly, the level 3 programmer can use the virtual memory without worrying about how it works. Only the operating system writers have to know how it works.

6.1.2. Implementation of Paging

One essential requirement for a virtual memory is a secondary memory in which to keep the complete program. It is conceptually simpler if one thinks of the copy of the program in the secondary memory as the original one and the pieces brought into main memory every now and then as copies rather than the other way around. Naturally, it is important to keep the original up to date. When changes are made to the copy in main memory, they should also be reflected in the original (eventually).

The virtual address space is broken up into a number of equal-sized pages. Page sizes ranging from 512 to 4096 addresses per page are common at present. The page size is always a power of 2. The physical address space is broken up into pieces in a similar way, each piece being the same size as a page, so that each piece of main memory is capable of holding exactly one page. These pieces of main memory into which the pages go are called **page frames**. In Fig. 6-3 the main memory only contains one page frame. In practical designs it will contain tens, hundreds, or even thousands in a large machine.

Figure 6-4 illustrates a possible way to divide up a 64K address space. The virtual memory of Fig. 6-4 would be implemented at level 2 by means of a 16-word **page table**. When the program tried to reference its memory, whether to fetch data, store data, fetch instructions or jump, it would first generate a 16-bit address corresponding to a virtual address between 0 and 65535. Indexing, indirect addressing, and all the usual techniques may be used to generate this address.

In this example, the 16-bit address is taken as a 4-bit virtual page number and a 12-bit address within the selected page, as shown in Fig. 6-5(a). In this figure the 16-bit address is 12310, which is regarded as address 22 of page 3. The relation between pages and virtual addresses for this example is shown in Fig. 6-5(b). If virtual address 0 of page 3 is at physical address 12288, virtual address 22 must be at physical address 12310.

Having discovered that virtual page 3 is needed, the operating system must find out where virtual page 3 is located. There are nine possibilities: eight page frames in main memory, or somewhere in secondary memory, because not all the virtual pages can be in main memory at once. To find out which of these nine possibilities is true, the operating system looks in the page table, which has one entry for each of the 16 virtual pages.

The example page table of Fig. 6-6 has three fields. The first is a bit which is 0 if the page is not in main memory and 1 if it is. The second gives the address where the virtual page is kept in secondary memory (e.g., a disk track and sector) when not in main memory. This address is needed so that the page can be found and brought in when necessary and later returned to its original place in secondary memory when no longer needed in main memory. The third is a 3-bit field giving the page frame where the page is located if it is in main memory. If the page is not in main memory, field 3 has no meaning so it is ignored.

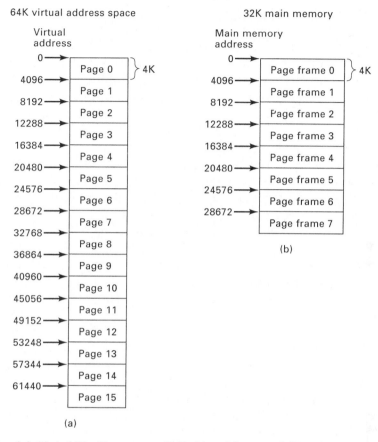

Fig. 6-4. (a) A 64K address space divided into 16 pages of 4K each. (b) A 32K main memory divided up into eight page frames of 4K each.

Assuming that the virtual page is in main memory, the 3-bit page frame specifies where the page is. The page frame number is then gated into the leftmost 3 bits of the MAR, and the address within the virtual page—that is, the rightmost 12 bits of the original address—are gated into the rightmost 12 bits of the MAR. In this way a main memory address can be formed, as shown in Fig. 6-7. The 3-bit page frame plus the 12-bit offset give a 15-bit address, which is precisely what is needed for the 32K main memory of Fig. 6-4 which we are considering. The hardware can now use this address and fetch the desired word into the MBR or it can store the MBR into the desired word.

Figure 6-8 shows a possible mapping between virtual pages and physical page frames. Virtual page 0 is in page frame 1. Virtual page 1 is in page frame 0. Virtual page 2 is not in main memory. Virtual page 3 is in page frame 2. Virtual page 4 is not in main memory. Virtual page 5 is in page frame 6, and so on.

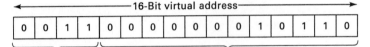

4-bit virtual page number = 3	12-bit address within the selected virtual page = 22

(a)

Page	Virtual address
0	0 - 4095
1	4096 - 8191
2	8192 - 12287
3	12288 - 16383
4	16384 - 20479
5	20480 - 24575
6	24576 - 28671
7	28672 - 32767
8	32768 - 36863
9	36864 - 40959
10	40960 - 45055
11	45056 - 49151
12	49152 - 53247
13	53248 - 57343
14	57344 - 61439
15	61440 - 65535

(b)

Fig. 6-5. (a) A virtual address consisting of a 4-bit virtual page number and a 12-bit offset. (b) Page numbers and their virtual addresses.

If the operating system had to convert every level 3 machine instruction's virtual address into an actual address, a level 3 machine with virtual memory would run many times slower than one without virtual memory, and the whole idea would be impractical. To speed up the virtual-to-physical address translation, the page table is usually maintained in special hardware registers, and the transformation from virtual address to actual address is done directly in hardware. Another way of

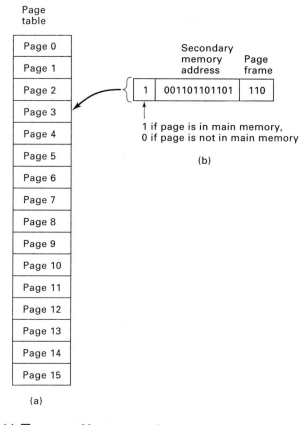

Fig. 6-6. (a) The page table must contain as many entries as there are virtual pages. (b) The example page table has three fields per entry: a present/absent bit, the disk address, and the page frame number.

doing it is to maintain the map in fast registers and let the microprogram do the transformation by explicit programming. Depending on the architecture of the microprogramming level, having the microprogram perform the transformation might be almost as fast as doing it directly in the hardware, and would require no special circuits or hardware modifications.

6.1.3. Demand Paging and the Working Set Model

In the preceding discussion it was assumed that the virtual page referenced was in main memory. However, that assumption will not always be true because there is not enough room in main memory for all the virtual pages. When a reference is made to an address on a page not present in main memory, it is called a **page fault**. After a page fault has occurred, it is necessary for the operating system to read in

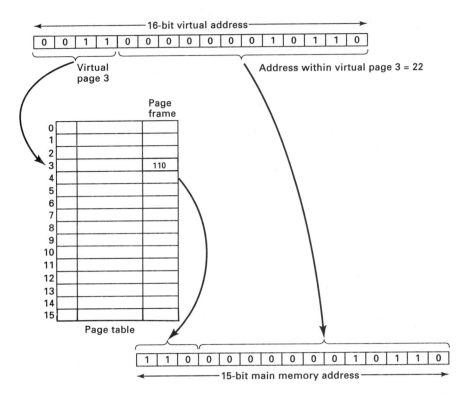

Fig. 6-7. Formation of a main memory address from a virtual address.

the required page from the secondary memory, enter its new physical memory location in the page table, and then repeat the instruction that caused the fault.

It is possible to start a program running on a machine with virtual memory even when none of the program is in main memory. The page table merely has to be set to indicate that each and every virtual page is in the secondary memory and not in main memory. When the CPU tries to fetch the first instruction, it immediately gets a page fault, which causes the page containing the first instruction to be loaded and entered in the page table. Then the first instruction can begin. If the first instruction has two addresses, with the two addresses on different pages, both different from the instruction page, two more page faults will occur, and two more pages will be brought in before the instruction can finally execute. The next instruction may possibly cause some more page faults, and so forth.

This method of operating a virtual memory is called **demand paging**, in analogy to the well-known demand feeding algorithm for babies: when the baby cries, you feed it (as opposed to feeding it at regular times of day). In demand paging, pages are brought in only when an actual request for a page occurs, not in advance.

The question of whether demand paging should be used or not is only relevant

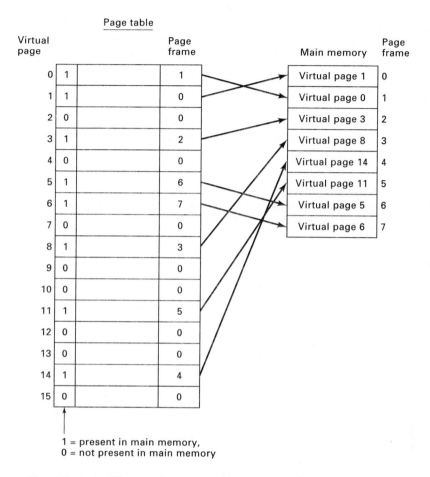

Fig. 6-8. A possible mapping of an address space with 16 pages onto a main memory with eight page frames.

when a program first starts up. Once it has been running for a while, the needed pages will already have been collected in main memory. If the computer is time-shared and users are swapped out after running 100 msec or so, each program will be restarted many times during the course of its run. Because the memory map is unique to each program, and is changed when programs are switched, for example, in a time-sharing system, the question repeatedly becomes a critical one.

The alternative approach is based on the observation that most programs do not reference their address space uniformly but that the references tend to cluster on a small number of pages. A memory reference may fetch an instruction, it may fetch data, or it may store data. At any instant in time, t, there exists a set consisting of all the pages used by the k most recent memory references. Denning (1968) has called this the **working set**, $w(k, t)$. Because the $k + 1$ most recent references must have used all the pages used by the k most recent references, and possibly others, $w(k, t)$ is a monotonically nondecreasing function of k. The limit of $w(k, t)$ as k becomes large is finite, because the program cannot reference more pages than its address space contains, and few programs will use every single page.

Figure 6-9 depicts the size of the working set as a function of k. The fact that most programs randomly access a small number of pages but that this set changes slowly in time explains the initial rapid rise of the curve and then the slow rise for large k. For example, a program that is executing a loop occupying two pages, using data occupying four pages, may reference all six pages every 1000 instructions, but the most recent reference to some other page may be a million references earlier, during the initialization phase. Because of this asymptotic behavior, the contents of the working set is not sensitive to the value of k chosen, or to put it differently, there exists a wide range of k values for which the working set is unchanged.

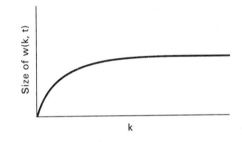

Fig. 6-9. The working set is the set of pages used by the k most recent memory references. The function $w(k, t)$ is the size of the working set at time t.

Because the working set varies slowly with time, it is possible to make a reasonable guess as to which pages will be needed when the program is restarted, on the basis of its working set when it was last stopped. These pages could then be loaded in advance before starting the program up (assuming they fit).

The argument in favor of bringing the working set into main memory in advance is that it can be brought in while some other program is running. When a program is started, it will not immediately generate a large number of time-consuming page faults, an event that may cause the CPU to be idle while the needed pages are being brought in. Remember that the time needed to read in a page from a disk is typically 20000 instruction times or more.

The argument against bringing the working set into main memory in advance is that if the program is in transition between one working set and another, and has not yet settled down, a lot of work will have been done bringing in pages that are not going to be referenced. With demand paging that situation cannot occur. The only pages that are loaded are those that are actually needed. The relative merits of these two strategies are still being debated.

6.1.4. Page Replacement Policy

Up to now, we have tacitly assumed that there is always a vacant page frame in which to put the newly loaded page. In general, this will not be true, and it will be necessary to remove some page (i.e., copy it back to the secondary memory) to make room. Thus an algorithm that decides which page to remove is needed.

Choosing a page to remove at random certainly is not a good idea. If the page containing the instruction should happen to be the one picked, another page fault will occur as soon as an attempt is made to fetch the next instruction. Most operating systems try to predict which of the pages in memory is the least useful in the sense that its absence would have the smallest adverse effect on the running program. One way of doing so is to make a prediction when the next reference to each page will occur and remove the page whose predicted next reference lies furthest in the future. In other words, rather than evict a page that will be needed shortly, try to select one that will not be needed for a long time.

One popular algorithm evicts the page least recently used because the a priori probability of its not being in the current working set is high. It is called the **least recently used** or LRU algorithm. Although it usually performs well, there are pathological situations, such as the one described below, where LRU fails miserably.

Imagine a program executing a large loop that extends over nine virtual pages on a machine with room for only eight pages in memory. After the program gets to page 7 the main memory will be as shown in Fig. 6-10(a). An attempt is eventually made to fetch an instruction from virtual page 8, which causes a page fault. A decision has to be made about which page to evict. The LRU algorithm will choose virtual page 0, because it has been used least recently. Virtual page 0 is removed and virtual page 8 is brought in to replace it, giving the situation in Fig. 6-10(b).

Virtual page 0		Virtual page 8		Virtual page 8
Virtual page 1		Virtual page 1		Virtual page 0
Virtual page 2		Virtual page 2		Virtual page 2
Virtual page 3		Virtual page 3		Virtual page 3
Virtual page 4		Virtual page 4		Virtual page 4
Virtual page 5		Virtual page 5		Virtual page 5
Virtual page 6		Virtual page 6		Virtual page 6
Virtual page 7		Virtual page 7		Virtual page 7
(a)		(b)		(c)

Fig. 6-10. Failure of the LRU algorithm.

After executing the instructions on virtual page 8, the program jumps back to the top of the loop, to virtual page 0. This step causes another page fault. Virtual page 0, which was just thrown out, has to be brought back in. The LRU algorithm chooses page 1 to be thrown out, producing the situation in Fig. 6-10(c). The program continues on page 0 for a little while. Then it tries to fetch an instruction from virtual page 1, causing a page fault. Page 1 has to be brought back in again and page 2 will be thrown out.

It should be apparent by now that here the LRU algorithm is consistently making the worst choice every time. If, however, the available main memory exceeds the size of the working set, LRU tends to minimize the number of page faults.

Another algorithm is **First-In First-Out**, or FIFO. FIFO removes the least recently loaded page, independent of when this page was last referenced. Associated with each page frame is a counter, possibly kept in the page table. Initially, all the counters are set to 0. After each page fault has been handled, the counter for each page presently in memory is increased by one, and the counter for the page just brought in is set to 0. When it becomes necessary to choose a page to remove, the page whose counter is highest is chosen. Since its counter is the highest, it has witnessed the largest number of page faults. This means that it was loaded prior to the loading of any of the other pages in memory and therefore (hopefully) has a large a priori chance of no longer being needed.

If the working set is larger than the number of available page frames, no algorithm that is not an oracle will give good results, and page faults will be frequent. A program that generates page faults frequently and continuously is said to be **thrashing**. Needless to say, thrashing is an undesirable characteristic to have in your system. If a program uses a large amount of virtual address space but has a small, slowly changing working set that fits in available main memory, it will give little trouble, even if, over its lifetime, it uses hundreds of times as many words of virtual memory as the machine has words of main memory.

If a page about to be evicted has not been modified since it was read in (a likely occurrence if the page contains program rather than data) it is not necessary to write it back into secondary memory, because an accurate copy already exists there. If it has been modified since it was read in, the copy in the secondary memory is no longer accurate, and the page must be rewritten.

If there is a way to tell whether a page has not changed since it was read in (page is clean) or whether it, in fact, has been stored into (page is dirty), all the rewriting of clean pages can be avoided, thus saving a lot of time. Some computers have 1 bit per page, in the page table, which is set to 0 when a page is loaded and set to 1 by the microprogram or hardware whenever it is stored into. By examining this bit, the operating system can find out if the page is clean or dirty, and hence whether it need be rewritten or not. Such a bit is sometimes referred to as a **dirty bit**.

It is obviously desirable to maintain a high ratio of clean pages to dirty pages to minimize the chance that a rewrite will be required at the next page fault. On nearly all computers, pages can be copied from main memory to secondary memory, while the CPU is computing, using DMA or data channels. Some operating systems take advantage of this parallelism whenever the disk is idle by picking a dirty page, preferably one likely to be written out shortly (due to its age), and issuing a command to copy it to the disk. Copying it to the disk does not alter or destroy the copy in main memory, of course.

If the page is made dirty again immediately after the copying process or even during it, the copying has been done in vain but because the disk was idle anyway, and the CPU was free to compute again as soon as it issued the disk command, the cost of performing the copy was not high. Writes to disk made with the intention of making dirty pages clean have been called **sneaky writes**. It is still an open issue whether the amount of time saved swapping is enough to counterbalance the administration involved in setting up the sneaky writes.

6.1.5. Page Size and Fragmentation

If the user's program and data accidentally happen to fill an integral number of pages exactly, there will be no wasted space when they are in memory. If, on the other hand, they do not fill an integral number of pages exactly, there will be some unused space on the last page. For example, if the program and data need 26000 words on a machine with 4096 words per page, the first six pages will be full, totaling $6 \times 4096 = 24576$ words, and the last page will contain 26000 - 24576 = 1424 words. Since there is room for 4096 words per page, 2672 words will be wasted. Whenever the seventh page is present in memory, those words will take up precious main memory but will serve no useful function. The problem of these wasted words is called **fragmentation**.

If the page size is n words, the average amount of space wasted in the last page of a program by fragmentation will be $n/2$ words—a situation that suggests using a small page size to minimize waste. On the other hand, a small page size means many pages, as well as a large page table. If the page table is maintained in hardware, a large page table means that more registers are needed to store it, which increases the cost of the computer. In addition, more time will be required to load and save these registers whenever a program is started or stopped.

Furthermore, small pages make inefficient use of secondary memories with long access times, such as disks. Given that one is going to wait 10 msec or more before the transfer can begin, one would like to transfer a large block of information, because the transfer time is usually shorter than the combined seek plus rotational delay time. Generally, it costs little extra time to read 1024 words as compared to 256 words. On the other hand, if a secondary memory with no rotational delay is being used, such as low-speed core or solid-state memory, the total transfer time is proportional to the block size.

Small pages do have the advantage that if the working set consists of a large number of small, separated regions in the virtual address space, there may be less thrashing with a small page size than with a big one. For example, consider a program that is randomly accessing 20 widely separated regions of 100 words each. If a 1000×20 matrix A is stored with $A[1, 1]$, $A[2, 1]$, $A[3, 1]$, and so on, in consecutive words, then $A[1, 1]$, $A[1, 2]$, $A[1, 3]$, and so on, will be 1000 words apart. A program performing some calculation on all the elements of the first 20 rows would use 20 regions of 20 words with 980 words separating these regions. If the page size were 2048 words, at least 10 pages, totaling 20480 words, would be in the working set. If the page size were 128 words, then even if each region occupied parts of two pages, only 40 pages, totaling 5120 words, would be needed to run the program. If the main memory available were more than 5120 words but less than 20480 words, the large page size would prohibit the complete working set from being in main memory, thereby causing thrashing, whereas the small page size would cause no problems.

6.1.6. Segmentation

The virtual memory discussed above is one-dimensional because the virtual addresses go from 0 to some maximum address, one address after another. For many problems, having two or more separate virtual address spaces may be much better than having only one. For example, a compiler has many tables that are built up as compilation proceeds, including

1. The source text being saved for the printed listing.

2. The symbol table, containing the names and attributes of variables.

3. The numeric constant table, containing all the integer and floating-point constants used.

4. The parse tree, containing the syntactic analysis of the program.

5. The stack used for procedure calls within the compiler.

Each of the first four tables grows continuously as compilation proceeds. The last one grows and shrinks in unpredictable ways during compilation. In a one-dimensional memory, these five tables would have to be allocated contiguous chunks of virtual address space, as in Fig. 6-11.

Consider what happens if a program has an exceptionally large number of variables. The chunk of address space allocated for the symbol table may fill up, but there may be lots of room in the other tables. The compiler could, of course, simply issue a message saying that the compilation cannot continue due to too many variables, but doing so does not seem very sporting when unused space is left in the other tables.

Another possibility is to play Robin Hood, taking space from the tables with much room and giving it to the tables with little room. This shuffling can be done,

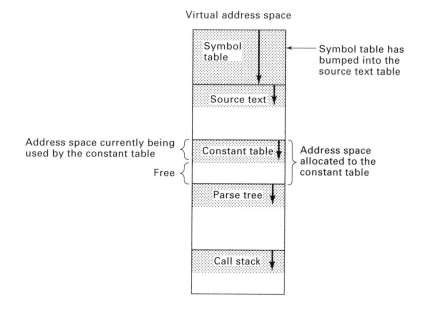

Fig. 6-11. In a one-dimensional address space with growing tables, one table may bump into another.

but it is analogous to managing one's own overlays—a nuisance at best and a great deal of tedious, unrewarding work at worst.

What is really needed is a way of freeing the programmer from having to manage the expanding and contracting tables, in the same way that virtual memory eliminates the worry of organizing the program into overlays.

A straightforward and extremely general solution is to provide the level 3 machine with many, completely independent address spaces, called **segments**. Each segment consists of a linear sequence of addresses, from 0 to some maximum. The length of each segment may be anything from 0 to the maximum allowed. Different segments may, and usually do, have different lengths. Moreover, segment lengths may change during execution. The length of a stack segment may be increased whenever something is pushed onto the stack and decreased whenever something is popped off the stack.

Because each segment constitutes a separate address space, different segments can grow or shrink independently, without affecting each other. If a stack in a certain segment needs more address space to grow, it can have it, because there is nothing else in its address space to bump into. Of course, a segment can fill up but segments are usually very large, so this occurrence is rare. To specify an address in this segmented or two-dimensional memory, the program must supply a two-part address, a segment number, and an address within the segment. Figure 6-12 illustrates a segmented memory being used for the compiler tables discussed earlier.

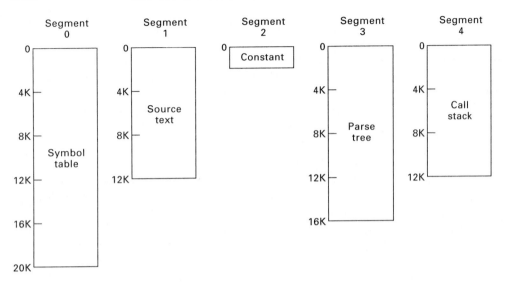

Fig. 6-12. A segmented memory allows each table to grow or shrink independently of the other tables.

We emphasize that a segment is a logical entity, which the programmer is aware of and uses as a single logical entity. A segment might contain a procedure, or an array, or a stack, or a collection of scalar variables, but usually it does not contain a mixture of different types.

A segmented memory has other advantages besides simplifying the handling of data structures that are growing or shrinking. If each procedure occupies a separate segment, with address 0 as its starting address, the linking up of procedures compiled separately is greatly simplified. After all the procedures that constitute a program have been compiled and linked up, a procedure call to the procedure in segment n will use the two-part address $(n, 0)$ to address word 0 (the entry point).

If the procedure in segment n is subsequently modified and recompiled, no other procedures need be changed (because no starting addresses have been modified), even if the new version is larger than the old one. With a one-dimensional memory, the procedures are packed tightly next to each other, with no address space between them. Consequently, changing one procedure's size can affect the starting address of other, unrelated procedures. This, in turn, requires modifying all procedures that call any of the moved procedures, in order to incorporate their new starting addresses. If a program contains hundreds of procedures, this process can be costly.

Segmentation also facilitates sharing procedures or data between several programs. If a computer has several level 3 machines running in parallel (either true or simulated parallel processing), all of which use certain library procedures, it is wasteful of main memory to provide each one with its own private copy. By making each procedure a separate segment, they can be shared easily, thus eliminating the need for more than one physical copy of any shared procedure to be in main memory. As a result, memory is saved.

Because each segment forms a logical entity of which the programmer is aware, such as a procedure, or an array, or a stack, different segments can have different kinds of protection. A procedure segment could be specified as execute only, prohibiting attempts to read from it or store into it. A floating-point array could be specified as read/write but not execute, and attempts to jump to it would be caught. Such protection is helpful in catching programming errors.

You should try to understand why protection makes sense in a segmented memory but not in a one-dimensional paged memory. In a segmented memory the user is aware of what is in each segment. Normally, a segment would not contain a procedure and a stack, for example, but one or the other. Since each segment contains only one type of object, the segment can have the protection appropriate for that particular type. Paging and segmentation are compared in Fig. 6-13.

Consideration	Paging	Segmentation
Need the programmer be aware that this technique is being used?	No	Yes
How many linear address spaces are there?	1	Many
Can the total address space exceed the size of physical memory?	Yes	Yes
Can procedures and data be distinguished and separately protected?	No	Yes
Can tables whose size fluctuates be accomodated easily?	No	Yes
Is sharing of procedures between users facilitated?	No	Yes
Why was this technique invented?	To get a large linear address space without having to buy more physical memory	To allow programs and data to be broken up into logically independent address spaces and to aid sharing and protection

Fig. 6-13. Comparison of paging and segmentation.

The contents of a page are, in a sense, accidental. The programmer is unaware of the fact that paging is even occurring. Although putting a few bits in each entry of the page table to specify the access allowed would be possible, to utilize this feature the programmer would have to keep track of where in his address space the page boundaries were, and that is precisely the sort of administration that paging was invented to eliminate. Because the user of a segmented memory has the illusion that all segments are in main memory all the time—that is, he can address them as though they were—he can protect each segment separately, without having to be concerned with the administration of overlaying them.

6.1.7. Implementation of Segmentation

The implementation of segmentation differs from paging in an essential way: pages are fixed size and segments are not. Figure 6-14(a) shows an example of physical memory initially containing five segments. Now consider what happens if segment 1 is evicted and segment 7, which is smaller, is put in its place. We arrive at the memory configuration of Fig. 6-14(b). Between segment 7 and segment 2 is an unused area—that is, a hole. Then segment 4 is replaced by segment 5, as in Fig. 6-14(c), and segment 3 is replaced by segment 6, as in Fig. 6-14(d). After the system has been running for a while, memory will be divided up into a number of chunks, some containing segments and some containing holes. This phenomenon is called **checkerboarding**, and, as a result, memory is wasted in the holes.

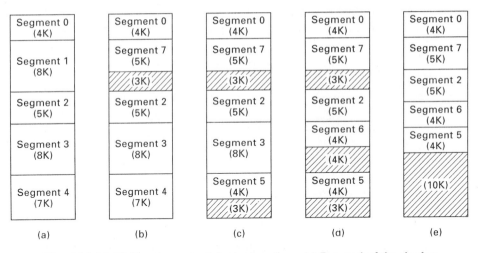

Fig. 6-14. (a)-(d) Development of checkerboarding. (e) Removal of the checkerboarding by compaction.

Consider what would happen if the program referenced segment 3 at the time memory was checkerboarded, as in Fig. 6-14(d). The total space in the holes is 10K, more than enough for segment 3, but because the space is distributed in small, useless pieces, segment 3 cannot simply be loaded. Instead, another segment must be removed first.

One way to avoid checkerboarding is as follows: every time a hole appears, move the segments following the hole closer to memory location 0, thereby eliminating that hole but leaving a big hole at the end. Alternatively, one could wait until the checkerboarding became quite serious (e.g., more than a certain percentage of the total memory wasted in holes) before performing the compaction. Figure 6-15(e) shows how the memory of Fig. 6-15(d) would look after compaction. The intention of compacting memory is to collect all the small useless holes into one big hole, into which one or more segments can be put. Compacting has the obvious drawback that some time is wasted doing the compacting. Compacting after every hole is created is usually too time consuming.

If the time required for compacting memory is unacceptably large, an algorithm is needed to determine which hole to use for a particular segment. Hole management requires maintaining a list of the addresses and sizes of all holes. One popular algorithm, called **best fit**, chooses the smallest hole into which the needed segment will fit. The idea is to match holes and segments so as to avoid breaking off a piece of a big hole, which may be needed later for a big segment.

Another popular algorithm, called **first fit**, circularly scans the hole list and chooses the first hole big enough for the segment to fit into. Doing so obviously takes less time than checking the entire list to find the best fit. Surprisingly, first fit is also a better algorithm in terms of overall performance than best fit, because the latter tends to generate a great many small, totally useless holes (Knuth, 1974).

First fit and best fit tend to decrease hole size. Whenever a segment is placed in a hole bigger than itself, which happens almost every time (exact fits are rare), the hole is divided in two parts. One part is occupied by the segment and the other part is the new hole. The new hole is always smaller than the old hole. Unless there is a compensating process recreating big holes out of small ones, both first fit and best fit will eventually fill memory with small useless holes.

One such compensating process is the following one. Whenever a segment is removed from memory and one or both of its nearest neighbors are holes rather than segments, the adjacent holes can be coalesced into one big hole. If segment 5 were removed from Fig. 6-14(d), the two surrounding holes and the 4K used by the segment would be merged into a single 11K hole.

6.1.8. The MULTICS Virtual Memory

For many years, computer scientists have realized that the ideal virtual memory consists of a large number of large segments. In the early 1960s, M.I.T., Bell Labs, and General Electric (later Honeywell) set up a joint project to construct an operating system that provided such an address space, as well as many other advanced features. This cooperation led to the MULTICS system (Corbató and Vyssotsky, 1965; Daley and Neumann, 1965; Organick, 1972), which, although not spectacularly successful in itself, had an enormous impact on the way people think about virtual memory. In many ways, no operating system built since MULTICS has approached its sophistication, although some have tried. For this reason, it is worth examining the MULTICS virtual memory in some detail.

MULTICS runs on the Honeywell 6000 machines and their descendants and provides each program with a virtual memory of up to 2^{18} segments (more than 250,000), each of which can be up to 65536 (36-bit) words long. To implement this, the MULTICS designers chose to treat each segment as a virtual memory and to page it, combining the advantages of paging (uniform page size and not having to keep the whole segment in memory if only part of it is being used) with the advantages of segmentation (ease of programming, modularity, protection, and sharing).

Each MULTICS program has a segment table, with one descriptor per segment. Since there are potentially more than a quarter of a million entries in the table, the segment table is itself a segment and is paged. A segment descriptor contains an indication of whether the segment is in main memory or not. If any part of the segment is in memory, the segment is considered to be in memory, and its page table will be in memory. If the segment is in memory, its descriptor contains a pointer to its page table [see Fig. 6-15(a)]. Because physical memory addresses are 24 bits, the low-order 6 bits of the address are assumed to be 0. The descriptor also contains the segment size, the protection bits, and a few other items. Figure 6-15(b) illustrates the MULTICS segment descriptor. The address of the segment in secondary memory is not in the segment descriptor but in another table used by the segment fault handler.

Each segment is an ordinary virtual address space and is paged in the same way as the nonsegmented paged memory described earlier in this chapter. The normal page size is 1024 words (although a few small segments used by MULTICS itself are not paged or are paged in units of 64 words).

An address in MULTICS consists of two parts: the segment and the address within the segment. The address within the segment is further divided into a page number and a word within the page, as shown in Fig. 6-16. When a memory reference occurs, the following algorithm is carried out.

1. The segment number is used to find the segment descriptor.

2. A check is made to see if the segment's page table is in memory. If it is not, a segment fault occurs. If there is a protection violation, a fault (trap) occurs. If the page table is in memory, it is located.

3. The page table entry for the requested virtual page is examined. If the page is not in memory, a page fault occurs. If it is in memory, the main memory address of the start of the page is extracted from the page table entry.

4. The offset is added to the page origin to give the main memory address where the word is located.

5. The read or store finally takes place.

This process is illustrated in Fig. 6-17. For simplicity, the fact that the descriptor segment is itself paged has been omitted. What really happens is that a register,

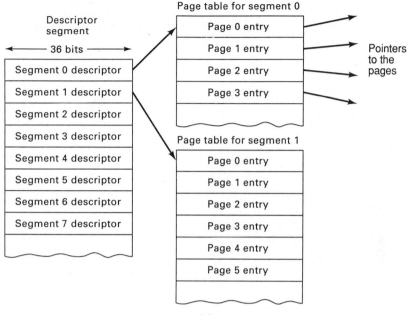

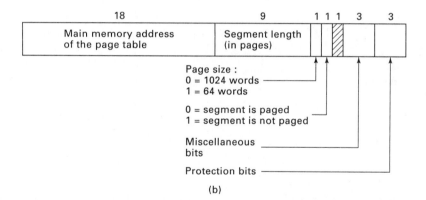

Fig. 6-15. The MULTICS virtual memory. (a) The descriptor segment points to the page tables. (b) A segment descriptor. The numbers are the field lengths.

called the descriptor base register, is used to locate the descriptor segment's page table, which, in turn, points to the pages of the descriptor segment. Once the descriptor for the needed segment has been found, the addressing proceeds as shown in Fig. 6-17.

As you have no doubt guessed by now, if the preceding algorithm were actually carried out by the operating system on every instruction, programs would not run

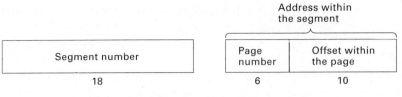

Fig. 6-16. A 34-bit MULTICS virtual address.

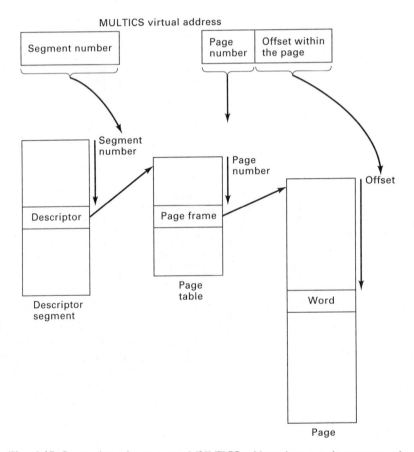

Fig. 6-17. Conversion of a two-part MULTICS address into a main memory address.

very fast. In reality, the MULTICS hardware contains a 16-word high-speed **associative memory** that can search all its entries in parallel for a given key. It is illustrated in Fig. 6-18. When an address is presented to the computer, the addressing hardware first checks to see if the virtual address is in the associative memory. If so, it gets the page frame number directly from the associative memory and forms the actual address of the referenced word without having to look in the descriptor segment or page table.

Comparison field					Is this entry used?
Segment number	Virtual Page	Page frame	Protection	Age	
4	1	7	Read / write	13	1
6	0	2	Read only	10	1
12	3	1	Read / write	2	1
					0
2	1	0	Execute only	7	1
2	2	12	Execute only	9	1

Fig. 6-18. A simplified version of the MULTICS associative memory. The existence of two page sizes makes the actual associative memory more complicated.

The addresses of the 16 most recently referenced pages are kept in the associative memory. Programs whose working set is smaller than the size of the associative memory will come to equilibrium with the addresses of the entire working set in the associative memory and therefore will run efficiently. If the page is not in the associative memory, the descriptor and page tables are actually referenced to find the page frame address, and the associative memory is updated to include this page, the least recently used page being thrown out. The age field keeps track of which entry has been least recently used. The reason that an associative memory is used is that segment and page number of all the entries can be compared simultaneously, for speed.

6.1.9. Virtual Memory on the Intel 80386

The 8088 does not have virtual memory, so we cannot examine it. The 80286 does have it, but the 80386 is much more interesting, so we will concentrate on the 80386. In many ways, the virtual memory on the 80386 resembles MULTICS, including the presence of both segmentation and paging. Whereas MULTICS has 256K independent segments, each up to 64K 36-bit words, the 80386 has 16K independent segments, each holding up to 1 billion 32-bit words. Although there are fewer segments, the larger segment size is far more important, as few programs need more than 1000 segments, but many programs need segments holding megabytes.

The heart of the 80386 virtual memory consists of two tables, the **LDT (Local Descriptor Table)** and the **GDT (Global Descriptor Table)**. Each program has its own LDT, but there is a single GDT, shared by all the programs on the computer. The LDT describes segments local to each program, including its code, data, stack, and so on, whereas the GDT describes system segments, including the operating system itself.

As we described in Chap. 5, to access a segment, an 80386 program first loads a selector for that segment into one of the six segment registers. During execution, CS holds the selector for the code segment, DS holds the selector for the data segment, and so on. Each selector is a 16-bit number, as shown in Fig. 6-19.

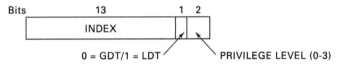
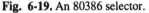

Fig. 6-19. An 80386 selector.

One of the selector bits tells whether the segment is local or global (i.e., whether it is in the LDT or GDT). Thirteen other bits specify the LDT or GDT entry number, so these tables are each restricted to holding 8K (2^{13}) segment descriptors. The other 2 bits relate to protection, and will be described later. Descriptor 0 is forbidden. It may be safely loaded into a segment register to indicate that the segment register is not currently available, but it causes a trap if used.

At the time a selector is loaded into a segment register, the corresponding descriptor is fetched from the LDT or GDT and stored in microprogram registers, so it can be accessed quickly. A descriptor consists of 8 bytes, including the segment's base address, size, and other information, as depicted in Fig. 6-20.

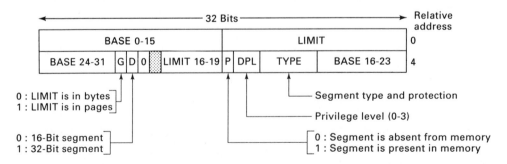

Fig. 6-20. 80386 Code segment descriptor. Data segments differ slightly.

The format of the selector has been cleverly chosen to make locating the descriptor easy. First either the LDT or GDT is selected, based on selector bit 2. Then the selector is copied to a microprogram scratch register, and the 3 low-order bits set to 0. Finally, the address of either the LDT or GDT table is added to it, to give a direct pointer to the descriptor. For example, selector 72 refers to entry 9 in the GDT, which is located at address GDT + 72.

Let us trace the steps by which a (selector, offset) pair is converted to a physical address. As soon as the microprogram knows which segment register is being used, it can find the complete descriptor corresponding to that selector in its internal registers. If the segment does not exist (selector 0), or is currently paged out (P is 0), a trap occurs.

It then checks to see if the offset is beyond the end of the segment, in which case a trap also occurs. Logically, there should simply be a 32-bit field in the descriptor giving the size of the segment, but there are only 20 bits available, so a different scheme is used. If the G (Granularity) field is 0, the LIMIT field is the exact segment size, up to 1 MB. If it is 1, the LIMIT field gives the segment size in pages instead of bytes. The 80386 page size is fixed at 4K bytes, so 20 bits is enough for segments up to 2^{32} bytes.

Assuming that the segment is in memory and the offset is in range, the 80386 then adds the 32-bit BASE field in the descriptor to the offset to form what is called a **linear address**, as shown in Fig. 6-21. The BASE field is broken up into three pieces and spread all over the descriptor for compatibility with the 80286, in which the BASE is only 24 bits. In effect, the BASE field allows each segment to start at an arbitrary place within the 32-bit linear address space.

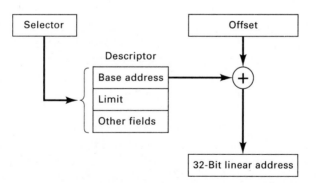

Fig. 6-21. Conversion of a (selector, offset) pair to a linear address.

If paging is disabled (by a bit in a global control register), the linear address is interpreted as the physical address and sent to the memory for the read or write. Thus with paging disabled, we have a pure segmentation scheme, with each segment's base address given in its descriptor. Segments are permitted to overlap, incidentally, probably because it would be too much trouble and take too much time to verify that they were all disjoint.

On the other hand, if paging is enabled, the linear address is interpreted as a virtual address and mapped onto the physical address using page tables, pretty much as in our examples. The only complication is that with a 32-bit virtual address and a 4K page, a segment might contain 1 million pages, so a two-level mapping is used to reduce the page table size for small segments.

Each running program has a **page directory** consisting of 1024 32-bit entries. It is located at an address pointed to by a global register. Each entry in this directory points to a page table also containing 1024 32-bit entries. The page table entries point to page frames. The scheme is shown in Fig. 6-22.

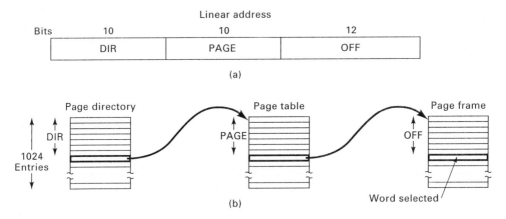

Fig. 6-22. Mapping of a linear address onto a physical address.

In Fig. 6-22(a) we see a linear address broken up into three fields, DIR, PAGE, and OFF. The DIR field is first used as an index into the page directory to locate a pointer to the proper page table. Then the PAGE field is used as an index into the page table to find the physical address of the page frame. Finally, OFF is added to the address of the page frame to get the physical address of the byte or word addressed.

The page table entries are 32 bits each, 20 of which contain a page frame number. The remaining bits contain access and dirty bits, set by the hardware for the benefit of the operating system, protection bits, and other utility bits.

Each page table has entries for 1024 4K page frames, so a single page table handles 4 megabytes of memory. A segment shorter than 4M will have a page directory with a single entry, a pointer to its one and only page table. In this way, the overhead for short segments is only two pages, instead of the million pages that would be needed in a one-level page table.

To avoid making repeated references to memory, the 80386, like MULTICS, has a small associative memory to directly map the most recently used DIR–PAGE combinations onto the physical address of the page frame. Only when the current combination is not present in the associative memory is the mechanism of Fig. 6-22 actually carried out and the associative memory updated.

A little thought will reveal the fact that when paging is used, there is really no point in having the BASE field in the descriptor be nonzero. All that BASE does is cause a small offset to use an entry in the middle of the page directory, instead of at the beginning. The real reason for including BASE at all is to allow pure (nonpaged) segmentation, and for compatibility with the 80286, which always has paging disabled (i.e., the 80286 only has pure segmentation, but not paging).

It is also worth mentioning that if a particular application does not need segmentation, but is content with a single, paged, 32-bit address space (Motorola mode), that is easy to obtain. All the segment registers can be set up with the same selector, whose descriptor has BASE = 0 and LIMIT set to the maximum. The instruction offset will then be the linear address, with only a single address space used—in effect, traditional paging.

All in all, one has to give credit to the 80386 designers. Given the conflicting goals of implementing pure paging, pure segmentation, and paged segments, while at the same time being compatible with the 80286, and doing all of this efficiently, the resulting design is surprisingly simple and clean.

Although we have covered the complete architecture of the 80386 virtual memory, albeit briefly, it is worth saying a few words about protection, since this subject is intimately related to the virtual memory. Just as the virtual memory scheme is closely modeled on MULTICS, so is the protection system. The 80386 supports four protection levels (called **rings** in MULTICS), with level 0 being the most privileged and level 3 the least. These are shown in Fig. 6-23. At each instant, a running program is at a certain level, indicated by a 2-bit field in its PSW. Furthermore, each segment in the system also belongs to a certain level.

As long as a program restricts itself to using segments at its own level, everything works fine. Attempts to access data at a higher level are permitted. Attempts to access data at a lower level are illegal and cause traps. Attempts to call procedures at a different level (higher or lower) are allowed, but in a carefully controlled way. To make an interlevel call, the CALL instruction must contain a selector instead of an address. This selector designates a descriptor called a **call gate**, which gives the address of the procedure to be called. Thus it is not possible to jump into the middle of an arbitrary code segment at a different level. Only official entry points may be used. Like the ring mechanism itself, this concept was also pioneered in MULTICS.

A typical use for this mechanism is suggested in Fig. 6-23. At level 0, we find the kernel of the operating system, which handles I/O, memory management, and other critical matters. At level 1, the system call handler is present. User programs may call procedures here to have system calls carried out, but only a specific and protected list of procedures may be called. Level 2 contains library procedures, possibly shared among many running programs. User programs may call these

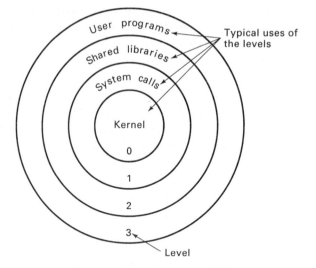

Fig. 6-23. Protection on the 80386.

procedures and read their data, but they may not modify them. Finally, user programs run at level 3, which has the least protection.

Traps and interrupts use a mechanism similar to the call gates. They, too, reference descriptors, rather than absolute addresses, and these descriptors point to
specific procedures to be executed. The DIR field in Fig. 6-20 distinguishes
between code segments, data segments, and the various kinds of gates.

6.1.10. Virtual Memory on the Motorola 68030

Like the 8088, the 68000 does not support virtual memory, but like the 80386,
the 68030 does, so we will study it. The 68020 can support virtual memory with
the help of an external **MMU (Memory Management Unit)** chip, but the differences between the 68020 and 68030 memory management are minimal.

Virtual memory on the 68030 is conceptually simple—straight paging—but the
implementation is somewhat elaborate to provide maximum flexibility. A good
starting place is Fig. 6-22, which shows how the 80386 maps a 32-bit virtual
address onto a 32-bit physical address via two page tables. The 68030 does not
have segmentation, so the lookup process begins with a 32-bit virtual address
directly generated by the CPU (e.g., direct addressing, register indirect, or indexed
mode), and ends with a 32-bit physical address that can be sent to the memory over
the bus.

Unlike the 80386, which has exactly two levels of page tables, the 68030 has a
variable number, between 0 and 4, controlled by software. Instead of the fixed (10,
10, 12) division of Fig. 6-22, the number of bits in each level can be determined by
the operating system by setting fields in a global register, the **TCR (Translation**

Control Register). Furthermore, since many programs need far less than 2^{32} bytes of memory, it is possible to tell the MMU to ignore the uppermost n bits.

As a (somewhat simplified) example, consider Fig. 6-24(a), which shows one of the many ways of breaking up 32-bit virtual addresses. Here we have decided to ignore the upper 12 bits (meaning that virtual addresses must be below 1M), followed by three levels of table lookup, A, B, and C. A potential fourth level, D, is not used in this example. Page sizes can be set by the operating system. All the powers of two from 256 to 32K are permitted. In this example, we have chosen to allocate 11 bits to OFFSET, which implies a page size of 2K.

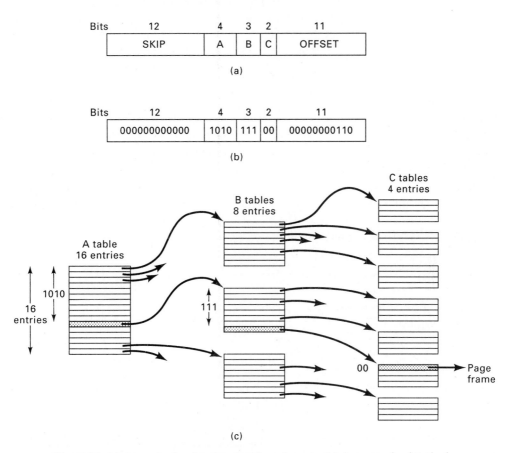

Fig. 6-24. (a) An example of a virtual address format. (b) An example virtual address. (c) Page tables corresponding to (a) and (b).

In Fig. 6-24(b) we show a virtual address, 000AE006H, split up according to the division of Fig. 6-24(a). In this format, 4 bits are allocated to the first table, which has up to 16 entries (but it may have fewer). The first entry in this table applies to virtual addresses in the range 0000H to FFFFH. The second one maps address 10000H to 1FFFFH, and so on. When presented with the virtual address of Fig. 6-24(b), the on-chip MMU ignores bits 20 through 31, and uses bits 16 through 19 as an index into the *A* table, as shown in Fig. 6-24(c).

The result of this lookup is a pointer to a *B* table, with eight entries (because the *B* fields of Fig. 6-24(a) and (b) are 3 bits). Next, the contents of the *B* field, bits 13 through 15 (with binary value 111) are used as an index into the *B* table, to get a pointer to one of the four-entry *C* page tables. This time we select entry 00, which contains a page descriptor, giving the page frame number and some other information. By combining the page frame number and the contents of the OFFSET field, we can construct the physical address of the byte or word needed.

Although in this example we only used three levels of page tables, we could have gone on to a fourth one by having the *C* table point to a *D* table, instead of a page frame. A field in each table entry tells whether it points to a page frame or to another table, and if the latter, which of the available table entry formats that table uses.

The final table at the end of the tree (the *C* table, in Fig. 6-24), contains page descriptors rather than pointers to yet another level of table. Figure 6-25 illustrates the simplest form of a page descriptor. It contains a 24-bit field for the page frame number. Recall that we mentioned earlier that the minimum page size is 256 bytes. With 256 byte pages, offsets are 8 bits, so the combination of 24 bits from the PAGE FRAME field and the 8-bit offset from the right-hand end of the virtual address together make up a 32-bit physical address. With larger page sizes, fewer than 24 bits are needed to specify a page frame number, so the appropriate number of low-order bits of the PAGE FRAME field are not used.

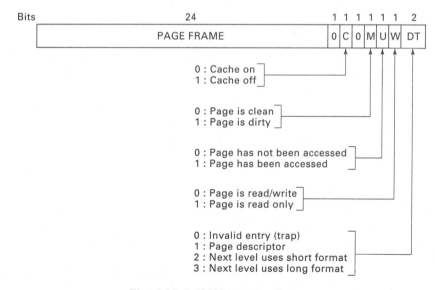

Fig. 6-25. A 68030 page descriptor.

The meaning of the five other fields are as follows. The 2-bit DT (Descriptor Type) field tells whether this entry is a page descriptor (i.e., the end of the line), simply another pointer to yet another level of tables (and if so, short or long), or an invalid entry.

The C bit is used to disable caching of the page pointed to. This facility is essential for pages that contain memory-mapped I/O device registers. Suppose that caching could not be disabled. Consider what would happen with programmed I/O. The first time that a device register was read, the register would be put into the cache. Subsequent reads would just pull the word out of the cache, so that changes in any of the bits of the real device register would not be seen. A loop waiting for a bit to change would wait forever.

The M and U bits are set by the hardware when the page is modified or just accessed, respectively. They are used by the operating system to keep track of clean and dirty pages, and for determining which page to throw out when a page frame is needed. These bits can be reset to 0 by the operating system after they have been read.

Finally, the W bit can be set to mark a page as read only. An attempt to write on a read-only page will cause a trap.

It may not be initially obvious what the value of so many levels of page tables is, so let us point out one use. Consider a group of programs that share a large data structure. If multiple entries in the A table of these processes all point to the same B table, then the entire page tree below that point is shared. If the processes also share a small data structure, their C or D tables may also point to the same page. Using this and other 68030 features and techniques, complex sharing schemes can be implemented.

It probably goes without saying, but the 68030, like the 80386 and MULTICS, has a small (22 entry), on-chip, associative memory to bypass the multilevel page table lookup for frequently used pages. Due to the potentially large number of memory references for each page lookup, this feature is essential for achieving good performance.

So far, we have not said how the MMU locates the A table. It is not pointed to by a single global register, as one might at first expect. Instead, the hardware maintains an array of eight registers, corresponding to the FCx function code lines present on the pins of the chip. Depending on the function code, one of potentially eight different A tables can be selected to start the page search. These tables correspond to instruction and data space references for the current user program, instruction and data space fetches for the operating system (i.e., kernel mode program), and a special address space for communicating with coprocessors and similar devices. The other three address spaces are not currently used; they are reserved for future versions of the chip.

Because the hardware distinguishes between instruction and data space references, a program on the 68030 may use 2^{32} bytes for its code, and an additional 2^{32} bytes for its data, for a total of 2^{33} bytes. The concept of separate instruction and data space was invented on the PDP-11/45, where the difference between 64K and 128K was important (it is not difficult to fill up 64K). For the 68030, there are not many *current* programs that are limited by being restricted to 2^{32} bytes, but someday that may also be perceived as hopelessly small, and programmers may thank their lucky stars for an extra address space, just as PDP-11/45 programmers once did.

One feature that the 68030 does not have is call gates. Thus it is generally not safe to have the operating system appear in user programs' address spaces, since they can jump to arbitrary operating system addresses. The reverse situation, having user programs appear in the operating system's address space is safe and perfectly reasonable.

6.1.11. Comparison of the 80386 and 68030

Since the 80386 and 68030 were both designed at roughly the same time, it is interesting to compare them to see how different people came up with different designs. Figure 6-26 lists some of the major differences between the two memory management schemes. The list is by no means complete; many minor differences also exist.

Item	80386	68030
Virtual address space size (in bytes)	2^{46}	2^{33}
Are separate instruction and data spaces possible?	No	Yes
Is pure segmentation available?	Yes	No
Is pure paging available?	Yes	Yes
Is segmentation plus paging available?	Yes	No
# Levels of page tables	2	4
Page size	4K	256–32K
Page table size	4K	variable
Does each page have access and modified bits?	Yes	Yes
Are call gates available?	Yes	No
# Protection levels	4	2

Fig. 6-26. Some differences in memory management between the 80386 and 68030.

The most significant difference is the presence of a huge (2^{46}-byte) segmented address space on the 80386, versus a merely large (2^{32}-byte) linear address space on the 68030 (2^{33} bytes if separate I & D space is used). The segmentation allows each object to be individually managed and protected, but brings with it the price of longer pointers. Although large segments will normally be paged, if most segments are small the option to have each one stored as a consecutive sequence of bytes may be viable. In any event, having a choice between segmentation and paging is better than not having a choice.

On the other hand, in practice, paging is the more important of the two, and the 68030 has a more flexible paging scheme. The use of multilevel tables and a programmable page size allow the operating system designers to tune the system to their work load and minimize page table overhead.

Another significant difference between the two machines is the protection structure. The 80386 has four protection levels, versus only two for the 68030. The additional levels make it easier to separate the system call handler from the operating system kernel, and also easier to implement shared libraries.

Furthermore, if segmentation is enabled, it is possible to include the operating system within the address space of every user process, so that making a system call can be done by calling a procedure (using a call gate), rather than causing a trap. Although going through a call gate is slightly more expensive than making an ordinary procedure call, it is at least an order of magnitude faster than trapping to the kernel.

As we shall see later in this chapter, the OS/2 operating system for the 80286 and 80386 uses this approach, thus greatly reducing the overhead required to make system calls. Because it lacks the call gate mechanism, there is no way for the 68030 to allow user programs to invoke protected operating system functions without trapping to the kernel. On the other hand, most operating systems, such as UNIX, do not use this feature, so its presence on the 80386 is not an advantage and its absence on the 68030 is not a handicap.

6.2. VIRTUAL I/O INSTRUCTIONS

Normally, the level 2 instruction set is completely different from the level 1 instruction set. Both the operations that can be performed and the formats for the instructions are quite different at the two levels. The existence of a few instructions that are the same at both levels is essentially accidental.

In contrast, the level 3 instruction set contains most of the level 2 instructions, with a few new, but important, instructions added and a few potentially damaging instructions removed. Input/output is one of the areas where level 2 and level 3 machines differ considerably. The reason for this difference is simple: a user who could execute the real level 2 instructions could read confidential data stored in the system, write on other users' terminals, and, in general, make a big nuisance of himself as well as being a threat to the security of the system. Second, normal, sane programmers do not want to write their own level 2 I/O programs themselves.

Device registers for disks typically have bits to detect the following errors:

1. An attempt to write on a protected cylinder was aborted.

2. Disk arm failed to seek properly.

3. Nonexistent memory specified as buffer.

4. Disk I/O started before previous one finished.

5. Read timing error.

6. Nonexistent disk addressed.

7. Nonexistent cylinder addressed.

8. Nonexistent sector addressed.

9. Checksum error on read.

10. Write check error after write operation.

When one of these errors occurs, the corresponding bit in a device register is set. Few users want to be bothered keeping track of all these error bits and the other status information.

6.2.1. Sequential Files

One way of organizing the virtual I/O is to conceive of data that is to be read or written as a sequence of logical records, where a **logical record** is some unit of information meaningful to the programmer. In the simplest case, a logical record might be a single character or an integer. For another application, a logical record might be a 10×10 matrix. For still another application, it might be a data structure consisting of five items: two character strings, "name," and "supervisor"; two integers, "department" and "office"; and a 1-bit string, "sex." A sequence of logical records is called a **file**. The records of a file need not all be the same length, in which case they are called **variable-length records**.

The basic virtual input instruction reads the next record from the specified file and puts it into consecutive cells in main memory beginning at a specified address, as illustrated in Fig. 6-27. To perform this operation, the virtual instruction must directly or indirectly specify (at least) two items of information:

1. The file to be read.

2. The main memory address into which the record is to be put.

No address within the file is specified. Consecutive sequential READ instructions get consecutive logical records from the file. This situation will be contrasted with random access files in the next section, in which the virtual instruction also specifies which logical record is to be read.

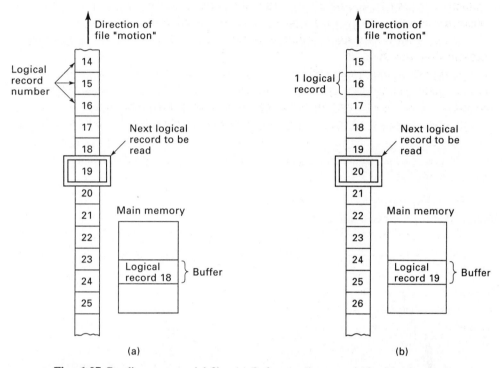

Fig. 6-27. Reading a sequential file. (a) Before reading record 19. (b) After reading record 19.

The basic virtual output instruction writes a logical record from memory onto a file. Consecutive sequential WRITE instructions produce consecutive logical records on the file. There is also a virtual REWIND instruction that repositions the file at the beginning so that the next logical record read or written will be the first one. The usual sequence is for a program first to create a file by writing a series of logical records onto it. The file is then rewound and read back one record at a time. In this manner, a file can be used to store large quantities of information that are too big for the main memory. In addition, if the file is stored on a magnetic tape or removable disk pack, it can be transported to another computer and read there.

Many operating systems require a file to be opened before it can be used, in which case an instruction OPEN is provided. The OPEN checks to see if the user is allowed to access the file, and if so, fetches information about the file into main memory. Then the file can be read or written. When the program is finished with a file it must close the file; an instruction is also provided for this operation.

Certain files can be permanently assigned to particular I/O devices. For example, there might be a file called OUTPUT, which consists of a series of 132-character strings and is associated with the printer. To print a line, the level 3 program writes a 132-character string onto the file OUTPUT, and somehow or other that string later appears on the printed output. The details of how that happens and how the printer actually works are of no concern to the level 3 programmer, although they are, of course, of great concern to the level 2 programmers who must write the software that carries out the virtual instructions (i.e., the operating system writers).

Another example might be a file called "INPUT", which consists of 80-character strings. Whenever a read from INPUT is performed, the contents of the next card are copied to memory. As far as the level 3 programmer is concerned, every instruction to read from input causes the next card in the deck to be read. In fact, the entire card deck may have been read all at once a while back and kept on the disk until needed, at which point one card at a time is copied to the user's buffer in main memory.

6.2.2. Random Access Files

The sequential files discussed previously are not addressable. A virtual READ instruction simply reads the next logical record. The program need not supply the logical record number. Many I/O devices, such as card readers, are by nature sequential. The level 3 instruction to read from the file associated with the card reader reads the next card. The program cannot say "Now read the 427th card" unless, by accident, it happens to have already read the first 426 cards. A sequential file is therefore a good model of such a device.

For some applications the program needs to access the records of a file in a different order from the order in which they have been written. As an example, consider an airline reservation system in which the passenger list for each flight forms a logical record and all the flights for one day form a file. A person may call up the airline's ticket agent and inquire about the availability of a seat on a flight to White Plains next Wednesday. The ticket agent enters the question into an on-line terminal. If the passenger list for that flight is record 26 of a certain file, the program needs only record 26. It clearly should not have to read sequentially starting at record 1 until it gets to record 26. The program needs to be able to access a specific record from the middle of a file by giving its record number.

Similarly, it is sometimes necessary to rewrite a particular logical record on a file without rewriting any logical records before or after it. In the preceding example, the person might want to make a reservation on the flight he inquired about. In order for this action to be performed, the program must rewrite the logical record containing the reservation list, adding the caller's name to the passenger list. It is neither necessary nor desirable to change any other logical records, however.

Most operating systems provide a virtual instruction to read the nth logical record of a file. These virtual instructions must provide (at least) three items of information:

1. The file to be read.

2. The main memory address into which the record is to be put.

3. The position of the logical record within the file.

The corresponding WRITE instructions must also provide this information.

Another form of file organization is one in which logical records are addressed not by their position in the file but by the contents of some field within each logical record, called the **key**. For example, a file containing a company's personnel data will have one field in each record containing the employee's name. A virtual instruction might be provided that allowed the program to give the name of an employee and have his logical record read in. It is the responsibility of the operating system to search the file for the needed logical record, saving the programmer the effort necessary to write the search procedure personally. This situation is analogous to a level 2 multiplication instruction, which spares the programmer the effort of (micro)programming his own multiplication procedure.

On some computers, a distinction is made between files that may be addressed by record number or key and files on which only the next record may be read. The former are called **random access** files, to distinguish them from the latter, the **sequential** files. On other computers, no such distinction is made, and both kinds of virtual instructions (with and without addressing) are allowed on all files.

6.2.3. Implementation of Virtual I/O Instructions

To understand how virtual I/O instructions are implemented on the level 2 machine, it is necessary to examine how files are organized and stored. In the following discussion we will assume that a disk is being used to hold the files, but similar considerations apply to other media.

A basic issue that must be dealt with by all file systems is allocation of storage. A disk consists of a series of arm positions or cylinders, each of which has one or more tracks, equal to the number of surfaces (typically from 2 to 20). Tracks are divided into sectors, each of which holds a certain number of words. On some disks, the sector size is adjustable. For example, the programmer may choose to format a track as 10 sectors of 600 bytes, 12 sectors of 500 bytes, or 15 sectors of 400 bytes. On other disks, the sector size is fixed.

A fundamental property of a file system implementation is the size of the unit in which space is allocated. A disk has three reasonable candidates: the sector, the track, or the cylinder. Allocating space in units of 2.93 tracks is absurd. The difference can be most clearly seen in the case of a file consisting initially of only a single character. If the sector is the allocation unit, only one sector will be reserved for the file, and the other sectors on the same track will be available for use by other files. If the track is the allocation unit, one entire track will be reserved for the file but the other tracks in the same cylinder will be available for other files. If disk space is allocated by the cylinder, an entire cylinder will be reserved even for a file of only one character.

Another fundamental property of a file system implementation is whether a file is stored in consecutive allocation units or not. Figure 6-28 depicts a simple disk with one surface consisting of five tracks of 12 sectors each. Figure 6-28(a) shows an allocation scheme in which the sector is the basic unit of space allocation and in which a file consists of consecutive sectors. Figure 6-28(b) shows an allocation scheme in which the sector is the basic allocation unit but in which a file need not occupy consecutive sectors.

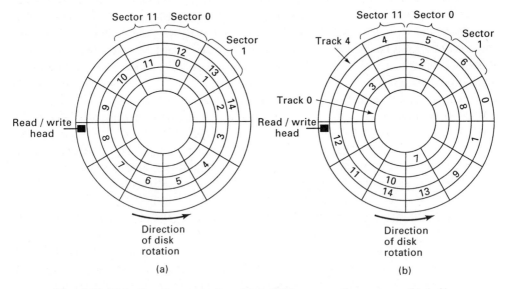

Fig. 6-28. Disk allocation strategies. (a) A file in consecutive sectors. (b) A file not in consecutive sectors.

If the track is the allocation unit, a consecutively allocated file will occupy consecutive tracks. As a rule, all the tracks in a cylinder will be allocated before the next cylinder is allocated. If a file is allocated in units of tracks but is not consecutively allocated, the tracks may be chosen anywhere on the disk, without regard to proximity to one another.

There is an important distinction between the level 3 view of a file and the operating system's view of a file. The level 3 program sees the file as a linear sequence of logical records, card images, print lines, arrays, and so on. The operating system sees the file as an ordered, although not necessarily consecutive, collection of allocation units.

In general the logical record size will be different from the allocation unit size, possibly being smaller and possibly being larger. A file may consist of a sequence of 80-byte strings stored on a disk on which space is allocated in units of 16384-byte tracks. Bytes 0 to 79 of track 0 will contain the first logical record, bytes 80 to 159 will contain the second logical record, and so on. The tracks are regarded as logically contiguous, even if they are not physically contiguous, and a logical record may be split over two tracks. It is the task of the operating system to make the physical allocation unit size transparent to the level 3 program. When the level 3 program asks for logical record n, it gets logical record n, without regard to which track or tracks that record may occupy.

In order for the operating system to deliver logical record n of some file on request, it must have some method for locating the record. If the file is allocated consecutively, the operating system need only know the location of the start of the file and the sizes of the logical and physical records in order to calculate the position of the logical record. For example, if a logical record consists of eight words and a track consists of 100 sectors of 64 words apiece, logical record 5000 will be in sector 25 of track 6. From its knowledge of the location of the first track, the level 2 software can calculate the exact disk address of the needed sector and issue a disk command to read it.

If the file is not allocated consecutively, it is not possible to calculate the position of an arbitrary logical record from the position of the start of the file alone. In order to locate any arbitrary logical record, a table called a **file index** giving the allocation units and their actual disk addresses is needed. The file index can be organized either in terms of the logical records, giving the disk address of each one, or simply as a list of the allocation units and their disk addresses. To illustrate how the file index is used, consider a disk allocated in sectors as in Fig. 6-28(b), with 512 bytes per sector. The file consists of 132-byte logical records (print lines) with bytes 0 to 131 constituting logical record 0, bytes 132 to 263 logical record 1, and so forth. Logical record 21 occupies bytes 2772 to 2903, which are in sector 5. By using the file index, the operating system can look up the address of the required sector, no matter which file index organization is used.

An alternative method of locating the allocation units of a file is to organize the file as a linked list. Each allocation unit contains the address of its successor. This can be done most efficiently if the hardware provides an extra word in each allocation unit for storing this address. This method is equivalent to dispersing the file index throughout the file. On a disk file allocated by sectors, each sector would contain the address of the succeeding sector. Such a file can only be read sequentially and cannot be accessed randomly.

Up until now we have discussed both consecutively allocated files and nonconsecutively allocated files but we have not specified why both kinds are used. A user who creates a file sometimes knows the maximum size that the file will later attain and sometimes does not. As an example of the latter, consider the computerized accounting system of the Ecology Manufacturing Company, which has just announced its latest product, a wind-up toothbrush. Their computer has a file listing the names and addresses of all their customers, but at the time the wind-up toothbrush is put on sale, they have no idea how many customers they will eventually have, and consequently, do not know how large the customer file will eventually become.

When the maximum file size is not known in advance, it is usually impossible to use a consecutively allocated file. If the file is started at track j and allowed to grow into consecutive tracks, it may bump into another file at track k and have no room to expand. If the file is not allocated consecutively, this situation presents no problem, because succeeding tracks can be put in any available cylinder. If a disk contains a number of "growing" files, none of whose final sizes is known, storing each of them as a consecutive file will be impossible. Moving an existing file is sometimes possible but always expensive.

If the maximum file size is known in advance, a region of the disk can be allocated when the file is created, even if the data are not yet available. For example, daily weather data for 1991 will require 365 records and can be allocated on or before December 31, 1990, even though none of the data are known at file-creation time. Consecutively allocated files are less flexible than nonconsecutively allocated files, because their maximum sizes must be known in advance. On the other hand, they are simpler to implement because no file index is needed. Note that both consecutively and nonconsecutively allocated files can be used as sequential access and as random access files.

In order to allocate space on the disk for a file, the operating system must keep track of which allocation units are available, and which are already in use storing other files. One method consists of maintaining a list of all the holes, a hole being any number of contiguous allocation units. This list is called the **free list**. Figure 6-29(a) illustrates the free list for the disk of Fig. 6-28(b).

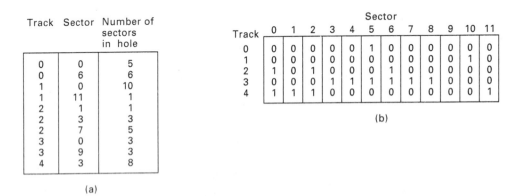

Track	Sector	Number of sectors in hole
0	0	5
0	6	6
1	0	10
1	11	1
2	1	1
2	3	3
2	7	5
3	0	3
3	9	3
4	3	8

(a)

	Sector											
Track	0	1	2	3	4	5	6	7	8	9	10	11
0	0	0	0	0	0	1	0	0	0	0	0	0
1	0	0	0	0	0	0	0	0	0	0	1	0
2	1	0	1	0	0	0	1	0	0	0	0	0
3	0	0	0	1	1	1	1	1	1	0	0	0
4	1	1	1	0	0	0	0	0	0	0	0	1

(b)

Fig. 6-29. Two ways of keeping track of available sectors. (a) A free list. (b) A bit map.

An alternative method is to maintain a bit map, with one bit per allocation unit, as shown in Fig. 6-29(b). A 1 bit indicates that the allocation unit is already occupied and a 0 bit indicates that it is available.

The first method has the advantage of making it easy to find a hole of a particular length, but it has the disadvantage of being variable sized. As files are created and destroyed the length of the list will fluctuate, an undesirable characteristic. The bit table has the advantage of being constant in size. In addition, changing the status of an allocation unit from available to occupied is just a matter of changing one bit. However, finding a block of a given size is difficult. Both methods require that when any file on the disk is allocated or returned, the allocation list or table be updated.

Before leaving the subject of file system implementation, it is worth commenting about the size of the allocation unit. Few files will occupy exactly an integral number of allocation units. Therefore, some space will be wasted in the last allocation unit of nearly every file. If the file is much larger than the allocation unit, the average space wasted will be half of an allocation unit. The larger the allocation unit, the larger the amount of wasted space.

If the expected file size is short, it is inefficient to allocate disk space in large units. For example, if most users of a proposed file system will be students with short programs averaging about 3000 characters, and a disk track contains 100 sectors of 640 characters apiece (i.e., 64000 characters), it would be foolish to allocate space in units of a track or, worse yet, a cylinder.

A disadvantage of allocating space in small chunks is that the file index and bit map (if used) will be large. Furthermore, if the file is nonconsecutively allocated, it will, in general, be necessary to do one disk seek per allocation unit. Disk seeks are slow; having to seek every 640 characters is less desirable than having to seek every 64000 characters. Of course, the strategy used to allocate new space to growing files can take this into consideration and try to assign allocation units close to the existing ones.

6.2.4. Directory Management Instructions

In the early days of computing, people kept their programs and data on punched cards in their offices. As the programs and data grew in size and number, this situation became less and less desirable. It eventually led to the idea of using the computer's secondary memory (e.g., disk) as a storage place for programs and data as an alternative to people's offices. Information that is directly accessible to the computer without the need for human intervention is said to be **on-line**, as contrasted with **off-line** information, which requires human intervention (e.g., reading in a card deck) before the computer can access it.

On-line information is stored in files, making it accessible to programs via the file I/O instructions discussed in Secs. 6.2.1 and 6.2.2. However, additional instructions are needed to keep track of the information stored on line, collect it into convenient units, and to protect it from unauthorized use.

The usual way for an operating system to organize on-line files is to group them into **directories** or **catalogs**. Figure 6-30 shows an example directory organization. Level 3 instructions are provided for at least the following functions:

1. Create a file and enter it in the owner's directory.

2. Delete a file from the directory.

3. Rename a file.

4. Change the protection status of a file.

File 0		File name:	Rubber-ducky	
File 1		Length:	1840	
File 2		Type:	Pascal program	
File 3		Creation date:	March 16, 1066	
File 4		Last access:	September 1, 1492	
File 5		Last change:	July 4, 1776	
File 6		Total accesses:	144	
File 7		Block 0:	Track 4	Sector 6
File 8		Block 1:	Track 19	Sector 9
File 9		Block 2:	Track 11	Sector 2
File 10		Block 3:	Track 77	Sector 0

Fig. 6-30. (a) A user file directory. (b) The contents of a typical entry in a file directory.

Various protection schemes are in use. The simplest one is for the owner of each file to specify a secret password for each file. When attempting to access a file, a program must supply the password, which the operating system then checks to see if it is correct before permitting the access. Another protection method is for the owner of each file to provide an explicit list of people whose programs may access that file.

Most operating systems allow users to maintain more than one file directory. Each directory is typically itself a file and, as such, may be listed in another directory, thus giving rise to a tree of directories. Multiple directories are particularly useful for programmers working on several projects. They can then group all the files related to one project together in one directory. While working on that project, they will not be distracted by unrelated files. Directories are also a convenient way for people to share files with members of their department or group.

6.3. VIRTUAL INSTRUCTIONS USED IN PARALLEL PROCESSING

Some computations can be most conveniently programmed for two or more cooperating processes, running in parallel (i.e., simultaneously, on different processors) rather than for a single process. Other computations can be divided into pieces, which can then be carried out in parallel to decrease the elapsed time required for the total computation. In order for several processes to work together in parallel, certain virtual instructions are needed. These instructions will be discussed in the following sections.

The laws of physics provide yet another reason for the current interest in parallel processing. According to Einstein's special theory of relativity, it is impossible to transmit electrical signals faster than the speed of light, which is nearly 1 ft/nsec. This limit has important implications for computer organization. For example, if a CPU needs data from the main memory 1 ft away, it will take at least 1 nsec for the request to arrive at the memory and another nanosecond for the reply to get back to the CPU. Consequently, subnanosecond computers will need to be extremely tiny. An alternative approach to speeding up computers is to build machines with many CPUs. A computer with a thousand 1-nsec CPUs may have the same computing power as one CPU with a cycle time of 0.001 nsec, but the former may be much easier and cheaper to construct.

On a computer with more than one physical processor, each of several cooperating processes can be assigned to its own processor, to allow the processes to progress simultaneously. If only one physical processor is available, the effect of parallel processing can be simulated by having the processor run each process in turn for a short time. In other words, the processor can be shared among several processes.

Figure 6-31 shows the difference between true parallel processing, with more than one physical processor, and simulated parallel processing, with only one physical processor. Even when parallel processing is simulated, it is useful to regard each process as having its own dedicated virtual processor. The same communication problems that arise when there is true parallel processing also arise in the simulated case.

6.3.1. Process Creation

When a program is to be executed, it must run as part of some process. This process, like all other processes, is characterized by a state and an address space through which the program and data can be accessed. The state includes the program counter and possibly, a program status word, a stack pointer, and general registers.

Simple operating systems usually support a fixed number of processes, all of which are created when the computer is started up in the morning and all of which remain in existence until the computer is stopped at night. On these computers a

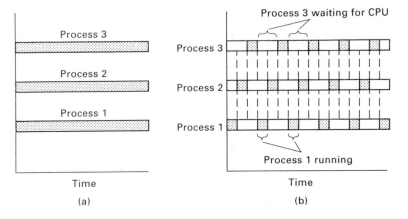

Fig. 6-31. (a) True parallel processing with multiple CPUs. (b) Parallel processing simulated by switching one CPU among three processes.

program must wait in the input queue until a process becomes available before it can be loaded into the process's address space and executed.

More sophisticated operating systems allow processes to be created and terminated without stopping the computer. A computer with this kind of operating system can support a variable number of level 3 machines, each process corresponding to one virtual machine. To take full advantage of parallel processing, a level 3 program needs a virtual instruction to create new processes, to which it can delegate work. Some operating systems provide a level 3 instruction for creating a new process, allowing the creating process to specify the initial state of the new process, including its program, data, and starting address. With some IBM 370 programming systems, for example, a procedure can call another procedure in a special way so as to have the caller and callee run in parallel as separate processes.

In some cases, the creating (parent) process maintains complete control over the created (child) process. To this end, virtual instructions exist for a parent to stop, restart, examine, and terminate its children. In other cases, a parent has less control over its children: once a process has been created, there is no way for the parent to forcibly stop, restart, examine, or terminate it. The two processes then run independently of one another.

6.3.2. Race Conditions

In this section the difficulties involved in synchronizing parallel processes will be explained by means of a detailed example. A solution to these difficulties will be given in the following section. Consider a situation consisting of two independent processes, process 1 and process 2, which communicate via a shared buffer in main memory. For simplicity we will call process 1 the **producer** and process 2 the **consumer**. The producer computes prime numbers and puts them into the buffer one at a time. The consumer removes them from the buffer one at a time and prints them.

These two processes run in parallel at different rates. If the producer discovers that the buffer is full, it goes to sleep; that is, it temporarily suspends its operation awaiting a signal from the consumer. Later, when the consumer has removed a number from the buffer, it sends a signal to the producer to wake it up—that is, restart it. Similarly, if the consumer discovers that the buffer is empty, it goes to sleep. When the producer has put a number into the empty buffer, it wakes up the sleeping consumer.

In this example we will use a circular buffer for interprocess communication. The pointers *in* and *out* will be used as follows: *in* points to the next free word (where the producer will put the next prime) and *out* points to the next number to be removed by the consumer. When *in* = *out*, the buffer is empty, as shown in Fig. 6-32(a). After the producer has generated some primes, the situation is as shown in Fig. 6-32(b). Figure 6-32(c) illustrates the buffer after the consumer has removed some of these primes for printing. Figure 6-32(d)-(f) depict the effect of continued buffer activity. The top of the buffer is logically contiguous with the bottom; that is, the buffer wraps around. When there has been a sudden burst of input and *in* has wrapped around and is only one word behind *out* (e.g., *in* = 52, and *out* = 53), the buffer is full. The last word is not used; if it were, there would be no way to tell if *in* = *out* meant a full buffer or an empty one.

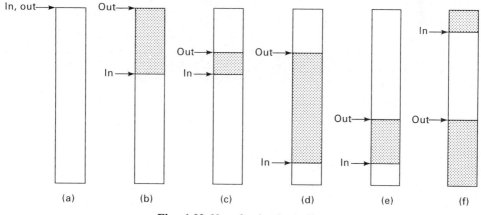

Fig. 6-32. Use of a circular buffer.

Figure 6-33 shows some declarations and the procedures used by the producer and the consumer in pseudo Pascal. Pascal does not allow parallel processing, so we have invented two "library" procedures: *sleep*, which puts a process to sleep, and *wakeup*, which wakes up the process named by its parameter (if it was asleep).

After appropriate initialization ($in = 1$ and $out = 1$), the producer and consumer should be started in parallel.

After the producer has found the next prime number in statement P1, it checks (in P2) to see if in is one behind out. If it is (e.g., $in = 62$ and $out = 63$), the buffer is full and the producer goes to sleep. If the buffer is not full, the new prime is inserted into the buffer (P3) and in is incremented (P4). If the new value of in is 1 ahead of out (P5) (e.g., $in = 17$ and $out = 16$), in and out must have been equal before in was incremented. The producer concludes that the buffer was empty and that the consumer was, and still is, sleeping. Therefore, the producer sends a signal to wake the consumer up. Finally, the producer begins looking for the next prime.

The consumer's program is structurally similar. First, a test is made (C1) to see if the buffer is empty. If it is, there is no work for the consumer to do, so it goes to sleep. If the buffer is not empty, it removes the next number to be printed (C2) and increments out ($C3$). If out is two positions ahead of in at this point (C4), it must have been one position ahead of in before it was just incremented. Because $in = out - 1$ is the "buffer full" condition, the producer must have been sleeping, and thus the consumer sends a signal to wake up the producer. Finally, the number is printed (C5) and the cycle repeats.

Unfortunately, this design contains a fatal flaw, as shown in Fig. 6-34. Remember that the two processes run asynchronously and at different, possibly varying, speeds. Consider the case where only one number is left in the buffer, in word 21, and $in = 22$ and $out = 21$, as shown in Fig. 6-34(a). The producer is at statement P1 looking for a prime and the consumer is busy at C5 printing out the number in position 20. The consumer finishes printing the number, makes the test at C1, and takes the last number out of the buffer at C2. It then increments out. At this instant, both in and out have the value 22. The consumer prints the number and then goes to C1, where it fetches in and out from memory in order to compare them, as shown in Fig. 6-34(b).

At this very moment, after the consumer has fetched in and out but before it has compared them, the producer finds the next prime. It puts the prime into the buffer at P3 and increments in at P4. Now $in = 23$ and $out = 22$. At P5 the producer discovers that $in = next(out)$. In other words, in is one higher than out, signifying that there is now one item in the buffer. The producer therefore (incorrectly) concludes that the consumer must be sleeping, so it sends a wakeup signal, as shown in Fig. 6-34(c). Of course, the consumer is still awake, so the wakeup signal is lost. The producer begins looking for the next prime.

At this point in time the consumer continues. It has already fetched in and out from memory before the producer put the last number in the buffer, Because they both have the value 22, the consumer goes to sleep. Now the producer finds another prime. It checks the pointers and finds $in = 24$ and $out = 22$, therefore it assumes that there are two numbers in the buffer (correct) and that the consumer is awake (incorrect). The producer continues looping and eventually it fills the buffer up and goes to sleep. Now both processes are sleeping and will remain so forever.

```
const MaxPrime = ...;                        {largest prime to look for}
      BufSize = 100;                         {number of buffer slots}

type index = 1 .. BufSize ;                  {buffer slots numbered from 1 to BufSize}

var in : index ;                             {next free slot for a prime to go into}
    out : index ;                            {next prime to be fetched and printed}
    buffer : array[index ] of integer ;      {shared buffer}

function next (k : index ): index ;
{ Compute the successor to k taking wraparound into account.}
begin
  if k < BufSize then next := k + 1 else next := 1
end; {next}
```

```
procedure producer ;
{ The producer computes prime numbers and puts them in a shared buffer for
  subsequent printing . When the buffer is full , the producer goes to sleep .
  When the consumer sends a wakeup signal , the producer continues at P3.}

var prime : integer ;
begin
  prime := 2;
  while prime < MaxPrime do
    begin
      {P1}  ComputeNextPrime(prime);
      {P2}  if next(in) = out then sleep;
      {P3}  buffer[in] : = prime;
      {P4}  in : = next(in);
      {P5}  if next(out) = in then wakeup(consumer)
    end
end; {producer}
```

```
procedure consumer ;
{ The consumer takes numbers out of the buffer and prints them. If the buffer
  becomes empty , the consumer goes to sleep . When the producer sends a wakeup
  signal , the consumer continues at C2.}
var emirp : integer ;
begin
  emirp := 2;
  while emirp < MaxPrime do
    begin
      {C1}  if in = out then sleep;
      {C2}  emirp := buffer[out];
      {C3}  out := next(out);
      {C4}  if out = next(next(in)) then wakeup(producer);
      {C5}  writeln(emirp)
    end
end; {consumer}
```

Fig. 6-33. Parallel processing with a fatal race condition.

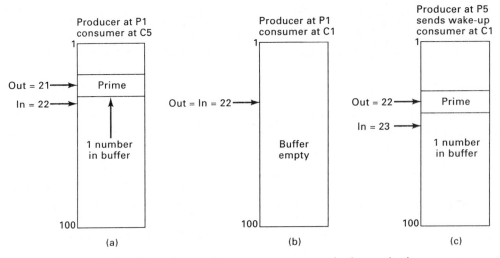

Fig. 6-34. Failure of the producer-consumer communication mechanism.

The difficulty here is that between the time when the consumer fetched *in* and *out* and the time it went to sleep, the producer snuck in, discovered that *in* = *out* + 1, assumed that the consumer was sleeping (which it was not yet), and sent a wakeup signal that was lost because the consumer was still awake. This difficulty is known as a **race condition**, because the method's success depends on who wins the race to test *in* and *out* after *out* is incremented.

6.3.3. Process Synchronization Using Semaphores

The race condition can be solved in at least two ways. One solution consists of equipping each process with a "wakeup waiting bit." Whenever a wakeup is sent to a process that is still running, its wakeup waiting bit is set. Whenever the process goes to sleep when the wakeup waiting bit is set, it is immediately restarted and the wakeup waiting bit is cleared. The wakeup waiting bit stores the superfluous wakeup signal for future use.

Although this method solves the race condition when there are only two processes, it fails in the general case of *n* communicating processes because as many as *n* − 1 wakeups may have to be saved. Of course, each process could be equipped with *n* − 1 wakeup waiting bits to allow it to count to *n* − 1 in the unary system, but this solution is rather clumsy.

Dijkstra (1968b) proposed a more general solution to the problem of synchronizing parallel processes. Somewhere in the memory are two nonnegative integer variables called **semaphores**. Two level 3 instructions that operate on semaphores, UP and DOWN, are provided by the operating system. UP adds 1 to a semaphore and DOWN subtracts 1 from a semaphore.

If a DOWN instruction is performed on a semaphore that is greater than 0, the semaphore is decremented by 1 and the process doing the DOWN continues. If, however, the semaphore is 0, the DOWN cannot complete; the process doing the DOWN is put to sleep and remains asleep until the other process performs an UP on that semaphore.

The UP instruction checks to see if the semaphore is 0. If it is and the other process is sleeping on it, the semaphore is increased by 1. The sleeping process can then complete the DOWN operation that suspended it, resetting the semaphore to 0 and allowing both processes to continue computing. An UP instruction on a nonzero semaphore simply increases it by 1. In essence, a semaphore provides a counter to store wakeups for future use, so that they will not be lost. An essential property of semaphore instructions is that once a process has initiated an instruction on a semaphore, no other process may access the semaphore until the first process has either completed its instruction, or been suspended trying to perform a DOWN on a 0. Figure 6-35 summarizes the essential properties of the UP and DOWN instructions.

Value of the semaphore before the instruction

Instruction	Semaphore = 0	Semaphore > 0
UP	Semaphore = semaphore + 1 If the other process was halted attempting to complete a DOWN instruction on this semaphore, it may now complete the DOWN and continue running	Semaphore = semaphore + 1
DOWN	Process halts until the other process UP's this semaphore	Semaphore = semaphore − 1

Fig. 6-35. The effect of a semaphore instruction.

Figure 6-36 shows how the race condition can be eliminated through the use of semaphores. Two semaphores are used, *available*, which is initially 100 (the buffer size), and *filled*, which is initially 0.

The producer starts executing at P1 in Fig. 6-36 and the consumer starts executing at C1. The DOWN instruction on *filled* halts the consumer processor immediately. When the producer has found the first prime, it executes a DOWN instruction on *available*, setting it to 99. At P5 it does an UP on *filled*, making it 1. This action releases the consumer, which is now able to complete its DOWN instruction. At this point, *filled* is 0 and both processes are running.

Let us now reexamine the race condition. At a certain point in time, $in = 22$, $out = 21$, the producer is at P1, and the consumer is at C5. The consumer finishes what it was doing and gets to C1 where it DOWNs the semaphore, which had the value 1 before the DOWN instruction and 0 after it. The consumer then takes the last number out of the buffer and UPs *available*, making it 100. The consumer

```
const MaxPrime = ...;                     {largest prime to look for}
      BufSize = 100;                      {number of buffer slots}

type index = 1 .. BufSize;                {buffer slots numbered from 1 to BufSize}

var in : index;                           {next free slot for a prime to go into}
    out : index;                          {next prime to be fetched and printed}
    buffer : array[index] of integer;     {shared buffer}

function next (k : index): index;
{ Compute the successor to k taking wraparound into account.}
begin
  if k < BufSize then next := k + 1 else next := 1
end; {next}


procedure producer;
{ In this improved version, the producer puts the primes in the buffer for
  subsequent printing. When the buffer is full, the producer goes to sleep
  by doing a DOWN on available. When the consumer does an UP on available,
  the producer continues at P3. DOWN and UP are level 3 instructions that
  are invoked by the library procedures down and up, respectively.}

var prime : integer;
begin
  prime := 2;
  while prime < MaxPrime do
    begin
      {P1}  ComputeNextPrime(prime);
      {P2}  down(available);
      {P3}  buffer[in] := prime;
      {P4}  in := next(in);
      {P5}  up(filled)
    end
end; {producer}


procedure consumer;
{ The consumer takes numbers out of the buffer and prints them. If the buffer
  becomes empty, the consumer goes to sleep. When the producer sends a wakeup
  signal, the consumer continues at C2.}
var emirp : integer;
begin
  emirp := 2;
  while emirp < MaxPrime do
    begin
      {C1}  down(filled);
      {C2}  emirp := buffer[out];
      {C3}  out := next(out);
      {C4}  up(available);
      {C5}  writeln(emirp)
    end
end; {consumer}
```

Fig. 6-36. Parallel processing using semaphores.

prints the number and goes to C1. Just before the consumer can perform the DOWN instruction, the producer finds the next prime and in quick succession executes statements P2, P3, and P4.

At this point, *filled* is 0. The producer is about to UP it and the consumer is about to DOWN it. If the consumer executes its instruction first, it will be suspended until the producer releases it (by performing an UP). On the other hand, if the producer executes its instruction first, the semaphore will be set to 1 and the consumer will not be suspended at all. In both cases, no wakeup is lost. This, of course, was our goal in introducing semaphores in the first place.

The essential property of the semaphore operations is that they are indivisible. Once a semaphore operation has been initiated, no other process can use the semaphore until the first process has either completed the operation or been suspended trying. Furthermore, with semaphores, no wakeups are lost. In contrast, the **if** statements of Fig. 6-33 are not indivisible. Between the evaluation of the condition and the execution of the selected statement, another process can send a wakeup signal.

In effect the problem of process synchronization has been eliminated by declaring the UP and DOWN instructions to be indivisible. In order for these level 3 instructions to be indivisible, the operating system must prohibit two or more processes from using the same semaphore at the same time.

Synchronization using semaphores is a technique that works for arbitrarily many processes. Several processes may be sleeping, attempting to complete a DOWN instruction on the same semaphore. When some other process finally performs an UP on that semaphore, one of the waiting processes is allowed to complete its DOWN instruction and continue running. The semaphore value remains 0 and the other processes continue waiting.

An analogy may make the nature of semaphores clearer. Imagine a picnic with 20 volleyball teams divided into 10 games (processes) each playing on its own court, and a large basket (the semaphore) for the volleyballs. Unfortunately, only seven volleyballs are available. At any instant, there are between zero and seven volleyballs in the basket (the semaphore has a value between 0 and 7). Putting a ball in the basket is an UP instruction because it increases the value of the semaphore. Taking a ball out of the basket is a DOWN instruction, because it decreases the value of the semaphore.

At the start of the picnic, each court sends a player to the basket to get a volleyball. Seven of them successfully manage to get a volleyball (complete the DOWN instruction); three are forced to wait for a volleyball (i.e., fail to complete the DOWN instruction). Their games are suspended temporarily. Eventually, one of the other games finishes and puts a ball into the basket (executes an UP instruction). This operation allows one of the three players waiting around the basket to get a ball (complete an unfinished DOWN instruction), allowing one game to continue. The other two games remain suspended until two more balls are put into the basket. When two more balls come back (two more UPs), they too can proceed.

6.4. EXAMPLE OPERATING SYSTEMS

In this chapter we have studied three features that many operating systems provide: virtual memory, virtual I/O, and parallel processing. In almost no real system are things quite as neat and simple as we have described. Therefore, it is worth taking a more detailed look at the real operating systems used by our example machines to see how these ideas are applied in practice.

However, before we can start studying about our example operating systems, we have to decide which ones to study. Both the Intel and Motorola lines have a variety of operating systems available from which we can choose. The choice for the 680x0 CPUs is relatively easy. Although some 68000 systems, like the Macintosh, Atari ST, and Amiga, run proprietary operating systems, most 68020- and 68030-based computers run UNIX. Thus we will use UNIX as our example here.

The choice for the Intel family is much harder. Most 8088s are in IBM PCs and clones, and these usually run MS-DOS. Unfortunately for our purposes, MS-DOS is an obsolete, primitive, and not very interesting system, despite its widespread use. (Who ever said that you had to be good to be popular? Look at BASIC.) However, two other operating systems are also available for the 80286 and 80386, namely UNIX and OS/2. Since we have already decided to treat UNIX because it is the system of choice on the 68020 and 68030, we will use OS/2 as the example for the Intel line. Although it is not nearly as popular as MS-DOS, it is much more interesting, and has some ideas not even found in UNIX. Since UNIX came first, and OS/2 was clearly influenced by it, we will start with UNIX and then look at OS/2 afterward. However, before getting into the technical aspects of each, it is worth saying a few words about their respective backgrounds.

In the mid 1960s, M.I.T., Bell Labs and General Electric decided to jointly develop an advanced time-sharing system, MULTICS, which we have described in some detail already. To make a long story short, MULTICS was twenty years ahead of its time in many ways, and the project did not go as well as the designers had hoped. For starters, the hardware was much too small and slow, and the compiler for the language MULTICS was written in (PL/I) never really worked. Eventually Bell Labs pulled out, and GE got out of the computer business altogether.

One of the Bell Labs people working on MULTICS, Ken Thompson, suddenly found himself with nothing to do. However, he soon noticed an old PDP-7 that nobody was using, and decided to write a stripped down, single-user version of MULTICS for the PDP-7 all by himself. Despite the tiny size of the PDP-7, the system (UNIX) showed remarkable promise, so Thompson, later joined by his colleague Dennis Ritchie, moved it to better hardware, rewriting it several times in the process.

At a certain point, they had a version running on the PDP-11/45. By a stroke of good luck, the PDP-11/45 was the machine of choice at most university computer science departments, and most users perceived the DEC operating systems as dreadful. When Bell Labs agreed to license UNIX to universities for 300 dollars (including all the source code), hundreds of them jumped at the chance and UNIX became an instant cult item. Meetings were held all over the world, where distinguished speakers would get up in front of the room and discuss how they had fixed an obscure kernel bug, showing the kernel code itself on overhead sheets.

The word spread, and within a few years UNIX had been moved to dozens of computers, large and small. By the early 1980s it was available on more machines than any other operating system in history. Its popularity is steadily increasing, and it will certainly continue to be one of the most widely used systems for years to come.

OS/2 has quite a different history. When IBM introduced the IBM PC in 1981, it simultaneously introduced a primitive operating system for it, MS-DOS, written by Microsoft. While MS-DOS is arguably adequate for the 8088, on the 80286 (let alone the 80386) it makes no use of the improved hardware. It supports a single user running a single program, and does that in real mode, using only 640K of memory, no matter how much the machine has. There is no multiprogramming, no swapping, no protection, and no virtual memory, all of which are perfectly reasonable things to have on the 80286. Furthermore, the operating system services are so inadequate, that many applications programs bypass MS-DOS altogether, and do their own I/O directly on the bare metal. Nevertheless, the PC was an enormous commercial success, so MS-DOS was dragged to a fame it never deserved.

Half a decade later, when IBM decided to put the PC line out to pasture and replaced it with the PS/2, the limitations of MS-DOS could not be ignored any more, and a new operating system was needed. This new system, developed jointly by IBM and Microsoft, was OS/2. Rather than making a half-hearted attempt at patching up MS-DOS, the designers took a good look around to see what the state-of-the art was in operating systems. Lo and behold, they discovered MULTICS. Twenty years later, personal computers powered by an 80286 were able to do what a great 1960s mainframe was too weak for. The design of OS/2 is completely new, but in many key areas, the influence of MULTICS, and its descendant, UNIX, is unmistakable. More information about OS/2 can be found in (Krantz et al., 1988; Iacobucci, 1988; Schildt, 1988; and Schmitt, 1989).

Figure 6-37 shows some of the critical areas in which OS/2 is superior to MS-DOS. In nearly all of them, the MULTICS influence is clearly visible.

Much as they probably would have liked to, the OS/2 designers were not permitted to simply treat MS-DOS as a bad dream and start all over. They were told that OS/2 must support running old MS-DOS binary programs. Furthermore, as an additional concession, the OS/2 file system had to be MS-DOS compatible, even down to the diskette format. While this support is of great commercial importance, it is of little interest to us because, basically, what OS/2 does, is put the 80286 into real mode to trick the software into thinking it is running on an 8088. Since OS/2 does not run DOS programs in protected mode, bugs in these programs are capable of crashing the entire system. While this lack of security is undesirable, there was little choice. We will not discuss MS-DOS compatibility much here.

Item	MS-DOS	OS/2
Available address space	640K	16M
Usable physical memory	640K	16M
Virtual memory?	No	Yes
Swapping?	No	Yes
Multiprogramming?	No	Yes
Protection?	No	Yes
# Environments	1	Many
Services	Primitive	Sophisticated
System calls made by	Trap	Call

Fig. 6-37. Comparison of MS-DOS and OS/2.

6.4.1. Examples of Virtual Memory

UNIX and OS/2 take diametrically opposed approaches to the issue of memory management. UNIX tries to hide the question entirely, providing a very simple memory model, so that the system could be ported to large numbers of very different machines. OS/2, in contrast, was designed specifically for the 80286 processor (although it also runs on the 80386, ignoring all features not present on the 80286). The operating system is so tightly tied to the details of the 80286's architecture, that it will never be ported to anything except the 80286 and its direct descendants.

There is something to be said for each approach. UNIX has become enormously popular precisely because it has been ported to so many machines, from personal computers to supercomputers. The widespread availability of UNIX means that an application program can be written once and then recompiled for a dozen different machines without being modified. This porting has only been possible because UNIX makes so few assumptions about the hardware and so few demands on it. The consequence of this way of doing things is that UNIX does not always make optimum use of the hardware, but it is not bad, either.

OS/2 does not have this problem. It squeezes every last drop of power out of the 80286. However, programs written for OS/2 are difficult, if not impossible, to move to other computers and operating systems, especially if they make heavy use of OS/2's advanced features. Some day the 80286 will become obsolete, and that will be a day of reckoning for many programs and users. In contrast, many UNIX programs have survived a dozen radical changes in the hardware and architecture with nothing more than a recompilation, and many other programs have been moved to other operating systems with little effort.

UNIX Virtual Memory

The UNIX memory model is simple. Each process has three segments: code, data, and stack, as illustrated in Fig. 6-38. In a machine with a single, linear address space, such as the 68030, the code is generally placed near the bottom of memory, followed by the data. The stack is placed at the top of memory. The code size is fixed, but the data and stack may each grow, in opposite directions. This model is easy to implement on almost any machine.

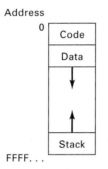

Fig. 6-38. The address space of a single UNIX process.

Furthermore, if the machine has paging, the entire address space can be paged, without user programs even being aware of it. The only thing they notice is that it is permitted to have programs larger than the machine's physical memory. UNIX systems that do not have paging generally swap entire processes between memory and disk to allow an arbitrarily large number of processes to be timeshared.

OS/2 Virtual Memory

The OS/2 memory model is closely matched to the 80286 architecture. An OS/2 program may have as many segments as it wants (up to 8192 of them), and each segment may be any size, up to a maximum of 64K bytes. So-called **huge segments** also exist, which span multiple 64K hardware segments. These are treated differently than ordinary segments.

Both global and local segments are used. Global segments contain the operating system itself. Local segments contain user code and data. System calls are available for creating segments, deleting segments, and changing segment sizes, as well as for other segment functions.

Processes are permitted to share segments, both read-only and writable. Thus a simple way for two processes to communicate is to set up a shared segment, and have one process write data into it and the other one take it out. Segments may also be shared among more than two processes.

A process may have more segments than memory can hold. In other words,

OS/2 implements virtual memory using pure segmentation. Paging is not used, not even when OS/2 runs on the 80386. If there is insufficient room in memory to hold all the segments owned by a running process, some of them are kept on disk. When a process references a segment that is on disk, the hardware causes a fault, and OS/2 brings in the required segment, possibly swapping out one or more other segments to make room for it. The system also can compact memory to combat checkerboarding.

When a program is executed, the question arises of which segments to bring into memory. This problem is solved in OS/2 by providing a way to mark segments as being **load on demand**. Segments with this bit on are not brought into memory when the program is started up. Instead they are only brought in if they are referenced. Load on demand segments are normally used to hold error routines and other code and data that are not likely to be used, but which must be available under certain unusual circumstances.

Segments can be protected, and all four protection levels are used by OS/2. The operating system kernel segments run at level 0. Level 1 holds the file system, interprocess communication, and the I/O device drivers. In level 2 we find I/O subsystems, such as the code for handling the video display and windowing software. Finally, user programs run at level 3.

6.4.2. Examples of Virtual I/O

The heart of any operating system is providing services to user programs, mostly I/O services such as reading and writing various I/O devices. Both UNIX and OS/2 offer a wide variety of I/O services to user programs. Some of these, such as reading and writing files, are similar, but other services are not. Furthermore, the way the services are invoked is radically different in the two systems. In this section we will look at virtual I/O and similar services in UNIX and OS/2.

UNIX Virtual I/O

Much of the popularity of the UNIX system can be traced directly to its simplicity, which, in turn, is a direct result of the organization of the file system. An ordinary file is a linear sequence of 8-bit bytes starting at 0 and going up to a maximum of over 1000 megabytes. The operating system itself imposes no record structure on files, although many user programs regard ASCII text files as sequences of lines, each line terminated by a line feed.

Associated with every file currently in use (i.e., every open file) is a pointer that points to the next byte to be read or written. The READ and WRITE calls read and write data starting at the file position indicated by the pointer. Both calls advance the pointer after the operation by an amount equal to the number of bytes transferred. The LSEEK call moves the pointer to an arbitrary byte number, either absolute, relative to the current position, or relative to the end of the file. By first moving the pointer and then calling READ or WRITE, any byte in the file can be accessed randomly.

Figure 6-39 is a fragment of a Pascal program that illustrates how the major file I/O calls work. Before entering the loop, the program opens an existing file, *data*, and creates a new file, *newf*. The second parameters to the two calls specify that the files are to be read and written, respectively. Both calls return a small positive integer called a **file descriptor** that is used to identify the file in subsequent calls. If either OPEN or CREAT fails, a negative file descriptor is returned, telling that the call failed.

The call to READ has three parameters: a file descriptor, a buffer, and a byte count. The call tries to read the desired number of bytes from the indicated file into the buffer. The number of bytes actually read is returned in *count*, which will be smaller than *bytes* if the file was too short. The WRITE call deposits the newly read bytes on the output file. The loop continues until the input file has been completely read, at which time the loop terminates and both files are closed.

```
infd:=open ("data", 0);                          {open existing file data}
outfd:=creat ("newf", ProtectionBits);           {create new file newf}
repeat
    count := read (infd, buffer, bytes);         {read buffer}
    if count > 0 then write (outfd, buffer, count)   {write buffer}
until count <= 0;

close (infd);                                    {close input file}
close (outfd);                                   {close output file}
```

Fig. 6-39. A fragment of a Pascal program for copying a file using the UNIX system calls.

In addition to ordinary files, the UNIX system also has special files, which are used to access I/O devices. Each I/O device typically has one or more special files assigned to it. By reading and writing from the associated special file, a program can read or write from the I/O device. Magnetic tapes, paper tapes, terminals, and many other devices are handled this way.

Closely related to the file system is the directory system. Each user may have multiple directories, with each directory containing both files and subdirectories. UNIX systems normally are configured with a main directory, called the **root directory**, containing subdirectories *bin* (for frequently executed programs), *dev* (for the special I/O device files), *lib* (for libraries), and *usr* (for user directories), as shown in Fig. 6-40. In this example, the *usr* directory contains subdirectories for *ast* and *jim*. The *ast* directory contains two files, *data* and *foo.p*, and a subdirectory, *bin*, containing four games.

Files can be named by giving their **path** from the root directory. A path

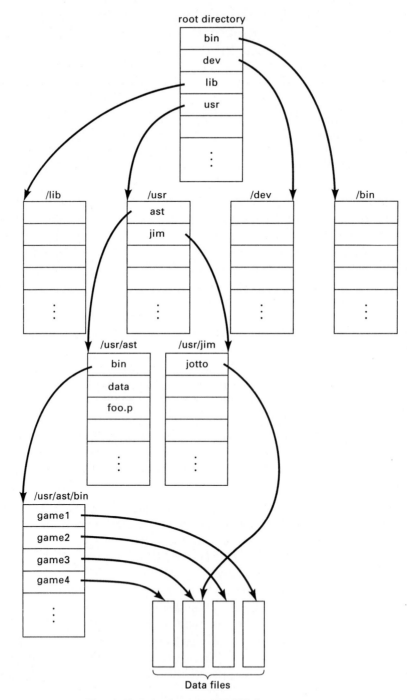

Fig. 6-40. Part of a typical UNIX directory system.

contains a list of all the directories traversed from the root to the file, with directory names separated by slashes. For example, the absolute path name of *game2* is */usr/ast/bin/game2*.

At every instant, each running program has a **working directory**. Path names may also be relative to the working directory, in which case they do not begin with a slash, to distinguish them from absolute path names. When */usr/ast* is the working directory, *game3* can be accessed using the path *bin/game3*. A user may create a **link** to someone else's file using the LINK system call. In the above example, */usr/ast/bin/game3* and */usr/jim/jotto* both access the same file. To prevent cycles in the directory system, links are not permitted to directories. The calls OPEN and CREAT take either absolute or relative path names as arguments.

Associated with every file (including directories, because they are also files) is a bit map telling who may access the file. The map contains three RWX fields, the first controlling the Read, Write, eXecute permissions for the owner, the second for others in the owner's group, and the third for everybody else. Thus RWX R-X --X means that the owner can read the file, write the file, and execute the file (obviously, it is an executable program, or execute would be off), whereas others in his group can read or execute it and strangers can only execute it. With these permissions, strangers can use the program but not steal (copy) it because they do not have read permission. The assignment of users to groups is done by the system administrator, usually called the **superuser**. The superuser also has the power to override the protection mechanism and read, write, or execute any file.

The major file and directory calls in the UNIX system are listed in Fig. 6-41. ACCESS determines if a potential read, write, or execute on a file is permitted. CHDIR switches to a new working directory, the name of which can be specified either absolutely or relative to the current one. CHMOD allows the owner of a file to change the RWX protection bits. STAT deposits information about a file in a buffer so the program can inspect it. The information comes from the i-node (see below). LINK makes a new directory entry with the new entry pointing to an existing file. For example, the entry */usr/jim/jotto* might have been created by the call

LINK("/usr/ast/bin/game3", "/usr/jim/jotto")

or an equivalent call using relative path names, depending on the working directory of the program making the call. UNLINK removes a file. If the file has only one link, the file is deleted. The call

UNLINK("/usr/ast/bin/game3")

makes *game3* only accessible via the path */usr/jim/jotto* henceforth. LINK and UNLINK can be used in this way to "move" files from one directory to another.

Let us now briefly examine how files and directories are implemented in UNIX. For a more complete treatment, see (Thompson, 1978). Associated with each file (and each directory, because a directory is also a file) is a 64-byte block of information called an **i-node**. The i-node tells who owns the file, what the permissions are,

File calls	Description
creat (name, mode)	Create a File; mode gives protection
open (name, mode)	Open a File; return file descriptor
close (fd)	Close a File
read (fd, buffer, count)	Read count bytes into buffer
write (fd, buffer, count)	Write count bytes from buffer
l seek (fd, offset, w)	Move the file pointer according to offset, w

Directory calls	
access (name, mode)	Check access permission; mode = read/write/execute
chdir (dirname)	Change working directory
chmod (name, mode)	Change protection mode
stat (name, mode)	Put file status in buffer
link (name1, name2)	Create directory entry name2 pointing to name1
unlink (name)	Remove a directory entry

Fig. 6-41. Some of the UNIX file and directory system calls.

where to find the data, and similar things. The i-nodes for the files on each disk are located in numerical sequence at the beginning of the disk. Thus given an i-node number, the UNIX system can locate the i-node by simply calculating its disk address.

A directory entry consists of 16 bytes: 14 bytes for the file (or subdirectory) name and a 2-byte i-node number. When a program executes

OPEN("foobar",0)

the system searches the working directory for the file name, "foobar," in order to locate the i-node number for that file. Having found the i-node number, it can then read in the i-node, which tells it all about the file.

When a longer path name is specified, the basic step outlined above is repeated several times. For example, to locate the i-node number for /usr/ast/data, the system first searches the root directory for an entry usr. Having found the i-node for usr, it can read the file (remember that a directory is a file, and as such, can be read the usual way). In this file it looks for an entry ast, thus locating the i-node number for the file /usr/ast. By reading /usr/ast, the system can then find the entry for data, and thus the i-node number for /usr/ast/data. Given the i-node number for the file, it can then find out everything about the file from the i-node.

The format, contents, and layout of an i-node varies somewhat from system to system (especially when networking is in use), but the following items are typically found in each i-node.

1. The file type, the 9 RWX protection bits, and a few other bits.

2. The number of links to the file (number of directory entries for it).

3. The owner's identity.

4. The owner's group.

5. The file length in bytes.

6. Thirteen disk addresses.

7. The time the file was last read.

8. The time the file was last written.

9. The time the i-node was last changed.

The file type distinguishes ordinary files, directories, and two kinds of special files, for block-structured and unstructured I/O devices, respectively. The number of links and the owner identification have already been discussed. The file length is a 32-bit integer giving the highest byte that has a value. It is perfectly legal to create a file, do an LSEEK to position 1,000,000 and write one byte, which yields a file of length 1,000,001. The file would *not*, however, require storage for all the "missing" bytes.

The first 10 disk addresses point to data blocks. With the usual block size of 512 bytes, files up to 5120 bytes can be handled this way. Address 11 points to a disk block, called an **indirect block**, which contains 128 disk addresses. Files up to $5120 + 128 \times 512 = 70656$ bytes are handled this way. For still larger files, address 12 points to a block containing the addresses of 128 indirect blocks, which takes care of files up to $70656 + 128 \times 128 \times 512 = 8,459,264$ bytes. If this **double indirect block** scheme is still too small, disk address 13 is used to point to a **triple indirect block** containing the addresses of 128 double indirect blocks. The largest file that can be handled is 1,082,201,088 bytes. Free disk blocks are kept on a linked list. When a new block is needed, the next block is plucked from the list. As a result, the blocks of each file are scattered randomly around the disk.

To make disk I/O more efficient, when a file is opened, its i-node is copied to a table in main memory and is kept there for handy reference as long as the file remains open. In addition, a pool of recently referenced disk blocks is maintained in memory. Because most files are read sequentially, it often happens that a file reference requires the same disk block as the previous reference. To strengthen this effect, the system also tries to read the *next* block in a file, before it is referenced, in order to speed up processing. All this optimization is hidden from the user; when a user issues a READ call, the program is suspended until the requested data are available in the buffer.

With this background information, we can now see how file I/O works. OPEN causes the system to search the directories for the specified path. If the search is successful, the i-node is read into an internal table. READs and WRITEs require the system to compute the block number from the current file position. The disk addresses of the first 10 blocks are always in main memory (in the i-node); higher-numbered blocks require one or more indirect blocks to be read first. LSEEK just changes the current position pointer without doing any I/O.

LINK and UNLINK are also simple to understand now. LINK looks up its first argument to find the i-node number. Then it creates a directory entry for the second argument, putting the i-node number of the first file in that entry. Finally, it increases the link count in the i-node by one. UNLINK removes a directory entry and decrements the link count in the i-node. If it is zero, the file is removed and all the blocks are put back on the free list.

OS/2 Virtual I/O

The most interesting aspect of OS/2 virtual I/O services is not what they do, but how they are invoked. In UNIX, MS-DOS, and all other operating systems except MULTICS and OS/2, virtual I/O and other operating system services are obtained by executing a TRAP instruction. This instruction causes the CPU to switch into kernel mode, and start running the operating system. The operating system first saves the registers and other state information, and then looks around to see what has been requested of it. Finally it carries out the call and returns from the trap back to user mode. This sequence of events is depicted in Fig. 6-42(a).

It is used because the operating system is not part of the user program's address space. The user's virtual address space, from 0 to some maximum is filled entirely with the user program and its data. No part of the operating system is located in it.

In OS/2, in contrast, the entire operating system *is* part of the user's address space. It occupies global segments pointed to by the GDT. User programs may directly call procedures located in operating system segments, without trapping to the kernel or going through any interrupt vectors, as illustrated in Fig. 6-42(b).

To prevent malicious user programs from calling operating system procedures that they have no business calling, all calls to operating system procedures use call gates. For example, to read from a file, a user might execute a CALL instruction with global selector 15 and some offset as the address of the called procedure. The 80286 hardware then finds entry 15 in the GDT, sees that it is a call gate, ignores the offset in the instruction, and extracts the segment number and starting address from global descriptor 15. It then calls this procedure, which in OS/2 will operate at level 1. The entire switch from the calling program to the operating system procedure that actually does the work takes one instruction.

And that is not all. Most system calls have parameters, such as the file

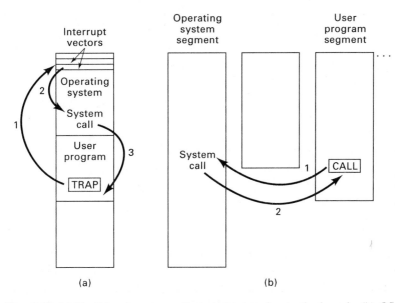

Fig. 6-42. (a) Traditional system call made by trapping to the kernel. (b) OS/2 system call made by calling an operating system procedure.

descriptor to be used and the address of the data buffer. With the TRAP mechanism, these parameters either have to be put in registers, which is not always convenient, or on the user stack, where the kernel cannot get to them easily. Some machines have special instructions to allow the kernel to read and write user space, but these can only be called from assembly code procedures. All in all, the overhead required to make a system call via the TRAP mechanism is typically several thousand instructions.

In OS/2, the operating system is called as an ordinary procedure, so it has direct access to the parameters within its own address space. Parameter access does not cause any extra overhead, and both the user program and the operating system can be written in a high level language, without any assembly code to handle the trap or parameter transfer.

The set of system calls provided by OS/2 is called the **API (Application Program Interface)**. These calls define the set of virtual I/O and other instructions provided by OS/2. When the Presentation Manager, OS/2's window system, is used, another 500 or so API calls are provided, for creating, deleting, and otherwise managing windows, menus, and icons. Not all of these procedures run at level 1. Some run at level 2 or 3.

The basic API calls are divided into four categories, listed in Fig. 6-43. The main calls, for memory management, file I/O, directory management, and process management are part of the DOS group (which has nothing to do with MS-DOS). The VIO group relates to writing information to the screen. The KBD group deals with input from the keyboard. The final calls, the MOU group, handle interaction with the mouse, including getting the mouse position and button status, as well as drawing mouse pointers on the screen.

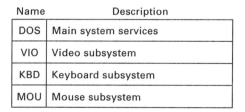

Name	Description
DOS	Main system services
VIO	Video subsystem
KBD	Keyboard subsystem
MOU	Mouse subsystem

Fig. 6-43. OS/2 API categories.

The OS/2 file system is structurally similar to that of UNIX, including the presence of a tree of directories. To use a file, it must first be opened, which results in a file descriptor (called a **file handle** in OS/2) being returned to the caller. Using the file handle, the file can be read and written, both sequentially and randomly, pretty much the same way as in UNIX.

OS/2 also supplies a number of directory management calls, including ones to create and delete directories, and change the working directory. It does not, however, have the LINK and UNLINK calls that UNIX has.

Another difference between UNIX and OS/2 is the issue of how multiple disks are dealt with. In UNIX, the file tree can span multiple disks. The directory tree on a diskette can be attached to the main tree on the hard disk by issuing a system call called MOUNT. Until it is unmounted, the diskette tree is simply part of the main tree, and can be referred to by giving its path from the root directory or elsewhere. In OS/2, directory trees cannot be mounted, and each call must explicitly or implicitly (via a default) tell which disk is being referenced. This nuisance is a leftover from MS-DOS.

Although the user interface to the OS/2 file system is similar to UNIX, its implementation is quite different. It is implemented the same way as the MS-DOS file system, in order to make it possible to write a diskette on one of them and read it on the other. The heart of the implementation is a table per disk called the **FAT (File Allocation Table)**. It is illustrated in Fig. 6-44.

Like UNIX, OS/2 maintains directories, whose purpose is to map symbolic (ASCII) names onto internal identifiers. UNIX directories map file names onto i-node numbers; OS/2 directories map file names onto the number of the first disk sector that the file occupies. Subsequent sectors can be found by following the chain in the FAT, which is kept in memory at all times. For example, the directory entry for file A maps the name A onto sector 5, because the first sector of data for this file is sector 5. The second sector, 8, can be found by looking in entry 5 in the FAT. Similarly, the next sector is 3 and finally 14.

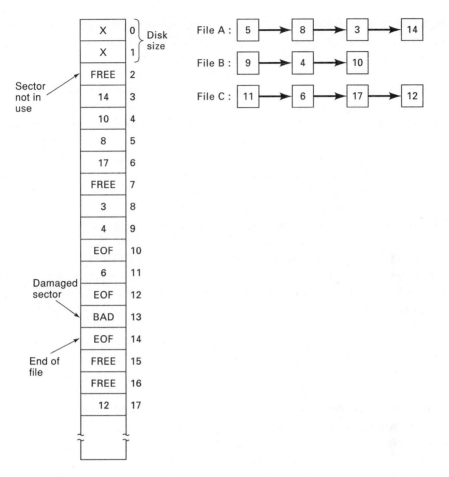

Fig. 6-44. The OS/2 FAT (File Allocation Table).

One of the lessons that was learned from MS-DOS is that much commercial software for it bypassed the system calls altogether and wrote directly to the hardware in order to gain speed. While the need for this sort of trickery is much less on the 80286 than on the 8088 (because the CPU is 10 times as fast), it was decided to provide general mechanisms for application programs to get fast access to the hardware when needed. One of the mechanisms chosen is the **I/O subsystem**. An I/O subsystem provides a lower-level (i.e., closer to the hardware) interface than the standard file I/O system calls. Standard I/O subsystems provided are the video subsystem, the keyboard subsystem, and the mouse subsystem. The VIO, KBD, and MOU API calls of Fig. 6-43 are in fact calls to these subsystems. New I/O subsystems can be added by users as they need them.

To give an example of the difference between the standard file I/O and an I/O subsystem, let us consider the screen. Like UNIX, OS/2 has special files that correspond to I/O devices. In fact, when a program is started up in either system, it is given file descriptors called STDIN and STDOUT for reading from the terminal and writing to the terminal, respectively. Using STDOUT it is possible to write a character stream to the screen.

However, many interactive programs need to do much fancier things, such as having a menu pop up when a certain key is struck. For these programs, the character stream model provided by the file system is inadequate. This is where the video subsystem comes in. It provides system calls that directly manipulate the screen image. Typical calls allow programs to read and write characters anywhere on the screen, scroll the screen in any direction, manipulate the shape and position of the cursor, and so on. Similarly, the KBD and MOU calls provide direct access to the keyboard input queue and the state of the mouse.

For programs that need even faster interaction, it is possible to declare that a certain segment is to be a shadow image of the video RAM. The program can then read and write this segment using ordinary machine instructions. When the image has been fully constructed, OS/2 can be asked to copy it byte-for-byte to the real video RAM, thus making it possible to update the entire screen in under 1 msec.

Although OS/2 took many ideas from MULTICS, there is one important area where it did not go as far as MULTICS. This subject is quite interesting, so it is worth at least mentioning here. The availability of a large segmented address space has important implications for file I/O. By making each file into a segment, a program can directly reference any part of any file without having to make system calls. For example, a program could directly add a constant to a word in a file using the ordinary ADD instruction, without first having to "read in" the relevant part of the file, do the addition, and then write it back

In a sense, I/O on files and virtual memory are competing mechanisms for transferring information from secondary memory to main memory. Virtual memory is by far the more convenient of the two from the programmer's point of view, because it does not require the programmer to issue any special instructions to access the data, or even be aware of whether the data are in main memory or not. Furthermore, it is wasteful to have two distinct mechanisms in the operating system, both of which perform the same function (transferring information from secondary memory to main memory).

The MULTICS system carries the correspondence between files and segments to its logical extreme: no distinction is made between files and segments. When a process is started up, all the files it initially needs (both procedures and data) are given segment numbers in order to make them directly addressable without the need for any I/O instructions. If it is discovered later that other files are needed, they are mapped into the virtual address space as new segments.

Because all the parts of all the files that a program needs can be accessed directly simply by using the proper virtual address, a typical MULTICS program never does any explicit I/O, even if it is processing large amounts of data.

Although OS/2 supports a segmented virtual memory, it uses conventional file

I/O instructions instead of mapping files into the address space. The reason for this decision is the small size (64K) of the 80286 segments. If OS/2 had been designed initially for the 80386, where the segments can be up to 4G, it might have been possible to eliminate all file I/O and just have files mapped onto segments.

6.4.3. Examples of Process Management

Both UNIX and OS/2 allow a job to be split up into multiple processes that can run in (pseudo)parallel and communicate with each other, in the style of the producer-consumer example discussed earlier. In this section we will discuss how processes are managed in both systems, and how they communicate.

UNIX Process Management

At any time, a UNIX process can create a subprocess that is an exact replica of itself by executing the FORK system call. The original process is called the **parent** and the new one is called the **child**. Right after the FORK, the two processes are identical, and even share the same file descriptors. Thereafter, each one goes its own way and does whatever it wants to, independent of the other one.

In many cases, the child process juggles the file descriptors in certain ways, and then executes the EXEC system call, which replaces its program and data with the program and data found in an executable file specified as parameter to the EXEC call. For example, when a user types a command *xyz* at a terminal, the command interpreter, called the **shell**, executes FORK to create a child process. This child process then executes EXEC to run the *xyz* program.

The two processes run in parallel (with or without EXEC), unless the parent wishes to wait for the child to terminate before continuing. If the parent wishes to wait, it executes the WAIT system call, which causes it to be suspended until the child finishes by executing EXIT. After the child finishes, the parent continues.

Processes can execute FORK as often as they want, giving rise to a tree of processes. In Fig. 6-45, for example, process *A* has executed FORK twice, creating two children, *B* and *C*. Then *B* also executed FORK twice, and *C* executed it once, giving the final tree of six processes.

Processes in UNIX communicate with each other via a structure called a **pipe**. A pipe is a kind of buffer into which one process can write a stream of data and another can take it out. Bytes are always retrieved from a pipe in the order they were written. Random access is not possible.

OS/2 Process Management

OS/2 has more sophisticated parallel processing than UNIX. The FORK and EXEC calls are not present as separate calls, but a combined call is available that creates a child process and runs a specified program in it. Process trees, such as

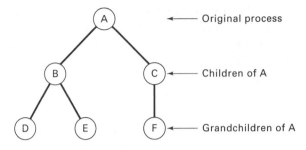

Fig. 6-45. A process tree in UNIX.

that of Fig. 6-45 also exist, as do pipes and **queues**, which are an alternative form of pipe, that handle message streams rather than byte streams. The difference between a pipe and a queue is that a queue remembers message boundaries and only returns one message on each read, whereas a pipe just contains a byte stream without regard to how many writes it took to get the bytes into the pipe.

More important, however, is the fact that a UNIX process has a single thread of control. In other words, a UNIX process is strictly sequential, with one program counter, one stack and one set of registers. OS/2, in contrast, allows multiple **threads** in a process, each with its own program counter, stack, and registers, but sharing the same address space. Threads in a process can communicate easily because they can read and write the same memory. New threads can be created dynamically, and they can be assigned priorities so that more critical threads get better service.

Semaphores are available to allow two threads in the same process or in different processes to synchronize. Unlike the examples in the text, in which a process doing a DOWN in principle will wait forever until another process does an UP on the semaphore, in OS/2 a maximum wait time can be specified.

Another important parallel processing feature present in OS/2 is the **session**. Conceptually, each session has its own virtual terminal, with keyboard, mouse and screen. A session may contain multiple processes (each with multiple threads), but all the processes and threads in a session share the same keyboard input queue, mouse input queue, and screen. Sessions are a way to simulate a multiwindow environment on a dumb terminal. A session can create a child session, just as a process can create a child process. The relationship between sessions, processes, and threads is shown in Fig. 6-46.

For example, consider a situation in which a user starts up a compilation in one session in the background, a file transfer in a second session, also in the background, and an editor in a third session in the foreground. Since the editor is in the foreground, all typed input goes to it, and all output that it displays appears on the screen. The output from the background sessions is invisible.

Nevertheless, the output produced by background sessions is not lost. By

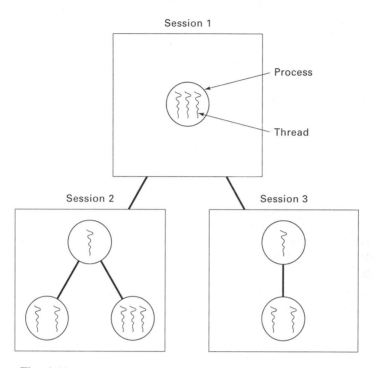

Fig. 6-46. Three sessions, six processes, and twelve threads in OS/2.

hitting the **hot key** (by depressing the ALT and ESC keys together), OS/2 puts the foreground session into the background and brings the first background session into the foreground, displaying its virtual terminal on the screen and sending keyboard and mouse input to it. By repeatedly hitting the hot key, the user can cycle through all the sessions.

This facility can also be used to make it easy to get at simple utility programs, like pocket calculators, appointment calendars, and notepads. The user just keeps hitting the hot key until the right utility appears on the screen.

6.4.4. Comparison of UNIX and OS/2

UNIX and OS/2 are alike in many ways, but they differ in other ways. Both have files consisting of sequences of 8-bit bytes, with system calls to create, destroy, read and write files. A hierarchical tree of directories is present in both, with similar properties. They both allow multiple processes that form a tree and have pipes for interprocess communication. Both were directly inspired by MULTICS.

The differences are perhaps more interesting than the similarities. UNIX supports multiple users; OS/2 only supports one. UNIX is portable; OS/2 is tied very tightly to the 80286 architecture. UNIX has a linear model of memory; OS/2 has a segmented model. UNIX supports virtual memory via paging; OS/2 supports it with segmentation. UNIX allows multiple links to a file and allows a collection of disks to be mounted into a single tree; OS/2 allows neither. UNIX processes make system calls by trapping to the kernel; OS/2 processes make system calls by making procedure calls through call gates. UNIX has only a single level of access—the file system; OS/2 has this and also I/O subsystems. UNIX has neither threads nor sessions; OS/2 has both.

One last difference is in a sense more important than all the others combined. Because the UNIX source code is widely available, many companies and organizations are working on their own versions of UNIX, which may cause some confusion in the marketplace, but may also lead to rapid adaptation as the world changes. The OS/2 source code is a closely guarded secret held by IBM and Microsoft, which leads to a more stable system, but one which may not be able to respond to user demands as quickly as UNIX.

As a simple example, when RISC computers came out, UNIX was the unanimous choice of all RISC vendors. Nobody chose OS/2. If RISC machines come to dominate the market in the next few years, UNIX will become the dominant operating system and OS/2 will vanish without a trace. Time will tell.

6.5. SUMMARY

The operating system can be regarded as an interpreter for certain architectural features not found at level 2. Chief among these are virtual memory, virtual I/O instructions, and facilities for parallel processing.

Virtual memory is an architectural feature whose purpose is to allow programs to use more address space than the machine has physical memory, or to provide a consistent and flexible memory protection mechanism. It can be implemented as pure paging, pure segmentation, or a combination of the two. Page replacement algorithms and demand paging were explained. Memory management on the 80386 and 68030 was described in some detail.

The most important I/O abstraction present at level 3 is the file. It consists of a sequence of logical records that can be read and written without knowledge of the how disks, tapes, and other secondary memory and I/O devices work. Files can be accessed sequentially, randomly by record number, or randomly by key. Directories can be used to group files together. Various implementation issues were discussed.

Parallel processing is often present at level 3 and is implemented by simulating multiple processors by time sharing a single CPU. Uncontrolled interaction between processes can lead to race conditions. To solve this problem, synchronization primitives are introduced, of which semaphores are a simple example. Using semaphores producer-consumer problems can be solved in a simply and elegantly.

As examples of two operating systems, UNIX and OS/2 were used. The memory architecture, file systems, I/O, and process structure of the two systems were briefly explained. The implementation of the file systems were briefly touched upon.

PROBLEMS

1. Why does an operating system only interpret some of the level 3 instructions, whereas a microprogram interprets all the level 2 instructions?

2. A virtual memory has a page size of 1024 words, eight virtual pages and four physical page frames. The page table is as follows:

Virtual Page	Page Frame
0	3
1	1
2	not in main memory
3	not in main memory
4	2
5	not in main memory
6	0
7	not in main memory

a. Make a list of all virtual addresses that will cause page faults.

b. What are the physical addresses for 0, 3728, 1023, 1024, 1025, 7800, and 4096?

3. A computer has 16 pages of virtual address space but only 4 page frames. Initially, the memory is empty. A program references the virtual pages in the order:

   0, 7, 2, 7, 5, 8, 9, 2, 4

a. Which references cause a page fault with LRU?

b. Which references cause a page fault with FIFO?

4. In Sec. 6.1.4 an algorithm was presented for implementing a FIFO page replacement strategy. Devise a more efficient one. *Hint:* It is possible to update the counter in the newly loaded page, leaving all the others alone.

5. In the paged systems discussed in the text, the page fault handler was part of the level 2 machine and thus was not present in any level 3 program's address space. In reality, the page fault handler also occupies pages, and might, under some circumstances (e.g., FIFO page replacement policy), itself be removed. What would happen if the page fault handler was not present when a page fault occurred? How could this be prevented?

6. A segmented memory has paged segments. Each virtual address has a 2-bit segment number, a 2-bit page number, and an 11-bit offset within the page. The main memory contains 32768 words. Each segment is either read only, read/execute, read/write, or read/write/execute. The page tables and protection are as follows.

Segment 0		Segment 1		Segment 2	Segment 3	
Read only		Read / execute		Read / write / execute	Read / write	
Virtual page	Page frame	Virtual page	Page frame		Virtual page	Page frame
0	9	0	On disk	Page table not in main Memory	0	14
1	3	1	0		1	1
2	On disk	2	15		2	6
3	12	3	8		3	On disk

For each of the following accesses to virtual memory, tell what physical address is computed. If a fault occurs, tell which kind.

Access	Segment	Page	Offset within page
1. fetch data	0	1	1
2. fetch data	1	1	10
3. fetch data	3	3	2047
4. store data	0	1	4
5. store data	3	1	2
6. store data	3	0	14
7. jump to it	1	3	100
8. fetch data	0	2	50
9. fetch data	2	0	5
10. jump to it	3	0	60

7. A computer system uses segmentation and paging. The mean segment size is s words and the page size is p words. When a segment is in memory, some words are wasted in the last page. In addition, s/p words are "wasted" because they comprise the page table (one word per entry). The smaller the page size, the less waste in the last page of the segment, but the larger the page table. What page size minimizes the total waste?

8. Some computers allow I/O directly to user space. For example, a program could start up a disk transfer to a buffer inside a user process. Does this cause any problems if compaction is used to implement the virtual memory? Discuss.

9. Suppose you were a systems programmer working for a company making a 32-bit computer. It had been decided to implement a MULTICS-like segmented virtual memory and it was up to you to determine how many of the 32 address bits were to be used for the segment number and how many for the offset within the segment. What would you recommend and why?

10. When a segment register is loaded on the 80286 or 80386, the corresponding descriptor is fetched and loaded into an invisible part of the segment register. Why do you

think the 80286 and 80386 designers decided to do this? Does the 68030 have anything analogous?

11. A program on the 80386 references local segment 10 with offset 8000. The BASE field of LDT segment 10 contains 10000. Which page directory entry does the 80386 use? What is the page number? What is the offset?

12. If the 68030 memory management registers are set up to skip s bits of each virtual address, and they use a, b, c, and d bits for each of the four page-table levels, how many words of memory are occupied with page tables if each entry takes one word?

13. Discuss some possible algorithms for removing segments in an unpaged, segmented memory such as the 80286's.

14. Compare fragmentation to checkerboarding. What can be done to alleviate each?

15. Supermarkets are constantly faced with a problem similar to page replacement in virtual memory systems. They have a fixed amount of shelf space to display an ever increasing number of products. If an important new product comes along, say, 100% efficient dog food, some existing product must be dropped from the inventory to make room for it. The obvious replacement algorithms are LRU and FIFO. Which of these would you prefer?

16. Why do many file systems require that a file be explicitly opened with an OPEN instruction before being read?

17. Compare the bit map and hole list methods for keeping track of free space on a disk with 800 cylinders, each one having 5 tracks of 32 sectors. How many holes would it take before the hole list would be larger than the bit map? Assume that the allocation unit is the sector and that a hole requires a 32-bit table entry.

18. To be able to make some predictions of disk performance, it is useful to have a model of storage allocation. Suppose that the disk is viewed as a linear address space of $N \gg 1$ sectors, consisting of a run of data blocks, then a hole, then another run of data blocks, and so on. If empirical measurements show that the probability distributions for data and hole lengths are the same, with the chance of either being i sectors as 2^{-i}, what is the expected number of holes on the disk?

19. On a certain computer, a level 3 program can create as many files as it needs, and all files may grow dynamically during execution without giving the operating system any advance information about their ultimate size. Do you think that files are stored in consecutive sectors? Explain.

20. Consider the following method by which an operating system might implement semaphore instructions. Whenever the CPU was about to do an UP or DOWN on a semaphore (an integer variable in memory), it first sets the CPU priority or mask bits in such a way as to disable all interrupts. Then it fetches the semaphore, modifies it, and branches accordingly. Finally, it enables interrupts again. Does this method work if:

a. There is a single CPU that switches between processes every 100 msec?
b. Two CPUs share a common memory in which the semaphore is located?

21. The Nevercrash Operating System Company has been receiving complaints from some of its customers about its latest release, which includes semaphore operations. They feel it is immoral for processes to block (they call it "sleeping on the job"). Since it is company policy to give the customers what they want, it has been proposed to add a third operation, PEEK, to supplement UP and DOWN. PEEK simply examines the semaphore without changing it or blocking the process. In this way, programs that feel it is immoral to block can first inspect the semaphore to see if it is safe to do a DOWN. Will this idea work if three or more processes use the semaphore? If two processes use the semaphore?

22. Make a table showing which of the processes P1, P2, and P3 are running and which are blocked as a function of time from 0 to 1000 msec. All three processes perform UP and DOWN instructions on the same semaphore. When two processes are blocked and an UP is done, the process with the lower number is restarted, that is, P1 gets preference over P2 and P3, and so on. Initially, all three are running and the semaphore is 1.

    At $t = 100$ P1 does a DOWN
    At $t = 200$ P1 does a DOWN
    At $t = 300$ P2 does an UP
    At $t = 400$ P3 does a DOWN
    At $t = 500$ P1 does a DOWN
    At $t = 600$ P2 does an UP
    At $t = 700$ P2 does a DOWN
    At $t = 800$ P1 does an UP
    At $t = 900$ P1 does an UP

23. In an airline reservation system, it is necessary to ensure that while one process is busy using a file, no other process can also use it. Otherwise, two different processes, working for two different ticket agents, might each inadvertently sell the last seat on some flight. Devise a synchronization method using semaphores that makes sure that only one process at a time accesses each file (assuming that the processes obey the rules).

24. To make it possible to implement semaphores on a computer with multiple CPUs that share a common memory, computer architects often provide a Test and Set Lock instruction. TSL X tests the location X. If the contents are zero, they are set to 1 in a single, indivisible memory cycle, and the next instruction is skipped. If it is nonzero, the TSL acts like a no-op. Using TSL it is possible to write procedures LOCK and UNLOCK with the following properties. LOCK(X) checks to see if X is locked. If not, it locks X and returns control. If X is already locked, it just waits until it becomes unlocked, then it locks X and returns control. UNLOCK releases an existing lock. If all processes lock the semaphore table before using it, only one process at a time can fiddle with the variables and pointers, thus preventing races. Write LOCK and UNLOCK in assembly language. (Make any reasonable assumptions you need.)

25. Show the values of *in* and *out* for a circular buffer of length 65 words after each of the following operations. Both start at 0.

    a. 22 words are put in.
    b. 9 words are removed.
    c. 40 words are put in.
    d. 17 words are removed.
    e. 12 words are put in.
    f. 45 words are removed.
    g. 8 words are put in.
    h. 11 words are removed.

26. Why did IBM go to such lengths to carefully define the API, print manuals about it, and generally treat it as if it were very important.

27. Although disk addresses in UNIX are 3-byte numbers, only 128 of them are put in the indirect blocks. If all the indirect blocks were changed to hold $512 / 3 = 170$ disk addresses instead of 128, what would the maximum file size become?

28. Suppose that the UNIX system call

    UNLINK("/usr/ast/bin/game3")

were executed in the context of Fig. 6-40. Describe carefully what changes are made in the directory system.

29. Imagine that you had to implement the UNIX system on a microcomputer where main memory was in short supply. After a considerable amount of shoehorning, it still did not quite fit, so you picked a system call at random to sacrifice for the general good. PIPE lost. Is it still possible to implement I/O redirection somehow? What about pipelines? Discuss the problems and possible solutions.

30. The Committee for Fairness to File Descriptors is organizing a protest against the UNIX system because whenever the latter returns a file descriptor, it always returns the lowest number not currently in use. Consequently, higher-numbered file descriptors are hardly ever used. Their plan is to return the lowest number not yet used by the program rather than the lowest number currently not in use. They claim that it is trivial to implement, will not affect existing programs, and is fairer. What do you think?

31. A personal computer has a 20M hard disk, allocated in 512-byte sectors. How big does the i-node table for UNIX have to be? How big does the FAT for OS/2 have to be? What conclusions can you draw from these numbers?

32. Write a procedure to simulate the 80386 memory management, including the descriptors and page tables. The procedure should take as parameters a selector and an offset within that segment, and should return the physical address to use. The LDT, GDT, and page tables should be available as global variables.

33. Write a procedure to simulate the 68030 paging. The procedure should take a 32-bit virtual address as input, and produce a 32-bit physical address as output, using the page tables found in memory.

34. Write a set of procedures to manage files using the OS/2 FAT and a single directory. One procedure, *create*, should create a new file and make a directory entry for it, returning an index into the directory to identify it. Another procedure, *append*, should take an index and a size as parameters, and grow the file by the specified number of bytes. A third procedure, *delete*, should delete the file specified by the index parameter and free its disk space.

7

THE ASSEMBLY LANGUAGE LEVEL

In Chapters 4, 5, and 6 we discussed three different levels present on most contemporary computers. This chapter is concerned primarily with another level that is also present on nearly all modern computers: the assembly language level. The assembly language level differs in a significant respect from the microprogramming, conventional machine, and operating system machine levels—it is implemented by translation rather than by interpretation.

Programs that convert a user's program written in some language to another language are called **translators**. The language in which the original program is written is called the **source language** and the language to which it is converted is called the **target language**. Both the source language and the target language define levels. If a processor that can directly execute programs written in the source language is available, there is no need to translate the source program into the target language.

Translation is used when a processor (either hardware or an interpreter) is available for the target language but not for the source language. If the translation has been performed correctly, running the translated program will give precisely the same results as the execution of the source program would have given had a processor for it been available. Consequently, it is possible to implement a new level for which there is no processor by first translating programs written for that level to a target level and then executing the resulting target-level programs.

It is important to note the difference between translation, on the one hand, and interpretation, on the other. In translation, the original program in the source language is not directly executed. Instead, it is converted to an equivalent program called an **object program** or **object module** whose execution is carried out only after the translation has been completed. In translation, there are two distinct steps:

1. Generation of an equivalent program in the target language.

2. Execution of the newly generated program.

These two steps do not occur simultaneously. The second step does not begin until the first has been completed. In interpretation, there is only one step: executing the original source program. No equivalent program need be generated first. Interpretation has the advantage of smaller program size and more flexibility, but translation has the advantage of faster execution.

While the object program is being executed, only three levels are in evidence: the microprogramming level, the conventional machine level, and the operating system machine level. Consequently, three programs—the user's object program, the operating system, and the microprogram—can be found in the computer's memory at run time. All traces of the original source program have vanished. Thus the number of levels present at execution time may differ from the number of levels present before translation. It should be noted, however, that although we define a level by the instructions and linguistic constructs available to its programmers (and not by the implementation method), other authors sometimes make a greater distinction between levels implemented by execution-time interpreters and levels implemented by translation.

7.1. INTRODUCTION TO ASSEMBLY LANGUAGE

Translators can be roughly divided into two groups, depending on the relation between the source language and the target language. When the source language is essentially a symbolic representation for a numerical machine language, the translator is called an **assembler** and the source language is called an **assembly language**. When the source language is a high-level language such as C or Pascal and the target language is either a numerical machine language or a symbolic representation for one, the translator is called a **compiler**.

7.1.1. What Is an Assembly Language?

A pure assembly language is a language in which each statement produces exactly one machine instruction. In other words, there is a one-to-one correspondence between machine instructions and statements in the assembly program. If each line in the assembly program contains one assembly statement and each machine word contains one machine instruction, then an *n*-line assembly program will produce an *n*-word machine language program.

The reason that people use assembly language, as opposed to programming in machine language (octal or hex), is that it is much easier to program in assembly language. The use of symbolic names and symbolic addresses instead of binary or octal ones makes an enormous difference. Most people can remember that the abbreviations for add, subtract, multiply, and divide are ADD, SUB, MUL, and DIV, but few can remember that the machine instructions (for the PDP-11) are 24576, 57344, 28672, and 29184. The assembly language programmer need only remember the symbolic names ADD, SUB, MUL, DIV, because the assembler translates them to the machine instructions, but the machine language programmer must remember, or constantly look up, the numerical values.

The same remarks apply to addresses. The assembly language programmer can give symbolic names to memory locations and have the assembler worry about supplying the correct numerical values. The machine language programmer must always work with the numerical values of the addresses. As a consequence, no one programs in machine language today, although people did so years ago, before assemblers had been invented.

Assembly languages have another property, besides the one-to-one mapping of assembly language statements onto machine instructions, that distinguishes them from high-level languages. The assembly programmer has access to all the features and instructions available on the target machine. The high-level language programmer does not. For example, if the target machine has an overflow bit, an assembly language program can test it, but a Pascal program cannot directly test it. If there are switches on the operator console, an assembly language program can read their status. Such a program can execute every instruction in the instruction set of the target machine, but the high-level language program cannot. In short, everything that can be done in machine language can be done in assembly language, but many instructions, registers, and similar features are not available for the high-level language programmer to use. Languages for system programming are often a cross between these types, with the syntax of a high-level language but the access to the machine of an assembly language.

One final difference that is worth making explicit is that an assembly language program can only run on one family of machines, whereas a program written in a high-level language can potentially run on many machines. For many applications, this ability to move software from one machine to another is of great practical importance.

7.1.2. Format of an Assembly Language Statement

Although the structure of an assembly language statement closely mirrors the structure of the machine instruction that it represents, assembly languages for different machines and different levels have sufficient resemblance to one another to allow a discussion of assembly language in general. Figure 7-1 shows fragments of assembly language programs for the 80386 and 68030, both of which perform the computation $N = I + J + K$. In both examples, the statements above the dots perform the calculation. The statements below the dots are commands to the assembler to reserve memory for the variables I, J, K, and N and are not symbolic representations of machine instructions. Statements that are commands to the assembler are called **pseudoinstructions**.

Label field	Operation field	Operands field	Comments field
FORMUL:	MOV	EAX, I	; LOAD I INTO EAX
	ADD	EAX, J	; ADD J TO EAX
	ADD	EAX, K	; ADD K TO EAX
	MOV	N, EAX	; STORE I + J + K IN N
	.		
	.		
I:	DW	2	; RESERVE 4 BYTES INITIALIZED TO 2
J:	DW	3	; RESERVE 4 BYTES INITIALIZED TO 3
K:	DW	4	; RESERVE 4 BYTES INITIALIZED TO 4
N:	DW	0	; RESERVE 4 BYTES INITIALIZED TO 0

(a)

Label field	Operation field	Operands field	Comments field
FORMUL:	MOVE. L	I, D 0	; LOAD I INTO D 0
	ADD. L	J, D 0	; ADD J TO D 0
	ADD. L	K, D 0	; ADD K TO D 0
	MOVE. L	D 0, N	; STORE I + J + K IN N
	.		
	.		
	DC. L	2	; RESERVE 4 BYTES INITIALIZED TO 2
	DC. L	3	; RESERVE 4 BYTES INITIALIZED TO 3
	DC. L	4	; RESERVE 4 BYTES INITIALIZED TO 4
	DC. L	0	; RESERVE 4 BYTES INITIALIZED TO 0

(b)

Fig. 7-1. Computation of the formula $N = I + J + K$. (a) 80386. (b) 68030.

Assembly language statements have four parts: label field, operation field, operands field, and comments field. Labels, which are used to provide symbolic names for memory addresses, are needed on executable statements so that the statements can be jumped to. They are also needed on memory allocation pseudoinstructions (e.g., DD and DC) to permit the data stored there to be accessible by symbolic name. If a statement is labeled, the label (usually) begins in column 1.

Figure 7-1(a) shows five labels: *FORMUL*, *I*, *J*, *K*, and *N*. Figure 7-1(b) shows the same five labels. Notice that the Intel assembly language requires a colon after each label, whereas the Motorola assembly language does not. There is nothing fundamental about this difference. The designers of the two assemblers simply had different taste. If they had each worked for the other company, the Intel assembly language would have used a colon and the Motorola one would not have. The designer of an assembler for either machine is perfectly free to choose any convention in this area that he wants to. Nothing in the underlying architecture suggests one choice or the other.

It is an unfortunate characteristic of some assemblers that labels are restricted to six or eight characters. In contrast, most high-level languages allow the use of arbitrarily long names. Long, well-chosen names make programs much more readable and understandable by other people (see Fig. 2-2 for an example of this point).

The operation field contains either a symbolic abbreviation for the opcode—if the statement is a symbolic representation for a machine instruction—or a pseudoinstruction if the statement is a command to the assembler. The choice of an appropriate name is just a matter of taste, and different assembly language designers often make different choices. The Intel designers liked MOV; the Motorola ones preferred MOVE.

Both the 80386 and 68030 allow byte, word, and long operands. How does the assembler know which length to use? Again, the two designers chose different solutions. Intel gave the registers different names, so EAX is used to move 32-bit items, AX is used to move 16-bit items, and AL or AH is used to move 8-bit items. Motorola, in contrast decided to add a suffix .L for long, .W for word, or .B for byte to each opcode. Both ways are valid, but they point out the arbitrary nature of language design.

The two assemblers also differ in the name of the pseudoinstruction used to reserve space for data. Intel chose DW (Define Word); Motorola liked DC (Define Constant). Once again, it is simply a matter of taste.

The operands field of an assembly language statement is used to specify the addresses and registers used as operands by the machine instruction. The operand field of an integer addition instruction tells what is to be added to what. The operands field of a jump instruction tells where to jump to. The operands field of a pseudoinstruction depends on the pseudoinstruction, for example, how much memory space to reserve.

The comments field provides a place for programmers to put helpful explanations of how the program works for the benefit of other programmers who may subsequently use or modify the program. An assembly language program without such documentation is nearly incomprehensible to all programmers, frequently including the author as well. The comments field is solely for human consumption; it has no effect on the assembly process or on the generated program.

7.1.3. Comparison of Assembly Language and High-Level Languages

A popular myth is that programs that will be used a great deal should, for efficiency, be written entirely in assembly language. Although true at one time, it is no longer. It is instructive to compare the MULTICS system with the IBM time-sharing system for the 360/67, TSS/67. Both operating systems were started around the same time and are roughly the same size (huge). MULTICS was written, for the most part (95%), in a high-level language, PL/I, whereas TSS/67 was written entirely in assembly language.

A large operating system such as MULTICS is a stringent test for a high-level language. Because an operating system must control all the I/O devices, deal with critical timing situations, handle large data bases, and do many other tasks, good performance is crucial. If high-level languages can pass this critical test, there are few large applications indeed where one could demonstrate the advantages to be gained by using assembly language. (Programming the microprocessor inside a washing machine is a different story, however, due to the large number sold.)

The results of these two projects can be summed up nicely by pointing out that each took about the same length of time to get running. However, MULTICS was written by 50 people at an estimated cost of 10 million dollars whereas TSS/67 needed 300 people at an estimated cost of 50 million dollars (Graham, 1970). Furthermore, MULTICS eventually worked. The conclusion that the use of PL/I saved the MULTICS project millions of dollars is inescapable.

Studies have shown that the number of lines of debugged code a programmer can produce per month on a project over a period of several years is approximately 100 to 200 lines, independent of the programming language used (Corbató, 1969). Only on small programs can higher productivity be expected. Since one PL/I statement is equivalent to 5 or 10 assembly language statements, the productivity of a PL/I programmer will be 5 or 10 times that of an assembly language programmer. The same holds for any other high-level language.

Another strong argument against programming in assembly language is that understanding someone else's assembly language program is nearly impossible. A complete listing of MULTICS in PL/I is about 3000 pages, hardly something one digests in an evening. Nevertheless, absorbing that amount is trivial compared to reading 30,000 pages of assembly code. Although no one ever tries to read the entire MULTICS listing, people have tried to understand particular procedures, about four pages of PL/I on the average. Personnel turnover on large projects often averages 15% per year; consequently, after 5 years few of the original programmers are still around. If the new programmers cannot understand their predecessors' programs, the project will be in big trouble.

7.1.4. Program Tuning

Studies have shown that, in most programs, a small percentage of the total code is responsible for a large percentage of the execution time (Darden and Heller, 1970). It is common to have 1% of the program be responsible for 50% of the execution time and 10% of the program be responsible for 90% of the execution time. A common situation is in a compiler, where searching the symbol table can eat up more time than the rest of the compiler combined.

Assume, for example, that it requires 10 man-years to write some big compiler in a high-level language and that the resulting compiler requires 100 sec to compile a certain test program. Writing the whole compiler in assembly language would require about 50 to 100 man-years, due to the lower productivity of assembler language programmers; the final program would, however, perform the test in about 33 sec, because a clever programmer can outdo a clever compiler by a factor of 3. This situation is illustrated in Fig. 7-2.

	Man-years needed to produce program	Program execution time in seconds
Assembly language	50	33
Problem-oriented language	10	100
Mixed approach before tuning		
Critical 10%	1	90
Other 90%	9	10
Total	10	100
Mixed approach after tuning		
Critical 10%	6	30
Other 90%	9	10
Total	15	40

Fig. 7-2. Comparison of assembly language and high-level language programming, with and without tuning.

Based on the above observation that only a tiny fraction of the code is responsible for most of the execution time, another approach is possible. The program is first written in a high-level language. Then a series of measurements is performed to determine which parts of the program account for most of the execution time. Such measurements would normally include using the system clock to compute the amount of time spent in each procedure, keeping track of the number of times each loop is executed, and similar steps.

As an example, let us assume that 10% of the total program accounts for 90% of the execution time. This means that for a 100-sec job, 90 sec is spent in this critical 10% and 10 sec is spent in the remaining 90% of the program. The critical 10% can now be improved by rewriting it in assembly language. This process is called **tuning** and is illustrated in Fig. 7-2. Here an additional 5 man-years are needed to rewrite the critical procedures but their execution time is reduced from 90 sec to 30 sec.

It is instructive to compare the mixed high-level language/assembly language approach with the pure assembly language version (see Fig. 7-2). The latter is about 20% faster but at more than triple the price. Furthermore, the advantage of the mixed approach is really more than indicated, because recoding an already debugged high-level language procedure in assembly code is, in fact, much easier than writing the same assembly code procedure from scratch. In other words, the estimate of 5 man-years to rewrite the critical procedures is exceedingly conservative. If this recoding actually took only 1 man-year, the cost ratio between the mixed approach and the pure assembly language approach would be more than 4 to 1 in favor of the mixed approach.

A programmer who uses a high-level language is not immersed in moving bits around, and sometimes obtains insights into the problem that allow *real* improvements in performance. This situation occurs much less often with assembly language programmers, who are usually trying to juggle instructions to save a few microseconds. Graham (1970) reports a PL/I procedure in MULTICS that was rewritten in 3 months with the new version 26 times smaller and 50 times faster than the original, as well as another that became 20 times smaller and 40 times faster with 2 months of work.

Corbató (1969) describes a PL/I drum management procedure that was reduced from 50,000 to 10,000 words of compiled code in less than a month and an I/O controller that shrank from 65,000 to 30,000 words of compiled code, with an improvement in speed of a factor of 8 in 4 months. The point here is that because high-level language programmers have a more global view of what they are doing, they are far more likely to obtain insights leading to totally different and vastly better algorithms.

After this introduction, you may be wondering: "Why bother studying assembly language programming at all, when it is so awful?" At least three good reasons exist. First, because the success or failure of a large project may depend on being able to squeeze a factor of 5 or 10 improvement in performance out of some critical procedure, it is important to be able to write good assembly language code when it is really necessary. Second, assembly code is sometimes the only alternative due to lack of memory (pocket calculators contain a CPU, but few have a megabyte of memory, and fewer yet have a hard disk). Third, a compiler must either produce output used by an assembler or perform the assembly process itself. Thus understanding assembly language is essential to understanding how compilers work.

7.2. THE ASSEMBLY PROCESS

In the following sections we will briefly describe how an assembler works. Although each machine has a different assembly language, the assembly process is sufficiently similar on different machines that it is possible to describe it in general terms.

7.2.1. Two-Pass Assemblers

Because an assembly language program consists of a series of one-line statements, it might seem natural to have an assembler that read one statement, translated it to machine language, and then output the generated machine language onto a file, along with the corresponding piece of the listing, if any, onto another file. This process would then be repeated until the whole program had been translated. Unfortunately, this method does not work.

Consider the situation where the first statement is a jump to L. The assembler cannot assemble this statement until it knows the address of statement L. Statement L may be near the end of the program, making it impossible for the assembler to find the address without first reading almost the entire program. This difficulty is called the **forward reference problem**, because a symbol, L, has been used before it has been defined; that is, a reference has been made to a symbol whose definition will only occur later.

Forward references can be handled in two ways. First, the assembler may in fact read the source program two times. Each reading of the source program is called a **pass**; any translator which reads the input program two times is called a **two-pass translator**. On pass one of a two-pass assembler, the definitions of symbols, including statement labels, are collected and stored in a table. By the time the second pass begins, the values of all symbols are known; thus no forward reference remains and each statement can be read, assembled, and output. Although this method requires an extra pass over the input, it is conceptually straightforward.

The second method consists of trying to do the assembly in one pass anyway. Whenever a statement is encountered that cannot be assembled because it contains a forward reference, no output is generated; instead, an entry is made in a table indicating that the statement with the forward reference has not yet been assembled. At the end of the assembly, all symbols will have been defined, so all statements in the not-yet-assembled table can be assembled.

The latter method generates output in a different order than the two-pass method. If the assembly is followed by loading, the loader can put the pieces of output back in the right order. Hence this objection is not a serious one. The one-pass assembler does have the problem that if many statements contain forward references, the table containing the statements not yet assembled may become too large to fit in memory. It also suffers from considerable greater complexity, and has difficulty printing a listing including the actual object code produced. For these reasons, most assemblers are two pass.

7.2.2. Pass One

The principal function of pass one is to build up a table called the **symbol table**, containing the values of all symbols. A symbol is either a label or a value that is assigned a symbolic name by means of an explicit pseudoinstruction such as

BUFSIZE EQU 100

In assigning a value to a symbol in the label field of an instruction, the assembler must know what address that instruction will have during execution of the program. To keep track of the execution-time address of the instruction being assembled, the assembler maintains a variable during assembly, known as the **instruction**

location counter or ILC. This variable is set to 0 at the beginning of pass one and incremented by the instruction length for each instruction processed, as shown in Fig. 7-3. This example is for the 80386. We will not give Motorola examples henceforth since the difference between the two assembly languages is not very important, and one example should be enough.

Label field	Operation field	Operands field	Comments field	Instruction length	ILC before statement
⋮					
SUZANNE:	MOV	EAX,I	EAX = I	5	100
	MOV	EBX,J	EBX = J	6	105
MARIA:	MOV	ECX,K	ECX = K	6	111
	IMUL	EAX,EAX	EAX = I*I	2	117
	IMUL	EBX,EBX	EBX = J*J	3	119
	IMUL	ECX,ECX	ECX = K*K	3	122
MARILYN:	ADD	EAX,EBX	EAX = I*I + J*J	2	125
	ADD	EAX,ECX	EAX = I*I + J*J + K*K	2	127
CAROL:	MOV	N,EAX	N = I*I + J*J + K*K	5	129
	JMP	DONE	JUMP TO DONE	5	134

Fig. 7-3. The instruction location counter (ILC) keeps track of the address where the instructions will be loaded in memory. In this example, the statements prior to SUZANNE occupy 100 bytes.

Some assemblers allow programmers to write instructions using immediate addressing even though no corresponding target language instruction exists. Such "pseudo-immediate" instructions are handled as follows. The assembler allocates memory for the immediate operand at the end of the program and generates an instruction that references it. For instance, the IBM 370 has no immediate instructions. Nevertheless, programmers may write

    L 14,=F'5'

to load register 14 with a Full word constant 5. In this way, the programmer avoids explicitly writing a DC pseudoinstruction to allocate a word initialized to 5. Constants for which the assembler automatically reserves memory are called **literals**. In addition to saving the programmer a little writing, literals improve the readability of a program by making the value of the constant apparent in the source statement. Pass one of the assembler must build a table of all literals used in the program. Both of our example families have immediate instructions, so their assemblers do not provide literals. Immediate instructions are quite common nowadays, but formerly they were unusual. It is likely that the widespread use of literals made it clear to machine designers that immediate addressing was a good idea.

Pass one of most assemblers uses at least two tables: the symbol table and the opcode table. If needed, the literal table is also kept. The symbol table has one entry for each symbol, as shown in Fig. 7-4. Symbols are defined either by using them as labels or by explicit definition (e.g., EQU on the 386). Each symbol table entry contains the symbol itself (or a pointer to it), its numerical value, and some-times other information. This additional information may include:

1. The length of data field associated with symbol.

2. The relocation bits. (Does the symbol change value if the program is loaded at a different address than the assembler assumed?)

3. Whether or not the symbol is to be accessible outside the procedure.

Symbol	Value	Other information
SUZANNE	100	
MARIA	111	
MARILYN	125	
CAROL	129	

Fig. 7-4. A symbol table for the program of Fig. 7-3.

The opcode table contains at least one entry for each symbolic opcode (mnemonic) in the assembly language. Figure 7-5 shows part of an opcode table. Each entry contains the symbolic opcode, two operands, the opcode's numerical value, the instruction length, and a class number that separates the opcodes into groups depending on the number and type of operands.

Opcode	First operand	Second operand	Hexadecimal opcode	Instruction length	Instruction class
AAA	—	—	37	1	6
ADD	EAX	IMMED32	05	5	4
ADD	REG	REG	01	2	19
AND	EAX	IMMED32	25	5	4
AND	REG	REG	21	2	19

Fig. 7-5. A few excerpts from the opcode table for an 80386 assembler.

As an example, consider the opcode ADD. If an ADD instruction contains EAX as the first operand and a 32-bit constant (IMMED32) as the second one, then opcode 05H is used and the instruction length is 5 bytes. (Constants that can be expressed in 8 or 16 bits use different opcodes, not shown.) If ADD is used with two registers as operands, the instruction is 2 bytes, with opcode 01H. The (arbitrary) instruction class 19 would be given to all opcode-operand combinations that follow the same rules and should be processed the same way as ADD with two register operands. The instruction class effectively designates a procedure within the assembler that is called to process all instructions of a given type.

If literals are needed, a literal table is maintained during assembly, with a new entry made each time a literal is encountered. After the first pass this table is sorted to remove duplicates.

Figure 7-6 shows a procedure that could serve as a basis for pass one of an assembler. The style of programming is noteworthy in itself. The procedure names have been chosen to give a good indication of what the procedures do. Most important, Fig. 7-6 represents an outline of pass one which, although not complete, forms a good starting point. It is short enough to be easily understood and it makes clear what the next step must be—namely, to write the procedures used in it.

Some of these procedures will be quite short, such as *CheckForSymbol*, which returns the label as a character string if there is one and a blank string if there is not. Other procedures, such as *type0* and *type1*, may be longer and may call other procedures. In general, the number of classes will not be two, of course, but will depend on the language being assembled.

Structuring programs in this way has other advantages in addition to ease of programming. If the assembler is being written by a group of people, the various procedures can be parceled out among the programmers. All the (nasty) details of getting the input are hidden away in *ReadNextStatement*. If they should change— for example, due to an operating system change—only one subsidiary procedure is affected, and no changes are needed to the *PassOne* procedure itself.

In some assemblers, after a statement has been read in, it is stored in a table. If the table should fill up, it must be written out onto disk, possibly several times. On the other hand, if the program being assembled is short enough to fit in the table, pass two can get its input directly from the table, thus eliminating the disk I/O.

When the END pseudoinstruction is read, pass one is over. The symbol table and literal tables can be sorted at this point if needed. The sorted literal table can be checked for duplicate entries, which can be removed.

7.2.3. Pass Two

The function of pass two is to generate the object program and possibly print the assembly listing. In addition, pass two must output certain information needed by the linker for linking up procedures assembled at different times. Figure 7-7 shows a procedure for pass two.

The procedure for each class knows how many operands that class may have and calls the *EvaluateExpression* procedure (not shown) the appropriate number of times. The *EvaluateExpression* procedure must convert the symbolic expression to a binary number. It must first find the values of the symbols and the addresses of

```
procedure PassOne;
{This procedure is an outline of pass one of a simple assembler}

const size = 8; EndStatement = 99;

var LocationCounter, class, length, value : integer;
    MoreInput: boolean;
    literal, symbol, opcode: array [1.. size] of char;
    line: array [1..80] of char;

begin
  LocationCounter := 0;                            {init instruction location counter}
  MoreInput: = true;                               {set to false at END statement}
  InitializeTables;                                {call a procedure to set up tables}

  while MoreInput do
  begin                                            {loop executed once per line}
    ReadNextStatement(line);                       {go get some input}
    SaveLineForPassTwo(line);                      {save the line}

    if LineIsNotComment(line) then                 {is it a comment?}
      begin
        CheckForSymbol (line, symbol);             {is there a symbol?}
        if symbol [1] <> ' ' then                  {if column 1 blank, no symbol}
          EnterNewSymbol (symbol, LocationCounter);
        LookForLiteral (line, literal);            {literal present?}
        if literal [1] <> ' ' then                 {blank means no literal present}
          EnterLiteral (literal);

        {Now determine the opcode class. -1 used to signal illegal opcode.}
        ExtractOpcode (line, opcode);
        SearchOpcodeTable(opcode, line, class, value);
        if class < 0 then TryPseudoInstr (opcode, class, value);
        length : =0;                               {compute instruction length}
        if class < 0 then IllegalOpcode;
        case class of
          0: length := type0 (line);               {compute instruction length}
          1: length := type1 (line);               {ditto}

              {Other cases here}

      end;

    LocationCounter := LocationCounter + length;
    if class = EndStatement then
      begin
        MoreInput := false;
        RewindPassTwoInput;
        SortLiteralTable;
        RemoveRedundantLiterals
      end
  end
end; {PassOne}
```

Fig. 7-6. Pass one of a simple assembler.

the literals from the respective tables. Once the numerical values are known, the expression can be evaluated. Numerous techniques for evaluating arithmetic expressions are known. One method (described in Chap. 5) is to convert the expression to reverse Polish and evaluate it by using a stack.

Once the numerical value of the opcode and the values of the operands are all

```
procedure PassTwo;
{This procedure is an outline of pass two of a simple assembler}

const size = 8; EndStatement = 99;

var code, class, value, LocationCounter, length: integer;
    MoreInput: boolean ;
    opcode: array [1.. size] of char:
    line:array [1..80] of char
    operands:array [1..3] of integer;

begin
    MoreInput := true;                              {set to false at END statement}
    LocationCounter:= 0;

while MoreInput do
begin
    GetNextStatement (line);                        {get input saved by pass one}
    if LineIsNotComment (line) then
        begin
            ExtractOpcode (line, opcode);
            SearchOpcodeTable (opcode, line, class, value);
            if class < 0 then TryPseudoInstr(opcode, class, value);
            length :=0;                             {compute instruction length}
            if class < 0 then BadOpcode;
            case class of
                0: length := eval0 (line, operands);
                1: length := eval1 (line, operands);

                {Other cases here}

        end;

    AssemblePieces (code, class, value, operands);
    OutputCode (code);
    LocationCounter := LocationCounter + length;
    if class = EndStatement then
        begin
            MoreInput := false
            FinishUp
        end
    end
end;{PassTwo}
```

Fig. 7-7. Pass two of a simple assembler.

known, the complete instruction can be assembled. The assembled instruction is then placed in an output buffer that is written to disk when it fills up.

The original source statement and the object code generated from it (in octal or hexadecimal) are either printed or put into a buffer for later printing. After the ILC has been adjusted, the next statement is fetched.

Up until now it has been assumed that the source program does not contain any errors. Anyone who has ever written a program, in any language, knows how realistic that assumption is. Some of the common errors are as follows:

1. A symbol has been used but not defined.

2. A symbol has been defined more than once.

3. The name in the opcode field is not a legal opcode.

4. An opcode is not supplied with enough operands.

5. An opcode is supplied with too many operands.

6. An octal number contains an 8 or a 9.

7. Illegal register use (e.g., a jump to a register).

8. The END statement is missing.

Programmers are most ingenious at thinking up new kinds of errors to make. Undefined symbol errors are frequently caused by typing errors, so a clever assembler could try to figure out which of the defined symbols most resembles the undefined one and use that instead. Little can be done about correcting most other errors. The best thing for the assembler to do with an errant statement is to print an error message and try to continue assembly.

7.2.4. Symbol Table

During pass one of the assembly process, the assembler accumulates information about symbols and their values that must be stored in the symbol table for lookup during pass two. Several different methods are available for organizing the symbol table. We will briefly describe some of them below. All the methods attempt to simulate an **associative memory**, which conceptually is a set of (symbol, value) pairs. Given the symbol, the associative memory must produce the value.

The simplest implementation method is indeed to implement the symbol table as an array of pairs, the first element of which is (or points to) the symbol and the second of which is (or points to) the value. Given a symbol to look up, the symbol table routine just searches the table linearly until it finds a match. This method is easy to program but is slow, because, on the average, half the table will have to be searched on each lookup.

Another way to organize the symbol table is to sort it on the symbols and use the **binary search** algorithm to look up a symbol. This algorithm works by comparing the middle entry in the table to the symbol. If the symbol comes before the middle entry alphabetically, the symbol must be located in the first half of the table. If the symbol comes after the middle entry, it must be in the second half of the table. If the symbol is equal to the middle entry, the search terminates.

Assuming that the middle entry is not equal to the symbol sought, we at least know which half of the table to look for it in. Binary search can now be applied to the correct half, which yields either a match, or the correct quarter of the table. Applying the algorithm recursively, a table of size n entries can be searched in about $\log_2 n$ attempts. Obviously, this method is much faster than searching linearly, but it requires maintaining the table in sorted order.

A completely different way of simulating an associative memory is a technique known as **hash coding**. This method requires having a "hash" function that maps symbols onto integers in the range 0 to $k - 1$. One possible function is to multiply the ASCII codes of the characters in the symbols together, ignoring overflow, and taking the result modulo k. In fact, almost any function of the input that gives a uniform distribution of the hash values will do. Symbols can be stored by having a table consisting of k **buckets** numbered 0 to $k - 1$. All the (symbol, value) pairs whose symbol hashes to i are stored on a linked list pointed to by slot i in the hash table. With n symbols and k slots in the hash table, the average list will have length n/k. By choosing k approximately equal to n, symbols can be located with only about one lookup on the average. By adjusting k we can reduce table size at the expense of slower lookups. Hash coding is illustrated in Fig. 7-8.

7.3. MACROS

Assembly language programmers frequently need to repeat sequences of instructions several times within a program. The most obvious way to do so is simply to write the required instructions wherever they are needed. If a sequence is long, however, or must be used a large number of times, writing it repeatedly becomes tedious.

An alternative method is to make the sequence into a procedure and call it wherever it is needed. This strategy has the disadvantage of requiring a procedure call instruction and a return instruction to be executed every time a sequence is needed. If the sequences are short—for example, two instructions—but are used frequently, the procedure call overhead may significantly slow the program down. Macros provide an easy and efficient solution to the problem of repeatedly needing the same or nearly the same sequences of instructions.

7.3.1. Macro Definition, Call, and Expansion

A **macro definition** is a method for giving a name to a piece of text. After a macro has been defined, the programmer can write the macro name instead of the piece of program. A macro is, in effect, an abbreviation for a piece of text. Figure 7-9(a) shows an assembly language program for the 80386 that exchanges the contents of the variables P and Q twice. These sequences could be defined as macros, as shown in Fig. 7-9(b). After its definition, every occurrence of SWAP causes it to be replaced by the four lines:

```
MOV EAX,P
MOV EBX,Q
MOV Q,EAX
MOV P,EBX
```

Symbol	Value	Hash code
andy	14025	0
ceriel	45012	5
ed	34004	2
hans	45019	2
henri	45009	7
jaco	15015	0
jim	14013	2
john	25014	1
marja	34101	3
martin	25014	3
peter	25018	1
reind	14004	4
ruud	34004	6
sape	24005	6
wiebren	24014	1

(a)

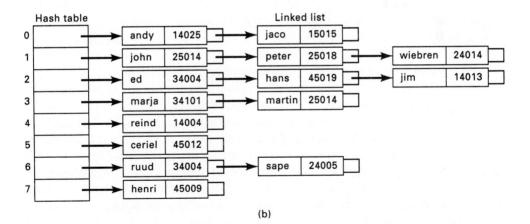

(b)

Fig. 7-8. Hash coding. (a) Symbols, values, and hash codes derived from symbols. (b) Eight-entry hash table with linked lists of symbols and values.

The programmer has defined SWAP as an abbreviation for the four statements shown above.

```
MOV   EAX,P          SWAP   MACRO
MOV   EBX,Q                 MOV EAX,P
MOV   Q,EAX                 MOV EBX,Q
MOV   P,EBX                 MOV Q,EAX
  ⋮                         MOV P,EBX
MOV   EAX,P                 ENDM
MOV   EBX,Q                  ⋮
MOV   Q,EAX                 SWAP
MOV   P,EBX                  ⋮
                           SWAP
```

              (a)   (b)

Fig. 7-9. Intel 80386 assembly language code for interchanging *P* and *Q* twice. (a) Without a macro. (b) With a macro.

Although different assemblers have slightly different notations for defining macros, all require the same basic parts in a macro definition:

1. A macro header giving the name of the macro being defined.

2. The text comprising the body of the macro.

3. A pseudoinstruction marking the end of the definition (e.g., ENDM).

When the assembler encounters a macro definition, it saves it in a macro definition table for subsequent use. From that point on, whenever the name of the macro (SWAP in the example of Fig. 7-9) appears as an opcode, the assembler replaces it by the macro body. The use of a macro name as an opcode is known as **a macro call** and its replacement by the macro body is called **macro expansion**.

Macro expansion occurs during the assembly process and not during execution of the program. This point is important. The program of Fig. 7-9(a) and that of Fig. 7-9(b) will produce precisely the same machine language code. Looking only at the machine language program, it is impossible to tell whether or not any macros were involved in its generation, because the macro expansion has been completed and the macro definitions discarded by the time the program has been assembled.

Macro calls should not be confused with procedure calls. The basic difference is that a macro call is a signal to the assembler to replace the macro name with the macro body. A procedure call is a machine instruction that is inserted into the object program and that will later be executed to call the procedure. Figure 7-10 compares macro calls with procedure calls.

Although macros are generally expanded on pass one of the assembly process, it may be conceptually simpler to think of the assembler as having an extra pass before pass one during which macro definitions are saved and macros are expanded. In this view, the source program is read in and is then transformed into another

Item	Macro call	Procedure call
When is the call made?	During assembly	During execution of the object program
Is the body inserted into the object program every place the name appeared ?	Yes	No
Is a procedure call instruction inserted into the object program and later executed ?	No	Yes
Must a return instruction be used to return control to the statement following the call ?	No	Yes
How many copies of the body appear in the object program?	One for each macro call	1

Fig. 7-10. Comparison of macro calls with procedure calls.

program from which all macro definitions have been removed, and in which all macro calls have been replaced by their bodies. The resulting output, an assembly language program containing no macros at all, is then fed into the assembler.

It is important to keep in mind that a program is a string of characters including letters, digits, spaces, punctuation marks, and "carriage returns" (change to a new line). Macro expansion consists of replacing certain substrings of this string with other character strings. A macro facility is a method of manipulating character strings, without regard to their meaning.

7.3.2. Macros with Parameters

The macro facility first described can be used to shorten programs in which precisely the same sequence of instructions occurs repeatedly. Frequently, however, a program contains several sequences of instructions that are almost but not quite identical, as illustrated in Fig. 7-11(a). Here the first sequence exchanges P and Q, and the second sequence exchanges R and S.

Macro assemblers handle the case of nearly identical sequences by allowing macro definitions to provide **formal parameters** and by allowing macro calls to supply **actual parameters**. When a macro is expanded, each formal parameter appearing in the macro body is replaced by the corresponding actual parameter. The actual parameters are placed in the operand field of the macro call. Figure 7-11(b) shows the program of Fig. 7-11(a) rewritten using a macro with parameters.

```
MOV  EAX,P        CHANGE MACRO  P1, P2
MOV  EBX,Q               MOV   EAX,P1
MOV  Q,EAX              MOV   EBX,P2
MOV  P,EBX             MOV   P2,EAX
  ⋮                         MOV   P1,EBX
MOV  EAX,R              ENDM
MOV  EBX,S               ⋮
MOV  S,EAX              CHANGE P, Q
MOV  R,EBX               ⋮
                        CHANGE R, S
```

(a)   (b)

Fig. 7-11. Nearly identical sequences of statements. (a) Without a macro. (b) With a macro.

The symbols $P1$ and $P2$ are the formal parameters. Each occurrence of $P1$ within a macro body is replaced by the first actual parameter when the macro is expanded. Similarly, $P2$ is replaced by the second actual parameter. In the macro call

CHANGE P,Q

P is the first actual parameter and Q is the second actual parameter. Thus the executable programs produced by both parts of Fig. 7-11 are identical.

7.3.3. Implementation of a Macro Facility in an Assembler

To implement a macro facility, an assembler must be able to perform two functions: save macro definitions and expand macro calls. We will examine these functions in turn.

The assembler must maintain a table of all macro names and, along with each name, a pointer to its stored definition so that it can be retrieved when needed. Some assemblers have a separate table for macro names and some have a combined opcode table in which all machine instructions, pseudoinstructions, and macro names are kept.

When a macro definition is encountered, a table entry is made giving the name of the macro, the number of formal parameters, and a pointer to another table—the macro definition table—where the macro body will be kept. A list of the formal parameters is also constructed at this time for use in processing the definition. The macro body is then read and stored in the macro definition table. Formal parameters occurring within the body are indicated by some special symbol. As an example, the internal representation of the macro definition of CHANGE with semicolon as "carriage return" and ampersand as the formal parameter symbol is shown below:

MOV EAX,&P1; MOV EBX,&P2; MOV &P2,EAX; MOV &P1,EBX;

Within the macro definition table the macro body is simply a character string.

During pass one of the assembly, opcodes are looked up and macros expanded. Whenever a macro definition is encountered, it is stored in the macro table. When a macro is called, the assembler temporarily stops reading input from the input device, and starts reading from the stored macro body instead. Formal parameters extracted from the stored macro body are replaced by the actual parameters provided in the call. The presence of an ampersand in front of the formal parameters makes it easy for the assembler to recognize them.

7.4. LINKING AND LOADING

Most programs consist of more than one procedure. Compilers and assemblers generally translate one procedure at a time and put the translated output on disk. Before the program can be run, all the translated procedures must be found and linked together properly. If virtual memory is not available, the linked program must be explicitly loaded into main memory as well. Programs that perform these functions are called by various names, including **linker**, **loader**, **linking loader**, and **linkage editor**. The complete translation of a source program requires two steps, as shown in Fig. 7-12:

1. Compilation or assembly of the source procedures.

2. Linking of the object modules.

The first step is performed by the compiler or assembler and the second one is performed by the linker.

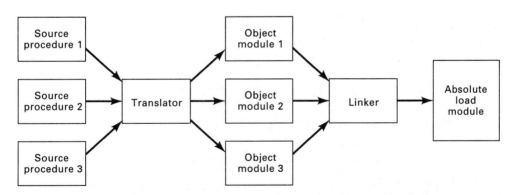

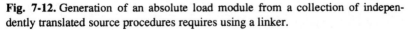

Fig. 7-12. Generation of an absolute load module from a collection of independently translated source procedures requires using a linker.

The translation from source procedure to object module represents a change of level because the source language and target language have different instructions and notation. The linking process, however, does not represent a change of level, since both the linker's input and the linker's output are programs for the same virtual machine. The linker's function is to collect procedures translated separately and link them together to be run as a unit, usually called an **absolute load module**. The loader's function is to load the absolute load module into main memory. These functions are often combined.

Compilers and assemblers translate each source procedure as a separate entity for a good reason. If a compiler or assembler were to read a series of source procedures and directly produce a ready-to-run machine language program, changing one statement in one source procedure would require that all the source procedures be retranslated.

If the separate-object-module method of Fig. 7-12 is used, it is only necessary to retranslate the modified procedure and not the unchanged ones, although it is necessary to relink all the object modules again. Linking is usually much faster than translating, however; thus the two-step process of translating and linking can save a great deal of time during the development of a large program.

7.4.1. Tasks Performed by the Linker

At the start of pass one of the assembly process, the instruction location counter is set to 0. This step is equivalent to assuming that the object module will be located at (virtual) address 0 during execution. Figure 7-13 shows four object modules. In this example, each module begins with a JUMP instruction to a MOV instruction within the module.

In order to run the program, the loader brings the object modules into main memory, as shown in Fig. 7-14(a). Typically, a small section of memory starting at address zero is used for interrupt vectors, communication with the operating system, or other purposes, so programs must start above 0. In this figure we have (arbitrarily) started programs at address 100.

The program of Fig. 7-14(a), although loaded into main memory, is not yet ready for execution. Consider what would happen if execution began with the instruction at the beginning of module A. The program would not jump to the MOVE instruction as it should, because that instruction is now at 300. In fact, all memory reference instructions will fail to operate properly for exactly the same reason.

This problem, called the **relocation problem**, occurs because each object module in Fig. 7-13 represents a separate address space. On a machine with a segmented address space, such as that provided by MULTICS, each object module can have its own address space by being placed in its own segment. On a machine with a linear, one-dimensional memory, the object modules must be merged into a single address space. The two-dimensional nature of the MULTICS virtual memory eliminates the need for merging object modules and greatly simplifies the task of the

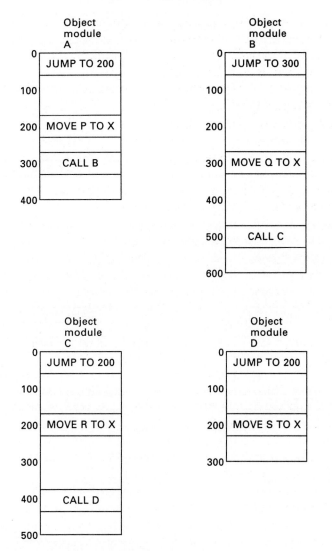

Fig. 7-13. Each module has its own address space, starting at 0.

linker. The separate address spaces of the object modules must also be merged on a machine with a paged, one-dimensional virtual memory.

Furthermore, the procedure call instructions in Fig. 7-14(a) will not work either. At address 400, the programmer had intended to call object module B, but because each procedure is translated by itself, the assembler has no way of knowing what address to insert into the CALL instruction. The address of object module B is not known until linking time. This problem is called the **external reference** problem. Both of these problems can be solved by the linker.

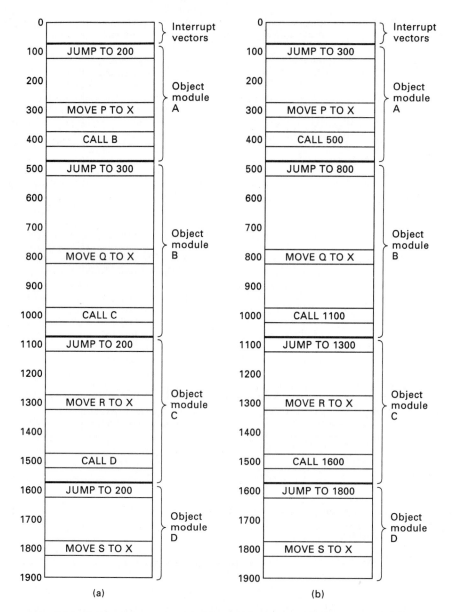

Fig. 7-14. (a) The object modules of Fig. 7-13 after being loaded but before being linked. (b) The same object modules after linking. Together they form an absolute load module, ready to run.

The linker merges the separate address spaces of the object modules into a single linear address space in the following steps:

1. It constructs a table of all the object modules and their lengths.

2. Based on this table, it assigns a load address to each object module.

3. It finds all the instructions that contain a memory address and to each one adds a **relocation constant** equal to the starting address of the module in which it is contained.

4. It finds all the instructions that reference other procedures and inserts the address of these procedures in place.

The object module table constructed in step 1 is as follows for the modules of Fig. 7-14.

Module	Length	Starting Address
A	400	100
B	600	500
C	500	1100
D	300	1600

Figure 7-14(b) shows how the address space of Fig. 7-14(a) looks after the linker has performed these steps.

7.4.2. Structure of an Object Module

Object modules contain six parts, as shown in Fig. 7-15. The first part contains the name of the module, certain information needed by the linker, such as the lengths of the various parts of the object module, and sometimes the assembly date.

The second part of the object module is a list of the symbols defined in the module that other modules may reference, together with their values. For example, if the module consists of a procedure named BIGBUG, the entry point table will contain the character string "BIGBUG" followed by the address to which it corresponds. The assembly language programmer indicates which symbols are to be declared as **entry points** or **external symbols** by using a pseudoinstruction.

The third part of the object module consists of a list of the symbols used in the module but defined in other modules, along with a list of which machine instructions use which symbols. The linker needs the latter list in order to be able to insert the correct addresses into the instructions that use external symbols. A procedure can call other independently translated procedures by declaring the names of the called procedures to be external. The assembly language programmer indicates which symbols are to be declared as external by using a pseudoinstruction. On

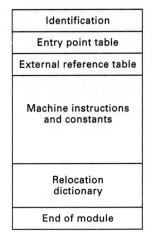

Fig. 7-15. The internal structure of an object module produced by a translator.

some computers the entry point table and the external reference table are combined into a single table.

The fourth part of the object module is the assembled code and constants. This part of the object module is the only one that will be loaded into memory to be executed. The other five parts will be used by the linker and then discarded before execution begins.

The fifth part of the object module is the relocation dictionary. As shown in Fig. 7-14, instructions that contain memory addresses must have a relocation constant added. Since the linker has no way of telling by inspection which of the data words in part 4 contain machine instructions and which contain constants, information about which addresses are to be relocated is provided in this table. The information may take the form of a bit table, with 1 bit per potentially relocatable address, or an explicit list of addresses to be relocated.

The sixth part is an end-of-module indication, sometimes a checksum to catch errors made while reading the module, and the address at which to begin execution.

Most linkers require two passes. On pass one the linker reads all the object modules and builds up a table of module names and lengths, and a global symbol table consisting of all entry points and external references. On pass two the object modules are read, relocated, and linked one module at a time.

7.4.3. Binding Time and Dynamic Relocation

In a time-sharing system, a program can be read into main memory, run for a little while, written to disk, and then read back into main memory to be run again. In a large system, with many programs, it is difficult to ensure that a program is read back into the same locations every time.

Figure 7-16 shows what would happen if the already relocated program of Fig. 7-14(b) were reloaded at address 400 instead of address 100 where the linker put it originally. All the memory addresses are incorrect; moreover, the relocation information has long since been discarded. Even if the relocation information were still available, the cost of having to relocate all the addresses every time the program was swapped would be too high.

The problem of moving programs that have already been linked and relocated is intimately related to the time at which the final binding of symbolic names onto absolute physical memory addresses is completed. When a program is written it contains symbolic names for memory addresses, for example, JUMP L. The time at which the actual main memory address corresponding to L is determined is called the **binding time**. At least six possibilities for the binding time exist:

1. When the program is written.

2. When the program is translated.

3. When the program is linked but before it is loaded.

4. When the program is loaded.

5. When a base register used for addressing is loaded.

6. When the instruction containing the address is executed.

If an instruction containing a memory address is moved after binding, it will be incorrect (assuming that the object referred to has also been moved). If the translator produces an absolute load module as output, the binding has occurred at translation time, and the program must be run at the address the translator expected it to be run at. The linking method described in the preceding section binds symbolic names to absolute addresses during linking, which is why moving programs after linking fails, as shown in Fig. 7-16.

Two related issues are involved here. First, there is the question of when symbolic names are bound to virtual addresses. Second, there is a question of when virtual addresses are bound to physical addresses. Only when both operations have taken place is binding complete. When the linker merges the separate address spaces of the object modules into a single linear address space, it is, in fact, creating a virtual address space. The relocation and linking serve to bind symbolic names onto specific virtual addresses. This observation is true whether or not virtual memory is being used.

Assume for the moment that the address space of Fig. 7-14(b) were paged. It is clear that the virtual addresses corresponding to the symbolic names A, B, C, and D have already been determined, even though their physical main memory addresses will depend on the contents of the page table at the time they are used. An absolute load module is really a binding of symbolic names onto virtual addresses.

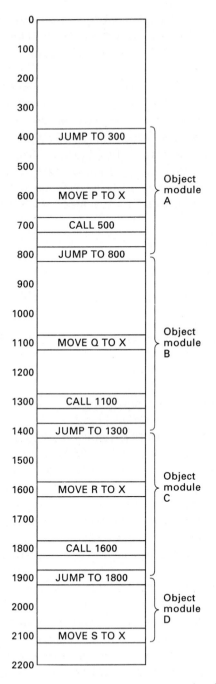

Fig. 7-16. The absolute load module of Fig. 7-14(b) moved up 300 addresses.

Any mechanism that allows the mapping of virtual addresses onto physical main memory addresses to be changed easily will facilitate moving programs around in main memory, even after they have been bound to a virtual address space. One such mechanism is paging. After a program has been moved in main memory, only its page table need be changed, not the program itself.

A second mechanism is the use of a run-time relocation register, such as CS on the Intel CPUs. On machines using this relocation method, the register always points to the physical memory address of the start of the current program. All memory addresses have the relocation register added to them by the hardware before being sent to the memory. The entire relocation process is transparent to the user programs. They do not even know that it is occurring. When a program is moved, the operating system must update the relocation register. This mechanism is less general than paging because the entire program must be moved as a unit (unless there are separate code and data relocation registers, in which case it has to be moved as two units).

A third mechanism is possible on machines that can refer to memory relative to the program counter, such as the 680x0 CPUs. Whenever a program is moved in main memory only the program counter need be updated. A program, all of whose memory references are either relative to the program counter or absolute (e.g., to I/O device registers at absolute addresses) is said to be **position-independent**. A position-independent procedure can be placed anywhere within the virtual address space without the need for relocation.

7.4.4. Dynamic Linking

The linking method discussed in Sec. 7.4.1 has the property that all procedures that a program might call are linked before the program can begin execution. On a computer with virtual memory, completing all linking before beginning execution does not take advantage of the full capabilities of the virtual memory. Many programs have procedures that are only called under unusual circumstances. For example, compilers have procedures for compiling rarely used statements, plus procedures for handling error conditions that seldom occur.

A more flexible method for linking separately compiled procedures is to link each procedure at the time it is first called. This process is known as **dynamic linking**. It was pioneered by MULTICS and is used by OS/2. The two implementations are somewhat different, so we will discuss both.

In MULTICS, associated with each program is a segment, called the **linkage segment**, which contains one block of information for each procedure that might be called. This block of information starts with a word reserved for the virtual address of the procedure and it is followed by the procedure name, which is stored as a character string.

When dynamic linking is being used, procedure calls in the source language are translated into instructions that indirectly address the first word of the corresponding linkage block, as shown in Fig. 7-17(a). The compiler fills this word with either an invalid address or a special bit pattern that forces a trap.

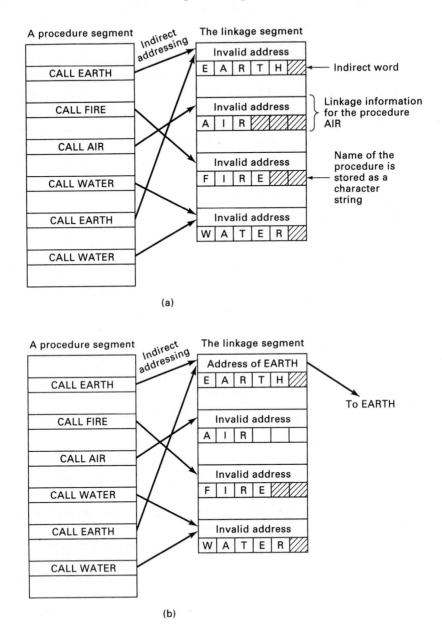

Fig. 7-17. Dynamic linking. (a) Before EARTH is called. (b) After EARTH has been called and linked.

When a procedure in a different segment is called, the attempt to address the invalid word indirectly causes a trap to the dynamic linker. The linker then finds the character string in the word following the invalid address and searches the user's file directory for a compiled procedure with this name. That procedure is then assigned a virtual address, usually in its own private segment, and this virtual address overwrites the invalid address in the linkage segment, as indicated in Fig. 7-17(b). Next, the instruction causing the linkage fault is reexecuted, allowing the program to continue from the place it was before the trap.

All subsequent references to that procedure will be executed without causing a linkage fault, for the indirect word now contains a valid virtual address. Consequently, the dynamic linker is invoked only the first time a procedure is called and not thereafter.

The OS/2 dynamic linking scheme is more general than that of MULTICS. An OS/2 programmer does not even have to know the names of all the procedures his program will ultimately call. Consider the following example. In a distributed banking system, a central machine receives requests from distant terminals to perform certain transactions. At the time the system is designed, it is expected that new types of transactions will be added as the system evolves.

To allow the system to develop, it is decided in advance that each transaction shall have a name, and that each transaction shall be carried out by a procedure named after the transaction. The executable code for this procedure will be stored as a file with the same name, in a special directory.

When a remote terminal sends a message to the central computer, it includes the name of the transaction in the message. The transaction program then constructs the name of the file containing the relevant code, and makes a system call asking the operating system to locate this file and bring it into memory. It then makes a second call asking the operating system to find and return to it the starting address of the procedure it needs (the file may contain multiple procedures). Armed with this address (really a segment selector and an offset), the main program calls the procedure. Subsequent calls to the same procedure are done in the normal way, without any system calls.

It should be clear that this scheme makes it possible to add new procedures to a running program just by compiling the relevant object code and putting it on the disk somewhere. It is not even necessary that the running program knows in advance where the procedure is, since this information can be contained in a message sent to it. It is not even required that the program stop executing, let alone be recompiled.

7.5. SUMMARY

Although most programs can and should be written in a high-level language, occasional situations exist in which assembly language is needed, at least in part. An assembly language program is a symbolic representation for some underlying machine language program. It is translated to the machine language by a program called an assembler.

Various studies have shown that even when fast execution is needed, a better approach than writing everything in assembly language is to first write the whole program in a high-level language, then measure where it is spending its time, and finally rewrite only those portions of the program that are heavily used. In practice, a small fraction of the code is usually responsible for a large fraction of the execution time.

Most assemblers are two pass. Pass one is devoted to building up a symbol table for labels, literals, and explicitly declared identifiers. The symbols can either be kept unsorted and then searched linearly, first sorted and then searched using binary search, or hashed. If symbols do not need to be deleted during pass one, hashing is usually the best method. Pass two does the code generation. Some pseudoinstructions are carried out on pass one and some on pass two.

Many assemblers have a macro facility that allows the programmer to give commonly used code sequences symbolic names for subsequent inclusion. Usually, these macros can be parameterized in a straightforward way. Macros are implemented by a kind of literal string-processing algorithm.

Independently assembled programs can be linked together to form an absolute load module. This work is done by the linker. Its primary tasks are relocation and binding of names. Dynamic linking is a technique in which certain procedures are not linked until they are actually called.

PROBLEMS

1. For a certain program, 1% of the code accounts for 50% of the execution time. Compare the following three strategies with respect to programming time and execution time. Assume that it would take 100 man-months to write it in Pascal, and that assembly code is 10 times harder to write and four times more efficient.

   a. Entire program in Pascal.
   b. Entire program in assembler.
   c. First all in Pascal, then the key 1% rewritten in assembler.

2. Do the considerations that hold for two-pass assemblers also hold for compilers?

   a. Assume that the compilers produce object modules, not assembly code.
   b. Assume that the compilers produce symbolic assembly language.

3. Suggest a method for allowing assembly language programmers to define synonyms for opcodes. How could this be implemented?

4. All the assemblers for the Intel CPUs have the destination address as the first operand and the source address as the second operand. What problems would have to be solved to do it the other way?

5. Can the following program be assembled in two passes? EQU is a pseudoinstruction that equates the label to the expression in the operand field.

```
A EQU B
B EQU C
C EQU D
D EQU 4
```

6. The Dirtcheap Software Company is planning to produce an assembler for a computer with a 48-bit word. To keep costs down, the project manager, Dr. Scrooge, has decided to limit the length of allowed symbols so that each symbol can be stored in a single word. Scrooge has declared that symbols may consist only of letters, except the letter Q, which is forbidden (to demonstrate their concern for efficiency to the customers). What is the maximum length of a symbol? Describe your encoding method.

7. What is the difference between an instruction and a pseudoinstruction?

8. What is the difference between the instruction location counter and the program counter, if any? After all, both keep track of the next instruction in a program.

9. Can you envision circumstances in which an assembly language permits a label to be the same as an opcode (e.g., MOV as a label)? Discuss.

10. Show the symbol table after the following 8088 statements have been encountered. The first statement is assigned to address 1000.

EVEREST:	POP BX	(1 BYTE)
K2:	PUSH BP	(1 BYTE)
WHITNEY:	MOV BP,SP	(2 BYTES)
MCKINLEY:	PUSH X	(3 BYTES)
FUJI:	PUSH SI	(1 BYTE)
KIBO:	SUB SI,300	(3 BYTES)

11. Show the steps needed to look up Berkeley using binary search on the following list: Ann Arbor, Berkeley, Cambridge, Eugene, Madison, New Haven, Palo Alto, Pasadena, Santa Cruz, Stony Brook, Westwood, and Yellow Springs. When computing the middle element of a list with an even number of elements, use the element just below the middle index.

12. Is it possible to use binary search on a table whose size is prime?

13. Compute the hash code for each of the following symbols by adding up the letters (A = 1, B = 2, etc.) and taking the result modulo the hash table size. The hash table has 19 slots, numbered 0 to 18.

ELS, JAN, JELLE, MAAIKE

Does each symbol generate a unique hash value? If not, how can the collision problem be dealt with?

14. The hash coding method described in the text links all the entries having the same hash code together on a linked list. An alternative method is to have only a single *n*-slot

table, with each table slot having room for one key and its value (or pointers to them). If the hashing algorithm generates a slot that is already full, a second hashing algorithm is used to try again. If that one is also full, another is used, and so on, until an empty is found. If the fraction of the slots that are full is r, how many probes will be needed, on the average, to enter a new symbol?

15. As VLSI technology progresses, it may one day be possible to put thousands of identical CPUs on a chip, each CPU having a few words of local memory. If all the CPUs can read and write three shared registers, how can an associative memory be implemented?

16. The 80386 has a segmented architecture, with multiple independent segments. An assembler for this machine might well have a pseudoinstruction SEG N that would direct the assembler to place subsequent code and data in segment N. Does this scheme have any influence on the ILC?

17. If a macro definition contains a label, that label will be generated every time the macro is called, leading to multiply defined labels. Because macros may contain loops, labels are sometimes needed. Devise a solution to this problem.

18. Can a register be used as the actual parameter in a macro call? How about a constant? Why or why not?

19. You are to implement a macro assembler. For esthetic reasons, your boss has decided that macro definitions need not precede their calls. What implications does this decision have on the implementation?

20. Think of a way to put a macro assembler into an infinite loop.

21. A linker reads five modules, whose lengths are 200, 800, 600, 500, and 700 words, respectively. If they are loaded in that order, what are the relocation constants?

22. One of the UNIX system calls is FORK, which creates an exact copy of the calling process, including program text, data, and stack. The two processes are called the parent and the child. Suppose the compiler for this system, a 68000 without an MMU, produces position-independent code. Is it possible to run the child process by just transferring control to it? Discuss.

23. Can MULTICS-style dynamic linking be implemented on the 80386? If so, explain how. If not, tell why not.

24. Write a symbol table package consisting of two routines: ENTER(SYMBOL, VALUE) and LOOKUP(SYMBOL, VALUE). The former enters new symbols in the table and the latter looks them up. Use some form of hash coding.

25. Write a simple assembler for the Mac-1 computer of Chap. 4. In addition to handling the machine instructions, provide a facility for assigning constants to symbols at assembly time, and a way to assemble a constant into a machine word. See Fig. 4-11(b) for an example program.

26. Add a simple macro facility to the assembler of the preceding problem.

8

ADVANCED COMPUTER ARCHITECTURES

Although the machines we have been studying for the past seven chapters are in a certain sense brand new, in a more fundamental way they are merely smaller versions of the big mainframes introduced in the early 1960s. Like the original IBM 360 family, the 80386, 68030 and many other current computers have a single CPU, an external memory, 8 to 16 registers, hundreds of instructions, and a dozen or more complex addressing modes. It is as though computer architecture has been sleeping for 30 years.

Nothing could be further from the truth. There has been an enormous amount of activity among computer architects recently. Some of them have produced innovative new designs that may revolutionize computer architecture. In this chapter we will study two alternative approaches that hold great promise for the future: RISC machines and parallel processors.

8.1. RISC MACHINES

We will start our study of new developments in computer architecture with **RISC machines**. RISC is an acronym for **Reduced Instruction Set Computer**, and is intended as a contrast with **CISC machines**, which are **Complex Instruction Set Computers**. The IBM 360 and all other mainframes, DEC VAX, Intel 80386, and Motorola 68030 are examples of CISC machines.

To make a long story short, the supporters of the RISC philosophy say that a complete overhaul is needed in the way we think about computer architecture, and that nearly all conventional computers are architecturally obsolete. They argue that computers have gotten much too complicated over the years, and that we should throw them all out (the designs, at least) and start over. Not surprisingly, this opinion has generated a certain amount of controversy and discussion, and the final word is by no means in. In this section we will look at RISC machines in detail, and present both sides of the great RISC versus CISC debate.

8.1.1. Evolution of Computer Architecture

The earliest digital computers were extremely simple. They had to be. It was hard enough to get them to work at all. From the ENIAC, through the IBM 7094, and on to the CDC 6600, computers had relatively few instructions and only one or two addressing modes.

All of that changed abruptly with the introduction of the IBM 360 series in 1964. All models of the 360 series were microprogrammed. Although the microarchitectures of the various 360 models were straightforward enough, the microprograms that ran on them presented the users with a highly complex instruction set at the conventional machine level, which is what everyone perceived as the "machine language," of course, since the microprograms were in ROM and could not be modified. Within a few years, even minicomputers, like the VAX, typically had well over 200 instructions and a dozen addressing modes, all implemented by a microprogram running on what was still a simple piece of hardware.

As time went on, even microprocessors, which started out with minimal architectures, rapidly approached or even exceeded the complexity of minicomputers and mainframes. This trend was encouraged by the widespread use of high-level languages. These languages contained constructs like **if**, **while**, and **case**, whereas the assembly languages to which programs in these languages had to be translated contained instructions like MOVE, ADD, and JUMP. The resulting **semantic gap** made writing compilers difficult.

Since lowering the level of the languages was out of the question, a popular approach to reducing this gap was to raise the level of the "machine language." New instructions for handling **case** statements were added, as were special addressing modes for dealing with arrays and records. Large parts of the procedure call mechanism, including parameter passing, stack adjustment, and register saving, migrated into the microcode. Almost everyone viewed this trend as positive. Foster (1972) even wrote that he expected future machines to have instructions with up to six fields and no registers, greatly reducing the semantic gap.

Another factor that encouraged the spread of these CISC machines was the relatively slow speed of main memory compared to the CPU. To see why this matters, think about COBOL applications that require decimal (as opposed to binary) arithmetic. Internally, all computers are binary, so there were two ways to simulate decimal arithmetic. The first way was to have the COBOL programs call library routines located in main memory. The second way was to put these routines into the microprogram, and add new instructions such as ADD DECIMAL to the architecture. The first approach required many (slow) memory references to fetch the instructions of the library routine; the second one fetched the routine from fast ROM inside the CPU. Under these conditions, the temptation to put more and more complexity in the microprogram was irresistible.

In the 1970s, the technology began to change. Semiconductor RAM memory was no longer ten times slower than ROM. Furthermore, writing, debugging, and maintaining all that microcode was beginning to become a major headache. After all, fixing a microcode bug meant equipping the customer service engineers with large boxes of new ROMs and lists of thousands of computer installations to install them in.

Worse yet, academic gadflies began examining real programs to see what kinds of statements they actually contained. Knuth (1971) measured FORTRAN programs. Wortman (1972) looked at system programs in a PL/I-like language called XPL. Tanenbaum (1978) examined the code of an operating system written in a Pascal-like language called SAL. Patterson (1982) measured system programs written in C and Pascal. These results are shown in Fig. 8-1. The last column gives the average of the five languages.

Statement	SAL	XPL	Fortran	C	Pascal	Average
Assignment	47	55	51	38	45	47
If	17	17	10	43	29	23
Call	25	17	5	12	15	15
Loop	6	5	9	3	5	6
Goto	0	1	9	3	0	3
Other	5	5	16	1	6	7

Fig. 8-1. Studies of five programming languages, giving the percentage of each statement type in a measured sample of programs. The column giving the averages does not sum to 100 percent due to roundoff.

What is abundantly clear is that most programs consist of assignments, **if** statements, and procedure calls (together, 85 percent). Even more interesting is the distribution of the number of terms in an assignment, number of local scalar variables, and number of parameters per procedure call. These are shown in Fig. 8-2 based on the figures in (Tanenbaum, 1978).

From the data of Fig. 8-2 we see that 80 percent of all assignments are of the form *variable := value*, such as assigning a constant, variable, or array element to a variable. Only 15 percent of all assignments involve a single operator on the right-

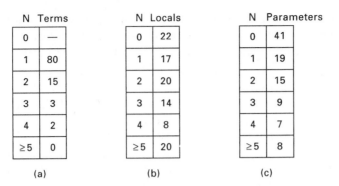

N Terms	
0	—
1	80
2	15
3	3
4	2
≥5	0

(a)

N Locals	
0	22
1	17
2	20
3	14
4	8
≥5	20

(b)

N Parameters	
0	41
1	19
2	15
3	9
4	7
≥5	8

(c)

Fig. 8-2. (a) Number of terms in assignment statements. (b) Number of local scalar variables per procedure. (c) Number of parameters in procedure calls. The sums do not necessarily add to 100 percent due to roundoff.

hand side, as in $v := a + b$ or $v := a - b[i]$. In other words, only 5 percent of all expressions involve two or more operators.

The distribution of local scalar variables is also interesting. Nearly a quarter of all procedures measured have none at all, and 80 percent have four or fewer. Finally, 41 percent of the measured procedures have no parameters, but only 8 percent have five or more.

The conclusion from these and other studies is clear and somewhat surprising. While *theoretically* people can write highly complex programs, the ones that they *actually* write consist of simple assignments, **if** statements, and procedure calls with a small number of parameters. This conclusion has enormous implications for the tendency to migrate more and more functionality into the microcode.

As the machine language gets larger and more complicated, its interpreter, the microprogram, gets bigger and slower. More instructions means more time spent decoding the opcodes. Even more important, a large number of addressing modes means that address analysis can no longer be done in-line because the same (lengthy) microcode would have to be repeated hundreds of times in the microprogram. Thus microprocedures are needed, and almost every instruction must call a microprocedure to analyze the addressing modes. On a machine (like the VAX) that has two general addressing modes per instruction, the address evaluation microprocedure must be called twice, once for the source operand and once for the destination operand.

The worst of it is that machines had been slowed down in order to permit the addition of all kinds of instructions and modes that, in practice, are hardly ever used. The stage had thus been set for someone to realize that computers could be made to run a lot faster by throwing out the interpreter altogether, and having each program compiled directly to microcode and executed out of fast semiconductor RAM memory.

Writing compilers that generate highly horizontal, parallel microcode, like that of the Mic-1 (Fig. 4-9) is exceedingly difficult, but producing code for the Mic-2 (Fig. 4-17) is not so hard. Each of the Mic-2 microinstructions performs only one function, and does it in a single data path (i.e., ALU) cycle. Generating code for a machine like this is not much harder than generating code for an early minicomputer or microcomputer, like the PDP-8 or 8080.

In short, a RISC machine is essentially just a computer with a small number of vertical microinstructions, not unlike the Mic-2. User programs are compiled into sequences of these microinstructions, and then directly executed by the hardware, with no intervening interpreter. The result is that the simple things that programs actually do, such as adding two registers, can now be completed in a single microinstruction. In contrast, in Figures 4-16 and 4-20, we see that the fastest machine language (i.e., Mac-1) instructions take 8 and 15 microinstructions, respectively. By winning a factor of 10 in the common case, we can afford to pay a penalty in the unusual case, and make a large net gain in performance.

In a sense, we have come full circle. Before Wilkes invented microprogramming, all computers were RISC machines, with simple instructions directly executed by the hardware. After microprogramming took hold, computers became more complex and less efficient. Now the industry is going back to its roots, and building simple, fast machines once again.

The critical breakthrough that made RISC machines feasible was, interestingly enough, a software advance and not a hardware one. It was the improvement in optimizing compiler technology that made it possible to generate microcode at least as good as, if not better than, handwritten microcode. Before this breakthrough it made sense to have a clever programmer write a microprogram by hand, and have it interpret user programs. Nowadays, it is possible to let the compiler produce the microcode directly, skipping the interpreter. In the past, no compiler could produce microcode that was good enough, although in all fairness, the hardware designers have helped too: RISC machines are somewhat simpler than even vertical microarchitectures.

The first modern RISC machine was the **801 minicomputer** built by IBM, starting in 1975. However, IBM did not publish anything about it until 1982 (Radin, 1982). In 1980, a group at Berkeley led by David Patterson and Carlo Séquin began designing VLSI RISC chips (Patterson, 1985; Patterson and Séquin, 1981, 1982). They coined the term RISC, and named their CPU chip the **RISC I** followed shortly by the **RISC II**. Slightly later, in 1981, across the San Francisco Bay at Stanford, John Hennessy designed and fabricated a somewhat different RISC chip he called the **MIPS** (Hennessy, 1984).

These three RISC machines are compared to three CISC machines in Fig. 8-3. Each of them has led directly to major commercial products. The 801 was the ancestor of the IBM PC/RT, the RISC I was the inspiration of Sun Microsystems' SPARC design, and the Stanford MIPS chip led to the formation of MIPS Computer Systems, which produces the CPU chips used in the RISC machines sold by DEC and other computer vendors. Some other relevant references to RISC work are (Birnbaum and Worley, 1986; Gimarc and Milutinović, 1987; Moussouris et al., 1986; Robinson, 1987; Steenkiste and Hennessy, 1988; Tabak, 1987; Wallich, 1985; Wilson, 1988).

	CISC			RISC		
	IBM 370/168	VAX 11/780	Xerox Dorado	IBM 801	Berkeley RISC I	Stanford MIPS
Year completed	1973	1978	1978	1980	1981	1983
Instructions	208	303	270	120	39	55
Microcode size	54K	61K	17K	0	0	0
Instruction size	2-6	2-57	1-3	4	4	4
Execution model	Reg-reg Reg-mem Mem-mem	Reg-reg Reg-mem Mem-mem	Stack	Reg-reg	Reg-reg	Reg-reg

Fig. 8-3. Comparison of three typical CISC machines with the first three RISC machines. The instruction and microcode sizes are in bytes.

8.1.2. Design Principles for RISC Machines

As a first approximation, we can think of the Mic-2 as being RISC-like, but in reality the situation is more complicated than that. In this section we will discuss the technical design of RISC machines in detail. However, let us first present the basic RISC design philosophy in a nutshell. Designing a RISC machine has five steps:

1. Analyze the applications to find the key operations.
2. Design a data path that is optimal for the key operations.
3. Design instructions that perform the key operations using the data path.
4. Add new instructions only if they do not slow down the machine.
5. Repeat this process for other resources.

The first step says the designer should find out what the intended programs actually do. For traditional algorithmic languages some statistics are shown in Fig. 8-1. However, for applications in COBOL, Smalltalk, or Lisp, one would have to start all over collecting statistical information about real programs in these languages. Similarly, when designing dedicated machines for banking, robotics, or computer-aided design applications, yet other information would be required.

The heart of any computer is the data path, which contains the registers, the

ALU, and the buses connecting them. This circuit should be optimized for the language or application in question. The time required to fetch the operands from their registers, run them through the ALU, and store the result back into a register, called the **data path cycle time**, should be made as short as possible.

The next step is to design machine instructions that make good use of the data path. Only a few instructions and addressing modes are typically needed. Additional instructions should only be added if they will be frequently used and do not reduce the performance of the most important ones. RISC Golden Rule number 1 states:

Sacrifice everything to reduce the data path cycle time

Whenever an attractive new feature rears its ugly head, it should be looked at in this light: how does it affect the data path cycle time? If it increases the cycle time, it is probably not worth having.

Finally, the same process should be repeated for other resources within the CPU, such as cache memory, memory management, floating-point coprocessors, and so on. As Antoine de St. Exupéry so aptly put it: "Perfection is achieved, not when there is nothing left to add, but when there is nothing left to take away."

RISC machines can differ from their CISC counterparts in eight critical ways, as listed in Fig. 8-4. Let us now examine each of these items in some detail.

	RISC	CISC
1	Simple instructions taking 1 cycle	Complex instructions taking multiple cycles
2	Only LOADS/STORES reference memory	Any instruction may reference memory
3	Highly pipelined	Not pipelined or less pipelined
4	Instructions executed by the hardware	Instructions interpreted by the microprogram
5	Fixed format instructions	Variable format instructions
6	Few instructions and modes	Many instructions and modes
7	Complexity is in the compiler	Complexity is in the microprogram
8	Multiple register sets	Single register set

Fig. 8-4. Characteristics of RISC and CISC machines.

One Instruction Per Data Path Cycle

In a sense the name Reduced Instruction Set Computer is something of a misnomer. While it is true that most RISC machines have relatively few instructions, the most important single characteristic that distinguishes them from CISC machines is that RISC instructions are completed in a single data path cycle. Looking at Fig. 4-10 or Fig. 4-18, we see that a data path cycle consists of fetching two operands from the register scratch pad, putting them on the internal buses, running them through the ALU, and finally storing the result back in the scratch pad. All of this activity takes one clock cycle. In this respect, a RISC instruction is very much like a microinstruction. In contrast, an interpreted instruction, such as the Mac-1 instructions interpreted in Figures 4-16 and 4-20, typically takes 10 clock cycles.

A consequence of the principle that every RISC instruction must take one cycle is that any operation that cannot be completed in one cycle cannot be included in the instruction set. Thus, many RISC machines lack instructions for multiplication or division. In practice, most multiplications are by small constants known at compile time, so they can be simulated by sequences of shifts and adds. The remaining multiplications and all divisions are handled by library procedures. Floating-point instructions are executed by a coprocessor.

LOAD/STORE Architecture

Given our desire to have every instruction take one clock cycle, it is clear that instructions that reference memory are going to be a problem. Instructions that fetch their operands from registers and store their results in registers can be handled in one cycle, but instructions that load from or store into memory take too long. Increasing the clock cycle by a factor of two or three to accommodate loads and stores violates Golden Rule number 1 of RISC design.

The solution is twofold. First, ordinary instructions may only have register operands. Thus, unlike on the 80386, 68030, and other CISCs, they do not have addressing modes for direct addressing, indexed addressing, or register or memory indirect addressing. Only register addressing is permitted.

However, some instructions must reference memory, so special LOAD and STORE instructions are added to the architecture. Only these instructions may reference memory. Figure 8-5 shows a typical set of LOAD/STORE instructions for a 32-bit RISC machine. The two signed LOAD instructions load 8 or 16 bits into the low-order part of the specified 32-bit register and fill all the remaining bits with sign bit (bit 7 or 15) to produce a 32-bit signed integer. The unsigned LOAD instructions do not propagate the sign bit. For full word LOADs and for STOREs, the issue does not arise.

It should be emphasized that the only instructions capable of addressing memory are those shown in Fig. 8-5. The instruction format used for ADD, MOVE, AND, and so on, typically contains 5-bit operand fields for addressing 32 registers, but no fields for memory addresses.

Pipelining

Of course, forbidding ordinary instructions from accessing memory does not solve the problem of how to make the LOADs and STOREs operate in one cycle. The solution lies in a bit of a trick. We are going to relax our goals ever so slightly.

Load signed byte	Store byte
Load unsigned byte	
Load signed halfword	Store halfword
Load unsigned halfword	
Load word	Store word

Fig. 8-5. LOAD and STORE instructions for a typical 32-bit RISC machine.

Instead of demanding that every instruction be executed in one cycle, we will merely insist that we be able to start one instruction in each cycle, without regard to when it finishes. If in n cycles we manage to start n instructions, on the average we have achieved one instruction per cycle, which is good enough.

In order to achieve this modified goal, all RISC machines are pipelined. We studied pipelining in Sec. 4.5.4, so we will only repeat the basic idea here. The CPU contains several independent units that work in parallel. One of them fetches the instructions, and other ones decode and execute them. At any instant, several instructions are in various stages of processing.

In Fig. 8-6 we show a simple pipeline with three stages, for fetching instructions, executing instructions, and performing memory references. Ordinary instructions are in the machine for two cycles, for fetching and executing. LOADs and STOREs require a third cycle for the memory reference. In cycle 1, instruction 1 is fetched. In cycle 2, instruction 2 is fetched and instruction 1 is executed. In cycle 3, instruction 3 (marked L for LOAD) is fetched and instruction 2 is executed. In cycle 4, the LOAD is started, but it cannot be completed in one cycle.

	Cycle									
	1	2	3	4	5	6	7	8	9	10
Instruction fetch	1	2	L	4	5	6	S	8	9	10
Instruction execution		1	2	L	④	5	6	S	⑧	9
Memory reference					L				S	

Fig. 8-6. A pipelined RISC machine with delayed LOAD, L, and STORE, S.

In cycle 5 something interesting happens (marked by the circle). Instruction 4 is executed, even though the LOAD started in the previous cycle has not yet completed. As long as instruction 4 does not try to use the register in the process of being LOADED, everything is fine and the machine continues execution at full speed. It is up to the compiler to make sure that the instruction following a LOAD does not use the item being fetched from memory. If the compiler cannot find any instruction to put after the LOAD, it can always insert a NO-OP instruction and waste one cycle. The analogous situation after a STORE (see cycle 9) does not cause a problem unless instruction 8 cannot operate properly until the STORE has completed.

The concept of having a LOAD instruction not take effect immediately is known as a **delayed load**. In our example the result is not available for one cycle, but longer delays are also possible, depending on the ratio of the processor speed to the memory speed. With some RISC machines it is up to the *compiler* to fill the slots following LOADs with something useful. The MIPS machine uses a somewhat different approach, however. Here the compiler generates ordinary sequential code, and a program called the **reorganizer** shuffles the assembly language instructions around, trying to fill up the slots behind the LOADs. This method not only keeps the compiler simpler, but allows the same reorganizer to be used with all compilers, so that the problem only has to be dealt with once.

In a sense, we have seen the concept of the delayed load before. In the Mic-2 (Fig. 4-17), the BEGRD microinstruction starts a memory operation, the result of which is not available for two cycles. In the Mic-2, the slot following the BEGRD must be filled with a CONRD, which is essentially a NO-OP. We could easily change the design to allow other instructions following the BEGRD, provided that they did not touch the register in the process of being loaded.

Even though it is not supposed to, what happens if a program tries to use a newly loaded register before it has arrived? RISC machines differ on this point. Most of them have a hardware interlock, effectively inserting automatic NO-OPs until the register has been loaded.

On the other hand, there are also RISC machines, like the MIPS, that simply use the incorrect value in the register. If the reorganizer cannot fill the slot, it must insert an explicit NO-OP, increasing the program length. The advantage of this approach is a simpler (and potentially faster) CPU, since the hardware does not have to check if the register being accessed is currently valid or not.

LOADs and STOREs are not the only instructions that can be delayed. As we saw in Sec. 4.5.4, conditional jumps wreak havoc with any pipelined machine. The RISC solution is the same as with the LOADs and STOREs, namely **delayed jumps**. The instruction following a JUMP is *always* executed, no matter whether the JUMP is ultimately taken or not. All the complicated predictive algorithms discussed in Chap. 4 are simply thrown out the window. In a RISC machine there is no time to run them. It is up to the compiler or reorganizer to find a useful instruction to put after each JUMP instruction. Failing that, a NO-OP is used.

No Microcode

The instructions generated by a compiler for a RISC machine are directly executed by the hardware. They are not interpreted by microcode. Eliminating this level of interpretation is the secret of the RISC machine's speed.

How these instructions are executed is not difficult to understand if we look again at Fig. 4-18. Instead of coming from the 256×12 control store shown in this figure, the "microinstructions" come from the output of the instruction fetch unit of the pipeline, that is, from main memory. They are not microinstructions at all, but user program instructions.

Their execution, however, is essentially the same as in Fig. 4-18. The OP decode box consists of hardwired logic (or a PLA) that takes the opcode field as input and generates all the control signals needed to drive the data path. As long as the instruction fetch unit is capable of providing one instruction every cycle, one data path operation can be done on each cycle.

CISC defenders often say that it is better to implement complex instructions in microcode, instead of user code. This statement leads us to RISC Golden Rule number 2:

Microcode is not magic

If a complex instruction (say, decimal addition), takes 10 microinstructions at 100 nsec each, it will take 1 µsec to execute on a CISC machine. On a RISC machine, the same instruction will take 10 RISC instructions instead of 10 microinstructions. If the RISC instructions also take 100 nsec, it will still take 1 µsec.

The only advantage to the CISC implementation is saving a little memory. However, if the operation occurs relatively often, it can be made into a library procedure at a minor cost in speed. Remember that most programs do simple things, so it is worthwhile accepting a small penalty on unusual instructions in return for getting the register moves and simple additions to go fast.

Fixed-Format Instructions

The need for fixed-format instructions is clear from Fig. 4-18. The individual bits in each instruction are used as inputs to the OP decode box and other parts of the hardware. Having variable-length instructions, ranging from 1 to 17 bytes (as on the 80386), just would not do here. That only works when there is a microprogram inside, sequentially pulling the bytes out of the instruction fetch queue and analyzing them one at a time in software.

Reduced Instruction Set

Finally, we come to the point for which RISC machines are named. Actually, there is no insurmountable objection to having many instructions, provided that each instruction executes in one cycle. The only real problem is that the complexity of the OP decode box grows exponentially with the number of instructions, and thus consumes increasingly large amounts of scarce chip area.

The situation with addressing modes is different. For reasons of speed and complexity, it is undesirable to have more than a minimal number of addressing modes. Figure 8-7 shows the basic instruction format used in the RISC I, as an example. It specifies an opcode, two 5-bit registers, a mode bit (immediate/not immediate), and an offset. Using this one format, and the fact that register 0 is hardwired to the constant 0, we can produce most of the useful addressing modes.

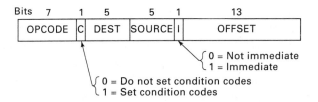

Fig. 8-7. RISC I basic instruction format.

For ordinary instructions, such as ADD, the operands depend on the *I* bit. If it is cleared, one operand is taken from the source register, the second is taken from the register specified by the low-order 5 bits of the OFFSET field, and the result is stored in the destination register. This combination gives register addressing. If the *I* bit is set, the second operand is a 13-bit constant, giving immediate addressing.

For LOAD and STORE instructions, the OFFSET is added to the source register to form the effective memory address (indexed addressing). If OFFSET is 0, this mode reduces to register indirect addressing. If register 0 is specified, we have direct addressing of the bottom 8K of memory, which is useful for accessing global variables. Other modes can be constructed at run time by building an address in a register and then using register indirect or indexed addressing. The RISC II design added a PC-relative conditional JUMP by concatenating the low-order three fields to form a 19-bit signed offset (the DEST field specifies the condition).

Put the Complexity in the Compiler

It should be clear by now that a great deal of effort has been made to keep the hardware as simple as possible, even at the price of making the compiler considerably more complicated. This strategy is in stark contrast to machines like the 80386 and 68030, with their highly complex addressing modes (see Figs. 5-36 and 5-39), allegedly devised to reduce the semantic gap discussed earlier. In practice, the existence of some of the more exotic addressing modes on the 80386 and 68030 make *both* the compiler *and* the microprogram very complicated.

Still, CISC machines do not have nasty features like delayed loads, stores, and jumps. These certainly add considerably to the complexity of the compiler or reorganizer. In addition, the fact that ordinary instructions cannot use memory operands means that it is essential for RISC compilers to go to great lengths to optimize register usage. The penalty for suboptimal use is much greater than for CISC compilers, which gives the compiler writer an additional burden.

Finally, the reduced instruction set itself also causes trouble. Some instructions that CISC compiler writers take for granted—MULTIPLY, for example—have to be synthesized in a variety of ways, depending on the operands.

Multiple Register Sets

By not having any microcode, a substantial amount of chip area is freed up on RISC chips for other purposes. Some, but not all, RISC machines use this new-found chip area for implementing a large number of CPU registers, to reduce the number of LOADs and STOREs. The subject of how these registers are organized is so important that we will devote the entire next section to the subject of registers.

Open Issues

Despite all these points of commonality, RISC designers do not agree on everything. A number of design issues are by no means settled. For one thing, a key question is how much of the hardware should be visible to the compiler writer. The problem of interlocks following a LOAD as discussed above is a typical one. One camp says that the machine simply cannot do a LOAD in one cycle, so the compiler writer should know about this property and learn to live with it. The other camp says it should be hidden by automatic interlocking.

If interlocking is visible, what about the cache? Can the compiler writer make the assumption that a variable just used will still be in the cache, and thus can be accessed more quickly than one in memory? Can he skip the delay slot following a LOAD and use the newly-loaded register in the very next instruction, or is this like playing Russian Roulette?

Byte ordering (little endian versus big endian) is still a hot topic. The MIPS chip finesses the problem by being configurable either way. Is this a good idea? It clearly costs some hardware and chip area that could be used for other things.

The RISC I has a bit in each instruction that tells whether the condition codes should be set. While setting the condition codes is frequently useful on arithmetic instructions, there is no consensus about whether MOVEs should set them. Adding a bit gives the compiler writer the choice on every MOVE. On the other hand, the MIPS chip does not have condition codes at all. It can test and jump in one instruction. Which way is better is a hotly debated issue. There are numerous other design issues that have not been settled.

8.1.3. Register Usage

The goal of every RISC machine is to execute one instruction per cycle on the average. Since LOADs and STOREs typically require two cycles, this average can only be achieved if the compiler or reorganizer is successful in filling 100 percent of the delay slots behind each of them (not to mention the delay slots following

JUMPs). It stands to reason that the fewer LOADs and STOREs there are, the fewer cycles will be wasted due to the compiler's inability to fill them with something useful.

For this reason, compilers for RISC machines make heavy use of registers in order to reduce the memory traffic (i.e., the number of LOADs and STOREs). Not only do RISC machines have substantially more registers than machines like the 80386 and 68030 (500 registers is not unusual), but more importantly, they are organized in a different way. Building a machine like the PDP-11 or 680x0, except with 512 registers instead of 8 or 16, would be counterproductive. Not only would the 16-bit instructions all become 32 bits to accommodate the 9-bit register fields, but the time to save all the registers on procedure calls would become prohibitively expensive.

In Sec. 8.1.2, we discussed several design principles for RISC machines, the first of which says to analyze the applications to see how they spend their time. People have done precisely that with respect to memory traffic. The most important conclusion is that a large percentage of the total memory traffic is related to procedure calls. Parameters must be passed, registers must be saved, and the return address must be stacked on the call and unstacked on the return. All of these actions generate memory traffic.

The designers of the RISC I (Patterson and Séquin, 1982) thought of an ingenious way to eliminate nearly all of this traffic. Their method, now known as **overlapping register windows,** has been adopted by other RISC machines as well. We will describe it in general terms below. The exact details vary slightly among implementations.

When overlapping register windows are used, the CPU contains a large number of registers, but at any instant only a subset of them, usually 32, is visible. These 32 registers are shown in Fig. 8-8, where they are designated R0 through R31. On most RISC machines the registers are 32 bits wide, but 64 bits or other widths are also possible.

The registers are divided into four distinct groups as illustrated in Fig. 8-8. In the RISC I, these groups consisted of 10, 6, 10, and 6 registers, respectively. However, more recent designs have made them all the same size (8 registers per group). For simplicity, in our discussion we will make this latter assumption.

The first group holds global variables and pointers. These are not specific to any one procedure, but are used by many procedures throughout the program. It is up to the compiler to decide what to put in each register. In some RISC machines, R0 is hardwired to the constant 0. Reads from it yield a 0 and writes to it have no effect.

The second group of registers, R8 through R15, holds the incoming parameters. Most procedures have parameters, supplied by the calling procedure. In traditional computers, these parameters are pushed onto the stack one at a time, just before the CALL instruction. When overlapping register windows are used, the procedure parameters are put into R8, R9, and so on up to R15 instead of being pushed onto

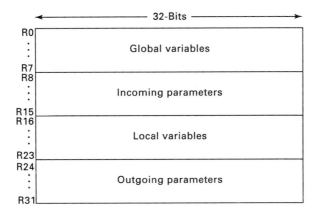

Fig. 8-8. The 32 registers visible to a program at any instant of time.

the stack. Not putting them on the stack eliminates STOREs when they are being passed and eliminates LOADs when they are accessed by the called procedure. If there are more than eight parameters, or if a parameter is more than one word, those parameters that cannot be passed in registers are passed on the stack in the conventional way. However, from Fig. 8-2(c) and similar measurements, we see that for most procedures eight parameters is probably overkill.

Registers R16 through R23 are available for local variables. From Fig. 8-2(b) and other measurements, it is clear that in most cases eight is enough. For those procedures that need more than eight words of local variables, the excess are kept on the stack, just as with excess procedure parameters. Still, if 80 or 90 percent of the procedures do not need to use the stack at all, either for accessing their parameters or for their local variables, we have made a substantial dent in the memory traffic and hence greatly reduced the numbers of LOADs and STOREs, and thus unfilled delay slots.

The final group of registers, R24 through R31, is used to pass outgoing parameters to called procedures. Instead of pushing these parameters onto the stack, they are put here. As usual, if we run out of registers, the excess parameters go on the stack.

By itself, this scheme is cute, but not terribly interesting. The real power comes from the presence of a large amount of on-chip storage, in this case in the form of a register file, say, 520 registers for this example. In Fig. 8-9(a) we have reproduced the situation of Fig. 8-8, with the addition of a variable *CWP* (Current Window Pointer) that points to register R8. When the current procedure, *A*, calls another procedure, *B*, the *CWP* pointer is incremented by 16 so that it points to 24.

When procedure *B* starts up, the situation is as shown in Fig. 8-9(b). References to R0 through R7 still use the eight global registers, as before, but R8 through R32 now refer to a different set of 24 registers. In particular, R8 (*B*'s first input parameter) now contains *A*'s first output parameter. Thus *A* can pass its parameters

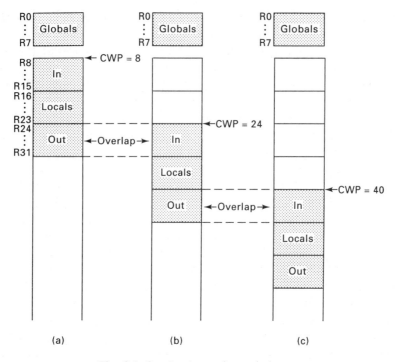

Fig. 8-9. Overlapping register windows.

to *B* without using memory, and *B* can access them without using memory. The reason that *A* and *B* can communicate this way is that eight of the registers overlap, as shown. When *B* calls *C*, *CWP* is advanced again, and the same relative situation holds.

In effect, the register file is being used as a kind of stack, with *CWP* being the stack pointer. Whenever a machine instruction references R0 through R7, the global registers are used, but R8 always means the register pointed to by *CWP*. Only the 24 registers starting at *CWP* (plus the eight globals) are accessible at any instant. *CWP* is advanced upon procedure calls and set back upon returns, but otherwise cannot be touched by ordinary user programs. (The operating system can save and restore it, however, when switching processes.)

To make the scheme of Fig. 8-9 work, the compiler must obey certain conventions, but these are not difficult to understand. When passing parameters to a called procedure, the caller must put the first one in R24, the second one in R25, and so on, with the seventh one in R30 and the eighth one, if any, as the first one on the real memory stack. R31 is reserved for the return address. Similarly, when the called procedure accesses its parameters, it must use R8 to access the first one, R9 to access the second one, and so on, with the seventh one coming from R14 and the eighth one, if any, from the real memory stack. The return address can be found in

R15. As long as all calling procedures and all called procedures obey the rules, there is no ambiguity and the scheme works fine.

When a parameter is longer than one word, it is up to the compiler to handle it, but a typical solution is to put the parameter itself onto the memory stack, and pass a pointer to it in the appropriate register. For long parameters after the seventh one, there is no need to pass a pointer in memory to a parameter in memory (even a one-word parameter); it is sufficient just to pass the parameter itself.

If the program gets nested deeply enough in calls (for example, due to recursion), the entire register file eventually will fill up. An additional call will have no place to put its registers. The usual solution is to design the hardware so that the attempt to advance *CWP* causes a trap. The trap handler then saves the first register window, starting at R8 in Fig. 8-9(a), by copying it to memory. If the calling continues, another trap occurs on the next call, and more registers are saved to memory. In this manner, the register file is used as a kind of circular buffer. Some administration is needed to keep track of what is in the registers and what is in memory, but that is not difficult to do. In practice, programs that are so deeply recursive that they overflow the register file are relatively rare.

By now it should be clear that overlapping register windows greatly reduce the number of memory references for parameters and the return address. It should also be clear that this scheme has little to do with RISC machines, and could equally well be implemented on a CISC chip. The reason, however, that it was invented in the RISC context is that such a large register file takes up a substantial amount of area on the CPU chip. On a conventional CPU, the chip is so full of microcode that there is no room for so many registers. Only by getting rid of the microcode is chip area freed up for the large register file.

Once we have gotten rid of the microcode, however, a large register file is not the only candidate for the empty chip real estate. Another possibility is a cache memory. A cache has the advantage that it holds not only data, but also recently used instructions. Furthermore, it does not enforce a rigid split with a fixed number of globals, a fixed number of parameters, and a fixed number of locals, as the register window scheme does. By adapting dynamically to the actual usage pattern, it is potentially more efficient.

Working against the cache is the fact that every cache entry has three parts, the valid bit, the tag, and the data (see Fig. 4-29). The first two take up chip area but cannot be used for storing data. They are a form of overhead and reduce the efficiency of chip usage.

In addition, given *CWP* and the register number (R0 through R31), it is easy for the hardware to find the proper register by a simple calculation. Using a cache, a full memory address must be calculated and moved around (instead of just a register number), and part of it must be extracted and compared with one or more tags, depending on the cache organization. The circuitry used for these comparisons also uses up chip area, and the comparisons themselves take time. All in all, the relative merits of register files versus on-chip caches are still being studied.

Register Allocation

The overlapping register window architecture presented above works best when all, or nearly all, of the local variables are in registers. For small procedures, there is often no problem, but for larger ones there may be more variables than there are registers available for them. In this case some must be spilled into memory, as described above.

To minimize this problem, and in keeping with the RISC design philosophy of pushing as much work as possible onto the compiler, most RISC compilers make a great effort to optimize register usage to reduce the number of variables that must be kept in memory. A common approach is to time-share individual registers over several variables that are used during disjoint intervals within a procedure. The basic idea is best illustrated by an example, such as the program of Fig. 8-10.

		n	num	$ones$	$zeros$	$half$	res
1	function $MostlyZero(n:integer):boolean$;	O					
2	var $num, ones, zeros, half:integer$;						
3	$res:boolean$;						
4	begin						
5	$num := n * n$;	●	O				
6	$ones := 0$;			O			
7	$zeros := 0$;				O		
8	while $num > 0$ do						
9	begin						
10	$half := num$ div 2;					O	
11	if $2*half = num$						
12	then $zeros := zeros + 1$						
13	else $ones := ones + 1$;						
14	$num := half$		●			●	
15	end;						
16	if $zeros > ones$			●	●		
17	then $res := true$						O
18	else $res :=false$;						
19	$MostlyZero := res$						●
20	end;						

Fig. 8-10. An example program and the state of its variables. The empty circles show when each variable becomes alive and the filled-in ones show when they become dead.

At the left of Fig. 8-10 is a (somewhat arbitrary) 20-line Pascal function that takes one parameter, n, computes n^2, and then counts the number of 0 bits and 1 bits in the binary representation of n^2. If there are more 0s than 1s, it returns *true*, otherwise it returns *false*. High-order 0s (i.e. 0s to the left of the most significant bit of n^2) are not counted. It operates by successively dividing the number being tested in half to see if it is odd or even, thus telling it the value of the low-order bit. The test for odd-even is done on lines 10 and 11 (remember that dividing an odd number in half, and then doubling the quotient, does not give the original number back, whereas doing this with an even number does).

The function uses six variables: *n, num, ones, zeros, half,* and *res* (it could obviously have been written with fewer, but that is not the point here). The first of these, n, is a parameter; the rest are locals. At each point during the execution of the function, each variable is in one of two states.

A variable is said to be **live** if the value it contains is needed. For example, if the compiler were to generate code to store random garbage in the variable *zeros* on line 12, the function would fail to work properly. However, the same garbling of *zeros* on line 5 would not matter, because *zeros* will be assigned to shortly.

More formally, a variable V is live at a point P if there is a control flow path from the procedure's entry point through a statement that assigns a value to V and then on through P to another statement U which uses V without an intervening assignment to V between P and U. In Fig. 8-11(a), for example, we see that V is live between P and U because its value matters. In Fig. 8-11(b), on the other hand, V is not live between P and Q because it is going to get a new value at Q anyway. A variable that is not live is said to be **dead**.

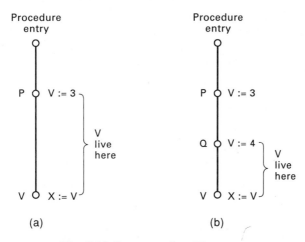

Fig. 8-11. Two examples of liveness.

The concept of liveness is important to register allocation because two or more variables can use the same register if they are never live simultaneously. Going back to Fig. 8-10 we see the live periods for each variable marked in the six columns at the right-hand side of the figure. In particular, note that n, *half*, and *res* are live in completely disjoint portions of the function. An optimizing compiler can assign all three variables to the same register. Because n is a input parameter, this register will be in the range R8 to R15 (see Fig. 8-8), but there is no problem with using an input register for local variables once the input parameter is dead. If there are unused input registers, they can be used for locals, too, of course.

A number of algorithms are known for maximizing the packing of variables into registers (Chaitin et al., 1981; Chow and Hennessy, 1984). The most popular of these use what is called **graph coloring**, in which each procedure is represented as a directed graph, with the statements as the nodes and the control paths between them as the arcs. Each variable is assigned a color in such a way that no two variables that are simultaneously live have the same color. The goal of the algorithm is to find the minimum number of colors required for the graph, the so-called **chromatic number**. If the chromatic number is less than or equal to the number of registers available, all variables can be kept in registers, and no LOADs or STOREs are needed.

8.1.4. The Great RISC versus CISC Debate

While RISC machines have increasingly many supporters, they also have no shortage of critics (e.g., see Colwell et al., 1985a, 1985b; Flynn et al., 1987; Patterson and Hennessy, 1985). Given the fundamental premise of the RISC camp—complex microprogrammed CPUs of the type that have dominated the computer industry for decades are a dead end and should be abandoned—it is not surprising that some people who are closely associated with CISC machines have taken a close and critical look at RISC technology and found problems that the RISC proponents have tried to sweep under the rug. In this section we will examine four key questions that go to the heart of the RISC-CISC controversy and present the arguments offered by both sides, to let the reader make an informed judgement.

Which Is Better for Running Programs Written in High-Level Languages?

No sane person programs in assembly language any more, so everyone wants to know whether RISC architectures are better than CISC architectures when it comes to running programs written in Ada, C, FORTRAN, Modula 2, Pascal, and other high-level languages. The question is simple, but the answer is not. To start with, what does "better" mean?

The obvious answer is: "faster." One could simply run a collection of important high-level language programs on RISCs and CISCs to see which is faster. Unfortunately, **benchmarking**, as this process is called, opens a real can of worms (Serlin, 1986). The first problem is: which language should the benchmark programs be written in? FORTRAN programs tend to be large and unstructured, with few procedure calls and many GOTOs. Since RISC machines are good at procedure calls and bad at jumps, would such a comparison be fair to the RISC side?

The next question is: what kind of programs should be included in the benchmarks? Small, highly recursive programs like the towers of Hanoi and Ackermann's function really fly on RISC machines, but are they representative of real work loads?

What about I/O? Experimental RISC machines typically have only rudimentary I/O, whereas many real programs are I/O limited. Is it fair to exclude I/O from the comparison?

Should floating-point programs be included, and if so, how much weight should they be given? Without special hardware assistance, RISC machines are not good at floating-point calculations. Many cannot even do integer multiplication and division, after all. And floating point comes in three varieties: single (32-bit), double (64-bit), and extended (128-bit) precision. Which should be used?

Another major factor that makes benchmarking tricky is factoring out the influence of the compiler. If a RISC machine outperforms a VAX or an 80386, who is to say that the RISC architecture is better? Maybe it simply has an optimizing compiler that does a great job on the graph coloring problem or otherwise makes much better use of the registers than the VAX or 80386 compiler.

In a similar vein, real programs use other resources than just the CPU. How can one tell if the result of running complex test programs reflects differences in the machine architecture, or perhaps differences in the performance of the underlying operating system, page size, or paging algorithm? Suppose a RISC machine beats a VAX when both of them run UNIX but suppose the same VAX then outperforms the RISC machine when running VMS. Which machine is really faster, and how much of the performance depends on the architecture, as opposed to the different compilers, operating systems, and the specific test programs chosen?

One final point regarding published comparisons is the old adage: "Figures don't lie, but liars figure." If the person or organization making the study (e.g., a computer vendor) has an axe to grind, one has to keep in mind the possibility that many programs were benchmarked and only the most favorable ones were included in the published results.

All this said, in Fig. 8-12 we present some comparisons of the Berkeley RISC I with popular CISC machines on a collection of UNIX benchmarks devised by the Department of Defense for comparing architectures (Patterson and Piepho, 1982). While one can quibble with many issues relating to benchmarking in general, it seems safe to say that if two professors and a class of graduate students at Berkeley can design and implement a RISC chip that outperforms a number of microprocessors and minicomputers designed by practicing professional engineers, the RISC idea undoubtedly has some merit.

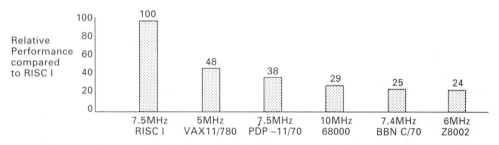

Fig. 8-12. Comparison of RISC I with five other computers. None of the others is even half as fast as the RISC I.

Given all the difficulties with running real programs, a commonly used approach is to create synthetic benchmark programs that have the same instruction mix as some measured sample of real programs. These artificial benchmarks typically do no I/O at all, so all they really test is the compiler and CPU performance. In the 1970s, Curnow and Wichman (1975) of the National Physical Laboratory in England developed a synthetic benchmark that measured floating-point performance in **whetstones** per second. (A whetstone is defined as a statistically "average" floating-point instruction.)

A successor to the whetstone, naturally called the **dhrystone** (Weicker, 1984), is now widely used to compare RISC and CISC machines. Unlike the whetstone, the dhrystone measures only integer computations. Although the results are still affected by factors such as compiler quality, register allocation, and cache performance, the number of dhrystones per second that a computer can execute gives at least a rough measure of its performance.

Figure 8-13 shows the number of dhrystones for several RISC and CISC machines. As usual, all benchmarks should be taken with a grain (or better yet, an imperial gallon) of salt. Still, when four RISC chips from four different vendors all outperform IBM's top-of-the-line 3090/200 mainframe, it becomes hard to deny that RISC machines are very fast.

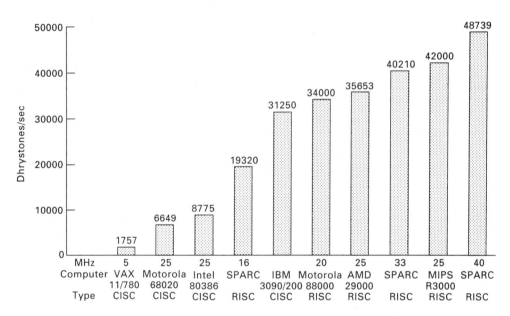

Fig. 8-13. Number of dhrystones/sec for a variety of RISC and CISC computers. As a rough approximation, 2000 dhrystones is 1 MIPs.

Perhaps the most difficult factor to remove when comparing two machines is the technology. Is an ECL RISC machine faster than a CMOS CISC machine? Probably. ECL transistors switch much faster than CMOS transistors. The RISC and CISC machines being compared invariably use different kinds of semiconductors, different clock rates, different buses, and different memory chips (not to mention different caches, different memory management units, different numbers of wait states, and different pipelining techniques). Under these conditions it is hard to compare the architectures independent of the implementations.

One measure that is sometimes used to factor out the implementation is program size. However, with memory getting cheaper every year, size is increasingly less important, and besides, it does not correlate well with speed. Another metric thought to be implementation independent is memory traffic. The idea here is that one can write a simulator for any computer and then have the simulator count the total number of memory references, both for code and data. If two simulated computers run the same benchmark program and one of them executes it in 1,000,000 memory references while the other needs only 800,000, all things being equal, the second computer is better.

However, even this seemingly technology-independent measure is not as foolproof as it first appears. The 80386 and many other computers prefetch instructions before they are needed. Every time a jump is taken, the contents of the prefetch buffer must be discarded. The memory cycles needed to prefetch these discarded instructions do not show up in the simulation runs, but can often add 25 percent extra to the bus load.

Although the performance figures given favor the RISC machines, in all fairness it should be pointed out that the CISC machines being benchmarked are greatly burdened by having to be compatible with ancient machines. When a group at IBM is told to build the fastest computer it can, the designers are all excited at the challenge. Several milliseconds later, when they are also told that this new wonder *must* run every program anybody, anywhere in the world has ever written for any IBM mainframe since 1964, their spirits may go down a bit. Likewise, if the 80486 did not have to be compatible with everything going back to the 8088, the Intel designers could have built a very different machine.

From this perspective, one of the main factors in the speed of RISC machines is that they are all brand new architectures, free of the mistakes of the past. If a design team is told to go out and design a new CISC from scratch specifically with the goal of running C and Pascal, the resulting machine will certainly be much faster than any existing CISC machine.

How Much of the Gain Is Due to the Large Register File?

It is abundantly clear that the overlapping register window scheme makes a major contribution to the performance of the RISC I, RISC II, and SPARC chips, among others. On the other hand, the MIPS chip does not use overlapping windows, and it also delivers high performance. Still, it is interesting to speculate about how much of the performance is due to the register file.

Hitchcock and Sprunt (1985) went further than that, and wrote simulators for the RISC I, 68000, and VAX. They made three versions of each simulator, one with overlapping register windows, one with nonoverlapping register windows, and one with a single set of registers. They then ran a standard set of benchmarks on all nine machines by hand-modifying the compiled assembly code to fit the register model. In this way the effect of the register file can be clearly separated from the large (VAX), medium (68000) or small (RISC I) instruction set. The performance metric used was the total volume of CPU-memory traffic.

On the whole, the results are as one might suspect. The modified VAX with overlapping register windows was up to twice as fast as a normal one, and the 68000 with overlapping windows was up to four times as fast. On the other hand, removing the window scheme from the RISC I slowed it down by as much as a factor of nine. The only counterintuitive result is that on extremely recursive programs, overlapping windows actually slow down execution due to insufficient windows (a full window has to be saved on almost every call and restored on every return). Their conclusion is that overlapping register windows are a good idea, but that this says little about RISC versus CISC architecture.

To this, the RISC supporters reply that a large register window is only possible due to the simplicity of the RISC chips, and especially the lack of microcode. At any point in time, it is possible to put n transistors on a chip. Some of them are needed for the basic control unit, but the rest are available for other use. They can be used for storing a large microprogram or for storing a large register file, but these two uses are clearly in competition for the same transistors.

Thus the reply to Hitchcock and Sprunt is that the comparison of an overlapping register VAX with an overlapping register RISC machine is not fair. The former would take up much more chip area than the latter. Put in other words, if a RISC designer were given the amount of chip area an overlapping register VAX would need, he could either include a much larger register file, an on-chip memory cache, or other features to improve performance.

How Good Are RISC Machines Overall?

The initial benchmark programs presented in the RISC literature tended to be very small. The longest test reported by Patterson and Piepho (1982), for example, ran less than 7 seconds. From these data it is clear that if your application consists of running tiny recursive functions like the towers of Hanoi all day, RISC is the way to go. But what if you want to run old fat COBOL programs? The results are less clear.

The initial attempts to run Smalltalk and Lisp programs on the RISC I were disappointing. This led Patterson to design the **SOAR (Smalltalk On A Risc)** and **SPUR (Symbolic Processing Using Risc)** chips (Ungar et al., 1984).

Even though these chips were more successful, the issue arises of whether RISC technology is suitable for computers that have to run multiple applications, and especially languages appreciably different from C. Some evidence comes from Coutant et al. (1986). They report on building a COBOL compiler for a RISC machine. Since no decimal arithmetic or other COBOL-type instructions were available, they wrote a library of procedures to do those things that a CISC machine normally does in microcode.

Furthermore, they were able to take advantage of compile-time information to enhance performance. For example, when moving a string, the compiler can call one procedure when the source and destination fields are the same size, and a different one when they are not. All in all, the resulting performance met the project's goals.

In addition to raw performance and language issues, other factors also are important to vendors and users. RISC chips are much simpler than CISC chips and use fewer transistors (even taking into account the large register file). This fact makes them easier to design and less likely to be subject to recall due to microcode bugs. It also reduces the time between design and shipment, a crucial issue in a rapidly moving and competitive industry.

Because RISC designs use relatively few transistors, they are well suited to very high-speed chips based on GaAs (Gallium Arsenide) instead of silicon. These fast chips have many fewer transistors than conventional silicon chips, so there is often not enough room for complex microprograms.

On the other hand, CISC machines lend themselves better to a complete family of machines spanning a wide range in price and performance, such as the 360 series. Computer vendors like the family idea because it makes it possible to provide personal computers, minicomputers, and mainframes that all run the same architecture. The smaller models can be microprogrammed and achieve their functionality in software (microcode) while the larger ones can be hardwired for speed. RISC architectures do not lend themselves as well to this concept.

Which Are Easier to Write: RISC Compilers or CISC Compilers?

Compilers for RISC machines clearly have some problems that conventional compilers do not have. Foremost among these are handling delayed loads, stores, and jumps.

When a compiler for a LOAD/STORE machine sees an assignment statement like

$A := B$

its natural reaction is to generate code like

```
LOAD B, R0                ; load B into register R0
STORE R0, A               ; store register R0 in A
```

With an interlocked delayed load machine, this code will work but will be inefficient due to the automatic delay slot introduced by the hardware. With a noninterlocked machine, it will give incorrect results because the register will not yet have the correct value at the time the STORE is executed.

Similarly, when the compiler is parsing an **if** statement, it normally generates code to evaluate the condition and jump to the **else** part (or the next statement) if the condition is false. The statement

if $A < B$ **then** $MIN := A$

normally would generate code like

```
    LOAD A, R0          ; load A into register R0
    LOAD B, R1          ; load B into register R1
    CMP R0, R1          ; compare A to B
    JGE L1              ; if A >= B, jump to label L1
    STORE R0, MIN       ; store A in MIN
L1:                     ; next statement begins here
```

For a RISC machine with delayed jumps, this code is incorrect because the statement following the JGE will be executed whether or not the jump is taken. Putting a NO-OP after the JGE makes the code correct, but inefficient. In this simple example, we see two things of note. First, of the five instructions, three of them are delayed. Second, there is not much opportunity for reorganizing the assembly code to fill any of the delay slots. Code from far away will have to be found.

For these examples, it should be clear that the RISC compiler has its work cut out for it trying to produce code that is both correct and reasonably efficient. None of these problems exist with CISC machines, thus making code generation easier.

Furthermore, nearly all RISC compilers have sophisticated register allocation algorithms such as the graph coloring one mentioned above. While these algorithms improve the code by packing more variables into a limited number of registers, they also greatly increase the complexity of the compiler. Squeezing the last drop of performance out of the registers is much less critical in CISC machines because the penalty for memory usage is much less. A simple assignment of one variable to another, as in $A := B$, can often best be done with a single memory-memory MOVE instruction, avoiding the registers altogether.

On the other hand, RISC architectures also have a property that makes life easier for the compiler writer. On most RISC machines, there is usually only one plausible way to compile any high-level language construction. The operands must be fetched into registers, the computation done, and the results returned to memory. CISC machines suffer from a multitude of choices. As an example, consider:

$A := B + C$

One way to compile this for a CISC with register-register, register-memory, and memory-memory instructions (like the PDP-11 or VAX) is:

```
    MOV B, R0           ; load B into register R0
    ADD C, R0           ; R0 is now equal to B + C
    MOV R0, A           ; store B + C in A
```

This code sequence requires three instructions to be fetched from memory and three memory references for data, one on each instruction. However, an alternative code sequence is:

MOV B, A	; copy B to A
ADD C, A	; add C to A to form B + C

Now we have performed the computation in only two instructions. Given the high interpretation overhead on a microprogrammed computer, getting rid of an instruction is always worth something.

However, interpretation overhead is not the only cost. The overall performance depends in part on how the ADD to memory works. If this instruction must first fetch A and C into the CPU, add them, and then store the result in memory, this code sequence requires two instruction fetches and five memory references for data. On the other hand, if a cache is present, only the first reference to A really counts; the others are satisfied out of the cache and are essentially free.

Because CISC machines have many ways of performing the same computation, the compiler has to devote a lot of effort to analyzing all of them. In the worst case, the algorithm may even be implementation dependent. For example, it is not inconceivable that on a family of CISC machines, the three-instruction sequence is better on the low-end machines that have no cache, but the two-instruction sequence is better on the high-end machines that have a cache.

As a final example, consider what would happen if the variable C in the original assignment statement were replaced by a constant. The analysis is completely different because immediate mode instructions are now applicable. Furthermore, if the constant happens to be −1 or +1, it may be best to use the machine's INCREMENT and DECREMENT instructions. The compiler must deal with all these possibilities if it is to generate the best code in all cases.

RISC machines have none of this complexity. The only way to do the computation is to fetch the operands into registers, perform the calculation there, and store the result.

8.1.5. An Example RISC Architecture: SPARC

In 1987, Sun Microsystems announced an open RISC architecture, called **SPARC (Scalable Processor ARChitecture)**, that would be the basis of future Sun products (e.g., Sun-4 series and SPARCstation). SPARC is an *architecture*, not a chip. The SPARC architecture reference manual describes what the machine looks like to the assembly language programmer or compiler writer, but does not specify how it is implemented. Sun also defined a standard memory management unit for use with SPARC chips.

About half a dozen semiconductor vendors were then licensed to produce SPARC chips using different technologies (CMOS, ECL, GaAs, gate array, custom VLSI, etc.). The intention was to encourage competition among chip vendors, in order to improve performance, reduce prices, and make an attempt at establishing the SPARC architecture as an industry standard.

For our purposes, SPARC is an interesting example because it is closely based on the pioneering RISC I, RISC II, and SOAR work of Patterson and Séquin at Berkeley. In this section we will describe the SPARC in some detail, starting with an overview, and then covering the registers, instructions, floating-point unit, interrupts, and memory management. After that we will give a simple example program for the SPARC. We will conclude by comparing the SPARC to the 80386 and 68030.

Technical Overview of the SPARC

The SPARC definition includes not only the CPU, called the **IU (Integer Unit)**, but also the **FPU (Floating Point Unit)** and an optional user-supplied **CP (CoProcessor)**. In addition, most SPARC-based systems will have also a memory management unit and cache, as illustrated in Fig. 8-14.

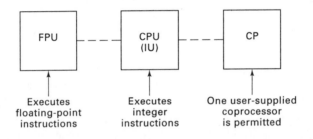

Fig. 8-14. A SPARC system may have an IU, FPU, and coprocessor.

The SPARC is basically a 32-bit design. It has a (paged) linear address space, consisting of 2^{32} individually addressable 8-bit bytes. Words are 32 bits long and must be aligned on word boundaries (i.e., addresses that are multiples of four). This alignment requirement not only improves performance, but allows certain useful optimizations in the instruction set. Memory is big endian, like the 680x0 family, with byte 0 on the left-hand (high-order) end of a 32-bit word.

All instructions and registers are 32 bits, even the floating-point registers. However, instructions are provided for loading and storing 8-, 16-, 32-, and 64-bit quantities into the 32-bit registers, the latter using two consecutive registers. Like other RISC machines, the SPARC is a LOAD/STORE architecture, so all operations take place on operands located in the 32-bit registers.

The SPARC is itself a uniprocessor architecture, but provision has been made for connecting up multiple SPARC chips to form a multiprocessor. Special instructions have been included for multiprocessor synchronization, for example.

The SPARC architecture has been carefully specified to allow for highly pipelined implementations. Among other aspects, it defines delayed loads, stores, branches, calls, and returns. A typical implementation has a four-stage pipeline, as shown in Fig. 8-15. During the first cycle, the instruction word is fetched from memory. During the second, it is decoded. During the third, it is executed. Finally, during the fourth, the results are written back.

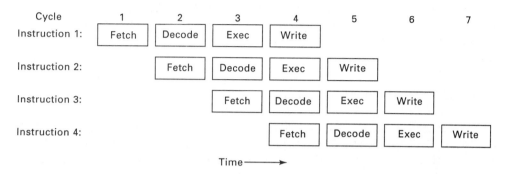

Fig. 8-15. Four-stage pipelining.

SPARC Registers

The SPARC has an overlapping register window scheme, very similar to the one described in Sec. 8.1.3. At any instant, 32 32-bit registers are visible. A *CWP* variable in the hardware points to the current set. The total size of the register file is not part of the architecture, allowing more registers to be added as the technology improves, up to a maximum of 32 windows (*CWP* is 5 bits). A maximum-length register file is then 32×16 for the windows plus eight for the globals, for a maximum of 520 registers. The initial implementations have about one-quarter of that.

The SPARC registers are shown in Fig. 8-16. The registers are numbered in the reverse order from Fig. 8-8 because *CWP* is *decremented* rather than *incremented* when a procedure is called. Thus the calling procedure puts the parameters in R8 through R15, and these registers become R24 through R31 in the called procedure. In other words, when a procedure is called, the window slides "upwards" rather than "downwards."

Some of the SPARC registers have specific functions, as shown in Fig. 8-16. All of them have alternative names, which are used by the compilers and assembly language programmers. G0 is hardwired to 0. Stores into it do not change its value. G1 through G7 are global, and may contain integer variables, pointers to tables, or other important data items.

O0 through O7 are the output registers, used by procedures to pass parameters to procedures being called. The first parameter goes in O0, the next in O1, and so on. O6 (SP) is used as a pointer to the memory stack. The stack is used for excess parameters, windows that have been spilled into memory due to register file overflow, dynamically allocated stack space, saved floating-point registers, pointers

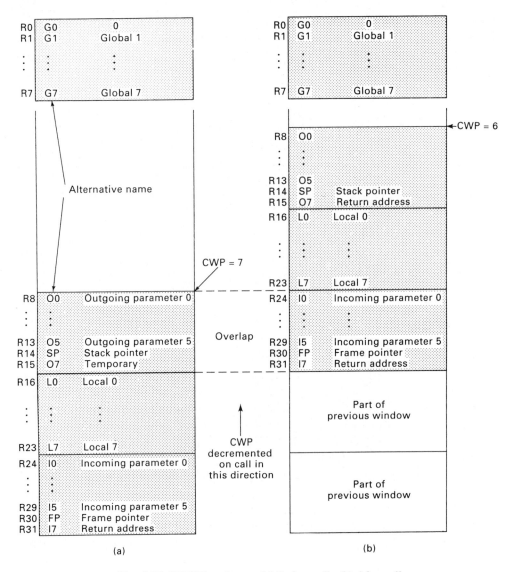

Fig. 8-16. SPARC registers. (a) Before call. (b) After call.

to buffers where called procedures can return structures and arrays, and so on. The CALL instruction deposits the return address in O7.

The eight registers for local variable, L0 through L7, can be used any way the programmer or compiler sees fit. The eight input variables, I0 through I7, are the parameters passed to the current procedure by its caller. Unused registers may be used for additional local variables. I6 (FP) is the frame pointer and is used to address variables in the stack frame. Unlike SP, which may change as the procedure executes, FP points at the same memory word during the entire procedure execution, thus making it more suitable for indexing from than SP. I7 contains the address to return to when the procedure has finished.

When a program first starts up, all the register windows are available for it to use. As procedures are called, windows are used up. Suppose that after a while, the program is so deep in calls that it has managed to use up all n windows. If another call has to be made, the oldest register window has to be saved to the stack. The question arises how the computer knows that all the windows are in use.

The solution lies in a special register, the **WIM (Window Invalid Mask)** that is visible only to the kernel. The WIM has one bit per window. When the *CWP* is decremented to advance to a new window, the hardware checks to see if the WIM bit for the new window is set. If so, a trap occurs. The trap handler then saves the window. In this manner, no software checking is needed on each call.

Normally, the WIM contains all 0 bits except for a single 1 bit marking the oldest register window currently in use. When that window is reached, a trap occurs, the oldest register window is saved on the stack, and the WIM is rotated one bit, to mark the next lowest window as the oldest.

A nontrivial amount of overhead is incurred when the windows wrap around. A trap occurs, registers must be saved, and the WIM must be updated. It is therefore useful to restrict window usage wherever possible.

One optimization that many SPARC compilers make is handling **leaf procedures** in a special way. A leaf procedure is one that does not call any other procedures (i.e., is a leaf of the call graph). If a leaf procedure can live with 6 registers for input parameters and locals combined, the compiler can cheat and have it use what is left of O0 through O5 for locals.

When this optimization is used, the caller puts the parameters in O0 through O5, as usual, and then issues a normal CALL, which deposits the return address in O7. The SAVE instruction, which is what actually advances the window, is omitted. The leaf procedure runs in the usual way, except that its local variables go in O5, O4, and so on, instead of in L0 through L7. When it is done, it jumps indirectly through O7, but does not execute the RESTORE instruction that normally increments *CWP*. Measurements have shown that something like 40 percent of all procedures are leaf procedures, so this optimization is frequently applicable.

SPARC Instruction Set

All SPARC instructions occupy a full word and start on a word boundary. Four formats are used, distinguished by the first two bits, as illustrated in Fig. 8-17. All arithmetic and logical instructions have three operands and calculate

dest := source1 *op* source2

In format 1a, both sources are registers; in format 1b, one source is a register and one is a constant in the range −4096 to +4095. Bit 13 selects between them. In both cases, the destination is always a register. Sufficient encoding space is provided for up to 64 instructions, some of which are currently reserved for future use. (Can it be long before we see some company advertising the "World's most complex RISC machine"?)

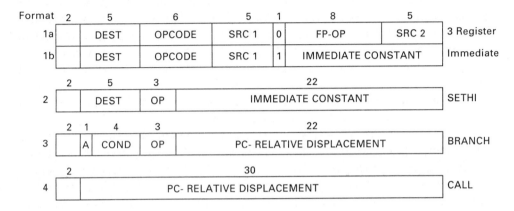

Fig. 8-17. SPARC instruction formats.

The other three formats are each used for one specific (but important) instruction. We will come back to them shortly.

As mentioned above, the SPARC is a LOAD/STORE architecture. Measurements have shown that about 20 percent of all instructions are LOADs, which on the SPARC require one delay slot. The instruction following a LOAD should not use the register being loaded. It is hardware interlocked, however, to prevent naughty instructions from wreaking havoc.

LOADs and STOREs may use either format 1a or 1b, with DEST being the register to be loaded or stored, respectively. The low-order 19 bits of the instruction determine how the effective memory address is calculated. Two addressing modes are provided (formats 1a and 1b):

1. Memory address = sum of SRC1 and SRC2

2. Memory address = sum SRC1 and a signed 13-bit constant

All 32 registers can be used for both source registers and destination registers.

In particular, if G0 (the constant 0) is used as SRC1, then the first addressing mode reduces to register indirect addressing, and the second one, which is normally indexed mode, becomes direct addressing for the bottom and top 4K of memory.

It is not possible to directly address an arbitrary word of memory in a single instruction. However, the compiler can arrange to use global registers to point to tables of 32-bit constants, addresses, or pointers to data structures. In this way, a memory address stored in a table accessible via a global register can be loaded into a register and then used in a subsequent register indirect LOAD instruction.

Although this method works, it requires two LOADs and necessitates that two delay slots be filled. A better way to access an arbitrary memory address is to use the SETHI instruction (format 2 in Fig. 8-17). This instruction copies its 22-bit immediate operand into the high-order 22 bits of any specified register, and sets each of the low-order 10 bits to 0. A following LOAD or STORE can now use index mode (format 1b) to supply the low-order 10 bits, thus making it possible to fetch any word in memory using direct addressing in two instructions. In practice, direct addressing rarely occurs, so it is in keeping with the RISC philosophy not to optimize it.

The user-mode integer SPARC instructions are listed in Fig. 8-18. Floating-point and coprocessor instructions are not given here.

The LOAD and STORE instructions are straightforward, with versions for 1, 2, 4, and 8 bytes. LDSTUB reads a byte from memory into a register, and simultaneously sets the byte in memory to eight 1s. This instruction is functionally similar to TSL on the 680x0, and serves the same purpose: synchronization in multiprocessor systems. SWAP exchanges a register and memory word, and is also used for multiprocessor synchronization.

The next group is for arithmetic. The instructions with CC in their name set the NZVC condition code bits. The others do not. On CISC machines, most instructions set the condition codes, but on a RISC machine that is undesirable because it restricts the compiler's freedom to move instructions around when trying to fill delay slots. If the original instruction order is A ... B ... C with A setting the condition codes and B testing them, the compiler cannot insert C between A and B if C sets the condition codes. For this reason, two versions of many instructions are provided, with the compiler normally using the one that does not set the condition codes, unless it is planning to test them later.

The SPARC does not have a multiplication instruction, but it does have MULSCC, which does one step of a multiplication, testing one bit and conditionally adding the multiplicand to the product. The advantage of MULSCC over a full MUL is that the former completes in one cycle, and the latter does not. Many multiplications are by small constants known at compile time. These are done by sequences of shifts and adds. The most general case is done by a library procedure that uses the operand with the fewest bits as the multiplier (to minimize the number of MULSCCs needed). The average multiplication (including ones where one factor is a constant) takes 6 cycles. When both are variables, the measured average is 24 cycles.

No division instruction is present. Divisions are done either using floating-point or entirely in software. Both are slow, but divisions are infrequent.

The next group consists of the tagged arithmetic instructions. In languages like C, Pascal, and Modula 2, the types of each variable are known at compile time. When the compiler sees two integer variables being added, it generates an integer

LDSB	Load signed byte
LDSH	Load signed halfword
LDUB	Load unsigned byte
LDUH	Load unsigned halfword
LD	Load word
LDD	Load double word

STB	Store byte
STH	Store halfword
ST	Store word
STD	Store double word

LDSTUB	Load/store unsigned byte
SWAP	Swap memory word with reg

ADD	Add
ADDCC	Add, set icc
ADDX	Add with carry
ADDXCC	Add with carry, set icc
SUB	Subtract
SUBCC	Subtract, set icc
SUBX	Subtract with carry
SUBXCC	Subtract with carry, set icc
MULSCC	Multiply step, set icc

TADDCC	Tagged add, set icc
TSUBCC	Tagged subtract, set icc
TADDCCTV	Tagged CC add, trap overflows
TSUBCCTV	Tagged CC sub, trap overflows

AND	Boolean AND
ANDCC	Boolean AND, set icc
ANDN	Boolean NAND
ANDNCC	Boolean NAND, set icc
OR	Boolean OR
ORCC	Boolean OR, set icc
ORN	Boolean NOR
ORNCC	Boolean NOR, set icc
XOR	Boolean exclusive OR
XORCC	Boolean exclusive OR, set icc
XNOR	Boolean excl. NOR
XNORCC	Boolean excl. NOR, set icc

SLL	Shift left logical
SRL	Shift right logical
SRA	Shift right arithmetic

Bxx	Conditional branch
Txx	Conditional trap
CALL	Procedure call
JMPL	Jump and link
SAVE	Advance register window
RESTORE	Move window backwards
RETT	Return from trap

SETHI	Set high 22 bits
UNIMP	Unimplemented instr (trap)
RD	Read a special register
WR	Write a special register
IFLUSH	Instruction cache flush

Fig. 8-18. SPARC integer instructions.

addition instruction. When it sees two floating-point variables being added, it generates a floating-point addition instruction. Simple as pie.

However, in dynamic languages, such as Smalltalk, Prolog, and Lisp, the compiler frequently does not know the type of the variables at compile time—assuming there is a compiler—as many of these languages are interpreted. Instead, variables are represented at run time as a tag and a value. Figure 8-19, for example, shows a representation with a 2-bit tag and a 30-bit value. An integer might have tag 00, a pointer tag 01, and so on.

Bits	30	2
	30-Bit value	Tag

Fig. 8-19. A tagged value.

One way to add two tagged values is to first inspect the tags, and then branch accordingly, depending on which of the 16 possible combinations occurred. The code for this is horrendously expensive. Since, in practice, most variables are integers (tag 00), the SPARC provides tagged ADD and SUB instructions that set the overflow bit or trap if either operand has a nonzero tag, or there is a genuine overflow. In this way, inspection of the tags has to be done much less often. Any CISC designer would be proud as a peacock to have these in his instruction set, but they can be carried out in one cycle and make a big performance difference, so they were included.

The Boolean group is analogous to the arithmetic group. It includes AND, OR, XOR, NAND, and NOR. The latter two are of questionable value, but they can be done in one cycle and require almost no additional hardware.

The shift group contains one left shift and two right shifts. The shifts are mostly used for simulating multiplication and division. Most CISC machines have a vast number of shift and rotate instructions, nearly all of them totally useless. Few compiler writers will spend restless nights mourning their absence.

The next instruction group contains the control transfers. The conditional branches use format 3 in Fig. 8-17. The COND field specifies the kind of branch (e.g., BLT, BLE, BEQ). The 22-bit DISPLACEMENT field gives the relative address of the target in *words* (not bytes), so conditional branches can go forward or backward by up to 8 megabytes. Remember that all instructions must be word-aligned in memory. Programmers who write procedures longer than 8 megabytes get what they deserve.

The ANNUL (A) bit is a trick to get rid of some delay slots. If it is 0 in a conditional branch, the delay slot is executed as usual. If it is 1, however, the delay slot is only executed if the branch is taken. If it is not taken, the instruction following the conditional branch is skipped.

The idea is that some taken-conditional-branches result from **if** statements and others from loops. In the latter case, the compiler can move the instruction at the top of the loop to the delay slot following the conditional branch at the end of the loop and set the ANNUL bit. This mechanism improves loop performance by filling an otherwise hard-to-fill delay slot.

The conditional traps are primarily used for overflow testing, but for reasons of symmetry, all 16 values of NZVC can be tested for.

Two ways are provided for calling procedures. The CALL instruction uses format 4 of Fig. 8-17 with a 30-bit PC relative *word* offset. This value is enough to reach any instruction within 4 gigabytes of the caller (i.e., the entire address space). The CALL instruction deposits the return address in O7.

The other way to call a procedure is by using JMPL, which uses format 1a or 1b, and allows the return address to be put in any register. This form is useful when the target address is computed during execution.

SAVE and RESTORE manipulate the register window and stack pointer. Both of them trap when the next (previous) window is not available. RETT is used to return from this or any other trap.

The last group contains some miscellaneous instructions. SETHI we have already discussed. UNIMP causes a trap when executed. It has a variety of somewhat arcane uses. RD and WR are used to read and write the special registers, such as the WIM. Some of these are only accessible in kernel mode. IFLUSH can be used to flush the internal instruction cache. Sometimes the operating system needs to do this.

A number of familiar CISC instructions that are missing from this list can be easily simulated using either G0 or a constant operand (format 1b). A few of these are given in Fig. 8-20. These **pseudoinstructions** are recognized by the SPARC assembler and are frequently generated by compilers.

Instruction	How to do it
MOV src,dst	OR src with G0 and store in dst
CMP src1,src2	SUBCC src1 from src2 and store in G0
TST src	ORCC src with G0 and store in G0
NOT dst	XNOR dst with G0
NEG dst	SUB dst from G0 and store in dst (2's complement)
INC dst	ADD 1 to dst
DEC dst	SUB 1 from dst
CLR dst	OR G0 with G0 and store in dst
NOP	SETHI G0 to 0

Fig. 8-20. SPARC pseudoinstructions.

SPARC Floating Point

Floating-point operations are usually (but not necessarily) done by a special coprocessor chip. The coprocessor is a passive device in the sense that it does not initiate instructions. When the CPU executes a floating-point instruction, the instruction is passed to the FPU for execution. As soon as the instruction has been handed off to the FPU, the CPU continues execution, in parallel with the FPU. Furthermore, the FPU may be able to perform multiple floating-point operations internally in parallel.

The FPU contains 32 32-bit registers. These can be used to hold 32 single-precision (i.e, 32-bit) floating-point operands, 16 double-precision (i.e., 64-bit) operands, or 8 extended-precision (i.e., 128-bit) operands. Double-precision operands occupy even-odd pairs, and extended ones occupy four consecutive registers.

The CPU has instructions to load and store the FPU's registers, but it has no direct path to the FPU itself. If it wants to transfer an operand between one of its registers and an FPU register, it must first store the operand in memory and then load it in the other device.

In addition to instructions for loading and storing the FPU's registers, the CPU can also test the FPU's registers and branch conditionally on the results. Like all other floating-point instructions, these are interlocked, so if the CPU tries to test a result before it is available, the CPU is simply delayed.

The FPU can execute about 20 floating-point instructions, most of them in single, double, or extended precision. All use format 1a in Fig. 8-17, with the floating-point opcode in the FP-OP field. Some of these do conversions between integers and the three floating-point formats, and the others do floating-point arithmetic, including addition, subtraction, multiplication, division, square root, exponent extraction, and comparison. The arithmetic instructions are all three-operand. The comparison instruction has two operands.

Provision is made for an additional coprocessor, but no instructions are defined for it, except for loading and storing its registers and testing its condition codes.

SPARC Interrupts and Traps

When a trap or interrupt occurs, the SPARC CPU advances the register window, stores the program counter and PSW in the new window, disables further interrupts, and transfers to the relevant handler. Each trap or interrupt has a number, and a dedicated kernel register (TBR) points to the base of the interrupt vector table. The interrupt handler may either run to completion and then return, or take care of its administration and then re-enable interrupts. In the latter case, it must explicitly check to see that the next window is also free, saving it if necessary before re-enabling. To avoid losing data, it is essential that the window following the current one be free at all times that interrupts are enabled or traps are possible.

The handler must be careful about which registers it uses. It may not touch either the input or output parameters, because these may overlap active windows. Only those locals that the interrupt hardware does not store values into may be used.

Three kinds of traps and one kind of interrupt are most frequent. The three traps are window overflow/underflow, page faults, and system call traps, and the interrupt is the I/O device completion interrupt. Window traps are handled quickly and without re-enabling interrupts. The contents of the next window is stored on the stack (or retrieved from the stack), the WIM is adjusted, and the handler returns from the trap. These operations are done by the operating system, without the user being aware of their existence.

The other traps and interrupts normally start with a generic handler. This routine saves the next window if need be, adjusts the WIM, and then dispatches to the appropriate code for handling the problem.

One other noteworthy trap is the floating-point trap. There is a bit present in the PSW that causes all floating-point operations to trap. When a program starts up, this bit is always set. When the first floating-point operation is performed, a trap occurs, and the operating system notes that the floating-point registers must henceforth be saved on every process switch. This scheme spares processes that do not use the FPU the overhead of having all 32 FPU registers saved on each trap to the operating system.

SPARC Memory Management

The MMU design is not formally part of the SPARC architecture, but Sun has defined a reference MMU to be used with SPARC chips. It is a relatively conventional device that supports a single paged 32-bit address space using three levels of tables, thus intermediate between the 80386 (two levels) and 68030 (four levels). The layout of the fields is shown in Fig. 8-21.

To avoid having to reload the tables when process switching occurs, the hardware can support multiple **contexts**, one per process. When a process is loaded into the machine, the operating system assigns it a unique context number. That context number is reserved for the process until it terminates. Current chips have 4096 contexts.

On every memory reference, the context number and the virtual address are presented to the MMU. Conceptually, the MMU uses the context number as an index into its context table to find the top-level page for that context (i.e., the process currently running). It then uses INDEX1 to select an entry from the top-level page table. That entry points to the next level of page table, and so on until the page is found. As usual in paging systems, to speed up the lookup, an associative memory is present.

SPARC-based computers normally support caching of memory words to reduce bus traffic. Less bus traffic means higher I/O throughput, and it also allows more

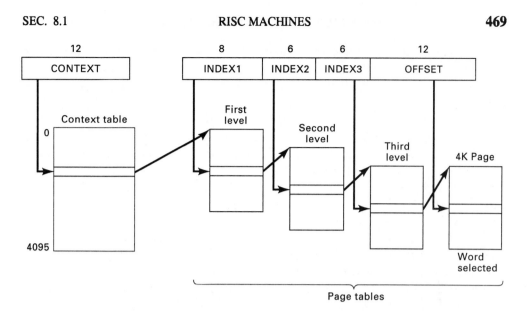

Fig. 8-21. SPARC memory management unit.

CPUs to share the same bus in a multiprocessor configuration. The position of the cache is somewhat unusual, and is illustrated in Fig. 8-22(a). When a virtual address is generated, it goes simultaneously to the MMU and the cache. On a cache hit, the MMU cycle is aborted and the cache provides the data to the CPU, FPU, or coprocessor.

This scheme can be contrasted with that of Fig. 8-22(b), in which all CPU-generated addresses first go through the MMU and then go to the cache, meaning that here the cache works with physical, rather than virtual addresses. All CPUs with an on-chip MMU, such as the 80386 and 68030, cache on physical addresses. The SPARC method has the advantage of potentially being faster, since the cache lookup and MMU mapping can proceed in parallel, instead of sequentially. In some SPARC machines, the MMU and cache controller are integrated into one chip, to reduce chip count and provide rapid communication between the two devices.

A Sample SPARC program

To give a better understanding of the SPARC architecture, we have translated the towers of Hanoi program of Fig. 5-48 to SPARC assembly language and listed it in Fig. 8-23.

For the most part, with the help of the comments in it, the program should be self-explanatory, but a few notes may be helpful. Symbols of the form %ix, %ox, and %lx are in, out, and local registers, respectively. For example, %l0 is local 0

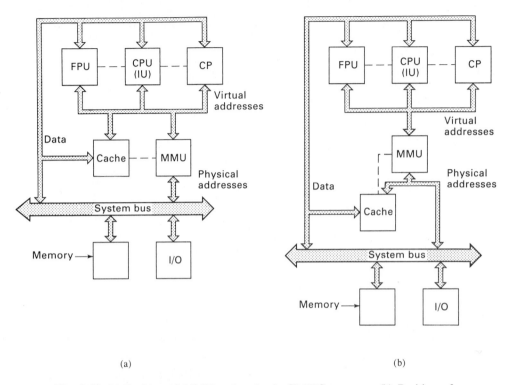

Fig. 8-22. (a) Position of MMU and cache in SPARC systems. (b) Position of MMU and cache in traditional systems.

(register 16). The notation %hi(*address*) tells the assembler to use the upper 22 bits of *address* as the operand for SETHI. Similarly, %lo(*address*) is the low-order 10 bits. The procedures .*writestr*, .*writenum*, and .*writecr* are library procedures that print a string, number and carriage return, respectively. By convention, library procedure names begin with a period and user procedure names have an underscore prepended to them.

The procedure begins with a SAVE instruction that advances the register window and also decrements the stack pointer by 112 bytes, reserving space for the register window (if it needs to be saved) and other administrative information. Not every procedure needs all this space, but it is easier to assume worst case on every entry than figure it out in detail.

Some of the instructions used by the program required delay slots. Those slots are marked as such. All but one have been filled with useful code. Although it takes some getting used to, setting up the last parameter of a procedure call *after* the CALL instruction is quite safe. Procedures are expected to begin with a SAVE instruction, by which time the parameter has been set up, even if setting it up references memory. Besides, hardware interlocking also prevents problems.

```
        .proc   4                  ! begin procedure
        .globl  _towers            ! define towers as an external symbol

_towers: save   %sp,-112,%sp       ! advance register window and stack pointer

! if n = 1 then                    ! IO = n, Il = i, I2 = j
        cmp     %IO,1              ! if n = 1
        bne     ELSE               ! if n <> 1 then goto ELSE

! writeln("move ", i, ' to ', j);
        sethi   %HI(A1),%OO        ! OO = high 22 bits of address A1 (delay slot)
        call    .writestr          ! output the string 'Move '
        or      %OO,%LO(A1),%OO    ! OO = address of A1 (delay slot)
        call    .writenum          ! print i
        mov     %I1,%OO            ! OO = i (delay slot)
        sethi   %HI(A2),%OO        ! OO = high 22 bits of address A2
        call    .writestr          ! output the string ' to '
        or      %OO,%LO(A2),%OO    ! OO = address of A2 (delay slot)
        call    .writenum          ! print j
        mov     %I2,%OO            ! IO = j (delay slot)
        call    .writecr           ! output carriage return
        nop                        ! (delay slot)
        b       DONE               ! jump around else part
        mov     0,%OO              ! return error code 0 (ok) to caller (delay slot)

! k = 6 - i - j;                   ! compute k in local register LO
ELSE:   mov     6,%LO              ! local register LO = 6
        sub     %LO,%I1,%LO        ! local register LO = 6 - i
        sub     %LO,%I2,%LO        ! local register LO = 6 - i - j

! towers(n - 1, i, k);
        sub     %IO,1,%OO          ! parameter 0: OO = n - 1
        mov     %I1,%O1            ! PARAMETER 1: O1 = i
        call    _towers,3          ! towers(n - 1, i, k)
        mov     %LO,%O2            ! parameter 2: O2 = k (delay slot)

! towers(1, i, j);
        mov     1,%OO              ! parameter 0: OO = 1
        mov     %I1,%O1            ! parameter 1: O1 = i
        call    _towers,3          ! towers(1, i, j)
        mov     %I2,%O2            ! parameter 2: O2 = j (delay slot)

! towers(n - 1, k, j);
        sub     %IO,1,%OO          ! parameter 0: OO = n - 1
        mov     %LO,%O1            ! parameter 1: O1 = k
        call    _towers,3          ! towers(n - 1, k, j)
        mov     %I2,%O2            ! parameter 2: O2 = j (delay slot)

        mov     0,%OO              ! return error code 0 (ok) to caller
DONE:   ret                        ! return to caller
        restore %g0,%OO,%OO        ! reset register window (delay slot)

        .seg    "data"             ! use data segment
A1:     .ascii  "Move \0"          ! allocate a string
A2:     .ascii  " to \0"           ! allocate a string
```

Fig. 8-23. Towers of Hanoi in SPARC assembly language.

8.1.6. A Second RISC Example: MIPS

At about the same time the Berkeley RISC chip was being developed, a similar RISC project was going on at Stanford. The Berkeley chip led directly to the SPARC, which we have just studied in some detail. The Stanford chip, slightly modified, led to the MIPS Computer Systems R2000 and R3000 chips. Since both chips originated as university research projects less than 100 km apart by professors who knew each other (Patterson and Hennessy) it is interesting to compare the respective designs to see on what points they are the same and on what points they differ. Therefore, in this section we will look at the MIPS chips and compare them to the SPARC. Since the R2000 and R3000 are architecturally identical, differing only in speed and price, we will just refer to them collectively as "the MIPS." For additional information see (Chow, 1988; Himelstein et al., 1987; Kane, 1988; and Moussouris et al., 1986).

Technical Overview of the MIPS

The basic idea of the MIPS is the same as that of the SPARC: a pipelined LOAD/STORE machine executing one simple instruction per data path cycle. As on the SPARC, the LOAD, STORE, JUMP, and procedure call instructions all have one delay slot. Both are 32-bit machines, with 32 32-bit registers and 32-bit, word-aligned instructions. The address space is 2^{32} bytes and byte addressable, although the upper 2 gigabytes of the MIPS address space are reserved for the operating system. Both machines support paged virtual memory, and both support an optional floating-point coprocessor, as well as additional user-supplied coprocessors (1 on the SPARC, 2 on the MIPS).

Nevertheless, the two chips also differ in some significant ways. The SPARC is big endian (to be compatible with Sun's existing line of 680x0 products), but the MIPS can be configured either as big endian or as little endian. This feature is extremely unusual, and was included to woo both big endian customers (680x0, IBM mainframes) and little endian customers (80x86, VAX). The endian-ness is selected by a pin on the chip; switching from one to the other in software, half-way through a program, would not be a good idea.

The next major difference is one of omission: the MIPS has a single set of 32 general-purpose registers. It does not have overlapping register windows as the SPARC does. We have already discussed the advantages of overlapping windows at some length. Let us now point out the disadvantages. First, overlapping register windows take up a lot of chip area. The MIPS designers decided to use this area for putting the MMU and cache controller on the CPU chip, as shown in Fig. 8-24. This decision not only reduces chip count, but allows faster communication between the CPU and these devices than putting them off chip does.

Second, in a multiprogramming system, when the operating system switches

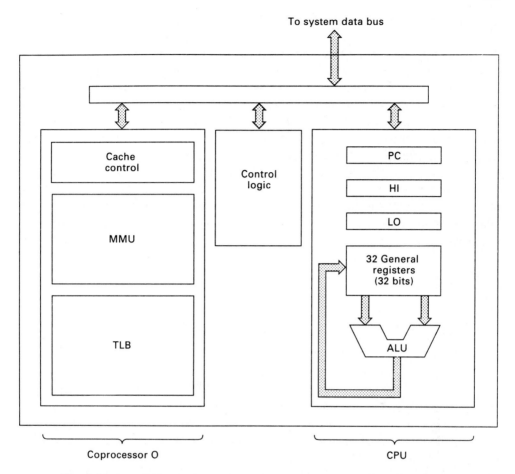

Fig. 8-24. The MIPS has the cache controller, MMU, and TLB (Translation Loo-kaside Buffer) on the CPU chip.

from one process to another, it is necessary to save the current process' registers in memory, and load the new process' registers from memory. When the CPU has hundreds of registers, as the SPARC does, process switching can be slow, unless the CPU contains multiple register files, which takes up even more chip area.

Third, the SPARC's rigid division of eight registers each for global, local, input parameters and output parameters is not optimal. By not earmarking any of the registers for special purposes, the MIPS compilers are free to use them in whatever way is best for the program currently being compiled. One program may need 20 local variables and another may need 20 global variables. The SPARC cannot put these in registers, but the MIPS can.

Of course, the other side of the coin is that procedure calls are potentially a lot slower on the MIPS than on the SPARC. The compilers must do extra work to win back in software what the SPARC gets for free in hardware. These procedure call optimizations are discussed below.

Another difference between the MIPS and SPARC is the complete absence of condition codes on the MIPS. Instead, special instructions are present to compare two registers, and write a 0 or 1 into a third register, depending on the outcome of the comparison. On some arithmetic instructions, overflows cause traps; on the rest, it is up to the software to check. In practice, nobody ever checks, so having overflows trap on at least some of the instructions is probably at least as good as having an overflow bit that is always ignored.

In contrast to the SPARC, the MIPS is not fully interlocked. In fact, MIPS is an acronym for **Microprocessor without Interlocking Pipe Stages**. If an instruction in the delay slot behind a LOAD reads the register being loaded, the results are unpredictable. It is up to the compiler to make sure that the delay slot is not misused.

One last general remark here is that the MIPS has a deeper pipeline than the SPARC, five stages versus four. The five stages are:

1. Instruction fetch.

2. Decode instruction and read operand registers.

3. ALU operation.

4. Start data write, if any, back to the cache and memory.

5. Store ALU output in the destination register.

In general, the MIPS designers made different trade-offs than the SPARC designers, more often accepting somewhat idiosyncratic hardware if they knew they could solve the resulting problems in software. The SPARC designers choose to keep the hardware clean to simplify the software, even at the expense of losing a little performance here and there. The SPARC approach tends to put more of the burden on the hardware designers, whereas the MIPS one tends to put it somewhat more on the software people.

MIPS Registers

The MIPS has 32 general-purpose 32-bit registers. As on the SPARC, R0 is permanently wired to 0 and cannot be changed. Although the compilers can use any of the 31 remaining registers any way they want, certain conventions have been established to facilitate linking together procedures written in different languages. The conventional register usage is shown in Fig. 8-25.

AT is used by the assembler as a temporary register for computing 32-bit direct addresses and other purposes. V0 and V1 are used as compiler temporaries, for

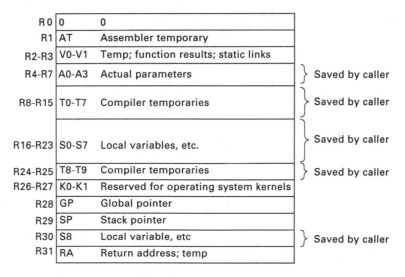

Fig. 8-25. MIPS Registers

function results, and for holding the static links for procedures nested within procedures (e.g., in Pascal). A0 through A3 are used for passing actual parameters from the calling procedure to the called procedure. If these four registers are insufficient, the stack is used for the rest.

Next come eight registers used by the compilers as scratch registers for evaluating expressions and other purposes. Called procedures are free to clobber (change) these, so if they contain anything useful at the time of a call, the caller must take care to save them. T8 and T9 are two more compiler temporaries. They are not consecutive with the first eight because the compiler writers changed their minds at the last minute and wanted two more.

The nine S0 through S8 registers are for local variables, global variables, and other items of a more permanent character than the temporaries. Called procedures must not clobber them. If the called procedure needs any of them, it must save them and then restore them later. K0 and K1 are reserved for the operating system. GP is a pointer into the middle of a 64K global table, not unlike the SPARC G1 through G7 registers. This table holds global variables, constants, and other useful items. The items in this table can be accessed in one instruction, so the most important ones are put here. Finally, we have SP, the stack pointer, and RA, the register used for holding the return address on calls. If a called procedure itself makes a call, it must first store RA on the stack.

Note that there is no frame pointer. On the SPARC and most other machines, upon procedure entry, one register, the frame pointer, is set to point to the base of the current stack frame. All references to local variables index off it, so that local variables maintain the same offsets, even if the stack pointer varies during procedure execution. On the MIPS, local variables are addressed relative to SP.

While this gives the compiler more work, it makes procedure calls faster by eliminating the need to manage the frame pointer.

Of course the big problem on the MIPS is how to minimize CPU-to-memory traffic, especially during procedure calls. To start with, a sophisticated graph coloring algorithm is used, to pack as many local variables into as few registers as possible. Furthermore, a lot of work has been done to avoid having to save them all when a procedure is called. Although this is not a book on compiler optimization techniques, let us at least take a brief look at the general approach.

Two basic strategies exist for saving registers at a call. In Fig. 8-26(a), each procedure begins with a **procedure prolog** that saves all the registers that need saving (S0 through S8), or better yet, only those S registers that the procedure clobbers. If the procedure does not use S4 through S8, it only has to save S0 through S3. It just leaves S4 through S8 alone. When it is finished, the **procedure epilog** restores the saved registers.

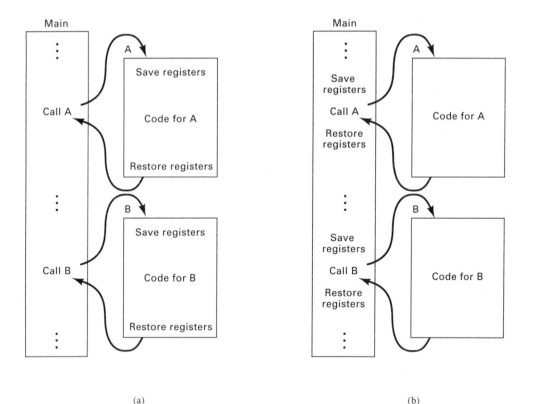

Fig. 8-26. (a) Callee saves the registers. (b) Caller saves the registers.

In Fig. 8-26(b), the other method is used. Here the caller saves the registers before the call, and restores them afterwards. The callee does nothing. Each method has its own strengths and weaknesses. When the callee does the saving, it does not know which of the S0 through S8 registers are live. It may well be that only S1 has anything useful in it, so saving all the registers it clobbers, say, S0 through S3, is wasteful. Why save dead registers? The problem is that the callee does not know which registers are live and which are dead.

When the caller does the saving, the reverse problem occurs. The caller knows very well which registers are live, so it only saves those. However, it does not know which registers the callee clobbers. Maybe it is carefully saving registers that the callee does not use at all. This is potentially just as wasteful as having the callee save dead registers.

The MIPS solution is to use what is called **interprocedural register allocation**. The compiler builds a graph of the procedures, one node per procedure, starting with the main program. Each procedure called by the main program is then added to the graph, with an arrow from the main program indicating that it is called. Then the compiler looks at each of the nodes just added to the graph and finds the procedures they call, adding them to the graph, and so on, until the full call graph has been constructed.

The compiler then starts at the bottom of the graph, at the leaf procedures (which call no one), and allocates registers to its variables, which have previously been packed using the graph coloring algorithm. It then propagates the register use information up the graph, so that when compiling, say, *main* in Fig. 8-26, it knows which registers A and B use. Armed with this information, the caller can save only those registers that are both live and going to be clobbered by the callee.

The key idea here is that the caller does the saving, but it only saves those registers that are (1) live at the call, and (2) clobbered by the callee. Registers that are either dead or left alone by the callee are not saved.

Furthermore, the compiler takes into account what callees use when allocating registers. As a simple example, consider the call graph of Fig. 8-27(a) in which each procedure uses three local variables. The compiler could decide to assign S0 through S2 to *main*, S3 through S5 to both A and B (which are never active simultaneously), and S6 through S8 to C, D, and E.

While *main* is running, it keeps its local variables in S0 through S2. When it calls A, it does not have to save any of these, because the compiler has carefully put A's local variables in different registers. Similarly, none of the other calls require saves or restores either. In practice, there are usually too few registers, so some saves and restores are needed, but by making judicious choices, their number can be minimized.

In effect, in Fig. 8-27 the compiler is simulating the run-time stack by the compile-time assignment of (packed) variables to registers. This scheme makes up to some extent for the lack of overlapping register windows. It fails for separately compiled procedures, recursive procedures, and some other cases, but by-and-large it does reduce CPU-memory traffic considerably at the price of increasing the complexity of the compilers. The designers considered this trade-off acceptable.

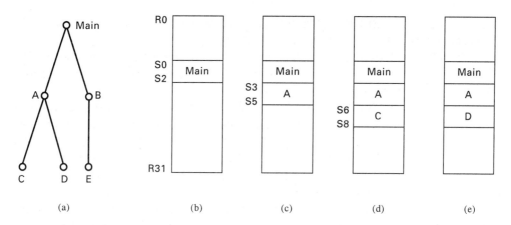

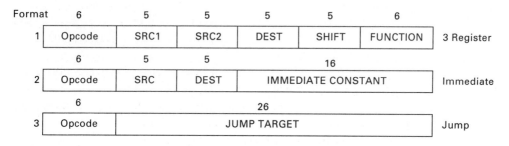

Fig. 8-27. (a) A call graph. (b) Registers at different points during execution. *Main*'s variables are statically assigned to S0–S2, *A*'s and *B*'s are statically assigned to S3–S5, and the other procedures' are statically assigned to S6–S8.

MIPS Instruction Set

The MIPS has only three instruction formats. They are illustrated in Fig. 8-28. All have a 6-bit opcode to define the instruction. The hardware can tell the format by looking at the opcode.

Fig. 8-28. MIPS instruction formats.

Format 1 has 6 more opcode bits at the other end, allowing for up to 4K instructions. That this is overkill hardly needs to be explained, but there were bits left over. The arithmetic, Boolean, and other computational instructions use format 1 to specify two registers as sources and one as a destination, just like the SPARC. The SHIFT field contains the count for SHIFT instructions.

Format 2 allows one of the source operands to be a constant, as in the SPARC. The only difference is that here the constant is a signed 16-bit constant (−32K to +32K) instead of a signed 13-bit constant. Not only does 16 bits give larger offsets, but it also means that a single global register gives access to 64K of memory. The SPARC needs eight registers to address 64K of global memory.

Format 3 is used by all the JUMP instructions. The meaning of the 26-bit operand is somewhat peculiar, as explained later.

The MIPS instructions are roughly similar to the SPARC instructions. The basic integer instructions are shown in Fig. 8-29. Floating-point and coprocessor instructions are not listed here.

The LOAD and STORE instructions are similar to those on the SPARC, with one major difference: indexed addressing is the only mode provided. The memory address to be loaded from is computed by adding a 16-bit signed constant to a register. As with the SPARC, by using R0 (0) we get a limited form of direct addressing, and by setting the constant to 0, we get register indirect addressing. All LOAD and STORE instructions use format 2.

A full 32-bit address can be constructed in a register by using the LUI instruction, which loads its 16-bit constant into the upper (high-order) 16 bits of the designated register. The lower 16 bits are cleared to 0. The next instruction can OR the low-order 16 bits into place, or more simply, just index off the register. In effect, LUI serves the same function on the MIPS that SETHI serves on the SPARC. Only the relative lengths of the upper and lower parts are different.

Unlike the SPARC, the MIPS does not have any instructions for loading or storing double words. On the other hand, the LWL, LWR, SWL, and SWR instructions can be used to fetch and store words that are not aligned on word boundaries. The SPARC just traps on such attempts.

Since the MIPS goes to great lengths to keep the instructions simple, it is a bit surprising that instructions like these were included. The reason is somewhat subtle and has to do with the way COMMON and EQUIVALENCE statements are used in FORTRAN. These can interact in such a way as to force many variables to be unaligned with respect to word boundaries. LWL and the other instructions were thus included to improve the performance of ancient FORTRAN programs. They are also useful for COBOL. The SPARC also has special instructions for specific languages (tagged arithmetic), only these are for LISP and Smalltalk, not FORTRAN and COBOL.

Addition and subtraction are straightforward. The only remark worth making is that because there is no mode bit to distinguish indexed from immediate mode, ADD and ADDI need different opcodes (actually, OPCODE is the same, but FUNCTION is different).

Now comes something surprising: non-RISC instructions. One of the things the designers did with the chip area saved by not having a large register file is add a special functional unit for multiplication and division. The MULT and MULTU instructions multiply two registers together and leave the 64-bit product in two special registers, LO and HI (see Fig. 8-24). The DIV and DIVU instructions use general registers for the divisor and dividend, and leave the quotient in LO and the remainder in HI. Transfers between LO and HI and the general registers use the MFHI, MTHI, MFLO, and MTLO instructions.

A multiplication or division takes multiple cycles, with the exact number

LB	Load byte (signed)
LBU	Load byte unsigned
LH	Load halfword (signed)
LHU	Load halfword unsigned
LW	Load word
LWL	Load word left
LWR	Load word right

SB	Store byte
SH	Store halfword
SW	Store word
SWL	Store word left
SWR	Store word right

ADD	Add
ADDI	Add immediate
ADDU	Add unsigned
ADDIU	Add immediate unsigned
SUB	Subtract
SUBU	Subtract unsigned
MULT	Multiply
MULTU	Multiply unsigned
DIV	Divide
DIVU	Divide unsigned
MFHI	Move from HI register
MTHI	Move to HI register
MFLO	Move from LO register
MTLO	Move to LO register

SLT	Set on < (less than)
SLTI	Set on < immediate
SLTU	Set on < unsigned
SLTIU	Set on < immediate unsigned

AND	Boolean AND
ANDI	Boolean AND immediate
OR	Boolean OR
ORI	Boolean OR immediate
XORI	Boolean EXCLUSIVE OR
XORI	Boolean XOR immediate
NOR	Boolean EXCLUSIVE NOR

SLL	Shift left logical
SRL	Shift right logical
SRA	Shift right arithmetic
SLLV	Shift left logical variable
SRLV	Shift right logical variable
SRAV	Shift right arithmetic variable

J	Jump
JR	Jump register
Bxx	Conditional branch
JAL	Jump and link
JALR	Jump and link register
BLTZAL	Branch if < 0 and link
BGEZAL	Branch if > = 0 and link

LUI	Load upper immediate
SYSCALL	System call
BREAK	Unconditional trap

Fig. 8-29. MIPS integer instructions.

depending on the operands. Once started, it does its work quietly in the background. Other instructions may continue in parallel. Attempts to read LO or HI before it is ready are interlocked, that is, suspended until the multiplication or division is finished. Thus, unlike the procedure call mechanism, where the SPARC uses a hardware solution and the MIPS a software solution, for multiplication and division, it is exactly the other way around.

The MIPS has no condition codes. Comparisons are done using the SLT instruction and its variants. All of these compare two registers and put a 0 in a third register if the first operand is less than the second; otherwise, a 1 is stored. The next instruction can test the result.

The Boolean instructions are what one might expect, except that NORI does not exist. Clearly, the MIPS designers did not accord a symmetric and uniform instruction set a high priority in their list of goals.

The six shift instructions are divided into two groups. The first three get their count from the SHIFT field in the instruction itself (really shift immediate). The other three get it from a general register. The SPARC does not have this dichotomy because its shift instructions, like almost all its instructions, can have either a register or a constant as the second source operand.

The J (jump) instruction is somewhat bizarre. It uses format 3, with a 26-bit TARGET field. The address to jump to is computed by shifting this 26-bit number left 2 bits, and then taking the upper 4 bits from the current program counter. What this does, is effectively split the 32-bit address space up into 16 "superpages" of 256M each. It is not possible to jump from one superpage to another. Thus a J instruction at address 0FFFFFFFH cannot jump a few bytes ahead to address 10000002 because the upper 4 bits differ.

In practice, of course, this hardly ever occurs, but the linker has to check for it nonetheless. If such a jump is detected, the present software essentially prints a message saying: "Guess what? You are the lucky owner of a program that by chance needs to jump across a superpage boundary. You lose. Program cannot be executed. Bye." In the future, when 256M programs become more common, MIPS will probably change the software to do emergency surgery on the program to work around the problem. Still, the MIPS philosophy is clear: make the hardware fast (a relative jump would have been slower) even if it creates problems for the software designers.

A comparison with the SPARC is instructive. The SPARC jumps use a 22-bit PC relative word offset. This means that jumps further than 8 megabytes either way cannot be handled. However, since jumps are only used *within* a single procedure, it would take a very unusual procedure indeed to cause trouble. With the MIPS, a perfectly ordinary, small procedure can run aground if it happens to be near the 256M mark of a large program.

An alternative way of jumping is to use JR, which just takes its target address from a register. All word-aligned addresses below 2^{31} are legal (in user mode).

The conditional branch instructions each compare two operands and branch if the condition is met. One delay slot is required, and it cannot be annulled as in the SPARC. Not all 16 Boolean conditions are provided for. Only BEQ, BNE, and four tests against zero (BLTZ, BLEZ, BGEZ, BGTZ) are provided. These six were chosen because none of them requires a subtraction. While the compiler can always manage to arrange its comparisons to live with this subset, it is a different approach than the SPARC. The SPARC designers chose to include all 16 Boolean tests to make the machine symmetric and simplify the software. The MIPS architects decided to go for speed and let the software people deal with the consequences of an asymmetric instruction set.

Procedures are called using JAL or JALR. JAL uses a 26-bit offset like J, and has the same problems as J. JALR takes its address from a register, like JR. JAL puts the return address in R31, because there are no bits available in the instruction to specify a register. JALR allows any register to be used.

BLTZAL is a conditional procedure call. If the specified register is less than zero, the call occurs and the return address is put in R31. BGEZAL is similar. We have already discussed LUI, and the last two instructions are self-explanatory.

MIPS Floating Point

Like the SPARC, the MIPS supports IEEE floating-point arithmetic using a coprocessor. Since real computer scientists rarely use numbers larger than 255, we will not go into it in detail, but one point is worth looking it. The MIPS has the ability to copy values from the CPU registers directly into the floating-point registers. The SPARC does not. Instead, it must first store the values in memory, and then load the floating-point registers from memory.

Is the ability to make direct transfers from the CPU to the floating-point coprocessor worth having extra instructions? The SPARC people undoubtedly think it is not; the MIPS people equally undoubtedly think it is. Both groups made numerous simulations, but still came to different conclusions. The lesson to be learned is that simulations and measurements are not everything. Computer design still requires some judgement calls.

MIPS Interrupt Handling

Interrupt handling on the MIPS is straightforward. Window overflow and underflow do not exist, but I/O interrupts and coprocessor traps certainly do. One interesting difference between the MIPS and the SPARC is how they deal with traps, as opposed to interrupts.

When the floating-point coprocessor gives a trap, the program counter is stored in an internal CPU register where the operating system can get at it. All instructions before the one pointed to have been executed. None of those after it have had any effect. Achieving this effect with a highly pipelined CPU running in parallel with an equally highly pipelined floating-point coprocessor is nontrivial. On the

SPARC, the hardware designers threw in the towel and said: "The saved program counter points somewhere in the general vicinity of the instruction that caused the trouble. You figure it out." This is an example where the MIPS hardware is clean and the SPARC hardware lets the software do all the work.

MIPS Memory Management

Virtual memory on the MIPS is handled in an interesting and quite unconventional way. The 32-bit virtual addresses are divided into a 20-bit virtual page number and a 12-bit offset within the page, as shown in Fig. 8-30(a).

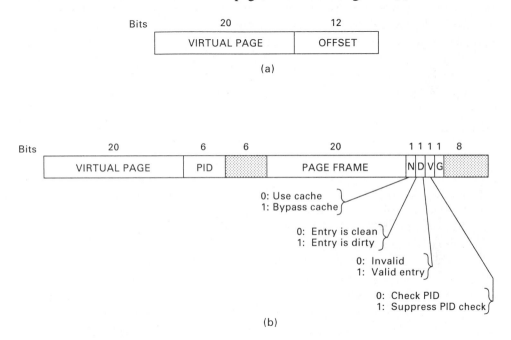

Fig. 8-30. (a) MIPS virtual address format. (b) TLB entry.

However, in contrast, to the SPARC, 68030, and 80386, all of which have conventional page tables, the MIPS has no page tables at all. Instead, it has a 64-word device called the **TLB (Translation Lookaside Buffer)** right on the CPU chip, as shown in Fig. 8-24.

The TLB is comparable to the associative memory used in most paging systems. Each TLB entry maps one virtual page onto a physical page frame. When the CPU generates an instruction, the high-order 20 bits are extracted and associatively compared to all the entries in the TLB. If a hit is found, the 20-bit page frame number replaces the virtual page to form a 32-bit physical address.

The MIPS was designed for multiprogramming, so it is possible that two or more processes will have a TLB entry for the same page. To avoid ambiguity, a 6-

bit field called PID (Process ID) is provided in each entry and compared to the current PID along with the virtual page number.

A bit is provided in each TLB entry to disable PID checking, for example, to allow all processes to share a common library at a fixed virtual address. Bits are also provided to mark entries as invalid or dirty, the latter set by the hardware on a write to the page. The fourth status bit is used by bypass the cache for the entries on that page, for example, for I/O device registers.

So far, so good. Nearly all MMUs have an associative memory that works more or less like this one. The unusual part is what happens on a TLB miss. On the SPARC, 68030, 80386, and other machines, the MMU uses the page tables to locate the page table entry for the virtual address just used, and then loads that entry into the TLB. On the MIPS, a TLB miss causes a trap to the operating system, which has to do the virtual-to-physical mapping in software. The operating system also updates the TLB in software, typically evicting an entry at random. A hardware register is provided for generating the random index. Actually it is not random, but the cumulative number of memory references so far, modulo 63. Also, it never selects entries 0 through 7, so these can safely be used by the page fault handler itself.

It should be clear that as long as all working sets are smaller than the size of the TLB, everything works fine. Once that size is exceeded, however, there is a performance penalty to be paid, since a TLB miss is akin to a page fault. With a more conventional design, a TLB miss just requires two or three memory references to the page tables, and takes under 1 μsec. On the MIPS, the operating system is invoked to update the TLB in software.

On the other hand, the scheme is highly flexible (any page table format can be used), and very little hardware is required, making it possible to put the TLB on the CPU chip, which makes it faster. In the long run, shaving a few nanoseconds from the basic cycle time may more than compensate for the extra overhead incurred on a TLB miss. Again we see the MIPS philosophy at work: make the hardware simple and fast in the normal case, even at the expense of more complexity in the software.

Comparison of SPARC, MIPS, 80386, and 68030

The SPARC and MIPS are typical RISC architectures and the 80386 and 68030 are typical CISC machines, so it is instructive to compare the two types. Figure 8-31 gives some of the major points of comparison in table form. To start with, a comparison of their respective instruction sets (Figures 5-5, 5-7, 5-11, 5-15, 5-16, 8-18, and 8-29) is illuminating. The SPARC and MIPS have fewer instructions, and the instructions that they have are much simpler.

Next, the SPARC has two basic addressing modes: sum of two registers and indexed mode. The MIPS has only indexed mode. Register indirect and absolute are special cases of indexed mode. The 80386 includes all the modes of Fig. 5-35

Item	SPARC	MIPS	80386	68030
Classification	RISC	RISC	CISC	CISC
Word length (bits)	32	32	32	32
User address space (bytes)	2^{32}	2^{31}	2^{46}	2^{32}
Separate I & D space?	No	No	No	Yes
Endian	Big	Both	Little	Big
User registers	32	32	8	16
Overlapping windows?	Yes	No	No	No
Addressing modes	4	3	8	18
Register indirect mode?	Yes	Yes	Yes	Yes
Sum of 2 registers mode?	Yes	No	Yes	Yes
Immediate constants (bits)	13	16	32	32
Indexed mode offsets	±4K	±32K	±2G	±2G
Direct addressing	Bottom 4K	Bottom 32K	32 Bits	32 Bits
Instruction length (bytes)	4	4	1-17	2-26
Instruction formats	4	3	Many	Many
Operands per instruction	3	3	2	2
Multiply?	Partial	Yes	Yes	Yes
Divide?	No	Yes	Yes	Yes
Absolute jumps?	No	No	Yes	Yes
PC relative jumps	Yes	No	Yes	Yes
Interlock?	Yes	No	Yes	Yes
Pipeline stages	4	5	3	3
Virtual memory?	Yes	Yes	Yes	Yes
On-chip MMU?	No	Yes	Yes	Yes
On-chip cache?	No	Controller	No	yes
Separate I & D cache?	No	Yes	No	Yes
Page size	4K	4K	4K	256-32K
Page tables	2	0	2	4
Floating-point coprocessor?	Yes	Yes	Yes	Yes
Other coprocessors	1	2	0	1

Fig. 8-31. Comparison of the SPARC, MIPS, 80386, and 68030.

and Fig. 5-36. The 68030 has those of Fig. 5-38 and Fig. 5-39. Some of the 68030 modes have 10 fields that have to be extracted and analyzed to compute the effective address.

In Fig. 8-13 we saw that a 25 MHz 68020 is one-third the speed of a 16 MHz SPARC, and one-sixth the speed of a 33 MHz SPARC. Even allowing for a 50 percent improvement of the 68030 over the 68020, at equal clock speeds, the SPARC is three times as fast. The MIPS is faster still. Given all those address fields, it is amazing the 68030 does as well as it does. The only thing that saves it is the fact that these esoteric modes are hardly ever used by most programs.

Another important difference between the SPARC and the two CISC machines is the register file. The SPARC has an overlapping register window system, with 32 registers visible at any instant. The 80386 has 8 user registers and the 68030 has 16. Neither of the latter has any form of overlap.

Both RISC machines have delayed instructions. While compiler writers do not jump with joy when presented with them, the Towers of Hanoi example showed that they are not as bad as one might first assume. Neither the 80386 nor the 68030 has any delayed instructions, which simplifies their compilers, but the possibility of doing almost anything in several ways complicates them again, at least if the goal is to produce optimal code.

Although these machines differ in the ways we have just pointed out, they also have many important similarities. All four are 32-bit machines and run at similar clock rates. All four support coprocessors, including floating point. All four provide paged virtual memory on a single 32-bit linear address space, although the 80386 also supports up to 2^{16} segments, which the other three do not. Finally, all four are designed to work with cache memories.

Although the SPARC and MIPS are both RISC machines, they also differ in a variety of ways. In general, the SPARC attempts to present a clean, orthogonal, symmetric interface to the compiler writer, whereas the MIPS is somewhat less so. For example, the MIPS does not have a complete set of conditional jump instructions, and the jump targets are restricted. In general, the respective designers made different trade-offs between what should go in hardware and what should go in software.

The SPARC uses overlapping windows to make procedure calls go fast, whereas the MIPS does it with with complex software. The SPARC has two basic addressing modes and four instruction formats, whereas the MIPS has one mode and three formats, making it slightly simpler. The instruction sets are roughly comparable, although the SPARC has double word LOAD/STORE, and tagged arithmetic, missing on the MIPS, which make it perhaps more suited to languages like Lisp and Smalltalk. On the other hand, the MIPS has full multiplication and division, missing on the SPARC, as well as the ability to read and write nonaligned memory words.

Another difference is the presence of condition codes on the SPARC and their absence on the MIPS. Correspondingly, the SPARC has two versions of many instructions, one that sets the condition codes and one that does not.

On the other hand, the MIPS needs special instructions for immediate-mode addressing, something that the SPARC does with an address bit. The trade-off here is an address bit versus a number of opcodes. If the MIPS had provided immediate mode addressing for *every* instruction, it also would have needed a bit, only located in the opcode instead of the address field. However, by not making immediate mode available for every instruction, some opcode space and hardware was saved at the cost of introducing some irregularity into the architecture.

Like all RISC machines, both the SPARC and the MIPS have delay slots, but the SPARC has the ability to annul some of them, which the MIPS does not. Furthermore, the SPARC has interlocking on LOADS and STORES and the MIPS does not.

Both machines have virtual memory. The SPARC implements it with a conventional paging scheme, whereas the MIPS requires traps to the operating system on TLB misses. For programs with working sets significantly larger than 64 pages, the MIPS performance may suffer appreciably.

The main thing to see here is that even within the constraints of RISC, there are many design choices to be made, and different, equally competent, experts can come to dissimilar conclusions. The field of RISC design is full of pitfalls and choices, and no doubt will be the subject of much activity in the years to come.

8.2. PARALLEL ARCHITECTURES

Although RISC machines hold the promise of winning a factor of 10 to 20 in performance by eliminating the microprogram, they are still traditional von Neumann machines, with all their inherent limitations. Chief among these is that circuit speed cannot be increased indefinitely. The speed of light is already a major problem for designers of high-end computers, and heat-dissipation issues are turning supercomputers into state-of-the-art air conditioners.

The most ironic aspect of the quest for ever-increasing speed is that most of the transistors are idle nearly all the time. Modern computers are dominated by memory chips. A typical computer has one CPU chip and over 100 memory chips. When the CPU issues a request to read a 32-bit word, either four chips (byte-organized static memory) or 32 chips (1-bit wide dynamic memory) respond. The rest do nothing.

The traditional structure of a computer with a single CPU that issues sequential requests over a bus to a memory that responds to one request at a time has become known as the **von Neumann bottleneck**. A great deal of research is currently taking place on how to eliminate this bottleneck, and a wide variety of radically different architectures have been proposed and built.

All the attempts to break the von Neumann bottleneck start with the assumption that a computer should consist of some number of control units, ALUs, and memory modules that can operate in parallel. Where they diverge is how many of each are present, what they are like, and how they are interconnected. Some designs use a relatively small number of powerful CPUs that are only weakly connected. Others use large numbers of ALUs that are strongly connected and work in unison, directed by a single control unit. Numerous intermediate architectures are also being experimented with. In the remainder of this section we will describe a few of the more interesting systems. Additional information can be found in (Almasi and Gottlieb, 1989; Athas and Seitz, 1988; Dongarra, 1987; Hwang and Briggs, 1984; Krajewski, 1985; and Veen, 1986).

8.2.1. Overview of Parallel Computers

When approaching a new parallel computer system, three fundamental questions to ask are:

1. Describe the nature, size, and number of the processing elements.

2. Describe the nature, size, and number of the memory modules.

3. Describe the strategy for interconnecting the processors and memories.

Let us examine each of these points briefly in turn. The processing elements can range from minimal ALUs through complete CPUs, with sizes ranging from a small portion of a chip to many cubic meters of electronics per element. As one might expect, when the processing element is a fraction of a chip, it is possible to equip a computer with thousands of such elements. Commercial systems with 65,536 processing elements are currently on the market; systems with a million processing elements are expected within a few years. When the processing element is a complete CPU chip, it is only possible to build systems containing up to about 1000 CPUs with current technology.

Memory systems are often split up into modules that can operate independently of one another and in parallel. At one extreme are systems with thousands of processing elements, each of which has its own memory of perhaps a few kilobytes. At the other are systems consisting of a few modules, each containing megabytes of memory. The relative speed of the memory and the processing elements is a critical issue. If the memory is relatively slow, the processors will have to wait for memory requests, and the designers will be tempted to pipeline multiple requests from the same processor to the memory system, to keep the processor busy. If the memory is fast, such pipelining can be dispensed with.

Although there is some variation among processor and memory designs, the area in which parallel systems differ most is how the pieces are put together. The interconnection schemes can be divided into two rough categories: static and dynamic. The static ones simply wire up all the components in a fixed way, such as a star, ring, or grid. In dynamic interconnection schemes, all the pieces are hooked up to a switching network that can dynamically route messages between components. Each has its own strengths and weaknesses, as we shall soon see.

Viewing parallel computers as a collection of chips that are wired up in one manner or another is essentially a bottom-up view of the world. In a top-down approach, one would ask: what is it that is to be run in parallel? Here again, we have a spectrum of possibilities. Some parallel computers are designed to run multiple independent jobs simultaneously. These jobs have nothing to do with one another and do not communicate. A typical example is a computer with 8 to 64 CPUs intended as a big UNIX time-sharing system for handling a few hundred users at remote terminals. Transaction processing systems used by large banks (e.g., automated teller machines) also fall into this category, as do independent simulation runs using different sets of parameters.

A different point on this spectrum is the parallel computer used for running a single job consisting of many parallel processes. As an example, consider a chess program that analyzes a given board by generating a list of legal moves that can be made from it, and then forking off parallel processes to (recursively) analyze each new board in parallel. The point of the parallelism here is not to accommodate more users, but to gain speedup on a single problem.

Continuing along this spectrum, we come to machines in which the parallelism comes from a high degree of pipelining or many ALUs operating on the same instruction stream at the same time. Numeric supercomputers with special hardware for vector processing fall in this category. Here we not only have one main problem being solved, but all parts of the computer are working very closely on almost the same aspect of the problem together (e.g., different elements of the same two vectors are being added in parallel).

Although it is hard to pin down exactly, these three examples differ in what is sometimes called **grain size**. In the multi-CPU time-sharing systems, the unit of parallelism is large: a complete user program. Running large pieces of software in parallel with little or no communication between the pieces is called **coarse-grained parallelism**. The opposite extreme, such as found in vector processing, is called **fine-grained parallelism**.

Grain size refers to the algorithms and software, but it has a direct analog in the hardware. Systems with a small number of large, independent CPUs that have low-bandwidth connections between the CPUs are called **loosely coupled**. Their opposite number are the **tightly-coupled** systems, in which the components are generally smaller, closer together, and interact with each other frequently over high-bandwidth communication networks. In most cases, problems with coarse-grained parallelism work best on loosely-coupled systems, and problems with fine-grained parallelism work best on tightly-coupled systems, but so much variety exists in the algorithms, software, and hardware, that this is a general guide at best.

Given this somewhat chaotic subject matter, numerous researchers have tried to produce classification schemes and taxonomies for parallel computing (Flynn, 1972; Gajski and Pier, 1985; Treleaven, 1985). Unfortunately, the Carolus Linnaeus† of parallel computing has yet to emerge. The only scheme that is used much is that of Flynn, and even his is, at best, a crude approximation.

Flynn's classification is based on two concepts—instruction streams and data streams. An instruction stream corresponds to a program counter. A system with n CPUs has n program counters, hence n instruction streams. An ILLIAC IV type machine (see Fig. 2-7) has one program counter and one instruction stream.

---

† Carolus Linnaeus (1707-1778) was a Swedish biologist who devised the system now used for classifying all plants and animals into kingdom, phylum, class, order, family, genus, and species.

Instruction Streams	Data Streams	Name	Examples
1	1	SISD	Classical Von Neumann machines
1	Multiple	SIMD	Vector supercomputers, array processors
Multiple	1	MISD	Arguably none
Multiple	Multiple	MIMD	Multiprocessors

Fig. 8-32. Flynn's taxonomy of parallel computers.

A data stream consists of a set of operands. A program computing the average of a list of temperatures has one data stream. A program computing the average temperature for each of 100 weather thermometers spread all over the world has 100 data streams.

The two streams are, to some extent, independent, so four combinations exist, as listed in Fig. 8-32. SISD is just the classical, sequential von Neumann computer. It has one instruction stream, one data stream, and does one thing at a time. SIMD machines have a single control unit that executes one instruction at a time, but they have multiple ALUs to carry out that instruction on multiple data sets simultaneously. The ILLIAC IV is the prototype of SIMD machines.

MISD machines are a somewhat strange category, with multiple instructions operating on the same piece of data. It is not clear if any such machines exist, although some people regard pipelined machines as MISD.

Finally, we have MIMD, which are just multiple independent CPUs operating as part of a larger system. Most parallel processors fall into this category.

Flynn's taxonomy stops here, but we have extended it in Fig. 8-33. SIMD has been split into two subgroups. The first one is for numeric supercomputers and other machines that operate on vectors, performing the same operation on each vector element. The second one is for parallel-type machines, such as the ILLIAC IV, in which a master control unit broadcasts instructions to many independent ALUs.

In our taxonomy, the MIMD category has been split into machines that have shared primary memory, called **multiprocessors**, and those that do not. The latter are variously called **multicomputers**, **private-memory** computers, or **disjoint-memory** computers. Two kinds of multiprocessors exist, distinguished by the way the shared memory is implemented. (The implementation method probably should not appear in an architectural classification, but so few distinct categories can be found, that it is a pity to throw away any valid criterion for dividing machines into disjoint groups.)

The distinction between machines with and without shared memory is a major one and is worth looking at a bit closer. In particular, one should distinguish between *physical* sharing and *logical* sharing (Bal et al., 1989). When two CPUs share physical memory, they have the same address space, and values written into a

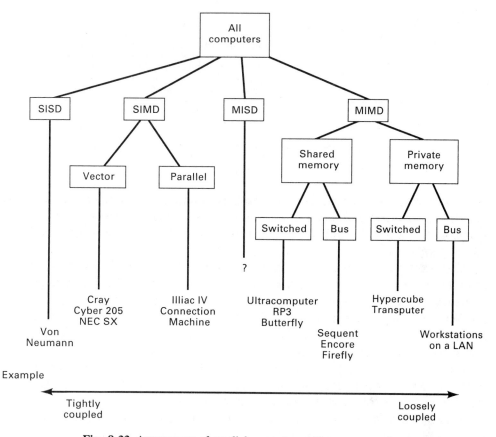

Fig. 8-33. A taxonomy of parallel computers with some examples.

word by one of them can be read by the other one. When two computers do not share physical memory, they must communicate by sending each other messages.

Logical sharing, in contrast, is determined by how the *software* views the world, as opposed to the *hardware*. When two processes share logical memory, information written into a data structure by one of them can be read by the other. When no logical sharing is present, processes must communicate by some form of I/O or message passing. For example, if WRITE(buffer) is executed by one process and READ(buffer) is executed by another, the contents of the buffer can be transferred between them. This mechanism is communication via I/O. These two concepts, physical sharing and logical sharing, are orthogonal, so again we have four categories, as given in Fig. 8-34.

The first category is obvious. If two processes on different computers use a language or system that supports logical message passing (e.g., pipes in UNIX), communication can most easily be accomplished by sending physical messages

Physical (hardware)	Logical (software)	Examples
Unshared	Unshared	Software message passing between disjoint computers
Unshared	Shared	Distributed virtual memory, Linda, Orca
Shared	Unshared	Message passing simulated by shared buffers
Shared	Shared	Shared-memory multiprocessors

Fig. 8-34. Combinations of physical and logical sharing.

between the two computers. The last category is equally obvious. If the language allows two processes to share variables and the hardware has physical shared memory, the shared variables can just be kept in the shared physical memory so both processes can access them.

If the software uses message passing but the hardware has physical shared memory, the software can simulate message passing by putting messages to be passed into a buffer in the shared memory.

The most interesting combination (from a research perspective) is simulating logically shared memory on machines that can only communicate by message passing, such as workstations on a local area network. This combination is particularly important because logically shared memory is much easier for programmers to use than message passing, but building large shared-memory computers is quite difficult, as we shall see shortly. If we can achieve logical sharing on top of physically disjoint computers, we will have obtained the best of both possible worlds—easy to write software on easy to build hardware.

Let us briefly look at three different approaches to simulating sharing on top of disjoint computers. Kai Li (1988) suggests having a single, paged, virtual address space encompassing all the processes that are working together. Pages are owned by a particular machine. When a process is started, its virtual memory map is set up so that those pages that are not resident on its processor cause a trap if referenced. Subsequently, when a process tries to use a nonresident page, a page fault occurs and the operating system sends a message to the machine where the page currently is located, asking it for the page. Thus instead of fetching nonresident pages from the disk, they are fetched over the network. When a processor gives up a page, it marks the page as nonresident, so that if that page is used again locally, the reference to it will be trapped.

If a page is heavily used by two or more processors, it will be ping-ponged over the network like crazy, but if most programs exhibit reasonable locality, the scheme may work acceptably well. An optimization that greatly reduces network traffic is to permit multiple copies of pages that are READ-ONLY. If a procedure library is shared, for example, there is no reason not to make a copy of it on every machine that uses it. A second useful optimization is to make sure that the local data belonging to different processes (including their stacks) are on distinct pages, so that these pages will never have to travel across the network.

A second approach is **Linda** (Carriero and Gelernter, 1989; Gelernter and Carriero, 1988), a programming model based on an abstract tuple space. Each tuple contains one or more data items, like a record in Pascal. All processes logically share the same tuple space, no matter where they reside.

Tuples are addressed by content, not by address. Operations are provided to insert tuples into the tuple space and take tuples out of the tuple space. Tuples may not be modified in place. Thus if a collection of processes all want to increment some value in a tuple, each one must first execute a primitive to remove the tuple, increment the appropriate field, and then put it back in the tuple space. In this way, no race conditions can occur.

Tuple space can be implemented by keeping all the tuples on one computer, by keeping each tuple on the processor that created it, or by hashing them over all the processors to balance the load. If programs exhibit reasonable locality in their tuple usage, and do not address tuples at random, these schemes, like Li's, can be made to perform reasonably well.

Our third and last example of implementing shared memory on disjoint computers is **Orca** (Bal and Tanenbaum, 1988; Bal et al., 1989). Orca is a language that allows programmers to define abstract objects along with operations on these objects. Consider, as an example, the traveling salesman problem, in which a salesman is given a starting point and a list of cities to visit, say, New York, Basel, Rio, Nairobi, Sydney, and Kuala Lumpur. He has to find the shortest path that visits each city exactly once and then returns to the starting point. In Orca one would define an object containing the shortest path found so far and its length. Two operations would be present: read the length of the shortest path and replace the current path (and its length) by a shorter one.

Processes would be started up on all the processors. Each process begins by examining a different flight from the starting point. Given a partial path and a list of k cities to visit, the algorithm is simple. First check to see if the length of the partial path exceeds the best total path found so far. If so, abandon the path. Otherwise, generate k new partial paths by concatenating each of the cities to the given path, and create processes to evaluate each one. It should be clear that the operation of reading the best path length found so far will be much more frequent than updating it.

Several implementations of Orca exist. The one we will describe here takes advantages of the fact that reading data is much more common than updating data. Each machine keeps a copy of all shared objects locally. Reading a shared object is then no more expensive than reading a local object. When an object has to be changed, an update protocol is used to synchronize independently generated changes. One possibility is to broadcast the new value to all machines. Alternatively, if hardware does not support broadcasting, the originator of the change can send individually acknowledged messages to each other process.

For more details, please consult the references, but it should be clear that a variety of ways exist to simulate shared memory on disjoint hardware. That said, let us now proceed to examine the various parallel architectures shown in Fig. 8-33, from most loosely coupled to most tightly coupled.

8.2.2. Disjoint-Memory MIMD Computers

Our first parallel system consists of computers in which each CPU has its own private memory. No memory is physically shared, so all communication is done by message passing. To pass these messages, communication channels are needed. In the simplest form, every computer has a direct link to every other computer. Figure 8-35(a) shows eight computers with such a full interconnection.

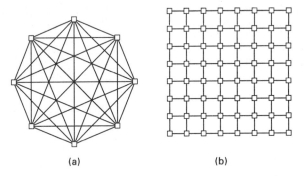

(a)   (b)

Fig. 8-35. (a) Full interconnection of eight computers. (b) Mesh interconnection of 64 computers.

A full interconnection of n computers provides a bandwidth that is proportional to n^2 and a minimal delay from any computer to any other. Unfortunately the cost also grows as n^2, making it unsuitable for large systems.

Since giving every computer a direct connection to every other computer is not feasible, let us try the other extreme—a single communication channel shared by all computers. For example, a collection of high-performance workstations connected by a local-area network, the rightmost leaf of the tree of Fig. 8-33. (A LAN is a special case of a bus; both are message passing serial devices.) Although parallel computation can be done on a network full of workstations, as the load grows, the bus saturates. Thus neither of the two extremes, full interconnect or a single channel, is entirely satisfactory. We need an intermediate solution that balances cost and performance.

A more practical topology is the **mesh** or **grid** of Fig. 8-35(b). Here the number of simplex (i.e., unidirectional) links, and hence the bandwidth and also the cost, is approximately $4n$ for large n. A linear growth in the cost as a function of size is usually acceptable, since the processor cost is also linear with n.

Transputers

An interesting system based on a rectangular grid is the INMOS **Transputer**, shown in Fig. 8-36. The Transputer (Homewood et al., 1987; Jesshope, 1988; Nicoud and Tyrrell, 1989; Whitby-Strevens, 1985) is a RISC machine designed especially for parallel computers built up from large numbers of Transputers arranged in a rectangular grid.

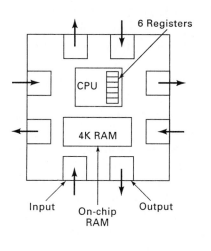

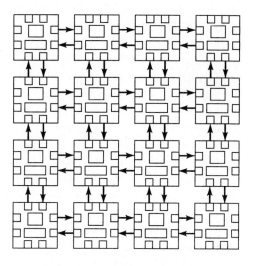

(a)   (b)

Fig. 8-36. (a) A Transputer. (b) A grid of 16 Transputers.

In contrast to most other RISC machines, the Transputer has a tiny register file (just three registers). The combination of an extremely reduced instruction set combined with the absence of a register file left a large amount of chip area unused. This area was filled with a block of RAM (e.g., 4K bytes, depending on the model) as well as four pairs of I/O channel interfaces. External memory can also be attached to each Transputer, increasing its capacity. The software does not see any distinction between on-chip and off-chip memory, other than speed.

In addition to the on-chip RAM, each Transputer has six 32-bit registers: the program counter, the stack pointer, an operand register, and the A, B, and C registers, which function as a 3-word stack. All instructions are 1 byte long, with 4 bits for the opcode and 4 bits for immediate data. The 16 instructions include LOAD, STORE, ADD, and so on. Some of the instructions use the immediate data field for addressing the bottom 16 words of the on-chip memory, somewhat like registers.

One special instruction is PREFIX, which loads its 4-bit immediate value into the operand register, and then shifts it left 4 bits. It is possible to build up an arbitrary value in the operand register in this way. Although a substantial number of instructions may be needed, these instructions are both very short and very fast, which is what RISC is all about, after all.

Expressions are evaluated in the three-register stack. In the rare cases that three registers are insufficient, the compiler stores the registers temporarily in memory. Again, moving work from run time to compile time is also typical RISC.

The most innovative aspect of the Transputer, however, is not the instruction set, but the inclusion of eight simplex, bit-serial I/O links on the chip. Transputers are normally programmed in the Occam language, which supports an unlimited number of processes that communicate by reading from and writing to **channels.** Each channel connects two processes, either on the same chip, on adjacent chips, or on distant chips. When two processes on the same chip communicate, the communication is handled entirely in software.

However, when two processes on adjacent chips want to communicate, the hardware provides the necessary synchronization. If the reader starts first, it is automatically blocked until the writer starts on the other chip. Similarly, if the writer begins first, it blocks until the reader also begins.

Once both have started, the first byte of the message is transmitted one bit at a time, preceded by a start bit and followed by a stop bit. When the receiver has gotten the stop bit, it sends back an acknowledgement signal, enabling the sender to transmit the next byte. This extremely simple hardware protocol provides for a very small delay for short messages (a 32-bit word can be sent in 6 μsec), and a fairly high bandwidth for long messages (megabytes/sec). It also means that the links need only contain buffer space for one byte.

Due to the small number of pins required (only eight pins are needed for the eight links), Transputers can be packed tightly on a printed circuit board. A board with a 16×8 processor grid can have 1000 MIPS of computing power and 512K of on-chip memory, plus as much off-chip memory as the board has room for. For computation-intensive problems that map well onto a two-dimensional grid (e.g., VLSI component placement and routing), this design is attractive.

Hypercubes

The biggest problem that the Transputer and similar grid-based systems have is the worst-case message delay. With a square $n \times n$ grid, if a message has to go from one corner to the diagonally opposite corner, it has to make about $2n$ hops. The average will be about half the worst case. If the transmission over the links is done in hardware, but the forwarding from, say, the incoming west link to the outgoing east link requires software intervention (as it does on the Transputer), the average message delay in a big system may become too large

For this reason, researchers have looked for topologies in which the average delay does not grow proportionally with n. One popular alternative topology is the **hypercube**, also called an **n-cube** (Athas and Seitz, 1988; Dally and Seitz, 1987;

and Seitz, 1985). In a hypercube, 2^n processors are connected in an n-dimensional cube. Three examples are shown in Fig. 8-37.

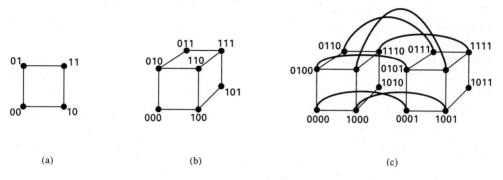

Fig. 8-37. Three examples of hypercubes. (a) Two dimensions. (b) Three dimensions (c) Four dimensions.

In an n-dimensional hypercube, each of the 2^n vertices is labeled with an n-bit binary integer giving its cartesian co-ordinates in n-space. The cube's side is of length 1, so each co-ordinate is either a 0 or a 1. Moving from any vertex to any adjacent vertex changes exactly one co-ordinate, so adjacent vertices differ in exactly one position.

The **diameter** of the hypercube, that is, the distance between the two furthest points, is n. For example, in the 4-dimensional cube of Fig. 8-37(c), to get from vertex 0000 to vertex 1111 requires four steps, each one changing one bit, such as the path 0000, 0001, 0011, 0111, 1111. Alternate paths are also possible. Put in other terms, the diameter of an n-node hypercube is $\log_2 n$, compared to $2\sqrt{n}$ for the grid. For $n = 1024$, for example, the diameter drops from 64 to 10.

The price paid for this enormous decrease in the diameter (hence in the mean delay) is an increase in fan-out. In a grid, each processor needs four links to other processors. In a hypercube with 2^n nodes, each one needs n lines to other processors. Thus with 1024 processors, each one needs 10 full-duplex links to other processors. More hardware is required at greater cost, but the performance improvement easily outweighs the cost increase.

Hypercubes provide multiple routes between any nonadjacent pairs, so a routing algorithm is needed. However, a simple one is available. First, compute the EXCLUSIVE OR of the current node with the destination node. The resulting number will have 1 bits corresponding to those axes on which the two nodes differ. The message should thus be sent along any one of them. For example, in Fig. 8-37(b), a message at 100 going to 111 would produce 011 when 100 and 111 are EXCLUSIVE ORed. Thus the message could go along either the second axis (to 110) or along the third axis (to 101). The two paths have the same length.

First-generation hypercubes (1983-1987) did all routing and forwarding of messages in software. Starting with the second generation, message handling was done nodes from a few milliseconds to a few microseconds. In general, a technique known as **wormhole routing** is now used. If a message is traveling from A through B onto C, as soon as the head of the message gets to B, it is immediately started on its way to C, even before the entire message arrives at B. In effect, this is a form of pipelining, and it greatly reduces the transit time for messages that have to make many hops.

The nice thing about hypercubes is that they are fairly easy to build. All you have to do is take a large number of standard single-board computers, add $\log_2 n$ I/O channels to each one, and wire them up. Athas and Seitz (1988) have predicted that by the mid 1990s we will have 1024-node hypercubes having 32 gigabytes of memory, 100,000 MIPS of processing power, and 500 nsec worst-case message delays.

8.2.3. Bus-Based Shared-Memory Multiprocessors

Transputers and hypercubes do not provide the logical shared memory that some applications need. Although Li's distributed virtual memory, Linda, and Orca can simulate shared memory reasonably well under certain circumstances, applications exist for which this simulation is not good enough. For applications that make heavy and random access to the shared address space, the hardware must actually support physical shared memory, so let us now turn our attention to how physical shared memory can be implemented.

The oldest and simplest approach is just to put a collection of CPUs and the memory onto a common bus, as illustrated in Fig. 8-38(a). However, since all memory traffic has to go over the same bus, we are rapidly faced with the von Neumann bottleneck again as soon as more than a handful of CPUs are present.

The first improvement is to add a cache to each processor, as in Fig. 8-38(b), to reduce the bus traffic. If the cache achieves a 90 percent hit rate, the bus traffic will be cut by a factor of 10, making systems with 16 to 32 processors feasible.

The next step is to realize that some data are inherently private to each processor (such as its code and stack), so they can be kept in private memory as in Fig. 8-38(c). In this way, bus traffic for code, the stack, and local variables can be reduced to zero.

Unfortunately, this arrangement leads to an asymmetric situation, in which some data cannot be accessed remotely at all. It often happens that certain data are mostly used by one processor, but that other processors need occasional access to it. This observation leads to the design of Fig. 8-38(d), which uses dual ported memories. Each on-board memory can be directly accessed by its own CPU, without going over the bus, but other CPUs can also get at it remotely.

In all four designs, we have drawn the global, shared memory as a single module. If the memory is as fast as the CPUs, this arrangement is fine. However, if the memory is appreciably slower than the CPUs, it may be better to split the memory up into multiple independent modules. In that way, after a CPU sends a

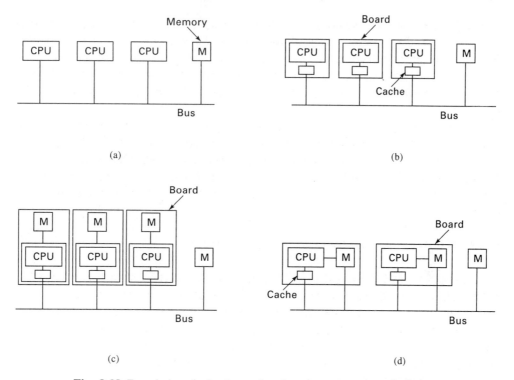

Fig. 8-38. Four designs for implementing shared memory over a single bus.

request to a memory module, it can release the bus and let other CPUs use it. When the memory is finally ready to respond, it acquires the bus itself and replies.

This method makes better use of the bus bandwidth by pipelining multiple requests to the memory system. On the other hand, it does have the disadvantage of making the memories active devices capable of requesting the bus. Normally, memories cannot become bus master, so additional logic has to be added to the memories to handle bus acquisition.

The Cache Coherence Problem

The method depicted in Fig. 8-38(a) is inefficient, but at least it is correct. The methods shown in the other three examples are fundamentally flawed. Consider what happens if processors A and B each read some word w from memory. Both will have local copies of w in their respective caches. Now suppose that A modifies w. The change is made entirely in A's cache; B knows nothing about it. If a process running in B uses w, it will get the old **stale data**, violating the semantics of shared memory (when one process changes a word, subsequent reads by other processes must return the new value). B will not be happy.

This problem, known in the literature as the **cache coherence problem**, is extremely serious. Without a solution, caching cannot be used, and bus-oriented multiprocessors would be limited to two or three CPUs. As a consequence of its importance and the fact that caching is easy to simulate, an extremely large number of papers have been written proposing solutions, most of them complete with simulation studies showing why the author's new one is the greatest thing since sliced bread. Although these protocols differ in the details, all of them prevent different versions of the same cache block from appearing simultaneously in two or more caches. Some of the many references are (Agarwal et al., 1988; Agarwal and Cherian, 1989; Bitar and Despain, 1986; Cheong and Veidenbaum, 1988; Eggers and Katz, 1989a, 1989b; Lee et al., 1987; Przybylski et al., 1988; Scheurich and Dubois, 1987; Vernon et al., 1988; Weber and Gupta, 1989; Wilson, 1987).

Solutions to the cache coherence problem can be divided into two general categories: software and hardware. We will now discuss each of these in turn. When the software approach to cache coherence is used, the programmer or compiler classifies each data item as shared versus not-shared and also as read-only versus writable (Owicki and Agarwal, 1989). Data that are not shared (i.e., are private to one process) cannot cause cache inconsistencies because they will never appear in two caches simultaneously. Similarly, data that are read-only cannot cause problems because they are never changed.

The category that causes all the trouble is shared, writable data. The solution thus lies in collecting all the shared, writable data together and putting them in a separate segment, page, or part of the address space. For example, the compiler could decide that for a particular program with a total of 16K of shared, writable data, all of it would be stored at vitual addresses below 16K.

At run time, caching would then be turned off for addresses between 0 and 16K. All references to memory below 16K would come directly from memory and be written back to memory, and would never be cached, no matter how often these words were used. Words above 16K would be cached in the usual way.

Of course to implement this "software" solution, the cache hardware needs the ability to disable caching for a range of addresses, so some hardware help is needed. On the other hand, all caches need the ability to disable some addresses anyway, in order to prevent caching of addresses corresponding to memory-mapped I/O devices. If a program is waiting for an I/O device to finish by sitting in a tight loop testing some status bit, it does not want the cache controller to read the I/O device register into the cache on the first read, and supply all subsequent reads from the cache.

Snooping Caches

While the software solution eliminates the cache coherence problem, it does so at the price of disabling caching for shared, writable data. For applications that happen to make especially heavy use of shared writable data, such as in some data base systems, this solution is inadequate. Consequently, we need to look at hardware solutions.

In all the hardware solutions, the cache controller is specially designed to allow it to eavesdrop on the bus, monitoring all bus requests from other CPUs and caches and taking action in certain cases. These devices are called **snooping caches** or sometimes **snoopy caches** because they "snoop" on the bus. The set of rules implemented by the caches, CPUs, and memory for preventing different versions of the same block from appearing in multiple caches is called the **cache consistency protocol**. Many of these have been proposed; below we will study a few of them.

The simplest, easiest to implement, and probably best known cache coherence protocol is called **write through**. It can best be understood by distinguishing the four cases shown in Fig. 8-39. When a CPU tries to read a word that is not in its cache (i.e., a read miss), its cache controller loads the block containing that word into the cache. The block size may be exactly one word, but it may also be several words, depending on the design of the cache. The block is supplied by the memory, which in this protocol is always up-to-date. Subsequent reads (i.e., read hits) can be satisfied out of the cache.

Action	Local request	Remote request
Read miss	Fetch data from memory	
Read hit	Use data from local cache	
Write miss	Update data in memory	
Write hit	Update cache and memory	Invalidate cache entry

Fig. 8-39. The *write through* cache coherence protocol. The empty boxes indicate that no action is taken.

On a write miss, the word that has been modified is written to main memory. The block containing the word referenced is *not* loaded into the cache. On a write hit, the cache is updated and the word is written through to main memory in addition. The essence of this protocol is that all writes are written through to memory, keeping memory up-to-date at all times.

Now let us look at all these actions again, but this time from the snooper's point of view, shown in the right-hand column of Fig. 8-39. Let us call the cache performing the actions, A, and the snooping cache, S. When A misses on a read, it makes a bus request to fetch a block from memory. S sees this but does nothing. When A has a read hit, the request is satisfied entirely locally, and no bus request occurs, so S is not aware of A's read hits.

Writes are more interesting. If A's CPU does a write, A will make a write request on the bus, both on misses and on hits. On all writes, S checks to see if it has the word being written. If not, from its point of view this is a remote request/write miss and it does nothing. (To clarify a subtle point, note that in

Fig. 8-39 a remote miss means that the word is not present in the snooper's cache; it does not matter whether it was in the originator's cache or not. Thus a single request may be a hit locally and a miss at the snooper, or vice versa.)

Now suppose that A writes a word that *is* present is S's cache (remote request/write hit). If S does nothing, it will have stale data, so it marks the cache entry containing the newly modified word as being invalid. In effect, it removes the item from the cache. Because all caches snoop on all bus requests, whenever a word is written, the net effect is to update it in the originator's cache, update it in memory, and purge it from all the other caches. In this way, inconsistent versions are prevented.

Of course, S's CPU is free to read the same word on the very next cycle. In that case, S will read the word from memory, which is up-to-date. At that point, A, S, and the memory will all have identical copies of it. If either CPU does a write now, the other one's cache will be purged, and memory will be updated.

Many variations on this basic protocol are possible. For example, on a write hit, the snooping cache normally invalidates its entry containing the word being written. It could equally well accept the new value and update its cache instead of marking it as invalid. Conceptually, updating the cache is the same as invalidating it followed by reading the word from memory.

Another variant is loading the snooping cache on write misses. The correctness of the algorithm is not affected by loading it, only the performance. The question is: "What is the probability that a word just written will be written again soon?" If it is high, there is something to be said for loading the cache on write misses. If it is low, it is better not to update on write misses. If the word is read soon, it will be loaded by the read miss anyway; little is gained by loading it on the write miss.

As with so many simple solutions to complex problems, the *write through* protocol is inefficient. In fact, it is only slightly better than the software solution. Although it eliminates the bus traffic on reads to shared, writable variables, it does not eliminate the traffic on writes. Our next protocol, **write once**, can eliminate bus traffic on both reads and writes in many cases (Goodman, 1983).

It is easiest to explain the *write once* protocol by means of the example of Fig. 8-40. Here we have three CPUs that are potentially interested in a word whose address is w, and whose current value, w_1, is cached by B. Memory is up-to-date.

In this protocol, each cache block is in one of four states:

1. INVALID   — This cache slot does not contain valid data

2. CLEAN   — Memory is up-to-date; block may be in other caches

3. RESERVED — Memory is up-to-date; no other cache holds this block

4. DIRTY   — Memory is incorrect; no other cache holds this block

If multiple CPUs read some word repeatedly, it will be present in all their caches in

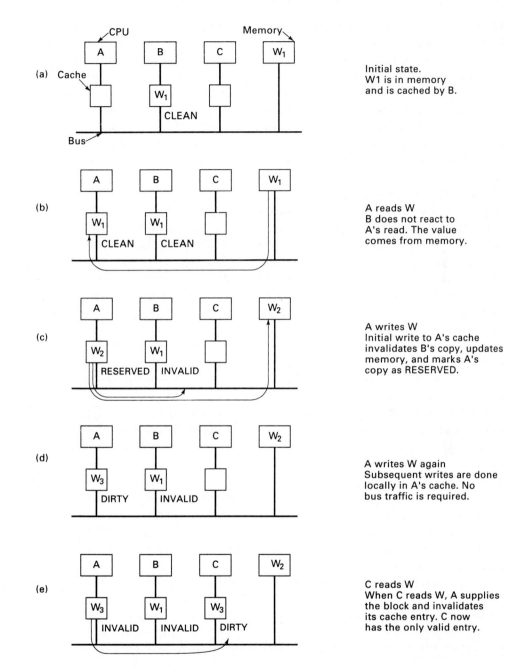

(a) — Initial state.
W1 is in memory
and is cached by B.

(b) — A reads W
B does not react to
A's read. The value
comes from memory.

(c) — A writes W
Initial write to A's cache
invalidates B's copy, updates
memory, and marks A's
copy as RESERVED.

(d) — A writes W again
Subsequent writes are done
locally in A's cache. No
bus traffic is required.

(e) — C reads W
When C reads W, A supplies
the block and invalidates
its cache entry. C now
has the only valid entry.

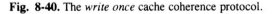

Fig. 8-40. The *write once* cache coherence protocol.

CLEAN state and memory will be correct. The RESERVED and DIRTY states come into play on writes, as described below.

Now A reads w from memory, resulting in Fig. 8-40(b), in which the value w_1 is present in two caches. Both entries are clean and memory is still up-to-date.

If A now does a write, it initially proceeds the same way as in *write through*: memory and A's cache entry are both updated, and B's cache entry is marked INVALID. One new aspect, however, is that the state of A's cache entry in Fig. 8-40(c) is now changed to RESERVED, to indicate that no other cache contains w and that memory is up-to-date. If w has to be removed from A's cache now (to make room for some other entry), the RESERVED state indicates that it does not have to be written back to memory.

On A's next write, in Fig. 8-40(d), the cache entry goes from RESERVED to DIRTY, but no bus traffic is generated. The fact that the state was RESERVED is a guarantee that no other cache holds the block containing w. All subsequent writes are also done locally. If the entry is forced out of the cache in order to make room for something else, it will first be rewritten to memory, as it is now out-of-date.

Now let us consider what happens if C suddenly reads (or writes) w. It gets a cache miss, so a bus request is made. A snoops on this request and sees that it has the entry and it is marked DIRTY, meaning that the memory word is stale. It immediately realizes that the full responsibility for making sure that C's request is satisfied lies with it, so it asserts a special bus signal to inhibit memory from replying, and provides the whole cache block to C itself. A then marks the entry as INVALID and C marks it as DIRTY.

The situation of Fig. 8-40(e) is, in fact, conceptually the same as Fig. 8-40(d). In both cases w is located in exactly one cache and is marked DIRTY. Memory will only be updated when w is purged from its current cache to make room for another entry.

The advantage of *write once* over *write through* is that if a CPU needs to make a large number of reads and writes in quick succession to a shared word, only the first write requires any bus traffic. Subsequent writes are handled internally.

Many variations of this protocol have been proposed, implemented and analyzed. We will briefly discuss two of them. See the paper by Archibald and Baer (1986) for more.

In the Firefly (Schroeder and Burrows, 1989), an experimental multiprocessor workstation built by researchers at DEC, the bus has a special signal SHARED, used to detect when a block is shared. Whenever a cache sees a reference to a word it is holding, it asserts SHARED so the originator can see that other caches hold the word too. Cache entries can be CLEAN, RESERVED, or DIRTY, like *write once*, but not INVALID.

On a read hit, the request is satisfied locally with no bus traffic. On a read miss, all caches that contain the block put it on the bus using a wired-OR. If there is only one cache entry, and that one is DIRTY, memory is also updated. If nobody has it, the originator goes to memory. At the end of the read miss cycle, there is one more cache copy than there was before it, all copies are marked CLEAN, and memory is up-to-date. Nothing is invalidated.

On a write hit, the action taken depends on the local state of the cache entry. If it is DIRTY, the cache is updated and that is all. If it is RESERVED, it is made DIRTY, the same as in *write once*. If it is CLEAN, the word is written to memory and snooped by all the caches containing the entry so they can do internal updates. If the originator sees that SHARED is not asserted, it knows that sharing has stopped. It then changes its entry to RESERVED so that subsequent writes will not require any bus traffic.

On a write miss, the block is supplied by other caches, if any, otherwise by memory. If the block came from memory (SHARED negated), it goes into the originator's cache as DIRTY. If it came from another cache, the originator writes the new word to the bus to allow everyone to update their entry and mark it CLEAN.

In both the *write once* and Firefly protocols, we saw that a block marked DIRTY is really "owned" by one specific cache, which takes responsibility for managing it. The concept of ownership can be generalized even further. Archibald and Baer (1984) suggest associating two bits with each memory block that give its status as ABSENT, CLEAN, RESERVED, or DIRTY. In this way, the SHARED bus line can be dispensed with. The bits are stored in memory, in addition to the status bits in the caches themselves.

As usual, read hits and write hits on RESERVED or DIRTY blocks can be done locally, since they do not require other caches or the memory to change their states. Read misses on ABSENT or CLEAN blocks fetch the needed data and change the status to CLEAN to signal that someone might have it. If the block is later discarded to make room for another entry, the memory bits need not be updated, so CLEAN does not guarantee that a cache has it, only that one might. Read misses on DIRTY blocks require the owner of the block to first update memory and mark the state as CLEAN. Then the read request can continue.

The action taken on write misses depends on the state. If no cache holds the block (ABSENT), the block is fetched and its state is marked DIRTY both in the cache and in the memory. If it is CLEAN or RESERVED, the competition has to update (or invalidate). If it is DIRTY, the new value is written to memory and the current owner, both of which now become CLEAN.

Finally we come to write hits. RESERVED and DIRTY blocks are updated locally. ABSENT is impossible on hits. Thus all that is left is CLEAN, in which case the new value is broadcast to the other caches for updating (or invalidating). The state remains CLEAN.

8.2.4. Multistage MIMD Shared-Memory Multiprocessors

Despite all these complicated cache coherence protocols, the bare fact remains that a single bus has a fixed and limited throughput. As more and more processors are added, the bus traffic grows linearly. At some point the bus will saturate.

Buses simply do not scale to large systems. Sixty-four processors is probably the practical limit for one bus. Multiple bus systems are conceivable, but they do not scale either, and have their own unique problems as well (Mudge et al., 1987).

The only practical way to implement a memory shared among a substantially larger number of CPUs is to split the memory up into numerous modules and provide multiple paths between the CPUs and the memories. Not only does this arrangement provide more bandwidth, but it also allows multiple requests to be handled in parallel. An essential property, of course, is that the access time from every processor to every memory is the same.

Crossbar Switches

The simplest circuit for connecting n CPUs to k memories is the **crossbar switch**, shown in Fig. 8-41 (Broomell and Heath, 1984; Sawchuk et al., 1987). Crossbar switches have been used for decades within telephone switching exchanges to connect a group of incoming lines to a set of outgoing lines in an arbitrary way.

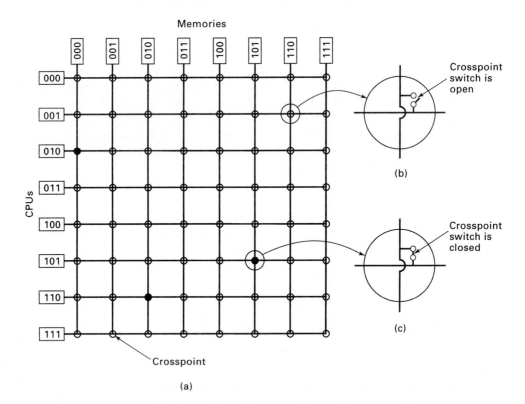

Fig. 8-41. (a) An 8×8 crossbar switch. (b) An open crosspoint. (c) A closed crosspoint.

At each intersection of a horizontal (incoming) and vertical (outgoing) line is a **crosspoint**. A crosspoint is a small switch that can be electrically opened or closed, depending on whether the horizontal and vertical lines are to be connected or not. In Fig. 8-41(a) we see three crosspoints closed simultaneously, allowed connections between the (CPU, memory) pairs (010, 000), (110, 010), and (101, 101). Many other combinations are also possible. In fact, the number of combinations is equal to the number of different ways eight rooks can be safely placed on a chess board.

One of the nicest properties of the crossbar switch is that it is a **nonblocking network**, meaning that no CPU is ever denied the connection it needs because some crosspoint or line is already occupied (assuming the memory module itself is available). Furthermore, no advance planning is needed. Even if seven arbitrary connections are already set up, it is always possible to connect the remaining CPU to the remaining memory. We will later see interconnection schemes that do not have these properties.

One of the worst properties of the crossbar switch is the fact that the number of crosspoints grows as n^2. With 1000 CPUs and 1000 memory modules we need a million crosspoints. Or better yet, we need a new design.

Omega Networks

The new design is based on the humble 2×2 switch shown in Fig. 8-42(a). This switch has two inputs and two outputs. Messages arriving on either input line can be switched to either output line. For our purposes, messages will contain up to four parts, as shown in Fig. 8-42(b). The *Module* field tells which memory to use. The *Address* specifies an address within a module. The *Opcode* gives the operation, such as READ or WRITE. Finally, the optional *value* field may contain an operand, such as a 32-bit word to be written. The switch inspects the *Module* field and uses it to determine if the message should be sent on X or on Y.

(a) (b)

Fig. 8-42. (a) A 2×2 switch. (b) A message format.

Our 2×2 switches can be arranged in many ways to build larger **multistage switching networks** (Adams et al., 1987; Bhuyan et al., 1989; Kumar and Reddy, 1987). Let us start with the no-frills, economy class **omega network**, illustrated in Fig. 8-43. Here we have connected eight CPUs to eight memories using 12 switches. More generally, for n CPUs and n memories we would need $\log_2 n$ stages, with $n/2$ switches per stage, for a total of $(n/2)\log_2 n$ switches, which is a lot better than n^2 crosspoints, especially for large values of n.

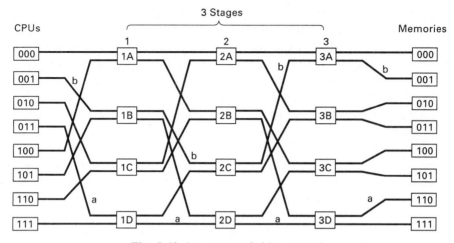

Fig. 8-43. An omega switching network.

The wiring pattern of the omega network is often called the **perfect shuffle**, since the mixing of the signals at each stage resembles a deck of cards being cut in half and then mixed card-for-card. To see how the omega network works, suppose that CPU 011 wants to read a word from memory module 110. The CPU sends a READ message to switch 1D containing 110 in the *Module* field. The switch takes the first (i.e., leftmost) bit of 110 and uses it for routing. A 0 routes to the upper output and a 1 routes to the lower one. Since this bit is a 1, the message is routed via the lower output to 2D.

All the second-stage switches, including 2D, use the second bit for routing. This, too, is a 1, so the message is now forwarded via the lower output to 3D. Here the third bit is tested, and found to be a 0. Consequently, the message goes out on the upper output and arrives at memory 110, as desired. The path followed by this message is marked in Fig. 8-43 by the letter *a*.

As the message moves through the switching network, the bits at the left-hand end of the module number are no longer needed. They can be put to good use by recording the incoming line number there, so the reply can find its way back. For path *a*, the incoming lines are 0 (upper input to 1D), 1 (lower input to 2D), and 1 (lower input to 3D), respectively. The reply is routed back using 011, only reading it from right to left this time.

At the same time all this is going on, CPU 001 wants to write a word to memory module 001. An analogous process happens here, with the message routed via the upper, upper, and lower outputs, respectively, marked by a *b*. When it arrives, its *Module* field reads 001, representing the path it took. Since these two requests do not use any of the same switches, lines, or memory modules, they can proceed in parallel.

Now consider what would happen if CPU 000 simultaneously wanted to access memory module 000. Its request would come into conflict with CPU 001's request at switch 3A. One of them would have to wait. Unlike the crossbar switch, the omega network is a **blocking network.** Not every set of requests can be processed simultaneously. Conflicts can occur over the use of a wire or over the use of a switch, as well as between requests *to* memory and replies *from* memory.

It is clearly desirable to spread the memory references uniformly across the modules. One common technique is to use the low-order bits as the module number. Consider, for example, a byte-oriented address space for a computer that mostly accesses 32-bit words. The 2 low-order bits will usually be 00, but the next 3 bits will be uniformly distributed. By using these 3 bits as the module number, consecutively addressed words will be in consecutive modules. A memory system in which consecutive words are in different modules is said to be **interleaved.** Interleaved memories maximize parallelism because most memory references are to consecutive addresses.

Although interleaving does help distribute the references uniformly among the memories, it is not a cure-all. Consider the problem of **barrier synchronization**, which occurs in many parallel applications. Suppose that the program has two phases, and no processes may enter the second phase until all processes have finished the first phase. The straightforward solution is to initialize a counter to the number of processes. When each process finishes the first phase, it decrements the counter. When the counter gets to zero, everybody can start phase 2.

The trouble is that after each process except the last one decrements the counter, it will discover a value other than zero. Since it cannot proceed until the counter becomes zero, it then sits in a tight loop reading the counter. The consequence of, say, 100 processes each trying to read the same memory word a million times a second is a load of 100 million references per second to the same memory module. This module then becomes a **hot spot** (bottleneck), slowing down the entire system. We will discuss one approach to dealing with hot spots shortly.

Some multiprocessors use a clever trick to reduce the number of switches. Instead of having $\log_2 n$ stages, there is only one stage. The output of this stage is fed back into the input, with each message making $\log_2 n$ passes through the network. Such a design is called a **recirculating omega network**. The principal disadvantage is that pipelining is not possible. In a multistage omega network, up to $(n/2)\log_2 n$ messages can be switched at the same time. In a recirculating network, the maximum is $n/2$.

Benes Networks

The problem of blocking in omega networks can be solved by adding more hardware and more stages. The Benes network, depicted in Fig. 8-44, is a five-stage network that is nonblocking. Unlike the omega network, in which there is exactly one path from any CPU to any memory, in the Benes network there are many alternatives. For example, from CPU 000 to memory module 000, one could go via 1A, 2A, 3A, 4A, and 5A, but another route is 1A, 2C, 3C, 4C, 5A. If the complete list of (CPU, memory) pairs is given in advance, it is always possible to find a set of routes to satisfy all requests, provided, of course, that no two CPUs want to use the same memory module simultaneously. However, if the requests come in sequentially, it is not always possible to satisfy all of them due to choices already made. Furthermore, routing in a Benes network is more complicated than in an omega network because genuine choices have to be made at each step along the way. For these reasons, Benes networks are not used as much as omega networks for connecting CPUs to memories, although they are widely used in telephone switching and other, more static, applications.

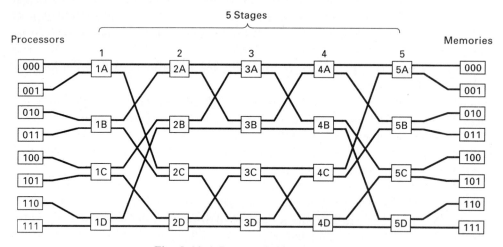

Fig. 8-44. A Benes switching network.

Examples of Multiprocessors

Several interesting shared-memory multiprocessors use omega networks for connecting the CPUs to the memories, including the BBN Butterfly (Crowther et al., 1985a, 1985b; Rettberg and Thomas, 1986), IBM RP3 (Pfister et al., 1987), and NYU Ultracomputer (Almasi and Gottlieb, 1989). We will briefly examine the NYU Ultracomputer as a typical example of this genre. The Ultracomputer is designed to connect up to 4096 CPUs to a large number of memory modules. At present eight Motorola 68010s are operational (universities have great goals, but small budgets). Each CPU has a cache to reduce memory traffic. Cache coherence is handled in software by not caching writable, shared variables (or in some cases by locking them, caching them, flushing the cache back to memory, and then unlocking them).

The omega switching network used has two important modifications. The first is that the switching elements have been greatly expanded and given considerable processing power. Messages that arrive simultaneously at a switch can be queued. Multiple requests for the same memory module can be combined and sent off in one message. In the hot-spot example given earlier, if multiple messages asking to read a specific memory word accumulate at a switch, it is sufficient to send one message further down the switching network toward the memory.

The other modification is the inclusion of a primitive operation called **FETCH-AND-ADD**. This instruction has two operands, a memory address and an integer. In one atomic action, the memory adds the integer to memory and returns the original value. As an example of its use, consider a program that has just built an array, each of whose entries is a pointer to some work that needs to be performed. The classical approach to dividing the work up among the processors is to establish a critical region, protected by a lock or semaphore. Processes in need of work first acquire the lock, then remove the next item from the array, and finally release the lock. The trouble with this algorithm is that time will be wasted busy waiting, and the lock will still be something of a hot spot, although combining will certainly help.

The Ultracomputer approach is to initialize a counter to 0, and then have each process do FETCH-AND-ADD, incrementing it by 1. The value returned is then the index into the array that the process is to use to find its work. Although the order in which the processes access memory is not defined, it is guaranteed that every process gets a unique index back. No critical regions, locks, semaphores or busy waiting are needed. Using generalized forms of FETCH-AND-ADD, such as FETCH-AND-OR, many ingenious synchronization primitives can be built.

Let us now compare bus-based shared-memory multiprocessors to those based on omega networks. Both are designed to allow each CPU to have access to the entire memory. The bus-based systems get most of their performance from snooping caches running complex cache coherence protocols. Omega network systems get theirs by physically increasing the bandwidth via multiple paths and switches.

Bus-based systems clearly do not scale to hundreds or thousands of processors. Omega network systems do scale to systems with several hundred nodes, but how much further they can go is an open issue. The main problem is the $\log_2 n$ delay introduced by the multiple layers of switches. If the switches are simple, with no queuing and combining, then hot spots may form, clogging the network like cars backing up at a toll plaza. If queuing and combining are used, then the switches need memory and begin to look like little microprocessors (Mizrahi et al., 1989).

If one of these devices takes even 100 nsec to accept, queue, analyze, combine, and ultimately forward a request, then in a 1024-node computer, 1 μsec will be needed to get a request to the memory and another 1 μsec will be needed to get the reply back. For a 100 nsec RISC CPU, this 2 μsec delay represents 20 instructions. Compiler writers will not be pleased when asked to fill 20 delay slots after each LOAD and STORE.

One approach is to do what IBM did with its experimental RP3 multiprocessor, designed for 512 nodes, of which 64 exist (IBM has smaller goals but more cash than NYU). A noncombining omega network used to access memory is built from 20-nsec water-cooled ECL chips packaged in special thermal conduction modules. A second, slower, combining CMOS omega network is used for synchronization operations. The full 512-node machine will consist of standard electronics cabinets occupying 75 square meters of floor space.

While the RP3 is only a prototype and the technology is constantly improving, it does seem to suggest that the interconnection network inherently has to use a much more exotic (and expensive) technology than the processors. The RP3 CPUs are 2-MIPS machines. The question of what kind of interconnection network one would need for 4096 machines at 20 MIPS each remains unanswered.

It is for this reason that much work is being done on parallel computers that do not have shared memory (Transputers, hypercubes, and so on), since these architectures have simple interconnection schemes. In this context, the research being done simulating shared memory in software takes on more meaning (see, for example, Bal, 1989; and Bal et. al, 1989).

8.2.5. SIMD Parallel Computers and the Connection Machine

Having finished our discussion of MIMD computers, let us now turn to SIMD ones. An SIMD computer executes the same program on a large number of different data sets simultaneously. Although this is less general than the MIMD model, it is simpler, cheaper, and for certain classes of problems, potentially much faster.

The first heavily used SIMD machine was the ILLIAC IV (see Fig. 2-7). It cost 30 million dollars and was used by NASA for years for computation-intensive problems. It was the most powerful computer in the world during the late 1970s, although it was notoriously difficult to program.

The ILLIAC IV was relatively straightforward, with 64 **PEs** (**Processing Elements**) arranged in a square 8×8 grid. Like all SIMD machines, it breaks the von Neumann bottleneck by having each PE consist of a small processor with its own local memory. The ILLIAC IV was not a commercial success, but it did have a major impact on hardware technology and the design of future SIMD computers. Let us now take a look at a modern SIMD computer that follows in the ILLIAC IV tradition.

The computer with the largest number of processors ever built is the **connection machine**, the brainchild of W. Daniel Hillis, who designed it as part of his Ph.D. research in artificial intelligence at M.I.T. (Hillis, 1985; Tucker and Robertson, 1988). Hillis and others formed a company, Thinking Machines Corporation, to manufacture and sell Connection Machines. The first delivery to a customer was in 1986. The machine described below is the CM-2, the successor to the original Connection Machine (CM-1), although the differences are few (primarily that the CM-2 has 16 times as much memory and much better I/O).

Structure of the Connection Machine

The architecture of the Connection Machine is shown in Fig. 8-45. It has four quadrants, each with 16,384 PEs. Each quadrant is divided into two 8K units for I/O and other purposes (note that 8K here means 8192 processors, not 8192 bytes of memory). Smaller systems can also be configured consisting of one, two, or three quadrants.

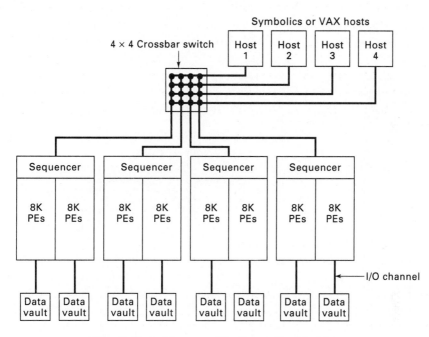

Fig. 8-45. Architecture of the Connection Machine.

The Connection Machine is not a complete system. It is really a back end machine with one or more **hosts**. Up to four hosts can be connected, either VAXes or Symbolics Lisp machines, or some combination of the two. Programs are edited, developed, and compiled on the hosts, and then downloaded to the Connection Machine via a 4 × 4 crossbar switch for execution. The compiled programs are executed on-the-fly by the **sequencers** (control units) as they are being downloaded. The Connection Machine has no program storage. Thus the hosts are needed not only for preparing programs, but also while the object programs are running.

The four quadrants can be run separately, to allow four different programs to run at once, each one being fed by a different host, if desired. In this way, one program can be debugged on a 16K quadrant while another quadrant is making a production run. It is also possible to have two or four quadrants ganged together to form a single 32K or 64K system in order to run very large problems.

The heart of the Connection Machine is the PE, of which up to 65,536 can be present. A PE consists of an ALU, 64 kilobits (8K bytes) of private memory, 4 flag bits, interfaces to the memory and I/O system and a router. The PEs are packaged in clusters of 16. Each cluster has one 68-pin custom VLSI chip containing 16 ALUs and a router, and four standard $32K \times 8$ static RAM chips. The megabit of memory is organized so that each ALU has a private chunk of $64K \times 1$ bits, with each bit (not byte) having a separate address. The ALU chip is sketched in Fig. 8-46.

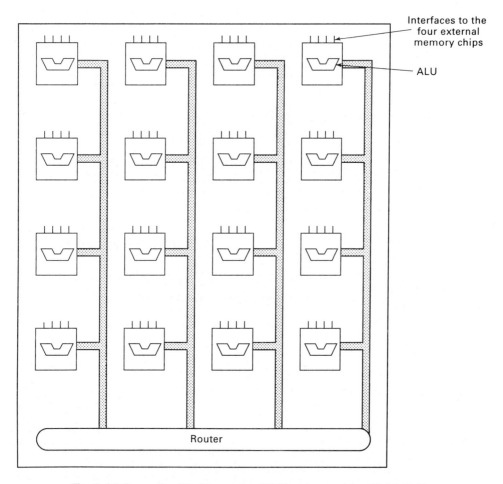

Fig. 8-46. Connection Machine custom VLSI processor chip with 16 ALUs.

The clusters are packaged 32 to a board (160 chips, plus some "glue" and interfacing chips). For numerical applications, 16 floating-point chips can also be included on the board. Sixteen boards fit into a backplane, called a **subcube**, for a total of 8K processors. Two subcubes are piled vertically to form a quadrant, and the four quadrants are put together to form a cube with an edge of about 1.5 meters. The complete system has about 25,000 chips, or about as many chips as the ENIAC had vacuum tubes. (The Connection Machine is millions of times faster than the ENIAC, so some progress has been made since 1946.)

Not all applications need 65,536 PEs. Some can live with fewer. However, there are also applications that need more. For this reason, the Connection Machine can be configured to time-share each PE into two or more virtual PEs, each with a proportional piece of the memory. If one million virtual PEs are needed, each physical PE can run a 16-way round-robin scheduling algorithm, and each virtual PE gets 4 kilobits of dedicated memory. The time sharing is done entirely in hardware, with the sequencer telling each physical PE which virtual PE to run, as the Connection Machine has no operating system. All applications run right down on the bare metal.

Operation of the Processing Elements

Programs for the Connection Machine are generally written in versions of C or Lisp that have been augmented with special features for expressing parallelism. These programs are then compiled on one of the hosts into a kind of machine language called **Paris** (**Parallel instruction set**). Paris consists of many conventional instructions, such as ADD and MOVE on 32-bit integers (or any other size integers, for that matter), but it also has some unusual instructions, mentioned below.

The binary programs in Paris are transmitted via the crossbar switch to one or more of the sequencers, where they are buffered and analyzed. The sequencers convert each Paris instruction into a sequence of **nanoinstructions**, which are broadcast to the PEs for execution. During any clock cycle (600 nsec), each PE executes the same nanoinstruction.

The reason that the host compilers do not generate the nanoinstructions themselves is to save bandwidth. If the hosts were to generate the nanoinstructions directly, they would have to put out about 8 bytes every 600 nsec, which requires a continuous bandwidth of over 13 MB/sec, something beyond their capability. By putting out a typical 8-byte Paris instruction every 20 μsec or so, the required bandwidth to the host is reduced by a factor of 32. Unfortunately, the Paris-to-nanoinstruction expansion takes time, resulting in a relatively long cycle time. Perhaps some day higher-bandwidth hosts will be available, so they can generate the nanoinstructions directly, eliminating the microprogrammed interpreter inside the sequencers (RISC Connection Machines?).

When a nanoinstruction is broadcast by the sequencer, all the PEs in its domain execute it simultaneously (SIMD principle). The details of this execution are shown in Fig. 8-47. During each nanoinstruction, the PE first fetches 2 bits from its private 64 kilobit memory, and 1 bit from its 4-bit flag register, giving a total of 3 input bits. These 3 bits are fed into the ALU, resulting in 2 output bits that can be stored in the memory and flags register, respectively.

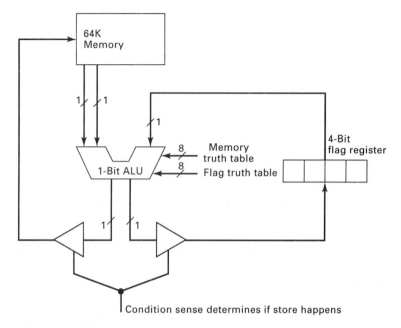

Fig. 8-47. Basic operation of a Connection Machine PE.

A Boolean function of three variables (e.g., the 3 input bits) has eight possible inputs: 000, 001, 010, 011, 100, 101, 110, and 111, where 0 is FALSE and 1 is TRUE. The function is completely described by giving the 8 result bits that correspond to each of the eight input combinations. For example, AND is 00000001, OR is 01111111, and XOR is 01101001. Since a Boolean function of three variables can be totally specified in an 8-bit number, 256 such functions exist, although many are not terribly interesting.

The PEs can compute all 256 functions, and they do it by looking the result up in a table. In fact, they do it twice in each cycle, with the first one yielding 1 bit that is stored back in memory and the second yielding 1 bit that goes back to the flag register. The value of having two results can be seen by looking at Fig. 3-19, where we see that a full 1-bit adder has 3 inputs (two data, one carry in) and 2 outputs (result and carry out). The Connection Machine can perform an n-bit addition in n cycles, 1 bit at a time, from right to left, preserving each intermediate carry for one cycle in the flag register. While it may seem slow to perform a 32-bit addition in 32 separate 600-nsec cycles (over 20 μsec per addition), remember that it can do 65,536 such additions simultaneously, for an aggregate rate of over 2500 MIPS.

The fields used in the nanoinstructions are shown in Fig. 8-48. The two 16-bit address fields are used to select 2 bits from the 64 kilobit memory to be operated on. The result overwrites the first bit, so we have two-operand addressing, like the 80386 and 68030 and most other traditional computers.

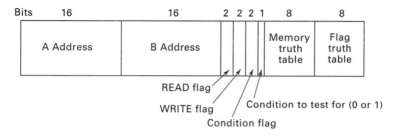

Fig. 8-48. Connection Machine nanoinstruction format.

The next two fields specify which flag bit is to be used as input and which is to be used as output. Unlike the memory operands, the result need not overwrite the input. The two 8-bit truth table fields specify which truth tables to use for the two results. In Fig. 3-19, again, we see that the truth table for the sum (memory result) is 01101001 and the truth table for the carry out (flag result) is 00010111.

The two condition fields have a special meaning. In many situations, it is desirable to have only a subset of all the PEs operate during a given cycle. For example, to calculate the mean age of all the children in a certain data sample (with one person per PE), the sequencer could instruct each PE to inspect the age field in its memory and set flag bit 0 to 1 if the age is less than 18, and to 0 otherwise. The next sequence of nanoinstructions could then be conditionally executed, with only those PEs having flag bit 0 set to 1 participating. Actually, all PEs work on every cycle, but the condition testing can be used to inhibit storing the results.

Armed with this knowledge of how the PEs work, we can now briefly describe Paris, the "machine language" produced by the compilers running on the hosts. Paris has a complete set of MOVE, arithmetic, Boolean and test instructions, on variable-sized data items, both signed and unsigned. Each instruction specifies the opcode, the source address, the destination address, and the length, for example, as four 16-bit quantities.

Consider, for example, the Paris instruction

S_ADD 480, 320, 32

to add the signed 32-bit integer at addresses 480 through 511 to the signed 32-bit integer at addresses 320 through 351. The sequencer first generates nanoinstructions to perform certain initializations, such as clearing two of the flag bits in preparation for their use as carry bit and overflow bits. Then it issues a nanoinstruction telling each PE to fetch bits 480 and 320, compute the sum and carry out, and store the results in bits 320 and one of the flags, respectively. The next nanoinstruction tells each PE to fetch bits 481 and 321 and perform the same calculation. This pattern is repeated a total of 32 times to form the full result.

In addition to these traditional operations, Paris directly supports vector and matrix operations. The Paris instruction for multiplying two $n \times n$ matrices is relatively short, but the number of nanoinstructions generated from it is enormous. The number of multiplications alone is n^3, and each multiplication may well require 32 additions, each of which may need 32 nanoinstructions. The sequencer knows how to multiply matrices because it is a CISC machine with a complex microprogram that includes the code for matrix multiply.

Another interesting class of Paris instructions are the global operations. The sequencer can ask each PE to announce the value of some number or field in its memory, and then compute the sum, minimum, maximum, AND, OR, or other function of all 65,536 values. Such an instruction takes many cycles to complete, but it can be specified in one Paris instruction.

Other Paris instructions are present for floating-point operations, sorting, sending messages, doing I/O, and communicating with the hosts, as well as some more exotic parallel operations for computing large numbers of partial sums and the like.

Message Routing

For many tasks, PEs need to communicate. With so many PEs, the interprocessor communication has great potential for being the system's undoing, just as the switching network does in shared-memory multiprocessors. Each chip contains a **router**, which handles the sending of messages between PEs, both on chip and off chip. The 4096 routers are connected by a 12-dimensional hypercube network, with each router having a unique 12-bit binary address. Two routers are adjacent if their addresses differ by exactly 1 bit. Adjacent routers have a physical wire between them, even if that wire has to run to another quadrant.

Each router can carry out five operations:

1. Injection   — Injecting a message from a local PE into the network.

2. Delivery   — Delivering a message to a local PE.

3. Forwarding— Moving a message for a remote PE one hop further.

4. Buffering   — Storing a message until the line it needs is free.

5. Referral   — Handing off a message when memory is full.

Together these form the routing system. Each message contains the number of the destination processor and the memory address where it is to be deposited when it arrives, as well as the data (e.g., a 32-bit integer).

When a Paris SEND instruction is executed, in principle, all 65,536 PEs can send messages to destinations determined by some field in each PE's memory. What happens if many messages go to the same destination? In the simplest form, the last one to arrive overwrites the rest. However, the instruction can also specify that the messages be combined in certain ways. For example, if each message contains one integer, a newly arriving message can be combined with what is already in memory using AND, OR, addition, minimum, or maximum.

Using this knowledge, the routers can do the combining on the way. For example, if a router has four messages containing 3, 6, 8, and 10 all destined for the same place, and the operation is sum, it can replace the four messages with one message containing 27. In this way, traffic can be greatly reduced. SEND operations, even with combining, take many cycles.

Parallel I/O

Since the Connection Machine can process data at such an enormous rate, getting the data into and out of the machine quickly is a very serious problem. What good is being able to search a huge data base in a fraction of a second, if it takes 10 minutes to load the data base? For this reason, the Connection Machine is equipped with an extremely powerful I/O system.

Each 8K subcube has its own I/O channel to which a mass storage system called a **data vault** can be attached, along with a graphics display and other peripherals. The I/O system regards the 8K subcube as two groups, each containing 4K PEs, contained in 256 chips. When doing I/O, each PE delivers or accepts 1 bit at a time, for a total of 256 bits in parallel. The I/O bus is 64 bits wide, so transferring 256 bits takes 4 bus cycles. For disk I/O, these 64 bits are split into two words of 32 bits each. Seven bits are added to form a 39-bit word with error correction.

Now comes the interesting part. Each data vault contains 39 disk drives. The 39-bit data word is written in parallel to the disks, one bit per drive. This technique increases the raw 1.25 megabyte/sec data rate of which each drive is capable to a total of 40 MB/sec. If each of the eight I/O channels is equipped with its own data vault, the aggregate data rate becomes 320 MB/sec, fast enough to load or store the 512 MB memory in 1.6 sec. Depending on whether one chooses 150 MB or 300 MB drives, the total storage capacity is then 40 gigabytes or 80 gigabytes (80,000 megabytes). For most applications this will do.

In addition to providing an impressive I/O bandwidth, the data vault construction also provides a high degree of fault tolerance. If a drive crashes, then one of the 39 bits in each word will be unavailable. However, due to the error correcting code used, the system can recover from one bad bit per word and continue operating. In addition, each data vault contains three spare drives that can be temporarily used to replace drives that are down.

Thus we see that massive parallelism is used not only within the computing part of the system, but also within the I/O subsystem. Some statistics about the Connection Machine's performance are given in Fig. 8-49. Although the PE's are individually small and slow, the total computation and I/O throughput is quite substantial, which is why there is considerable interest in SIMD architectures.

Property	Value
Number of processors	65,536
Memory size	512 megabytes
Memory bandwidth	300 gigabits/sec
I/O bandwidth	320 megabytes/sec
Interprocessor bandwidth	250 million words/sec
Integer addition (32-bits)	2,500 MIPS
Floating-point addition (32-bits)	4,000 megaflops
Power dissipation	28 kW
Weight	1,200 kg

Fig. 8-49. Some characteristics of the Connection Machine.

8.2.6. SIMD Vector Computers

The Connection Machine is intended for symbolic applications such as AI problems. Although it can do floating-point operations, it is not ideally suited for weather forecasting, analysis of seismic data, or processing 3-dimensional real-time CAT scan data. For number-crunching applications like these, **vector computers** (also called **numeric supercomputers**) are needed. In this section, we will examine the fundamental principles used by these high-performance computers.

A typical number-crunching application is full of statements like

for $i := 1$ **to** n **do** $a[i] := b[i] + c[i]$

where a, b, and c are **vectors**, that is, arrays of numbers, usually in floating point. The above **for** loop tells the computer to add the ith elements of b and c together and store the result in the ith element of a.

Technically, the program specifies that the elements should be added sequentially, but that is entirely due to the fact that Pascal does not have any other way to express the addition of the two vectors. Besides, an optimizing compiler can see that the order is irrelevant, and can generate code to add all n elements simultaneously, if the hardware has that capability.

A possible SIMD architecture well suited to this kind of vector processing is shown in Fig. 8-50. This machine takes two n-element vectors as input, and operates on the corresponding elements in parallel using a vector ALU that can operate on all n elements simultaneously.

Vector computers also need to do scalar (nonvector) operations and mixed vector-scalar operations. The basic types of vector operations are listed in Fig. 8-51. The first one, f_1, performs some operation, such as cosine or square root, on

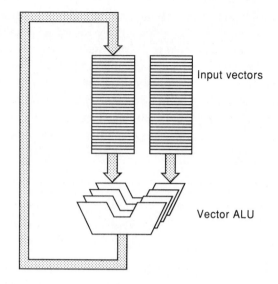

Fig. 8-50. A vector ALU.

each element of a single vector. The second one, f_2, takes a vector as input and produces a scalar as output. A typical example is adding up all the elements. The third one, f_3, performs a dyadic operation on two vectors, such as adding up corresponding elements. Finally, f_4 combines a scalar operand with a vector one. A typical example is multiplying each element of a vector by a constant. It is sometimes faster to convert the scalar to a vector, each of whose values is equal to the scalar, and then perform the operation on two vectors.

Operation	Examples
$A_i := f_1 (B_i)$	f_1 = cosine, square root
Scalar := $f_2 (A)$	f_2 = sum, minimum
$A_i := f_3 (B_i, C_i)$	f_3 = add, subtract
$A_i := f_4$ (scalar, B_i)	f_4 = multiply B_i by a constant

Fig. 8-51. Various combinations of vector and scalar operations.

All the usual vector operations can be built up using these forms. For example, the inner product (dot product) of two vectors consists of first multiplying the corresponding elements together (f_3) and then summing the result (f_2).

In practice, few supercomputers are actually built like Fig. 8-50 (although some slower attached array processors are). The reason is not technical—one could certainly build such machines—but is economic. A design with, say, 64 very high speed ALUs would be too expensive. The Connection Machine is able to afford so many because its ALUs are so simple and cheap. For a supercomputer we need extremely fast floating-point ALUs, which greatly raises the price tag.

The method that is normally used is to combine vector processing with pipelining. Floating-point operations are quite complex, requiring several steps to complete, and any multistep operation is a candidate for a pipelined implementation. If you are not familiar with floating-point arithmetic, please read Appendix B.

As an example of floating-point pipelining, consider the example of Fig. 8-52. In this example, a normalized number has a mantissa above or equal to 1, but below 10. The idea here is to subtract 9.212×10^{11} from 1.082×10^{12}.

Step	Name	Values
1	Fetch operands	$1.082 \times 10^{12} - 9.212 \times 10^{11}$
2	Adjust exponent	$1.082 \times 10^{12} - 0.9212 \times 10^{12}$
3	Execute subtraction	0.1608×10^{12}
4	Normalize result	1.608×10^{11}

Fig. 8-52. Steps in a floating-point subtraction.

To subtract two floating-point numbers, it is first necessary to adjust them so that their exponents are the same. In this example we can either convert the subtrahend to 0.9212×10^{12} or convert the minuend to 10.82×10^{11}. In general, each conversion has its risks. Raising an exponent might cause the mantissa to underflow, and lowering it might cause the mantissa to overflow. Underflow is the less serious of the two, because an underflowed number can be approximated by 0, so let us take the former route. After adjusting both exponents to 12, we have the values shown in step 2 of Fig. 8-52. Next we perform the subtraction, followed by normalizing the result.

Pipelining can be applied to the **for** loop given at the beginning of this section. In Fig. 8-53 we see a pipelined floating-point adder with four stages. In each cycle, the first stage fetches a pair of operands. Then the second stage adjusts the exponent of the smaller one to match that of the larger. The third stage performs the operation, and the fourth stage normalizes the result. In this manner, on every cycle, one result rolls out of the pipeline.

One big difference between using pipelining for operations on vectors and using it for general-purpose instruction execution is the absence of jumps when operating on vectors. Every cycle is fully utilized, and no slots are wasted.

Supercomputers typically have multiple ALUs, each specialized for some particular operation, and all capable of running in parallel. As an example, let us consider the Cray-1, the world's first supercomputer. Although it is not the most recent supercomputer, it has a simple RISC-like architecture that makes it a good subject

Cycle

	1	2	3	4	5	6	7
Fetch operands	B_1 , C_1	B_2 , C_2	B_3 , C_3	B_4 , C_4	B_5 , C_5	B_6 , C_6	B_7 , C_7
Adjust exponent		B_1 , C_1	B_2 , C_2	B_3 , C_3	B_4 , C_4	B_5 , C_5	B_6 , C_6
Execute operation			$B_1 + C_1$	$B_2 + C_2$	$B_3 + C_3$	$B_4 + C_4$	$B_5 + C_5$
Normalize result				$B_1 + C_1$	$B_2 + C_2$	$B_3 + C_3$	$B_4 + C_4$

Fig. 8-53. A pipelined floating-point adder.

to study. That the Cray-1 bears a striking resemblance to the CDC 6600 is not an accident. Both were designed by Seymour Cray, one of the founders of CDC and its chief architect until he left to form his own company, Cray Research.

Typical of all RISC machines, the Cray-1 is register-oriented, with mostly 16-bit instructions consisting of a 7-bit opcode and three 3-bit register numbers for the three operands. Five kinds of registers are present, as shown in Fig. 8-54. The eight 24-bit A registers are used to address memory. The 64 24-bit B registers are used to hold A registers when they are not needed, rather than writing them back to memory. The eight 64-bit S registers are for holding scalar quantities, both integer and floating point. Values in these registers can be used as operands for both integer and floating-point operations. The 64 64-bit T registers are extra storage for the S registers, again to reduce the number of LOADs and STOREs.

The most interesting part of the Cray-1 register set is the group of eight vector registers. Each register can hold a 64-element floating-point vector. Two vectors can be added, subtracted, or multiplied in one 16-bit instruction. Division is not possible, but reciprocals can be calculated. The vector registers can be loaded from, and stored into, memory, but such transfers are expensive, and best minimized. All vector operations use register operands.

Not all supercomputers have this RISC-like property of requiring all operands to be in registers. The CDC 205, for example, performs its vector operations on vectors in memory. This approach allows arbitrarily long vectors to be handled, but greatly slows down the machine since the memory is then a major bottleneck.

The Cray-1 has 12 functional units, as shown in Fig. 8-54. Two are for 24-bit address arithmetic, and four are for integer operations on 64-bit integer scalars. Like its ancestor, the CDC 6600, the Cray-1 does not have a unit for doing integer multiplication. The remaining six units all work on vectors, and are all highly pipelined. The addition, multiplication, and reciprocal units also work on scalar floating-point numbers as well as on vectors.

Like many other vector computers, the Cray-1 allows **chaining** of operations. For example, one way to compute

R1 := R1 * R2 + R3

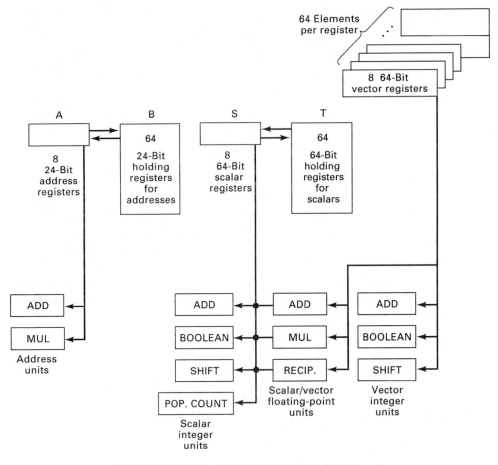

Fig. 8-54. Registers and functional units of the Cray-1

where R1, R2, and R3 are all vector registers, would be to do the vector multiplication, element by element, store the result somewhere, and then do the vector addition. With chaining, as soon as the first elements have been multiplied, the product can go directly to the adder, along with the first element of R3. No intermediate storage is required. This technique improves performance considerably.

8.2.7. Dataflow Computers

Our last model for parallel computation is so different from the ones we have presented so far that it defies classification. In this model the problem is described by a graph, with each node of the graph corresponding to a processor. Results are moved among the processors as messages. Whether this is MIMD or SIMD or something else is arguable. In any event, the concept is called **dataflow** and we will give a brief introduction to it here. For more information, see (Grafe et al., 1989; Nikhil and Arvind, 1989; and Veen, 1986).

The key idea behind a dataflow system is that there are no variables in the usual sense, that is, no addressable memory words that can be read from and stored into. Instead, values are represented by packets that are transmitted between processing units. Each processing unit has the task of computing some function of its inputs and producing an output containing the result. These functions are really functions in the strict mathematical sense: each function depends only on its inputs, and not on any global variables or other side information. Furthermore, the only thing a function does is produce an explicit result. It has no side effects such as modifying global variables, because there are none.

Because there are no variables or side effects, each processor may begin its computation as soon as its input packets have arrived. There is no program counter and no explicit sequencing of computations, other than that implicit in one calculation depending on the result of another one. For example, if $y = f(x)$ and $z = g(y)$, then f *must* run before g. It is precisely this ability of dataflow systems to operate without any artificially forced sequencing that makes them so attractive for distributed computing.

To make the idea of dataflow more concrete, we will now look at a detailed example. The problem we wish to tackle is how to use multiple processors to solve the ordinary differential equation

$$\frac{d^2y}{dx^2} + 2x\frac{dy}{dx} + 2y = 0$$

subject to the boundary conditions $y(0) = 1$ and $y'(0) = 0$.

To solve our equation numerically, let $u = dy/dx$, yielding two equations

$$\frac{du}{dx} + 2ux + 2y = 0 \qquad \text{and} \qquad u = \frac{dy}{dx}$$

Replacing the infinitesimal dx with the finite step Δx, we can solve for the changes in y and u respectively, as

$$\Delta u = -2ux\,\Delta x - 2y\,\Delta x \qquad \text{and} \qquad \Delta y = u\,\Delta x$$

We start out at the known boundary point $x_0 = 0$. From this point we move forward to the new x coordinate, given by $x + \Delta x$. The new u and y values at this point (call them u_1 and y_1) are

$$u_1 = u_0 - 2u_0x_0\,\Delta x - 2y_0\,\Delta x \qquad \text{and} \qquad y_1 = y_0 + u_0\,\Delta x$$

Having found x, u, and y at a new point, we have a new boundary condition, and we can repeat the whole process all over again. Eventually, we will have found the value of y at all x values that are a multiple of Δx. By choosing Δx small enough, we can solve the equation to high accuracy.

If you barely know what a differential equation is, let alone how to solve one, do not despair. The whole purpose of this exercise was to lead up to the program of Fig. 8-55. Having gotten there, we need the differential equation no more. The thing to notice about the program is that it is sequential; the statements are executed in the order written. The computer does not begin on the second iteration step until the first one has been completed. This statement may seem obvious, but it will not be true for the data flow version.

```
{Solve the differential equation: y"+ 2xy' + 2y =0.}
program diffeq (input, output);
var a, dx, x, u, y, x1, u1, y1: real;
begin
    {read in the ordinate, a, at which we want the value of the function,
    the step size, dx, and boundary condition}
    read (a, dx, x, u, y);
    while x < a do
        begin
            x1 := x + dx;
            u1 := u - 2*x*u*dx - 2*y*dx;
            y1 := y + u*dx;
            x :=x1; u :=u1; y := y1
        end;
        writeln (y: 13:9)
end.
```

Fig. 8-55. A program to solve a differential equation.

The equivalent dataflow program written in a dataflow language would look similar to Fig. 8-55. This similarity is hardly an accident. Dataflow languages have been carefully designed to make them look like traditional programming languages, to make dataflow more palatable to the masses. The dataflow graph of Fig. 8-56(a) is really the equivalent of the assembly language translation of Fig. 8-55.

The basic element in a dataflow graph (or machine) is a box (or processor) with one or more inputs and one or more outputs. Consider the box labeled "6" in Fig. 8-56. It has two inputs and an output. As soon as packets have arrived on each input line and the previously sent output packet has been absorbed by its destination, the processor can begin execution.

By requiring the previous output to already have been absorbed before the processor can generate more, we are sure there will be a place to put it. Some dataflow systems do not have this restriction, leading to a higher degree of parallelism but a much more complicated buffering strategy. We will stick to the simpler systems, known as **feedback interpreter** systems, so called because when a processor fires (executes), it must send acknowledgement packets back up its input lines to tell whoever generated those inputs that the lines are now free again. In effect, each processor has a buffer of size 1 for each input line, and any other processor planning to send an output packet must be kept informed of the status of the buffer.

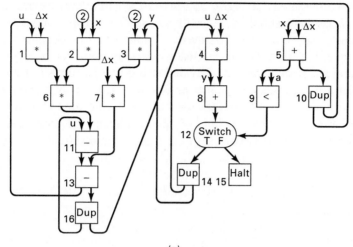

(a)

Processor	Opcode	Operand 1			Operand 2			Destination 1		Destination 2	
		Value	Sticky	Full	Value	Sticky	Full	Target	Port	Target	Port
1	*	u	0	1	Δx	1	1	6	1	0	0
2	*	2	1	1	x	0	1	6	2	0	0
3	*	2	1	1	y	0	1	7	2	0	0
4	*	u	0	1	Δx	1	1	8	2	0	0
5	+	x	0	1	Δx	1	1	9	1	10	1
6	*	0	0	0	0	0	0	11	2	0	0
7	*	Δx	1	1	0	0	0	13	2	0	0
8	+	y	0	1	0	0	0	12	1	0	0
9	<	0	0	0	a	1	1	12	2	0	0
10	Dup	0	0	0	0	1	1	2	2	5	1
11	−	u	0	1	0	0	0	13	1	0	0
12	Switch	0	0	0	0	0	0	14	1	15	1
13	−	0	0	0	0	0	0	1	1	16	1
14	Dup	0	0	0	0	1	1	8	1	3	2
15	Halt	0	0	0	0	1	1	0	0	0	0
16	Dup	0	0	0	0	1	1	11	1	4	1

(b)

Fig. 8-56. (a) A dataflow graph. (b) Initial values of the templates.

To see how the system of Fig. 8-56 operates, imagine that the input buffers of processors 1 through 5 are initialized with the values shown. Constant arguments are shown encircled; they are "hardwired" into their respective buffers. For simplicity's sake, we will assume that each operation requires one cycle. During cycle 1, processors 1 through 5 all fire, delivering results to processors 6 through 10, all of which fire during cycle 2. Processor 9 compares its two arguments. If the first is less than the second, it outputs a packet containing a 1 (for true); otherwise, it outputs a 0 (for false). Processor 10 simply duplicates its argument. The DUP function is useful to generate extra copies of a previous result. Note that processor 5 has two outputs, but that three are needed. (Again for simplicity, we have arbitrarily limited the number of outputs per processor to two.)

During the third cycle something amazing happens. While processor 11 is busy computing $2xu \, \Delta x - 2y \, \Delta x$, processor 5 is already busy working on the following iteration (i.e., $x = 2 \, \Delta x$), even though the previous one has not yet finished. Notice that this parallelism is completely automatic; any part of the computation that can proceed does proceed. Also during cycle 3, processor 12 uses its second argument to select one of the output lines onto which the first argument is passed. As long as processor 9 keeps generating "true" packets based on the condition $x < a$, the output from processor 12 will be directed to processor 14 and the computation will continue. However, as soon as processor 9 generates a single false packet, the computation will be terminated in two cycles by processor 15. Since our system has no input or output devices, let us assume that processor 15 prints its input prior to halting the system, with this packet being the answer to the problem.

Note that a certain amount of synchronization is inherent in the feedback interpreter. The loop consisting of processors 5 and 10 cannot go arbitrarily fast, because 5 cannot generate output unless processor 9 is willing to accept the value.

Associated with each processor in Fig. 8-56 is a **template** that contains enough information to allow the processor to function. The template contains the operation to be performed, because most processors can execute any one of several instructions, the input buffers, and a list of the output destinations. Associated with each input buffer are 2 bits, the *sticky* bit and the *full* bit. The full bit simply indicates whether or not there is a value in the buffer. The sticky bit tells what should be done with the buffer after firing. Normally, it is cleared, that is, the full bit is turned off. However, if the sticky bit is on, the buffer is not cleared after firing. This feature is useful for operands that are constant throughout the program, such as the left inputs of processors 2 and 7 and the right inputs of processors 4 and 9. The output destinations must tell not only which processor is to receive the output, but also whether it is the left or right line (port) on which it enters.

Figure 8-56(b) shows the initial values for all the templates in the system. By simply inserting the five input variables a, Δx, x, u, and y into the appropriate templates at the start of computation, we finesse the lack of input facilities. Given these initial templates, the calculation is deterministic and will run until $x \geq a$.

Please notice that in Fig. 8-56(a) a substantial part of the program logic is contained in the way the processors are wired, somewhat reminiscent of the plug-board machines that existed prior to von Neumann's invention of the internal stored program. What an irony. Our post von Neumann machine turns out to be a pre von Neumann machine.

In reality, the model of Fig. 8-56(a) is only a conceptual one; an actual dataflow system looks more like that of Fig. 8-57. The templates are stored in the program memory. As soon as a template is ready to fire (i.e., its inputs are loaded and its destinations are all free), the fetch unit can extract the opcode, operands, and destination addresses, make a packet from them, and send the packet to one of the processors. The output packets generated by the processors are stored in the appropriate templates by the store unit.

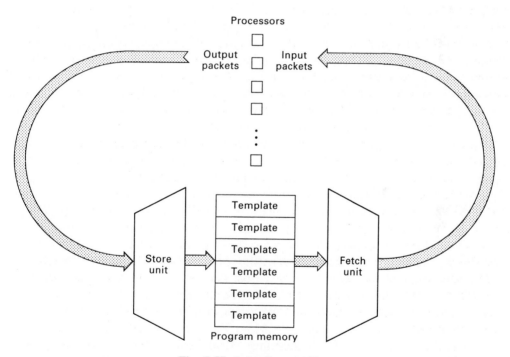

Fig. 8-57. A dataflow machine.

The assumption behind Fig. 8-57 is that the fetching and storing operations are much, much faster than the actual calculations. If this assumption is not true, the whole idea makes little sense. There is no point in spending 100 μsec in setting up a processor that will do its work in 100 nsec. In most dataflow machines, the fetch and store units are highly parallel combinatorial networks; they are not little microprocessors, for performance reasons.

Put in other terms, we assume that a cycle consists of fetching and dispatching all the fireable templates (limited only by the number of processors available), having them all executed, and then storing the results back in proper places. Under these conditions, it is clear that if we start out with a single processor and then add more, the performance of the machine will go up until all the inherent parallelism has been exploited. We finally come to the whole point of dataflow: once a problem has been compiled into a dataflow graph, it can run on a machine with many processors, or a machine with few processors, with no changes to the binary program. The execution automatically adjusts itself to the number of processors available, up to some maximum. All that the compiler must do is produce the original dataflow graph, which looks surprisingly like a collection of parse trees for the expressions in the program.

8.3. SUMMARY

In this chapter, we have examined two types of advanced architectures: RISC computers and parallel computers. Both are designed for high performance. The former gets its speed by eliminating the microcode and executing simple instructions very quickly. The latter's strength is doing many operations at the same time.

The essence of a RISC machine is that it executes one instruction per data path cycle, directly on the hardware, with no interpretation by an underlying layer of software. The basic instructions are simple, register-register operations like ADD and AND, and do not reference memory. The instruction set is always chosen to make it possible to execute instructions simply and quickly. There are few formats and fewer addressing modes.

We discussed two examples in detail, the SPARC and the MIPS. Together, these two examples illustrate most of the ideas found in contemporary RISC machines. Both are 32-bit machines with 3-address instructions. The SPARC has overlapping register windows and the MIPS does not, but at any instant, both have 32 registers addressable. Both support virtual memory with 4K pages and both are designed to work with a cache and a floating-point coprocessor. The two machines are far from identical, however, and the various differences and design trade-offs were discussed.

Parallel computers can be divided into MIMD and SIMD. MIMD computers can be further subdivided into disjoint memory systems such as Transputer grids and hypercubes, and shared memory systems. Disjoint memory computers use message passing for physical communication, although work has begun on simulating shared memory in software on top of them. Shared memory can be implemented over a bus, in which case caching and cache coherence protocols are needed, or over multistage switching networks such as the omega network.

Parallel SIMD computers have a single instruction stream that drives a large number of PEs, each with its own private memory. The Connection Machine has 64K PEs and a tremendous computing power and I/O power, despite the relatively simple nature of the PEs, which perform arithmetic serially, one bit at a time.

Vector SIMD computers also have high performance, but achieve it differently. They can perform operations on vectors at a great rate due to their highly pipelined and parallel ALUs. This architecture is popular for numeric supercomputers that are used for weather forecasting and other number-crunching applications.

Finally, we looked at dataflow computers, which do not fit neatly into any classification scheme. These are completely asynchronous, allowing operations to begin as soon as the operands are available.

PROBLEMS

1. An overlapping register window RISC machine has 32 registers, 8 of which are dedicated to global variables. The remaining 24 are split among incoming parameters, local variables, and outgoing parameters. List all the feasible ways the 24 registers can be allocated among these three categories.

2. Consider the execution of the Towers of Hanoi procedure of Fig. 5-48 on a RISC machine with overlapping register windows. The main program uses a register window itself and calls *towers*(3, 1, 2). How many times during the execution does a window have to be saved in order to allow a call to complete if three windows are available? What if there are four windows?

3. If a procedure makes no calls to other procedures, are the registers normally used for outgoing parameters simply wasted?

4. Of the 32 registers visible in the RISC I at any instant, 10 are globals, 6 are input parameters, 10 are locals and 6 are output parameters. How many registers should the window be advanced upon a procedure call?

5. In Fig. 8-5, there are five LOADs but only three STOREs. Why?

6. In our examples, there was only one delay slot behind each LOAD or JUMP. Suppose that the delay were n slots, that a fraction L of all instructions were LOADs and a fraction J were JUMPs. At what fraction of the full speed would the machine run if all the delay slots were filled with NO-OPs?

7. A procedure has 20 statements and 12 local variables, A through L. Below is a listing of the range of statements during which each local variable is live. What is the minimum number of registers needed to hold these variables, and how should they be packed to achieve this minimum?

A: 1–5	E: 6–10	I: 1–4
B: 3–12	F: 12–20	J: 5–8
C: 10–15	G: 14–19	K: 7–12
D: 13–20	H: 1–6	L: 16–19

8. A procedure consists of 17 consecutive assignment statements and no jumps. Variable x is assigned to in statements 4, 9, and 15, and is used in statements 7, 10, 12, and 17. Give a list of the statement ranges in which x is live.

9. Suppose a RISC machine has a large on-chip cache, with a hit rate of over 99 percent. Further suppose that LOAD instructions can complete in 1 cycle on a cache hit and 2 on a cache miss. Does it matter if this machine has hardware interlocking? Explain.

10. How many dhrystones/sec can the RISC I do? (*Hint*: The answer is not given in the text, but enough information is provided to allow you to calculate it.)

11. A RISC machine has a 100-nsec cycle time. Twenty percent of its instructions are LOADs or STOREs, half of whose delay slots are lost to NO-OPs. Suppose that a new model is brought out with a 90-nsec cycle time, but the price of the faster cycle time is that the LOADs and STOREs now have two delay slots each, and only one-fourth of these can be filled with useful instructions. Which machine is faster and by how much?

12. Give 5 ways to implement NO-OP on the SPARC.

13. The Pascal assignment statement $j := 2 * i$ can be compiled in two different ways on the SPARC. List them.

14. In the previous problem we saw that a single Pascal statement could be compiled in two different ways. Does this contradict our earlier statement that code generation on a RISC machine is easier than on a CISC machine because there is only one way to do everything?

15. In Fig. 8-23, the first thing the program does is test to see if n is 1. If it is not, a conditional branch is made to ELSE to do the recursion. However, the SETHI that follows the BNE is in a delay slot. If the branch is not taken, the BNE is effectively ignored and the SETHI is needed. However, consider the case that the branch *is* taken. The SETHI will still be executed. Does this cause a problem?

16. Probably the most common instruction in any assembly language program is moving a constant to a register. Can the SPARC do this in one instruction? If so, how? If not, how many does it take?

17. The SPARC has hardware interlock on delayed instructions like LOAD. Some other RISC machines do not. What implications does this decision have on the portability of programs to future models of the machine that might have more delay slots?

18. Suppose you were working for a company designing a successor to the SPARC. To make your machine more impressive, you have decided to make 64 registers visible at any instant, instead of the competition's 32. Is this approach feasible without a drastic overhaul of the SPARC instruction formats?

19. How can you load the 32-bit constant FFFFFF00H into a register on the MIPS in one cycle?

20. The MIPS has no condition codes. Does this mean that compiling code for

   if x < y **then** ...

takes more instructions on the MIPS than on the SPARC? Discuss.

21. The SPARC SETHI and MIPS LUI instructions are almost the same. Would it be possible to replace SETHI with LUI on the SPARC?

22. One morning, the queen bee of a certain beehive calls in all her worker bees and tells them that today's assignment is get collect marigold nectar. All the workers then buzz off in different directions looking for marigolds. Is this an SIMD or an MIMD parallel system?

23. Are dataflow machines loosely coupled or tightly coupled?

24. The 2D Computer company has a product consisting of n memory-disjoint computers arranged in a square grid. One night, the Vice President for Topology gets an idea for a new product: a 3-dimensional grid with the n processors arranged in a perfect cube (e.g., for 4096 this is possible).

   a. How is the worst case delay affected by this change?
   b. How is the total bandwidth affected by this change?

25. Consider a multiprocessor using a shared bus. What happens if two processors try to access the global memory at exactly the same instant?

26. Suppose that for technical reasons it is only possible for a snooping cache to snoop on address lines, not data lines. Would this change affect the *write through* protocol? How about the Firefly protocol?

27. In the text, we discussed what happens if a word on the Firefly is RESERVED and then written by its owner. What do you think happens if another processor sneaks in and reads it before it can be written?

28. Suppose that there are n CPUs on a common bus. The probability that any CPU tries to use the bus in a given cycle is p. What is the chance that

   a. the bus is idle (0 requests).
   b. exactly one request is made.
   c. more than one request is made.

29. Suppose the wire between switch 2A and switch 3B in the omega network breaks. Who is cut off from whom?

30. In the Benes network, list all the paths from CPU 000 to memory 000.

31. Give the paths in a Benes network to simultaneously connect the following (CPU, memory) pairs: (0, 1), (2, 2), (4, 6), and (7, 4).

32. Hot spots are clearly a major problem in multistage switching networks. Are they also a problem in bus-based systems?

33. An omega switching network connects 4096 RISC CPUs, each with a 60-nsec cycle time, to 4096 infinitely fast memory modules. The switching elements each have a 5-nsec delay. How many delay slots are needed by a LOAD instruction?

34. Consider a machine using an omega switching network, like the one shown in Fig. 8-43. Suppose that the program and stack for processor i is kept in memory module i. Propose a slight change in the topology that makes a large difference in the performance (the IBM RP3 and BBN Butterfly use this modified topology). What disadvantage does your new topology have compared to the original?

35. How critical is the switching speed of the crossbar that is used to connect the hosts to the Connection Machine?

36. Suppose the Connection Machine PEs took 2 flag bits and 2 memory bits as inputs to compute the 2 output bits. How many bits would the truth-table field have to be?

37. Compute the worst-case propagation time (in cycles) for a message whose total length is 32 bits. On each cycle, a PE can deliver a bit to its router (or accept one), and on each cycle, a router can give one bit to a neighboring PE. Assume no contention anywhere.

38. Give a lower bound to the number of nanoinstructions needed on the Connection Machine for a 32-bit multiply.

39. A vector processor like the Cray-1 has arithmetic units with four-stage pipelines. Each stage takes 1 nsec. How long does it take to add two 1024-element vectors?

40. How might one connect the templates and processors of Fig. 8-57?

41. Suppose the third term of the differential equation given in the text were $5y$ instead of $2y$. What changes would have to be made to the dataflow templates of Fig. 8-56(b)?

42. Write a SPARC simulator. To make this project slightly easier, assume that there are no delayed instructions. Do not simulate the traps, floating-point, or coprocessor instructions.

43. Write a dataflow program to compute square roots using the Newton-Raphson iterative algorithm. The inputs are the number whose square root is needed, and epsilon, the value which tells if two iterations are close enough to stop the calculation.

9

READING LIST AND BIBLIOGRAPHY

In the preceding eight chapters, a large number of topics were discussed in various degrees of detail. This chapter is meant to assist readers interested in pursuing further their study of computer organization. Section 9.1 contains a list of suggested readings arranged by chapter. Section 9.2 is an alphabetical bibliography of all books and articles cited in this book.

9.1. SUGGESTIONS FOR FURTHER READING

9.1.1. Introduction and General Works

Hamacher et al., *Computer Organization, 2nd ed.*
   A traditional textbook on computer organization including instruction sets, the CPU, microprogramming, I/O, arithmetic, memories, and digital logic.

Hayes, *Computer Architecture and Organization, 2nd ed.*
   Although the title is almost the same as Stallings' book (see below), the content is somewhat different. Hayes tends to emphasize the design and engineering aspects of the subject over the pure architectural ones. The book contains many detailed circuit diagrams.

Kain, *Computer Architecture: Software and Hardware*

This two-volume work contains over 800 pages of material on computer architecture. The choice and organization of the material is rather unconventional, but a number of topics, especially memory and parallelism, are treated in an interesting way.

Langholtz et al., *Elements of Computer Organization*

A general text on computer organization covering logic design, the CPU, I/O, memory, microprogramming, and other topics. The chapters on pipelined computers and parallel processing provide interesting introductions to these subjects.

Price, "A History of Calculating Machines"

Although modern computers started with Babbage in the 19th century, human beings have been computing since the dawn of civilization. This fascinating illustrated article traces the history of counting, mathematics, calendars, and computation from 3000 B.C. to the start of the 20th century.

Slater, *Portraits in Silicon*

Why didn't Dennis Ritchie turn in his Ph.D. thesis at Harvard? What is Seymour Cray's algorithm for buying new cars? Why did Steve Jobs become a vegetarian? The answers lie in this fascinating book that contains short biographies of 34 people who shaped the computer industry, from Charles Babbage to Donald Knuth.

Stallings, *Computer Organization and Architecture*

A general text on computer architecture. Some of the topics treated in this book are also covered in Stallings' book.

Wilkes, "Computers Then and Now"

A personal history of computers from 1946 to 1968 by pioneer computer designer and inventor of microprogramming, Maurice Wilkes. He tells of the early battles between the "space cadets," who believed in automatic programming (pre-FORTRAN compilers), and the traditionalists, who preferred to do their programming in octal.

9.1.2. Computer Systems Organization

Fujitani, "Laser Optical Disk: The Coming Revolution in On-Line Storage"

An introduction to optical disk technology and how it differs from magnetic disk technology. It deals with media, recording issues, and trends.

Humphrey and Smock, "High-Speed Modems"

As modems go above 9600 bps, the technology gets ever more intricate. This article describes the various competing approaches to modern high-speed modems, and compares a dozen modems.

Murray and Pappas, "Pick of the Litter"
A short introduction to computer mice that discusses interfacing and movement detection. Several personal computer mice are compared in various ways.

Shuford, "CD-ROMs and Their Kin"
An introduction to CD-ROMs, focusing on the drive structure and magneto-optical technology. Some of the problems are also discussed.

Smarte and Baran, "Face to Face"
Four display technologies are being used or considered for computer terminals. CRTs are currently the leader, but liquid crystal displays, gas plasma displays, and electroluminescent are all up-and-coming. This article provides an introduction to all four of them.

9.1.3. The Digital Logic Level

Borrill, "Microprocessor Bus Structures and Standards"
A nice introduction to component, backplane, system, parallel, and serial buses. In addition to discussing the various kinds of buses, the paper treats bus termination, software visibility, DMA, interrupts, and data representation.

Dailey, *Small Computer Theory and Applications*
The title notwithstanding, this book contains no theory and no applications. It does, however, tell a lot about the IBM PC CPU, memory, and I/O, how they work and how to interface to them. If you are interested in the hardware side of the IBM PC, this is a good reference.

Gustavson, "Computer Buses—A Tutorial"
This introduction to buses covers how buses work, bus mechanics, signal transmission, arbitration, protocols, reliability, and software aspects, among other topics. It also provides a list of references about specific buses.

9.1.4. The Microprogramming Level

Andrews, *Principles of Firmware Engineering in Microprogram Control*
A thorough treatment of many aspects of microprogramming, including microinstruction organization, sequencing, and control. Optimization and engineering techniques are discussed in detail and the relevant theory is covered.

Milutinović, *Microprogramming Firmware Engineering*
A discussion of the fundamentals of microprogramming, including hardware, architecture, horizontal and vertical microprogramming, optimization, and testing.

Tredennick, "The Impact of VLSI on Microprogramming"
Does microprogramming have a future? With the advent of RISC machines, some people have said it is dead. This paper by a leading microprogrammer (co-designer of the 68000) discusses the different cultures of microprogramming and presents the view that it will survive for at least two more chip generations.

Tredennick, *Microprocessor Logic Design*
Suppose you actually wanted to design a microprogrammed computer. Where would you begin? By reading this book. Tredennick was one of the architects of the Motorola 68000 and IBM Micro/370, so he knows what he is talking about.

9.1.5. The Conventional Machine Level

Bacon, "The Motorola MC68000"
An introduction to the 68000, with emphasis on I/O programming and device interfacing for the assembly language programmer.

El-Ayat and Agarwal, "The Intel 80386—Architecture and Implementation"
A programmer's introduction to the 80386 by the people who designed it. The base architecture and memory management are covered, and a little is said about the implementation. A labeled photograph of the chip is included.

Johnson, "A Comparison of MC68000 Family Processors"
An overview and comparison of the 680x0 chips, with an emphasis on how they differ from one another.

Leventhal, "Lance Leventhal's 80386 Programming Guide"
Having included his name in the title, his photograph on the front cover, and his biography inside, the author is apparently proud of this book. Of the various books on the 80386, it is one of the better ones, dispensing with assembly language programming in one chapter, and then going on to I/O, the MMU, task management, exceptions, and various hardware features.

9.1.6. The Operating System Machine Level

Corbató and Vyssotsky, "Introduction and Overview of the MULTICS System"
A general introduction to the design goals of MULTICS. This article introducing MULTICS to the world was written by two of its chief designers long before the system was completed. One of their intentions was to put their ideas into print

before carrying them out, to be able to see later how far the system drifted from its original plans.

Denning, "Virtual Memory"
    An excellent tutorial on virtual memory. Topics covered include segmentation, paging, storage utilization, replacement algorithms, page size, fragmentation, demand paging, and the working set model.

Finkel, *An Operating Systems Vade Mecum*
    A good introductory text on operating systems. Chapter 3 on memory management and Chap. 8 on concurrency treat in more depth topics that we have provided an introduction to.

Horner, *Operating Systems Concepts and Applications*
    A breezy text on operating systems. In addition to the usual theory, short introductions are given to MS-DOS, OS/2, the Macintosh, UNIX, VMS, and a few of IBM's mainframe operating systems.

Iacobucci, *OS/2 Programmers Guide*
    If this 1100 page book on OS/2 written by one of its designers does not tell you everything you ever wanted to know about OS/2, you are more curious than most people. It describes memory management, multitasking, the file system, resource management, device drivers, I/O, sessions, and much more, as well as describing all the system calls in detail.

Pinkert and Wear, *Operating Systems Concepts, Policies, and Mechanisms*
    A fairly standard, up-to-date textbook on operating systems.

Ritchie and Thompson, "The UNIX Time-Sharing System"
    This is the original published paper on UNIX. It is still well worth reading. From this small seed has grown a great operating system.

Tanenbaum, *Operating Systems: Design and Implementation*
    Unlike most books on operating systems that only deal with the theory, this one covers all the relevant theory and illustrates it by discussing the actual code of a UNIX-like operating system, MINIX, that runs on the IBM PC and other computers. The heavily annotated source code is listed in a 250-page appendix.

9.1.7. The Assembly Language Level

Darden and Heller, "Streamline Your Software Development"
    This paper discusses measurements of program performance showing that in many programs a very large fraction of the execution time is accounted for by a

very small fraction of the program. This strongly suggests writing programs in a higher-level language, testing them, and rewriting only the critical parts in assembly language, instead of writing everything in assembly language.

Gorsline, *Assembly and Assemblers*

Although most of this book is about how to program the 68000 in assembly language, Chap. 8 discusses in some detail how a macro assembler works. In Chap. 9, the authors tells how to design a linker.

Presser and White, "Linkers and Loaders"

Since the field of linking and loading changes very slowly, this survey article, although written many years ago, is still a useful reference.

9.1.8. Advanced Architectures

Almasi and Gottlieb, *Highly Parallel Computing*

An attempt to cover the entire state of the art in parallel computing in 500 pages. The last 200 pages are most interesting, and deal with interconnection networks, SIMD, MIMD, and hybrid parallel architectures. The typography, page layout, and figure design are also interesting, but for a different reason: they clearly show that with the aid of a computer it is possible for a pair of computer scientists to set printing back 500 years.

Athas and Seitz, "Multicomputers: Message-Passing Concurrent Computers"

An overview of parallel computers that do not have shared memory. Both hardware and software aspects of hypercube-type systems are discussed.

Desrochers, *Principles of Parallel and Multiprocessing*

An introductory text on parallel processing, covering general principles, implementations, and case studies.

Gajski et al., *Tutorial on Computer Architecture*

This tutorial covers a variety of advanced architectures, including RISC, parallel processors, multiprocessors, numeric supercomputers, and others.

Gimarc and Milutinović, "A Survey of RISC Processors and Computers of the Mid-1980s"

An introduction to RISC technology along with a comparison of about 20 existing RISC processors. Collectively, these machines violate every fundamental RISC principle. The moral of the story is that the design space is very large, and different architects, with different goals, make different choices. The authors do a good job of pointing out the various trade-offs that exist.

Hinnant, "Accurate UNIX Benchmarking: Art, Science, or Black Magic?"
     With all the excitement about fast RISC chips, benchmarks are becoming big business. It is a pity that most are worthless. Read this article to find out why.

Huck and Flynn, *Analyzing Computer Architectures*
     An approach to computer architecture based on measurements is described. Benchmarks and compiler effects are examined, and various machines are compared.

Hwang and Briggs, *Computer Architecture and Parallel Processing*
     A wide-ranging book on the architecture of parallel computers. Pipelined computers, vector computers, array processors, SIMD and MIMD computers, multiprocessors and data flow machines are all covered in detail in this 846-page work.

IEEE Computer Magazine, June 1987
     A special issue on the interconnection networks used in shared-memory multiprocessors. The six articles cover an introduction, fault tolerance, multistage networks, buses, optical crossbars, and performance analyses.

Lipovski and Malek, *Parallel Computing*
     For readers interested in the theory behind parallel processor architectures, this is a good place to look. The emphasis is on the graph-theoretic properties of omega and other switching networks. Eight lengthy appendices describe actual systems as well.

Melear, "The Design of the 88000 RISC Family"
     In Chap. 8 we have described the SPARC and MIPS chips in some detail. Another interesting RISC processor is the Motorola 88000. Melear's article discusses the architecture and instruction set of the 88000 in roughly the same level of detail as we have used for our examples.

Piepho and Wu, "A Comparison of RISC Architectures"
     Three of the more popular RISC designs, the SPARC, the Motorola 88000, and the Intel i860 are discussed and compared with respect to branches, registers, addressing modes, data types, floating point, and memory management.

Robinson, "How Much of a RISC?"
     A short history of RISC, treating both university and commercial designs. The paper covers processors designed by Berkeley, AMD, Stanford, HP, and Acorn.

Stenstrom, "Reducing Contention in Shared-Memory Multiprocessors"
     An overview of multiprocessor systems using buses, crossbars, and multistage switching networks. A short summary is given of ten different multiprocessors:

C.mmp, CM*, RP3, Alliant, Cedar, Butterfly, SPUR, Dragon, Multimax, and Balance. These systems are then compared with one another.

9.1.9. Binary and Floating-Point Numbers

Cody, "Analysis of Proposals for the Floating-Point Standard"
Some time ago, IEEE designed a floating-point architecture that is becoming widespread on smaller machines. Cody discusses the various issues, proposals, and controversies that came up during the standardization process.

Garner, "Number Systems and Arithmetic"
A tutorial on advanced binary arithmetic concepts, including carry propagation, redundant number systems, residue number systems, and nonstandard multiplication and division. Strongly recommended for anyone who thinks he learned everything there is to know about arithmetic in sixth grade.

IEEE, *Proc. of the n-th Symposium on Computer Arithmetic*
Contrary to popular opinion, arithmetic is an active research area with many scientific papers written by and for arithmetic specialists. In this symposium series, advances in high-speed addition and multiplication, VLSI arithmetic hardware, coprocessors, fault tolerance, and rounding, among other topics, are presented.

Knuth, *Seminumerical Algorithms*
A wealth of material about positional number systems, floating-point arithmetic, and multiple-precision arithmetic. All algorithms are specified carefully, both in English and in the assembly language of a hypothetical computer called MIX. This material requires and deserves careful study.

Perlmutter and Yuen, "The 80387 and Its Applications"
An introduction to the 80386's floating-point coprocessor. The article treats the hardware, architecture, programming, software, and applications of this chip.

Stein and Munro, *Introduction to Machine Arithmetic*
A thorough treatment of computer arithmetic in a general radix. Although the emphasis is primarily on the theory of machine arithmetic, there are also a large number of carefully worked problems and examples illustrating the algorithms covered.

Wilson, "Floating-Point Survival Kit"
A nice introduction to floating-point numbers and standards for people who think that the world ends at 65,535. Some popular floating-point benchmarks, such as *Linpack*, are also discussed.

9.2. ALPHABETICAL BIBLIOGRAPHY

ADAMS, G.B. III, AGRAWAL, D.P., and SIEGEL, H.J.: "A Survey and Comparison of Fault-Tolerant Multistage Interconnection Networks," *IEEE Computer Magazine*, vol. 20, pp. 14-27, June 1987.

AGARWAL, A., HOROWITZ, M., and HENNESSY, J.: "An Analytical Cache Model," *Trans. on Computer Syst.*, vol. 7, pp. 184-215, May 1989.

AGARWAL, A., and CHERIAN, M.: "Adaptive Backoff Synchronization Techniques," *Proc. 16th Ann. Int'l Symp. on Computer Arch.*, ACM, pp. 396-406, 1989.

AGARWAL, A., SIMONI, R., HENNESSY, J., and HOROWITZ, M.: "An Evaluation of Directory Schemes for Cache Coherence," *Proc. 15th Ann. Int'l Symp. on Computer Arch.*, ACM, pp. 280-289, 1988.

ALMASI, G.S., and GOTTLIEB, A.: *Highly Parallel Computing*, Redwood City, CA: Benjamin/Cummings, 1989.

ANDREWS, M.: *Principles of Firmware Engineering in Microprogram Control*, Rockville, Md.: Computer Science Press, 1980.

ARCHIBALD, J., and BAER, J.-L.: "Cache Coherence Protocols: Evaluation Using a Multiprocessor Simulation Model," *ACM Trans. Prog. Comp. Syst.*, vol. 4, pp. 273-298, Nov. 1986.

ARCHIBALD, J., and BAER, J.-L.: "An Economical Solution to the Cache Coherence Problem," *Proc. 11th Ann. Int'l Symp. on Computer Arch.*, ACM, pp. 355-362, 1984.

ATHAS, W.C., and SEITZ, C.L.: "Multicomputers: Message-Passing Concurrent Computers," *IEEE Computer Magazine*, vol. 21, pp. 9-24, Aug. 1988.

BACON, J.: *The Motorola 68000*, Englewood Cliffs, NJ: Prentice-Hall, 1986.

BAL, H.E.: *The Shared Data-Object Model as a Paradigm for Distributed Programming*, Ph.D. dissertation, Vrije Universiteit, 1989.

BAL, H.E., KAASHOEK, M.F., and TANENBAUM, A.S.: "A Distributed Implementation of the Shared Data-Object Model," IR-189, May 1989.

BAL, H.E., STEINER, J.G., and TANENBAUM, A.S.: "Programming Languages for Distributed Computing Systems," *Computing Surveys*, 1989.

BAL, H.E., and TANENBAUM, A.S.: "Distributed Programming with Shared Data," *Proc. 1988 Int'l Conf. on Computer Languages*, IEEE, pp. 82-91, 1988.

BHUYAN, L.N., YANG, Q., and AGRAWAL, D.P.: "Performance of Multiprocessor Interconnection Networks," *IEEE Computer Magazine*, vol. 22, pp. 25-37, Feb. 1989.

BIRNBAUM, J.S., and WORLEY, W.S. Jr.: "Beyond RISC: High Precision Architecture," *Proc. Spring COMPCON 1986*, IEEE, pp. 40-47, 1986.

BITAR, P., and DESPAIN, A.M.: "Multiprocessor Cache Synchronization: Issues, Innovations, Evolution," *Proc. 13th Ann. Int'l Symp. on Computer Arch.*, ACM, pp. 424-433, 1986.

BORRILL, P.L.: "Microprocessor Bus Structures and Standards," *IEEE Micro Magazine*, vol. 1, pp. 84-95, Feb. 1981.

BORRILL, P.L.: "A Comparison of 32-bit Buses," *IEEE Micro Magazine*, vol. 5, pp. 71-79, Dec. 1985.

BROOMELL, G., and HEATH, J.R.: "An Integrated-Circuit Crossbar Switching System," *Proc. 4th Int'l Conf. on Distr. Computing Systems*, IEEE, pp. 278-287, 1984.

CARRIERO, N., and GELERNTER, D.: "Linda in Context," *Commun. ACM*, vol. 32, pp. 444-458, April 1989.

CHAITIN, G.J., AUSLANDER, M.A., CHANDRA, A.K., COCKE, J., HOPKINS, M.E., and MARKSTEIN, P.W.: "Register Allocation via Coloring," *Computer Languages*, vol. 6, pp. 47-57, 1981.

CHEONG, H., and VEIDENBAUM, A.V.: "A Cache Coherence Scheme with Fast Selective Invalidation," *Proc. 15th Ann. Int'l Symp. on Computer Arch.*, ACM, pp. 299-307, 1988.

CHOW, F.: "Minimizing Register Usage Penalty at Procedure Calls," *Proc. ACM SIG-PLAN 88 Symp. on Prog. Lang. Design and Impl.*, ACM, pp. 85-94, 1988.

CHOW, F., and HENNESSY, J.: "Register Allocation by Priority-based Coloring," *Proc. of the ACM Sigplan '84 Symp. on Compiler Construction*, pp. 222-232, 1984.

CODY, W.J.: "Analysis of Proposals for the Floating-Point Standard," *IEEE Computer Magazine*, vol. 14, pp. 63-68, Mar. 1981.

COHEN, D.: "On Holy Wars and a Plea for Peace," *IEEE Computer Magazine*, vol. 14, pp. 48-54, Oct. 1981.

COLWELL, R.P., HITCHCOCK, C.Y. III, JENSEN, E.D., SPRUNT, H.M.B., and KOLLAR, C.P.: "Computers, Complexity, and Controversy," *IEEE Computer Magazine*, vol. 18, pp. 8-19, Sept. 1985a.

COLWELL, R.P., HITCHCOCK, C.Y. III, JENSEN, E.D., and SPRUNT, H.M.B.: "More Controversy about 'Computers, Complexity, and Controversy'," *IEEE Computer Magazine*, vol. 18, p. 93, Dec. 1985b.

CORBATO, F.J.: "PL/1 as a Tool for System Programming," *Datamation*, vol. 15, pp. 68-76, May 1969.

CORBATO, F.J., and VYSSOTSKY, V.A.: "Introduction and Overview of the MULTICS System," *Proc. FJCC*, pp. 185-196, 1965.

COUTANT, D.S., HAMMOND, C.L., and KELLY, J.W.: "Compilers for the New Generation of Hewlett-Packard Computers," *Proc. COMPCON Spring 1986*, IEEE, pp. 48-61, 1986.

CROWTHER, W., GOODHUE, J., GURWITZ, R., RETTBERG, R., and THOMAS, R.: "The Butterfly Parallel Processor," *IEEE Computer Arch. Tech. Committee Newsletter*, pp. 18-45, Sept. 1985a.

CROWTHER, W., GOODHUE, J., STARR, E., THOMAS, R., MILLIKEN, W., and BLACKA-DAR, T.: "Performance Measurements on a 128-Node Butterfly Parallel Processor," *Proc. 1985 Int'l Conf. on Parallel Proc.*, IEEE, 1985.

CURNOW, H.J., and WICHMAN, B.A.: "A Synthetic Benchmark," *Computer Journal*, vol. 19, Jan. 1975.

DAILEY, D.J.: *Small Computer Theory and Applications*, New York: McGraw-Hill, 1988.

DALLY, W.J., and SEITZ, C.L.: "Deadlock-Free Message Routing in Multiprocessor Inter-connection Networks," *IEEE Trans. on Computers*, vol. C-36, pp. 547-553, May 1987.

DARDEN, S.C., and HELLER, S.B.: "Streamline Your Software Development," *Computer Decisions*, vol. 2, pp. 29-33, Oct. 1970.

DASGUPTA, S.: "The Organization of Microprogram Stores," *Computing Surveys*, vol. 11, pp. 39-65, Mar. 1979.

DENNING, P.J.: "The Working Set Model for Program Behavior," *Commun. ACM*, vol. 11, pp. 323-333, May 1968.

DENNING, P.J.: "Virtual Memory," *Computing Surveys*, vol. 2, pp. 153-189, Sept. 1970.

DEROSA, J.A., and LEVY, H.M.: "An Evaluation of Branch Architectures," *Proc. 15th Ann. Int'l Symp. on Computer Arch.*, ACM, pp. 10-16, 1988.

DESROCHERS, G.R.: *Principles of Parallel and Multiprocessing*, New York: McGraw-Hill, 1987.

DIJKSTRA, E.W.: "GOTO Statement Considered Harmful," *Commun. ACM*, vol. 11, pp. 147-148, Mar. 1968a.

DIJKSTRA, E.W.: "Co-operating Sequential Processes," in *Programming Languages*, F. Genuys (ed.), New York: Academic Press, 1968b.

DONGARRA, J.J. (ed.): *Experimental Parallel Computing Architectures*, Amsterdam: North Holland, 1987.

EGGERS, S.J., and KATZ, R.H.: "The Effect of Sharing on the Cache and Bus Performance of Parallel Programs," *Proc. 3rd Int'l Conf. on Arch. Support for Prog. Lang. and Operating Syst.*, ACM, pp. 257-271, 1989a.

EGGERS, S.J., and KATZ, R.H.: "Evaluating the Performance of Four Snooping Cache Coherency Protocols," *Proc. 16th Ann. Int'l Symp. on Computer Arch.*, ACM, pp. 2-15, 1989b.

EL-AYAT, K.H., and AGARWAL, R.K.: "The Intel 80386—Architecture and Implementa-tion," *IEEE Micro Magazine*, vol. 5, pp. 4-22, Dec. 1985.

FARRENS, M.K., and PLESZKUN, A.R.: "Improving Performance of Small On-Chip Instruction Caches," *Proc. 16th Ann. Int'l Symp. on Computer Arch.*, ACM, pp. 234-241, 1989.

FINKEL, R.A.: *An Operating Systems Vade Mecum*, Englewood Cliffs, NJ: Prentice-Hall, 1986.

FLYNN, M.J.: "Some Computer Organizations and Their Effectiveness," *IEEE Trans. on Computers*, vol. C-21, pp. 948-960, Sept. 1972.

FLYNN, M.J.: "Directions and Issues in Architecture and Language," *IEEE Computer Magazine*, vol. 13, pp. 5-22, Oct. 1980.

FLYNN, M.J., MITCHELL, C.L., and MULDER, J.M.: "And Now a Case for More Complex Instruction Sets," *IEEE Computer Magazine*, vol. 20, pp. 71-83, Sept. 1987.

FOTHERINGHAM, J.: "Dynamic Storage Allocation in the Atlas Computer Including an Automatic Use of a Backing Store," *Commun. ACM*, vol. 4, pp. 435-436, Oct. 1961.

FUJITANI, L.: "Laser Optical Disk: The Coming Revolution in On-line Storage," *Commun. ACM*, vol. 27, pp. 546-566, June 1984.

GAJSKI, D.D., MILUTINOVIC, V.M., SIEGEL, H.J., and FURHT, B.P.: *Tutorial on Computer Architecture*, Washington, D.C.: IEEE Computer Society Press, 1989.

GAJSKI, D.D., and PIER, K.-K.: "Essential Issues in Multiprocessor Systems," *IEEE Computer Magazine*, vol. 18, pp. 9-27, June 1985.

GARNER, H.L.: "Number Systems and Arithmetic," in *Advances in Computers*. Vol. 6, F. Alt and M. Rubinoff (eds.), New York: Academic Press, 1965, pp. 131-194.

GELERNTER, D., and CARRIERO, N.: "Applications Experience with Linda," *Proc. PPEALS Conf.*, ACM, pp. 173-187, 1988.

GIMARC, C.E., and MILUTINOVIC, V.M.: "A Survey of RISC Processors and Computers of the Mid-1980s," *IEEE Computer Magazine*, vol. 20, pp. 59-69, Sept. 1987.

GOODMAN, J.R.: "Using Cache Memory to Reduce Processor Memory Traffic," *Proc. 10th Ann. Int'l Symp. on Computer Arch.*, ACM, pp. 124-131, 1983.

GORSLINE, G.W.: *Assembly and Assemblers*, Englewood Cliffs, NJ: Prentice-Hall, 1988.

GRAFE, V.G., DAVIDSON, G.S., HOCH, J.E., and HOLMES, V.P.: "The Epsilon Dataflow Processor," *Proc. 16th Ann. Int'l Symp. on Computer Arch.*, ACM, pp. 36-45, 1989.

GRAHAM, R.: "Use of High Level Languages for System Programming," Project MAC Report TM-13, Project MAC, MIT, Sept. 1970.

GUSTAVSON, D.: "Computer Buses—A Tutorial," *IEEE Micro Magazine*, vol. 4, pp. 7-22, Aug. 1984.

HAMACHER, V.V., VRANESIC, Z.G., and ZAKY, S.G.: *Computer Organization, 2nd ed.*, New York: McGraw-Hill, 1984.

HAMMING, R.W.: "Error Detecting and Error Correcting Codes," *Bell Syst. Tech. J.*, vol. 29, pp. 147-160, Apr. 1950.

HAYES, J.P.: *Computer Architecture and Organization, 2nd ed.*, New York: McGraw-Hill, 1988.

HENNESSY, J.L.: "VLSI Processor Architecture," *IEEE Trans. on Computers*, vol. C-33, pp. 1221-1246, Dec. 1984.

HILL, M.D.: "A Case for Direct-Mapped Caches," *IEEE Computer Magazine*, vol. 21, pp. 25-40, Dec. 1988.

HILLIS, W.D.: *The Connection Machine*, Cambridge, MA: MIT Press, 1985.

HIMELSTEIN, M., CHOW, F., and ENDERBY, K.: "Cross-module Optimizations: Its Implementation and Benefits," *Proc. USENIX Conf.*, USENIX Association, pp. 347-356, 1987.

HINNANT, D.F.: "Benchmarking: Art, Science, or Black Magic?," *IEEE Micro Magazine*, vol. 8, pp. 64-75, Oct. 1988.

HITCHCOCK, C.Y. III, and SPRUNT, H.M.B.: "Analyzing Multiple Register Sets," *Proc. 12th Ann. Int'l Symp. on Computer Arch.*, ACM, pp. 55-63, 1985.

HOMEWOOD, M., MAY, D., SHEPHERD, D., and SHEPHERD, R.: "The IMS T800 Transputer," *IEEE Micro Magazine*, vol. 7, pp. 10-26, Oct. 1987.

HOPPER, A., JONES, A., and LIOUPIS, A.: "Multiple vs. Wide Shared Bus Multiprocessors," *Proc. 16th Ann. Int'l Symp. on Computer Arch.*, ACM, pp. 300-306, 1989.

HORD, R.M.: *The ILLIAC IV*, Berlin: Springer-Verlag, 1982.

HORNER, D.R.: *Operating Systems: Concepts and Applications,* Glenview, IL: Scott Foresman, 1989.

HUCK, J.C., and FLYNN, M.J.: *Analyzing Computer Architectures*, Washington, D.C.: IEEE Computer Society Press, 1989.

HUMPHREY, J.H., and SMOCK, G.S.: "High-Speed Modems," *Byte*, vol. 13, pp. 102-113, June 1988.

HWANG, K., and BRIGGS, F.A.: *Computer Architecture and Parallel Processing*, New York: McGraw-Hill, 1984.

IACOBUCCI, E.: *OS/2 Programmer's Guide*, New York: McGraw-Hill, 1988.

HWU, W.W., CONTE, T.M., and CHANG, P.P.: "Comparing Software and Hardware Schemes for Reducing the Cost of Branches," *Proc. 16th Ann. Int'l Symp. on Computer Arch.*, ACM, pp. 224-233, 1989.

IEEE: *Binary Floating-Point Arithmetic*, IEEE Standard 754, New York: IEEE, 1985.

JESSHOPE, C.: "Building and Binding Systems with Transputers," in *Parallel Systems and Computation*, G. Paul and G.S. Almasi (eds.), Amsterdam: North Holland, pp. 205-218, 1988.

JOHNSON, T.L.: "A Comparison of MC68000 Family Processors," *Byte*, vol. 11, pp. 205-218, Sept. 1986.

KABAKIBO, A., MILUTINOVIC, V. SILBEY, A., and FURHT, B.: "A Survey of Cache Memory in Modern Microcomputer and Minicomputer Systems," in *Tut. Comp. Arch.*, Washington, D.C.: IEEE Computer Society Press, pp. 210-227, 1987.

KAIN, R.Y.: *Computer Architecture: Software and Hardware*, Englewood Cliffs, NJ: Prentice-Hall, 1989.

KANE, G.: *MIPS RISC Architecture*, Englewood Cliffs, NJ: Prentice-Hall, 1988.

KESSLER, R.E., JOOSS, R., LEBECK, A., and HILL, M.D.: "Inexpensive Implementations of Set Associativity," *Proc. 16th Ann. Int'l Symp. on Computer Arch.*, ACM, pp. 131-139, 1989.

KNUTH, D.E.: "An Empirical Study of FORTRAN Programs," *Software—Practice & Experience*, vol. 1, pp. 105-133, 1971.

KNUTH, D.E.: *The Art of Computer Programming: Fundamental Algorithms,* 2nd ed., Reading, Mass.: Addison-Wesley, 1974.

KNUTH, D.E.: *The Art of Computer Programming: Seminumerical Algorithms,* 2nd ed. Reading, Mass.: Addison-Wesley, 1981.

KRAJEWSKI, R.: "Multiprocessing: An Overview," *Byte,* vol. 10, 171-181, May 1985.

KRANTZ, J.I., MIZELL, A.M., and WILLIAMS, R.L.: *OS/2 Features, Functions, and Applications,* New York: Wiley, 1988.

KUMAR, V.P., and REDDY, S.M.: "Augmented Shuffle-Exchange Multistage Interconnection Networks," *IEEE Computer Magazine,* vol. 20, pp. 30-40, June 1987.

LANGHOLZ, G., FRANCIONI, J., and KANDEL, A.: *Elements of Computer Organization,* Englewood Cliffs, NJ: Prentice-Hall, 1989.

LEE, R.L., YEW, P.-C., and LAWRIE, D.H.: "Multiprocessor Cache Design Considerations," *Proc. 14th Ann. Int'l Symp. on Computer Arch.,* ACM, pp. 253-262, 1987.

LEVENTHAL, L.: *Lance Leventhal's 80386 Programming Guide,* New York: Bantam Books, 1987.

LI, K.: "IVY: A Shared Virtual Memory System for Parallel Computing," *Proc. 1988 Int'l Conf. on Parallel Proc. (Vol. II),* IEEE, pp. 94-101, 1988.

LI, K., and HUDAK, P.: "Memory Coherence in Shared Virtual Memory Systems," *Proc. 5th Ann. ACM Symp. on Prin. of Distr. Computing,* ACM, pp. 229-239, 1986.

LILJA, D.J.: "Reducing the Branch Penalty in Pipelined Processors," *IEEE Computer Magazine,* vol. 21, July 1988.

LIPOVSKI, G.J., and MALEK, M.: *Parallel Computing,* New York: John Wiley, 1987.

LUKASIEWICZ, J.: *Aristotle's Syllogistic,* 2nd ed., Oxford: Oxford University Press, 1958.

MACGREGOR, D., MOTHERSOLE, D., and MOYER, B: "The Motorola 68020," *IEEE Micro Magazine,* vol. 4, pp. 101-118, Aug. 1984.

MACGREGOR, D., and RUBINSTEIN, J.: "A Performance Analysis of MC68020-based Systems," *IEEE Micro Magazine,* vol. 5, pp. 50-70, Dec. 1985.

MCFARLING, S., and HENNESSY, J.L.: "Reducing the Cost of Branches," *Proc. 13th Ann. Int'l Symp. on Computer Arch.,* ACM, pp. 396-403, 1986.

MCKEVITT, J., and BAYLISS, J.: "New Options from Big Chips," *IEEE Spectrum,* pp. 28-34, March 1979.

MELEAR, C.: "The Design of the 88000 RISC Family," *IEEE Micro Magazine,* vol. 9, pp. 26-38, April 1989.

MILUTINOVIC, V.: *Microprogramming Firmware Engineering,* Washington, D.C.: IEEE Computer Society Press, 1989.

MIZRAHI, H.E., BAER, J.-L., LAZOWSKA, E.D., and ZAHORJAN, J.: "Introducing Memory into the Switch Elements of Multiprocessor Interconnection Networks," *Proc. 16th Ann. Int'l Symp. on Computer Arch.,* ACM, pp. 158-166, 1989.

MOUSSOURIS, J., CRUDELE, L., FREITAS, D., HANSEN, C., HUDSON, E., MARCH, R., PRZYBYLSKI, S., RIORDAN, T., ROWEN, C., and VAN'T HOF, D.: "A CMOS RISC Processor with Integrated System Functions," *Proc. Spring COMPCON 1986*, IEEE, pp. 126-131, 1986.

MUDGE, T.N., HAYES, J.P., and WINSOR, D.C.: "Multiple Bus Architectures," *IEEE Computer Magazine*, vol. 20, pp. 42-48, June 1987.

MURRAY, W.H., and PAPPAS, C.H.: "Pick of the Litter," *Byte*, vol. 12, pp. 238-242, June 1987.

NICOUD, J.-D., and TYRRELL, A.M.: "The Transputer T414 Instruction Set," *IEEE Micro Magazine*, vol. 9, pp. 60-75, June 1989.

NIKHIL, R.S., and ARVIND: "Can Dataflow Subsume von Neumann Computing," *Proc. 16th Ann. Int'l Symp. on Computer Arch.*, ACM, pp. 262-272, 1989.

ORGANICK, E.: *The MULTICS System,* Cambridge, Mass.: MIT Press, 1972.

OWICKI, S., and AGARWAL, A.: "Evaluating the Performance of Software Cache Coherence," *Proc. 3rd Int'l Conf. on Arch. Support for Prog. Lang. and Operating Syst.*, ACM, pp. 230-242, 1989.

PATTERSON, D.A.: "Reduced Instruction Set Computers," *Commun. ACM*, vol. 28, pp. 8-21, Jan. 1985.

PATTERSON, D.A., and HENNESSY, J.L.: "Response to 'Computers, Complexity, and Controversy'," *IEEE Computer Magazine*, vol. 18, pp. 142-143, Nov. 1985.

PATTERSON, D.A., and PIEPHO, R.S.: "RISC Assessment: A High-Level Language Experiment," *Proc. 9th Int'l Symp. on Computer Arch.*, ACM, 1982.

PATTERSON, D.A., and SEQUIN, C.H.: "RISC I: A Reduced Instruction Set VLSI Computer," *Proc. 8th Int'l. Symp. on Computer Arch.*, ACM, pp. 443-457, 1981.

PATTERSON, D.A., and SEQUIN, C.H.: "A VLSI RISC," *IEEE Computer Magazine*, pp. 8-22, Sept. 1982.

PERLMUTTER, D., and YUEN, A.: "The 80387 and Its Applications," *IEEE Micro Magazine*, vol. 7, pp. 42-56, Aug. 1987.

PFISTER, G.F., BRANTLEY, W.C., GEORGE, D.A., HARVEY, S.L., KLEINFELDER, W.J., MCAULIFFE, K.P., MELTON, E.A., NORTON, V.A., and WEISS, J.: "The IBM Research Parallel Processor Prototype (RP#)," in *Parallel Computing*, G.J. Lipovski and M. Malek (eds.), New York: Wiley, pp. 270-280, 1987.

PIEPHO, R.S., and WU, W.S.: "A Comparison of RISC Architectures," *IEEE Micro Magazine*, vol. 9, pp. 51-62, Aug. 1989.

PINKERT, J.R., and WEAR, L.L.: *Operating Systems Concepts, Policies, and Mechanisms*, Englewood Cliffs, NJ: Prentice-Hall, 1989.

POHM, A., and AGARWAL, O.: *High Speed Memory Systems*, Reston, VA: Reston Publ. Co., 1983.

PRESSER, L., and WHITE, J.: "Linkers and Loaders," *Computing Surveys*, vol. 4, pp. 150-167, Sept. 1972.

PRICE, D.: "A History of Calculating Machines," *IEEE Micro Magazine*, vol. 4, pp. 22-52, Feb. 1984.

PRZYBYLSKI, M., HOROWITZ, J., and HENNESSY, J.: "Performance Tradeoffs in Cache Design," *Proc. 15th Ann. Int'l Symp. on Computer Arch.*, ACM, pp. 290-298, 1988.

PRZYBYLSKI, M., HOROWITZ, J., and HENNESSY, J.: "Characteristics of Performance-Optimal Multilevel Cache Hierarchies," *Proc. 16th Ann. Int'l Symp. on Computer Arch.*, ACM, pp. 114-121, 1989.

RADIN, G.: "The 801 Minicomputer," *Computer Arch. News*, vol. 10, pp. 39-47, March 1982.

RETTBERG, R., and THOMAS, R.: "Contention is No Obstacle to Shared-Memory Multiprocessing," *Commun. ACM*, vol. 29, pp. 1202-1212, Dec. 1986.

RITCHIE, D.M., and THOMPSON, K.: "The UNIX Time-Sharing System," *Commun. ACM*, vol. 17, pp. 365-375, July 1974.

ROBINSON, P.: "How Much of a RISC?," *Byte*, vol. 12, pp. 143-159, April 1987.

ROSIN, R.F.: "The Significance of Microprogramming," *SIGMICRO Newsletter*, vol. 4, pp. 24-39, Jan. 1974.

SAWCHUK, A., JENKINS, B.K., RAGHAVENDRA, C.S., and VARMA, A.: "Optical Crossbar Networks," *IEEE Computer Magazine*, vol. 20, pp. 50-60, June 1987.

SCHEURICH, C., and DUBOIS, M.: "Correct Memory Operation of Cache-Based Multiprocessors," *Proc. 14th Ann. Int'l Symp. on Computer Arch.*, ACM, pp. 234-24, 1987.

SCHILDT, H.: *OS/2 Programming: An Introduction*, New York: McGraw-Hill, 1988.

SCHMITT, D.A.: *The OS/2 Programming Environment*, Englewood Cliffs, NJ: Prentice-Hall, 1989.

SCHROEDER, M.D., and BURROWS, M.: "Performance of the Firefly RPC," *Proc. 12th ACM Symp. on Oper. Syst. Prin.*, ACM, 1989.

SEITZ, C.L.: "The Cosmic Cube," *Commun. ACM*, vol. 28, pp. 22-33, Jan 1985.

SERLIN, O: "MIPS, Dhrystones, and Other Tales," *Datamation*, pp. 112-118, June 1, 1988.

SHORT, R.T., and LEVY, H.M.: "A Simulation Study of Two Level Caches," *Proc. 15th Ann. Int'l Symp. on Computer Arch.*, ACM, pp. 81-88, 1988.

SHUFORD, R.S.: "CD-ROMs and Their Kin," *Byte*, vol. 10, pp. 137-146, Nov. 1985.

SLATER, R.: *Portraits in Silicon*, Cambridge, MA: MIT Press, 1987.

SMARTE, G., and BARAN, N.M.: "Face to Face," *Byte*, vol. 13, pp. 243-252, Sept. 1988.

SMITH, A.J.: "Cache Memories," *Computing Surveys*, vol. 14, pp. 473-530, Sept. 1982.

SMITH, A.J.: "Bibliography and Readings on CPU Cache Memories and Related Topics," *Computer Arch. News*, vol. 14, pp. 22-42, Jan. 1986.

SMITH, A.J.: "Line (Block) Size Choice for CPU Caches," *IEEE Trans. on Computers*, vol. C-36, pp. 1063-1075, Sept. 1987.

STALLINGS, W.: *Computer Organization and Architecture*, New York: Macmillan, 1987.

STEENKISTE, P., and HENNESSY, J.: "Lisp on a Reduced Instruction Set Processor: Characterization and Optimization," *IEEE Computer Magazine*, vol. 21, pp. 34-45, July 1988.

STEIN, M.L., and MUNRO, W.D.: *Introduction to Machine Arithmetic*, Reading, Mass.: Addison-Wesley, 1971.

STENSTROM, P.: "Reducing Contention in Shared-Memory Multiprocessors," *IEEE Computer Magazine*, vol. 21, pp. 26-37, Nov. 1988.

STRITTER, S., and TREDENNICK, N.: "Microprogrammed Implementation of a Single Chip Microprocessor," *Proc. 11th Annu. Microprogr. Workshop*, ACM and IEEE, pp. 8-16, 1978.

TABAK, D.: *RISC Architecture*, New York: John Wiley, 1987.

TANENBAUM, A.S.: "Implications of Structured Programming for Machine Architecture," *Commun. ACM*, vol. 21, pp. 237-246, Mar. 1978.

TANENBAUM, A.S: *Operating Systems: Design and Implementation*, Englewood Cliffs, NJ: Prentice-Hall, 1987.

THOMPSON, K.: "UNIX Implementation," *Bell Syst. Tech. J.*, vol. 57, pp. 1931-1946, July-Aug. 1978.

TREDENNICK, N.: "The Impact of VLSI on Microprogramming," *Proc. 19th Annual Workshop on Microprogramming*, ACM, pp. 2-7, 1986.

TREDENNICK, N.: *Microprocessor Logic Design*, Bedford, MA: Digital Press, 1987.

TRELEAVEN, P.: "Control-Driven, Data-Driven, and Demand-Driven Computer Architecture," *Parallel Computing*, vol. 2, 1985.

TUCKER, L.W., and ROBERTSON, G.G.: "Architecture and Applications of the Connection Machine," *IEEE Computer Magazine*, vol. 21, pp. 26-38, Aug. 1988.

UNGAR, D., BLAU, R., FOLEY, P., SAMPLES, D., and PATTERSON, D.: "Architecture of SOAR: Smalltalk on a RISC," *Proc. 11th Ann. Int'l Symp. on Computer Arch.*, ACM, pp. 188-197, 1984.

VAN DER POEL, W.L.: "The Software Crisis, Some Thoughts and Outlooks," *Proc. IFIP Congr. 68*, pp. 334-339, 1968.

VEEN, A.H.: "Dataflow Machine Architecture," *Computing Surveys*, vol. 18, pp. 365-396, Dec. 1986.

VERNON, M.K., LAZOWSKA, E.D., ZAHORJAN, J.: "Snooping Cache-Consistency Protocols," *Proc. 15th Ann. Int'l Symp. on Computer Arch.*, ACM, pp. 308-317, 1988.

WALLICH, P.: "Toward Simpler, Faster Computers," *IEEE Spectrum*, pp. 38-45, Aug. 1985.

WANG, W.-H., BAER, J.-L., LEVY, H.M.: "Organization and Performance of a Two-Level Virtual-Real Cache Hierarchy," *Proc. 16th Ann. Int'l Symp. on Computer Arch.*, ACM, pp. 140-148, 1989.

WEBER, W., and GUPTA, A.: "Analysis of Cache Invalidation Patterns in Multiprocessors," *Proc. 3rd Int'l Conf. on Arch. Support for Prog. Lang. and Operating Syst.*, ACM, pp. 243-256, 1989.

WEICKER, R.P.: "A Synthetic Systems Programming Benchmark," *Commun. ACM*, vol. 27, pp. 1013-1090, Oct. 1984.

WHITBY-STREVENS, C.: "The Transputer," *Proc. 12th Ann. Int'l Symp. on Computer Arch.*, ACM, pp. 292-300, 1985.

WILKES, M.V.: "Computers Then and Now," *J. ACM*, vol. 15, pp. 1-7, Jan. 1968.

WILSON, A.W. Jr.: "Hierarchical Cache/Bus Architecture for Shared Memory Multiprocessors," *Proc. 14th Ann. Int'l Symp. on Computer Arch.*, ACM, pp. 244-252, 1987.

WILSON, P.: "Floating-Point Survival Kit," *Byte*, vol. 13, pp. 217-226, March 1988.

WILSON, P.: "The CPU Wars," *Byte*, vol. 13, pp. 213-248, May 1988.

WORTMAN, D.B.: "A Study of Language Directed Computer Design," Report CSRG-20, University of Toronto, 1972.

A

BINARY NUMBERS

The arithmetic used by computers differs in some ways from the arithmetic used by people. The most important difference is that computers perform operations on numbers whose precision is finite and fixed. Another difference is that most computers use the binary rather than the decimal system for representing numbers. These topics are the subject of this appendix.

A.1. FINITE-PRECISION NUMBERS

While doing arithmetic, one usually gives little thought to the question of how many decimal digits it takes to represent a number. Physicists can calculate that there are 10^{78} electrons in the universe without being bothered by the fact that it requires 79 decimal digits to write that number out in full. Someone calculating the value of a function with pencil and paper who needs the answer to six significant digits simply keeps intermediate results to seven, or eight, or however many are needed. The problem of the paper not being wide enough for seven-digit numbers never arises.

With computers, matters are quite different. On most computers, the amount of memory available for storing a number is fixed at the time that the computer is designed. With a certain amount of effort, the programmer can represent numbers two, or three, or even many times larger than this fixed amount, but doing so does not change the nature of this difficulty. The finite nature of the computer forces us to deal only with numbers that can be represented in a fixed number of digits. We call such numbers **finite-precision numbers.**

In order to study properties of finite-precision numbers, let us examine the set of positive integers representable by three decimal digits, with no decimal point and no sign. This set has exactly 1000 members: 000, 001, 002, 003, ..., 999. With this restriction, it is impossible to express several important sets of numbers, such as:

1. Numbers larger than 999.

2. Negative numbers.

3. Fractions.

4. Irrational numbers.

5. Complex numbers.

One important property of arithmetic on the set of all integers is **closure** with respect to the operations of addition, subtraction, and multiplication. In other words, for every pair of integers i and j, $i + j$, $i - j$, and $i \times j$ are also integers. The set of integers is not closed with respect to division, because there exist values of i and j for which i / j is not expressible as an integer—for example, 7/2 and 1/0.

Finite-precision numbers unfortunately are not closed with respect to any of these four basic operations, as shown below, using three-digit decimal numbers as an example:

$$600 + 600 = 1200 \qquad \text{(too large)}$$
$$003 - 005 = -2 \qquad \text{(negative)}$$
$$050 \times 050 = 2500 \qquad \text{(too large)}$$
$$007 / 002 = 3.5 \qquad \text{(not an integer)}$$

The violations can be divided into two mutually exclusive classes: operations whose result is larger than the largest number in the set (overflow error) or smaller than the smallest number in the set (underflow error), and operations whose result is neither too large nor too small but is simply not a member of the set. Of the four violations above, the first three are examples of the former, and the fourth is an example of the latter.

Because computers have finite memories and therefore must of necessity perform arithmetic on finite-precision numbers, the results of certain calculations will be, from the point of classical mathematics, just plain wrong. A calculating device that gives the wrong answer even though it is in perfect working condition may appear strange at first, but the error is a logical consequence of its finite nature. Some computers have special hardware that detects overflow errors.

The algebra of finite-precision numbers is different from normal algebra. As an example, consider the associative law:

$$a + (b - c) = (a + b) - c$$

Let us evaluate both sides for $a = 700$, $b = 400$, $c = 300$. To compute the left-hand side, first calculate $(b - c)$, which is 100, and then add this amount to a, yielding 800. To compute the right-hand side first calculate $(a + b)$, which gives an overflow in the finite arithmetic of three-digit integers. The result may depend on the machine being used but it will not be 1100. Subtracting 300 from some number other than 1100 will not yield 800. The associative law does not hold. The order of operations is important.

As another example, consider the distributive law:

$$a \times (b - c) = a \times b - a \times c$$

Let us evaluate both sides for $a = 5$, $b = 210$, $c = 195$. The left-hand side is 5×15, which yields 75. The right-hand side is not 75 because $a \times b$ overflows.

Judging from these examples, one might conclude that although computers are general-purpose devices, their finite nature renders them especially unsuitable for doing arithmetic. This conclusion is, of course, not true, but it does serve to illustrate the importance of understanding how computers work and what limitations they have.

A.2. RADIX NUMBER SYSTEMS

An ordinary decimal number with which everyone is familiar consists of a string of decimal digits and, possibly, a decimal point. The general form and its usual interpretation are shown in Fig. A-1. The choice of 10 as the base for exponentiation, called the **radix**, is made because we are using decimal, or base 10, numbers. When dealing with computers, it is frequently convenient to use radices other than 10. The most important radices are 2, 8, and 16. The number systems based on these radices are called **binary, octal,** and **hexadecimal** respectively.

A radix k number system requires k different symbols to represent the digits 0 to $k - 1$. Decimal numbers are built up from the 10 decimal digits

    0 1 2 3 4 5 6 7 8 9

In contrast, binary numbers do not use these ten digits. They are all constructed exclusively from the two binary digits

    0 1

Octal numbers are built up from the eight octal digits

    0 1 2 3 4 5 6 7

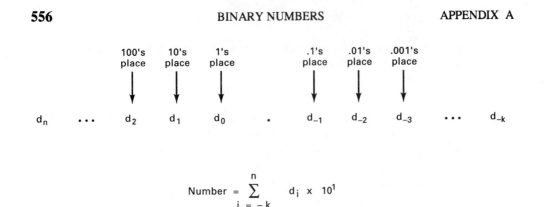

$$\text{Number} = \sum_{i = -k}^{n} d_i \times 10^i$$

Fig. A-1. The general form of a decimal number.

For hexadecimal numbers, 16 digits are needed. Thus six new symbols are required. It is conventional to use the uppercase letters A through F for the six digits following 9. Hexadecimal numbers are then built up from the digits

   0 1 2 3 4 5 6 7 8 9 A B C D E F

The expression "binary digit" meaning a 1 or a 0 is usually referred to as a **bit**. Figure A-2 shows the decimal number 2001 expressed in binary, octal, and hexadecimal form. The number 7B9 is obviously hexadecimal, because the symbol B can only occur in hexadecimal numbers. However, the number 111 might be in any of the four number systems discussed. To avoid ambiguity, people use a subscript of 2, 8, 10, or 16 to indicate the radix when it is not obvious from the context.

Binary   1   1   1   1   1   0   1   0   0   0   1

$1 \times 2^{10} + 1 \times 2^9 + 1 \times 2^8 + 1 \times 2^7 + 1 \times 2^6 + 0 \times 2^5 + 1 \times 2^4 + 0 \times 2^3 + 0 \times 2^2 + 0 \times 2^1 + 1 \times 2^0$
1024 + 512 + 256 + 128 + 64 + 0 + 16 + 0 + 0 + 0 + 1

Octal   3   7   2   1

$3 \times 8^3 + 7 \times 8^2 + 2 \times 8^1 + 1 \times 8^0$
1536 + 448 + 16 + 1

Decimal   2   0   0   1

$2 \times 10^3 + 0 \times 10^2 + 0 \times 10^1 + 1 \times 10^0$
2000 + 0 + 0 + 1

Hexadecimal   7   D   1

$7 \times 16^2 + 13 \times 16^1 + 1 \times 16^0$
1792 + 208 + 1

Fig. A-2. The number 2001 in binary, octal, and hexadecimal.

As an example of binary, octal, decimal, and hexadecimal notation, Fig. A-3 shows a collection of numbers expressed in all four systems. Perhaps some archaeologist thousands of years from now will discover this table and regard it as the Rosetta Stone to late 20th Century number systems.

Decimal	Binary	Octal	Hexadecimal
0	0	0	0
1	1	1	1
2	10	2	2
3	11	3	3
4	100	4	4
5	101	5	5
6	110	6	6
7	111	7	7
8	1000	10	8
9	1001	11	9
10	1010	12	A
11	1011	13	B
12	1100	14	C
13	1101	15	D
14	1110	16	E
15	1111	17	F
16	10000	20	10
17	10001	21	11
18	10010	22	12
19	10011	23	13
20	10100	24	14
30	11110	36	1E
40	101000	50	28
50	110010	62	32
60	111100	74	3C
70	1000110	106	46
80	1010000	120	50
90	1011010	132	5A
100	1100100	144	64
200	11001000	310	C8
300	100101100	454	12C
400	110010000	620	190
500	111110100	764	1F4
600	1001011000	1130	258
700	1010111100	1274	2BC
800	1100100000	1440	320
900	1110000100	1604	384
1000	1111101000	1750	3E8
2989	101110101101	5655	BAD

Fig. A-3. Decimal numbers and their binary, octal, and hexadecimal equivalents.

A.3. CONVERSION FROM ONE RADIX TO ANOTHER

Conversion between octal or hexadecimal numbers and binary numbers is easy. To convert a binary number to octal, divide it into groups of 3 bits, with the 3 bits immediately to the left (or right) of the decimal point (often called a binary point) forming one group, the 3 bits immediately to their left, another group, and so on. Each group of 3 bits can be directly converted to a single octal digit, 0 to 7, according to the conversion given in the first lines of Fig. A-3. It may be necessary to add one or two leading or trailing zeros to fill out a group to 3 bits. Conversion from octal to binary is equally easy. Each octal digit is simply replaced by the equivalent three-bit binary number. Hexadecimal-to-binary conversion is essentially the same as octal-to-binary except that each hexadecimal digit corresponds to a group of 4 bits instead of 3 bits. Figure A-4 gives some examples of conversions.

Example 1

| Hexadecimal | 1 | 9 | 4 | 8 | . | B | 6 |

Binary 0 0 0 1 1 0 0 1 0 1 0 0 1 0 0 0 . 1 0 1 1 0 1 1 0 0

| Octal | 1 | 4 | 5 | 1 | 0 | . | 5 | 5 | 4 |

Example 2

| Hexadecimal | 7 | B | A | 3 | . | B | C | 4 |

Binary 0 1 1 1 1 0 1 1 1 0 1 0 0 0 1 1 . 1 0 1 1 1 1 0 0 0 1 0 0

| Octal | 7 | 5 | 6 | 4 | 3 | . | 5 | 7 | 0 | 4 |

Fig. A-4. Examples of octal-to-binary and hexadecimal-to-binary conversion.

Conversion of decimal numbers to binary can be done in two different ways. The first method follows directly from the definition of binary numbers. The largest power of 2 smaller than the number is subtracted from the number. The process is then repeated on the difference. Once the number has been decomposed into powers of 2, the binary number can be assembled with 1s in the bit positions corresponding to powers of 2 used in the decomposition, and 0s elsewhere.

The other method (for integers only) consists of dividing the number by 2. The quotient is written directly beneath the original number and the remainder, 0 or 1, is written next to the quotient. The quotient is then considered and the process repeated until the number 0 has been reached. The result of this process will be two columns of numbers, the quotients and the remainders. The binary number can now be read directly from the remainder column starting at the bottom. Figure A-5 gives an example of decimal-to-binary conversion.

Binary integers can also be converted to decimal in two ways. One method consists of summing up the powers of 2 corresponding to the 1 bits in the number. For example,

$$10110 \text{ is } 2^4 + 2^2 + 2^1 = 16 + 4 + 2 = 22$$

In the other method, the binary number is written vertically, one bit per line, with the leftmost bit on the bottom. The bottom line is called line 1, the one above it line 2, and so on. The decimal number will be built up in a parallel column next to the binary number. Begin by writing a 1 on line 1. The entry on line n consists of

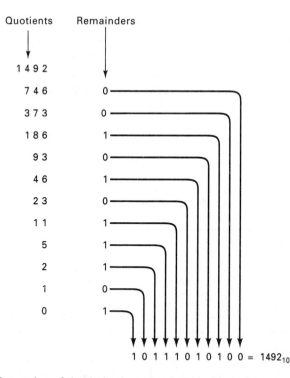

Fig. A-5. Conversion of the decimal number 1492 to binary by successive halving, starting at the top and working downward. For example, 93 divided by 2 yields a quotient of 46 and a remainder of 1, written on the line below it.

two times the entry on line $n - 1$ plus the bit on line n (either 0 or 1). The entry on the top line is the answer. Figure A-6 gives an example of this method of binary to decimal conversion.

Decimal-to-octal and decimal-to-hexadecimal conversion can be accomplished either by first converting to binary and then to the desired system or by subtracting powers of 8 or 16.

A.4. NEGATIVE BINARY NUMBERS

Four systems for representing negative numbers have been used in digital computers. The first one is called **signed magnitude**. In this system the leftmost bit is the sign bit (0 is + and 1 is −) and the remaining bits hold the absolute magnitude of the number.

The second system, called **one's complement**, also has a sign bit with 0 used for plus and 1 for minus. To negate a number, replace each 1 by a 0 and each 0 by a 1. This holds for the sign bit as well. One's complement is obsolete.

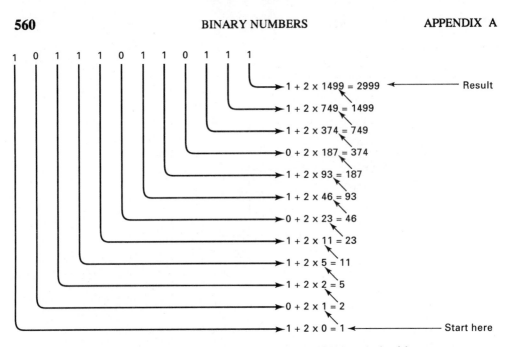

Fig. A-6. Conversion of the binary number 101110110111 to decimal by successive doubling, starting at the bottom. Each line is formed by doubling the one below it and adding the corresponding bit. For example, 749 is twice 374 plus the 1 bit on the same line as 749.

The third system, called **two's complement**, also has a sign bit that is 0 for plus and 1 for minus. Negating a number is a two step process. First, each 1 is replaced by a 0 and each 0 by a 1, just as in one's complement. Second, 1 is added to the result. Binary addition is the same as decimal addition except that a carry is generated if the sum is greater than 1 rather than greater than 9. For example, converting 6 to two's complement is done in two steps:

```
00000110  (+6)
11111001  (−6 in one's complement)
       1  (add 1)
11111010  (−6 in two's complement)
```

If a carry occurs from the leftmost bit, it is thrown away.

The fourth system, which for m-bit numbers is called **excess 2^{m-1}**, represents a number by storing it as the sum of itself and 2^{m-1}. For example, for 8-bit numbers, $m = 8$, the system is called excess 128 and a number is stored as its true value plus 128. Therefore, −3 becomes $-3 + 128 = 125$, and −3 is represented by the 8-bit binary number for 125 (01111101). The numbers from −128 to +127 map onto 0 to 255, all of which are expressible as an 8-bit positive integer. Interestingly enough, this system is identical to two's complement with the sign bit reversed. Figure A-7 gives examples of negative numbers in all four systems.

N (decimal)	N (binary)	-N (signed mag.)	-N (1's compl.)	-N (2's compl.)	-N (excess 128)
0	00000000	10000000	11111111	00000000	10000000
1	00000001	10000001	11111110	11111111	01111111
2	00000010	10000010	11111101	11111110	01111110
3	00000011	10000011	11111100	11111101	01111101
4	00000100	10000100	11111011	11111100	01111100
5	00000101	10000101	11111010	11111011	01111011
6	00000110	10000110	11111001	11111010	01111010
7	00000111	10000111	11111000	11111001	01111001
8	00001000	10001000	11110111	11111000	01111000
9	00001001	10001001	11110110	11110111	01110111
10	00001010	10001010	11110101	11110110	01110110
11	00001011	10001011	11110100	11110101	01110101
12	00001100	10001100	11110011	11110100	01110100
13	00001101	10001101	11110010	11110011	01110011
14	00001110	10001110	11110001	11110010	01110010
15	00001111	10001111	11110000	11110001	01110001
16	00010000	10010000	11101111	11110000	01110000
17	00010001	10010001	11101110	11101111	01101111
18	00010010	10010010	11101101	11101110	01101110
19	00010011	10010011	11101100	11101101	01101101
20	00010100	10010100	11101011	11101100	01101100
30	00011110	10011110	11100001	11100010	01100010
40	00101000	10101000	11010111	11011000	01011000
50	00110010	10110010	11001101	11001110	01001110
60	00111100	10111100	11000011	11000100	01000100
70	01000110	11000110	10111001	10111010	00111010
80	01010000	11010000	10101111	10110000	00110000
90	01011010	11011010	10100101	10100110	00100110
100	01100100	11100100	10011011	10011100	00011100
127	01111111	11111111	10000000	10000001	00000001
128	--------	--------	--------	10000000	00000000

Fig. A-7. Negative 8-bit numbers in four systems.

Both signed magnitude and one's complement have two representations for zero: a plus zero, and a minus zero. This situation is highly undesirable. The two's complement system does not have this problem because the two's complement of plus zero is also plus zero. The two's complement system does, however, have a different singularity. The bit pattern consisting of a 1 followed by all 0s is its own complement. The result is to make the range of positive and negative numbers unsymmetric; there is one negative number with no positive counterpart.

The reason for these problems is not hard to find: we want an encoding system with two properties:

1. Only one representation for zero.

2. Exactly as many positive numbers as negative numbers.

The problem is that any set of numbers with as many positive as negative numbers and only one zero has an odd number of members, whereas m bits allow an even number of bit patterns. There will always be either one bit pattern too many or one bit pattern too few, no matter what representation is chosen. This extra bit pattern can be used for −0 or a large negative number, or something else, but it will always be a nuisance.

A.5. BINARY ARITHMETIC

The addition table for binary numbers is given in Fig. A-8.

Addend	0	0	1	1
Augend	+0	+1	+0	+1
Sum	0	1	1	0
Carry	0	0	0	1

Fig. A-8. The addition table in binary.

Two binary numbers can be added, starting at the rightmost bit and adding the corresponding bits in the addend and the augend. If a carry is generated, it is carried one position to the left, just as in decimal arithmetic. In one's complement arithmetic, a carry generated by the addition of the leftmost bits is added to the rightmost bit. This process is called an end-around carry. In two's complement arithmetic, a carry generated by the addition of the leftmost bits is merely thrown away. Examples of binary arithmetic are shown in Fig. A-9.

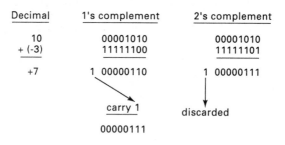

Fig. A-9. Addition in one's complement and two's complement.

If the addend and the augend are of opposite signs, overflow error cannot occur. If they are of the same sign and the result is of the opposite sign overflow error has occurred and the answer is wrong. In both one's and two's complement arithmetic, overflow occurs if and only if the carry into the sign bit differs from the carry out of the sign bit. Most computers preserve the carry out of the sign bit, but the carry into the sign bit is not visible from the answer. For this reason, a special overflow bit is usually provided.

PROBLEMS

1. Convert the following numbers to binary: 1984, 4000, 8192.

2. What is 1001101001 (binary) in decimal? In octal? In hexadecimal?

3. Which of the following are valid hexadecimal numbers? BED, CAB, DEAD, DECADE, ACCEDED, BAG, DAD.

4. Express the decimal number 100 in all radices from 2 to 9.

5. How many different positive integers can be expressed in k digits using radix r numbers?

6. Most people can only count to 10 on their fingers; however, computer scientists can do better. If you regard each finger as one binary bit, with finger extended as 1 and finger touching palm as 0, how high can you count using both hands? With both hands and both feet? Now use both hands and both feet, with the big toe on your left foot as a sign bit for two's complement numbers. What is the range of expressible numbers?

7. Perform the following calculations on 8-bit two's complement numbers.

00101101	11111111	00000000	11110111
+ 01101111	+ 11111111	- 11111111	- 11110111

8. Repeat the calculation of the preceding problem but now in one's complement.

9. Consider the following addition problems for 3-bit binary numbers in two's complement. For each sum, state:
   a. Whether the sign bit of the result is 1.
   b. Whether the low-order 3 bits are 0.
   c. Whether an overflow occurred.

000	000	111	100	100
001	111	110	111	100

10. Signed decimal numbers consisting of n digits can be represented in $n + 1$ digits without a sign. Positive numbers have 0 as the leftmost digit. Negative numbers are formed by subtracting each digit from 9. Thus the negative of 014725 is 985274. Such numbers are called nine's complement numbers and are analogous to one's complement binary numbers. Express the following as three-digit nine's complement numbers: 6, −2, 100, −14, −1, 0.

11. Determine the rule for addition of nine's complement numbers and then perform the following additions.

$$
\begin{array}{cccc}
0001 & 0001 & 9997 & 9241 \\
+\ 9999 & +\ 9998 & +\ 9996 & +\ 0802 \\
\hline
\end{array}
$$

12. Ten's complement is analogous to two's complement. A ten's complement negative number is formed by adding 1 to the corresponding nine's complement number, ignoring the carry. What is the rule for ten's complement addition?

13. Construct the multiplication tables for radix 3 numbers.

14. Multiply 0111 and 0011 in binary.

B

FLOATING-POINT NUMBERS

In many calculations the range of numbers used is very large. For example, a calculation in astronomy might involve the mass of the electron, 9×10^{-28} grams, and the mass of the sun, 2×10^{33} grams, a range exceeding 10^{60}. These numbers could be represented by

0000000000000000000000000000000000.0000000000000000000000000009
2000000000000000000000000000000000.0000000000000000000000000000

and all calculations could be carried out keeping 34 digits to the left of the decimal point and 28 places to the right of it. Doing so would allow 62 significant digits in the results. On a binary computer, multiple-precision arithmetic could be used to provide enough significance. However, the mass of the sun is not even known accurately to five significant digits, let alone 62. In fact few measurements of any kind can (or need) be made accurately to 62 significant digits. Although it would be possible to keep all intermediate results to 62 significant digits and then throw away 50 or 60 of them before printing the final results, doing this is wasteful of both CPU time and memory.

What is needed is a system for representing numbers in which the range of expressible numbers is independent of the number of significant digits. In this appendix, such a system will be discussed. It is based on the scientific notation commonly used in physics, chemistry, and engineering.

B.1. PRINCIPLES OF FLOATING POINT

One way of separating the range from the precision is to express numbers in the familiar scientific notation

$$n = f \times 10^e$$

where f is called the **fraction**, or **mantissa**, and e is a positive or negative integer called the **exponent**. The computer version of this notation is called **floating point**. Some examples of numbers expressed in this form are

$$
\begin{array}{lll}
3.14 & = 0.314 \times 10^1 & = 3.14 \times 10^0 \\
0.000001 & = 0.1 \times 10^{-5} & = 1.0 \times 10^{-6} \\
1941 & = 0.1941 \times 10^4 & = 1.941 \times 10^3
\end{array}
$$

The range is effectively determined by the number of digits in the exponent and the precision is determined by the number of digits in the fraction. Because there is more than one way to represent a given number, one form is usually chosen as the standard. In order to investigate the properties of this method of representing numbers, consider a representation, R, with a signed three-digit fraction in the range $0.1 \leq |f| < 1$ or zero and a signed two-digit exponent. These numbers range in magnitude from $+0.100 \times 10^{-99}$ to $+0.999 \times 10^{+99}$, a span of nearly 199 orders of magnitude, yet only five digits and two signs are needed to store a number.

Floating-point numbers can be used to model the real-number system of mathematics, although there are some important differences. Figure B-1 gives a grossly exaggerated schematic of the real number line. The real line is divided up into seven regions:

1. Large negative numbers less than -0.999×10^{99}.

2. Negative numbers between -0.999×10^{99} and -0.100×10^{-99}.

3. Small negative numbers with magnitudes less than 0.100×10^{-99}.

4. Zero.

5. Small positive numbers with magnitudes less than 0.100×10^{-99}.

6. Positive numbers between 0.100×10^{-99} and 0.999×10^{99}.

7. Large positive numbers greater than 0.999×10^{99}.

One major difference between the set of numbers representable with three fraction and two exponent digits and the real numbers is that the former cannot be used to express any numbers in region 1, 3, 5, or 7. If the result of an arithmetic operation yields a number in regions 1 or 7—for example, $10^{60} \times 10^{60} = 10^{120}$—overflow error will occur and the answer will be incorrect. The reason is due to the

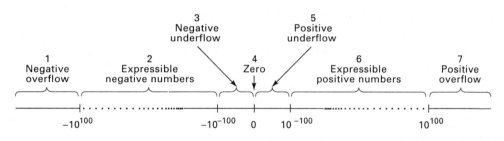

Fig. B-1. The real number line can be divided into seven regions.

finite nature of the representation for numbers and is unavoidable. Similarly, a result in region 3 or 5 cannot be expressed either. This situation is called underflow error. Underflow error is less serious than overflow error, because 0 is often a satisfactory approximation to numbers in regions 3 and 5. A bank balance of 10^{-102} dollars is hardly better than a bank balance of 0.

Another important difference between floating-point numbers and the real numbers is their density. Between any two real numbers, x and y, is another real number, no matter how close x is to y. This property comes from the fact that for any distinct real numbers, x and y, $z = (x + y)/2$ is a real number between them. The real numbers form a continuum.

Floating-point numbers, in contrast, do not form a continuum. Exactly 179,100 positive numbers can be expressed in the five-digit, two-sign system used above, 179,100 negative numbers and 0 (which can be expressed in many ways), for a total of 358,201 numbers. Of the infinite number of real numbers between -10^{+100} and $+0.999 \times 10^{99}$, only 358,201 of them can be specified by this notation. They are symbolized by the dots in Fig. B-1. It is quite possible for the result of a calculation to be one of the other numbers, even though it is in region 2 or 6. For example, $+0.100 \times 10^3$ divided by 3 cannot be expressed *exactly* in our system of representation. If the result of a calculation cannot be expressed, in the number representation being used, the obvious thing to do is to use the nearest number that can be expressed. This process is called **rounding**.

The spacing between adjacent expressible numbers is not constant throughout region 2 or 6. The separation between $+0.998 \times 10^{99}$ and $+0.999 \times 10^{99}$ is vastly more than the separation between $+0.998 \times 10^0$ and $+0.999 \times 10^0$. However, when the separation between a number and its successor is expressed as a percentage of that number, there is no systematic variation throughout region 2 or 6. In other words, the **relative error** introduced by rounding is approximately the same for small numbers as large numbers.

Although the preceding discussion was in terms of a representation system with a three-digit fraction and a two-digit exponent, the conclusions drawn are valid for other representation systems as well. Changing the number of digits in the fraction or exponent merely shifts the boundaries of regions 2 and 6 and changes the number of expressible points in them. Increasing the number of digits in the fraction increases the density of points and therefore improves the accuracy of approximations. Increasing the number of digits in the exponent increases the size of regions 2 and 6 by shrinking regions 1, 3, 5, and 7. Figure B-2 shows the approximate boundaries of region 6 for floating-point decimal numbers for various sizes of fraction and exponent.

Digits in fraction	Digits in exponent	Lower	Upper
3	1	10^{-12}	10^{9}
3	2	10^{-102}	10^{99}
3	3	10^{-1002}	10^{999}
3	4	10^{-10002}	10^{9999}
4	1	10^{-13}	10^{9}
4	2	10^{-103}	10^{99}
4	3	10^{-1003}	10^{999}
4	4	10^{-10003}	10^{9999}
5	1	10^{-14}	10^{9}
5	2	10^{-104}	10^{99}
5	3	10^{-1004}	10^{999}
5	4	10^{-10004}	10^{9999}
10	3	10^{-1009}	10^{999}
20	3	10^{-1019}	10^{999}

Fig. B-2. The approximate lower and upper bounds of expressible (unnormalized) floating-point decimal numbers.

A variation of this representation is used in computers. For efficiency, exponentiation is usually to base 2, 4, 8, or 16 rather than 10, in which case the fraction consists of a string of binary, base-4, octal, or hexadecimal digits. If the leftmost of these digits is zero, all the digits can be shifted one place to the left and the exponent decreased by 1, without changing the value of the number (barring underflow). A fraction with a nonzero leftmost digit is said to be **normalized**.

Normalized numbers are generally preferable to unnormalized numbers, because there is only one normalized form, whereas there are many unnormalized forms. Examples of normalized floating-point numbers are given in Fig. B-3 for two bases of exponentiation. In these examples a 16-bit fraction (including sign bit) and a 7-bit exponent using excess 64 notation are shown. The radix point is to the left of the leftmost fraction bit—that is, to the right of the sign bit.

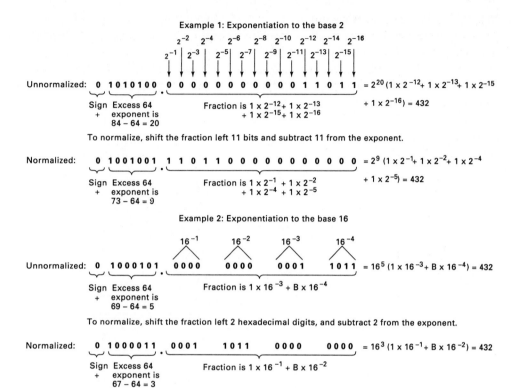

Fig. B-3. Examples of normalized floating-point numbers.

B.2. IEEE FLOATING-POINT STANDARD 754

Until about 1980, each computer manufacturer had its own floating-point format. Needless to say, all were different. Worse yet, some of them actually did arithmetic incorrectly because floating-point arithmetic has some subtleties not obvious to the average hardware designer.

To rectify this situation, in the late 1970s IEEE set up a committee to standardize floating-point arithmetic, not only to permit floating-point data to be exchanged among different computers, but to also to provide hardware designers with a model known to be correct. The resulting work led to IEEE Standard 754 (IEEE, 1985). Most CPUs these days (including the Intel, Motorola, SPARC, and MIPS ones studied in this book) have a floating-point coprocessor chip, and all of them conform to the IEEE floating-point standard. Unlike many standards, which tend to be wishy-washy compromises that please no one, this one is not bad. The standard will be described in the remainder of this section.

The standard defines three formats: single precision (32 bits), double precision (64 bits), and extended precision (80 bits). The extended-precision format is intended to reduce roundoff errors. It is used primarily inside floating-point arithmetic units, so we will not discuss it further. Both the single- and double-precision formats use radix 2 for fractions and excess notation for exponents. The formats are shown in Fig. B-4.

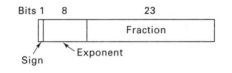

(b)

Fig. B-4. IEEE floating-point formats. (a) Single precision. (b) Double precision.

Both formats start with a sign bit for the number as a whole, 0 being positive and 1 being negative. Next comes the exponent, using excess 127 for single precision and excess 1023 for double precision. The minimum (0) and maximum (255 and 2047) exponents are not used for normalized numbers; they have special uses described below. Finally, we have the fractions, 23 and 52 bits, respectively.

A normalized fraction begins with a binary point, followed by a 1 bit, and then the rest of the fraction. Following a practice started on the PDP-11, the authors of the standard realized that the leading 1 bit in the fraction does not have to be stored, since it can just be assumed to be present. Consequently, the standard defines the fraction in a slightly different way than usual. It consists of an implied 1 bit, an implied binary point, and then either 23 or 52 arbitrary bits. If all 23 or 52 fraction bits are 0s, the fraction has the numerical value 1.0; if all of them are 1s, the fraction is numerically slightly less than 2.0. To avoid confusion with a conventional fraction, the combination of the implied 1, the implied binary point, and the 23 or 52 explicit bits is called a **significand** instead of a fraction or mantissa. All normalized numbers have a significand, s, in the range $1 \le s < 2$.

The numerical characteristics of the IEEE floating-point numbers are given in

Fig. B-5. As examples, consider the numbers 0.5, 1, and 1.5 in normalized single-precision format. These are represented in hexadecimal as 3F000000, 3F800000, and 3FC00000, respectively.

Item	Single precision	Double precision
Bits in sign	1	1
Bits in exponent	8	11
Bits in fraction	23	52
Bits, total	32	64
Exponent system	Excess 127	Excess 1023
Exponent range	−126 to +127	−1022 to +1023
Smallest, normalized	2^{-126}	2^{-1022}
Largest, normalized	approx. 2^{+128}	approx. 2^{+1024}
Decimal range	approx. 10^{-38} to 10^{+38}	approx. 10^{-308} to 10^{+308}
Smallest, denormalized	approx. 10^{-45}	approx. 10^{-324}

Fig. B-5. Characteristics of IEEE floating-point numbers.

One of the traditional problems with floating-point numbers is how to deal with underflow, overflow, and uninitialized numbers. The IEEE standard deals with these problems explicitly, borrowing its approach in part from the CDC 6600. In addition to normalized numbers, the standard has four other numerical types, described below and shown in Fig. B-6.

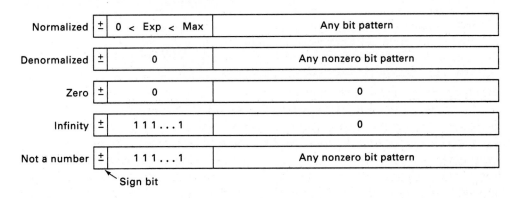

Fig. B-6. IEEE numerical types.

A problem arises when the result of a calculation has a magnitude smaller than the smallest normalized floating-point number that can be represented in this system. Previously, most hardware took one of two approaches: just set the result to zero and continue, or cause a floating-point underflow trap. Neither of these is really satisfactory, so IEEE invented **denormalized numbers**. These numbers have an exponent of 0 and a fraction given by the following 23 or 52 bits. The implicit 1 bit to the left of the binary point now becomes a 0. Denormalized numbers can be distinguished from normalized ones because the latter are not permitted to have an exponent of 0.

The smallest normalized single precision number has a 1 as exponent and 0 as fraction, and represents 1.0×2^{-126}. The largest denormalized number has a 0 as exponent and all 1s in the fraction, and represents about $0.9999999 \times 2^{-127}$, which is almost the same thing. One thing to note however, is that this number has only 23 bits of significance, versus 24 for all normalized numbers.

As calculations further decrease this result, the exponent stays at 0, but the first few bits of the fraction become zeros, reducing both the value and the number of bits in the fraction. The smallest nonzero denormalized number consists of a 1 in the rightmost bit, with the rest being 0. The exponent represents 2^{-127} and the fraction represents 2^{-23} so the value is 2^{-150}. This scheme provides for a graceful underflow by giving up significance instead of jumping to 0 when the result cannot be expressed as a normalized number.

Two zeros are present in this scheme, positive and negative, determined by the sign bit. Both have an exponent of 0 and a fraction of 0. Here too, the bit to the left of the binary point is implicitly 0 rather than 1.

Overflow cannot be handled gracefully. There are no bit combinations left. Instead, a special representation is provided for infinity, consisting of an exponent with all 1s (not allowed for normalized numbers), and a fraction of 0. This number can be used as an operand and behaves according to the usual mathematical rules for infinity. For example infinity plus anything is infinity, and any finite number divided by infinity is zero. Similarly, any finite number divided by zero yields infinity.

What about infinity divided by infinity? The result is undefined. To handle this case, another special format is provided, called **NaN** (**Not a Number**). It too, can be used as an operand with predictable results.

PROBLEMS

1. Convert the following numbers to IEEE single-precision format. Give the results as eight hexadecimal digits.

   (a) 9
   (b) 5/32
   (c) -5/32
   (d) 6.125

2. Convert the following IEEE single-precision floating-point numbers from hex to decimal:

(a) 42E48000H
(b) 3F880000H
(c) 00800000H
(d) C7F00000H

3. The format of single-precision floating-point numbers on the 370 has a 7-bit exponent in the excess 64 system, and a fraction containing 24 bits plus a sign bit, with the binary point at the left end of the fraction. The radix for exponentiation is 16. The order of the fields is: sign bit, exponent, fraction. Express the number 7/64 as a normalized number in this system in hex.

4. The following binary floating-point numbers consist of a sign bit, an excess 64, radix 2 exponent, and a 16-bit fraction. Normalize them:

(a) 0 1000000 0001010100000001
(b) 0 0111111 0000001111111111
(c) 0 1000011 1000000000000000

5. To add two floating-point numbers, you must adjust the exponents (by shifting the fraction) to make them the same. Then you can add the fractions and normalize the result, if need be. Add the single-precision IEEE numbers 3EE00000H and 3D800000H and and express the normalized result in hexadecimal.

6. The Tightwad Computer Company has decided to come out with a machine having 16-bit floating-point numbers. The Model 0.001 has a floating-point format with a sign bit, 7-bit, excess 64 exponent, and 8-bit fraction. The Model 0.002 has a sign bit, 5-bit, excess 16 exponent, and 10-bit fraction. Both use radix 2 exponentiation. What are the smallest and largest positive normalized numbers on both models? About how many decimal digits of precision does each have? Would you buy either one?

7. There is one situation in which an operation on two floating-point numbers can cause a drastic reduction in the number of significant bits in the result. What is it?

8. Some floating-point chips have a square root instruction built in. A possible algorithm is an iterative one (e.g., Newton-Raphson). Iterative algorithms need an initial approximation, and then steadily improve it. How can one obtain a fast approximate square root of a floating-point number?

9. Write a procedure to add two IEEE single-precision floating-point numbers. Each number is represented by a 32-element Boolean array.

10. Write a procedure to add two single-precision floating-point numbers that use radix 16 for the exponent and radix 2 for the fraction but do not have an implied 1 bit to the left of the binary point. A normalized number has 0001, 0010, ... 1111 as the leftmost 4 bits of the fraction, but not 0000. A number is normalized by shifting the fraction left 4 bits and adding 1 to the exponent.

INDEX